DYING, DEATH, AND BEREAVEMENT

Third Edition

Editors

George E. Dickinson
College of Charleston

George E. Dickinson is professor of sociology at the College of Charleston in Charleston, South Carolina. He received a B.A. in biology from Baylor University, an M.A. in sociology from Baylor, and a Ph.D. in sociology from Louisiana State University. His research and publications focus on physicians' treatment of terminally ill patients, children and death, physician-assisted suicide, and health treatment for the elderly.

Michael R. Leming
St. Olaf College

Michael R. Leming is professor of sociology and anthropology at St. Olaf College. He holds a B.A. degree from Westmont College, an M.A. degree from Marquette University, and a Ph.D. degree from the University of Utah, and he has done additional graduate study at the University of California in Santa Barbara. Dr. Leming serves on numerous boards of directors, and he serves as a hospice educator, volunteer, and grief counselor.

Alan C. Mermann
Yale University School of Medicine

Alan C. Mermann received an A.B. degree in biology from Lehigh University, an M.D. degree from Johns Hopkins University, and M.Div. and S.T.M. (Master of Sacred Theology) degrees from Yale University. Dr. Mermann is a clinical professor of pediatrics and a chaplain at Yale University School of Medicine. He counsels and teaches courses on homelessness, death and dying, and coping with chronic illness.

Cover illustration by Mike Eagle

Annual Editions
A Library of Information from the Public Press

Dushkin Publishing Group/
Brown & Benchmark Publishers
Sluice Dock, Guilford, Connecticut 06437

The Annual Editions Series

Annual Editions is a series of over 65 volumes designed to provide the reader with convenient, low-cost access to a wide range of current, carefully selected articles from some of the most important magazines, newspapers, and journals published today. Annual Editions are updated on an annual basis through a continuous monitoring of over 300 periodical sources. All Annual Editions have a number of features designed to make them particularly useful, including topic guides, annotated tables of contents, unit overviews, and indexes. For the teacher using Annual Editions in the classroom, an Instructor's Resource Guide with test questions is available for each volume.

Printed on Recycled Paper

VOLUMES AVAILABLE

Abnormal Psychology
Africa
Aging
American Foreign Policy
American Government
American History, Pre-Civil War
American History, Post-Civil War
American Public Policy
Anthropology
Archaeology
Biopsychology
Business Ethics
Child Growth and Development
China
Comparative Politics
Computers in Education
Computers in Society
Criminal Justice
Developing World
Deviant Behavior
Drugs, Society, and Behavior
Dying, Death, and Bereavement
Early Childhood Education
Economics
Educating Exceptional Children
Education
Educational Psychology
Environment
Geography
Global Issues
Health
Human Development
Human Resources
Human Sexuality

India and South Asia
International Business
Japan and the Pacific Rim
Latin America
Life Management
Macroeconomics
Management
Marketing
Marriage and Family
Mass Media
Microeconomics
Middle East and the Islamic World
Multicultural Education
Nutrition
Personal Growth and Behavior
Physical Anthropology
Psychology
Public Administration
Race and Ethnic Relations
Russia, the Eurasian Republics, and
   Central/Eastern Europe
Social Problems
Sociology
State and Local Government
Urban Society
Western Civilization,
   Pre-Reformation
Western Civilization,
   Post-Reformation
Western Europe
World History, Pre-Modern
World History, Modern
World Politics

Cataloging in Publication Data
Main entry under title: Annual Editions: Dying, death, and bereavement. 3/E.
      1. Death—Psychological aspects—Periodicals. 2. Bereavement—Periodicals. I. Dickinson, George E., *comp.* II. Leming, Michael R., *comp.* III. Mermann, Alan C., *comp.* IV. Title: Dying, death, and bereavement.
ISBN 1-56134-439-7   155.937′05
BF789.D4

Third Edition

Printed in the United States of America

To the Reader

In publishing ANNUAL EDITIONS we recognize the enormous role played by the magazines, newspapers, and journals of the *public press* in providing current, first-rate educational information in a broad spectrum of interest areas. Within the articles, the best scientists, practitioners, researchers, and commentators draw issues into new perspective as accepted theories and viewpoints are called into account by new events, recent discoveries change old facts, and fresh debate breaks out over important controversies.

Many of the articles resulting from this enormous editorial effort are appropriate for students, researchers, and professionals seeking accurate, current material to help bridge the gap between principles and theories and the real world. These articles, however, become more useful for study when those of lasting value are carefully *collected, organized, indexed,* and *reproduced* in a *low-cost format,* which provides easy and permanent access when the material is needed. That is the role played by *Annual Editions.* Under the direction of each volume's *Editor,* who is an expert in the subject area, and with the guidance of an *Advisory Board,* we seek each year to provide in each *ANNUAL EDITION* a current, well-balanced, carefully selected collection of the best of the public press for your study and enjoyment. We think you'll find this volume useful, and we hope you'll take a moment to let us know what you think.

Though dying, death, and bereavement have been around for as long as humankind, as topics of discussion they have been "offstage" for decades. Indeed, dying in the United States currently takes place away from the arena of familiar surroundings of kin and friends, with approximately 70 percent of deaths occurring in institutional settings of hospitals and nursing homes. Americans have developed a paradoxical relationship with death: We know more about the causes and conditions surrounding death, but we have not equipped ourselves emotionally to cope with dying, death, and bereavement. The purpose of this anthology is to provide an understanding of dying, death, and bereavement that will assist individuals to better cope with and understand their own deaths and the deaths of others.

Articles in this volume are taken from professional publications, semi-professional journals, and popular lay publications aimed at both special populations and a general readership. The selections are carefully reviewed for their currency and accuracy. On some issues, opposing viewpoints are presented. The current edition has changed approximately two-thirds of its articles from the previous editions through updating and responding to comments from reviewers regarding earlier editions.

These articles are drawn from many different periodicals, thus exposing the reader to a diversity of publications in the library. With stimulated interest from a particular article, the student is encouraged to pursue other related articles in that particular journal.

The reader will note the tremendous range of approaches and styles of the writers from personal, firsthand accounts to more scientific and philosophical writings. Some are more practical and applied, while others are more technical and research-oriented. If "variety is the very spice of life," this volume should be a spicy venture for the reader.

This anthology is organized into six units to cover many of the important aspects of dying, death, and bereavement. Though the units are arranged in a way that has some logical order, one can determine from the brief summaries in the *table of contents* and the cross-references in the *topic guide* whether another arrangement would best fit a particular teaching situation. The first unit provides an overview of the American way of dying and death. Unit 2 takes a life-cycle approach and looks at the developmental aspects of dying and death at different age levels. Unit 3 concerns the process of dying, and unit 4 addresses ethical issues of dying, death, and suicide. In the fifth unit, the articles deal with death rituals and funerals, and unit 6 presents articles on bereavement.

Annual Editions: Dying, Death, and Bereavement is meant as a supplement to augment selected areas or chapters of regular textbooks on dying and death. The articles in this volume can also serve as a basis for class discussion about various issues in dying, death, and bereavement.

Annual Editions: Dying, Death, and Bereavement is revised periodically to keep the materials timely as new social concerns about dying, death, and bereavement develop. Your assistance in the revision effort is welcome. Please complete and return the article rating form at the back of the book. We look forward to your input.

George E. Dickinson

Michael R. Leming

Alan C. Mermann
Editors

Contents

Unit 1

The American Way of Dying and Death

Eight selections discuss definitions of death, focusing on the denial and causes of death, the current status of death education, and the relationship of religion and death.

The concepts in bold italics are developed in the article. For further expansion please refer to the Topic Guide and the Index.

Unit 2

Developmental Aspects of Dying and Death

Eight articles examine how the experience of watching friends and relatives die can affect individuals at various periods of their lives.

The concepts in bold italics are developed in the article. For further expansion please refer to the Topic Guide and the Index.

Unit 3

The Dying Process

Nine articles examine the various stages of the dying process, how physicians view dying, near-death experiences, and the dynamics of hospice.

The concepts in bold italics are developed in the article. For further expansion please refer to the Topic Guide and the Index.

Unit 4

Ethical Issues of Dying, Death, and Suicide

Seven selections discuss euthanasia, organ donations, and the economics of dying and death.

The concepts in bold italics are developed in the article. For further expansion please refer to the Topic Guide and the Index.

Unit 5

Funerals and Burial Rites

Nine articles discuss the American funeral, cross-cultural burial rites, and cremation.

The concepts in bold italics are developed in the article. For further expansion please refer to the Topic Guide and the Index.

Unit 6

Bereavement

Eight articles discuss the grieving process, the loss of a significant other, and bereavement from a cross-cultural perspective.

The concepts in bold italics are developed in the article. For further expansion please refer to the Topic Guide and the Index.

Topic Guide

This topic guide suggests how the selections in this book relate to topics of traditional concern to students and professionals involved with the study of dying, death, and bereavement. It is useful for locating articles that relate to each other for reading and research. The guide is arranged alphabetically according to topic. Articles may, of course, treat topics that do not appear in the topic guide. In turn, entries in the topic guide do not necessarily constitute a comprehensive listing of all the contents of each selection.

TOPIC AREA	TREATED IN:	TOPIC AREA	TREATED IN:
AIDS	3. Constructing AIDS Policy	Dying Patients	5. Rewriting the End
Bereavement	8. Organizational Responses to Death in the Military		17. Conversation with My Mother
	10. Death of a Friend		19. Art of Dying
	12. Detachment Revisited		20. Dimensions of Dying
	34. Rituals		21. Decade beyond Medical School
	43. Coping with Bereavement		22. Attitudes to Death and Bereavement among Cultural Minority Groups
	47. Adolescent Mourning		24. Spiritual Aspects of Death and Dying
	48. Solace and Immortality		
Brain Dead	7. Sunny Side Up	Elderly Persons	15. Old No More
Burial	2. American Death and Burial Custom Derivation from Medieval European Cultures		16. Naturalness of Dying
		Euthanasia	27. Medicine's Position . . . in Assisted-Suicide Debate
Caregivers	22. Attitudes to Death and Bereavement among Cultural Minority Groups		28. Always to Care, Never to Kill
			29. Euthanasia
	23. Spiritual Needs of the Dying	Faith	24. Spiritual Aspects of Death and Dying
Children	9. Communication among Children	Fear	6. Psychology and Death
	10. Death of a Friend	Funerals	2. American Death and Burial Custom Derivation from Medieval European Cultures
	11. First Childhood Death Experiences		
	12. Detachment Revisited		9. Communication among Children
	32. "We Have a Problem"		33. Contemporary American Funeral
	48. Solace and Immortality		34. Rituals
	49. Effects of a Child's Death on the Marital Relationship		37. She Plans Funerals That Celebrate Life
Comatose	7. Sunny Side Up		38. It's Your Funeral
Communication	9. Communication among Children		39. Burying the Ungrateful Dead
	17. Conversation with My Mother		40. Burying Tradition, More People Opt for 'Fun' Funerals
	21. Decade beyond Medical School		41. Mourners Will Please Pay Respects at Speeds Not Exceeding 15 MPH
Coping	4. Current Models of Death, Dying, and Bereavement		43. Coping with Bereavement
	10. Death of a Friend	Grief	4. Current Models of Death, Dying, and Bereavement
	13. Reflections on the Death of My Daughter-in-Law		6. Psychology and Death
Counseling	32. "We Have a Problem"		10. Death of a Friend
Cultural Differences	22. Attitudes to Death and Bereavement among Cultural Minority Groups		12. Detachment Revisited
			32. "We Have a Problem"
	34. Rituals		34. Rituals
Death	1. Death and Dying		42. Grieving Process
	2. American Death and Burial Custom Derivation from Medieval European Cultures		43. Coping with Bereavement
			44. Disenfranchised Grief
			45. Increasing Prevalence of Complicated Mourning
	6. Psychology and Death: Meaningful Rediscovery		46. Spiritual Crisis of Bereavement
			47. Adolescent Mourning
			48. Solace and Immortality
			49. Effects of a Child's Death on the Marital Relationship

TOPIC AREA	TREATED IN:	TOPIC AREA	TREATED IN:
Health Care	4. Current Models of Death, Dying, and Bereavement 12. Detachment Revisited 45. Increasing Prevalence of Complicated Mourning 46. Spiritual Crisis of Bereavement	**Pets** **Physicians**	11. First Childhood Death Experiences 5. Rewriting the End 16. Naturalness of Dying 17. Conversation with My Mother 21. Decade beyond Medical School 26. Doctor, I Want to Die 27. Medicine's Position . . . in Assisted-Suicide Debate
History	1. Death and Dying	**Religion**	23. Spiritual Needs of the Dying 36. How Different Religions Pay Their Final Respects 46. Spiritual Crisis of Bereavement
Hospice	25. Hospice Care for the 1990s		
Life Expectancy	15. Old No More		
Marriage	49. Effects of a Child's Death on the Marital Relationship	**Rituals**	34. Rituals 36. How Different Religions Pay Their Final Respects 37. She Plans Funerals That Celebrate Life 38. It's Your Funeral 39. Burying the Ungrateful Dead 40. Burying Tradition, More People Opt for 'Fun' Funerals 43. Coping with Bereavement 46. Spiritual Crisis of Bereavement
Medical Ethics	17. Conversation with My Mother 18. Planning to Die 19. Art of Dying 26. Doctor, I Want to Die 27. Medicine's Position . . . in Assisted-Suicide Debate		
Medical Students	20. Dimensions of Dying		
Mourning	2. American Death and Burial Custom Derivation from Medieval European Cultures 34. Rituals 43. Coping with Bereavement 47. Adolescent Mourning 48. Solace and Immortality	**Spiritual**	23. Spiritual Needs of the Dying 24. Spiritual Aspects of Death and Dying
		Suicide	27. Medicine's Position . . . in Assisted-Suicide Debate 28. Always to Care, Never to Kill 30. Suicide 31. Attitudes toward Suicidal Behavior
Multicultural	22. Attitudes to Death and Bereavement among Cultural Minority Groups 34. Rituals 35. Psychocultural Influences on African-American Attitudes 36. How Different Religions Pay Their Final Respects	**Survivors**	8. Organizational Responses to Death in the Military
		Taboo	1. Death and Dying
Parents	12. Detachment Revisited 14. Feeling Something 32. "We Have a Problem" 48. Solace and Immortality 49. Effects of a Child's Death on the Marital Relationship	**Teachers**	10. Death of a Friend
		Timing of Death	17. Conversation with My Mother 18. Planning to Die 19. Art of Dying 26. Doctor, I Want to Die

The American Way
of Dying and Death

The topic of death is like sex in that both are taboo subjects. Socialization into the American way of life has not traditionally prepared us to cope with dying and death. Sex and death have "come out of the closet" in recent decades, however, and now are issues discussed and presented in formal educational settings. Though these topics frequently make news headlines, we still have a long way to go in educating the public about these rather "forbidden" subjects.

We are beginning to recognize the importance of education in dying and death at an earlier age. Like sex education, death education is an approved topic for presentation in elementary and secondary school curricula in many states, but the topics (especially thanatology) are "optional" and therefore seldom receive high priorities when educational funds are limited. The essay "Constructing AIDS Policy in the Public Schools" addresses the issue of a student entering school with AIDS and shows how an educational community reacted. If our population were better educated regarding dying and death, perhaps a student with AIDS or cancer would not cause such a controversy.

Social "causes" of death, a brief history of thanatology, and new norms for dying are presented in the article "Death and Dying." We do not really have any well-established norms for dying or relating to a dying person, since the latter is not something that most Americans typically encounter. In "Current Models of Death, Dying, and Bereavement," Charles Corr and Kenneth Doka address this problem by presenting "task-based" models for coping with dying and death. Paul Bartone and Morten Ender, in their article "Organizational Responses to Death in the Military," relate coping strategies of the military in assisting survivors to adjust to a death.

Ernest Becker, in his Pulitzer Prize-winning book, *The Denial of Death,* argues that fear and denial of death are basic dynamics for everyone. Herman Feifel's article, "Psychology and Death: Meaningful Rediscovery," addresses changing death attitudes and the fear of death. Even determining when a person is actually dead is not clear-cut, an issue Jim Holt presents in "Sunny Side Up."

Looking Ahead: Challenge Questions

In a society with limited resources, is it acceptable for some individuals to have access to better medical care than others?

Since socioeconomic status is related to death rates, should something be done to correct this inequity in our society?

Some health professionals argue that there simply is no room in the curriculum for thanatology. Yet, health professionals, especially physicians, have a high probability of relating to dying patients and their families. Should more emphasis be placed on presenting the topic of dying, death, and bereavement to health professionals?

How can society help to reduce death anxiety? Do you personally see any relationship between religion and death attitudes or death experience?

When is a person really dead? Though one may have "signs" of being dead, our society does not deem the death "official" until proclaimed by a physician. Should a uniform definition of death be established in the United States? Why or why not?

DEATH AND DYING

DEATH AND DYING In the 1930s a U.S. encyclopedic entry on the topic might well have focused on the economic plight of the bereaved family (Eliot 1932). In the 1950s the focus might have been on the high cost of dying and the commercialization of funerals (Bowman 1959). Twenty years later, it could have shifted to the social implications of relaxing the taboo on death (Riley 1970). This 1990 article will (1) review what sociologists have learned to date and (2) predict that the main focus of sociological interest over the proximate future will be on the process of dying. Two trends make this prediction plausible. Greater longevity dictates that most deaths will continue to occur in the later years of life, and continuing use of life-sustaining technologies dictate that the circumstances of dying will be increasingly controllable and negotiable.

GENERAL BACKGROUND

There is today no well-developed sociology of "death and dying." The phrase was first celebrated in 1969 in the title of a psychologically oriented best-seller (Kübler-Ross). Sociologists tended to be critical but recognized the appeal of the subject matter. During the subsequent decade a spate of popular literature appeared, but no major sociological work (Charmaz 1986). One sociologist termed the literature of that modern-day "discovery" of death as "a collective bustle" and summarized the ideas as "the happy death movement" (Lofland 1978).

A scattered body of sociological knowledge, however, tells us that death, in all known societies, imposes imperatives. A corpse must be looked after; property must be reallocated; vacated roles must be reassigned; the solidarity of the deceased's group must be reaffirmed (Blauner 1966; Riley 1968). A volume by Kearl (1989) makes notable contributions to the sociological perspective, relating death and dying to politics, the military, religion, war, and popular culture. Throughout this literature death is typically viewed as a transition, as a *rite de passage*.

Several threads running through the research literature also tell us that death and dying can be thought about and talked about quite openly in American society; various "arrangements" are increasingly being negotiated prior to death; dying persons are generally more concerned about their survivors than they are about themselves; dying individuals are able to exercise a significant degree of control over the timing of their deaths; tensions often exist between the requirements of formal care and the wishes of dying patients; and similar tensions almost always exist between formal and informal caregivers—between hospital bureaucracies and those significant others who are soon to be bereaved (Glaser and Strauss 1965, 1968; Riley 1983; Kalish 1985b).

No Systematic Sociology. Despite this background of knowledge and research, death has received surprisingly little systematic attention from sociologists. There are only two indexed references in the 1988 *Handbook of Sociology* (Smelser 1988): one to poverty resulting from death of breadwinners, the other to the role of death in popular religion. The *Encyclopedia of the Social Sciences* (Sills 1968) contains two entries, both on the social meanings of death. Furthermore, sociologists have failed to generate any overarching theory, although there have been many attempts.

Several kernels illustrate the range of these theoretical efforts. Talcott Parsons (1963) related the changing meanings of death to basic social values; Karl Mannheim (1928, 1952) used mortality to explain social change; Renée Fox (1980, 1981) finds that "life and death are coming to be viewed less as absolute . . . entities . . . and more as different points on a meta-spectrum . . . a new theodicity." Dorothy and David Counts (1985) specify the role of death in the various social transformations from preliterate to modern societies; Paul Baker (1990), following Warner (1959) and others, is beginning to elaborate the long-recognized theory that images of the dead exert profound influences on the living; Victor Marshall is engaged in a sustained effort—both theoretical and empirical—to link aging and dying. His basic postulate is that "awareness of finitude" operates as a trigger that permits socialization to death (Marshall 1980; Marshall and Levy 1990).

TOPICAL SOCIOLOGICAL FINDINGS

A review of the empirical literature tells us that sociological research on death has been largely topical, ranging from a taboo on death to suicide.

A Taboo on Death. In contemporary American society, death has, until recently, been viewed as a taboo topic. By the early 1960s, however, a national survey reported that the great majority of Americans (85 percent) are quite realistic and consider it important to "try to make some plans about death" and to talk about it with those closest to them (Riley 1970). Recent studies have shown that bereavement practices, once highly socially structured, are becoming increasingly varied and individually therapeutic; dying is feared primarily because it eliminates the opportunities for self-fulfillment; and active adaptations to death increase as one approaches the end of the life course (the making of wills, leaving instructions, negotiating interpersonal conflicts, etc.).

Social Organization of Death. Most deaths in the United States occur in hospitals. Two aspects have been studied sociologically. First, a detailed account of the social organization of death in a public hospital focuses on the corpse. According to the rules, the body must be washed, cataloged, and ticketed. Dignity and bureaucratic efficiency are at odds (Sudnow 1967). A contrasting account of public and private rules governing disposition of the body in contemporary Ireland is even more sociological in emphasis (Prior 1989). Second, the caring issue has been studied more as a social problem. The dying person has often been treated according to rigid rules, and selfhood is put at risk in a hospital setting that is essentially dedicated to efficiency. Changes, however, have been noted, stressing the need for caring attitudes (Kalish 1985b).

Hospice Care. The major contemporary response to care of the dying in the United States is found in programs of hospice care, now well over 1,600 in number (Bass 1985). While its definitive sociological significance is still to be documented, several studies have noted that the hospice team "mediates between the families and formal institutions that constitute the social organization of death and dying" (Marshall and Levy 1990; Levy 1982).

The Funeral. Sociologists have studied the funeral mainly as a social institution. A massive cross-cultural study attests to its worldwide function in marking a major social transition (Habenstein and Lamers 1963). Although Durkheim had emphasized its ceremonial role in facilitating social regrouping, later sociologists have shown that elaborate and extravagant funeral rites are more reflective of commercial interests than of human grief or mourning (Parsons and Lidz 1967).

Bereavement. A now classic study (Eliot 1932) of the bereaved family stimulated a large literature that documents the general proposition that survivors—particularly significant others—require various types of social supports to "get through" the period of intense personal grief and the more publicly expressed mourning. In today's societies, the time devoted to bereavement activities generally becomes shorter (Pratt 1981). This is consistent with Parsons' position that in societies characterized by an "active" orientation, the bereaved are expected to carry out their grief work quickly and privately.

Widowhood. It is estimated that by the year 2000 there will be sixty-five men for every 100 women over age sixty-five and that most of the women will be widows. Many studies (e.g., Lopata 1973, 1979) have detailed the negative aspects of widowhood: loneliness, poor health, loss of personal identity, anxiety about the future. A somewhat different picture has emerged from an analysis of data (Hyman 1983) from the General Social Surveys. Samples of widows (who were not interviewed as widows) were compared with control samples of married and divorced women. Although somewhat controversial, this study reported that widowhood does not produce the negative and enduring consequences that the earlier studies had documented.

Social Stressors and Death. Sociologists have investigated many social "causes" of death: individually experienced stressors such as retirement and bereavement, and collectively experienced stressors such as economic depressions, wars, and technological revolutions. By and large all such studies have been inconclusive. For example, the hypothesis that a bereaved spouse is at higher risk of death (that death causes death) has been widely investigated but with no conclusive results, although recent and as yet unpublished research suggests that bereavement may have a negative mortality effect for older spouses. Retirees in some longitudinal studies have been shown to experience excess mortality, whereas other investigations have reported opposite results. (Retirement is a complex process, not a simple or single event.) In an era in which nursing homes play an important role in the lives of many older people, the consequences of residential relocation have come under critical scrutiny. Several studies have reported that the "warehousing" of the frail elderly results in increased mortality, while in other studies feelings of security in the new "home" are reported to enhance both a sense of well-being and lower mortality. (Obviously the nursing home population is far from homogeneous.) Similar caveats apply to macro-level studies that attempt to relate economic and technological change to trends in mortality. Recent advances in mathematical modeling and the increasing availability of relevant data sets make this problem an attractive area for continuing sociological research (Riley 1983).

Suicide. Durkheim's studies of suicide spawned a wide, diverse, and sometimes confusing research literature. In most such studies social integration is the operative concept. If the theoretical relationship is believed to be relatively unambiguous, the empirical relationship is far from tidy. For example, war has been found to heighten integration, both economic and political, but it also diminishes the availability of beverage alcohol, which, in turn, reduces suicides triggered by alcohol consumption (Wasserman 1989). Various other types of intervening variables have been studied (e.g., "suggestion") (Phillips 1974).

FOCUS ON DYING

Apart from suicide, it is a sociological truism that individuals are often socially motivated to try to influence the time of their own deaths. Several studies, for example, have tested the hypothesis of a "death dip"—that social events of significance are preceded by lower than expected mortality (Phillips and Feldman 1973). These studies rest on Durkheim's insight that if some are so detached from society that they commit suicide, others may be so attached to society that they postpone their deaths in order to participate in events in which they are involved (Phillips and Smith 1990). The same hypothesis has been extended to studies of a "birthday dip" in which the event is more personal and local in its significance for death (Phillips 1972). Along similar lines, several sociological investigations have explored the proposition that some people die socially before they die biologically. These studies center on the notion of levels of "awareness" of death (Glaser and Strauss 1965). When both the dying person and his significant others are cognizant of death as a soon-to-be-experienced event, an ensuing "open" awareness may enable them to negotiate various aspects of the final phase of life. Further research on "dying trajectories" involves certainties and uncertainties as to the time of death (Glaser and Strauss 1968).

Recently, this question has been asked: Does the individual, in a society deeply committed to the preservation of life, have a "right" to die? The U.S. Supreme Court has answered this in the affirmative but with limitations. The issue has become one of the most profound, complex, and pressing questions of our time. It involves the "rights" and wishes of the dying person; the "rights" and responsibilities of his or her survivors; the "rights" and obligations of attending physicians; and the "rights" and constraints of the law. And the human side of the issue is producing a tidal wave of public interest: television documentaries, opinion surveys, radio talk shows. The issue is openly debated in leading medical journals, which now carry editorials on euthanasia—an unthinkable topic only a few years ago. It is altering age-old hospital rules in which resuscitation orders were written on blackboards, then quickly erased. A major book proposes rationing medical resources (Callahan 1987). Radical movements have sprung up that advocate active euthanasia. The mounting costs of the last days of life have been dramatized. All this ferment reflects powerful ideas that potentially fuel social change (M. W. Riley 1978).

New Norms for Dying. Demography dictates that a substantial proportion of the 5,500 or so deaths that occur each day in the United States will be at the later years of life, but medical technology now offers options as to timing. The period of dying can be lengthened or shortened. Sociology has identified three elements in the process of dying: (1) depending on the "level of awareness," the dying person is able to "negotiate" to some degree both the course of dying and the consequences of death (Glaser and Strauss 1965); (2) depending on "awareness of finitude," dying persons are able to be socialized to death and to prepare themselves for it (Marshall 1980); (3) depending on the quality of care, both the physical pain of dying and the psychosocial pain of separation and loss can be mitigated (Kalish 1985a; Levy forthcoming; Bass 1985).

Today, moreover, the problems and dilemmas inherent in the "management" of death have captured both popular and scientific attention. The reality of the extreme case is starkly clear. Many dying persons have given written or oral instructions that they do not want to go on living under certain conditions, often specified in "living wills." Similarly, many kin of nonsentient or hopelessly ill and suffering persons may not want to have the lives of such patients prolonged. In both instances doctors and lawyers play ambiguous but critical roles. It is, however, the "negotiation" that is of sociological interest. Norms designed to reduce the perplexities in wrenching decisions or to reassure the decision makers (including dying persons) are generally lacking. The need for relevant norms governing "the dying process" has been noted (Riley and Riley 1986), and the main considerations have been specified (Logue 1989). The U.S. Office of Technology Assessment (1987) and the Hastings Center (1987) have issued medical and ethical guidelines, respectively, on the use of life-sustaining procedures. In the 1970s sociologists developed research models for studying the social aspects of heroic operations and the treatment of nonsalvageable terminal patients (Fox and Swazey 1974; Crane 1975). Yet models necessary to the formation of norms capable of handling the "rights" and wishes of the various parties to the process of dying are still clearly needed. Today such models are yet to be developed, although human "rights" are being recognized as basic components in the development of social theory (Coleman 1990).

While a sociology of "dying" is yet to be developed, at least three aspects of norms and "rights" governing the dying process have been identified: timing and level of awareness, socialization to death, and quality of care. These suggest for sociological research a demanding agenda that should carry well into the twenty-first century.

REFERENCES

Baker, Paul M. 1990 "Socialization After Death: The Might of the Living Dead." In Beth Hess and Elizabeth Markson, eds., *Growing Old in America.* New Brunswick, N.J.: Transaction Books.

Bass, David M. 1985 "The Hospice Ideology and Success of Hospice Care." *Research on Aging* 7:1.

Blauner, Robert 1966 "Death and Social Structure." *Psychiatry* 29:378–394.

Bowman, L. 1959 *The American Funeral: A Study in Guilt, Extravagance, and Sublimity.* Washington, D.C.: Public Affairs Press.

Callahan, Daniel 1987 *Setting Limits: Medical Goals in an Aging Society.* New York: Simon and Schuster.

Charmaz, K. C. 1986 *Social Reality of Death.* Reading, Mass.: Addison-Wesley.

Coleman, James P. 1990 *Foundations of Special Theory.* Cambridge, Mass.: Harvard University Press.

Counts, D. A., and D. C. Counts 1985 *Aging and Its Transformations: Moving Toward Death in Pacific Societies.* Lanham, MD.: University Press of America.

Crane, D. 1975 *The Sanctity of Social Life: Physicians' Treatment of Critically Ill Patients.* New York: Russell Sage Foundation.

Eliot, T. 1932. "The Bereaved Family." Special issue, *The Annals* 160.

Fox, R. C. 1980 "The Social Meaning of Death." *The Annals* 447.

—— 1981 "The Sting of Death in American Society." *Social Service Review* March:42–59.

——, and Swazey, T. P. 1974 *The Courage to Fail: A Social View of Organ Transplantation and Dialysis.* Chicago: University of Chicago Press.

Glaser, B. G., and A. O. Strauss 1965 *Awareness of Dying.* Chicago: Aldine.

—— 1968 *Time for Dying.* Chicago: Aldine.

Habenstein, R. W. 1968 "The Social Organization of Death." In D. L. Sills, ed. *International Encyclopedia of the Social Sciences.* New York: Macmillan and Free Press.

——, and M. W. Lamers 1963 *Funeral Customs the World Over.* Milwaukee, Wisc.: Bulfin.

Hastings Center, The 1987 *Guidelines on the Termination of Life-Sustaining Treatment and the Care of the Dying.* Bloomington: Indiana University Press.

Hyman, H. H. 1983 *Of Time and Widowhood: Nationwide Studies of Enduring Effects.* Durham, N.C.: Duke University Press.

Kalish, R. A. 1985a *Death, Grief and Caring Relationships.* Monterey, Calif.: Brooks/Cole.

—— 1985b "The Social Context of Death and Dying." In R. H. Binstock and E. Shanas, eds., *Handbook of Aging and the Social Sciences.* New York: Van Nostrand Reinhold.

Kearl, Michael C. 1989 *Endings: A Sociology of Death and Dying.* Oxford, Eng.: Oxford University Press.

Kübler-Ross, E. 1969 *On Death and Dying.* New York: Macmillan.

Levine, S., and N. A. Scotch 1970 "Dying as an Emergent Social Problem." In O. G. Brim, Jr., et al., eds., *The Dying Patient.* New York: Russell Sage Foundation.

Levy, Judith A. 1982 "The Staging of Negotiations Between Hospice and Medical Institutions." *Urban Life* 11.

—— Forthcoming "Hospice in an Aging Society." *Journal of Aging Studies.*

Lofland, L. 1978 *The Craft of Dying: The Modern Face of Death.* Beverly Hills, Calif.: Sage Publications.

Logue, B. 1989 *Death Control and the Elderly: The Growing Acceptability of Euthanasia.* Providence, R.I.: Population Studies and Training Center, Brown University.

Lopata, H. Z. 1973 *Widowhood in an American City.* Cambridge, Mass.: Schenkman.

—— 1979 *Women as Widows: Support Systems.* New York: Elvesier.

Mannheim, K. (1928) 1952 "The Problem of Generations." In P. Keeskemeti, ed., *Essays in Sociological Knowledge.* London: Routledge and Kegan Paul.

Marshall, V. W. 1980 *Last Chapters: A Sociology of Aging and Dying.* Belmont, Calif.: Wordsworth.

——, and J. A. Levy 1990 "Aging and Dying." In R. H. Binstock and L. George, eds., *Handbook of Aging and the Social Sciences,* 3rd ed. San Diego, Calif.: Academic Press.

Parsons, T. 1963 "Death in American Society: A Brief Working Paper." *American Behavioral Scientist.*

——, and V. W. Lidz 1967 "Death in American Society." In E. S. Shneidman, ed., *Essays in Self-Destruction.* New York: Science House.

Phillips, D. P. 1972 "Deathday and Birthday: An Unexpected Connection." In J. Tanur, ed., *Statistics: Guide to the Unknown.* San Francisco: Holden-Day.

—— 1974 "The Influence of Suggestion on Suicide: Substantive and Theoretical Implications of the Werther Effect." *American Sociological Review* 39:340–354.

——, and L. L. Carstensen 1986 "Clustering of Teenage Suicides After Television Stories About Suicide." *New England Journal of Medicine* 315 (11).

——, and K. A. Feldman 1973 "A Dip in Deaths Before Ceremonial Occasions: Some New Relationships Between Integration and Mortality." *American Sociological Review* 38:678–696.

——, and D. G. Smith 1990 "Postponement of Death Until Symbolically Meaningful Occasions." *Journal of the American Medical Association* 203 (14).

Pratt, L. V. 1981 "Business Temporal Norms and Bereavement Behavior." *American Sociological Review* 4:317–333.

Prior, Lindsay 1989 *The Social Organization of Death: Medical Discourses and Social Practices in Belfast.* New York: St. Martin's Press.

Riley, J. W., Jr. 1968 "Death and Bereavement." In D. L. Sills, ed., *International Encyclopedia of the Social Sciences.* New York: Macmillan and Free Press.

—— 1970 "What People Think About Death." In O. G. Brim, Jr., et al., eds., *The Dying Patient.* New York: Russell Sage Foundation.

—— 1983 "Dying and the Meanings of Death: Sociological Inquiries." *Annual Review of Sociology* 9:191–216.

Riley, M. W. 1978 "Aging, Social Change and the Power of Ideas." *Daedalus* 107:39–52.

———, A. Foner, and J. Waring 1988 "Sociology of Age." in N. J. Smelser, ed., *Handbook of Sociology*. Newbury Park, Calif.: Sage Publications.

———, and J. W. Riley, Jr. 1986 "Longevity and Social Structure: The Added Years," *Daedalus* 115:51–75.

Sills, David L. (ed.) 1968 *International Encyclopedia of the Social Sciences*. New York: Macmillan and Free Press.

Smelser, Neil J. (ed.) 1988 *Handbook of Sociology*. Newbury Park, Calif.: Sage Publications.

Stroebe, W., and M. E. Stroebe 1987 *Bereavement and Health: The Psychological and Physical Consequences of Partner Loss*. Cambridge: Cambridge University Press.

Sudnow, D. 1967 *Passing On: The Social Organization of Dying*. Englewood Cliffs, N.J.: Prentice-Hall.

U.S. Congress, Office of Technology Assessment 1987 *Life-Sustaining Technologies and the Elderly*. Washington, D.C.: U.S. Government Printing Office.

Warner, W. L. 1959 *The Living and the Dead*. New Haven, Conn.: Yale University Press.

Wasserman, I. M. 1989 "The Effects of War and Alcohol Consumption Patterns on Suicide: United States (1910–1953)." *Social Forces* 66: 513–533.

JOHN W. RILEY, JR.

American Death and Burial Custom Derivation from Medieval European Cultures

Dr. J. Mack Welford

Dr. J. Mack Welford is with the Department of Education at Roanoke College in Salem, Virginia.

Lynne DeSpelder and Albert Lee Strickland, in their book entitled *The Last Dance*, state the following: "Death is a universal human experience, yet the response it elicits is shaped by the attitudes towards it and beliefs about it that are prevalent in a particular culture. This shared consciousness among its members makes a culture distinct; it gives a particular cast to experiences and the meanings ascribed to them, and death is such an experience." (DeSpelder and Strickland, p. 41)

In teaching an interdisciplinary course entitled Perspectives on Death and Dying during the past 13 years, I have encountered a genuine interest on the part of many of my students in the social and culture changes in the United States from the nineteenth century to the present and how those century-old customs have affected and shaped present custom and practice in regard to death, burial, and mourning rituals within modern day culture. In a recent class about two years ago the question arose as to how contemporary customs were affected by ancient and medieval history and practice. I found that I had neither the knowledge nor information at hand to respond. A limited search of the literature available revealed that very little such information existed in an organized fashion related to that particular topic. Consequently, I sought funding for research, and as a result I have spent periods of time during the past two summers (1990 and 1991) researching the topic at the British Library and Museum and at the University of London Library. I have also visited several sites of ancient and medieval burial in various parts of England and Scotland. That research, still unfinished, has resulted in two papers devoted to the topic, emphasizing how archeological evidence from the time which predates the advent of written history through the early historical period of Western civilization, the Middle Ages, and post-Renais-

sance periods have all influenced contemporary death ritual and practice in the United States. In these papers and subsequent papers to follow, I wish to identify the social, economic, political, and cultural influences that have helped to shape present day culture in regard to death practices.

Hope of an Afterlife

The Middle Ages view of death in the Western world was one of acceptance, one in which people viewed death as part of the natural law and process of God's law at work in the world. Theologically church teaching gave hope of an afterlife with God in heaven if a person was good and sought God's will through faith. Philip Aries has divided the historical period into two periods or parts. The early period (500-1100) is described as the idea that "All people die." Death was a part of the natural law and process of God, and the person saw him/herself as a part of the group of mankind of God's creation. The later Middle Ages period and beyond (1100-1700), in the Aries scheme, is described as "One's own death." The collective view of mankind by the individual changed to a perception of an individual standing individually and being judged based on his/her own individual "good or bad" life.

In St. Augustine's *City of God*, Book I, Chapter 11, is found the following: "All these ceremonies concerning the dead, the care of the burial, the fashions of the sepulchers, the pomp of the funerals, are rather solaces to the living than furtherance to the dead...The family of that rich, gorgeous glutton prepared him a sumptuous funeral unto the eyes of men: but one far more sumptuous did the ministering angels prepare for the poor ulcerated beggar in the sight of God; they bore him not unto any sepulcher

of marble but placed him in the bosom of Abraham." (St. Augustine, p. 193).

During the Middle Ages burial was either in the ground or in vaults. The body was wrapped in a shroud, knotted at the head and foot. In many cases it was laid directly into the grave, but from an early date stone, wooden, or lead chests were employed. Much importance was attached to the place of burial. Funeral masses were occasions of great solemnity. In descriptions of Middle Age burial we find the source of several contemporary death and funeral practices. These include the use of a specially prepared burial garment, the use of a casket or coffin to be buried underground to protect the body from the elements of nature. We also see the continuance of the ceremonies and particularly the religious rites that had predated the Middle Ages by thousands of years, but these rites have become almost universally Christian/Roman Catholic in nature.

In medieval Britain before the Reformation we find that shrouds were utilized almost universally from the richest to the poorest, although many of the richer classes were buried in elaborate and elegant garments. Even among the poorest class, babies who died before the age of one month were buried in swaddling clothes. The shrouds were usually of linen and were wrapped and tied at the top and bottom. For the poor often a sheet from the house supply was utilized in place of a linen shroud, and the body was put into the grave thusly with the body tied inside the sheet. Some brides even included a shroud in their trousseaus. This was also the case for children. This practice was due to the high death rate of both young wives and babies at the time of childbirth.

At the beginning of the thirteenth century there was a widely held belief within the church that masses said on behalf of the dead would shorten the time that a soul spent in

From *The Forum*, September/October 1992, pp. 6-9. Reprinted with permission from *The Forum*, newsletter of The Association for Death Education and Counseling, Hartford, CT.

11

purgatory. A funeral liturgy included a mass for the dead. This mass was also sung on the third, seventh and thirtieth days following burial, and to complete the calendar of commemoration on the first year anniversary of the death. (Seventh, thirtieth, and first year anniversary dates are also important in contemporary Jewish mourning ritual.) Sometimes this singing of the masses went on until the tenth year on each anniversary. It also provided a good business from purchases of fresh candles to burn, the renting or purchase of mourning cloaks, and a requirement that an invitation be issued to the poor. It was customary to use poor people as part of the body of mourners. It was good and laudable to remember them at one's death, and the family bought the poor clothes to wear for the ceremonial procession and funeral and fed them a mourning meal.

Poor Clothed, Fed and Paid

Poor people were given a new set of clothing and marched in the funeral procession, often carrying candles. The poor flocked in droves to attend funerals of their social superiors, and they were often given a small amount of money as well as possibly food and drink. Sometimes they were given the smallest denomination of coin, receiving one for each year of the age of the deceased, and sometimes thirteen coins were given representing the number of people present at the Last Supper. Some of the poor made a good living at this and an efficient "telegraph" system of an impending "rich" death developed. There was also a priest's fee to be paid and a donation made to the church. There was much burning of candles, and the funerals were often held at night. The body was sometimes kept for weeks or months because of the fear of being buried alive. Even the poor and the condemned prisoners generally desired a Christian burial. Paupers' funerals were paid for by the parish from a tax or rate levied on all property owners. Food and drink were also provided by the parish at pauper funerals. Even unknown strangers were given the same burial. Food and drink was a vital ritual whereby the community coped with the death, and this continues today. Poors holes or Poors graves were holes or pits dug in the churchyard (due to lack of space). Coffins three or four across and up to six or seven deep were stacked for the paupers. The Poors holes or graves were then filled and another pit was dug.

The business aspect that arose during the Middle Ages can be seen in the fact that some priests left the parish ministry to become chantry priests, those who chanted, sang, or said the funeral masses, thus often gaining a lucrative income for little work.

A charnel house was often maintained in the smallest village church and in large cathedrals. This was a subterranean chamber where bones were placed when disturbed by interments in the churchyard. Burial was nearly always done in the churchyard, and when the churchyard became completely filled with graves, the oldest graves were often disinterred, and the bones kept in the charnel house due to the Christian teaching or belief in the physical resurrection of the body and the consequent necessity that the bones or whatever remained of the physical body must be kept intact in the hope of that physical resurrection. Many so-called crypts beneath churches were these. Sometimes chantry altars were set up in the charnel and priests said masses there. This particular practice ended with Henry VIII's repression of the Roman Catholic Church and was not reintroduced into the Anglican Church until 1873. After the Reformation it was not unusual for these charnels to be cleared and taken over by prominent local families to be used for their own personal burial vaults. There were often parochial guilds and fraternities organized to arrange and service the funeral procession. They kept the parish coffin, the pall, mourning cloaks, candles, hearses, and, for the impoverished, also paid the mass fee to the priest. They also arranged the funeral feast that followed the burial ceremonies and burial itself. The laying out and preparation of the body was the responsibility of the family. Issuing of the mourning candles to mourners began to decline in the early 1500s, but it was reintroduced in the late 1600s for nighttime funerals. A parish coffin was utilized for the poor until the mid-seventeenth century. This coffin was used to "lay out" the body for the wake or watch over the body during the night prior to the funeral itself, and the body was removed at the graveside and generally placed into the ground wrapped in a linen shroud or sheet and covered with dirt. The coffin was used again and again. Mourning clothes were used during the Middle Ages, but their use declined in the late 1500s. A chief mourner was designated, usually a close relative or close family friend. The chief mourner led the funeral processions and was generally the most elegantly dressed of those attending the funeral rites. One's funeral rites depended entirely on one's status. These various practices which were found to different degrees throughout the Middle Ages in Western Europe continued through the seventeenth century.

Beside the coffin, some would eat and drink, some would drink and smoke, and often during a day or two of the "wake" there would be sports and mimical plays held in honor of the dead person. White was the mourning color for bachelors and virgins,

children, and women dying in childbirth. The mourning color for all others was black. The sound of bells was important to mark the funeral, and the bellringers and clergy were paid.

Symbolic Grave Placement

Bodies were always buried in the church or churchyard, and the graves were dug traditionally six feet deep from east to west with the head lying to the west, so a person would rise up with his/her face to the east. The symbolism involved in the placement of the grave was twofold: the biblical teaching that Jesus Christ would return from heaven to earth in a cloud in the east, so the person during physical resurrection on leaving the grave would first be facing Jesus; the second symbolism is that of the setting sun in the west and the head facing west symbolized the end of life. When old graves were disturbed, as was necessary after the churchyard was filled with graves, the old bones were put in the charnel house (or bone house). The practice of burying the dead in the churchyard seems to have begun to decline in the first half of the seventeenth century.

Another common practice of the Middle Ages, particularly among the rich and powerful, was to remove one or more organs, usually the heart, to be buried at the place of death. Sometimes monasteries demanded it, since many of the rich had died in their infirmaries. The body was returned to be buried in the deceased's parish church.

The practice of embalming, carried out to such a high art of sophistication during the time of the Egyptians and then falling into disuse, was revived during the Middle Ages. Dr. Vanderlyn Pine, past president of the Association for Death Education and Counseling, describes it thusly in an article entitled "The Care of the Dead":

"During the Middle Ages the Christian version of embalming included removing some body organs, washing the body with water, alcohol, and pleasant smelling oils, chemically drying and preserving the flesh, wrapping the body in layers of cloth sealed with tar or oak sap, and mummifying in a way similar to the Egyptians. These tasks were performed by specialists who acted solely as embalmers. Apparently, there was relatively little bureaucratic handling of formal arrangements, and most funerary services were kin-provided and essentially personal in nature.

"Leonardo da Vinci developed a system of venous injection for preservation of the dead body to enable him to draw anatomical plates. His method served as an inspiration to the early medical embalmers whose practices later gave rise to many modern embalming procedures. . .'' (Pine, Fulton, et al, p. 274)

Embalming decreased in the late 1500s and early 1600s, and it was not commonly used again, except in the case of royalty and nobility, until the late 1800s.

Embalming seems to have been lost after the Egyptians until it was resumed for royalty and nobility in the late 1200s. Embalming was done on royalty in England from the 1200s to the 1700s. The bowels and heart were often removed and put in a separate container and carried on top of the coffin or buried elsewhere. The body was wrapped, encased in lead, and placed in a wood coffin.

In small towns and rural areas there was often a board placed between two chairs, and the body was draped in a sheet or shroud. During the time immediately prior to the religious funeral ceremony, people passed by to view the corpse which had never been alone since death, with people sitting with the body all night. The shroud or burial sheet would then be tied at both ends, placed in a closed coffin, usually the parish coffin, and the procession set off for the churchyard. Visitation and viewing of the body continue today.

Coffin: A Status Symbol

Coffins were and are status symbols. No thirteenth, fourteenth, or fifteenth century peasant or artisan expected to be buried in a coffin. By contrast, no nobleman would have been subjected to shroud burial in a churchyard. Introduction of the reusable parish coffin in the 1400s was a marked improvement, but it was abandoned in the 1600s due to the Black Death, pestilence and plague. The body of a rich person was often put in a lead body coffin for vault interment, from the 1400s to the 1600s, and then sometimes was put into a wooden coffin as well. By 1700-1725 the funeral furnishing trade was firmly established and supplied coffins.

Among non-Christian pagans of Western Europe in the earlier Medieval period, some idea of a continuing life of the individual after physical bodily death seems universal, though it is often nebulous. It is improbable that the gloomy view of souls of the dead confined to their tombs or grave was ever generally held, and more likely to be have been considered was the idea that death was merely a line between the living and the soul of the dead, wherever it was. The soul journeyed to a far land, either a shadowy and gloomy land beneath the earth (the tomb, Sheol of the Old Testament Jewish tradition, etc.) or, more cheerfully, a happy land beyond the seas (Isle of the Blessed, Avalon, Valhalla, etc.) or in the sky (heaven).

Many practices or ceremonies within the funeral services themselves seem to represent various ways to assist and speed the movement of the dead person into the afterlife. There were also various rites during the Middle Ages to prevent the dead from returning to interfere with the living. Many of these rites, and the mixing of the two generalized traditions of speeding the soul to its place of final afterlife destination and preventing the soul to return to interfere with the dead, can be seen intertwined in the ritualistic dance of the dead practiced from the fourth century until the sixteenth century. Ivan Illich, founder of the Center for International Documentation in Cuernavaca, Mexico describes the dance of the dead as follows:

''From the fourth century onwards, the Church had struggled against the pagan tradition of crowds dancing in cemeteries: naked, frenzied, and brandishing swords. Nevertheless, the frequency of ecclesiastical prohibitions testifies that they were of little avail, and for a thousand years Christian churches and cemeteries remained dance floors. Death was an occasion for the renewal of life. To dance with the dead over their tombs was an occasion for affirming the joy of being alive and a source of many erotic songs and poems. By the late fourteenth century, the sense of these dances seems to have changed: from an encounter between the living and those who were already dead, it was transformed into a meditative, introspective experience. In 1424 the first 'Dance of the Dead' was painted on a cemetery wall in Paris. The original of the 'Cimetiere des Innocents' is lost, but good copies allow us to reconstruct it: king, peasant, pope, scribe and maiden each dance with a corpse. Each partner is a mirror image of the other in dress and feature. In the shape of his body Everyman carries his own death with him and dances with it through his life. During the late Middle Ages, indwelling death faces man; each death comes with a symbol of rank corresponding to his victim: for the king a crown, for the peasant a pitchfork. After dancing with dead ancestors over their graves, people turn to representing a world in which everyone dances through life embracing his own mortality. Death is not represented as an anthropomorphic figure but has a macabre self-consciousness, a constant awareness of the gaping grave. It is not yet the skeleton man of the next century to whose music men and women soon dance through the autumn of the Middle Ages, but rather each one's own aging and rotting self. At this time the mirror becomes important in everyday life, and in the grip of the 'mirror death,' life acquires a hallucinating poignancy. With Chaucer and Villon death becomes as intimate and sensual as pleasure and pain. . .'' (Illich, in Fulton, et al, p. 112).

Reincarnation Attacked by Justinian

Reincarnation, another aspect of the belief that an afterlife exists continues to the present time in most Eastern religions and was also found in Christianity until the early Middle Ages. It seems to have existed in Christianity until it was attacked in A.D. 543 by the Byzantine emperor, Justinian. Reincarnation had been introduced to early Christianity by Origen (A.D. 185?-254?) an early Christian philosopher and writer who developed the complex system of thought. He believed that all knowledge comes from God and finds its highest and most complete expression in Christianity. He had great influence in early times, and was said to have written 6,000 books on religious subjects. He was born and educated in Alexandria, Egypt, and died as a result of torture by the Roman Emperor Decius. The emperor Justinian also attacked many of the other teachings of Origen as well. Origen was considered the most prominent of all the Church fathers with the exception of Augustine. In *De Principiis*, Origen wrote the following:

''The soul has neither beginning nor end. . .every soul comes to this world strengthened by the victories or weakened by defeats of its previous life. Its place in this world as a vessel appointed to honor or dishonor is determined by its previous merits or demerits. Its work in this world determines its place in the world which is to follow this.'' (Grof, in Fulton, et al, p. 107)

The concept of reincarnation was also condemned by the Second Council in A.D. 553 in Constantinople; consequently, the concept of reincarnation seems to have been removed as a type of belief in afterlife during the very early Middle Ages.

Burial, entombment, cremation, and other means of body disposal have taken place as long as mankind has existed. Throughout the world three basic methods of disposal have generally been used: (1) by exposure and consumption by scavengers, such as in the Towers of Silence in the Parsees and in some African tribes such as in Nandi in Kenya and among some North American Indians; (2) by burial, the method most familiar to us and the one leaving the most archeological evidence; (3) and by cremation.

Grave gods excavated from graves hundreds and even thousands of years old have indicated an almost universal belief in some type of afterlife throughout recorded history, even in pre-historic times in every culture studied through archeological examination. Neanderthal, Cro-Magnon, and Paleolithic men have all indicated that belief through flowers, food, clothing and tools that have been found in grave sites, just as humankind continues to indicate such a belief today through special religious or natural ceremonies associated with the disposal of the body. Consequently, funeral, burial, and other body disposal customs can give us a mirror to view our own reflected practices, traditions, and customs.

Prior to 1500, during the Middle Ages, the cosmos of Western culture was essentially Roman Catholic from the time of post-Roman society. The upheavals of the Protestant Reformation undermined the unity of European Catholicism and its system, but one of the great influences during the time between, the Middle Ages, was that of death, mourning, and funeral ritual during the Middle Ages. The Christian belief of universal resurrection, as so often evidenced in mourning and funeral practice, marked a vast improvement upon the ancient Egyptian belief in the restriction of resurrection to a well-preserved body kept alive through the funeral offering ritual. For the Egyptians life after death was of paramount importance, and they believed that spiritual survival depended absolutely on the bodies' physical survival, so they devoted a great deal of ingenuity into the art of preserving dead bodies. The Christian teaching which arose during the Roman Empire based upon the teachings of Jesus, and continuing into the Middle Ages of post-Roman times, did away with the necessity of physical preservation of the body. Consequently, embalming fell into general disuse until the late Middle Ages when it arose again in a more preservation context.

Funeral as Religious Statement

The means by which individual and societal reactions to death are most often seen is through the funeral ritual or tradition. The funeral has not only been used as a commemoration of an individual life, it has also been used as a religious statement and as a means of allowing the social group to establish its presence and support. The funeral also serves in the role of ritualistic body disposal. Again, consequently, in our own reactions to death, we can ascertain how our grief and mourning practices have evolved. Why study death, grief, and burial customs from a historical perspective? A quotation from James J. Farrell can probably best answer this:

"Death is a cultural event, and societies as well as individuals reveal themselves in their treatment of death. Historians, therefore, can profitably discover important patterns of social and cultural life by examining ideas and institutions associated with death. By studying death as a cultural event, we add an important historical dimension to those studies of the meaning of management of death by sociologists, psychologists, and social critics." (Farrell, p. 14)

Through the described medieval practices of death, funeral, burial, and mourning practices, we see reflected many of our contemporary practices and traditions. In conclusion, different concepts of deaths and the associated beliefs related to death have contributed to our understanding and experience of contemporary practices. By comparing the situation of a person's death in contemporary western civilization with that of the death of individuals from ancient and medieval worlds, it is possible to ascertain in some ways how and why we view death as we do today.

References

Aires, Phillippe, *Western Attitudes Toward Death from the Middle Ages to the Present*. Baltimore: Johns Hopkins University Press, 1974.

Augustine, St. Aurelius, *Treatise on the City of God*. New York: Macmillan, 1922.

Bendann, Effie, *Death Customs: An Analytical Study of Burial Rites*. New York: Alfred A. Knopf, 1930; republished by Gale Research Company, Detroit, 1974.

Boase, Thomas Sherrer Ross, *Death in the Middle Ages: Mortality, Judgment, and Remembrance*. London: Thames and Hudson, 1972.

Braet, Herman and Webeke, Werner, Eds. *Death in the Middle Ages*. Leuven: Leuven University Press, 1983.

Choron, Jacques, *Death and Western Thought*. New York: Collier Books, 1963.

Clark, J.M., *The Dance of Death in the Middle Ages and the Renaissance*. Glasgow: University of Glasgow Press, 1950.

DeSpelder, Lynne Ann and Strickland, Albert Lee, *The Last Dance: Encountering Death and Dying*. Palo Alto: Mayfield Publishing Company, 1992.

Farrell, James J., *Inventing the American Way of Death, 1830-1920*. Philadelphia: Temple University Press, 1980.

Farrell, James, "The Dying of Death: Historical Perspectives," *Death Education*, 6:2 (1982): 108-122.

Fulton, Robert; Markusen, Eric; Owen, Greg; and Scheiber, Jane L. Editors, *Death and Dying: Challenge and Change*. Reading, Massachusetts: Addison-Wesley Publishing, 1984.

Gittings, Claire, *Death, Burial, and the Individual in Early Modern England*. London: Croom Helm, 1984.

Litten, Julian, *The English Way of Death (The Common Funeral since 1450)*. London: Robert Hall, 1984.

Meyer-Baer, K., *Music of the Spheres and the Dance of Death*. Princeton, New Jersey: Princeton University Press, 1970.

Puckle, Bertram Saward, *Funeral Customs: their Origins and Development*. London: Singing Tree, 1968.

CONSTRUCTING AIDS POLICY IN THE PUBLIC SCHOOLS

A Multimethod Case Study

**Tiffani Mari Schmitt and
Raymond L. Schmitt**

Tiffani Mari Schmitt received her BA degree from the University of Iowa and her master's degree from the University of Illinois at Champaign-Urbana. She is presently employed as a school social worker for the Woodford County Special Education Association.

Raymond L. Schmitt is Professor of Sociology at Illinois State University in Normal. His most recent research has involved symbolic interactional studies of emotion, having published chapters on emotion and the female body, the Holocaust as "emotional reminder," and the bereavement act as a mesostructure in Studies in Symbolic Interaction: A Research Annual. *His statements on Reference Ground and on Erving Goffman are in* The Encyclopedia of Language and Linguistics (*Elsevier, 1993*).

A male hemophiliac, who had contracted AIDS through a contaminated blood product, enrolled as a senior student in an Illinois public high school. The disruptive reactions that had emerged in similar situations were averted. The 13 processes that were primarily responsible for the successful integration of the student into the school system are delineated, illustrated, documented, and interpreted. Four methods—inside participant observation, analysis of documents, interviews, and survey questionnaires—were used to investigate the situation. The

AUTHORS' NOTE: *Jeff's parents and the superintendent of the Sherrard School District gave permission to have their son and school district, respectively, identified. The private school is not identified because permission was not requested. Our sincere appreciation is expressed to Jeff Proctor and his parents; Dr. Max Redmond, Sherrard School District Superintendent; Harry Hunt, Principal of Sherrard High School; JoAnn Watson, the school's nurse; Donna Wolf, the school's social worker; the Sherrard School Board; and the numerous students, teachers, and parents who participated in this research.*

findings have implications for three areas: (a) the use of multiple methods in researching large social systems, (b) the sociological understanding of "overt ambiguous awareness contexts," and (c) policies for the management of schoolchildren with AIDS. This study appears to be the first to intensively examine the reaction of an educational community to a student with AIDS while the reaction was actually emerging. Other studies have been retrospective.

A major consequence of the appearance of the human immunodeficiency virus (HIV) in America has been the controversies that have developed over schoolchildren with the acquired immunodeficiency syndrome (AIDS). The Ryan White and the Louise and Clifford Ray incidents attracted national attention (Kirp et al. 1989). Ryan White was denied permission to continue attending the local high school in Kokomo, Indiana, during fall 1985. Ryan had been infected with HIV during his treatment for hemophilia. The Rays, who had fought to have their three sons, all hemophiliacs with AIDS, admitted into the grade school of a small farming town in Arcadia, Florida, had their home burned to the ground in 1987. Some communities, however, have reacted sympathetically to students with AIDS (Kirp et al. 1989). One father was so moved by the response to his hemophiliac son's 6-month struggle against AIDS that he wrote a book describing his town's compassion (Hoyle 1988).

The most noteworthy sociological aspect of the controversies over schoolchildren with AIDS is that similar processes seem to occur irrespective of whether communities respond harshly or compassionately to them. An array of emotions, ranging from shock and fear to sympathy and support, appear. Physicians, lawyers, educators, and other experts are consulted. Formal and informal discussions are held. These reactions occur, fundamentally, because communities are caught in the throes of an "overt ambiguous awareness context" (Schmitt 1985). Such contexts usually involve two oppositional, but linked, categories of some identity that promote overt controversy (Schmitt 1985). Regarding students with AIDS, feelings and debates emerge because it is unclear whether such students pose a severe health threat to others.

This study describes the reaction of the students, parents, and teaching and nonteaching staffs within the Sherrard High School Community to Jeff Proctor, the first known student with AIDS to enroll in the school district. The reaction to Jeff, a senior and a hemophiliac, was exceptionally favorable. There was neither violence nor significant interpersonal difficulties. Jeff did well in his studies and graduated. Furthermore, the community took pride in its accomplishment. This favorable reaction provided an opportunity to identify the processes that reduced the fear and ambiguity associated with persons with AIDS. Fortuitously, one of the two investigators was employed at the high school over the entire academic year and was able to observe and to experience the reaction to Jeff as it unfolded. Other studies of schoolchildren with AIDS have been entirely retrospective (see Kirp et al. 1989).

Our findings have significant policy implications for educators who have to make decisions regarding schoolchildren with AIDS. The State Board of Education in Illinois, for example, has found the results instructive in the education of their HIV trainees who are preparing every school district in Illinois for students with AIDS. Policy implications are considered, following the discussion of methodology and the research findings.

THE TRAJECTORY OF A TRIANGULATED RESEARCH ACT

Ethnographers are becoming aware of the need to employ "across-method triangulation," that is, two or more different methods in single studies, because the flaws of one method are often the strengths of another (Denzin 1989, 244). Our experience addresses the *dynamics* of triangulation. Such knowledge is essential if ethnographers are to become proficient in investigating large systems. Depictions of the ethnographer's story should be useful to critics who are concerned with how the experiences of the subject are portrayed (see Denzin 1989, 156–81).

Inception of the Study

The student investigator had just begun her full-time internship at the high school as part of the requirements for a master's degree in social work from the University of Illinois at Champaign-Urbana when Jeff asked to be enrolled. Her supervisor requested her to participate in the activities that Jeff's request precipitated. Since the intern had to complete a research project for a graduate class, she considered focusing on the reaction to Jeff. Her professor approved the study.

The student had consulted her father regarding her proposed research. He had previously engaged in "inside participant observation" (Schmitt 1982, 1990) and encouraged her to begin making covert notes. She was present while community reaction to the first student with AIDS to enroll in the district was unfolding. The student and her father agreed to coinvestigate this unique situation more fully than required by the course instructor.

Hurdles to Triangulation

The virtues of triangulation have been emphasized (Denzin 1989, 234–47), but such studies breed difficulties because of their intensiveness. We learned to interpret emerging problems as "hurdles"—rather than obstacles—that had to be overcome, circumvented, or acknowledged. The process of confronting hurdles ultimately enhanced the quality of the study. Three such hurdles are considered.

One hurdle concerned the ability of the student investigator to make valid observations due to her inexperience as a participant observer. This hurdle was met. First, the student was intelligent, having completed a BA degree from the University of Iowa in 3 years and 1 year of graduate study by age 21. She was able to learn quickly and implement observational techniques. Second, AIDS-related experiences were clearly identifiable and recordable. Third, both researchers jointly interpreted observational data. Fourth, participant observations were compared to findings from other methods. Experience level had no bearing on the validity of documentary data. Both investigators were involved in questionnaire and interview decisions. Fifth, the student could uniquely describe and interpret observations because she observed and experienced them as they unfolded.

Another hurdle involved going public with the research. The student investigator was afraid that the principal would not approve the study once he learned about it. Yet she had developed good rapport with the district superintendent through her visits to the grade school in which his office was located in order to counsel students. The superintendent approved the project, reviewed the questionnaires, and provided $200 to encourage students to return their parents' questionnaires. The superintendent's approval satisfied the protection of the Human Subject's Code at the University of Illinois. The student investigator subsequently obtained permission from the high school principal.

Another hurdle concerned the revelation of findings that some might regard as manipulative. We learned that we felt appreciative of having the opportunity to conduct the research and did not wish to unnecessarily embarrass anyone. However, manipulative-type incidents were reported because they were particularly illustrative of the policy implementation stance of the school board and its advisory task force. Our intent is to provide a sociological analysis of the policy implementation procedures.

FOUR DATA-GATHERING METHODS

Documentary, inside participant observation, questionnaire or survey, and interview methods were employed. These four methods served various functions. The methods provided corroborative data, as others have stressed (Denzin 1989, 244), but they did more than this. The community reaction itself was expressed in different forms requiring different methods of investigation. Because the methods actually reflected emergent interaction, they were differentially important at various points during the process of the community reaction. Finally, the data elicited by an earlier employed method enabled us to more effectively plan for the implementation of a later method.

The documentary data included four long letters to parents by the pastor of the private school that Jeff attended, accounts in four newspapers, copies of state and local infectious disease policies and guidelines, printed and cinematic materials used at the in-service and educational sessions, and letters of acclamation from the media, educators, and community residents. These data provided insight into many events during the process of community reaction. The four letters described Jeff's experience at the private school, an event that occurred before the onset of our study.

The student investigator's observations included participation in two policy formation meetings and attendance at eight educational sessions and two school board meetings. Observations were made covertly and recorded on a data-gathering form. Also, interactions at three educational sessions were audiotaped. Inside participant observations were particularly critical in September and October. Only a few persons were privy to the dynamics of the task force interaction and the observer heard individuals voice fears about the student with AIDS at every educational session. Inside observations continued to be useful throughout the year. The student investigator never introduced an AIDS-related topic into a conversation in order to avoid contaminating interaction. *Insider status allowed the student unobtrusive access to interactions.*

Questionnaires were administered to four different groups exactly 4 months after Jeff started school. The questionnaires enabled us to elicit standardized information regarding the feelings of four groups about the enrollment, AIDS, and the high school training programs at the time Jeff began school and 4 months later. The groups were also asked "cross-check" type questions about each other. Each teacher was personally given a questionnaire and asked to return it anonymously to the observer's mailbox; 35 of 55 teachers (64%) responded. A questionnaire was given to a purposive sample of seven nonteaching staff members (e.g., a counselor). Six persons anonymously returned them. The school nurse also provided information regarding the reactions of nonteaching staff to her in-service sessions. The student investigator administered questionnaires to a stratified random sample of 178 seventh-through twelfth-grade students, all of whom anonymously completed them. These students were then asked to take home an envelope with two questionnaires in it for their parent(s) to anonymously complete. Ten students refused to take envelopes. Students were to return their sealed envelopes to the student investigator in order to receive a one-dollar cafeteria certificate. Of the 168 students 82 (49%) returned them. Since 36 returned envelopes contained two questionnaires, data were obtained from 118 parents.

Both investigators jointly interviewed the high school principal, school nurse, school social worker, and one of Jeff's teachers. Jeff's other teachers were given and returned questionnaires. His health teacher was interviewed because AIDS was covered in her class and hers was one of the first classes that Jeff took at Sherrard. The student investigator was not present when the superintendent, Jeff, and his parents were interviewed. The 1- to 2-hour interviews were conducted during the last 2 weeks in May because we wanted the reaction of these central participants to the entire year's events. Certain specific information was requested from each participant to fill in certain "gaps," but interviews were nonstandardized (Denzin 1989, 106). Respondents were asked to "tell us how things went this year." This strategy was very effective. Each respondent had a different "story" to tell and provided information that could not have been totally anticipated.

REACTION TO THE STUDENT WITH AIDS: A NATURAL HISTORY

Jeff's passage through the high school entailed six critical junctures (see Glaser and Strauss 1971). These junctures must be described before the processes that mediated against fear and ambiguity can be understood.

Biography Before Enrollment Request at Public High School

Jeff was 17 years old when he asked to be enrolled at Sherrard in late August 1988. The high school accommodated 845 students in the seventh through twelfth grades, most of whom were from working-class families. Although the high school is located in the Quad-City area, encompassing Bettendorf and Davenport, Iowa, and Moline and Rock Island, Illinois, its enrollment largely comes from four "feeder" elementary schools located in small, rural communities of less than 1,000 individuals.

Jeff lived in the same house in one of these communities for his entire life and attended a private religious school in the immediate area since kindergarten. However, after learning that Jeff had acquired AIDS through a contaminated blood product, he was not allowed to attend the private school during 1987/1988 for fear of a significant decrease in enrollment. Jeff's mother, who taught kindergarten at the private school, and his four siblings were also asked to leave the school. Jeff's mother instructed her five children at home during 1987/1988 (Walker-Baley 1988a). The following academic year, Jeff's parents enrolled four children in another private religious school in Davenport, Iowa. When asked why he didn't enroll Jeff in that school, Jeff's father said, " 'They didn't offer to have Jeff attend, and we didn't push' " (Walker-Baley 1988a). Consequently, Jeff enrolled at the public high school.

Enrollment Request and Consequent Preparation for Entry

Shortly after Jeff asked to be enrolled at the high school, the district superintendent negotiated an agreement with his parents that would provide the Sherrard School Board time to prepare the community for their first encounter with a student with AIDS. Jeff would begin school the first week in October, 6 weeks after the other students. The school board quickly completed an ongoing communicable and chronic infectious disease policy for the Sherrard Community Unit School District No. 200 and appointed the Communicable and Chronic Infectious Disease Task Force. The task force would serve in an advisory capacity to the school board and be responsible for preparing the community to successfully integrate Jeff into the school system. The task force consisted of the district superintendent, the high school's principal, nurse, and social worker, a physician with expertise in communicable diseases, and a public health educator.

The physician concluded that Jeff was not an undue health risk to others. The task force obtained the physician's conclusion in writing and tape recorded it as a legal precaution. Subsequently, the task force decided that its role was to implement the state educational policy that indicated a student with AIDS was to be admitted if the student did not pose an undue health threat to others (Naumer, Sanders, and Turnock 1986, 3–6). Jeff, for instance, was not an "external bleeder" and was too mature to deliberately bite anyone. The task force further decided that it would "take early positive control" by openly acknowledging that a student with AIDS would be attending the high school, rather than allowing a less favorable definition of the situation to emerge through rumor, secrecy, or deceit. The task force decided that by being completely open about Jeff, they could more effectively address any questions or fears that individuals had about persons with AIDS through a complex of educational activities.

The task force spent considerable time discussing who should educate the community about AIDS and delineating the specific targets, content, and scheduling of the proposed educational programs. The task force decided to work with health agencies that had effectively advised the high school regarding health problems in the past,

including the University of Iowa, the Rock Island County Council on Addictions, and the Rock Island County Public Health Department. The school nurse would provide in-service training. All staff members would be given gloves to reduce fears. Teachers would conduct follow-up sessions with those students taking health classes.

Everyone within the high school community was to be made aware of the facts, including students in the seventh through twelfth grades and their parents, and teaching and nonteaching staffs at the high school. The content of the training would focus on facts about AIDS and hemophilia. Educational materials, including a paperback book on AIDS, would be made available to everyone. Since it was felt that students would be more open-minded than parents, they would be seen first so that parents would obtain a positive image from their children before they attended an evening meeting. Questions from the audience at the evening meeting would be written on small cards so that the moderator could delete, control the order of, and rephrase them. The possibility of selectively eliciting reactions of parents favorable to the board's AIDS policy was suggested.

The task force decided the certain evaluative dimensions of the situation should be made salient. First, they would emphasize that "we are all in the same boat." The task force felt that the school nurse would be an effective spokesperson because she would be the individual most intimately exposed to Jeff over the school year, being responsible for his medical injections. They would underscore the fact that two of the high school principal's children were enrolled, and would remain, as students in the high school. Second, they would stress that the student with AIDS had contracted AIDS through a contaminated blood product rather than through "deviant activity." Third, although the law prevented the school from identifying Jeff by name, they decided to emphasize that the student with AIDS was an older mature person who was perfectly capable of managing his or her hemophiliac condition. Fourth, they would depict Jeff's enrollment as "an opportunity for growth" because of its problematic character. Fifth, they would counter the anticipated concern that Jeff's enrollment would encourage students with AIDS to move into the district by noting that Sherrard could bring legal action against a school district that discriminated against a student with AIDS.

Experts and Conferences

An in-service session was held for the teaching staff the afternoon of September 28. Students, nonteaching staffs, and parents were seen at various times the following day. Conferences with students were held for one hour with each grade level. Parents were alerted through the school paper, various local papers, and a large pink postcard. The meetings were characterized by numerous questions and discussion. Fears concerning contracting AIDS through casual contact and "blood spills" were expressed at every meeting.

An estimated 400 to 500 persons attended the evening meeting for parents. There were numerous questions during the question-and-answer period following the presentations. One parent was more openly emotional than the others, citing evidence from Masters, Johnson, and Kolodny (1988) regarding the transmission of HIV through casual contact that she felt contradicted the null position of the guest speakers. A typical question was, "But how can you be certain that a student won't contract AIDS through casual contact?"

Formal Approval and Identification of Student

The Sherrard school board voted on October 5 to allow the student with AIDS to attend the high school. This action came after the task force reported that he "was no risk to other students, if proper procedures for handling situations were followed" (Walker-Baley 1988b, A1). The school board had no choice but to reach this decision or they could be sued by Jeff's parents. The following day, the Proctors thanked the school board and voluntarily identified their son at a press conference, "hoping that doing it that way would help people get over being afraid" (Walker-Baley 1988b, A2).

Media Reaction During Initial Week of School

Jeff's first few days at school attracted considerable attention from the local media. Jeff did not attend school on October 6, as scheduled, in order to avoid the media. The three local television stations and a number of local newspapers and radio stations had representatives on the school grounds. The principal was particularly adamant in his interview with us regarding how dysfunctional it was to have the media on the grounds. The *Rock Island Argus* (Pearson and Berenger 1988, A1) also reported that "students thought the presence of the media was 'unfair to all of them,' said high school principal Harry Hunt. Media representatives were asked to leave." There was some resentment regarding the emphasis given to the few angry parents at the parents' informational meeting (see Schorpp 1988a), but the task force felt that the media was generally helpful. The *Rock Island Argus*, for example, ran a piece indicating that an AIDS suit filed against the Florida school that barred the three Ray brothers had cost that school $1.2 million (Associated Press 1988) alongside their report of the evening educational meeting for parents. The task force felt that the Ray news release illustrated what could happen to their school if they refused to enroll a student with AIDS without sufficient grounds. A local health agency had kept the media informed about HIV for more than a year prior to Jeff's enrollment.

Favorable Interaction and Accolades

Jeff's presence in the school the remainder of the year was quite "uneventful." The task force carefully mon-

itored the situation for possible problems, but none appeared. There were no "blood spills" or uncivil incidents. Members of the task force agreed that fear and ambiguity subsided within 2 to 4 weeks after Jeff began classes. Indeed, the school received accolades from the media, health, and educational units for successfully integrating Jeff into the school. These accolades were received in October after Jeff was admitted and again at the end of the school year. As a *Quad City Times* editorial noted:

> The people in the Sherrard, Ill., school district stand tall today. They have handled a sensitive, emotional, scary subject in a thoughtful, rational and responsible way.
>
> AIDS victim Jeff Proctor is now attending Sherrard High School after some upfront, frank public discussion that has reassured most people that he poses very little risk to others.
>
> In contrast to some communities elsewhere in the country—where protests against school attendance by AIDS victims have gotten ugly—Sherrard could serve as a model on how to handle such a situation. (Editorial 1988)

AWARENESS AND FEAR

Although everyone did not know Jeff's identity, every parent, student, teacher, and nonteaching staff person who completed a questionnaire, with the exception of one seventh grader, knew that a student with AIDS had enrolled in the high school. Moreover, 37%, 65%, and 67% of teachers, students, and nonteaching staff, respectively, stated that they had some type of contact with Jeff, ranging from passing him in the hall to being with him in a class.

Initial fears about the student were pervasive in all data forms. The *Quad-City Times* reported that school board members were fearful (Schorpp 1988b). Numerous concerns about the transmission of AIDS were observed at every training session. Regarding interviews, the health teacher confided that "the first time I checked Jeff's paper, I wondered if I would get AIDS." The principal related that two teachers who were going to have Jeff in class were particularly "uptight." He also estimated that 25% of all teachers were initially very concerned, that 50% took a "wait and see" attitude, while 25% were perfectly comfortable with the situation. The school nurse said that there were fears expressed in all of the in-service sessions that she conducted, particularly among the kitchen and custodial staffs.

Persons were asked early in the questionnaire if they had any fears when they first heard about the school's decision to enroll a student with AIDS. Percentages of students, parents, and teachers responding yes were similar, ranging from 44% to 49% (see Table 1). Respondents were asked to describe their initial fears, which included the possibility of acquiring AIDS specifically through casual contact, the student being hurt by negative reaction, accidents to Jeff involving blood, the uncertainty of scientific knowledge, and the risk that Jeff would die while in school.

TABLE 1: Initial and Residual Fears Among Four Groups Regarding Enrollment of a Student With AIDS (in frequencies and percentages)

Group	Had Initial Fears f (N)	%	Had Residual Fears F (N)	%
Students	79 (178)	44	18 (178)	10
Parents	54 (116*)	47	25 (117)	21
Teachers	17 (35)	49	4 (35)	11
Nonteaching staff	4 (6)	67	1 (6)	17

*N does not equal 118 due to no response.

Respondents were asked later in the questionnaire: "Thinking back, did you initially have any fears regarding your own health upon hearing that a student with AIDS would enroll at Sherrard High School?" Percentages of teachers, nonteaching staff, and students answering yes were very similar, ranging from 31% to 37% (Table 2). Only 10% of the parents responded yes. Parents may have been less fearful because they would not be in contact with Jeff at the high school.

There was ample evidence the fears of many persons subsided. Conversely, there were only three instances in which a person became more fearful or less approving of Jeff's enrollment. The school nurse acknowledged in her remarks to the Illinois Association of School Boards that Jeff had to remind her to wear her gloves when administering his injections. She felt her fear had subsided. Jeff's mother reported that Jeff was elated at the end of the year when his peers asked him before the school play, "Why do you have your own personal makeup?" "They forgot I had AIDS!" Jeff exclaimed to his mother. The health teacher had no fear the second time she graded Jeff's paper. The cooks eventually stopped saying that they were going to use bleach in the dishwater.

The questionnaire data unequivocally confirmed a reduction in the fears of many persons. Information was obtained regarding various "residual fears" that individuals had when they completed their questionnaires 4 months after Jeff had started classes:

1. There were substantial reductions in the percentages of students, parents, teachers, and nonteaching staff who indicated that they had any type of fear about Jeff's enrollment (Table 1).

2. There were substantial reductions in the percentages of, particularly, teachers, nonteaching staff, and students, who indicated they were concerned about their own health due to the enrollment (Table 2).

3. Approximately 36% of 152 codable open-ended answers indicated that students felt their parents were initially fearful; only 15% of 149 codable answers indicated that students felt their parents had these fears 4 months later,

4. Responses to two forced-choice questions regarding feelings about the board's decision to admit the student at the beginning of the year and feelings at the time the questionnaire was completed were compared. Among those answering the questionnaire, 77 persons initially selected the "very favorable" answer; 160 persons selected "very favorable" 4 months later.

REDUCING FEAR AND AMBIGUITY

Thirteen processes facilitated the reduction of the ambiguity and fear generated by Jeff's enrollment. These were "moving" processes that integrated with one another in complex and emergent ways (see Blumer 1956). Jeff entered, experienced, and helped shape a context that was a totality rather than a series of discrete variables.

Changing Climate

The American public is becoming more informed about how HIV is transmitted. The Ryan White case began in 1985. A more informed public certainly existed by fall 1987 because of the dissemination of new scientific evidence (Kirp et al. 1989, 280). Some persons studied were aware that AIDS is not acquired through casual contact. AIDS was discussed in health classes. Some teachers, students, parents, and nonteaching staff even volunteered in their open-ended questionnaire responses that they were not concerned because they were informed about AIDS:

> Most people have seen or heard enough from TV or newspapers to know you don't get AIDS by just touching someone with it. (Parent)
>
> AIDS is something that isn't that new anymore so when this happened we had already seen cases of where students went to school with AIDS and we saw the problems because people weren't educated. Now I think we are. (Senior student)

However, all four data forms (Tables 1 and 2) indicated that some fear of AIDS remained.

TABLE 2: Initial and Residual Fears Among Four Groups Regarding One's Own Health Due to Enrollment of a Student With AIDS (in frequencies and percentages)

Group	Had Initial Fears f (N)	%	Had Residual Fears F (N)	%
Parents	12 (117*)	10	6 (117*)	5
Teachers	11 (35)	31	4 (35)	11
Nonteaching staff	2 (6)	33	0 (6)	0
Students	66 (178)	37	17 (178)	10

*N does not equal 118 due to no response.

Law as Coercion

Law influences acceptance of schoolchildren with AIDS. The pastor of the private school that Jeff left wrote:

We must openly acknowledge the legal ramifications.
The courts have ruled that the public schools must take students who have the AIDS disease. This ruling places the public schools in a no-choice position and thus eliminates the danger of lawsuits. Private schools are in the opposite position. We do have a choice and that choice places us in danger of future lawsuits.

Sherrard, a public school, was mandated to accept Jeff. The superintendent often said, "It's not a question of whether we admit Jeff, but *when.*"

Equal Right to Education

Illinois state law had an informal counterpart in the value system of the Sherrard community. A significant number of persons, including 30 parents, 8 teachers, 2 nonteaching staff members, and 57 students volunteered the following type of statement in their open-ended questionnaire responses:

Again, this student should be allowed the same opportunity of education as any other child. As long as the AIDS student practices good hygiene, I see no problem. (Parent)

Innocent Victim

It was abundantly clear in every data form that many persons, including Jeff's parents, felt acceptance would have been much more difficult if Jeff had not acquired HIV through a contaminated blood product. A female senior wrote:

And I think it helped, though this may sound awful, and I don't feel this way, when everyone knew Jeff contracted it from hemophilia and not from being gay or sexually active or because of I.V. drugs.

Indeed, as planned, the superintendent told parents at their evening meeting: "This child is a victim. He received AIDS from a blood transfusion, not from sexual contact or deviate behavior" (Berenger 1988, A2).

Responsible Self-Management

The emphasis at the educational sessions on the student's maturity was effective. Positive remarks describing the student as older, responsible, and an "internal bleeder" were heard among parents and students at the sessions, mentioned in interviews, and volunteered on questionnaires. Some persons worried about accidents involving blood, but there was never any concern expressed about "irresponsible actions," such as deliberate biting (see Kirp et al. 1989, 198–227).

Familiarity

The fact that some individuals were friends of Jeff or his family and that Jeff was a long-time district resident,

even though he attended a private school, enhanced acceptance. A teacher wrote, "Some of the students already knew him and socialized with him regularly. They didn't know what the fuss was all about." The principal emphasized that Jeff's public identification was extremely helpful. Individuals, for example, could feel completely confident about Jeff's maturity. The task force did not have to worry as much about the legal implications of Jeff standing out" as the student with AIDS when he began classes late.

Prompt Planning

Integration was facilitated by the task force's prompt and effective planning and implementation. One of the external experts from the University of Iowa, who had considerable experience with initial AIDS cases in school districts, drew this conclusion, as did numerous parents, students, and teaching and nonteaching staff members. One parent wrote:

The school handled it in a very good way. First by informing the parents and students that it was going to happen, then by educating everyone about the disease, then by allowing the student to enroll after everyone had a chance to become familiar with the facts about the disease and the student and his family.

Some felt, however, that an AIDS policy should have been "in place" before the enrollment. Jeff's parents were dissatisfied that a tutor had not been provided for Jeff when he had to miss school.

Educational Strategies

At least 93% of students, parents, teachers, and nonteaching staff felt that the educational strategies employed to inform the community about AIDS were "effective" or "very effective." Persons with initial fears also often volunteered the following type of statement when asked, "Do you still have the above fears?"

No, the AIDS assembly with experts on AIDS took care of all my fears. It was just the fact that I didn't have previous knowledge of the things I had fears about. (Eleventh-grade student)

It is noteworthy that the respondents themselves concluded that the educational strategies had helped to alleviate their fears.

Respondents were also asked which educational procedures were the most effective. A content analysis revealed that most open-ended responses were captured under eight appealing features of the strategies. These features are explained here and illustrated in Table 3. The participation observations also helped to illuminate these features. The first feature, availability of experts, indicates that the speakers were specialists regarding AIDS or hemophilia. The school was extremely fortunate to be located in the Quad-City area where it could draw on credible authorities from the University of Iowa and Rock

TABLE 3: Illustrations of Eight Most Appealing Features of Educational Strategies Regarding AIDS

Appealing Feature of Educational Strategy	Illustrations From Open-Ended Questionnaire Responses
Availability of experts	"Outside authorities as speakers" (Teacher)
Concreteness	"The written booklets and materials made available" (Parent)
Factuality	"Explaining the facts both medically and the state laws" (Parent)
Openness	"That Dr. Redmond and the school board put out all the information and didn't hide anything" (Parent)
Opportunity for questions and answers	"There was a seminar about AIDS and a question-answer period. If anyone was unsure, they could ask their question and have it answered" (Student)
Postpresentation feedback	"Educational seminars followed by interaction with knowledgeable peers" (Parent)
	"I think it was the teachers *talking* to the kids about it to us, not lecturing, that way we knew teachers have fears too" (Student)
	"Kids coming home and telling what was told to them" (Parent)
Style of presentation	"In health our guest speaker Mike was the best" (Student)
	"The administration was very open and informative. Dr. Redmond is an extremely persuasive speaker. The medical panel also gave persuasive information." (Staff)
	"The large, bright pink postcard that announced the information meeting really got my attention" (Parent)
Universality	"Educating everyone—students, teachers, support staff, parents, and community" (Staff)

Island. The experts included two nurses, a social worker and AIDS coordinator in the Pediatrics Department at the University of Iowa Hospitals and Clinics, a public health educator, and an AIDS prevention coordinator from the Rock Island County Council on Addictions.

The second feature, concreteness, refers to informational items that could be transferred from place to place. Individuals did not have to rely on their notes or memories if they wanted to look something up about AIDS. A table with a variety of free informational items on AIDS was set up for parents at their evening meeting. They would stop at this table and inspect the items. Parents were observed discussing their contents at the break during the meeting. Some parents said that they were happy to have these items because they could take them home and look at them.

The third feature, factuality, indicates that the speakers emphasized factual aspects of AIDS and hemophilia by providing current local and national statistics and covering various topics: What is AIDS? What is HIV? How do you get the virus? Speakers were careful not to raise any value-related topics (e.g., using condoms) because the task force wanted to avoid generating any unnecessary controversy. The fact that the student with AIDS had internal bleeds was stressed.

Openness, the fourth feature, refers to a readiness of the speakers to address all aspects of AIDS and hemophilia in a comprehensive and objective manner. Some speakers did address issues that encompassed attitudes and values about persons with AIDS (e.g., How do you feel about a person with AIDS in your school? What role will you play?).

The fifth feature, opportunity for questions and answers, refers to the question-and-answer periods that were a part of every session. The participant observer concluded that the very process of forming, asking, and discussing a question was therapeutic for some. Postpresentation feedback, the sixth feature, refers to discussions that took place after a presentation, including question-and-answer periods, had ended. Students found it useful, for example, to talk to their homeroom teachers after a presentation. Parents also learned from their children.

Style of presentation, the seventh feature, indicates the capacity of the training strategy to generate and maintain appeal. Speakers tried to be interesting, organized, and use different techniques (e.g., slides were shown on hemophilia). The eighth feature, universality, indicates that the educational strategies were made available to everyone. This feature was widely recognized and positively interpreted.

Lack of Organized Opposition

There was no evidence of organized opposition in the four data sets. Although the task force discussed the possibility of a conservative organization from the Quad-

Cities raising objections about Jeff's enrollment, this never occurred. Also, while several families voiced opposition at the evening session for parents, they never joined in a united front. The presence and absence of organized opposition has been found to be important in contexts where students with AIDS have been rejected and accepted, respectively (Kirp et al. 1989, 83).

Auspicious Backlash

Acceptance was enhanced by a backlash toward the local media, the school Jeff left, and the Ryan White and similar incidents. The most frequently appearing backlash in the data was toward the local media for invading the school grounds. Others, however, pointed to the private school. The president of the Sherrard School Board told us: "I feel it helped us that the other school didn't take him." Eight persons volunteered in the open-end responses that Jeff should be treated better than had Ryan White and other students with AIDS.

Anticipated Interaction

Persons who did not anticipate interacting with Jeff were the least fearful. The principal, for example, made this observation about the teachers, and several teachers and students mentioned it in their open-ended responses. Jeff's health teacher was not initially worried because Jeff was not assigned to her class. She became much more concerned when she found out that a mistake had been made. A student wrote that he was not worried "because he wasn't going to be in my classes or my grade."

Favorable Interaction

Individuals who interacted with Jeff tended to interpret the interaction favorably and felt this favorable interaction reduced their fears. Three facets of the interaction accounted for the change: routinism, personalism, and emotional understanding. First, routinism occurred when persons forgot that Jeff had AIDS because they had become accustomed to him. Persons said, "We got used to him." Jeff's presence eventually lodged into routine social acts (see Denzin 1969). Routinism was greatly facilitated by the absence of negative incidents (e.g., a major external bleed) during the school year.

Second, personalism entails the realization that a person with AIDS is similar in most respects to individuals who do not have AIDS. Personalism erodes stereotypes and may ultimately include the more fundamental realization that the individual with AIDS is a person rather than a "disease entity." Jeff's health teacher and the school nurse achieved this realization, as did the following senior student:

I really don't think of him as the guy with AIDS, unlike other people. He's just a person like everyone else except

he's going to die. And that's the only thing that comes up sometimes in our conversations with him.

Third, emotional understanding encompasses persons who share authentic feelings about a social object (Denzin 1989, 160). A teacher wrote, "I have met and talked with Jeff. Now that I know him I can understand his situation."

Favorable Self/Community Image

Some persons did not want the high school or themselves to look bad. This desire for a positive image facilitated acceptance. The superintendent said, "We don't want to be another Kokomo." The backlash, discussed earlier, helped foster a sense of pride and motivation. A senior student wrote, "It made me feel proud that our school was opening up to him rather than pushing him away."

SOCIOLOGICAL AND POLICY IMPLICATIONS

This investigation (a) generated insights into the use of multiple methods in the study of large social systems, (b) elaborated the dynamics involved in the resolution of an overt ambiguous awareness context regarding the dangerousness of a student with AIDS, and (c) furnished one baseline regarding how private and public schools can manage students infected with HIV in the future.

Multiple methods provided the anticipated corroborative framework. We learned, however, that some methods were "natural indicators" of the various forms in which community reaction was expressed. Such data had to be obtained because of their de facto significance. Some methods proved more important at certain junctures than others because of the path community reaction had taken. Data acquired from an earlier method also proved useful in planning for the implementation of a later method. The inside participant observation method was particularly useful because the student investigator had a natural and ready access to situations, could observe, experience, and interpret interactions as they emerged, and was able to interpret later unfolding interactions within the context of her previous experiences. We learned that intensive methodologies themselves generate problems (Becker 1958), but that it was the very act of confronting these "hurdles" that matured the triangulated research act.

The overt ambiguous awareness context was resolved through social and emergent processes. Organizations, groups, and the media interacted and interpreted ambiguity. The social structure did not provide "ready-made" solutions. However, the 13 fear-reducing processes that were identified were clearly anchored within the institutionalized setting in which ambiguity and fear were debated. Perhaps only two processes, prompt planning and the decision to implement an educational campaign, were truly under the control of the task force. The task force interpreted but had not originated, for example, the manner in which Jeff contracted AIDS, Jeff's maturity, the excellent array of local medical resources, the improving climate regarding the communicability of HIV, and state directives concerning schoolchildren with AIDS. Luck, too, colored the fear-reducing processes. No major negative incidents occurred and the backlash helped solidify students behind Jeff.

In interpreting the fear-reducing processes at Sherrard, the nearby religious school that Jeff left constitutes a natural and meaningful comparison group, particularly regarding the impact of AIDS legislation. It is important to note that familiarity did not prevent Jeff's enrollment from being terminated, but, as previously discussed, the absence of legal mandate was critical as economic concerns surfaced! There is further evidence of the significance of the 13 fear-reducing processes identified here in other communities that have both accepted and rejected schoolchildren with AIDS (see Kirp et al. 1989). Also, regarding the impact of the training programs in this study, many respondents, themselves, felt that the educational training sessions had changed their feelings about AIDS.

Policy regarding the treatment of schoolchildren with AIDS has changed rapidly with the accumulation of evidence that AIDS is not transmitted through casual, everyday contact (Fraser 1989, 5), the decreased concern regarding transmission of HIV through biting behaviors and bodily functions (p. 3), and the September 1988 opinion of the U.S. Department of Justice that there is grounds for a lawsuit—under Section 504 of the Rehabilitation Act of 1973—if the education program of a student is changed simply because that person is infected with HIV (pp. 24–25). The National Association of State Boards of Education (NASBE) now recommends that school districts do not proceed precisely in the manner that the Sherrard School Board did. Although Sherrard did attempt to keep decision-making activities within a small group of individuals, as now recommended by the NASBE, educational programs regarding transmission of the HIV should take place "*before* there is an infected student or employee at school" (Fraser 1989, p. 17; italics added) and HIV infection "is not, in itself, a reason to remove a student or staff member from school" (p. 10). The fact that Sherrard did not have an AIDS policy in place prompted them to temporarily remove Jeff from the school. Although this removal did, in fact, help to integrate Jeff into the high school community, it would not have been necessitated if an AIDS policy had been in place and the community had been educated about the HIV.

The NASBE, however, recommends that educators develop their own "homegrown policy with a diverse group of community members and effectively educate the community about AIDS, HIV infection, and the rationale for the policy (Fraser 1989, pp. 3, 7). The present study illustrates the importance of establishing educational programs that extend beyond health classes. Moreover, if situations occur in which news of a student with AIDS becomes public, schools may decide to pursue a path similar to that taken by Sherrard. "Facts" about HIV are always interpreted politically (see Nelkin and Hilgartner 1986). Some policymakers, however, may be concerned that the term "innocent victim" implies that some persons with AIDS are less than "innocent." Policymakers must weigh the moralistic implications of using terms like "innocent victim" against the practical use of these terms for accomplishing effective student integration.

There is the further possibility that some parents may still decide, as did Jeff's, to identify their child in order to alleviate fear in the community, even though this open identification may cause the family some personal discomfort. The public identification of Jeff did facilitate positive feelings regarding the origin of the disease, self-management, familiarity, planning, backlash, anticipated interaction, and favorability of interaction. The integration that occurred was also beneficial for Jeff in many ways. For example, he was given considerable personal support throughout his final year. Unfortunately, the NASBE's current recommendations do not encourage people to benefit from favorable interaction with a person with AIDS through personalization, routinization, and emotional understanding. Furthermore, persons with AIDS will not experience full equality until they are able to interact openly in society.

REFERENCES

Associated Press. 1988. AIDS suit costs Florida school $1.1 million. *Rock Island Argus*, 30 September, A1.

Becker, H. S. 1958. Problems of inference and proof in participant observation. *American Sociological Review* 23:652–59.

Berenger, P. 1988. AIDS hearing draws only one objector. *Rock Island Argus*. 30 September. A1, A2.

Blumer, H. 1956. Sociological analysis and the variable. *American Sociological Review* 21:683–90.

Denzin, N. K. 1969. Symbolic interactionism and ethnomethodology: A proposed synthesis. *American Sociological Review* 34:922–34.

———. 1989. *The research act*. Englewood Cliffs, NJ: Prentice-Hall.

Editorial. 1988. Sherrard should be proud. *Quad-City Times*, 10 October, 8.

Fraser, K. 1989. *Someone at school has AIDS: A guide to developing policies for students and school staff members who are infected with HIV*. Alexandria, VA: National Association of State Boards of Education.

Glaser, B., and A. Strauss. 1971. *Status passage*. Chicago: Aldine.

Hoyle, J. 1988. *Mark*. South Bend, IN: Langford.

Kirp, D. L., with S. Epstein, M. S. Franks, J. Simon, D. Conaway, and J. Lewis. 1989. *Learning by heart: AIDS and schoolchildren in America's communities*. New Brunswick, NJ: Rutgers University Press.

Masters, W. H., V. E. Johnson, and A. C. Kolodny. 1988. *Crisis: Heterosexual behavior in the age of AIDS*. New York: Grove.

Naumer, W. W., Jr., T. Sanders, and B. J. Turnock. 1986. *Management of chronic infectious diseases in school children.* Springfield, IL: Illinois State Board of Education and Illinois Department of Public Health.

Nelkin, D., and S. Hilgartner. 1986. Disputed dimensions of risk: A public school controversy over AIDS. *Milbank Quarterly* 64:118–42.

Pearson, R., and P. Berenger. 1988. Students ready with welcome. *Rock Island Argus,* 6 October, A1, A2.

Schmitt, R. L. 1982. Grounded directives for research of the interracial act: The white syndrome as transformation. In *Studies in symbolic interaction,* edited by N. K. Denzin, 191–216. Greenwich, CT: JAI.

_____. 1985. Negative and positive keying in natural contexts: Preserving the transformation concept from death through conflation. *Sociological Inquiry* 55:383–401.

_____. 1990. The bereavement act as mesostructure: An ordinary person dies. In *Studies in symbolic interaction,* edited by N. K. Denzin. Greenwich, CT: JAI.

Schorpp, D. 1988a. AIDS fear prompts parents to give ultimatum. *Quad-City Times,* 30 September, 3.

_____. 1988b. Sherrard policy allows AIDS patients. *Quad-City Times,* 6 October, 13.

Walker, Baley, E. 1988a. Jeff outsmarted media on first day of school: But AIDS is constant companion. *Rock Island Sunday Argus.* 9 October, B1.

_____. 1988b. Sherrard High open to student with AIDS. *Rock Island Argus,* 8 October, A1, A2.

CURRENT MODELS OF DEATH, DYING, AND BEREAVEMENT

Charles A. Corr, PhD, and Kenneth J. Doka, PhD

From the School of Humanities, Southern Illinois University at Edwardsville, Edwardsville, Illinois (CAC); and Graduate Geronotology Program, College of New Rochelle, New Rochelle, New York (KJD)

Theoretic models in the field of death, dying, and bereavement have experienced a significant shift in character in recent years. *Stage-* and *phase-based models* have come under increasing criticism because they seem to lend themselves too easily and in too many applications to stereotyping of the very individuals whose experiences they should help to explicate. How often have we heard statements such as: "Oh, he's just in denial"; or "She can't get to the final stage of acceptance." Of course, there is some truth in characterizations of this sort; otherwise, they would have been without any justification. But there is also a fiendishness in this sort of labeling as Rosenthal[23] pointed out: "Being invisible I invite only generalizations." Accordingly, Attig[2] argued for the importance of conceiving grieving (in bereavement, but also in dying) not merely as a passive victimization which must be endured, gotten through, resolved, or completed, but as an active process whereby a person can regain some measure of control and meaning in living with loss.

In an effort to avoid the generalizations that obscure the unique individuality of persons who are coping with dying or bereavement, a number of contemporary writers have turned to *task-based models*. Such models emphasize the vital potential of task work and the specificity of individual tasks that are part of the larger coping efforts associated with dying and bereavement. This article is a review of recent task-based models in the field of death, dying, and bereavement. One of its premises is that such models are especially appropriate for nurses in general and for critical care nurses in particular. Task-based models have a natural affinity for a profession that has adopted as one of its fundamental paradigms—the nursing process—an approach that encourages helpers to develop goals and objectives not apart from but *together with* the individual client. And task-based models are well suited to critical care settings which emphasize present-tense concerns and which may not often have the luxury of long-term relationships.

FINAL GIFTS FROM DYING PERSONS

In 1992, two experienced hospice nurse-researchers published *Final Gifts: Understanding the Special Awareness, Needs, and Communications of the Dying*.[3] In this book, the authors argued on behalf of the thesis that communications from dying persons may contain significant messages about the experiences which those persons are undergoing. Quite frequently, such communications are dismissed as empty or enigmatic expressions of confusion. On the contrary, Callanan and Kelley[3] argued that these communications may actually reflect: (1) *special awareness of the imminence of death* and efforts to describe what dying is like as it is being experienced by the individual; and (2) *expressions of final requests* concerning that which is needed before the individual can experience a peaceful death.

Callanan and Kelley[3] described their research as a study of "nearing death awareness." Their book was given special recognition by the editors of the *American Journal of Nursing* in the form of a special Editor's Award conferred separately from that journal's familiar Book-of-the-Year awards.[1] According to the journal's editors, this book deserved this recognition for: (1) the encouragement that it

From *Critical Care Nursing Clinics of North America*, Vol. 6, No. 3, September 1994, pp. 545-552. © 1994 by W. B. Saunders. Reprinted by permission.

offered to caregivers to pay attention to the dying; and (2) the guidance that it provided to family members, friends, and others in responding to such communications.

In its most basic terms, Callanan and Kelley's research represents a systematic study of the efforts of dying persons to articulate and communicate their experiences and their needs. Callanan and Kelley have directed our attention to a special set of communicative tasks undertaken by dying persons. In this article, we suggest the value of pursuing that type of task-based perspective by attending to a series of task-based theoretic models that are intended to throw light on the experiences of individuals who are coping with dying or with bereavement.

WORDEN'S TASKS IN MOURNING

The task-based model that is best known in the literature on death, dying, and bereavement is an attempt to describe *four tasks that are involved in the processes of mourning*. According to Worden[30] the four tasks of mourning are:

Task I: To accept the reality of the loss.
Task II: To experience the pain of the grief.
Task III: To adjust to an environment in which the deceased is missing.
Task IV: To withdraw emotional energy from the deceased and to reinvest it in another relationship.

These four are tasks of what Worden called *uncomplicated mourning*. They are understood to be components of the healthy processes of coping with loss. Such processes have been termed *grief work* and have been said to involve working with one's loss and grief in order to integrate them into ongoing living. In the language of Scripture, tasks of this sort are part of the overall processes of mourning which are characterized as a blessing and which are described as essential in order for the bereaved to find comfort.

Worden revised the wording of the second and fourth of his tasks in mourning.[31] He reformulated these two tasks in the following way:

Task II: To work through to the pain of grief.
Task IV: To emotionally relocate the deceased and move on with life.

The reformulation of Task II was apparently intended as an appreciation of the difficulties involved in experiencing the pain of grief. That is, in light of personal and social obstacles, it may be too naive to speak so easily of simply "experiencing" the pain of grief. In fact, bereaved persons often find themselves struggling to work through to such pain in ways that respect the degree, nature, and timing of the pain that each individual is able to experience.

The reformulation of Task IV was prompted by criticism that the language of "withdrawing emotional energy" and "reinvesting it" elsewhere—classic psychoanalytic vocabulary for detachment/decathexis and reattachment/recathexis—appeared to be too facile and too mechanical. Many bereaved persons objected that the original formulation of Task IV seemed to require them to "give up," "forget," or "betray" the deceased loved one, just as it seemed to require them to enter into new relationships at a time when they were unsure of themselves or unwilling to do so. Against these undesirable interpretations of Task IV, in the second edition of his book Worden introduced quotations such as the following to support his reformulation of this dimension of a bereaved person's grief work:

. . . . a mourner never altogether forgets the dead person who was so highly valued in life and never totally withdraws his investment in his representation. We can never purge those who have been close to us from our own history except by psychic acts damaging to our own identity.[27]

What Worden seems to be striving to articulate in the original formulation and subsequent reformation of Task IV is two things. First, there is the need which faces the bereaved person to restructure his or her relationship with the deceased in ways that respect the harsh fact that death renders the deceased no longer available to the living as that person had been available in the past. This task imposes itself despite the equally important fact that the deceased still remains available to the living in ways such as those involved in a legacy of memories from the relationship. Second, healthy mourning does not shut down life; rather, it strives to enable ongoing life to be productive and rewarding despite the enduring pain of loss and grief. The important point is that this ongoing living may be carried out in many different ways by different individuals or at different times. And all of these modes of ongoing living may be equally healthy. No single prescription governs the life of persons after the death of a loved one, any more than a single prescription governed that individual's life before the death.

MODIFICATIONS OF WORDEN'S TASKS OF MOURNING

Since the publication of Worden's description of these tasks of mourning, other authors have suggested two different ways of modifying his contributions. One author[12] has suggested the value of adding a *fifth task*.

> Task V: To rebuild faith and philosophical systems challenged by loss.

This proposal respects the distinct and special *spiritual dimension in mourning*. It implies that an account of task work in mourning that confines itself to the psychologic or psychosocial is not sufficient to the complexities of grief work in human beings.

Other authors[28, 29] have suggested the need to take account of *family systems in bereavement*. According to these authors, mourning processes are not confined to individuals. On the contrary, the small social networks within which most human beings find themselves must also engage in mourning processes. If that is true, one can modify in the following ways the original formulation of Worden's tasks in order to bring out more fully their systemic social aspects:[28]

> Task I: To share acknowledgement of the reality of the death.
> Task II: To share experience of the pain of grief.
> Task III: To reorganize the family system.
> Task IV: To reinvest in other relationships and life pursuits.

Note that this family systems version of Worden's work drew upon the original formulation of his task and was published before the reformulation of Worden's tasks appeared in the second edition of his book. However, if one accepts Worden's arguments for rewording his original Task II and Task IV, presumably it would not be difficult to modify these family systems tasks similarly along the following lines:

> Task II: To share in the process of working through to the pain of grief.
> Task IV: To restructure the family's relationship with the deceased and to reinvest in other relationships and life pursuits.

For the sake of completeness, it may be useful to note that Walsh and McGoldrick[29] have also published an alternative version of their family systems perspective on Worden's tasks in mourning. However, that alternative does no more than to collapse the four tasks that these authors had originally proposed into the following two sets of compound mourning tasks:

> Task I: To share acknowledgement of the reality of death and to share the experience of loss.
> Task II: To reorganize the family system and to reinvest in other relationships and life pursuits.

TASKS FOR GRIEVING YOUNGSTERS

In work that has not been as well known as Worden's, Fox[13] described *four tasks for grieving youngsters*:

> Task I: To understand or begin to make sense out of what has happened or is happening.
> Task II: To grieve or express emotional responses to loss.
> Task III: To commemorate in some formal or informal manner the life of the person who has died.
> Task IV: To learn how to begin to integrate the loss into one's life in order to go on with the everyday activities of living and loving.

One can understand these four tasks in a broader framework by thinking of them in the following way. Task I is essentially *cognitive*, focusing as it does on assembling information and interpreting its meaning. Task II has to do with *emotions* or *other grief responses to loss*. To avoid a certain verbal circularity in depicting grief work as involving grieving, it might perhaps be better stated in the following way: "To identify, validate, and express in constructive ways strong reactions to the loss that has occurred." Task III has to do with *behavior* or the acting out of some way of commemorating the life that has been lost. And Task IV is concerned with *values* or the framework, and perhaps the permission from others, that a child may need in order to know that it is appropriate to find ways to go on with healthy living.

Like Worden's account, the description which Fox provided of tasks in mourning gives primary attention to the psychosocial aspects of bereavement and grief work.

TASKS IN COPING WITH DYING

Recently in the literature, task-based models have been developed not only to explain bereavement but also now to explicate *coping with dying*. Drawing on a well-established description[24] of four dimensions of pain in terminal illness, Corr[6] has proposed an account of task work in coping with dying as involving physical, psychologic, social, and spiritual dimensions. The important point about such task work is that it is always highly individualized even though the model which Corr has proposed is inevitably described in broad, general terms.

Within each of the four basic areas of task work in coping with dying, one can suggest that each set of tasks is likely to assume a general pattern or form along the following lines:

Physical tasks: To satisfy *bodily needs* and to minimize *physical distress,* in ways that are consistent with other values.

Psychologic tasks: To maximize *psychologic security, autonomy,* and *richness.*

Social tasks: To sustain and enhance those *interpersonal attachments* which are significant to the person concerned, and to address *social implications* of dying.

Spiritual tasks: To identify, develop, or reaffirm sources of *spiritual energy,* and, in so doing, to *foster hope.*

In other words, *physical tasks* in coping with dying usually address basic bodily needs, for example, nutrition, hydration, rest, exercise, and physical comfort, and physical distress or discomfort, for example, pain, nausea, diarrhea or constipation. The caution here is that sometimes physical tasks are made to give way to other concerns, as when an individual struggles to remain in his or her own home even at the risk of not benefiting from high standards of physical care that might be achieved under professional management in an institutional setting.

Psychologic tasks in coping with dying usually address the basic human concern for security (which can be achieved even when death is very near and one cannot be held safe from its imminent arrival), the desire among many individuals to exercise some degree of autonomy (even when the sphere of that autonomy or decision making is very limited, largely symbolic, or employed mainly to select someone else upon whose decisions the individual will rely), and the highly individualized matter of richness or dignity in living.

Social tasks in coping with dying address the individuals and the groups within my society that are important to me. They involve questions such as the following: Which individuals do I want to remain close to me or to help me?; Which individuals do I want to keep away from me?; And which individuals do I simply no longer have the energy with which to maintain a relationship?; Which groups in society do I still need (or no longer need) to draw upon for assistance?; And which groups in society do I still need (or no longer need) to contribute to or to meet their requirements?

Spiritual tasks in coping with dying are often incorrectly conflated with psychologic or religious tasks. But spiritual tasks are more than merely psychologic and they need not be exclusively religious. Spiritual tasks concern the sources from which the most fundamental values in one's life spring. They involve the foci or centers of meaning in one's life. For many, this is embodied in religious conviction

and community. But that need not always be the case. Philosophic or other value frameworks may be at the heart of one's spiritual tasks in coping with dying, just as hope is almost always central to this process. According to Doka,[11] in coping with dying one is challenged by three spiritual tasks:

Task I: To search for the meaning of one's life.
Task II: To die appropriately.
Task III: To find hope that extends beyond the grave.

Obviously, these are general descriptions of task work in coping with dying. To appreciate the actual living and dying of each individual who is involved in coping with dying, one would need to examine the specific tasks that are included in that coping, as well as the ways in which they are addressed in the individual's coping work. Moreover, in most concrete situations individuals who are coping with dying do not only face their own tasks; most often, they also are drawn into some relationship with the coping tasks of others who are involved in the same dying process. For example, a person who is dying may face tasks involved in preparing for death as well as tasks involved in taking leave of survivors-to-be. Similarly, a survivor-to-be may be coping with his or her desire not to experience the death of the loved one at this time, even as he or she is faced with the task of giving permission for the loved one to die.

TASKS IN COPING WITH LIFE-THREATENING ILLNESS

Doka[10] has taken the application of task-based models beyond the specifics of coping with dying by developing a task-based analysis that is meant to describe *living with life-threatening illness.* This model extends from the first recognition of a possible life-threatening illness throughout its course, that is, through diagnosis, the living-dying interval, recovery or death, and aftermath. Doka's description of the tasks that arise during this broad spectrum of coping with illness is presented in condensed form in Table 1. As can be seen, these include four general tasks, seven tasks associated with the acute phase of illness which is centered on diagnosis, 11 tasks that apply to the chronic phase of illness, and nine tasks relating to the terminal phase.

In addition to these, Doka's model also incorporates ways in which an individual responds to the threat of possible illness in the prediagnostic phase, as well as tasks that are involved in cases of recovery when one is coping with the aftermath of an encounter with life-threatening illness. Prediagnostic tasks include: (1) recognizing possible danger or risk; (2) coping with anxiety and uncertainty; and (3) developing and following through on a health-seeking strategy that may provide useful clues to the coping strategies of affected individuals. Tasks associated with recovery include: (1) dealing with psychologic, social, physical, spiritual, and financial aftereffects of illness; (2) coping with fears and anxieties about recurrence; (3) examining life and lifestyle issues and reconstructing one's life; and (4) redefining relationships with caregivers.

This is a broad and rich account of coping with life-threatening illness, one that can be applied in useful ways to education, clinical practice, and scholarly research in nursing and other health professions.

THEORETICAL MODELS IN THE FIELD OF DEATH, DYING, AND BEREAVEMENT

Perhaps the best known theoretic model in the field of death, dying, and bereavement is Kübler-Ross' account of *five stages* (denial, anger, bargaining, depression, and acceptance) in coping with dying.[17] One often finds this model presented in textbooks in nursing and other fields. Readers of such textbooks may be unaware that since its initial presentation in 1969 its author has advanced no further evidence in support of the claim that dying is a process involving five interlinked "stages." Moreover, this model has been sharply criticized in the professional literature, for example, by Corr and Kastenbaum[16], and has not been substantiated by later research, such as, Metzger[19], and Schulz and Aderman.[25]

This does not mean that the work of a pioneering theorist such as Kübler-Ross was not important. Nor does it mean that contemporary caregivers cannot still learn from her theoretic model if they approach this paradigm in the right way. For example, it is undeniable that Kübler-Ross played an important role in drawing the attention of professionals and lay persons to the subjects that she studied. She also drew attention to real possibilities for *hope* in coping with dying. In addition, Kübler-Ross taught three lessons that are of fundamental and lasting importance:[7]

Lesson 1: All who are coping with dying are still alive and often have unfinished needs which they want to address.

Lesson 2: We cannot be or become effective providers of care unless we listen actively to those who are coping with dying and identify with them their own needs.

Lesson 3: We need to learn from those who are dying and coping with dying in order to come to know ourselves better.

TASKS AND COPING

The notion of tasks is particularly well suited to draw upon the literature on coping.[18, 21] Coping with losses, including the losses involved in life-threatening illness, dying, and bereavement, is multifaceted and highly individual. Often, individuals will cope with death-related losses as they have coped with other crises in life. Nevertheless, different individuals can be expected to cope in different ways in similar situations. And specific individuals may be found to cope in different ways in different situations. Coping is not just a matter of a brief list of psychosocial responses; coping need not find optimal or even adequate representation in a pattern of stage- or phase-like progressions. Those who seek to understand or help individuals who are coping with dying, death, and bereavement must be sensitive to the complexities of all that is involved in such coping.

TASK-BASED MODELS

Task-based models of the sort described in this article represent an effort by a number of recent writers in the field of death, dying, and bereavement to listen carefully to those who are coping with dying or bereavement, to provide a useful framework for understanding their experiences, and to encourage an emphasis on attention to the particular qualities of each individual's experiences.

In the field of dying and bereavement, tasks appear to have particular advantages in capturing the central distinction in bereavement between *grief* (the reaction to loss) and *mourning* or "grief work" (processing or working with one's loss and grief in order to integrate them into ongoing living). Much the same can be said of the difference between reacting to the imminent prospect of death and the dynamic processes that are involved in coping with dying.

If this is correct, task-based models may meet four requirements that have been proposed as desirable (essential?) for theoretic models in the field of death, dying, and bereavement.[7] These four requirements are that such theoretic models should:

1. Help to improve our understanding of the complex processes that are involved in coping with dying and in coping with bereavement.
2. Foster empowerment on the part of those who are coping with death-related experiences.
3. Enhance appreciation of interactive participation among all of those who are involved in coping with a shared death-related experience.

Table 1. TASKS IN LIFE-THREATENING ILLNESS

General	Acute Phase	Chronic Phase	Terminal Phase
1. Responding to the physical fact of disease	1. Understanding the disease	1. Managing symptoms and side effects	1. Dealing with symptoms, discomfort, pain, and incapacitation
2. Taking steps to cope with the reality of disease	2. Maximizing health and lifestyle 3. Maximizing one's coping strengths and limiting weaknesses 4. Developing strategies to deal with the issues created by the disease	2. Carrying out health regimens 3. Preventing and managing health crisis 4. Managing stress and examining coping 5. Maximizing social support and minimizing isolation 6. Normalizing life in the face of the disease 7. Dealing with financial concerns	2. Managing health procedures and institutional stress 3. Managing stress and examining coping 4. Dealing effectively with caregivers 5. Preparing for death and saying goodbye
3. Preserving self concept and relationships with others in the face of disease	5. Exploring the effect of the diagnosis on a sense of self and others	8. Preserving self concept 9. Redefining relationships with others throughout the course of the disease	6. Preserving self concept 7. Preserving appropriate relationships with family and friends
4. Dealing with affective and existential/spiritual issues created or reactivated by the disease	6. Ventilating feelings and fears 7. Incorporating the present reality of diagnosis into one's sense of past and future	10. Ventilating feelings and fears 11. Finding meaning in suffering, chronicity, uncertainty, and decline	8. Ventilating feelings and fears 9. Finding meaning in life and death

4. Provide guidelines for persons who are helping those who are coping with death-related experiences.

A task-based approach also permits development of a schema of diverse coping skills which can be identified and taught, including those focused on the very different issues that arise in connection with appraisal, the problem, or one's reactions to the problem.[21]

CONCLUSION

In 1991, a record number of deaths—2,169,518—was recorded in the United States.[22] Approximately 60% of these deaths occurred in hospitals or medical centers. Other deaths occurred in long-term care facilities. Another significant group of deaths occurred among individuals who are in the care of hospice or other home care programs. Approximately 64% of all of these deaths resulted from three leading causes: diseases of the heart; malignant neoplasms (cancer); and cerebrovascular diseases (stroke).

In all of these settings and for most of these deaths, nurses are the health professionals who most often are in contact with dying persons and their family members. Nurses also frequently play significant roles in assisting bereaved persons, for example, in hospice and other forms of bereavement follow-up programs, in support groups for the bereaved, and as independent counselors or therapists.

Many students of the thanatologic implications of social change[5, 9] have noted the strong pressures in our society to move many death-related events out of the mainstream of life, to locate them in institutions, and to assign care for those who are coping with dying or with bereavement to professionals. In these circumstances, it is clear that nurses are playing and will continue to play prominent roles in the provision of this care.

Nurses will be able to fulfill their enhanced responsibilities in care of the dying and care of the bereaved most effectively if they are well prepared to do so.[20, 26] Not surprisingly, research has suggested two interrelated points. First, many nurses wish to enhance their competencies in care of the dying and care of the bereaved, and many baccalaureate nursing education programs have incorporated in their curricula some sort of education in this field.[4] Second, nurses who have been specifically prepared to meet the needs of the dying and their families reflect a more positive attitude when caring for the dying than those who have not been prepared in these specific ways.[14]

We consider that an understanding and appreciation of the role of task-based models in the field of death, dying, and bereavement may assist nurses in the important work that they undertake in this subject area. However, these models and a growing body of literature in the field[8] will only be helpful if they are correctly employed in sensitive and thoughtful ways. That is the moral of Jung's[15] comment that "theories in psychology are the very devil. It is true that we need certain points of view for their orienting and heuristic value; but they should always be regarded as mere auxiliary concepts that can be laid aside at any time."

References

1. American Journal of Nursing: Decoding the messages of the dying. Am J Nurs, 93:7, 1993
2. Attig T: The importance of conceiving of grief as an active process. Death Studies 15:385–393, 1991
3. Callanan M, Kelley P: Final Gifts: Understanding the Special Awareness, Needs, and Communications of the Dying. New York, Simon & Schuster, 1992
4. Collican MB, Stark J, Doka KJ et al: Education about death, dying, and bereavement in nursing programs. Nurse Education. In press
5. Corr CA: Reconstructing the changing face of death. In Wass H (ed): Dying: Facing the Facts. Washington, DC, Hemisphere, 1979, pp 5–43
6. Corr CA: A task-based approach to coping with dying. Omega 24:81–94, 1992
7. Corr CA: Coping with dying: Lessons that we should and should not learn from the work of Elisabeth Kübler-Ross. Death Studies 17:69–83, 1993
8. Corr CA, Morgan JD, Wass H (eds): International Work Group on Death, Dying, and Bereavement: Statements on Death, Dying, and Bereavement. Ontario, Canada, King's College, 1994
9. Corr CA, Nabe CM, Corr DM: Death and Dying, Life and Living. Pacific Grove, CA, Brooks/Cole Publishing Co., 1994
10. Doka KJ: Living with Life-Threatening Illness. Lexington, MA, Lexington Books, 1993
11. Doka KJ: The spiritual needs of the dying. In Doka KJ Morgan JD (eds): Death and Spirituality. Amityville, NY, Baywood Publishing, 1993, pp 143–150
12. Doka KJ: The spiritual crisis of bereavement. In Doka KJ, Morgan JD (eds): Death and Spirituality. Amityville, NY, Baywood Publishing, 1993, pp 185–193
13. Fox SS: Good Grief: Helping Groups of Children When a Friend Dies. Boston, The New England Association for the Education of Young Children, 1988
14. Frommelt KHM: The effects of death education on nurses' attitudes toward caring for terminally ill persons and their families. The American Journal of Hospice and Palliative Care 7(5):37–43, 1991
15. Jung C: The Development of Personality. In Read H, Fordham M, Adler G (eds): The Collected Words of C. G. Jung, vol 17. New York, Pantheon Books, Random House, 1954
16. Kastenbaum RJ: Death, Society, and Human Experience. ed 4, New York, Macmillan, 1991
17. Kübler-Ross E: On Death and Dying. New York, Macmillan, 1969
18. Lazarus RS, Folkman S: Stress, Appraisal, and Coping. New York, Springer Publishing Co., 1984
19. Metzger AM: A Q-methodological study of the Kübler-Ross stage theory. Omega 10:291–302, 1979
20. Miles MS: The effects of a course on death and grief on nurses' attitudes toward dying patients and death. Death Education 4:245–260, 1980
21. Moos RH, Schaefer JA: Life transitions and crises: A conceptual overview. In Moos RH, Schaefer JA (eds): Coping with Life Crises: An Integrated approach. New York, Plenum, 1986, pp 3–28
22. National Center for Health Statistics: Advance report of final mortality statistics, 1991. Monthly Vital Statistics Report 42(2), Supp. Hyattsville, MD, US Public Health Service, 1993
23. Rosenthal T: How Could I Not be Among You? New York, George Braziller, 1973
24. Saunders CM: The Management of Terminal Illness. London, Hospital Medicine, 1967
25. Schulz R, Aderman D: Clinical research and the stages of dying. Omega 5:137–144, 1974
26. Swain HL, Cowles KV: Interdisciplinary death education in a nursing school. Death Education 5:297–315, 1982
27. Volkan V: Complicated mourning. Annual of Psychoanalysis 12:323–348, 1985
28. Walsh F, McGoldrick M: Loss and the family life cycle. In Falicov CJ (ed): Family Transitions: Continuity and Change Over the Life Cycle. New York, Guildford Press, pp 311–336, 1988
29. Walsh F, McGoldrick M: Loss and the family: A systemic perspective. In Walsh F, McGoldrick M (eds): Living Beyond Loss: Death in the Family. New York, Norton, 1991, pp 1–29
30. Worden JW: Grief Counseling and Grief Therapy: A Handbook for the Mental Health Practitioner. New York, Springer Publishing Co., 1982
31. Worden JW: Grief Counseling and Grief Therapy: A Handbook for the Mental Health Practitioner, ed 2. New York, Springer Publishing Co., 1991

Rewriting the End

Elisabeth Kübler-Ross

**Her groundbreaking book made America face death.
Now she says it doesn't exist.**

Jonathan Rosen

*Jonathan Rosen is the associate editor of
The Forward.*

ELISABETH KÜBLER-ROSS, whose books are everywhere, isn't easy to find in the flesh. Before lighting out for new territory three months ago, she lived alone in a wooden house she'd built in rural Virginia as a refuge from the notoriety of a long and controversial career. I found her surrounded by sheep, cattle, pigs and llamas on a 300-acre farm, presiding like a priestess over the Elisabeth Kübler-Ross Center, a kind of Appalachian Lourdes where the sick, the troubled, the lame and the dying came to be healed by a doctor who made her name helping people die.

Twenty-five years ago, Kübler-Ross published "On Death and Dying: What the Dying Have to Teach Doctors, Nurses, Clergy and Their Own Families," and started a revolution in the sanitized corridors of the medical establishment. Before that book, the needs of the terminally ill—from proper pain medication to the chance to die at home—were virtually ignored. Kübler-Ross is largely responsible for bringing the modern hospice movement to this country from England, where it orig-

inated. A medical doctor, she wrote and lectured tirelessly, shattering the taboo surrounding terminal illness. "On Death and Dying," never out of print, was a declaration of war on the denial of death in America.

Which made it all the more shocking to pick up a copy of her latest book, "On Life After Death," and read: "My *real* job is, and this is why I need your help, to tell people that death does not exist." Finding that passage, and others like it (for example, the one describing how she was visited by a dead patient in a hallway at the University of Chicago), is like turning on the television and hearing Billy Graham declare that there is no God.

KÜBLER-ROSS'S HOUSE, HIDden by trees, was off-limits to guests. She received me in the white farmhouse she lived in when she first moved to the property, which she named Healing Waters Farm, 12 years ago. At 68, Kübler-Ross radiates a defiant vitality. Despite suffering a small stroke while lecturing in Paris last may and a major stroke eight years before, she bustled around the kitchen with brisk energy, throwing heavy logs into the woodburning stove and putting up the kettle for tea. Dressed in faded jeans and a turquoise sweater,

her loose gray hair uncombed, she is a small woman with a dowdily dramatic presence. A cigarette lighter hands around her neck on a leather strap decorated with Indian beads. A bumper sticker on her red Dodge pickup reads "Just Visiting This Planet" and another, "Wild Women Don't Get the Blues."

The first thing the author of "On Death and Dying" did when she had settled herself across from me was light up. "My spooks told me I have to stop smoking American cigarettes because they're full of toxic stuff," she explained, "but I can smoke as many as I want if they're pure tobacco. I asked them what is pure tobacco, and they said Dunhills."

I asked her to clarify the word "spooks."

"My spooks, my guardian angels, whatever you call them."

There is a blunt, matter-of-fact manner to the way Kübler-Ross explains her mysticism. She may believe in spirit guides, but she has retained the practical outlook of the Swiss village where she grew up and the Zurich medical school where she trained as a physician. She rails in heavily accented English against "extreme New Age people" and "tofu people," complaining about the volunteers who come to her farm in the summer: "They work for 40 minutes in the garden and then fall into a trance and meditate 10 minutes—every hour. And then *everybody* stops working. I can't have such kooks."

Despite her aversion to "kooks"— a favorite word—many people feel that Kübler-Ross herself has moved perilously far from the sober scientist she once was. Born in Zurich, she grew up in Meilen, nor far from the village where Carl Gustav Jung— "the only shrink I respect"—was then living. She decided to become a doctor after hitchhiking as a teenager through war-ravaged Europe, working in relief stations for refugees and visiting recently liberated concentration camps, an event she sees as formative to her later work.

"I would never have gone into the work on death and dying without Maidanek," she told me. "All the hospices—there are 2,100 in America alone—came out of that concentration camp. All work with dying patients, all the books that came out." While attending the prestigious medical school of the University of Zurich, she met Emanuel Ross, whom she eventually married and followed to America, where she trained as a psychiatrist.

Having worked as a country doctor in a Swiss village where most people died at home, their families and friends gathered round, Kübler-Ross was appalled by the isolation of the dying in America. When clergy were called in, she recalls, "they came with a little black book and they read a psalm and they took off quick as a bunny." Her own interest in how people died intensified and led to her legendary seminar at the University of Chicago, where she interviewed terminally ill cancer patients in front of an audience of medical students and members of the clergy.

During the classes Kübler-Ross formulated her now-famous stages of dying: denial, anger, bargaining, depression and acceptance. And from the seminar came "On Death and Dying," which she wrote in three months. Shortly before its publication, Life magazine wrote an article based on one of her classes. Cancer was a dirty word then, and the Life article, with its photographs of the young, attractive, terminally ill woman Kübler-Ross has on stage that day, struck a nerve worldwide, Kübler-Ross became famous virtually overnight. She estimates she receives 250,000 pieces of mail a year. "It just goes on and on and on and on," she says with a kind of horror, though she devotes a great deal of time to personally answering everything addressed to her.

But even as Kübler-Ross was transforming the American approach to death, her own thinking was beginning to change. More and more she heard from her patients about strange experiences they had on the brink of death and beyond, patients who floated above their bodies, who saw departed loved ones. Still, she was afraid to write about it. "At the time they would have thrown the whole book out on death and dying," she told me. "And I was only interested in helping dying patients, that they're not put in a bathroom, that somebody listens to them and treats them like a mensch. And they weren't treated like a mensch in the old days."

She nevertheless incorporated her findings into the nationwide workshops she led and the thousands of lectures she gave here and abroad. Those workshops began as an effort to help the dying and their families free themselves of pent-up feelings, but became a kind of therapy for anyone looking for emotional release. Techniques include pounding on a mattress with a length of rubber hose and tearing up the pages of a telephone book. Conventional therapy, as far as she is concerned, doesn't work. "I've been a shrink too long," she told me. "I've known too many shrinks. It's just talk talk talk talk. For the birds."

Kübler-Ross's impatience, her desire for quick results, is part of her contradictory appeal. One need not wait until illness to learn to face the end. One need not wait until death to learn what lies beyond. She offers Eastern answers delivered at Western speed. Despite her intense mysticism, she finds it impossible to meditate—"I have ants in my pants"—but she believes you can have any mystical experience you wish, just by asking.

Her appeal to an impatient and uncertain age has won her a wide following as the millennial clock ticks down. The shift in her work is emblematic of a transformation in the culture at large, and Kübler-Ross has clearly helped bring about that change. She bought her farm from Raymond Moody, the man many consider the father of near-death experiences and a major promoter of books testifying to encounters with the beyond. His book, "Life After Life," has sold more than 11 million copies since it was published in 1975—with a forward by Elisabeth Kübler-Ross.

Betty J. Eadie, whose account of her own near-death experience, "Embraced by the Light," made history by appearing simultaneously on the hardcover and paperback best seller list of the New York Times, helped Kübler-Ross present illustrations at a 1993 lecture she gave in New York. "She is a heroine," Eadie told me, "an idol of mine."

Melvin Morse, a pediatrician who wrote the introduction to "Embraced by the Light" and whose 1990 book about near-death experiences in children, "Closer to the Light," was a national best seller, began his research into the paranormal as a way to disprove claims he heard Kübler-Ross make on a Seattle television show in the 80's about the spiritual nature of dying. "I thought we could have some fun with her," he told me, though he has since become her greatest champion and is writing a book that begins with a tribute to Kübler-Ross's contributions not only to the field of death and dying but to the "next stage" as well.

Even less likely authors bear signs of her influence. James Redfield, who claims Kübler-Ross "influenced me tremendously," heard her lecture in Birmingham, Ala., and afterward showed her the manuscript of his novel, "The Celestine Prophecy," which Redfield had published himself a month before. Kübler-Ross wrote a glowing blurb that was immediately added to the cover. "That really gave us momentum," Mr. Redfield recalls, "because she's such a respected person in the field." The book, which offers celestial advice to earthbound mortals, sold nearly 150,000 copies before Warner Books, which paid $800,000 for the rights, republished it, complete with the Kübler-Ross blurb. It is currently on The New York Times best seller list.

'She is actively destroying the work she has done,' says Dr. Samuel Klagsbrun. 'She's killing her own work by denying death.'

Even now, years after "On Death and Dying," Kübler-Ross has published surprisingly little on the subject of life after death, though she says that before her last stroke she lectured about it to some 15,000 people a week. "Everyone knows what I believe," she told me. In general she has more faith in direct contact with audiences. "On Life After Death," published in 1991 by Celestial Arts, a Berkeley, Calif.-based press, is made up almost entirely of lectures. But Kübler-Ross's popularity is such that the book has sold 47,500 copies largely on word of mouth. It seems only a matter of time before a mainstream publisher will buy the rights and reissue the book—the fate of "Closer to the Light" and "The Celestine Prophecy."

"Mankind has finally learned to look at death, and when you look, you find," Kübler-Ross told me. "The time is right now." Whether these books represent the further evolution of our understanding of life and death, or a terrible betrayal, depends on whom you ask.

"She is actively destroying the work she has done, which I think will long live after her attempts to destroy it," says Dr. Samuel Klagsbrun, executive medical director of Four Winds Hospital in Katonah, N.Y., and a psychiatrist well known for his own work with the dying. "She's killing her own work by denying death."

Sherwin B. Nuland, a surgeon whose book "How We Die" received the 1994 National Book Award for nonfiction, laments bitterly: "It is impossible to deal with questions of death and dying without being bombarded on all sides by mystical concepts, and it's easy to pander to them. It's a terrifying phenomenon."

But many of Kübler-Ross's defenders are people like Nuland and Klagsbrun, who've worked directly with the dying. Nurses, social workers, hospice workers flock to her lectures. About one third of those who attend the "Life, Death and Transition" workshops conducted each month at the Elisabeth Kübler-Ross Center are health-care professionals. "You cannot work with dying patients over any period of time and leave the spiritual out," Kübler-Ross maintains. "Otherwise you're a phony baloney."

Without doubt her ideas have filtered deep into the world of hospice care. Lee Hayner, the program coordinator of palliative care at Stratton Veterans Administration Medical Center at Albany, says she often shares with dying patients and their families Kübler-Ross's notion that "no one dies alone," an idea based on the belief that the dead come to greet the dying. Though Kübler-Ross's views, so long on the margin, have become somewhat more mainstream, she insists she has no desire to convert doubters. "Don't worry," she told me, lighting up another Dunhill. "You'll get there soon enough, and you'll be pleasantly surprised."

Kübler-Ross speaks with utter certainty about what lies in store for all of us. "It's just the most beautiful thing that can ever happen to you," she told me, a look of beatific conviction on her creased face. Later she showed me the framed picture of an attractive young woman, a patient of hers who had died. "She's on the other side now, dancing and singing," Kübler-Ross told me casually. "She was paralyzed from the waist down."

UNEXPECTEDLY, KÜBLER-Ross granted my request to see the inside of her house, a crowded multicultural emporium featuring a collection of E.T. dolls, African masks, an Indian headdress with real eagle feathers and a peace pipe wrapped in cloth, used only on the last day of workshops in a special ceremony. There was an enormous loom on which she weaved her own rugs, and an entire room reserved for her mail.

There were photographs everywhere—of her family, of patients, of deceased pets. I asked about a photograph of her husband, who died last year. He and Kübler-Ross had been divorced for many years, but she still cared for him as he lay dying and expects to be with him in the next life. "To my mind, when you're married, you're married for life. That's my philosophy. So even after he married that young Lou-Lou, he was still my husband. That was his problem, not mine."

I toured the grounds and took a closer look at the llamas, bought in anticipation of the arrival of 20 AIDS babies Kübler-Ross hoped to adopt. "I wanted to have a Noah's ark," she said, but the project fell through nine years ago when neighbors protested that she was bringing AIDS to the area.

Near the house was a large garage; when I peeked inside, I saw an old-fashioned horse-drawn carriage, with the harness ropes hanging loose before it. I asked what it was for.

"That's for after the earth changes," she said. Then she asked if I had seen the future map of America.

As we drove back to her house to get it, she asked where I live. When I told her I was from New York, she shook her head sadly. "You should move," she said blandly. "That's one of the places that isn't going to make it."

Back at the farmhouse, I sat in front of the wood-burning stove with "The Future Map of the United States" unscrolled before me. Dated 1998–2001 and mailed out by something called the Earth Changes Report, the glossy map features the "Islands of California," a truncated East Coast and vast empty tracts of missing America destroyed in an unspecified cataclysm. Kübler-Ross is particularly taken with the fact that Nevada is missing. "My spooks told me that's because it's where all the nuclear testing took place; we destroyed so much," she said.

This apocalyptic aspect of Kübler-Ross's thinking throws a dark shadow over her undeniably enormous achievements, and it is difficult to avoid the conclusion that all those years watching men, women and children die have made her drunk on death. It was only when she told me that her work with the dying grew out of what she saw while visiting Maidanek concentration camp that I felt a possible explanation. If her mission was partly formed by an effort to provide a redemptive answer to the ravages of World War II, it makes sense that she would come to see death as a gateway to life. It is disturbing but somehow logical that the underside of her noble work would be a vision of destruction. In her efforts to provide an answer to the Holocaust, she is calmly envisioning another one.

Kübler-Ross, who knits scarves to raise money for terminally ill patients who can't afford her workshop, was reading about sweater patterns while I studied her grim map.

"Doesn't it horrify you that all these people will die?" I finally asked her.

"Why should it be horrifying?" she answered serenely, looking up from her knitting book. "Death isn't the end. They'll just be somewhere else."

Two days after my visit, Kübler-Ross's imagination for diaster eerily became reality. Her house was burned to the ground and one of her llamas was shot. The fire was so severe, police have not yet determined its origin. The killing of the llama also remains a mystery. The episode has sparked another change in Kübler-Ross and she has since quit the Virginia farm for Arizona, where her son lives and where she plans to buy a house. The Elisabeth Kübler-Ross Center will continue operating under an executive director while its enigmatic founder makes another transition.

MY LAST ENCOUNTER with Kübler-Ross was unplanned. It was at the Shenandoah Valley Airport, the day after our interview. She was headed for Hershey, Pa., where George M. Leader, a former Governor, was presenting her with a health-care achievement award; the 1993 recipient was C. Everett Koop.

After the ceremony she was slated to speak to doctors and nurses at the Milton S. Hershey Medical Center of Pennsylvania State University. Dressed in a tweed herring-bone suit, her hair neatly combed, she looked like the eminent, aging physician they were no doubt expecting. There was no more talk of the coming "earth changes," only complaints that the airport had recently banned smoking.

Before the flight, her assistant, Cindy Simmons, bought her breakfast while Kübler-Ross headed outside for a quick smoke. I watched her cross the floor with slow but purposeful steps. People kept rushing over to embrace her, from the woman at the Avis car rental desk to the baggage handler.

"Isn't Dr. Ross wonderful?" the woman X-raying my suitcase asked with a look of genuine awe.

Kübler-Ross doesn't ask for this adulation. She complained that her isolated farm was "like Grand Central Station," with all the seekers dropping by. But it is easy to understand the enormous appeal she holds for people in this unmoored age. She cheerfully offers an answer to the greatest mystery of human existence.

There were only 6 of us on the 21-seat plane that day, and as we took off I saw 6 looking out the window, watching the Earth vanish below us. The day before, I'd asked if she was afraid to fly and she broke into a girlish smile.

"I'm not afraid to *die*," she'd said, laughing. "I just await orders from above."

Psychology and Death

Meaningful Rediscovery

Herman Feifel
U.S. Department of Veterans Affairs
Outpatient Clinic, Los Angeles

ABSTRACT: *The place of death in psychology is reviewed historically. Leading causes for its being slighted as an area of investigation during psychology's early years are presented. Reasons for its rediscovery in the mid-1950s as a legitimate sector for scientific inquiry are then discussed, along with some vicissitudes encountered in carrying out research in the field. This is followed by a description of principal empirical findings, clinical perceptions, and perspectives emerging from work in the thanatological realm. The probability that such urgent social issues as abortion, acquired immunodeficiency syndrome (AIDS), and euthanasia, and such destructive behaviors as drug abuse, alcoholism, and certain acts of violence are associated with attitudes toward death offers a challenge to psychology to enhance the vitality of human response to maladaptive conduct and loss. Recognition of personal mortality is a major entryway to self-knowledge. Although death is manifestly too complex to be the special sphere of any one discipline, psychology's position as an arena in which humanist and physicist-engineer cultures intersect provides us with a meaningful opportunity to advance our comprehension of how death can serve life.*

To die is the human condition, and reflection concerning death exists practically among all peoples. From the beginnings of recorded history, realization of finitude has been a powerful concern and shaping force. Indeed, many feel that one of humanity's most distinguishing characteristics, in contrast to other species, is its capacity to grasp the concept of a future—and inevitable—death.

Yet, except for a few sporadic forays (e.g., Fechner, 1836/1904; Hall, 1915; James, 1910), the place of death in psychology was practically *terra incognita* and an off-limits enterprise until the mid-20th century.

There were a number of influential reasons for psychology's inordinate delay in coming to grips with such a universal matter. One was 17th-century Western individuals' transfer of their intellectual inquisitiveness and libido from theology to science (Toynbee et al., 1968). We witnessed a shift from spiritual mastery over self to physical conquest of nature. A major consequence was that we became impoverished in possessing religious or philosophic conceptual creeds, except nominally, with which to transcend death. Death became a "wall" rather than a "doorway." A taboo of considerable measure was placed on death and bereaved persons. Death and its concomitants were sundered off, isolated, and permitted into society only after being properly decontaminated. In this context, further circumstances making the area uncomfortable to deal with were (a) an expanding industrial, impersonal technology that steadily increased fragmentation of the family and dismantled rooted neighborhoods and kinship groups with more or less homogeneous values—what sociologists call a change from *gemeinschaft* to *gessellschaft*—thus depriving us of emotional and social supports with which to cushion the impact of death when it intruded into our lives; (b) a spreading deritualization of grief, related to criticism of funerary practices as being overly expansive, baroque, and exploitive of the mourner's emotions; (c) a gradual expulsion of death from everyday common experience; death has developed into a mystery for many people, increasingly representing a fear of the unknown, and has become the province of the "professional," whose mastery, unfortunately, is more technical than human these days; and (d) in a modern society that

Reprinted from *American Psychologist*, Vol. 45, No. 4, April 1990, pp. 537-543.

37

has emphasized achievement, productivity, and the future, the prospect of no future at all, and loss of identity, has become an abomination. Hence, death and mourning have invited our hostility and repudiation (Feifel, 1977).

A second powerful reason was psychology's natal need to raise its flag independently of mental philosophy and metaphysics. Steered by the burgeoning fields of experimental psychophysiology and psychophysics evolving in Europe, American psychologists moved to declare the independence of their new science. Scientific respectability meant occupying oneself with measurable stimuli and responses that were repeatable and public. Experimental and objective study of behavior became psychology's commanding posture, and logical positivism became its dominant notion of the scientific undertaking. Areas such as love, will, values, and death, elusive to operational definition and measurement, were slighted in favor of such spheres as memory, reaction time, size constancy, and perception of form and color. This, it was felt, would bring psychology in line with physics and mathematics (Feifel, 1964).

The sway of logical positivism on psychology was unquestionably wholesome, in part. It was responsible for producing imposing diagnostic instruments, discrediting anecdotal data, and stimulating the demand for more exacting standards of evidence. Additionally, it was responsible for more intelligible communication because of its emphasis on operational clarity. But it also brought stultifying effects, for example, tending to exclude explanation in terms of inner traits, purposes, or interests. Explanatory efforts were mainly confined to events lying outside the organism. Interest in the existential richness of life was muted (Feifel, 1964). Even the emerging role of psychoanalysis on the American scene, with its attention to processes of mind, undervalued the import of death in the psychic economy by interpreting death attitudes and fears as being essentially derivative and symbolic of other mainsprings such as castration fear and separation anxiety (Feifel, 1969).

Death Reconsidered

This was the regnant state of affairs until World War II. Events of that war, with its defense of democratic values, the Holocaust, challenge of racism, and ensuing press of urgent social problems, forced psychology to look beyond its traditional positivism. A waxing humanism, the growing prominence of existential psychology in Europe with its accentuation of death as a philosophical theme, and Piaget's work in cognitive development all contributed to fostering the view that a vital psychology must be rooted in human beings not in a mathematical physics model.

Most compelling, perhaps, was the legacy of the A-bomb with its potential for providing us all with a common epitaph. Not only the individuality of death, but posterity and social immortality, were now at risk. Physical science had made it possible for us to destroy not only society but history as well. Issues of meaning, purpose, and temporality started to move center stage. In this juncture of psychology's expanding interest in the pulse of human life and intensified awareness of life's transience, attention to and research in the area of dying and death began to emerge as an authentic and fertile undertaking (Feifel, 1969).

Early Years of the Death Movement

Although a few empirical articles by psychologists had been published in the mid-1950s relating mental illness and old age to death and measuring affective responses to death-related words (e.g., Alexander, Colley, & Adlerstein, 1957; Feifel, 1955, 1956), psychology's first organized approach to death was a symposium titled, *The Concept of Death and Its Relation to Behavior,* which I initiated and chaired and which was presented at the 1956 annual meeting of the American Psychological Association (APA) in Chicago. Other participants were Irving E. Alexander, Jacob Taubes, Arnold A. Hutschnecker, and Gardner Murphy. The symposium served as the basis for the 1959 book, *The Meaning of Death,* which I edited. Authorities agree that the book was seminal in galvanizing regard for the field and in familiarizing the scholarly community with the issues and concerns of dying, death, and grief. The same year I received what was probably the first research grant awarded to an individual by the National Institute of Mental Health (NIMH) to study attitudes toward death. Despite these initial signs of recognition of the legitimacy of investigating the thanatological domain, numerous scientific Grundys still felt that the topic of death was not appropriate for psychology. *Contemporary Psychology,* for instance, rejected considering *The Meaning of Death* because the book had just received a review by *Time* magazine and, hence, had attained its allotted morbid fascination exposure. More significant was the communication that the subject was not germane to genuine scientific inquiry.

The attempt to implement my NIMH research mandate relating attitudes toward death and behavior was also beset with manifold tribulations and frustrations. Some of the professional personnel with whom I was working told me that at no time did they ever inform patients that they had a serious illness from which they could die. "The one thing you never do," it was emphasized, "is to discuss death with a patient." Along this same line, after a three-month delay in responding to my request for permission to gather data from some of his patients, the chief physician-in-charge of a leading metropolitan hospital finally replied, "Excuse my immoderate delay in answering, but you have to be a staff member,"

Editor's note. This article was originally presented as a Distinguished Professional Contributions award address at the meeting of the American Psychological Association in Atlanta in August 1988.

Award-based manuscripts appearing in the *American Psychologist* are scholarly articles based in part on earlier award addresses presented at the APA convention. In keeping with the policy of recognizing these distinguished contributors to the field, these submissions are given special consideration in the editorial selection process.

Author's note. Preparation of this manuscript was facilitated by a U.S. Department of Veterans Affairs grant.

I thank the American Psychological Association for presenting me with this broad base from which to share developments in the "death movement," and Stephen Strack for assisting me in preparing the article.

Correspondence concerning this article should be addressed to Herman Feifel, Psychology Service (116B), VA Outpatient Clinic, 425 South Hill St., Los Angeles, CA 90013.

a lack known to him at the inception of our discussion about obtaining patients. The commissioner of hospitals of a major city responded to my request for subjects by saying, "It is not consonant with our policy to set aside patients for this purpose." Then there was the chief research psychiatrist of a prominent medical center who "knew" that the research project would induce what he termed "test toxicity" in the patients, despite already demonstrated results to the contrary (Feifel, 1963, p. 12).

The realization soon began to sink in that what I was up against were not idiosyncratic personal quirks, the usual administrative vicissitudes, pique, or nonacceptance of an inadequate research design. Rather, it was personal position, bolstered by cultural structuring, that death is a dark symbol not to be stirred—not even touched—an obscenity to be avoided. I must admit to more than passing vagaries about chucking the whole thing. Two things, though, held me to the task. One was my ego. I had made a dent or two, *mirabile dictu,* here and there, using "gamesmanship" of an order that would have warmed Stephen Potter (no date). Second was my sentiment, albeit occasionally dampened by repeated rejections, that study of the area was important and, come hell or high water, should be implemented. Fortunately, as I have noted, there were exceptions to the situation I have been describing. I did find congenial colleagues and professional personnel who perceived what I was striving to do, acknowledged its importance, and helped me get my work off the ground (Feifel, 1963, pp. 11–13).

Succeeding years saw a burst of activity in the field. The 1960s and 1970s were characterized by the introduction of workshops and courses on dying, death, and mourning in various universities and professional schools. There were also noteworthy pioneering books by Kastenbaum and Aisenberg (1972), the psychiatrists Eissler (1955), Hinton (1967), Kübler-Ross (1969), Parkes (1972), and Weisman (1972), sociologists Fulton (1965) and Glaser and Strauss (1965), the nurse–sociologist Quint-Benoliel (1967), the philosopher Choron (1963), and cultural anthropologist Gorer (1965), among others. Journals such as *OMEGA* (1969; Robert Kastenbaum, editor), *Death Education* (1977; now called *Death Studies,* Hannelore Wass, editor), and the *Journal of Thanatology* (1973; Austin H. Kutscher, editor) came into being. Additionally, a number of scientific and professional associations devoted specifically to thanatological matters were founded. Among the more prominent were the International Work Group on Death, Dying, and Bereavement, the Forum for Death Education and Counseling, and Foundation for Thanatology. Bolstering these groups were several self-help and lay groups, for example, Make Today Count (1973), The Society of Compassionate Friends (1969), and widow-to-widow programs sparked by Phyllis Silverman (1969).

Empirical Findings and Clinical Perceptions

What are some empirical findings and clinical perceptions issuing from work already carried out in the field?

1. Death is for all seasons. Its directive force is present from the very beginning in all of us, young and old, healthy and sick. It is not just for the combat soldier, dying person, elderly individual, or suicidal person. It is an ingredient of import throughout the entire life span. In this frame, we do not serve children well by shielding them from the experience of death. We only hinder their emotional growth. We are learning that children are more capable of withstanding the stress brought on by their limited understanding of death than by its mystery and implied abandonment (Wahl, 1959).

2. Death fear can be a secondary phenomenon reflecting, for example, clinical displacement of separation anxiety. Incoming findings, however, increasingly suggest that the reverse may be more to the point. Apprehensiveness and concern about dying and death can themselves assume dissembling guises and gain expression in such symptoms as insomnia, depression, above-average fears of loss, and sundry psychosomatic and even psychotic manifestations (Gillespie, 1963; Searles, 1961).

3. Fear of death is not a unitary or monolithic variable. Various subcomponents are evident, for example, fear of going to hell, loss of identity, loneliness. For a good number of persons, negative connotations of death are associated substantially with feelings of rootlessness and having to face the "unknown" with minimal mastery. These features appear to be more prominent than even such aspects as "I may not have lived completely" or "My family may suffer." For many, death no longer signals the possibility of atonement and salvation, or a point in time on the road to eternity, but isolation and loss of self (Feifel, 1977; Feifel & Nagy, 1981).

4. Significant discrepancies exist in many people between their conscious and nonconscious fear of death. Fear of death evidences itself as a lockstitching phenomenon with little reported fear of death on a verbal conscious level, coupled with one of ambivalence at a fantasy or imagery level, and outright negativity at the nonconscious level. This apparent counterbalance of coexisting avoidance–acceptance of personal death appears to serve powerful adaptational needs. In the face of personal death, the human mind ostensibly operates simultaneously on various levels of reality, or finite provinces of meaning, each of which can be somewhat autonomous. We, therefore, need to be circumspect in accepting at face value the degree of fear of death affirmed at a conscious level (Feifel & Branscomb, 1973).

5. Coping with a life-threatening illness or death threat varies in significant fashion not only among differing groups but among situations. Meaningful disparities seem to exist in how cancer patients, heart patients, and elderly individuals contend with their serious illness and old age compared to the way they deal with nonlife-threatening stresses such as competition, marital discord, decision making, or loss of a job. Differences noted in these situations suggest not so much the employment of new coping strategies as modifications in the patterning or configuration of an individual's more usual coping modes. This is in contrast to much of the clinical literature, which reports that coping efforts used in the face of severe threat and impending death reflect but an intensified or more pervasive employment of an individual's coping deportment previously applied to generally aversive situations in personal life (Feifel & Nagy, 1986; Feifel & Strack, 1989; Feifel, Strack, & Nagy, 1987a, 1987b; Silver & Wortman, 1980).

6. Most dying patients do not expect "miracles" concerning their biological condition. Their essential communication is the need for confirmation of care and concern. When emotional and psychosocial needs of dying patients are attended to, we discover competence in many of them for responsible and effective behavior. Moreover, when appreciation of their integrity and recognition of their input in decision making are major features in the treatment process, there is reduced depression, less projection of blame onto others, and diminished feelings of guilt and inadequacy not only in the patient but also in the helping care professionals and family members involved with that patient. The patient, in this type of context, moves toward the death of a person rather than of an illness. And, as professionals, we end up not merely as voyeurs of another's pain and tribulations but are prodded by the process to probe our own values and aspirations (Feifel, 1977).

One of the superb responses to this understanding has been the hospice movement. Its alertness to the problem of chronic pain, involvement of the family and friends as part of the caring team, and value of the meaningfulness of life are resulting in a prolonging of *living* rather than dying for many terminally ill persons. Being in a dying state does not veto respect for the sanctity and affirmation of life (Saunders, 1977).

7. Grief is not a sign of weakness or self-indulgence. Rather, it demonstrates a necessary and deep human need most of us have in reacting to the loss of a significant person in our lives, and it recognizes no age boundaries. Furthermore, it is multifaceted, arises from differing types of loss, and manifests itself in numerous representations: anticipatory grief, high-low grief, self-grief, survival grief, or anniversary grief (Feifel, 1977; Fulton & Gottesman, 1980).

Increasing privatization of death and grief needs to be undercut. There is a traditional Jewish proverb that "to grieve alone is to suffer most." The community needs to expand its current institutional networks and communal resources in responding to grief. Suppressing or minimizing it, and failure to acknowledge the healing process of grief are maladaptive not just for the individual and immediate family but for the larger community. Indeed, there is growing comprehension that community sharing of grief decreases feelings of guilt and depression in survivors and minimizes the break in the societal fabric (Feifel, 1977).

Bereavement lacks precise criteria as a clinical entity, and the line between healthy and unhealthy grief, at times, can become blurry and difficult to distinguish. An instructive criterion in this circumstance seems to be that unhealthy grief may reveal itself in deviant behavior that violates conventional expectations or imperils the health and safety of self and others (Weisman, 1975).

We need to be cautious in encouraging survivors to abandon grief prematurely, or to wallow in it for that matter, because of our own painful and uncomfortable feelings. We are learning that if mourning is neglected or short-circuited, or does not take place close in time to a serious loss, its expression may occur later on in a more inappropriate and regressive manner. We are now aware that grief can gain expression in such masked appearances as school absenteeism and bed-wetting in children, drug abuse and delinquency in adolescents, and promiscuity, suicide, and diverse physical and mental illnesses in adults. We are also now more keenly informed about the "high-risk" group status of the bereaved in the area of somatic and emotional illness, particularly during the first year or two after a loved one's death; the well-being of one who mourns is itself in a kind of jeopardy. Additionally, we increasingly realize that the grieving person not only can experience deprivation of sex, companionship, and economic support but is further vulnerable to a loss of social role, autonomy, and power. Moreover, it is being reestablished that the funeral ceremony and mourning rituals can be liberating as well as enslaving for survivors in their grief (Parkes, 1972).

8. We are discovering that just as there are multitudinous ways of living, there are numerous ways of dying and grieving. Despite the equanimity of sorts that it offers, and a prevailing chic, the hard data do not support the existence of any procrustean stages or schedules that characterize terminal illness or mourning. This does not mean that, for example, Kübler-Ross's (1969) "stages of dying" and Bowlby's (1980) "phases of mourning" cannot provide us with implications and insights into the dynamics and process of dying and grief, but they are very far from being inexorable hoops through which most terminally ill individuals and mourners inevitably pass. We should beware of promulgating a coercive orthodoxy of how to die or mourn. In the last analysis, applying Weisman's (1975) wise admonition, an "appropriate" dying or mourning is one acceptable to or tolerated by the dying person or mourner, not one so designated by either the helping professions, significant others, or the community. Individual differences and esteem for personhood must be our principal guides.

9. It is important for members of the health care team working with severely ill and terminally ill patients, and mourners, to be alert to signs of personal denial, avoidance, or antipathy in themselves concerning the reality of death. The more nonaccepting and unresolved helping care personnel tend to be about their own fears concerning personal death, the less likely they are to provide the optimal assistance of which they are capable. Ministry to the dying and bereaved is extremely difficult if we ourselves are not comfortable with the idea of personal death. Even if the professional's anxieties in the field are not completely resolved they, at least, have to be looked at and contended with. Grappling with our own somber feelings about death and grief will tend to moderate our disposition to seek refuge in the technical functions of disease, skulk behind theological dogmas, and equivocate with intellectual words in order to evade open encounter with the dying patient or grief of the mourner (Feifel, 1977).

10. Redefinition is called for concerning the function of the helping professional, particularly that of the physician. When cure is definitely not in the cards, the provision of comfort and care is just as valid and authentic a contribution in meeting the real needs of the dying patient. In a significant sense, the growing hospice movement is a reaction to this prevailing lack in much of cure-oriented modern medicine (Feifel, 1977).

Perspectives From the Death Movement

What are some of the perspectives advanced by the death movement?

1. Dying is not only a biological affair but a human one. The movement has underscored the importance of healing the humanity of the person wounded by illness and oncoming death. It has indicated that technology and competence have to be infused with compassion and benevolence and that life is not just a matter of length but of depth and quality as well. In this regard, the movement has emphasized the importance of controlling chronic pain in the dying so that terminal patients can use their full potential and has also stressed the moral, spiritual, and ethical dimensions inherent in health-care giving.

2. It has refocused attention on the role of the future in steering conduct. Just as the past, the future abides dynamically in the present. How we anticipate future events—and death—governs our "now" in substantive fashion and provides an important organizing principle in determining how we behave in life. This is providing us with a needed corrective to a widespread vogue of being mesmerized by the moment (Feifel, 1963).

3. It is forwarding the realization that we must be at home with fear of death and with the enigma of death if we are not to become alienated from our nature and destiny and lose basic contact with who we are and what we are about. Acceptance of personal mortality is one of the foremost entryways to self-knowledge. Human maturity brings along with it a recognition of limit. In truth, we have a legitimate need to face away from death. Unfortunately, too many of us resort to unhealthy expulsion and camouflage of the actuality of death, resulting in self-estrangement and social pathology. If we accepted death as a necessity and did not try to demote it to the level of mischance or fortuity, if we accepted death as lodged in our bowels from the very beginning, energies now bound up in continuing strivings to shelve and subdue the idea of death could be available to us for the more constructive and positive aspects of living, perhaps even fortifying our gift for creative splendor against our genius for destruction (Feifel, 1969).

As time-ridden beings, we are faced with the task of identifying ourselves with history and eternity. I think our most viable response will issue from basic philosophic, religious, or psychological deliberations about death already in our possession. This is difficult for a generation that finds itself dislodged from time-honored anchors. But we must establish bearings with the idea of death. Whether we do so via faith, love, art, or intelligence is a matter of *de gustibus*. In pondering death, the agony of selfhood is not endurable for most of us without resources, be they transcendental, inspirational, or existential. The evolution of an *ars moriendi* prior to the advent of death is needed (Feifel, 1969, p. 294).

4. Clearly, life can be menaced and compromised in many ways short of death and on varying levels of experience. In this context, such notions as "partial death," "symbolic death," and mourning over deprivation other than life such as a limb, sense, marriage, or old neighborhood will also profit from a more comprehensive theory of death and grief (Feifel, 1977, p. 354).

5. It is evident that death and grief are too multi-splendored and complex to be trussed up in the conceptual straitjacket of any one discipline. We must be more cognizant of the positive synergistic effect of a transdisciplinary rather than unilateral approach in dealing with the dying and survivors.

6. The time is overdue for death education to assume a rightful role in our cultural upbringing as a preparation for *living*. We have disabused ourselves of the fancy that sex first comes to life at puberty, as a kind of full-bodied Minerva emerging from Jupiter's head. In a similar vein, it is fitting that we now concede the psychological presence of death in ourselves from childhood on and attend to it at all stages of life development, not merely at its beginning and end. Naturally, its qualitative form of expression will embody such variables as individual differences, values and belief systems, social context, and differing developmental periods. But, just as it is belated to start reading sex manuals on the marriage bed, it is rather tardy to begin developing a philosophy of life and death when one is terminally ill or newly bereaved. The pertinence of death education is not only for those of us in the health care professions who deal with dying, death, and bereavement but for all—in the home, school, religious institution, and general culture. The mandate is to alter cultural perspective, not just achieve a palliative concern (Feifel, 1977).

Implications for Psychologists

We must expand our information base so that application does not outrun knowledge. William James once stated that he was no lover of disorder but feared to lose the truth by pretensions to wholly possessing it. Knowledge of the specified links and interactive bonds of widespread variables to the meaning of death, for example, "will to live," life-style, coping strategies, need for achievement, and ethnic background, among others, is still not available to us in an organized fashion because of methodological complexities. Inconsistent findings reported in the death literature mirror the use of differing populations, ages, assessment devices, "conditions under which," and failure to fully appreciate the untidy nature of attitudes toward death. Some pitfalls, already alluded to, are nonconsideration of the multimeanings that death acquires for people and perception of fear of death as a homogeneous variable. Another shortcoming has been neglect of the discrepancies that exist in individuals between conscious and nonconscious levels of death anxiety. Analysis of these incongruities may prove more instructive than merely noting the presence or degree of death concern (Feifel & Nagy, 1981; Kastenbaum & Costa, 1977; Schulz, 1978).

Experimental manipulation of variables has also been sparse. Case-based offerings continue to be informative in identifying phenomena and in suggesting leads for theory and practice. Nevertheless, although the medley of human responses to death-related situations is often noted by the clinician, these discernments do not, per se, provide a robust foundation for empirical generalizations.

At this stage of development, major desiderata for the field are more generative theory-based formulations, conversion of major assumptions into operationalized empirical inquiry, longitudinal studies, cross-validation and reliability analyses of prevailing procedures, more astute incorporation of multilevel aspects, and extended examination of functional and behavioral correlates of attitudes toward death. Psychotherapeutic functioning and models of personality and psychopathology require amplified representation of the future and death in their horizons. There is a definite need to integrate the clinician's admiration for individuality and complexity with the researcher's demand for precise and vigorous documentation (Feifel, 1969). We require comprehension and images that are more applicable to contemporary death and grief.

Refinement in the pursuit of our craft, however, will not be sufficient unless it is carried on in the context of healing the humanity of the dying patient and wounded mourner. Our model of understanding and treatment must be the humanity of the person. The requisite is not just to succor the body but also to speak to the soul. The humanities, ethics, and the spiritual dimension must be in our ken along with biology and the behavioral sciences. Death and grief bring with them a preoccupation with a vision of life.

Our field of regard should focus on the individual as purposive and striving: one whose scope is not made parochial by a limiting philosophy of science, and whose concepts are not derived essentially from methods of study but rather from the functioning of human life. Too often have we worked with portions of the human individual and tried to make a virtue of this. The challenge is to enlarge horizons without sacrificing our gains. Humanity cannot be grasped in its totality by a view that exempts personhood, meaning, and redemption from its purview, by a perspective whose criterion is the machine rather than man (Feifel, 1964).

Leaving the mountain top for more earthly ground, it is becoming plain that power is needed along with scholarship and learning. It is not enough to offer advice, instructive as it may be. The call is to integrate existing knowledge concerning death and grief into our communal and public institutions. There is no way in a dynamic society that a strict line can be drawn between scholarship and *wissenschaft* and the tides of social change. The glorious Apollo program in the United States to put an American on the moon, for example, for all its benefits, was more the child of politics than of the craving for exploration. Like it or not, political motives have been telling in driving science and technology these past decades. In other words, we must be valid participants in helping formulate public policy or else be its victims. Power can be enabling as well as corrupting.

Conclusion

A discipline is defined by the questions it asks as well as the validity of its measuring instruments. Recognition of death and knowledge of finiteness has contributed to psychology's progression into adulthood. It betokens a certain loss of innocence and youth and has probably introduced a repressive element into relationships. At the same time, however, it can serve positively as a galvanizing force—an Aristotelian *vis-a-tergo*—pushing us toward creativity and accomplishment. No less a person than Michelangelo said, "No thought is born in me that has not 'Death' engraved upon it" (Feifel, 1977, p. 11).

In final consideration, the death movement and social engineering will obviously never exorcize death of its demonic power. Still, the movement has been a major force in broadening our grasp of the phenomenology of illness, in helping humanize medical relationships and health care, and in advancing the rights of the dying. It is highpointing values that undergird the vitality of human response to catastrophe and loss. Furthermore, it is contributing to reconstituting the integrity of our splintered wholeness. More important, perhaps, it is sensitizing us to our common humanity, which is all too eroded in the present world (Feifel, 1977). It may be somewhat hyperbolic, but I believe that how we regard death and how we treat the dying and survivors are prime indications of a civilization's intention and target.

Concern with death is not the fixation of a cult indifferent to life. Conversely, in emphasizing awareness of death, we sharpen and intensify our appreciation of the uniqueness and preciousness of life. In responding to our temporality, we shall find it easier to define values, priorities, and life goals.

Because of advances in medical technology and an expanding aging population, the years ahead will behold increasing numbers of people wrestling with chronic and life-threatening illness and prolonged dying. Furthermore, such urgent social issues as abortion, AIDS, euthanasia, and capital punishment, and such behaviors as alcoholism, drug abuse, and certain acts of violence, may well have links to overt and latent meanings that death holds for us. After all, life-threatening behaviors involve confrontation, in one way or another, with the threat of possible injury or ultimate death to self and others.

Death possesses many faces and meanings, and perceptions of it vary in divergent cultures and in differing epochs. It is obviously too intricate to be the special province of any one discipline. Nevertheless, psychology's contributions in the past to thanatology have succeeded in increasing understanding of and coping with dying, death, and bereavement. Our future mandate is to extend our grasp of how death can serve life.

REFERENCES

Alexander, I. E., Colley, R. S., & Adlerstein, A. M. (1957). Is death a matter of indifference? *Journal of Psychology, 43,* 277–283.

Bowlby, J. (1980). *Loss: Sadness and depression.* New York: Basic Books.

Choron, J. (1963). *Death and Western thought.* New York: Collier Books.

Eissler, K. R. (1955). *The psychiatrist and the dying patient.* New York: International Universities Press.

Fechner, G. T. (1904). *The little book of life after death.* Boston, MA: Little, Brown. (Original work published 1836)

Feifel, H. (1955). Attitudes of mentally ill patients toward death. *Journal of Nervous and Mental Disease, 122,* 375–380.

Feifel, H. (1956). Older persons look at death. *Geriatrics, 11,* 127–130.

Feifel, H. (Chair). (1956, September). *The concept of death and its relation to behavior.* Symposium presented at the meeting of the American Psychological Association, Chicago.

Feifel, H. (1959). (Ed.). *The meaning of death.* New York: McGraw-Hill.

Feifel, H. (1963). Death. In N. L. Farberow (Ed.), *Taboo topics* (pp. 8–21). New York: Atherton Press.

Feifel, H. (1964). Philosophy reconsidered. *Psychological Reports, 15,* 415–420.

Feifel, H. (1969). Attitudes toward death: A psychological perspective. *Journal of Consulting and Clinical Psychology, 33,* 292–295.

Feifel, H. (1977). (Ed.). *New meanings of death.* New York: McGraw-Hill.

Feifel, H., & Branscomb, A. B. (1973). Who's afraid of death? *Journal of Abnormal Psychology, 81,* 82–88.

Feifel, H., & Nagy, V. T. (1981). Another look at fear of death. *Journal of Consulting and Clinical Psychology, 49,* 278–286.

Feifel, H., & Nagy, V. T. (1986). *Coping with life-threat and general life conflict: Two diverse beasts.* Ann Arbor: University of Michigan. (ERIC Document Reproduction Service No. ED 266 362)

Feifel, H., & Strack, S. (1989). Coping with conflict situations: Middle-aged and elderly men. *Psychology and Aging, 4,* 26–33.

Feifel, H., Strack, S., & Nagy, V. T. (1987a). Degree of life-threat and differential use of coping modes. *Journal of Psychosomatic Research, 31,* 91–99.

Feifel, H., Strack, S., & Nagy, V. T. (1987b). Coping strategies and associated features of medically ill patients. *Psychosomatic Medicine, 49,* 616–625.

Fulton, R. (1965). (Ed.). *Death and identity.* New York: Wiley.

Fulton, R., & Gottesman, D. J. (1980). Anticipatory grief: A psychosocial concept reconsidered. *British Journal of Psychiatry, 137,* 45–51.

Gillespie, W. H. (1963). Some regressive phenomena in old age. *British Journal of Medical Psychology, 36,* 203–209.

Glaser, B. G., & Strauss, A. L. (1965). *Awareness of dying.* Chicago: Aldine.

Gorer, G. (1965). *Death, grief, and mourning.* New York: Doubleday.

Hall, G. S. (1915). Thanatophobia and immortality. *American Journal of Psychology, 26,* 550–613.

Hinton, J. (1967). *Dying.* Baltimore, MD: Penguin Books.

James, W. (1910). *The varieties of religious experience.* Boston, MA: Longmans, Green.

Kastenbaum, R., & Aisenberg, R. (1972). *The psychology of death.* New York: Springer.

Kastenbaum, R., & Costa, P. T. (1977). Psychological perspectives on death. *Annual Review of Psychology, 28,* 225–249.

Kübler-Ross, E. (1969). *On death and dying.* London: Macmillan.

Parkes, C. M. (1972). *Bereavement: Studies of grief in adult life.* New York: International Universities Press.

Potter, S. (no date). *The theory and practice of gamesmanship.* New York: Holt, Rinehart & Winston.

Quint-Benoliel, C. (1967). *The nurse and the dying patient.* New York: Macmillan.

Saunders, C. (1977). Dying they live: St. Christopher's hospice. In H. Feifel (Ed.), *New meanings of death* (pp. 153–179). New York: McGraw-Hill.

Schulz, R. (1978). *The psychology of death, dying, and bereavement.* Reading, MA: Addison-Wesley.

Searles, H. (1961). Schizophrenia and the inevitability of death. *Psychiatric Quarterly, 35,* 634–665.

Silver, R. L., & Wortman, C. B. (1980). Coping with undesirable life events. In J. Garber & M. E. P. Seligman (Eds.), *Human helplessness: Theory and applications* (pp. 279–375). New York: Academic Press.

Toynbee, A., Mant, A. K., Smart, N., Hinton, J., Yudkin, S., Rhode, E., Heywood, R., & Price, H. H. (1968). *Man's concern with death.* New York: McGraw-Hill.

Wahl, C. W. (1959). The fear of death. In H. Feifel (Ed.), *The meaning of death* (pp. 16–29). New York: McGraw-Hill.

Weisman, A. D. (1972). *On dying and denying: A psychiatric study of terminality.* New York: McGraw-Hill.

Weisman, A. D. (1975). Thanatology. In A. M. Friedman, H. J. Kaplan, & B. J. Sadock (Eds.), *Comprehensive textbook of psychiatry* (Vol. 2, 2nd ed., pp. 1748–1759). Baltimore, MD: William & Wilkins.

Sunny side up

Jim Holt

Jim Holt is a New York writer.

In the course of a dinner party the other night, the conversation somehow reached the intersection of necrophilia and Hollywood. Seizing the chance, I observed that *Sunset Boulevard* was the only film in history narrated by a corpse. At this several other guests sharply demurred: What about *Reversal of Fortune?* Wasn't that narrated by the corpse of Sunny von Bulow? Well, I replied, as a matter of fact, no. While Sunny did supply the voice-over in that dramatized retelling of *l'affaire von Bulow,* she was not actually dead. She was merely in an irreversible coma. There is, after all, a difference. I mean, isn't there?

In 1982, you will recall, Sunny von Bulow's Danish-born socialite husband, Claus, was convicted of attempting to murder her with an insulin-loaded hypodermic needle, and was sentenced to a long prison term. Two years later the verdict was overturned, and in a retrial Mr. von Bulow was acquitted. There had been no insulin injection, his lawyers contended; rather, Sunny's coma was induced by barbiturates and alcohol, complicated by hypothermia as she lay unattended on a cold bathroom floor at Clarendon Court, the couple's great stone pile in Newport.

At the time the trials of Claus von Bulow divided the international beau monde as deeply as the Dreyfus trials divided the Third Republic. Today they are a faint memory. Few realize that more than thirteen years after she was precipitated into a coma, Mrs. von Bulow survives in her deeply oblivious state. This beautiful and storied heiress is living out her days in a slummy quarter of northern Manhattan, at Columbia-Presbyterian hospital. Though her room is not large, it offers a fabulous view of the Hudson river and the New Jersey Palisades. She is dressed daily by around-the-clock attendants who also see to her hair, makeup and nails. A small stereo, I am told, fills the room with her favorite music.

All this, one might protest, for a breathing cadaver. At no time in the last thirteen years has Sunny evinced any sign of self-awareness. She cannot respond to stimuli—sights, sounds, touch. She is artificially nourished via a food tube. Neurological experts who have examined the damage to her brain declare that her loss of consciousness is irreversible. And yet: she *is* capable of breathing on her own, with no need of a respirator. She shows sleep-wake sequences. Now and then her lips curl into a smile. Her eyes open periodically, and have been said to tear when her two children by her first marriage, Ala and Alexander Auersperg, visit.

Improbably enough, Ala and Alex's father, Prince Alfie von Auersperg, also went into a coma, shortly after Sunny did, as a result of a car accident in Austria. He remained comatose for almost a decade until his recent death. The children were understandably perplexed by the shared condition of their parents, in whose memory they later established the Sunny von Bulow Coma and Brain Trauma Foundation in New York. "They're neither typically alive nor dead," Ala told *Vogue* in 1988. "What are they thinking? Are they thinking anything? Where is their 'I'? Where is their soul?"

Across this nation as many as 10,000 people are at any given moment in the same state as Sunny, according to Laurence J. Schneiderman, director of the program in medical ethics at the University of California–San Diego. They are being maintained in a coma (from the Greek word for "deep sleep"), or, as doctors now put it, in a "persistent vegetative state." The causes that brought about their PVS are various: boxing injuries, dental anesthesia, strokes, car accidents, police choke-holds, heart attacks and on and on. The longest comatose survivor ever, according to the *Guinness Book of World Records,* was Elaine Esposito: she lapsed into the state after surgery in 1941 and remained that way for

From *The New Republic,* February 21, 1994, pp. 23-24, 26-27. © 1994 by The New Republic, Inc. Reprinted by permission.

thirty-seven years, until her death in 1978. The most famous—at least until Sunny—was Karen Quinlan, the New Jersey "sleeping beauty" who, in the mid-'70s, became the object of a protracted and much publicized legal battle when her parents tried to have her respirator turned off.

What all coma victims have in common is a severely damaged cerebral cortex. This is the "upper brain," responsible for cognition, perception, language and purposeful movement. If there is a cut-off of oxygen to the brain, it will lay waste to the cerebral hemispheres well before it damages the "lower brain," or brain stem, which controls respiration, blood pressure and the sleep-wake cycle, as well as certain involuntary reflexes. The brain stem remains largely intact in comatose patients. Thus they will occasionally yawn, chew, swallow, sigh, grimace, laugh and cry. They open their eyes and seem to glance about; on closer inspection, however, their eyeballs are seen to be moving in uncoordinated, random directions, and there is no visual input to the brain.

The comatose sorely test our intuitions about the boundary between life and death. What precisely does "death" mean? Is it primarily a biological, philosophical or religious concept? How can we tell for sure if someone has been grimly reaped? Is there some metaphysical event, analogous to the departure of the soul from the body, that marks the moment? Today the need for organ transplants gives these questions practical urgency, just as in previous centuries the danger of premature burial did. People used to harbor a very real fear that they might be declared dead and put in the ground while still alive. And the macabre eighteenth-century tales about exhumed corpses found to have clawed at the interior of the casket were not wholly fanciful: graveyard excavations reveal that nearly 2 percent of those interred before the advent of embalming in the twentieth century were buried alive. One of the first physicians to agitate for a clear index of death was the Englishman Jean-Jacques Winslow, who in 1740 proposed putrefaction as the sure sign. It is notable that Winslow himself was prematurely interred twice as a child.

Whatever death is, it ought to be permanent and irreversible. And if there is anything on which thanatologists have always agreed, it is that the state of death is characterized by the irreversible cessation of something or other. For centuries the "something" was obvious enough: breathing and heartbeat. The permanent loss of breath was held to mark the disunion of soul and body. (Both the Greek and the Latin terms for soul—"*anima*" and "*pneuma*"—mean "breath"; the etymology of "soul" itself is unknown.) But in the late 1950s new medical gadgetry began to be developed that could take over the functions of the heart and lungs. With the artificial respiration of brain-damaged patients now possible, the continuance of breathing and circulation became disjoined from the continuance of faculties linked with the soul: thought,

feeling, memory, rationality. The seat of these, of course, is the brain, which is also the locus of personal identity. "I left my heart in San Francisco"—that is a conceptual possibility; "I left my *brain* in San Francisco"—not likely.

Clearly, the boundary between life and death would have to be redrawn, with neurological criteria taking the place of cardio-respiratory ones. Who would do it? The Catholic Church, for one, proved reluctant; in the 1958 proclamation "The Prolongation of Life," Pope Pius XII submitted that this was rather a matter for physicians to decide. A decade later, a clear concept emerged: "brain death." The 1968 Harvard Medical School Ad Hoc Committee to Examine the Definition of Brain Death defined it as a state entailing a total unawareness of external stimuli, no spontaneous breathing and a flat brain wave. "Our primary purpose," said the committee's report, "is to define irreversible coma as a new criterion of death."

This is where matters get a bit confusing. Being in a coma, even an irreversible one, turns out to be not the same thing as being brain-dead by the Harvard criteria. Comatose patients typically have "slow" brain waves, not flat ones. Moreover, unless there is substantial damage elsewhere in the body, they are always able to breathe spontaneously, without the use of ventilators. When the plug was pulled on Karen Quinlan, for instance, she surprised everyone by wheezing along on her own for more than a decade.

In fact, there are two different concepts of brain death: "whole-brain death," where both the cerebral cortex (upper brain) and the brain stem (lower brain) irreversibly cease to function; and "higher-brain death," where only the cerebral cortex has sustained terminal damage and the brain stem is largely intact. What the Harvard criteria were aiming at was the more conservative of these, whole-brain death. This state is tantamount to decapitation. Once the brain stem stops functioning, traditional heart-lung death invariably follows within a week or so, even with the most aggressive support of life-sustaining gadgetry. Thus it is not possible for someone to be both whole-brain dead and at the same time in a persistent coma. The whole-brain standard was endorsed in 1983 by the President's Commission for the Study of Ethical Problems in Medicine, and has since become statue law in more than thirty states. Only a few states have adopted the broader higher-brain criterion. As for the rest of the world, virtually every industrialized country has accepted the whole-brain criterion as legal death, except, weirdly, Japan.

By one interpretation of brain death, Sunny von Bulow is indisputably alive. By the other, she is presumably dead. Which standard ought we to embrace? Reflecting on this question tends to bubble the intuition. The image of a permanently comatose but still breathing human in a coffin or crematory *is* a distasteful one. If the breathing is spontaneous, there is no respirator to be unplugged so that the patient can be "allowed" to die before burial/cremation. She must be suffocated, or starved to death by the removal of nourishment—which, unlike a respirator, cannot be deemed an "extraordinary" means of sustaining life. This may be excused as morally inconsequential, but it is still killing. (The preferred form of euthanasia today is somewhat subtler: since the comatose patient typically must be given medication to maintain his heart rate, and since required dosage increases over time, all one needs to do is set fixed levels of such medication; death ensues even though no treatment was actually withdrawn.) When, in 1986, the American Medical Association pronounced it ethical for physicians to withdraw care from comatose patients who met the criteria of higher-brain death, there was no implication that such patients were actually dead.

On the other hand, the destruction of the higher brain is thought not only to strip the individual of all psychological attributes—to wit, of personhood—but also to entail the irreversible loss of consciousness. And it is certainly plausible to maintain, as Schopenhauer did, that "death itself consists merely in the moment that consciousness vanishes." (On second thought, this can't be *exactly* right; if Jones suffers brain death while he is asleep, his death does not date from the moment he falls asleep.) Can a life of permanent unconsciousness—where the very possibility of having experiences is irretrievably lost—really be considered a *human* life? From the subjective point of view, is it in any way distinguishable from death?

Sunny von Bulow was lucky enough to inherit a fortune of about $75 million. There is plenty of money to pay for her hospital room, her around-the-clock nursing care and so forth, and her heirs are willing to see it spent in this way. When, by contrast, in one Veterans Administration hospital an irreversibly comatose patient survived ten years and ran up a bill for millions of dollars, the bill was paid with public money. Even if some small, intrinsic value were attributed to maintaining the vegetative functions of a human organism when the person formerly incarnated in it has vanished, it would hardly justify this sort of expenditure. Some go as far as to argue that such maintenance has a *negative* ethical value, inasmuch as it is an affront to human dignity, condemning the human person to what one ethicist described as "an eternity of exile," like the Flying Dutchman or the Wandering Jew.

Suppose, then, we were to redefine death to mean the irreversible loss of consciousness, the (earthly) extinction of the person, as opposed to the organism. Two snags remain. First, how can we make sure the loss is in fact irreversible? Two kinds of coma are known to be reversible: those resulting from drug overdose and those caused by the lowering of the body temperature below ninety degrees. Judging the odds of reversibility in other cases can be tricky. Even with the help of external brain scans, making a diagnosis of higher-brain death (as distinct from widespread cortical damage) is scarcely infallible. People *do* snap out of comas from time to time, a fact that raises doubts about whether PVS suffices for a diagnosis of brain death.

Item. In 1984 a Long Island youth named David Gribin went into a coma after sustaining severe head injuries in a horse-riding accident, and was placed on a respirator. After a month of unconsciousness, though, he revived. Eight years later, in 1992, he became the first coma victim to complete the New York City marathon.

Item. On March 5, 1991, a High Point, North Carolina, man who had been comatose since he had been beaten with a log more than eight years earlier suddenly regained consciousness and revealed to authorities the identities of his two assailants.

Item. In 1981 Artur Lundkvist, a Swedish poet, novelist and member of the committee that awards the Nobel Prize for literature, suffered a massive heart attack while delivering a lecture on Anthony Burgess, and fell into a coma. The doctors did not expect him to regain his faculties. Two months later he woke up and related a fantastic series of visions he had had while supposedly unconscious. These were later described in his book *Journeys in Dream and Imagination* (1992). While his body was lying immobile in intensive care, Lundkvist's spirit flew over Vietnam, to an alien planet where cows produced blue milk, to a Chicago train station where doctors operated on white people to make them black. He watched green saplings emerge from between his toes, saw cubist birds and met people who were long dead.

Lundkvist's case raises a second problem with redefining death to mean higher-brain death. How extensive must the damage to the cerebral cortex be before the constituents of consciousness and personhood—faculties such as imagination, feeling and desire—are actually obliterated? Must both hemispheres be destroyed, or only one? Must all electrical activity in the higher brain cease, or only the appearance of certain characteristic brain waves correlated with conscious thought? The danger here is the slippery slope, as the dire need for transplant organs pressures doctors to be more and more liberal about declaring potential donors dead.

Because of ethical obstacles to experimenting on human brains, not a great deal is known about the neural locale of consciousness. It is certainly possible that, even with the cessation of higher-brain function, some rudimentary cognitive capacity remains as long as the brain stem and other systems deeper in the brain are working. And even if consciousness does turn out to reside exclusively in the cerebral cortex, some opponents of the higher-brain death standard refuse to concede that personal identity can be defined purely in terms of consciousness. One such, the British philosopher David Lamb, maintains that uncertainty over which mental processes are constitutive of personhood "can only be avoided by accepting the proposal that the point where loss of personhood is certain is when the brain as a whole, and hence the organism as a whole, no longer functions." And that moment, he adds, is "when the brain stem dies."

In the face of these difficulties, it is tempting to adopt a thanatological agnosticism. Some maintain, for example, that death is simply the name we give to a person's condition when certain social "death behaviors" come to be considered appropriate: mourning, reading of the will, arranging for the Social Security checks to stop and so on. Perhaps, the logic goes, there is no need to impose a single standard of mortality on everyone, and each person should be allowed to choose his own, specifying it in advance. This proposal would require some minimal neurological sophistication on the part of every citizen, of course. It would require reflection on what kind of mental or biological functions constitute one's personhood; and some glancing consideration of the many unfortunate people who are short a liver or a kidney. It would require each person to contemplate his death with a cold clarity, like a mathematical theorem. What standard of death would *you* choose?

What standard would Sunny von Bulow have chosen? She was decisive when it came to flowers, caviar and Parisian couture, but she was also pathologically shy, and musing on the precise moment when one checks out is a rather shy-making proposition. So it remains for us to consider: On which side of the mortal brink is she frozen in time? Perhaps there is still a guttering flame of consciousness within her ruined brain, whose fluid-bearing ventricles have by now almost entirely usurped the place of the cerebral cortex. Perhaps, utterly abstracted from empirical reality, she is having endless hallucinatory visions in which she presides over grand, glittering parties at Clarendon Court, with—or possibly without—Claus at her side. The very thought makes her opening line in *Reversal of Fortune* almost unbearably poignant: "Brain-dead—body better than ever!"

ORGANIZATIONAL RESPONSES TO DEATH IN THE MILITARY

**Paul T. Bartone, Ph.D., and
Morten G. Ender, M.A.**

*Walter Reed Army Institute of Research, Washington,
DC, USA*

*When a friend or loved one dies, the challenge for sur-
vivors is to somehow cope effectively with the loss and go
on living and functioning. This is true not only for family
members, but also for friends and coworkers of the
deceased. How organizations respond to a death can
influence coping in either a positive or negative direction.
Military organizations have long experience with death,
and have developed programs and policies aimed at
assisting survivors to adjust positively to loss. This report
reviews how casualty policies have developed in the U.S.
Army, and draws on the Army's casualty experience to
suggest some ways in which organizational responses to
death might facilitate healthy adjustment for survivors.*

The sudden, unexpected death of family members,
relatives, and close friends can be disturbing in a way
unmatched by other stressful life events. Death con-
fronts the survivors with a variety of issues and challenges for which they are often unprepared. In addition
to the grief associated with loss of a loved one, death
can generate persistent thoughts and concerns about
one's own mortality. Within organizations, the adaptive challenge for individuals is compounded when
death creates vacancies in key positions or roles. Such
"role vacuums" often require major readjustments for
the survivors, while duties are reallocated and/or re-
placements sought. A critical (though infrequently contemplated) question for managers, counselors,
educators, and policy makers concerns how survivors
cope with the challenges presented by the death of a
coworker, and what organizations might do to encourage healthy adjustment. This article examines programs and policies related to casualties and death in
the military and attempts to extract useful lessons of
wider applicability. Drawing on military casualty experience and relevant research, we suggest some ways
in which individual and group recovery might be facilitated by organizational responses to death.

Military organizations regularly must address issues related to death, during peacetime as well as war.
A recent study shows that despite generally lower
mortality rates in the peacetime U.S. Army than in
comparable U.S. civilian groups, still significant numbers of service members are killed each year in training accidents, as well as by other external causes
(Rothberg, Bartone, Holloway, & Marlowe, 1990). The
military must also be prepared to respond to death on a
large scale in the event of hostilities or disasters, and
to do so in a context that places a premium on rapid
recovery of individual and group functioning (Bartone
& Wright, 1990). For these reasons, and also out of
humane concern for grieving family members, many
military organizations have established comprehensive programs to foster effective and sensitive handling of death-related matters. These programs are
typically managed by a special "casualty branch,"
which develops, coordinates, and implements policies
and procedures on issues related to casualties. Casualty affairs include such things as the notification of
family members, recovery and transport of human
remains, respectful and appropriate disposition of per-

Thanks are due to Joseph M. Rothberg, James E. McCarroll,
Jocelyn V. Bartone, and two anonymous reviewers for helpful
comments on the manuscript.

The views of the authors are not necessarily those of the
Department of the Army or of the Department of Defense
(para. 4–3, AR 360–5).

Address correspondence to Paul T. Bartone, Ph.D., U.S.
Army Medical Research Unit-Europe, HQ, 7th Medical Com-
mand, Nachrichten Kaserne, Karlsruher Str. 144, D-W-6900
Heidelberg, Germany.

sonal effects, helping families plan funeral arrangements and memorial services, and facilitating claims for insurance and other benefits.

Military casualty activities also serve important social and psychological functions. Policies and practices related to casualty processing are likely to impact on (a) individual mental health—how persons exposed to death cope with their reactions of grief, horror, loss and fear; (b) unit morale—how quickly and fully the military unit recovers its capacity to function effectively; and (c) the broader world of civil-military relations (Bartone, Ursano, Wright, & Ingraham, 1989; Wright, 1987; Ender, 1991). For example, Army officers who assisted bereaved family members after the Army's Gander, Newfoundland air disaster (a charter airline crash that killed 248 soldiers returning from peacekeeping duty in 1985) had a positive impact on many family members. As official representatives of the organization, these assistance officers came to personify a responsive and caring military for many grieving families (Bartone, 1987).

The military casualty affairs office or branch is the agency responsible for planning and implementing institutional responses to death. As such, it is in a unique position to influence the course of adjustment or adaptation to loss. Through their programs and policies, such agencies can facilitate healthy psychological recovery following trauma by establishing a context in which normal, positive adjustment processes can occur. Formal organizational responses to death shape the environment within which individuals and groups respond to death, or what might be termed the "organizational recovery context." It is now understood that situational or environmental factors are important determinants of the coping processes people use to manage stress in their lives (McCrae, 1984; Lazarus, DeLongis, Folkman & Gruen, 1985). While all organizations can influence both physical and psychological aspects of the work environment, this is even more true for highly structured organizations like the military (Moos, 1975; Bartone, 1988; Bartone & Kirkland, 1991). In fact, a recent study found that the "recovery context" established by leaders of military units experiencing fatal training accidents appears to influence individual and unit adjustment to loss, in either a positive or negative direction (Tyler & Gifford, 1991).

In what follows, we briefly discuss the nature of death in the military, not only in war but also during peacetime. Next, we give a short historical overview of casualty operations and services in the U.S. Army. Finally, we consider how casualty programs and policies may speed healthy recovery for both individuals and organizations.

DEATH IN THE MILITARY

Death in the military occurs in times of peace as well as war. A peacetime military must train for war if it is to be effective, and such training is inherently dangerous. For example, in one typical recent year there were 483 accidental deaths in the Army alone (Washington Headquarters Service, 1988). Occasionally, large-scale disasters push this number even higher. For example in 1985, 248 Army soldiers died in the Gander air crash just before Christmas (Bartone et al., 1989).

Although the number of fatal training accidents has been decreasing since 1977 (Washington Headquarters Service, 1988), the risk of death and injury remains a prominent demand of the military occupation (M. W. Segal, 1989). In addition to the approximately 12,000 military retiree deaths each year, Department of Defense casualty centers process an average of 2,100 active duty deaths per year (based on 1979–1988 data; Washington Headquarters Service, 1988). Those who die while on active duty are generally quite young, with an average age of 26 for enlisted service members and 33 for officers (Department of Defense, 1988). Although the safety record of the U.S. Army is good, fatal accidents continue to occur as soldiers train with heavy, dangerous equipment. Terrorism poses another peacetime risk for soldiers. As military units are utilized more commonly in peacekeeping operations, soldiers can make convenient targets for terrorist attack (D. R. Segal, 1989). For example, 241 U.S. Marines died in 1983 when a terrorist truck-bomb crashed into their Beirut barracks. So even in the absence of combat, military organizations must be prepared to respond effectively to the sudden death of service members.

U.S. ARMY CASUALTY OPERATIONS: AN OVERVIEW

The story of U.S. Army casualty operations since World War II is one of continued growth and expansion of services to the families of dead, wounded, or seriously ill soldiers. In order to obtain an historical perspective on casualty services provided to families, we examined eleven editions of the Army's handbook for survivors published since 1950 (e.g., Department of Army, 1950; 1989), and identified the number of distinct services or entitlements listed in each. Results show that the number of services and benefits provided by the Army and other federal agencies approximately doubled from 22 in 1950 to 46 in 1989. The Appendix lists the current benefits available to survivors. While some of these are actually paid by government agencies other than the Army (e.g., Veterans Administration, Social Security Agency, Internal Revenue Service), the Army provides detailed information to survivors on benefits available, and extensive help in applying for them.

During World War II, the families of soldiers who died were informed by telegram from the Army Adjutant General. The telegram was directed to whoever the soldier had designated as the "emergency addressee" or person to notify in case of emergency. The message stated the basic facts of the death as known at the time, and offered a brief statement of regret. Not uncommonly, the telegram did not arrive until weeks after the death. Following the telegram, the Army sent the family a letter of condolence and a pamphlet outlining survivor benefits. It was the family member's responsibility to apply for most of these benefits (Department of the Army, 1950).

Shortly after the Korean War ended in 1956, the Army sought to improve the death notification process by providing a personal visit by an Army officer to the family's home to confirm the soldier's death. The initial notification of death still came by telegram, but this was followed by an officer who verified the death, and provided additional details to the family when possible. The personal visit was meant to convey a greater sense of organizational appreciation and respect for the sacrifice of the deceased soldier and his/her family.

During the Vietnam conflict, the Army made additional substantial changes to its casualty notification and assistance policies. In an effort to further humanize the process, the initial notification was now made in person by a "casualty notifier," with a confirming telegraph to follow. Financial benefits to family members were increased significantly. Written policy statements more clearly delineated the eligibility criteria for survivor benefits. While there was no stated requirement that the casualty notifier be from the same unit as the deceased soldier, it was recommended that notifying officers be of equal or higher rank to the deceased. Only officers or senior ranking non-commissioned officers were to make death notifications. Again, this was meant to convey greater respect and appreciation for the deceased soldier, and to symbolize the importance vested by the Army in each soldier's life. In the interest of lessening the shock for family members, the new policy also stipulated that death notifications not be made after 10:00 p.m. or before 6:00 a.m. local time. The personal notification was still followed by a telegram confirming the details of the death.

Also during the Vietnam era, the Army initiated an expanded Casualty Assistance Program. Under this program, which persists in its basic form today, commissioned officers, warrant officers and senior ranking non-commissioned officers are placed on unit duty rosters for possible service as casualty notifiers or casualty assistance officers (CAOs). Before 1987, the casualty assistance officer was known as the survivor assistance officer. When a soldier dies, his unit contacts the Army's central casualty records office in Washington, DC. There, the soldier's emergency data card is checked to obtain the name and location of his/her next-of-kin. This information, as well as a factual statement on the death, is forwarded to the subordinate casualty office that is geographically closest to

the home of the soldier's next-of-kin. This office assigns a casualty notifier and a casualty assistance officer, drawing names from local unit duty rosters. Experience has shown it is helpful to separate these roles, since many families seem to be more receptive to ongoing support when it comes from a person other than the one who made the initial notification of death. Many surviving family members report persistent negative images and associations to the casualty notifier (F. R. Lange, personal communication, April 26, 1989).

The casualty notifier has the task of first locating the next-of-kin, and then telling them of the soldier's death. This is done in a careful, formal manner. The following paragraph is recommended:

"The Secretary of the Army has asked me to express his deep regret that your (relationship) (died/was killed in action) in (country/State) on (date). (State the circumstances.) The Secretary extends his deepest sympathy to you and your family in your tragic loss." (Dept. of the Army PAM 608-33, 1987, p. 5)

The notifier informs the family member(s) that a telegram confirming the death will come within 24 hours, and that a casualty assistance officer will visit soon to provide assistance. Unless the family member requires immediate help, the notifier departs once the notification is complete. The notifier immediately informs the CAO that notification was made, and relays any information about the family that might help in providing support. Next the CAO contacts the family, usually by phone, and arranges a time to meet. By policy, this meeting should occur within 24 hours of the initial death notification. During their first visit the CAO provides the family with phone numbers for contacting him/her, and solicits the family's wishes for funeral arrangements and disposition of remains. These and other duties of the CAO are detailed in a Casualty Assistance Handbook that has undergone several revisions over the years (e.g., Department of the Army, 1971; 1987). The general guidance given to CAOs is "to help the family in any way possible,' An important aspect of the job is to function as liaison between the family and the Army, facilitating the flow of information to the family and providing them with practical assistance on administrative matters.

The next major change in Army casualty policies occurred in 1970, when personalized notification of death was extended to "secondary next-of-kin" (SNOK), as well as primary. Although usually listing a parent as their SNOK, soldiers can name anyone they choose on their emergency data cards, including siblings, spouses or ex-spouses, grandparents or friends. The responsibilities of the CAO remained the same.

The Army's 1985 Gander crash provided the impetus for another series of changes in casualty assistance programs. Just before Christmas in 1985, a plane carrying 248 U.S. Army soldiers crashed at Gander, Newfoundland. The flight was returning soldiers from peacekeeping duty in the Sinai to their home post, Fort Campbell, Kentucky. Everyone aboard was killed. For the United States, it was the largest military mass casualty event since Vietnam. Useful lessons were learned in the aftermath of the crash, leading to greater elaboration and refinement of services for families of dead soldiers. Where earlier editions of the Army pamphlet for next-of-kin emphasize the survivors' own responsibility to pursue entitlements, the latest (twelfth) edition specifies the CAO's role in helping the family obtain even more extensive entitlements, from funeral expenses to movie theater, transportation, and recreation privileges (Department of the Army, 1989). Furthermore, services to the secondary next-of-kin are no longer limited to simple notification. Anyone designated by a service member as a SNOK is now entitled to a wide range of services, including regular briefings by the CAO, and government-funded travel to and from funerals and memorial services. As new experiences accumulate, the Army continues to improve its casualty programs and policies. For example, efforts are currently underway to apply computer-based technologies to the transmission of casualty data and messages, in order to provide family members with more accurate and timely information.

DISCUSSION AND IMPLICATIONS

As an organization that must deal on a regular basis with death, the U.S. Army has developed a variety of programs and policies aimed at helping bereaved survivors. This article has outlined the Army's casualty procedures, and documents how casualty services have grown over the last 40 years. Although these services still focus mainly on providing administrative and financial assistance to families, Army casualty programs reflect an increased sensitivity to emotional and psychological issues surrounding death. The current policy of assigning a CAO to help a family for an extended period is indicative of the general trend to make casualty programs more personalized and supportive than they have been in the past.

An often unstated assumption that underlies many Army casualty assistance efforts is that the course of individual adjustment for a survivor may be influenced positively or negatively by how the organization responds to a death. If the organization seems cold and uncaring, the anger, grief, and frustration of family members is exacerbated, and the sense of meaninglessness regarding the death can be increased. On the other hand, if the organization responds with concern and dignity, a family's pain may be eased somewhat. It is largely this desire to reduce the family's grief, and facilitate healthy recovery that leads the Army on an organizational level to attend so carefully to the details

of casualty operations, from how the initial notification is performed, to arranging funeral and memorial services, and providing ongoing personal support and assistance to family members. These programs have developed largely without the benefit of research or theory to support their effectiveness. Instead, they are the result of long and hard experience with casualties, and the slow accumulation of wisdom regarding what is effective and what is not.

Recent research on coping with traumatic loss indeed supports the potential psychological value of many military casualty policies. For example, a variety of studies have shown that programs/activities that increase a sense of positive meaning regarding the trauma or loss can facilitate healthy psychological adjustment for survivors (e.g., Pennebaker, Colder; & Sharp, 1990). While many questions remain, there is a growing consensus among professionals that healthy adjustment to major loss involves a cognitive/emotional process of "working-through" the traumatic event, through which the loss is understood and integrated into one's total life experience (Horowitz, 1978; Ursano & Fullerton, 1990). This involves finding some acceptable explanation for the loss, and attributing meaning that is generally positive and coherent in nature (Frankl, 1959; Antonovsky, 1979; Dollinger; 1986). To the extent casualty assistance programs facilitate positive cognitive constructions of meaning for survivors, a healthy grief and coping process may be accelerated. Anecdotally at least, many family members appear to have less trouble adjusting to the death of a loved one when the loss is construed as serving a noble or "good cause," such as defending one's country or family, as opposed to a senseless event like a car accident or natural disaster. In Operation Desert Storm, for example, several Army deaths resulted from preventable motor vehicle accidents completely unrelated to combat. In more than one such case, surviving family members requested that the death be officially recorded as combat-related rather than non-combat-related. In research interviews, the CAOs working with these families reported that family members had a strong desire to believe the death was for a worthy cause (Bartone, Gifford, & Tyler, 1991). The vast majority of family members also choose to have a funeral with full military honors, including honor guard, 21-gun salute, and the flag-draped coffin. For many, this seems to enhance the sense that the death was in the service of some noble, higher purpose.

U.S. Army casualty assistance programs are aimed almost exclusively at bereaved family members. But some of the wisdom accumulated in casualty operations might be usefully applied to other groups affected by death, such as surviving members of the military unit. Whether unit losses are the result of combat, training accidents, or some other cause, the survivors can be profoundly affected (Bartone & Wright, 1990;

Gifford & Tyler, 1989). Recognizing this, a potential pitfall for agencies that must respond somehow to death within their ranks is that they will fail to provide an organizational context that encourages and supports healthy acceptance and integration of loss. Worse yet, organizational policies might actually interfere with healthy coping processes. Ideally, organizations will provide programs, policies, and practices that assist individuals and groups to transform loss, suffering, and death into a psychological asset instead of a liability, a source of strength and commitment rather than of prolonged mental distress. Tyler & Gifford (1991) observed several ways in which this may occur in military units following fatal training accidents. For example, surviving soldiers apparently adjust more effectively to the accidental death of comrades when leaders take time to eulogize the deceased, and relate the loss in positive terms to the pursuit of broader mission goals.

Casualty workers themselves, such as casualty notifiers and casualty assistance officers, may be deeply affected by their experiences, and can benefit from supportive organizational policies. Several studies have documented the special stressors and related ill effects that casualty workers often experience (Bartone et al., 1989, 1992). While these duties must be performed with the highest professionalism, most of those assigned receive no special training. They are typically thrust into the role with only several hours notice, do it as a duty in addition to their regular jobs, and are encouraged to complete the process promptly (Department of the Army, 1987). Following submission of the CAOs' final report (anywhere from 1 week to 1 year after the death), there is no further organizationally sanctioned contact between the bereaved family and the Army.

While no amount of preparation is likely to remove the stress from casualty work, some kind of advance training or preparation should help casualty workers to cope more effectively with the special demands of the job. Rosenbaum & Ballard (1990) recently described an effective training program for Air Force officers who specialize in casualty affairs. In the Army, the need to train casualty personnel is complicated by the fact that most Army casualty workers are not specialists, but perform casualty assistance as extra duty. Although families of the deceased have been well-served by this system, Army casualty workers themselves can pay a heavy psychological price (Bartone et al., 1989; Bartone & Fullerton, 1992). Large organizations such as the Army that confront death with some regularity might benefit by adopting the Air Force strategy of training personnel to specialize in casualty affairs.

It is an unpleasant fact that military organizations have extensive experience with death, and with trying to assist survivors in various ways. But useful lessons with application beyond the military can be taken from military casualty operations. This brief review of casualty programs in the U.S. Army shows that on an organizational level many programs and policies aim to encourage healthy coping of survivors after the death of a soldier. While the Army's casualty support programs are still being improved, they do represent an unusually high level of organizational commitment to assist those affected by death, and may thus provide a policy template for other organizations that want to assist survivors following a "death within the ranks."

REFERENCES

Antonovsky, A. (1979). *Health, stress and coping.* San Francisco: Jossey-Bass.

Bartone, P. T. (October, 1987). Boundary crossers: The role of Army family assistance officers in the Gander disaster. Paper presented at the Biennial Meetings of the Inter-University Seminar on Armed Forces and Society, Chicago, IL.

Bartone, P T. (April, 1988). Persons, environments, and the management of stress. Paper presented at the 11th Biennial Symposium on Psychology in the Department of Defense, Colorado Springs, CO.

Bartone, P. T. & Fullerton, T. D. (August, 1992). Psychological effects of war stress on casualty operations personnel. Paper presented at the Annual Convention of the American Psychological Association, Washington, DC.

Bartone, P. T., Gifford, R. K., & Tyler, M. P. (October, 1991). Casualty Assistance Officers to families of Desert Storm dead. Presented at the annual meeting of the International Society for Traumatic Stress Studies, Washington, DC.

Bartone, P. T., Gifford, R. K., Tyler, M. P, & Lowell, A. M. (April, 1992). Stress and illness in wartime casualty workers. Paper presented at the Annual Meeting of the Eastern Psychological Association, Boston, MA.

Bartone, P. T. & Kirkland, F. R. (1991). Optimal leadership in small army units. In R. Gal and A. D. Mangelsdorff (Eds.). *Handbook of military psychology* (pp. 393–409). New York: Wiley and Sons.

Bartone, P. T., Ursano, R. J., Wright, K. M., & Ingraham, L. H. (1989). The impact of a military air disaster on the health of assistance workers: A prospective study. *Journal of Nervous & Mental Disease, 177,* 317–328.

Bartone, P. T. & Wright, K. M. (1990). Grief and group recovery following a military air disaster. *Journal of Traumatic Stress, 3,* 523–539.

Department of the Army (1950). *For your guidance.* Headquarters, Department of the Army, Pamphlet No. 20-15, Washington, DC.

Department of the Army (1971). *Survivor assistance officer and family services and assistance handbook.* Headquarters, Department of the Army, Pamphlet No. 608-33, Washington, DC.

Department of the Army (1987). *Casualty assistance handbook.* Headquarters, Department of the Army, Pamphlet No. 608-33, Washington, DC.

Department of Defense (1988). *Defense almanac.* Superintendent of Documents. U.S. Government Printing Office, Jacket No. 202-262/80002, Washington, DC.

Department of the Army (1989). *Personal affairs: A guide for survivors of deceased Army members.* Washington, DC: Headquarters, Department of the Army Pamphlet No. 608-4.

Dollinger, S. J. (1986). The need for meaning following disaster: Attributions and emotional upset. *Personality & Social Psychology Bulletin, 12,* 300–310.

Ender, M. G. (1991). Associated strains of a temporary role: The case of the Army Casualty Assistance Officer. Unpublished master's thesis, University of Maryland, College Park, MD.

Frankl, V. (1959). *Man's search for meaning.* New York: Pocket Books.

Gifford, R. K. & Tyler, M. P. (1989). Consulting in grief leadership: A practical guide. *Disaster Management, 2,* 218–224.

Horowitz, M. (1978). *Stress response syndromes.* New Jersey: J. Aronson.

Lazarus, R. S., DeLongis, A., Folkman, S., & Gruen, R. (1985). Stress and adaptation outcomes. *American Psychologist, 40,* 770–779.

McCrae, R. R. (1984). Situational determinants of coping responses: Loss, threat, and challenge. *Journal of Personality and Social Psychology, 46,* 919–928.

Moos, R. H. (1975). *Evaluating correctional settings.* New York: Wiley.

Pennebaker, J. W., Colder, M., & Sharp, L. K. (1990). Accelerating the coping process. *Journal of Personality and Social Psychology 58,* 528–537.

Rosenbaum, S. D., & Ballard, J. A. (1990). Educating Air Force mortuary officers. *Death Studies, 14,* 135–145.

Rothberg. J. M., Bartone, P. T., Holloway, H. C., & Marlowe, D. H. (1990). Life and death in the U.S. Army: In corpore sano. *Journal of the American Medical Association, 264,* 2241–2244.

Segal, D. R. (1989). *Recruiting for Uncle Sam.* Lawrence, KS: University Press of Kansas.

Segal, M. W. (1989). The nature of work and family linkages: A theoretical perspective. In G. L. Bowen & D. K. Orthner (Eds.), *The organization family: Work and family linkages in the U.S. military* (pp. 3–36). New York: Praeger.

Tyler, M. P. & Gifford, R. K. (1991). Fatal training accidents: The military unit as a recovery context. *Journal of Traumatic Stress, 4,* 233–249.

Ursano, R. J. & Fullerton, C. S. (1990). Cognitive and behavioral responses to trauma. *Journal of Applied Social Psychology, 20,* 1766–1775.

Washington Headquarters Service (1988). *Worldwide U.S. active duty military personnel casualties.* Pamphlet #DIOR/M07-88-02, Superintendent of Documents, U.S. Government Printing Office, Washington, DC.

Wright (Saczynski), K. M. (Ed.). (1987). The human response to the Gander military air disaster: A summary report. Department of Military Psychiatry, Walter Reed Army Institute of Research. Washington, DC.

APPENDIX

Army/Government Benefits & Entitlements for Survivors of Deceased Army Members, as Described in Department of Army Pamphlet No. 6084 (1989 Edition).

1. General Report of Death: All available facts are provided to family during personal visit by casualty notifier
2. Report of Casualty: 10 certified copies of "certificate of death" provided to next-of-kin
3. Reports of Investigation: autopsy & death investigation reports provided to family on request
4. Care of remains by military: includes embalming, metal casket, clothing, burial, transport, & other expenses
5. Private arrangements for shipment of remains: Army will reimburse for transportation arranged by family
6. Private arrangements for preparation of remains: Army pays if family prefers private arrangements
7. Care of remains if death occurs overseas—Army pays for preparation & transport
8. Burial in Arlington National Cemetery authorized (if space available)
9. Burial in other national cemeteries is authorized (if space available)
10. Headstone or marker supplied
11. Full military honors provided at funeral
12. Army funds travel of dependents to/from funeral
13. Army funds movement of household goods
14. Army funds movement of a mobile home
15. Army funds the shipment of an automobile
16. Family can remain in government housing for 90 days & more
17. Personal effects are collected, safeguarded, & returned to family
18. Army Emergency Relief provides financial support as needed
19. American Red Cross provides emergency financial assistance
20. "Death Gratuity" payment of $6,000 made within 72 hours
21. Family receives any pay or allowances due the soldier
22. Soldier contributions to Veterans Education Assistance Program are returned to family
23. Social security lump-sum death payment to surviving spouse
24. Eligible family members receive social security benefits
25. Dependency & Indemnity Compensation paid to family through the Veterans Administration
26. Survivor Benefit Plan provides annuity to spouse if soldier was retirement eligible
27. Reinstated Entitlement Program for Survivors, extends some Social Security benefits for spouses & children
28. Serviceman's Group Life Insurance, now pays up to $200,000 to survivors if soldier was enrolled
29. Home mortgages insured by FHA are paid by Army for 2 years beyond date of death
30. Continued medical care provided to spouse (if unmarried) & children under age 21
31. Commissary privileges for unremarried spouse
32. Unremarried spouse & dependent children may continue to shop at post exchange
33. Unremarried spouse & dependent children may continue to use post movie theaters & recreational facilities
34. Unremarried spouse & dependent children are entitled to government identification card
35. Unremarried spouse receives preference for civil service jobs
36. Federal income taxes cancelled for year in which death occurred (under some circumstances)
37. Federal estate taxes are reduced if death was combat related
38. Army will pay claims for loss or destruction of personal property (e.g., household goods, personal effects)
39. Posthumous promotions are made under some circumstances
40. Posthumous awards/medals are granted on commander's approval, & presented to family
41. Unremarried spouses are entitled to V.A. secured home loans
42. V.A. Dependents' Education Assistance program provides educational benefits to spouses & children
43. Army Emergency Relief program gives college loans & grants to spouses & children of deceased soldiers
44. Dependent children may attend Dept. of Defense Overseas Dependents Schools (if space available)
45. Free legal advice & assistance from Army lawyers is available to family members
46. Government benefits & life insurance proceeds are generally exempt from attachment by creditors

Developmental Aspects of Dying and Death

Though no one really understands death, it is something we must accept. We can talk about death, learn from each other, and help each other. By better understanding death conceptualizations at various stages and in different relationships within the life cycle, we can better help each other. It is not our intent to suggest that age should be viewed as the sole determinant of one's death concept. Many other factors influence this cognitive development such as level of intelligence, physical and mental well-being, previous emotional reactions to various life experiences, religious background, other social and cultural forces, personal identity and self-worth appraisals, and exposure to or threats of death. Nonetheless, we will discuss death and death perceptions at various stages from the cradle to the grave or the womb to the tomb.

Research on very young children's conceptions of death still does not have an adequate understanding of their responses. Yet a need exists to look more carefully at the dynamics of the young and to their families relating to the concept of death. Adults tend to remember their first experience with death occurring around the average age of 8, as is noted in the article "First Childhood Death Experiences." Many adults recall vivid details about this event decades later, and for many it was a traumatic experience filled with fear, anger, and frustration. Bruce Duffy, as an adult, reflects back on the death of his mother when he was 11, and how he and his father had struggled in "Feeling Something: When a Father Dies." These feelings of misunderstanding surfaced with the death of his father some 27 years later.

As parents, we need to recognize the insecurity often found with children at the time of a death and to deal with the situation accordingly. Children can generally take about as much as we can "dish out" to them; the problem is that we adults are often rather inept about dying and death ourselves, and thus may practice avoidance in relating to children. We must remember that children, too, have feelings. They especially need emotional support during a time of crisis such as a death. The essay "Death of a Friend" is a good account of how teachers and children worked through the death of a 7-year-old student. "Detachment Revisited: The Child's Reconstruction of a Dead Parent," based on interviews of children following a parent's death, discusses how an inner construction of the dead parent had developed. Doctor and social work educator Vanda Manahan shares her observations of how others react to death in her article "Reflections on the Death of My Daughter-in-Law."

While life expectancy tends to be extended more today than in the past, as noted in "Old No More," the naturalness of dying with the very elderly actually conflicts with the medicalization and legalization of death in Jack McCue's article, "The Naturalness of Dying."

Looking Ahead: Challenge Questions

Since children are experiencing death situations at a relatively early age (average age is 8 years), what societal steps can be taken to help children better cope with the death of a person or pet?

What can our society do to enhance an acceptance of the "naturalness of dying" with the very elderly, or should prolongation of life be our goal?

Are the elderly in America "warehoused" and put away to die? Can you present evidence of such "warehousing"? How might the image of the elderly be improved in our society? Is growing old really "the best to be," or is growing old really "hell"?

Communication Among Children, Parents, and Funeral Directors

Daniel J. Schaefer

Daniel J. Schaefer is a funeral director, Brooklyn, NY.

I have been a funeral director for the last twenty-five years. My family has been in the funeral service for one hundred and seven years. We have buried our friends; I have buried parents of my friends and children of my friends. Over the last ten years or so, I have found that something is missing: there have been fewer children attending funerals than I knew were in my friends' families. I began to ask parents, very simply, "What are you saying to your kids about this death in your family?" The replies of 1,800 sets of the parents of more than 3,600 children proved that they were basically unprepared to talk with their children about death and terribly uneasy about doing so, but not unwilling to say something once they were prepared by someone or given appropriate information.

The bits of information that I am going to present are not a standard message. They are building materials. The blueprint is individual to each family, so what we do is to take the family's blueprint, which has their particular death circumstance, then take the building materials, and build a message that parents can give to their children. For the families that I serve, I do this on an individual basis.

TALKING TO CHILDREN ABOUT DEATH

Thinking about talking to children about death is upsetting. It makes many parents anxious. It has been helpful for parents to know how many other parents feel. On Memorial Day two years ago, at three in the morning, I received a call that my brother had been killed in an automobile accident. I have five children, and I knew that four hours from then I was going to have to explain to them about their uncle. I said to my wife, "It's unusual—I've done this with hundreds of families, but I have this thing in the pit of my stomach. I *know* what to say to these kids; I know exactly what I'm going to do. Can you imagine how it must be for somebody who doesn't know what to say?"

What do people say about speaking to children about death? Some are sure that they do have to talk to their children and some say they are not sure that it is necessary. Some parents who believe that something should be said are told by others that they should avoid upsetting their children. Parents naturally tend to build a protective wall around their children. What I say to them is "Let's look at the wall, let's see if it works, and if it does work, who is it working for? Is it working for you, to protect you from your child's grief? If we look over the wall, what do we see on the other side? Do we see a kid who is comfortable or do we see, in fact, a kid who is a solitary mourner?"

When parents plan to speak to their children about death, they have to understand that what they are about to do is not easy, that they are going to be upset and stressed, that they are probably going to lack energy, and that they are going to feel unable to concentrate. They are going to be afraid of their own emotions and the effect that these emotions will have on their children. They are not going to know what their children understand, and basically they have to realize that they want to protect their children from pain. It is important that parents know ahead of time that they are going to feel this way.

What do other people say to them? They say, "Your kids don't know what's going on," "Wait until later," "Tell them a fairy tale," "Don't say anything," "Send them away until the funeral is over," or "Do you really want to put your kids through all this?" implying that no loving parent would. It is almost frightening to talk with one's children on this subject, but I believe that it is dangerous not to.

From Chapter 5 of *Loss, Grief and Care*, by Daniel J. Schaefer, 1988, pp. 131-142. © 1988 by Haworth Press, Inc., 10 Alice Street, Binghamton, New York.

Almost all parents will agree that children are surprisingly perceptive. They overhear conversations, read emotions and responses around them, and ask questions, directly and indirectly. They *will* receive messages; it is impossible not to communicate. No matter how hard parents try not to, they are going to communicate their grief to their children. Without some explanation, the children will be confused and anxious. What I say to parents is, "Since you're going to be sending a message out anyway, why don't you try to control the message?" A message is controlled by making sure that the information is true, geared for the age of the child, and, if possible, delivered in surroundings that make the child's reception of the message a little easier to handle.

For parents, feeling in control is important at a time when feeling out of control is routine and common, and when helping the child—the most dependent person in the family at that time—is also critical. The discussion between parent and child may be the child's only chance to understand what is happening. Sometimes, however, the pressure and enormity of this task, along with the advice of others, really proves too great for parents. They choose a short-term covering for themselves, without realizing the long-term effect on their children.

Explaining the How and Why of Death

Children have to know from the beginning what sad is. They have to know why their parents are sad and why they themselves are sad. So parents can begin with, "This is a very sad time," or "A very sad thing has happened," or "Mommy and Daddy are sad because...." Children have to know that it is a death that has made the parents sad: with no explanation, they may think that they have caused the sadness. They also have to know that it is appropriate to feel sad.

The next stage involves an explanation of death and what it means. Death basically means that a person's body stops working and will not work any more. It won't do any of the things it used to do. It won't walk, talk, or move; none of its parts work; it does not see and it does not hear. This foundation is what parents feel comfortable referring back to when children ask questions like "Will Grandpa ever move again?" "Why can't they fix him?" "Why isn't he moving?" "Is he sleeping?" "Can he hear me?" "Can he eat after he's buried?" If parents come up with different answers to all of these questions, it becomes confusing, but when they have a foundation, they can come back to it repeatedly. The notion that something has stopped working is a firm foundation for children, and parents feel comfortable in not lying or deceiving in using this type of explanation.

Because death is a form of abandonment, the words "passed away," "gone away," or "left us," that many people use hold out to the child the hope that the deceased will return, which of course causes tremendous frustration while they wait for the person to return. Appropriate explanations to children of why a particular death happened might be, for example, in a case of terminal illness, "Because the disease couldn't be stopped. The person became very, very sick, the body wore out, and the body stopped working"; in a case of suicide, "Some people's bodies get sick and don't work right, and some people's minds don't work right. They can't see things clearly, and they feel that the only way to solve their problems is to take their own life"; in a case of miscarriage, "Sometimes a baby is just starting to grow; something happens and makes it stop. We don't know what it was—it wasn't anything that anyone did."

CHILDREN'S REACTIONS TO DEATH

When people start to take this information and relate it to their own family situations in preparation for confronting their families, they want to know what they need to be concerned about and what to look for. Even newborn infants and toddlers know when things are different. The smaller they are, the less likely it is that they will be able to figure out why. Children respond to changes in behavior; they sense when life patterns change. Infants may alter their nursing patterns; toddlers become cranky, and change their sleeping and eating patterns. Excitement at home, new people around, parents gone at odd times, a significant person missing, a sad atmosphere—children know that something is different and react accordingly. When parents expect these changes in their children, they can respond to them more sensibly.

Piaget says that children between the ages of three and six years see death as reversible. The way this translates for parents (and for children) is that people will come back, that dead is not forever. Parents have said to me, "How could a child think that somebody will return?" From a child's point of view, ET returns, Jesus and Lazarus returned, and Road Runner returns constantly. And children may misinterpret the rise-again eulogies often given by clergy.

Several years ago (1978), "Sesame Street" produced a program dealing with the death of Mr. Hooper. The program was written up in newspapers and other publications as being an advance for the education of children. The problem is that Mr. Hooper has returned in reruns of the show, so that children who experienced his death now find that Mr. Hooper is back again.

People may say, "My child isn't affected by his grandfather's death—he's only four years old." I say, "Why should he be affected? As far as he's concerned, Grandpa's only going to be dead for a little while." Knowing how children perceive death helps parents to understand their children better, so that they will not become upset when a child continues to ask questions. They know that children in that age range can be expected to ask more questions.

Children also tend to connect events that are not connected. Does this death mean that someone else is going to die? "Grandpa died after he had a headache. Mommy has a headache. Does that mean that she is going to die?" "Old people die. Daddy is old [he is thirty]. Is he going to die?" This means that we have to explain the difference between being very, very sick and just sick like Mommy or Daddy might be; the difference between being very, very old and over twenty; and the difference between being very old and very sick and being very old but not very sick.

Children ages six to nine know that death is final, but they still think about return. They need a more detailed explanation of why a person has died than younger children do. With these children, it is much more important to distinguish between a fatal illness and just being sick—to say, "It's not like when you get sick, or when Mommy or Daddy get sick." If a parent tells a child, "Grandpa had a pain in his stomach, went to the hospital, and died," what is the child to think the next time that Mommy has menstrual cramps? What are children to think when a grandparent dies from lung cancer after a tremendous bout of coughing and then find that their father has a cough? It is normal for children in that situation to start to cling to the father and ask, "Are you okay?"

Children of this age may not want to go to a house where a person has died because "it's spooky." They also have to deal with and understand their emotions, to know that crying, feeling bad, and being angry are all acceptable behaviors.

Children ages nine to twelve move much closer to an adult sense of grieving. They are more aware of the details of an illness and more aware of the impact of a death on them. Consequently, they need more emotional support. They need to know that their feelings are acceptable and that someone is supportive of those feelings.

Teenagers also need support with their new feelings. Parents may find it better to share their own feelings with their adolescent children. Teenagers also have to understand why a person has died.

At the funeral of a friend, I met a man I used to know, another funeral director. He said to me, "It's strange. When I grew up in Queens with my grandfather, we lived in a two-family house for ten-and-a-half years. When my parents had enough money, they bought a house on Long Island, and we moved there. That was in the summer. On my birthday, in October, Grandpa didn't send me a card. I was a little concerned about that, but when Grandpa didn't come for Thanksgiving, and then when he didn't come for Christmas, I asked my mother where Grandpa was. She said he couldn't come." My friend went on: "I couldn't think what I could possibly have done to this dear man that I had spent my childhood with that would cause him not to like me any more. Then it went on again. Grandpa never came in the summer, then it was another Thanksgiving and another Christmas. It wasn't until I was thirteen that they told me that my grandfather had died. I thought that was bizarre until a woman came into my funeral home three weeks ago and when I said to her, as I say to everybody, 'What did you say to your kids about the death of your mother?' she said, 'I haven't told them. I just told them she went on vacation in Vermont.'" So the difference between ten years ago, or fifteen, or twenty years ago and today is not so great for uninformed parents.

Responsibility

People say, "How can a child feel responsible for the death of another person?" Yet, they will say to their children, "You're driving me crazy," "You'll be the death of me yet," or "Don't give me a heart attack!" Adults may say such things as figures of speech, but children do not always see it that way. "If only I had prayed harder," they may say. Children basically see God as a rewarder or punisher; He rewards good behavior and punishes bad. Therefore, if a child does a bad thing that only he or she knows about, God may punish the child by the death of someone in the child's family. If illness or death follows a misdeed, the child can feel really responsible for this. For example, when a parent leaves the home, a child may say, "If I had cleaned my room (done my chores, hadn't wet my pants, done better in school), maybe he (or she) wouldn't have left." This is what happens when no explanation is given to a child about why a person has died. When a grandparent stops visiting, the child again may say, "What did I do?"

Magical Thinking

Some children believe that by wishing that a person will die, they can cause the person's death. They sometimes also believe that if they think about the death of a person who is dying, they themselves may die.

Anger

This is a common response at the time of a death and one that is extremely damaging to families. Understanding it and anticipating its presence helps families deal with anger from both sides, the parent's and the children's. Children can be angry at parents for not telling them that the deceased was sick, for having spent so much time with the deceased and not enough time with them, for not allowing them to attend the funeral, or just because they need someone to be angry at.

I offer two examples of children's anger at parents. When my brother died, two days after the funeral there was a tremendous downpour. There were two inches of water in the back yard, and my ten-year-old son came to me and said, "I want to pitch my tent in the back yard." I said, "David, you can't pitch a tent. There are two inches of water in the yard!" He became angry, threw the tent down, and walked away. I said to him, "Look, I'll tell you why you're angry: you don't have anyone to be angry at. You can't be angry at your uncle because he was in an automobile accident. He wasn't drunk and he wasn't driving fast. It was a wet road, he didn't know it, and the car turned over and he was killed. You can't be angry at the doctors or the hospital because he was dead when he arrived there." I said, "There's nobody else to be angry at, so the next possibility is to be angry at me. As long as you understand that, it's okay." He came back a while later and said, "You know, after thinking about it, I don't know why I ever wanted to pitch my tent in the yard."

The second example came a few days ago when I spoke to a woman about coming to a funeral. She said, "You know, I was seven years old when they took me to my grandfather's funeral. I could go to the funeral, I could sit outside—my parents even bought me a brand new dress—but I was not allowed to go in and say goodbye to Grandpa. So you know what? I never wore the dress again and I never talked about Grandpa again."

Children can also be angry at themselves for wishing that a person would die or for not visiting or helping a dying person. One young boy had seen his grandfather walking down the street carrying some packages and noticed that his grandfather was not doing so well. But Grandfather did not do well a lot of the time, so the boy helped his grandfather take the packages inside, went on home, and did not say anything to his father about his grandfather. The grandfather died of a heart attack in the house. Later, the boy's father came to me and asked, "What am I going to say? My son said, 'If only I'd told you this time that Grandpa didn't look well, maybe we could have done something.'" Two weeks ago a mother came to me and said, "My daughter thinks that my mother may have died because she failed to send her a get-well card. She thought that maybe it would have saved her if she had sent it."

The driver of a car, the doctor at a hospital, the deceased for putting themselves in dangerous situations, even the event that caused a death—these are just a few examples of the legitimate targets of children's anger. When parents know that children are responding with anger or that they may do so, the parents will do best if they address it directly with the children. The important point for parents is that they feel much more in control when they can anticipate this kind of anger. They know the historical background of their old circumstances, their own blueprint,

and if they consider these they can help their children through their anger.

Guilt

This is another aspect of grief and grieving. Knowing that a child may feel guilt, or having it pointed out, lets parents know that their children can, on one hand, be angry at the deceased and, on the other, feel guilty about being angry. Children may express their guilt in statements such as "I didn't do enough," "I should have visited him before he died," and "If only I hadn't gone to the movies last week instead of going to see Grandpa, I would have been able to say goodbye before he died." All of these "shoulds" and "if onlys" can have a tremendous impact on a family if they are not directed, if nobody anticipated them, and if nobody explains them to the children.

CHILDREN AND FUNERALS

People feel the need to know how to explain what is going to happen next: "After I've explained to my children that this person has died, what do I say to them about what's going to happen now?" I have some material in script form that I offer to families, but basically parents have to start from the beginning with a child. They can say, "Grandpa will be taken from where he died to a funeral home; it's a place where they'll keep him for a few days until he's buried. He'll be dressed in clothes he liked and put into a casket— that's a box we use so that no dirt gets on him when he's buried. People will come to the funeral home to visit and say how sorry they are that Grandpa has died. Because his body isn't working any more, it won't move or do any of the things it used to do, but if you want to come and say some prayers, you can."

The basic premise here is that people will ask whether or not they should bring a child to the funeral home. People are surprised when I say, "Never! Don't ever bring children to a funeral home if you're not going to prepare them for it ahead of time." My son had cardiac surgery a year and a half ago. Before his operation, they showed him the operating room, the recovery room, and the intensive care unit. He knew everything that was going to happen to him before he went into the hospital for the surgery. His doctor even drew a diagram of the operation for him and made a model of the surgical repair out of clay for him. But people will still waltz children into a funeral home and say, "We're just going to see Grandma." Then they wonder why the children are upset when they walk in and find out that Grandma is lying down in a casket and not moving.

Children should be treated like people and given the same concern we give anyone else. They should hear an explanation of what will happen and then be given the opportunity to come to the funeral home or not, but they cannot make that decision without information. If children decide to come, they should be prepared further. They should be told the color of the rugs and walls, whether there are plants or paintings, whether there are flowers, what color the casket is, what color clothing the deceased is wearing, and that the deceased is lying down and not moving. The children should be informed so completely that when they walk into the funeral home it is almost as if they have been there before. Does it work? Children have walked into my funeral home and checked off exactly the points that I covered with their parents three hours before—"Oh, there's a green rug, there's the painting on the wall, there are the flowers." When this happens, I know that the parents have used the information I have provided, and I know that the children are comfortable because the place is not strange to them. All of this draws a child into the family support network on the same side of the wall, rather than putting the child alone on the other side of the wall.

We cannot assume that parents speak to their children about death or that they know how to do so. We cannot assume that if a death occurs suddenly in the middle of the night the parents will be prepared to talk to their children about it at seven o'clock in the morning when they get up. We cannot assume that "user-friendly" information is available, that if parents were given a booklet it would apply, or even that they would read it. I used to think that talking to children about death was only the concern of parents, but another funeral director who is using my program told me that a senior citizen came to him and said, "I'm here because I want to make sure that when I die my children will provide my grandchildren with this type of information."

We cannot assume that children are not talking or thinking about a death, that they are not affected when a family pet dies or by the deaths they see every day on television, or by the death of a neighbor or classmate. We cannot assume that children are prepared in any way to come to a funeral. We cannot assume that their parents have answered their questions or that the children have asked questions. For example, I have found that about 85 percent of the children between the ages of four and twelve who come to a funeral home and see a half-closed casket do not realize or believe that the deceased's legs are in the bottom of the casket. How do I know? Because I have said to parents, address that issue with children: Walk into the funeral home and up to the casket, and say, "You know, some kids think that the whole person isn't there, so if you want us to, we'll show you the rest of the person." Some parents respond by saying "No, I don't want to do that, I don't want to deal with that." But I have found that their children will accept my invitation to have the bottom part of the casket opened so that they can look inside. I have been putting a family into a limousine and heard a child ask, "Why did they cut Grandma up?" and heard the mother say, "What do you mean they cut Grandma up?" So I have said, "She only saw half of Grandma; let's go back inside." We have gone back in, opened the bottom of the casket, and the child has said, "Oh, yes, she is all there."

Children constantly ask for this type of information. A mother said to me, "Why does my child ask if that's a dummy inside the casket? And why does she ask me how they got the dummy to look so much like Grandpa?" And I say, "What did you say to your child? And she says that she told the child that her grandfather had died and gone to heaven. So I say, "If Grandpa died and went to heaven, who's inside the casket?"

A psychiatrist told me that he had one patient, a five-year-old boy who had been very close to his grandmother. When she died, the boy was told that Grandma had gone right up to heaven. His mother later found the boy standing on the windowsill of the apartment, about to jump out. After the boy was safely on the floor again, his mother asked him why he had been going to jump and what he thought would happen if he did. The boy said, "I would go up, just like Grandma."

So many of the points that seem like separate, discrete bits of information are actually the building materials to be fitted into a family blueprint. When I present this information to parents, they ask, "How do you expect us to put all of this together in our grief? How do you expect us to do that?" I say, "I don't expect you to do that; I expect your funeral director to do it."

Death of a Friend

Eva L. Essa, Colleen I. Murray and Joanne Everts

Eva L. Essa is Professor and Colleen I. Murray and Joanne Everts are Associate Professors, Human Development and Family Studies, University of Nevada, Reno.

On September 23, 1989, Tommy died, just two weeks before his seventh birthday.

Not quite a year before, in December, Tommy told a teacher that he did not feel well. Then, after Christmas, the news came that he was in the Oakland Children's Hospital, diagnosed as having a particularly virulent and rare form of cancer. Shock, anger, helplessness and dismay hit everyone at the Child and Family Research Center, where Tommy was enrolled. Tommy? That bright, cheerful, mischievous, wonderful little boy? How could that be? Why could that be? As the adults probed their own hurt, they realized they would also have to tell Tommy's friends. Although Tommy was absent, he was still very much a part of his class.

The teachers first informed the other children's parents about Tommy's illness. Then they talked to the children. "Tommy is very sick and is in the hospital. He has a special type of illness, not like catching a cold. It is called cancer and makes him very sick." The children asked a lot of questions. They wanted to know why Tommy got this illness, if they could catch it and if he would be back. Someone asked if he would die.

Tommy's class talked about him often. While Tommy was in the hospital, his classmates frequently made pictures, cards, stories and videotapes to send to him. The children's preoccupation with illness was also reflected in their play. They used the doctor props in the dramatic play area almost daily, they built a hospital out of blocks and they frequently read books about illness and death. Some children talked about Tommy every day while others never mentioned him at all.

Sometimes the teachers cried and shared their feelings with the children. All of the staff at the Center talked among themselves, both in staff meetings and informally. For some, Tommy's illness reminded them of their own childhood experiences with the death of a sibling or friend. Likewise, many of the parents frequently discussed Tommy's illness among themselves and with the teachers. One parent, a clinical psychologist, offered her counseling services to staff and parents who wanted to discuss their feelings with a professional.

After Tommy came home from the hospital, he was invited to visit his friends at school. For several days before his visit, the teachers discussed Tommy with the other children. They told the children that although he might look a little different, the Tommy who would visit was the same Tommy they already knew. He might, they said, have lost his hair. He would also be more tired and the children would have to be especially gentle with him. They all talked about how they remembered Tommy and looked at some old photographs.

The day Tommy first visited his class was difficult. Tommy was hesitant, as were some of his friends. But the children's natural curiosity about what had happened to Tommy helped break the ice. They wanted to see where the tubes that disappeared under Tommy's shirt went and to know what they did. They wanted to know why his head was covered with a cap. Tommy was pleased to lift his shirt, but embarrassed to show his bald head. Tommy's friends reacted in different ways; Diana, for instance, was looking forward to playing with Tommy while Christopher, who used to love rough-and-tumble play with Tommy, did not want to be around him at all.

When he felt well enough, Tommy also visited some of his school friends at their homes. Ben particularly treasured these visits from his good friend. Ben's mother recalls one occasion when Ben and Tommy laughingly compared a spaghetti dinner to intravenous tubes and blood.

Tommy visited his classmates a few more times during the spring and summer. When he died in the fall, a palpable sense of sadness fell over those who had known him. Although many of his classmates had moved on to kindergarten and 1st grade, the children who had known Tommy, as well as younger siblings of his former classmates, needed to be told about his death. The staff at the Child and Family Research Center also telephoned parents of former classmates who were no longer at the Center.

Many children and teachers attended the grave-side funeral service. A slight breeze ruffled the fall foliage on that beautiful, sunny day and a children's choir, of which Tommy had been a member, sang sweetly. Some of the children wandered to the edge of the group and played near a grove of pine trees. Some looked at a scrapbook full of pictures and other mementos of Tommy. "It was a calming experience," recalled one of Tommy's teachers, "sad, but not overwhelmingly sad. I felt soothed by the experience, not oppressed."

The topic of Tommy's death was brought up repeatedly at school and home, and, according to some of the parents, continues to be raised even now, more than 5 years later. Katie, who was 4 when Tommy died, at first frequently asked, "Tommy is dead, right? He won't ever come back, right?" Now she remembers that he is dead and talks about the fact that Tommy is under the ground. Sometimes she wonders if he is up in the air and she speculates about whether he still has bones.

To this day, Ben declares "Tommy is my best friend." Teachers and parents still talk about him. Tommy's picture is posted on the bulletin board in his former classroom, along with pictures of other children. When a child asks, "Who is that?" the teacher answers, "That's Tommy. He was in our class. He was a friend of ours and we like to remember him."

Unfortunately, the death of a child is not an unusual occurrence. Life-threatening illnesses and accidents take the lives of thousands of young children in the United States each year, leaving behind family, peers and adults who must cope with grief and a sense of loss. When a friend dies, teachers must come to terms with their own feelings, as well as those of the children and their parents. The experiences of the Child and Family Research Center staff in the wake of Tommy's illness and death can provide some insights and guidelines that may be helpful to others coping with a similar situation.

Honest communication helped everyone deal with Tommy's illness and subsequent death. In

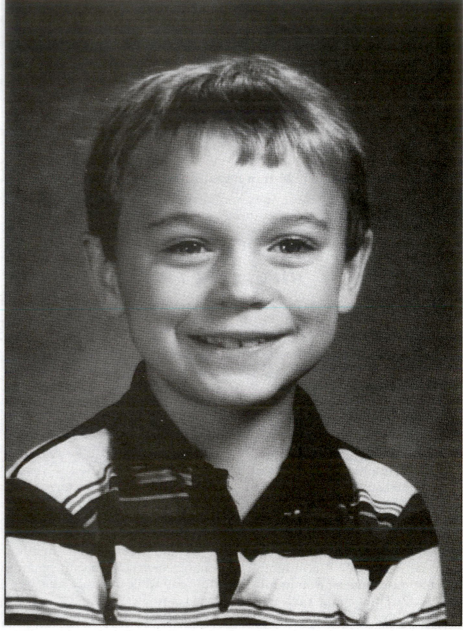

Tommy Irwin, 1982-1989

Photo courtesy of the authors

spite of social norms that often prevent open discussion of death and dying, teachers from the Center consciously maintained an open environment. They talked freely among themselves, with the parents and with the children. Children need an accepting atmosphere that allows them to discuss such sensitive topics. They should never be "protected" from the facts of serious illness and death. Experiencing the disappearance of a friend without knowing what happened to him can be more distressing than hearing about his death (Fox, 1985; Wolfelt, 1983).

Communication also meant the adults acknowledged and faced their own feelings. Many relived past experiences that compounded the reality and emotion surrounding Tommy's death. One teacher, reminded of her brother's death, found herself recalling how she and her mother reacted. She felt that Tommy's death helped her gain a new, adult perspective on a painful childhood experience.

The teachers were not afraid of acknowledging Tommy's illness and death or sharing their own feelings with the children. By showing their genuine reactions, they sent the message to the children that it is all right to be sad, to grieve or to feel uncertainty. Children also find it reassuring to know that someone would care if they became seriously ill or died.

The teachers talked to the parents about Tommy's illness and death first in order to prepare them in case their children brought up the topic or asked questions. Knowing the situation helps parents understand any changes in their children's behavior resulting from feelings of fear, anger, loss or distress (Fox, 1985).

The teachers tried to keep their explanations simple and honest. They did not overwhelm the children with a lot of detail or technical terminology. They presented the basic facts and then allowed the children to ask questions.

Many of the children's questions were concrete and reflected concern about themselves: whether, for instance, they could also become sick (Fox, 1985; Grollman, 1967; Wass & Corr, 1984).

By listening to the children and reflecting their questions and comments, the teachers gained insight into the children's thoughts and feelings and were better equipped to help them understand. The teachers sometimes asked, "What do you think?" The responses helped them discern the children's emotional and cognitive grasp of Tommy's illness and death.

Once the children knew about Tommy's illness, they reacted in different ways. Teachers should recognize that children will not react in the same way and some may not appear to react at all (Wolfelt, 1983). Some reactions may even seem to be callous. Children employ different coping strategies. Diana and Ben were eager to play with Tommy and looked forward to his visits. Christopher remained aloof. The teachers speculated that their admonitions to "be gentle" with Tommy frightened Christopher because he generally communicated in physical ways. The humor Tommy and Ben exhibited by comparing spaghetti to intravenous tubing is a healthy reaction to stress.

Adults also responded in various ways, depending upon how comfortable they felt answering the children's questions, interacting with Tommy and talking about their own feelings. Teachers rarely receive sufficient information or training in dealing with death or dying (Pratt & Hare, 1985). Teachers who have not adequately resolved their own misgivings about death will be less able to help children and parents deal with the issue. A professional can ease the situation by discussing attitudes, values and concerns about death and dying—either with individual teachers or at a staff meeting. Tommy's teachers benefited

from their talks with the clinical psychologist.

In addition to facilitating open discussions, the teachers allowed the children to work through their feelings in indirect ways. They equipped the dramatic play area with medical props and encouraged the children to express their feelings and concerns artistically. The children used the materials often (Tait & Depta, 1993).

Books about illness and death also can be helpful. Teachers should be careful, however, to review the books in advance, as some books can be more confusing than helpful. For example, books about the death of a grandparent or a pet are probably too removed from the reality of losing a friend. Furthermore, teachers should not use such stories to help children cope with the death of a friend because instead of feeling better, the children may become fearful of losing another important person. Children's books about death need to be carefully screened for age-appropriateness, situation-appropriateness and religious overtones. Only a few books are appropriate for young preschoolers. While some books for preschoolers deal with the deaths of parents or grandparents, animals and plants, books specific to the death of siblings or peers are missing for this age group (Ordal, 1983).

The teachers caringly supported Tommy and his family in a number of ways. They kept in touch throughout his illness by sending special messages from themselves and the other children, such as cards, pictures and videotapes. Many attended the funeral. Staff members should continue to consider an ill child as being part of the class and should express their feelings to the family.

Although children's concrete responses to illness and death can seem ghoulish to adults, they reflect children's curiosity and a need to know. The questions Tommy's classmates asked about the tubes under his shirt or Katie's speculation about whether Tommy still has bones are typical. Children of different ages respond to death in different ways. Preschoolers tend to conceptualize death in an immature way. Ben, who was 7 when Tommy died, seemed to understand that his friend's death was permanent and irreversible. He grieved for the loss of his close friend, realizing that he would never see him again. Katie, at 3, did not yet recognize the finality of death. She continues to bring up Tommy's death and now, at the age of 8, she is working through the experience from a more mature understanding of death. A sizable body of research supports the belief that the ages between 5 and 7 are pivotal to the development of an understanding about death (Speece & Brent, 1984; Stambrook & Parker, 1987). During this stage, children begin "to grasp that death is not temporary, that one cannot come back to life under any circumstances, and that death happens to everyone" (Essa & Murray, 1994).

The children continued to talk about Tommy, both at school and at home. They asked questions about his illness and wanted to know what happened to him after he died. Such persistent conversations are not unusual. Teachers should expect that children will ask many questions about illness and death and can tell parents to expect the recurring conversations and questions. By continuing to help children process their questions, teachers can help them deal with their fears, anger or confusion in a healthy manner.

Thus, the death of a child is not an end. The child continues to live on in the memories of all who knew him or her. Dealing with death is a deeply felt experience that, while inevitable, is particularly difficult for young children who still have a rather limited capacity for comprehending its finality. Teachers have an important role in helping a deceased child's friends understand and cope with the death.

References

Essa, E. L., & Murray, C. I. (1994). Young children's understanding and experience with death. *Young Children, 49*(4), 74-81.

Fox, S. S. (1985). *Good grief: Helping groups of children when a friend dies.* Boston: The New England Association for the Education of Young Children.

Grollman, E. A. (Ed.). (1967). *Explaining death to children.* Boston: Beacon Press.

Ordal, C. C. (1983). Death as seen in books suitable for young children. *Omega, 14*(3), 249-277.

Pratt, C. C., & Hare, J. (1985). Death anxiety and comfort in teaching about death among preschool teachers. *Death Studies, 9*, 417-425.

Speece, M. W., & Brent, S. B. (1984). Children's understanding of death: A review of three components of a death concept. *Child Development, 55*, 1671-1686.

Stambrook, M., & Parker, K. C. (1987). The development of the concept of death in children: A review of the literature. *Merrill-Palmer Quarterly, 33*, 133-157.

Tait, D. C., & Depta, J. (1993). Play therapy group for bereaved children. In N. B. Webb (Ed.), *Helping bereaved children: A handbook for practitioners* (pp. 169-185). New York: Guilford Press.

Wass, H., & Corr, C. A. (1984). *Helping children cope with death: Guidelines and resources* (2nd ed.). New York: Hemisphere Publishing.

Wolfelt, A. (1983). *Helping children cope with grief.* Muncie, IN: Accelerated Development, Inc.

Some Helpful Resources

Buckingham, R. W. (1989). *Care of the dying child: A practical guide for those who help others.* New York: Continuum.

Fox, S. S. (1985). *Good grief: Helping groups of children when a friend dies.* Boston: The New England Association for the Education of Young Children.

Grollman, E.A. (1976). *Talking about death: A dialogue between parent and child.* Boston: Beacon Press.

Kubler-Ross, E. (1983). *On children and death.* New York: Macmillan.

Lonetto, R. (1980). *Children's conceptions of death.* New York: Springer Publishing Co.

Schaefer, D., & Lyons, C. (1986). *How do we tell the children?* New York: Newmarket.

Smilansky, S. (1987). *On death: Helping children understand and cope.* New York: Peter Lang Publishing.

Wass, H., & Corr, C. A. (1984). *Childhood and death.* New York: Hemisphere Publishing.

Wass, H., & Corr, C. A. (1984). *Helping children cope with death: Guidelines and resources* (2nd ed.). New York: Hemisphere Publishing.

Webb, N. B. (1993). *Helping bereaved children: A handbook for practitioners.* New York: Guilford Press.

Wolfelt, A. (1983). *Helping children cope with grief.* Muncie, IN: Accelerated Development, Inc.

Selected Children's Books About Death

Brown, M. W. (1985). *The dead bird.* New York: Harper and Row.

Clifton, L. (1983). *Everett Anderson's goodbye.* New York: Holt, Rinehart & Winston.

DePaola, T. (1973). *Nana upstairs and Nana downstairs.* New York: Putnam.

McGraw, S. (1986). *Love you forever.* Scarborough, Ontario: Firefly Books.

Mellonie, B., & Ingpen, R. (1983). *Lifetimes: The beautiful way to explain death to children.* New York: Bantam Books.

Tresselt, A. (1972). *The dead tree.* New York: Parents' Magazine Press.

Viorst, J. (1971). *The tenth good thing about Barney.* New York: Atheneum.

Zolotow, C. (1974). *My grandson Lew.* New York: Harper and Row.

FIRST CHILDHOOD DEATH EXPERIENCES

George E. Dickinson

College of Charleston, South Carolina

ABSTRACT

A child's first experience with death may be met with a variety of responses. The objective of this research was to determine what adults remember about these early death experiences. Students in college death-and-dying classes were asked to write an essay about their first death experience. The average age of the respondents (N = 440) was 23.79 years, and their average age at the time of their first death experience was 7.95 years. Content analysis was used to analyze the essays. Over half of all first experiences with death involved relatives, 28 percent involved a pet. Children's responses to death showed emotions similar to those expressed by adults. Over one-third mentioned that crying occurred. Details of the funeral were remembered by many respondents some sixteen years later. Adults need to be sensitive to the needs of children when a significant other or pet dies. It is clear that childhood experiences flavored with death, loss, or separation can become important influences on the way one sees life and copes with death.

A fascinating aspect of children is the naive, simplistic way in which they approach the unknown. That very naivete often makes their questions hard for adults to answer [1]. Children can ask especially difficult questions about death. Most people encounter death for the first time in childhood. Because children often do not understand the concept of death, each child's reaction to death will be unique. The memory of the death experience and the manner in which the child is treated by adults may last beyond childhood into adulthood.

Some children may find their first death experience to be a traumatic happening, while others may seem less affected. Children may feel alone and frightened. Some may cry. Others may not know if they should cry. Whether a child's first experience with death involves a person or an animal, most children are ill-prepared to handle the realities of death. They may shy away from the dead body of a grandparent or pet dog. Other death-related "rituals" such as funeral home activities and interment at the cemetery will likely leave the child with numerous questions.

The objective of this research is to determine the impact a person's first death experience has on him or her as an adult. What does the adult remember about this event? At what age did the event occur? How vivid are the memories about the death? Who or what died? If recollections are rather clear about this first death experience, the findings could certainly suggest the significance of such an event in the mind of the now-adult child. Parents should notice a child's reaction to death, and then strive to learn as much as they can in order to assist the child in coping with it.

METHOD

Students enrolled in death-and-dying courses between 1979 and 1991 in two universities in the southeastern United States were asked to write a brief essay on their first childhood death experiences. They were instructed in this in-class assignment to relate how old they were at the time, to recollect who or what died, and to recall what they could remember about the event.

The number of respondents writing essays was 440. Content analysis was used to analyze the essays. The average age of the students at the time of their response was 23.79 years. Average age at first death experience was 7.95 years. The majority of students were female (82%).

RESULTS

The most frequently cited first death experience involved the death of a relative (57%). Forty-two percent of all first experiences with death were with a grandfather or grandmother (see Table 1). Although the majority of student responses highlighted the death of another human (either a relative or non-relative), twenty-eight percent of the students first experienced death with the loss of a pet. Besides being the "child's best friend," the dog was also cited as the pet most often involved in the students' first experience with death (14%), followed by the cat (5%).

Responses to Death

The students' reactions upon learning of the death of a loved one encompassed a wide range of feelings and emotions: relief,

Table 1. First Death-Related Experience of College Students[a]

Relation to Respondent	Percentage of Respondents	
Relative	57	
Aunt		1
Cousin		1
Father		3
Grandfather		23
Grandmother		19
Mother		1
Sibling		2
Uncle		4
Other person, not a relative	15	
Pets	28	2
Bird		5
Cat		<1
Caterpillar		<1
Chicken		<1
Cow		<1
Crab		<1
Deer		14
Dog		<1
Duck		1
Fish		<1
Gerbil		1
Hamster		1
Mouse		<1
Pig		<1
Rabbit		<1
Squirrel		<1
Toad		1
Turtle		

[a]N = 440. Percentages do not add to 100 due to rounding.

confusion, disbelief, fear, happiness, anger, sadness, emptiness, shock, and guilt. Confusion and fear followed when the child seemed uninformed as to what was occurring. One ten-year-old "had extreme fear" until someone explained to her about what would happen to the body. Disbelief usually followed a sudden death. A nine-year-old girl felt "empty, scared, and totally alone" when her father died. Some children were upset because they had been unable to go to the hospital and say goodbye to the deceased.

One six-year-old girl was afraid of her great-grandmother who had "big brown moles all over her face and sat in a wheelchair." When told that she had died, the little girl became "infatuated with her ghost." When the television shows went off the air at night and the "black and white fuzzy stuff came on," she used to imagine that she would hear her great-grand-mother's voice or see her face in the television screen.

Almost without exception, anger was the response of children whose pet had died in an accident. The anger, outright hatred at times, was directed toward the one who had killed the animal, whether it was a parent who had accidentally run over the animal or the vet who "put the animal to sleep." Guilt was another common denominator in many of the students' responses. One four-year-old girl's responsibility was to feed the dog, Charlie, every night. One night she forgot to feed Charlie, and the next day Charlie did not come home. She said:

I just knew he had run away because I had not fed him. I felt terribly guilty, but I kept my mouth shut and did not tell my parents of my grave mistake. A few days passed, and Charlie still did not come back, even though every night I tried to call him to feed him. I can literally remember calling his name and crying and yelling that I was sorry. My parents finally told me that Charlie would never be coming back because he had been run over. Well, this information devastated me. I put all the blame on myself. I just knew that Charlie had been run over because I had failed to feed him that night. I kept all this to myself until recently when my family was discussing the history of our family pets. My parents got a good laugh out of this, but to a four-year-old child, this was devastating. Even though now I know I am not responsible for Charlie's death, I still wish that I would have fed him that night.

Thus, guilt from a death experienced at an early age can stay with a person into adulthood.

A similar account of guilt occurred with an eight-year-old female who put her pet turtle out in the garage in a shoebox with food and water. *Two weeks later,* when the girl was puttering around in the garage, she spotted the shoebox. She slowly opened the box and saw her turtle's empty shell, dried up grass, and an empty water bowl. She convinced herself that she was a turtle murderer. It took her mother two weeks to convince her that "turtle murdering was an intentional deed" and that her forgetfulness was just an accident.

Responses at the Death Scene

Of those stating their responses at the death scene, the following fears and dislikes were noted: "Disliked having a dead body in the living room"; "Afraid grandmother's ghost was going to get me"; "Grandfather seemed as if he were asleep"; "Ran out of the room"; "Resented others trying to be helpful"; "disappointed because she only looked asleep"; "Looked to see if grandfather's spirit rose from his body at the time of death"; and "Afraid buzzards would eat my daddy."

The children who saw someone die felt puzzled and became excited about the event. One six-year-old was confused because people talked about how nice her deceased aunt looked: how could someone who suffered so much pain look pretty when dead? Another child was afraid her dead uncle would come back and bother her, so she slept with the covers over the head at night. In the case of a dead pet, one child noted a positive response—the closeness of the family in sharing grief by sitting down and crying together. Some students remembered that they did not know what to do or how to act.

Explanations of Death

Of those respondents given explanations of death, the response most frequently given was that the deceased "went to heaven." Since heaven was described to the children as a "happy place," most felt reassured by such an explanation. The father of one four-year-old girl, however, told her that her kitten "went to heaven to be with God." She responded, "Why does God want a dead kitten?" A three-year-old became angry when told that her grandmother had gone to heaven, and responded, "I don't want her in heaven, I want her here!"

A seven-year-old girl felt that her parents had prepared her for her grandfather's funeral when they told her that he had gone to heaven and that she would meet him there someday. However, when they went to the funeral home and saw his body, she said: "You told me that Grandaddy was in heaven. No he is not, he is right here." She was upset that her grandfather was lying there not talking to anyone. Her mother quickly pulled her aside and "explained" that his soul was in heaven. The student noted that it was "quite a few years later" before she understood what her mother was saying.

In explaining death to children, it is important to be careful what we say. For example, one nine-year-old girl remembered the day a classmate died in an automobile accident. A nun came in and said that the girl had been "called by God home to heaven." The student remembered asking the nun how God called her: "Did she get a phone call, or what?" The student was punished for her "smartness" and had to sit in the corner. That night she asked her father if he thought it was the girl's day to die, and if God really called her. He answered:

> We don't know why she died in that car yesterday. We do not know if it was supposed to happen or if it was a mistake. It doesn't matter. We just know she is dead now and we are alive.

Years later, this nine-year-old girl noted that she really did appreciate her father's wisdom.

When a four-year-old's younger sister died, the child's parents told her that the sister was "too sick to live with us so she went to visit grandmother in heaven and would never come home again." The surviving child was frightened for months afterward. "Whenever anyone did not feel well, I thought they would go away forever too."

One child was told, "Grandfather's heart was bad and stopped working." Another parent said, "Grandfather can breathe easier now." (This child noted he wanted to join his grandfather because he had asthma and would welcome an opportunity to "breathe easier." He was informed, however, that he was too young!)

A six-year-old boy did not need an "explanation" of his grandfather's death. He explained it as follows:

> I figured out that Grandfather had gone to join my pet cow who had died. I thought they both had just gone back into the hills behind my house for a rest, since they both were so old.

Thus, some explanations of death given to children seem to suffice, while others miss the mark entirely.

Traumatic Experiences with Death

Many respondents also related traumatic experiences of death. An eight-year-old girl had been afraid of her great-grandmother because she was so old:

> At the funeral home my cousins and I were ushered up for a closer look at her. An older female picked me up and made me kiss my dead great-grandmother. Never in all my life was I so scared! For the longest time after that I had nightmares of my great-grandmother grabbing me and putting me in the casket with her! At the gravesite I remember being happy that the lid was closed and that she was being put into the ground.

Another child watched her cat die a violent death and "cannot to this day" even stroke a pet for fear of becoming emotionally

attached again. One female is afraid of fire because her neighbor's infant burned to death when she was a little girl. After seeing her uncle's tongue and neck eaten away by cancer, one little girl had nightmares for weeks. A four-year-old girl was not told about her puppy's traumatic death by a mowing machine until two or three weeks after the event. She was allowed to search for him "frantically" every day. She even put out food and would worry at night that he was cold or hungry. Another child had a negative post-Easter experience with his pet:

> As a young child, I would receive ducks and chickens as an Easter present. One of these chicks was able to survive the playing and was able to grow into a nice white hen. She was my pride and joy, following me and coming when I called. The hen stayed at my grandmother's. One Sunday dinner the main course was "fried chicken." It took me several minutes to realize just what had happened. To say the least, I was devastated and do not each chicken to this day.

A seventeen-year-old was taking care of her nineteen-year-old sister-in-law who died in the bed with her. Her mother asked her to bathe the deceased before the undertaker came since she did not want him to see her naked. A six-year-old recalls the death of a neighbor's son by drowning. While viewing the body in the casket, water came up out of the mouth of the deceased. The funeral home personnel were called "to change his clothes and clean up the coffin."

Crying and Death

Many of the respondents (37%) mentioned crying in their essays about their first experiences with death. While most simply stated that crying occurred, others indicated that their crying was not found acceptable and even that it had negative consequences. For example, a fifteen-year-old was spanked with a hairbrush for crying over the death of her puppy. A ten-year-old was "smacked" by her uncle to "make her stop crying at a funeral." Some noted that they were "scared" and "upset" at seeing their parents and others cry. For many, it was the first time they had seen their fathers cry. One ten-year-old girl was told by her mother that their daddy did not want the children to see him cry "because he had to be strong during grandfather's funeral." Some said they cried because others were crying.

At the funeral of her aunt, one nine-year-old girl recalled the following scene:

> Everyone else was crying softly, except me. I felt badly because I couldn't cry. Even my cousin was crying. I kept trying to cry but no tears would come. I remember seeing my mom cry. I hated to see her cry because when she did she had to take her glasses off, and I liked her better with them on. After the funeral, I went back to my grandmother's, and that night I threw up!

(Thus, the trauma and uncertainty of a funeral for a child may contribute to physical illness.)

Some children associated crying with childish behavior, as noted by these comments: "I was the only one of my classmates who did not cry at the funeral"; "I acted like a big girl and didn't cry"; and "I did not cry since I had to act grown-up." Perhaps some felt embarrassed to cry in front of others, as if shame were associated with crying: "I tried hard not to cry"; "I cried in my pillow, not in front of anyone"; "I hid my face so no one would see me crying"; "I hid in the closet so Mom would not see me crying"; "I was not allowed to show emotion because Daddy's family was unemotional"; "Grandfather had made everyone promise there would be no tears at his funeral"; and "My neighbor told me not to cry because Pop wouldn't want to see me sad."

Yet, not all parents impressed the negative aspects of crying upon their children, as indicated by this account of a nine-year-old boy on the death of his grandfather:

> The day of my grandfather's death, my dad came over to my aunt and uncle's house where my brother and I were staying. He took us into one of the bedrooms and sat us down. He told us Grandaddy Doc had died. He explained to us that it was okay if we needed to cry. He told us he had cried, and that if we did cry we wouldn't be babies, but would just be men showing our emotions.

After observing her father's sudden death from an acute heart attack while sitting in his favorite chair, one five-year-old girl remembered crying, but her real concern was that her friends not have pity on her. Thus, at school she did not want to tell her elementary school friends about her father's death.

Recollections of the Funeral

One of the most frequently-cited recollections of funerals was the deceased person appearing to be asleep. One child was puzzled that grandma was sleeping with her glasses on! Another was afraid her uncle would open his eyes. Several students noted the lighting and color of the room, the casket and clothing, and the flowers. Others remembered the body itself: the body was "cold and unalive," "looked too real because of cosmetics," and had "long fingernails." One child remembers "a funny white statue in a pretty box." Several students said they could see nothing in the casket but a nose sticking up.

Some students recalled experiencing the fun of the family reunion (certainly a eufunction of a funeral is the bringing together of the extended family), feeling important because so many people gathered, not wanting to look at the corpse, and thinking of things to do to "avoid thinking of grandmother." An eight-year-old was frightened to see his grandmother put into the ground. One five-year-old's little brother got a shovel and was planning to dig up his grandmother after the funeral. Another girl noted a sense of finality at her grandfather's funeral when the casket was closed. She tried to go near the casket, but could not make her legs move. Finally, she succeeded and touched the casket.

Some students recalled the funerals of their pets, yet could not grasp the finality of death:

> When I was seven years old, I had a goldfish named Goldilocks. She lived in a fishbowl with my younger brother's fish, Wolfie. One afternoon I came home from school to find Goldilocks floating instead of swimming. We had a proper service for her in my backyard underneath a tree. I buried her in a plastic pimento cheese container filled with water and a little bit of fish food in case she got hungry and decided to wake up. Wolfie died a few days later, and we had a similar service for him. I recall digging

them up the next week to see if they may have been ready to go back and swim in their bowl.

A six-year-old's account of her pet's death and burial suggests that many children feel death is not a permanent condition:

> I had a cute little hamster. I think we had been talking about hibernation in school because when I came home and found the hamster lying there, I thought he was hibernating! My next door neighbor, Sharon, came over and said that if we warmed him up then he would come back to life. So I put him in my electric blanket to see if he would wake up. He never did and by that time my mom realized what had happened, so we had to bury him. My brother and I put him in the shoebox, put a blanket in there to keep him warm and a picture of us to keep him company. Then we buried him in the backyard.

Some children "play funeral director" at an early age. A seven-year-old boy had a pet black-and-white mouse named Squeaky. One day the little boy came home from school and found that "Squeaky was no longer with us." He decided it was necessary to dispose of Squeaky properly so he put him in a "little shoebox lined with tissue paper and took him out to the backyard and buried him." He even made a cross out of sticks and string to serve as a grave marker.

In describing the burials of their pets, children reveal a strong element of drama, imitation, and play, as noted by Boris Levinson [2]. They also reveal genuine grief and tenderness, and a desire that the dead pet be gently cared for and that respect be shown to its memory.

DISCUSSION

As noted above, children often must confront death at a relatively early age (an average of eight years with these respondents). Their vivid recollections of these first death experiences at an average age of nearly twenty-four years—nearly sixteen years after the actual events—testify to the impact that such experiences had on these individuals. In the 1920s, distinguished psychologist G. Stanley Hall verified the significance of early childhood memories of death on children, evidenced by the vivid detail used in recalling these events [3]. Of special note is that Hall found that funeral and burial scenes sometimes were the very earliest of all memories of the adults he studied. More recent studies also find death experiences common among adults' earliest memories [4, 5].

Children's and adults' responses to death have remarkable similarities: emotions range from fear to happiness. As Kavanaugh suggests, children differ from adults mainly in size, as a subcompact car differs from a full-size model [6]. They are basically the same; one is simply larger than the other. Adults, however, often fail to give children enough credit and try to shelter them from the reality of death.

John Bowlby states that young children can mourn just as healthy adults can [7]. For this mourning to happen, the child needs to be fully aware of what is taking place during the time of death and after the death. Adults should not withhold information from a child; questions should be welcomed and thoughtfully answered. The child should participate in the funeral rites and should also be supported in a "comforting way" with an assurance of a continued relationship with the surviving adult(s).

Crying

Because of the way some of these children were treated regarding death, many have difficulty coping with death as adults. For example, punishing a child for expressing grief through crying does not allow that child to mourn the loss so that he or she can then go on with life. Perhaps learning to express sadness and happiness as children would loosen our inhibitions as adults.

Earl Grollman defines crying as the sound of anguish at losing a part of oneself in the death of one whom he or she loves [8]. Tears and sorrowful words help the child feel relieved. Displaying emotions makes the dead person or pet seem more worthy. Tears are a natural tribute to the deceased; the child misses the deceased and wishes that he or she were not gone. As Sesame Street's Big Bird said at the end of the show's special tribute following the death of groceryman Mr. Hooper, "Mr. Hooper, we're going to miss you."

The child must also feel that he or she has the right to grieve when a pet dies. As S. H. Fraiberg notes [9, p. 274]:

> Mourning, even if it is mourning for a dead hamster, is a necessary measure for overcoming the effects of loss. A child who is not allowed feelings of grief over a pet or a more significant loss is obliged to fall back on more primitive measures of defense, to deny the pain of loss, for example. If a child were consistently reared on this basis . . . he would become an impoverished person, without quality or depth in his emotional life.

Unlike a person who loses a friend or relative and receives outpourings of sympathy and support, someone who suffers the death of a pet often receives ridicule for overreacting, for being foolishly emotional, and for expressing grief over the death of "a mere" animal [10]. To a child, to whom a pet offers the most secure and certain acceptance, such a loss can be especially painful. Well-meaning adults who try to assuage the child's feelings by promising to buy an immediate replacement are denying the reality of the child's feelings [11].

Grollman notes that a person should not be afraid of causing tears, as they are like a safety valve [12]. Parents often deliberately attempt to veer the conversation away from the deceased. They are apprehensive of the tears that might follow. We need to understand that expressing grief through tears is normal and helpful.

Several children in this study noted that they watched for others' reactions at the death scene and then responded accordingly. Since children are watching adults, a parental role model for expressing one's self in front of children just might be beneficial to the socialization of children in the long run. Children then might not feel a need to hide in the closet to cry, or to cry into their pillows at night. The child who noted the positive experience of his family's sharing a good cry at the death of his pet emphasized the warmth of the family in sharing this common experience. He did not carry his burden alone; his family grieved with him. It is comforting to know that others care.

Respondents who noted that although others were crying they did not feel like crying themselves—they indeed tried but were unable to cry—should be made to feel that it is also okay not to cry, if one does not feel the need to cry. Grollman notes that parents should not urge children to display unfelt feelings [12]. The child is likely to feel confused and hypocritical when told that he or she ought to express a sentiment that he or she does not honestly feel. Other outlets can be used to release emotion, and the child should express those emotions in a way that most naturally meets his or her needs.

Euphemisms

Such unrealistic explanations about death as "merely sleeping" or "gone away" are not only untruthful, they can lead to sleep disturbances and produce anxiety about normal trips that anyone might take. Adults should try to avoid euphemisms when talking to a child about death. Adults should use words such as dead, stopped working, and wore out—simple words to establish the fact that the body is biologically dead [13]. The parents should make it clear that life stops with death, that the deceased cannot return, and that the body will be buried or disposed of in some other way. Euphemisms can cause the child a "bad trip" if, for example, the child observes that the "sleeper" is locked away in a box and buried in the ground. While attending her first funeral and observing the attendants closing the casket, the author's five-year-old daughter asked "But Daddy, how can Mrs. Kirby breathe in there?" To her, the deceased was only sleeping; closing the casket presented a problem.

Such misconceptions in using euphemisms may cause problems for the child later in life. In a story related by Jacob Antelyes one child whose pet had recently been euthanized was about to undergo surgery and was told that he would be "put to sleep" for the procedure. He was terror-stricken because this was exactly the term used by his parents and the veterinarian when their pet's life was ended [14, p. 39]. Fortunately, his terror was allayed when the differences between euthanasia and anesthesia was explained in clear language.

A child between the ages of six and ten (the age of most of these respondents at the time of their first death experience) is just beginning to understand that death is a permanent cessation of life. However, the permanency of death is still unclear, and the cognitive obstacles to abstract thought prevent its completion. Children see death as a taker, something violent that comes and gets you like a burglar or a ghost.

Communication

Interviews with 100 mothers confirmed the belief that parents find it difficult to talk with their young children about death [15]. They tend to feel inadequate in knowing what to say or how to say it. Nonetheless, most parents feel obligated to respond to their children's questions in an appropriate fashion, and these mothers welcomed the opportunity to improve their ability to do so. The mothers had more difficulty dealing with questions on particular deaths that involved an actual situation than with questions posed out of normal curiosity.

Concerns expressed about the death scene could perhaps be diminished by open communication with children. An explanation of the funeral and what happens to the body could help alleviate some of these fears. Wass and Shaak note that parents can help children most merely by being available and assuring the child that he or she is loved and will not be abandoned [16]. Waiting for days or weeks to tell children of a death only increases the trauma and may create serious problems of trust between parent and child. It is important to be honest and answer the child's questions as they surface.

Opportunities to discuss death with children will present themselves. For example, dead flies, mosquitoes, birds, and animals beside the road offer unthreatening occasions to discuss the finality of death. To bury a deceased pet, as several of these students did, is a good exercise in relating to death. The animal is cold, still, and unalive: it is dead. That is reality. A pet is usually considered a significant member of the family. The death of a pet is a traumatic experience for family members and leaves a big void in the family circle. Giving children an opportunity to experience and express their feelings about a pet's death, and to ask questions, helps them to come to terms with their own and everyone else's mortality, notes Boris Levinson [2].

To tell a young child of an ill-defined place where everyone goes after death could be frightening. However, the majority of these children seemed content with the explanation that the deceased had gone to a "happy place." Given a small child's world of fantasy, the magic world of Disney mentality, the response may suffice. Harold Kushner cautions, however, that trying to make a child feel better by stating how beautiful heaven is and how happy the deceased is to be with God may deprive the child of a chance to grieve [17]. By doing this, we ask a child to deny and mistrust his or her own feelings; to be happy when sadness is desired. The child's right to feel upset and angry should be recognized, notes Kushner.

Support

While the greatest number of earliest death memories involved grandparents, occasionally a classmate or teacher died. It is important that teachers and counselors deal with the issue of death. One day Johnny is in class, the next day he is dead. Do we just ignore his absence? The teacher or counselor must prepare to cope with death so that the students can also deal with the issue. The adult must be a good role model. Avoidance of the topic is not the solution.

Like it or not, death is a recurring event in the lives of human beings. We must face death as a "final stage of growth." Death education should be a significant part of formal education, as is the socialization of our children prior to school. Being kept informed about death matters should help children in coping with death. Awareness is an important first step in accepting death—one's own or the deaths of others.

As adults, we should strive to be good support persons for children when death occurs. A comforting word or a caring inquiry can go a long way for a bereaved child. In the end, both the child and the adult will be the better for sharing this meaningful experience. Though most of us are not professionally trained to handle death and dying situations, we can show that we care, as is noted in the following story told by Rabbi Kushner [18]:

A little boy had gone to the store, but was late in returning home. His mother asked, "Where were you?" He said, "I found a little boy whose bicycle was broken, and I stopped to help him." "But what do you know about fixing bicycles?" his mother asked. "Nothing," the little boy replied, "I sat down and cried with him."

Many times, we may not know how to fix the situation, but like the little boy in the story, we can give support to the individual in other ways.

Studies such as this one indicate that a child's experiences of death and loss may become life-long memories for the adult. As Robert Kastenbaum notes, however, it would be going much too far to say that a particular childhood experience "causes" us to behave or feel a particular way in adult life [5, p. 150]. Nevertheless, it is clear that childhood experiences tinged with death, loss, or separation can become significant influences on the way one sees life and copes with death.

REFERENCES

1. O. J. Sahler, *The Child and Death*, C. V. Mosby, St. Louis, 1978.
2. B. M. Levinson, Grief at the Loss of a Pet, in *Pet Loss and Human Bereavement*, W. J. Kay (ed.), The Iowa State University Press, Ames, Iowa, 1984.
3. G. S. Hall, *Youth: Its Education, Regimen and Hygiene*, D. Appleton and Company, New York, 1922.
4. S. Tobin, The Earliest Memory as Data for Research in Aging, in *Research, Planning, and Action for the Elderly*, D. P. Kent, R. Kastenbaum, and S. Sherwood (eds.), Behavioral Publications, Inc., New York, 1972.
5. R. J. Kastenbaum, *Death, Society, and Human Experience*, (4th Edition), Macmillan Publishing Company, New York, 1991.
6. R. E. Kavanaugh, *Facing Death*, Penguin Books, Baltimore, 1972.
7. J. Bowlby, *Attachment and Loss*, Vol. III, Basic Books, New York, 1980.
8. E. A. Grollman, *Explaining Death to Children*, Beacon Press, Boston, 1967.
9. S. H. Fraiberg, *The Magic Years: Understanding and Handling the Problems of Early Childhood*, Scribner's, New York, 1959.
10. J. E. Brody, Loss of a Pet Often Agonizing for Owners, *The News and Courier*, Charleston, South Carolina, p. 14E, October, 27, 1985.
11. R. A. Kalish, *Death, Grief and Caring Relationships*, (2nd Edition), Brooks/Cole Publishing Company, Monterey, California, 1985.
12. E. A. Grollman, *Concerning Death: A Practical Guide for the Living*, Beacon Press, Boston, 1974.
13. D. Schaefer and C. Lyons, *How Do We Tell the Children? A Parent's Guide to Helping Children Understand and Cope When Someone Dies*, Newmarket Press, New York, 1986.
14. J. Antelyes, When Pet Animals Die, in *Pet Loss and Human Bereavement*, W. J. Kay (ed.), The Iowa State University Press, Ames, Iowa, 1984.
15. J. N. McNeil, Young Mothers' Communication about Death with Their Children, *Death Education, 4*, pp. 323–339, 1983.
16. H. Wass and J. Shaak, Helping Children Understand Death Through Literature, in *Death: Current Perspectives*, (2nd Edition), E. S. Schneidman (ed.), Mayfield Publishing Company, Palo Alto, California, 1980.
17. H. S. Kushner, *When Bad Things Happen to Good People*, Schocken Books, New York, 1981.
18. H. S. Kushner, lecture given in Charleston, South Carolina, October 20, 1985.

Detachment Revisited: The Child's Reconstruction of a Dead Parent

During the year following a parent's death, children in a community-based sample were found to have developed an inner construction of the dead parent. This continued, though altered, relationship appeared to facilitate their coping with the loss and with accompanying changes in their lives. Implications for understanding the bereavement process and for interventions focusing on detachment are discussed.

Phyllis R. Silverman, Ph. D.,
Steven Nickman, M. D.,
J. William Worden, Ph. D.

The observation that children maintain a connection to deceased parents is not new *(Bowlby, 1980; Dietrich & Shabad, 1989; Jacobs, Koston, Dasl, & Ostfeld, 1987; Klass, 1988; Miller, 1971; Moss & Moss, 1981; Osterweis, Solomon, & Greene, 1984; Rubin, 1985; P.R. Silverman, 1986; Silverman & Silverman, 1979; Worden, 1991).* However, there are different interpretations of this observation and different theories about the nature of the connection. In their studies of parents whose children had died, Klass *(1988)* and Rubin *(1985)* concluded that remaining connected to the deceased seems to be a necessary part of the bereavement process—that it is adaptive and facilitates an accommodation to the death. Lifton *(1979)* described strategies that mourners used to provide the deceased with "symbolic immortality." Others *(Furman, 1984; Volkan, 1981)* have reported that for successful mourning to take place, the mourner must disengage from the deceased, that is, let go of the past. This experience of the deceased is often thought of as symptomatic of psychological problems *(Dietrich & Shabad, 1989; Miller, 1971).* In her study of bereaved preschool children attending a therapeutic nursery school, Furman *(1974)* noted that it is important for children to loosen their ties to their deceased parents and suggested that therapists should encourage detachment behavior. This formulation has its roots in Freud's *(1917/1957)* observations that patients best resolved their grief when they gradually withdrew the mental energy they had extended toward the lost love object and reinvested this energy in new relationships.

The conceptualizations that prescribe detachment were drawn primarily from clinical interactions with troubled people. Thus, they may be based on a sample that is overly representative of individuals who had recourse to relatively primitive defense mechanisms, such as denial. These people, who may have experienced greater than normal difficulty in accepting the reality of the death, were more likely to exhibit an inappropriate investment in the past *(Furman, 1974; Volkan, 1981).* The present paper,

A revised version of a paper submitted to the Journal in August 1991. Research was funded by grant MH41791 from the National Institute of Mental Health, and by grants from the National Funeral Directors Association and from the Hillenbrand Corporation. Authors are at the Department of Psychiatry, Massachusetts General Hospital, Boston.

based on interviews with children who had lost a parent, is an attempt to broaden our understanding of the bereavement process and the ways in which the deceased is experienced by a nonclinical population.

In the psychoanalytic literature on children, efforts to maintain a connection to the deceased parent are seen as internal representations of the dead parent (*Dietrich & Shabad, 1989; Jacobson, 1965; Rochlin, 1959, 1965; Schafer, 1968; Wolfenstein, 1973*). Identification and internalization are considered processes that the bereaved use to keep an aspect of the deceased with them forever (*Furman, 1984; Volkan, 1981*). These inner representations are described as unchanging. Dietrich and Shabad *(1989)* emphasized the paradoxical character of the inner representation of the deceased: one that is both frozen in time and timeless— immortalized and lost simultaneously. Schafer *(1968)* regarded a bereaved child's inner representations of the lost parent as persisting unmodified and inaccessible to secondary-process thinking.

The concept of internalization, however, does not fully describe the process that bereaved children undergo. What the authors observed was more colorful, dynamic, and interactive than the term *internalization* suggests. In fact, this inner representation was not buried in the unconscious or stable over time. The child was aware of the inner representation, and the representation seemed to change with time as the child developed. Playwright Robert Anderson *(1974)* used the word *relationship* to describe his experience of the deceased, as did such researchers as Klass *(1988)* and Rubin *(1985)*.

Rizzuto *(1979)* observed that the process of constructing inner representations involves the whole individual and that these representations are not static, but grow and change with the individual's development and maturation. She also noted the importance of the role of others in the construction of inner representations of significant people in her subjects' lives. Construction, she suggested, is partly a social activity. This observation is supported by the findings of Rosenblatt and Elde *(1990)*, who studied bereaved families and found that grief work included maintaining connections with memories of the deceased. Mourners kept these memories "alive" by remembering, both in solitude and in the company of others, while integrating their memories into the present and into relationships with others.

A helpful family environment has positive facilitating effects. While individual family members have their "internalization," or inner representation of the deceased, the family as a whole may also have communal or shared representations, which may be experienced by individual members as existing or proceeding from outside the self; these can be altered as people and relationships change. Klass *(1988)* made a similar observation about the importance of others in helping bereaved parents maintain an active "relationship" with their dead children.

An analogous situation may occur with the disclosure of the fact of adoption to a child who was placed in infancy (*Nickman, 1985*). How well the adoptive parents are able to remain in touch with the child's developing internal representation of the birthparents can affect the child's self-esteem, personality development, and overall level of functioning. How well the adoptive parents help their child build a realistic representation of the birthparents that is compatible with the child's changing ability to understand is also a factor. With a child who is adopted later, the experience is similar to that of the bereaved child because the child is old enough to remember his or her birthparents.

The authors propose that it may be normative for mourners to maintain a presence and connection with the deceased and that this presence is not static. Just as the adopted child faces the question, "How could they give me up?" and deals with the birthparents' motivation over a period of years, so the bereaved child must deal with how and why the parent died and what the parent's presence may have been like had it continued over time. One cannot deal with a loss without recognizing *what* is lost.

The construction of the lost parent is an ongoing cognitive process. The nature of the construction of the deceased is connected to the child's developmental level, with particular reference to children's changing ability to know themselves and to know others (*Kegan, 1982; Piaget, 1954*). For example, a critical developmental shift takes place when a child moves from seeing others in terms of how these others can meet his or her needs to seeing others as people with needs of their own and with whom some reciprocity is required for a relationship to be sustained. Although the deceased does not change, the child's ability to understand a given set of information about this person will change as the child matures.

The word *construction* derives from the Latin *struere,* to make something out of component parts; to construe is to analyze or set out logically the figurative aspects of a thing. In the psychological literature, constructivism refers to a theoretical position that regards persons or systems as constituting or constructing their own reality *(Gergen, 1985).* The authors see the child's attempt to maintain a connection to a dead parent as an active effort to make sense of the experience of loss and to make it part of the child's reality.

Data to be reported in this paper, drawn from a longitudinal study of the impact of a parent's death on school-age children, suggest a process of adaptation and change in the postdeath relationship and the construction and reconstruction of new connections. On the basis of these observations, the authors posit that learning to remember and finding a way to maintain a connection to the deceased that is consistent with the child's cognitive development and family dynamics are aspects of an accommodation process that allows the child to go on living in the face of the loss. The present paper investigates the elements from which this connection is made and describes what the connection looks like phenomenologically.

CHILD BEREAVEMENT STUDY

The Child Bereavement Study is a prospective study of children aged 6–17, one of whose parents has died. Families representing a range of socioeconomic and ethnic backgrounds were recruited from communities in the greater Boston area; 70% of the families were Catholic, reflecting the large concentration of Roman Catholics in this region. Interviews were conducted in the family home with each child and with the surviving parent at four months, one year, and then two years after the death *(Silverman & Worden, 1992).*

Seventy families with 125 children were interviewed. There were an almost equal number of boys and girls in the sample, with an average age of 11.6 years. Seventy-two percent of the children had lost a father and 28% a mother. The average age of the surviving parent was 41 years, with a range of 30 to 57 years for the surviving mothers and 33 to 50 years for the surviving fathers. In the case of 58% of the children (34 boys and 38 girls), the parent had died after a long illness.

For most couples (91%), this was their only marriage, and the mean length of their marriage had been 17 years. The modal number of children was two. In nine of the families, the child who participated in the study was an only child.

Family incomes after the death ranged from less than $10,000 a year to more than $50,000, with a median income range of $20,000–$29,000. Before the death, men were the primary breadwinners in the families. Many women worked part time outside the home, providing the family with a second income.

Data presented in this paper were taken primarily from the first two semistructured research interviews with these bereaved children and their surviving parents at four months and then at one year after the death. Where appropriate, data from the third interview were used. All the interviews were taped; if a tape was not transcribed, the authors listened to it. These interviews included questions regarding the parent's death, the child's mourning behavior, and the child's thoughts about the deceased, in part informed by one of the author's prior research on bereaved children *(Silverman, 1989; Silverman & Silverman, 1979).*

Additional qualitative data were drawn from the children's responses to the Child's Understanding of Death questionnaire *(Smilansky, 1987).* The analysis of data followed that recommended by Strauss *(1987),* leading to the development of a theory of the bereavement process that is grounded in the data *(Glaser & Strauss, 1967).* The authors studied a sample of these interviews to identify themes and then read additional records to determine whether the same themes were present *(Strauss, 1987).* The remainder of this paper describes the elements from which a connection to the deceased is constructed.

AWARENESS OF DEATH

The children's responses were initially examined to see if their efforts to connect with the deceased were the consequences of a faulty understanding of the concept of death. Findings from research on non-bereaved children raise questions about the age at which a child understands the irreversibility and finality of death (Lonetto, 1980). These bereaved children, regardless of their age, seemed aware of the meaning of death. One seven-year-old girl had no doubt about the finality of her father's death: "Sometimes I want to talk to him, but I go to sleep fast so I won't think about his being gone." A ten-year-old said: "He's not with me, and it hurts."

It was with great difficulty that these children accustomed themselves to the fact that their parents were dead. The contrast between presence and absence often seemed too difficult for them to contemplate, and their discomfort was apparent. In response to the standardized question, "What does it mean when someone dies?" a ten-year-old boy said, "I can't think about that." It seemed impossible to think that his father was gone. Some children, especially those whose parents died suddenly, talked about the shock they felt when they heard the news.

Their new reality required an understanding of death that is not typical of nonbereaved children of the same ages. A 12-year-old girl whose mother died after a long illness said that she could not talk about her mother because it "simply hurts too much." She added: "However, I don't want her to come back and be in such pain." When asked how he felt after his father's death, one 13-year-old boy said plaintively: "I don't know. . . . I just know he's not here anymore." The connection to the deceased cannot be dismissed as merely a way of denying the finality of the loss. The special tension in these children was clear. Although they were aware that their parents were dead, they experienced their parents as still existing in themselves and in their world. This duality caused cognitive dissonance for some and may have accounted for some of the inarticulateness seen shortly after the loss.

STRATEGIES OF CONNECTION

Five categories were identified that reflect the child's efforts to maintain a connection to the deceased parent during this period: 1) making an effort to locate the deceased, 2) actually experiencing the deceased in some way, 3) reaching out to initiate a connection, 4) remembering, and 5) keeping something that belonged to the deceased. The majority of the children reported some activity in each area. There seemed to be no significant relationship between the type of death or the gender or age of the child and any of these responses. These aspects are discussed next, along with anecdotal data from interviews with the children.

Locating the Deceased

When asked where they thought the dead parent was presently, most of the children were able to locate the deceased. Of the 125 children, 92 (74%) believed in a place called "heaven" and that once dead, this was where their parents were; the other 33 (26%) were uncertain what they believed. There was no relationship between a child's age and his or her belief about an afterlife, nor was there any relationship between a child's belief system and how frequently the child dreamed or thought about the dead parent.

Although 70% of the sample were Roman Catholic and Catholic theology encourages these children to believe in the existence of heaven and in a life after death, there was no statistical relationship between the children's expressed beliefs and their religious background. Many non-Catholic children shared a similar belief system in which their parents had some form of existence in a place called "heaven." Even children in their early teens, who were otherwise developmentally and cognitively sophisticated, did not always distinguish between the state of being of the spirit and the body. Many continued to endow the deceased, now residing in heaven, with concrete attributes of a living person, e.g., that dead people see, hear, feel, and move. Others acknowledged a difference between the body that was buried and the soul that was in heaven, but they still endowed the soul with living qualities of vision, hearing, and mobility.

By contrast, matched nonbereaved control children were less likely to endow a deceased person with living attributes. Locating the deceased in a distant place (heaven) seemed to help the bereaved children make sense of their experience: although the deceased cannot see, feel, and move here, they may be able to do so in the place to which they have gone (a place that cannot be seen from here).

The words of a 14-year-old Catholic boy whose father died reflected this belief:

I want my father to see me perform. If I said a dead person can't see, then I would not be able to have my wish that he see what I am doing. I believe that the dead see, hear, move. Don't ask me how, I just believe it. Heaven is a mysterious place. My father is with all the other relatives that died.

Belief in heaven allowed this boy to maintain a sense that his father was still in his life. A 17-year-old Jewish girl, two years after her father died, was clear about the permanency and finality of death, as would be expected, given her age. In her religious education the concept of heaven or an afterlife was not mentioned. However, in her response to a question about whether the dead can see or hear, she said:

Yes, the dead can see and hear. It's what I would *like* to think, so he could hear comforting words and . . . that maybe he can see significant events in my life.

A similar cognitive construction was made by a 15-year-old girl who both saw her father in heaven and recognized that some of what she was experiencing was of her own making:

I think heaven is not a definite place. . . . I know I'm not imagining him . . . it's not as if I actually see him standing there, but I feel him and, like, in my mind I hear his voice.

Experiencing the Deceased

Believing that their dead parents were watching them was an extension of this construction of the parents being in heaven and provided these children with yet another way of connecting with their dead parents. Of the 125 children, 101 (81%) felt that their deceased parents were watching them, and of those who felt watched, 71 (57%) were "scared" by this feeling. These children's uneasiness was related to their fear that their dead parent might not approve of what they were doing. As an 11-year-old boy said:

I sometimes think he is watching me. It scares me because sometimes he might see me do something he wouldn't like. Like, it's weird . . . it's not scary . . . like if you're doing something, like if someone's watching you, you don't do it, if it's bad. You don't do it if someone's watching.

This boy saw his father in the role of disciplinarian, and his feelings about his father included experiencing him as a helpful external control to supplement his incompletely formed superego. A teenage girl talked about how important good grades were for her mother. She said almost playfully that she could imagine her mother "yelling in heaven if I didn't do well in school."

In contrast, a child who did not have a good relationship with her father pictured him in a dream with a mean facial expression, but she could not make out his attitude toward her with any certainty. The dream frightened her and seemed to reflect an aspect of their relationship before his death that was not affirming of the child. It is apparent that, whether the parent was a disciplinarian, a nurturer, or one whose response might be unpredictable, the child experienced the parent in a way that reflected aspects of their relationship before the death.

Some children experienced their parents as communicating with them in a benevolent way that reflected the parents' status as spirits. One nine-year-old boy saw flashing colored dots in his bedroom at night and said he liked to think that it was his mother trying to be in touch with him. When he asked his father if it was possible, his father allowed the possibility and did not try to rationalize the experience away. An adolescent girl noticed a puff of wind blowing open the door of a restaurant where both she and her mother had worked and thought of it as her mother's presence coming to visit. This perception became a standing, good-natured joke between her and the others working in the restaurant.

Another way of experiencing the deceased was through dreams. Many children (56%, $N=69$) dreamed about their parents and, for almost all of them ($N=63$), the parents were alive in the dreams. As one child put it:

I dreamed he met me on the way home from school and that he hugged me. When I woke up, I felt so sad that I won't have that anymore.

Even though the children felt sad when faced with the fact that their parents' presence was only a dream, some children found these dreams comforting:

When I wake up from these dreams, I know she's gone, but when I dream, it feels like she is there and it's reality.

I'm not sure but I hear his voice at night. It's probably in my dreams. He tells me he likes what I did, that I did real good.

Experiencing the deceased in this way tempered the pain and provided an occasion for the child to get parental approval: "It feels good to remember, to feel that he is still part of the family."

Children who found their deceased parents available to them in this way attributed some initiative to the parents and saw themselves as recipients. At some level, they knew that this construction was probably coming from something within themselves. This understanding may be similar to what Weisman *(1972)* called "middle knowledge": a partial awareness of the reality of death that forms the best compromise between an unpleasant truth and a wished-for state of events.

Reaching Out to the Deceased

Children also took some initiative to keep a connection. Visiting the cemetery was one way of actively seeking a place where they could "find" the deceased. For many, the cemetery was the place where they had the last contact with their parents. A 12-year-old girl whose mother had died said: "I go to the cemetery when I feel sad and I need someone to talk with." "Going to the cemetery makes me feel close." A 15-year-old boy, who passed the cemetery on his way home from school, stated:

I don't talk about it much, but I stop by to visit about once a week. I tell him about my day and things I've done.

Speaking to the deceased was another way of bringing the parent into the child's life. Seventy-one children (57%) spoke to their deceased parents. The initiative to choose the place was clearly with the child. A teenage girl said: "I say 'Hi, how are you?' when I go by her picture in the house." A 10-year-old boy reported: "In my mind, I talk to him; I tell him what I did today, about the fish I caught and that I did real good." Although 43% ($N = 29$) of these children, mostly younger, felt they received an answer, they were not usually able to tell us what their parents said. A 15-year-old girl remarked: "It's not that I heard him, but in my head I felt he said, 'You'll be OK. Carry on.'" A 16-year-old described her experience one year after her mother died:

My mother was my friend. I could talk to her about anything. I talk to her, but she can't respond. She doesn't tell me what to do, but like she helps me—I can't explain it.

The ability to take an active role in relation to the death of their parents was reflected in the children's answers to the question, "What advice would you give another child who had lost a parent?" Some children could not answer this question and responded, "I don't know" or "I can't think of anything." These were the same children who did not dream about or talk to their deceased parents. They did not seem to have a place, as yet, for the deceased in their lives. The majority of children, however, did have suggestions, and most counseled fortitude. They said they would advise another child "not to let it get you down all the time" and that "it's possible to carry on." They also said, "It's best to think about the person who died and to remember the good times that you had." "Just think of them as often as you can." "It helps to go to the cemetery a lot to let them know." These responses reflected the ability of some children to organize their experience and to reflect on what would be helpful to others in the same plight.

Waking Memories

The dead parents were present in the children's waking thoughts as well. These waking thoughts involved both reflection and memory. At the four-month interview, 90% of those responding were still thinking about their deceased parents at least several times a week. When asked what they thought about, most children remembered in fairly literal and concrete terms what they did with their parents. A 15-year-old girl whose mother had died said: "I think about the stupid little things we did together." A seven-year-old said, in remembering her father: "I think about all the things that he used to bring me and how he used to flip me over."

A few children reported that they still could not believe the death was real and sometimes forgot their parents had died. Others, reflecting on their new reality, thought about how hard it was to get along without their parents and wished for them to come back. Such reflections were painful and contrasted to the comforting memories that some children counseled a hypothetical bereaved child to call upon.

Linking Objects

Having an object belonging to the deceased was an important means of maintaining a link to him or her. *Linking objects,* a term used by Volkan *(1981),* refers to an aspect of the relationship or an object from that relationship that keeps the mourner living in the past. A more positive link or connection can be found in the concept of *transitional objects*—those that connect one realm of experience with another *(Winnicott, 1953; Worden, 1991)*. These transitional objects provide comfort while one is engaged in the initial mourning process. Of the 125 children, 95 (77%) had something personal that belonged to their dead parents. They acquired these objects in different ways. Often it was something the deceased had given them or something belonging to the deceased that the child had taken after the death. Sometimes their surviving parents had given the objects to them or told them they could take what they wanted from the deceased parents' possessions. For the most part, the children kept these items either on their person or in their rooms. One teenage girl said: "It makes me feel good to wear his shirt to school." Another girl said: "I carry his key chain; it makes me feel good . . . the way some people use crystals or whatever."

As the first year of mourning progressed, some of these transitional objects became less powerful for the children and took on more of the characteristics of "keepsakes" *(Worden, 1991)*. A 13-year-old boy took his father's baseball hat and his cologne right after he learned that the father was dead. He did not understand why he did so, but he just reached out and took what was there and put it in his room. A year later both objects were still in his room. The hat now hung in a remote corner, rather than on the bedpost. Two years after the death, the boy was not sure what had happened to the hat. However, he said that he was reassured by his feeling that his father was always with him, making sure that "I am safe and stuff."

Role of the Surviving Parent

As was noted earlier, the authors see the process of constructing a connection to the deceased as part of an ongoing family dialogue. Not every parent was prepared to talk about the deceased, however. One father, who was primarily concerned with keeping his family going, remarked that his children had forgotten how often they were angry with their mother for being so involved outside the home. He acknowledged that he would listen to the children, but had little patience for their reminiscences. These children finally discovered that they could talk with each other about

their mother and thus felt less frustrated with their father's silence.

On the other hand, some parents were eager to talk, but were met with resistance from the children. As one boy said, "I know my father would listen, but I don't want to talk." One year later, the boy remarked: "Talking makes me sad, but it is better than thinking about it alone. My father listens, and it really helps."

A ten-year-old boy whose sadness was clear and who could not talk about his father told the interviewer that his mother helped him to develop a positive memory of his father:

She says we'll pray every night for Daddy and that he'll be able to see me. She says we have to remember Daddy outside in the sunshine laughing, not like he looked when he died. I asked if Daddy can help me now, if he'll always be with me. Mom said yes.

The children seemed to be comforted by being reminded of their dead parents, even when such reminders did not come from direct conversations with their surviving parents. Although he did not share his reaction with his mother, one 14-year-old commented: "It makes me feel good when I hear my mother talking to someone about how nice my father was."

Changes Over Time

By the second interview, some children who initially had reported no relevant dreams and who seemed to have little or no connection with the deceased found it easier to remember. An 11-year-old girl reported during the first interview that she did not dream about her mother, and she could not describe her to the interviewer. She was unable to concentrate at school because of her thoughts about her mother's absence. She did not possess anything that had belonged to her mother. Her sadness was palpable. She could not talk about her feelings, and she did not feel close to anyone in the family with whom she could talk about her mother.

By the end of the first year, this girl began to dream. She wanted to keep the dreams private, but said they went back to before her mother died. She visited the cemetery, where she talked to her mother; in her head, she could hear her mother's voice, giving her good advice. She took some of her mother's jewelry and kept it in her room. Her schoolwork improved, and her sadness seemed less pervasive. She talked to her friends and her father about her mother and what her mother was like:

This Christmas was hard, but I got through it because I got used to it. Just looking at her picture is hard because I miss her. I think about whether or not she can see me and she can hear me. Is she happy? I hear her voice in my head telling me it's OK. I talk to my friends I can trust and to my dad because he loved her, too, and understands what I am going through.

It is not clear if this girl was better able to confront the loss and tolerate sad feelings because she found a way of connecting with her deceased mother or if being able to tolerate her feelings enabled her to connect with her mother.

DISCUSSION

This paper has described an aspect of the bereavement process in children: the establishment of a set of memories, feelings, and actions that the authors have called "constructing" the deceased. This inner representation or construction leads the child to remain in a relationship with the deceased, and this relationship changes as the child matures and as the intensity of the grief lessens. The concept of identification is insufficient to describe what was observed. A child may construct a sense of the deceased and develop an inner representation of that person that does not involve (at either a conscious or an unconscious level) becoming like that person. Memorializing, remembering, and knowing who died are active processes that may continue throughout the child's entire life. Rubin (1985) noted that there seems to be a relationship between the comfort and fluidity with which the bereaved can relate to the representations of the deceased and their ability to cope effectively with the loss. Although the intensity of the relationship with the deceased must diminish with time, it does not disappear. This is not a matter of living in the past, but rather recognizing how the past informs the present.

These findings suggest a shift in our understanding of the bereavement process. Bereavement should not be viewed as a psychological state that ends or from which one recovers. The intensity of feelings may lessen and the child may become oriented more to the future than to the past, but a concept of closure that requires a determination of when the bereavement process ends does not seem compatible with the view suggested by these findings. The emphasis should be on negotiating and renegotiating the meaning of the loss over time, rather than on letting go. While the loss is permanent and unchanging, the process is not. Thus bereavement should be understood as a cognitive, as well as an emotional, process that takes place in a social context of which the deceased is a part.

Children's cognitive processes include their ability to experience complex feeling states, as well as their inborn qualities and their intellectual and social development. Piaget (1954) observed that development involves a push toward greater mastery of one's situation. In Kegan's view (1982), mastery emerges as children construct and reconstruct their world to find greater coherence and new meanings that can unify memories and feelings into a temporary coherent whole that prevails until the child moves to the next stage of development. The ability to call up memories of specific events; abstractions concerning the nature of past interactions; and, on the highest level, descriptions of the deceased's personality, likes, and dislikes depends on the child's level of development.

Accommodation may be a more suitable term than recovery or closure for what takes place as a result of a death in the family. However, in this context, accommodation should not be viewed as a static phenomenon. Rather, it is a continuing set of activities—related both to others and to shifting self-perceptions as the child's mind and body change—that affect the way the child constructs meaning. In this process, the child seeks to gain not only an understanding of the meaning of death, but a sense of the meaning of this now-dead parent in his or her life. To do so requires the development of a common language for talking about the death and the person who died.

When an experience is re-created in language, it may lose in immediacy, but it is more likely to be kept in memory. Critical to representation in language is the family's use of ritual that could legitimate the construction of an inner representation of the deceased. Most non-Western cultures have rituals that help their members acknowledge and cope with loss and with the sense of the deceased (Rosenblatt, Walsh, & Jackson, 1976; Silverman & Silverman, 1979). The need for such rituals is acknowledged less in contemporary Western thinking and worldviews. We may need to look anew at rituals that facilitate dialogue and other kinds of relationships to the past.

The interview data reported in this paper have identified ways in which the child maintains a connection to the deceased parent. These data challenge the traditional clinical practice of encouraging the bereaved to disengage from the deceased. In facilitating mourning, those who work with children may need to focus on how to transform connections and place the relationship in a new perspective, rather than on how to separate from the deceased.

REFERENCES

Anderson, R. (1974). Notes of a survivor. In S.B. Troop & W.A. Green (Eds.), *The patient, death and the family* (pp. 73–82). New York: Charles Scribner's Sons.

Bowlby, J. (1980). *Attachment and loss: Vol. 3. Loss, sadness, and depression*. New York: Basic Books.

Dietrich, D.R., & Shabad, P.C. (1989). *The problem of loss and mourning*. Madison, CT: International Universities Press.

Freud, S. (1957). Mourning and melancholia. In J. Strachey (Ed. and Trans.), *The standard edition of the complete psychological works of Sigmund Freud* (Vol. 14, pp. 237–258). London: Hogarth Press. (Original work published 1917)

Furman, E. (1974). *A child's parent dies: Studies in childhood bereavement*. New Haven, CT: Yale University Press.

Furman, E. (1984). Children's patterns in mourning the death of a loved one. In H. Wass & C. Corr (Eds.), *Childhood and death* (pp. 185–203). Washington, DC: Hemisphere Publishing.

Gergen, K.J. (1985). The social constructionist movement in modern psychology. *American Psychologist, 40*, 266–273.

Glaser, B., & Strauss, A. (1967). *The discovery of grounded theory*. Chicago: Aldine Publishing.

Jacobs, S.C., Koston, T.R., Dasl, S., & Ostfeld, A-M. (1987). Attachment theory and multiple dimensions of grief. *Omega, 18*, 41–52.

Jacobson, E. (1965). The return of the lost parent. In M. Schur (Ed.), *Drives, affects, and behaviors* (Vol. 2, pp. 193–211). New York: International Universities Press.

Kegan, R. (1982). *The evolving self: Problem and process in human development*. Cambridge, MA: Harvard University Press.

Klass, D. (1988). *Parental grief: Solace and resolution*. New York: Springer.

Lifton, R.J. (1979). *The broken connection: On death and the continuity of life*. New York: Simon & Schuster.

Lonetto, R. (1980). *Children's conceptions of death* (Vol. 3). New York: Springer.

Miller, J.B.M. (1971). Children's reactions to the death of a parent: A review of the psychoanalytic literature. *Journal of the American Psychoanalytic Association, 19*, 697–719.

Moss, M.S., & Moss, S.Z. (1981). The image of the deceased spouse in remarriage of elderly widowers. *Journal of Gerontological Social Work, 3*(2), 59–70.

Nickman, S.L. (1985). Loss in adoption: The importance of dialogue. *Psychoanalytic Study of the Child, 40*, 365–398.

Osterweis, M., Solomon, F., & Greene, M. (Eds.). (1984). *Bereavement: Reactions, consequences, and care*. Washington, DC: National Academy Press.

Piaget, J. (1954). *The construction of reality in the child* (M. Cook Trans.). New York: Basic Books.

Rizzuto, A.M. (1979). *The birth of the living God: A psychoanalytic study*. Chicago: University of Chicago Press.

Rochlin, G. (1959). Loss and restitution. *Psychoanalytic Study of the Child, 8*, 288–309.

Rochlin, G. (1965). *Griefs and discontents: The forces of change*. Boston: Little, Brown.

Rosenblatt, P., & Elde, C. (1990). Shared reminiscence about a deceased parent: Implications for grief education and grief counselling. *Family Relations, 39*, 206–210.

Rosenblatt, P.C., Walsh, R.P., & Jackson, D.A. (1976). *Grief and mourning in cross-cultural perspective* [Machine-readable data file]. Human Relations Area Files.

Rubin, S.S. (1985). The resolution of bereavement: A clinical focus on the relationship to the deceased. *Psychotherapy: Theory, Research, Training and Practice, 22*, 231–235.

Schafer, R. (1968). *Aspects of internalization*. New York: International Universities Press.

Silverman, P.R. (1986). *Widow to widow*. New York: Springer.

Silverman, P.R. (1989). The impact of the death of a parent on college age women. *Psychiatric Clinics of North America, 10*, 387–404.

Silverman, P.R., & Worden, J.W. (1992). Children's reactions to the death of a parent in the early months after the death. *American Journal of Orthopsychiatry, 62*, 93–104.

Silverman, S.M., & Silverman, P.R. (1979). Parent-child communication in widowed families. *American Journal of Psychotherapy, 33*, 428–441.

Smilansky, S. (1987). *On death: Helping children understand and cope*. New York: Peter Lang.

Strauss, A.L. (1987). *Qualitative analysis for social scientists*. Cambridge, England: Cambridge University Press.

Volkan, V.D. (1981). *Linking objects and linking phenomena*. New York: International Universities Press.

Weisman, A. (1972). *On dying and denying: A psychiatric study of terminality*. New York: Behavioral Publications.

Winnicott, D.W. (1953). Transitional objects and transitional phenomena. *International Journal of Psycho-Analysis, 34*, 89–97.

Wolfenstein, M. (1973). The image of the lost parent. *Psychoanalytic Study of the Child, 28*, 433–456.

Worden, J.W. (1991). *Grief counseling and grief therapy: A handbook for the mental health practitioner* (2nd ed.). New York: Springer.

Reflections on the Death of My Daughter-in-Law

Vanda Manahan, PhD, ACSW

Vanda Manahan is chairman of the Department of Social Work at Mankato State University, MN.

On February 21, one month after her 25th birthday, our daughter-in-law, Lea Anne Williams Hedges, died. There had been a 16 month ordeal: 14 rounds of aggressive chemotherapy, back-to-back bone marrow transplants, lung surgery, excision and radiation of the original tumor, pneumonias and bleeds into her lungs, until all her breathing space was exhausted.

During that time, she had spent 174 days, including two New Years' Eves in the hospital. But she had also watched Duke win the NCAA in the Metrodome, seen a play on Broadway, hiked on Chimney Rock where the Last of the Mohicans was filmed, donned costumes for the famed Chapel Hill Halloween celebration, had a song recorded in Dallas, appeared in a PBS documentary, finished coursework for her doctorate, presented a poster session at the American Psychological Association, and picnicked in the park. On her birthday she was riding in a convertible down the Florida coast, with the wind blowing her hair, observing, "I'm so happy. . . ."

But if I could find few to listen to her amazing feats as she tried to out distance the invading cancer, I can find fewer to tell of her death.

I now know concretely what I previously taught in the abstract—we are a society that can not deal with death, the dying, or the bereaved. I'm offering my observations as tips for encountering the bereaved and removing a little of the unnecessary pain in their lives.

The first rule, indeed, the only rule, for all the others are corollaries, is:

ACKNOWLEDGE THE LOSS

If you can't attend the memorial, or call at the visitation, the easiest way to acknowledge the death is to send a card. Those messages of sympathy meant so much. It told me that someone had noticed what for me was the only news: Lea had died.

While driving from Durham, N.C. where she died to Iowa City where she was buried, I half-expected the news to be on national radio. This was our Waco, our Bosnia, our deepest tragedy. I yearned to have her death noted. And only her death, for now, please. **Don't gather up other tragedies.** It won't help us establish rapport, it diminishes Lea's death, and I don't have the energy to deal with more evidence of nature's random cruelty.

Acknowledge the Loss at the Beginning of Our First Meeting

Don't leave me wondering if I must break this news to you. You can't finesse a death, but many acquaintances, colleagues, and friends have tried. The most bewildering response is the, "Other than that, Mrs. Lincoln . . . how did you enjoy the play?" technique. I'm greeted warmly, with determined good cheer. "How's your sabbatical going? I hear you're traveling a lot. I wish I were that lucky. I bet you're having a lot of fun!"

At first I assumed such people didn't know of Lea's death. After telling a few, who mumbled, "Yes, I heard about that . . ." I came to understand that they want to keep the conversation in comfortable territory. They insist that I am happy, and that I not tell them otherwise.

Acknowledge My Particular Loss Directly, Not Obliquely

Mention the relationship . . . I'm sorry about your daughter. Other mourners are always involved, and there may be hierarchies of grief, but acknowledge mine when you first speak to me. Then you might extend your condolences through me to my son, in the inner circle of grief.

It is hard to be perceived as a peripheral mourner, as though I am saddened only because of my son's loss. "Whither thou goest, I will go . . ." was a promise of love spoken by Ruth to her mother-in-law, I have lost a daughter, one of My People; I have a visceral grief.

Make Statements, Rather Than Ask Questions

The statements seem simple: What a tragic loss. It must be so hard. This is a difficult time.

And I can nod, and answer in words of one syllable, or give the phrases I've practiced saying. The grieving are inarticulate in the spoken word. Words *are* inadequate as the sympathy cards say and we are unable to pronounce the words that might describe how we feel.

But don't believe because an exchange was short or stilted that it was unimportant to me, for we must speak of this before we can speak of anything else.

Don't Try to Console

There really aren't words of comfort. Perhaps "time does heal." But right now it seems unthinkable that someday we will be both bereft of Lea *and* the pain that marks her loss. Just grasp the void we feel. If you know Lea, say one of the hundreds of wonderful things that could be said of her.

Don't Ask Me to Evaluate the Grief of Others

A most difficult question is: "How is your son doing?" Or, "How is Lea's mother doing?" How can I judge their grief?

I've settled on, "It's hard for us all. . . ." You want reassurance that the unbearable can be borne. It can . . . that is its curse.

A more appropriate inquiry is, "How is it that he does?" What is he doing to get through this time? *What* is easier to respond to than *how.* He's finished out his year of teaching, he's put their life in storage, and he's gotten in his car to find someplace where it doesn't hurt to look out the window.

Speak of Lea in Normal Conversation; Notice Her Pictures; Say What You Would Ordinarily Say

No one who has visited my home since Lea's death has voluntarily mentioned her name or noted her pictures that are decorating the refrigerator. Any other time, they would say, "My, isn't she beautiful. That's a great picture of Lea." We are asked to pretend that she never lived, so they can ignore that she died.

I've tricked them with baby pictures of Lea with her twin sister. Those who don't know that Lea had an identical twin fall into my trap of commenting on their mischievous toddler faces, and then I can point out the other pictures. I need to speak of Lea and to hear her name spoken.

Don't Be Afraid of Being Stuck; I Won't Tell You More Than You Can Handle

I'd like to tell of Lea's last days . . . of her good-bye before she went on the respirator; Of our agonized, but mercifully quick recognition of the medical futility of forcing oxygen into her tumor-filled lungs.

I'd like to tell you how tenderly we cared for her while she was unconscious. We held her hand, played her favorite music, massaged her feet, told her favorite memories and my genetically tuneless son even sang her a song. But I'll pass on those stories. Those are for the closest friends.

Don't Be Afraid of My Tears

I don't believe that people mean to be unkind. I must assume that they don't mention Lea's death because they think it will make me sad. Since the funeral's over, and the death was weeks or months past, they "don't want to remind me. . . ."

Don't think I've forgotten Lea's death for a minute.

I may cry when I speak of her, but it is not because you have created sadness. The sadness is there; you have permitted me briefly to share it.

Don't Be Afraid of Your Own Tears

Of course, you might cry, too. The most comforting calls were from friends who sobbed on the phone. After all, how little it is . . . to cry for a young woman who died, one month after her 25th birthday.

FEELING SOMETHING

When a father dies

Bruce Duffy

Bruce Duffy is the author of the novel The World As I Found It. *His last piece for Harper's Magazine, "Catching a Westbound Freight," appeared in the June 1989 issue. He is currently working on a new novel.*

In the fall of 1962 I was eleven, still submerged in that murk, or sump, between childhood and puberty. The mind at eleven is raw and mistrustful, forever explaining life to itself, ruthlessly scrutinizing it like something wriggling on the end of a stick. I can still hear that boy's summoning, inward voice crackling like a police radio, trying to unscramble knotted feelings and worries about so many things that to him seemed either unreal or phony, like brownnosing or closing your eyes real tight when you prayed after receiving Communion. Descending from age thirty-eight to the silty deeps of eleven, I can still hear him say, *Come on, how can I cry in front of everybody in public like that? That really stinks!*

How could I cry? I had just lost my mother, and now my father, my relatives, and the neighbors—everybody was watching me like I was supposed to sob or act some kind of way. But how was I supposed to act—even, say, if I almost *felt* like crying—without also "playacting"? I was stuck. For me, it was the scourged feeling of standing exposed before a wall of urinals in a packed men's room, a feeling of wanting to go real bad but being plugged and powerless to pee. *So everybody quit staring, huh!*

Even now, the intense self-scrutiny and impotence of those days seem like something dreamed. But no, I didn't imagine it. Several years ago, after meeting one of my favorite aunts, my wife playfully asked her what I was like as a boy. "Well, honey," said Aunt Rose coyly, with a darting smile at me. "Wellll, you might say he was one strange kid! One thing I remember. Nobody knew what in the dickens he felt when his poor mom died. He didn't seem to feel a thing."

Felt nothing!? Hearing this old slander, I wanted to fly back, *Christ, Rose, how could you presume that? Are you really that blind or naive?*

But I couldn't fight with my old aunt now. I didn't want to dredge up that old mess. So the matter of what I felt or didn't feel lay undisturbed until last summer, when a young man in a dark suit ushered me into the parlor where my father lay in an open coffin, looking smaller than his six feet three inches and clutching in his hairy, withered hands a black rosary.

His death had been sudden—a massive coronary—and I was his only child. His second wife, my stepmother, was on her way to the viewing, but mercifully for me, I had beaten her there, wanting a few minutes alone so that I might get used, like very deep, cold water, to the feeling of looking down on my father's shellacked face and the buzzing, black whorl inside his ear where the makeup so abruptly ended.

So odd, how we talk to the dead, trailing off, then resuming miles later in the bending force field of memory. Patting my father's immobile shoulder, I was saying squeakily, "Oh, Christ, Pop, why'd this have to happen, huh? Man, you didn't even have a chance to see your first grandchild."

Man. Suddenly, I'm calling him "man": Death forces us to take queer liberties, two minds suddenly thrust together, memory to memory. For five minutes I stood there, muttering or half praying in my head, when out of a kind of desperation to bring him closer, I did something impulsive, something inappropriate, perhaps, but to me intensely natural. This was an old impulse, something I used to do to him as a kid, whether to love or annoy him or both. Lightly, like a wing, I skipped my open palm like a Hellcat fighter plane over his bushy gray flattop, humming *NYYYYeeeerr-roowwwWWW*—

That's what got me. That dumb kid's love prank was what finally broke loose those jammed feelings—back to when his hair was bristly dark and tipped with light, back to 1958 and the summer in Maine, when, both wearing white bucks, really snazzy, we twanged two sprunged-out tennis rackets and wiggle-waggled our knees singing Elvis's "Hound Dog" and Mom got the hiccups, and it was such a riot—back when life was a given, and happiness ever youthful, the goodness surging in like a cold Maine tide.

From *Harper's*, June 1990, pp. 70-75, 78. © 1990 by Bruce Duffy. Reprinted by permission of International Creative Management.

NYYYYYeeeerrroowwwWWW, and I was too much feeling something. Lurching off to the men's room, I turned on the spigots, washing my face of this blackness because people were coming and I still didn't **understand a goddamned thing.**

The odd thing was, for months before this I'd had this peculiar, gathering sense of my life as something fated. Slowly, my past seemed to be rolling toward me, heaving down hard, then rushing back with the heavy, dark purgings of ocean waves.

But why this prickly, fated feeling? I wondered. Maybe it was the imminent birth of our first child after two miscarriages that made me feel so dangerously lucky. On the other hand, maybe it was the two good friends who had just lost parents that made me feel this dark breath on my neck. Then again, if I was seeing the emergence of a certain curious shape to my life, that was also because I was actively *seeking* it. I was nearing thirty-eight, the age my mother was when she died. I guess I had always imagined that at thirty-eight we would converge, my mother and I. Catching her in age after twenty-seven years of pursuit, I thought at last I might better understand her life and what she felt when she left: I awaited that day when we would be not just mother and son but simply Joan and Bruce, as if we'd met at some raucous party of the memory.

But all the while my mother had been changing. After dying once, she had been slowly dying out of me as I grew into adulthood, dying twice and a dozen times, never leaving for good or remaining what she was but receding ever further, growing ever more the mocking dream. When I look back through my youth, I see my mother vanish repeatedly, only to return like a comet, here darker and more obscure, there more brilliant, and yet always returning in the bending bow of memory. And me always struggling, either to evade or deny her, like a man confronting an old lover, insisting that I'm strong and independent, hardened and now immune to her sting. We don't know our own hearts. After a time, once the spell of grief is broken, the truth is, we don't *want* the dead to return, that's our dark secret and the bitter root of our confusion. Oh, Mother, so many

years I've spent running and never catching up, cursing you because I could neither catch you nor kill you as a memory, powerless ever to get free. Or so it has been until now, when the light shifts and suddenly I see I've surpassed you—when I must endure the cruel irony of growing older, perhaps even wiser, while remaining forever a captive child, ever subject to your fickle will.

But I wasn't just struggling with my mother all that time. For years after her death my father and I also fought, and fought bitterly. From my teens through my late twenties, my father and I were sucked through the undertow of a bitterness so progressive and consuming that I don't think either of us understood it, in either its unholy force or its prolonged and insidious effects. My chief consolation now is that when he died our days of warring were miraculously over—so resoundingly over that at times I still found it stunning that we could actually be friends, at times almost buddies. But this doesn't account for our former estrangement, those jumbled, tormented feelings of love, awe, contempt, and even hatred that I had for him when I was younger.

A premature death is never quite forgiven: After someone dies too messily, early, or pointlessly, someone else always gets blamed. I had, and still have, my mother's long nose and dark eyes, her small, insistent chin and bratty mouth. Maybe I was too much like her for him then, too flamboyant and playful, too cunning and desirous to put on airs and live, as she had, beyond our class and modest means. He was such a straight arrow, really. Maybe that's what he had found so alluring about her, the way she had so blithely lived the risky life he couldn't quite allow himself and certainly couldn't afford then—not when his business partner, taking advantage of his distraction, had screwed him and her hospital bills had all but wiped us out.

But what most irked him then was my "unfeelingness," as he put it. He hated the fact that her death seemed to have passed clean through me, leaving precious little grief that he could see and only my wild, obnoxious propensity to laugh at inappropriate times. I saw his pain. Yet why couldn't I give in, if only to ease his distress at watching our life unravel? I

see his red and silent face at supper, a glowering, slapped face that my hot ears could hear sneering, *Eat your food, you miserable little prick. Feel something.* And me in my willfulness, just staring him down in a so-go-cut-my-tongue-out way, hiding my true feelings while feeling such perverse contempt for him, that he shouldn't somehow have divined my obviously profound and courageous grief. And anyway, who was *he,* forcing me, like a criminal, to express remorse for a crime I didn't commit? He didn't know what I felt . . . *that was the point!*

Then, in a way, I guess, I irrationally blamed him for his failure to save her after the progressive botchings of a supposedly routine appendectomy. He always said he could have sued the hospital for malpractice, but as a matter of honor he said he wouldn't use the damaging information the doctors had given him against them in court. "Well, come on," he said, with that dour, mumps look he would take on when he felt beaten and intimidated by life. "Whatever else, the doctors acted in good faith." But hearing this intended note of reassurance, I only felt more frantic, outraged by his complacency and cowardice. "What do you mean, '*Good faith*'?" I stood there goggling at him. "They *killed* her, for Christ's sake!"

I thought he was a chump for swallowing that shit, for resolutely playing the gentleman while his partner bilked him and the doctors lost his wife. As a culprit, I craved culprits, yet even so the kid partly knew it was just a plain humiliation, to see his proud father crippled with grief and the bills so punctiliously submitted by the very idiots he said had killed her.

My father was a complex mixture of power and passivity, a tall, commanding presence, with his bushy dark flat-top. A former Eagle Scout and Navy lieutenant, he was an intense, compulsively active man, a mechanical engineer by profession and a man of intimidating prowess in the physical world—able to build a house or tear down an engine. In contrast to this powerful builder was the defeated man who emotionally would retreat, like a crab, into the ritual order of his workshop when life got too upsetting. This was the irascible man, the hopeless gumhand who, it seemed to me, could fix anything in the world but our life, the man who periodically would lash out at me as he did once about a year after she died: "What's wrong with you, you stupid kid! You never cried. Not one miserable tear for your mother. You faced me like a snowman—still do! Oh, sure, go on! Just gape at me with that sneaking, idiot grin smeared all across your face!"

Eight years later—a century later, the chasm between 1962 and 1970 —things between us were only worse. He couldn't stand me growing my hair and wasting his money studying English in college—this to him was "basket weaving," as deluded and impractical as my grandiose, gigolo plans of becoming a writer. ("Oh, sure! A big shot! Another way to run your mouth!") At nineteen, the day after I got my draft number (351, no chance of being drafted), I drove home from college and told him I wouldn't cut my hair, which was tantamount to saying I was leaving. But this familiar struggle wasn't merely about hair or values. For me, I think, it was about freedom from the past, one final expectoration of that swillish death-taste tinged with vileness and failure.

Yet was I really so ready to leave? I remember gently stopping him at the precipice, as he pulled the screen door shut, hopelessly asking if we might sit outside on the stoop and maybe *talk* for a while.

But it was way too late to talk. Mostly through sick silences we talked, the words sticking like fish bones in our throats, until I climbed into my faded blue VW and left. God, what a waste that was, the young, raw, pissed-off one driving away in stubbornness and the older one standing in stubbornness as if his feet were cast in cement.

For more than a year there was total silence, a contest, mano a mano, to see who could hold his breath longer. Then came years of brief, awkward reunions and holiday thaws engineered by my stepmother. In his stiff, resentful way he tried during these truces. In my sullen, arrogant way I suppose I tried, too, but it was still terrible. One way or another we always parted gored and heartbroken. After a curt, embarrassed hug I would walk into the cool darkness, feeling absolutely scalded before his all-too-evident bitterness about the waste and folly of my life,

about the women who inevitably left me, and about my pigheaded delusions of eventually being published.

By the time I was twenty-six—a promising unpublished writer—security guard—there was still too much bitterness and mistrust between us to sustain much more than a punishing twice-yearly visit. Pride dies slowly. Only years later, when I was well past thirty and happily married, could he admit how during our warring years he would sit out back on the patio under the big maple. "Yeah," he said, gritting his teeth in that way he did when about to hook a fish. "On Friday nights I'd sit out here, half bombed, just crying my damned eyes out, asking myself what I'd ever done to deserve you dumping me like that."

We both had tears in our eyes. Squeezing his shoulder, I said, "So why couldn't you ever pick up the phone? Do you think I ever would have wanted to put you through that? Do you, even for a second? I can't stand to think of you in pain, I can't. But how was I to know? With me you always acted like you were made of fucking stone."

Nothing is sadder for me than to think of him under that smothering tree, with the tears streaming down his stiff, red face. And, of course, he was deeply emotional. You can see this clearly in one unforgettable picture of him in our wedding album. There he is, sitting in the front row of the pine grove where my wife and I were married, his eyes wet, staring off into the trees, utterly oblivious to the camera and the people around him. It was my party-crashing mother, so long absent, who had visited him that day. Closing an ellipse of nineteen years, she returned to him as the ceremony was about to begin, intensely visible in the way that dust is illuminated by the spokes of noon, no ghost but rather a memory summoned by a power of memory. Later that evening, by the bar, he told my friend Steve, "You know, it's strange—I mean, to be with one wife while thinking about the old one. It's like getting stuck in a revolving door."

According to Steve, my father said only a few words before he took his drink and drifted outside, out into the evening wind, under the rushing locust trees. Between two wives he stood: two selves and two pasts at the great white confluence where riv-

ers marry the drowned to the living. So trapped he must have felt, so swamped between times, to have one wife inside, in that flushed warmth where everyone was dancing, while this other, younger one still abided in his mind, ageless and impervious in those rushing branches where the wind still stirred.

I think it's fair to say that three years ago, when I published my first novel, he was deeply shocked. Truly, he was strangely tickled that at last my thrashings and confusions had panned out. By then he had semi-retired from his heating and air-conditioning business. He'd had a mild heart attack, a good whiff of mortality, but he was still going hard, working part-time, testing an invention he was patenting, bicycling for miles, and traveling, first to the Mid-east, then to Australia, then the next summer to Ireland.

I remember him as being more relaxed then, happier than he'd been in years, actually. I could say, with a child's condescension, that he had mellowed, but the truth is, we both had. Over the last two summers, my wife and I had an annual weekend with him down at the beach. My dad and I also talked regularly and—unusual for us—had several long lunches together. Unmistakable resemblance, the tall, graying older man with the perennial flattop and the tall, short-haired ex-hippie in the suit, the two of them grabbing and laughing, then rather fastidiously eating dribbling bay oysters, two platters, followed by gamy shad roe and bacon washed down with schooners of beer.

In his quiet way he was especially excited about becoming a grandfather. Just two days before he died, he and my stepmother came to our house with gifts—baby clothes, bedding, and a new stroller. What hurts now is remembering him sitting in the freshly painted baby's room, rocking in the maple glider chair, peering around the room, just smiling and luxuriating in the sheer, uncanny idea of it, a granddaughter.

Two days later I was up in New York, deciding on a new publisher. For three hours that day I'd talked with editors in two different publishing houses about a new novel—one about, among other things, the queer, continuing relationship between a child and a dead parent. But, God, the timing was rotten. Why dig all this up now, especially when my father was still alive? For months I fought it like a seasickness, feeling guilty yet mindful that the book couldn't be deferred or avoided.

But at last I'd made my decision to publish, and as I boarded the train for Washington, I was excited by a suggestion my new editor had just made. No sooner did I find my seat on the train home than I began to write the scene of the father picking up his son at school, then evasively explaining, in those fumbling conditional tenses we use for death, how the boy's mother might possibly die. Ordinarily, I never write on trains, yet now I wrote steadily, propulsively. Over the next two hours I covered nearly six pages in my notebook, describing that mysterious feeling of coincidence that accompanies death—that whammy feeling that out of millions of possible targets death should strike you. Describing the boy's inner thoughts, I wrote: *But still it could happen. It could happen like a ball whizzing straight for your head.*

For more than two weeks the kid's mother has been in the hospital, worsening to the point that for days the boy hasn't seen her. Shunted from family to family, the boy has hardly seen his father either, what with him being all the time at the hospital, mixed up in some kind of conspiracy with the doctors. But then one morning the boy is called up to the principal's office. Singled out! All the other kids aghast, watching him as he rushes out, his head engulfed in flames. But, hey, what's his dad doing at the principal's? "I thought we'd go home for a while," he says evasively, quickly ushering the boy out. Yet once outside, as they're getting into the car, the father says, "You know, we've gotta be prepared. I hope I'm wrong, but your mother could die, she really might. It's real close and, to tell the truth—well, things don't look too good."

The boy nods, but he can't fathom this any more than he can understand why, when they have such a short way to go, his father should keep fiddling with the radio dial like he can't find the proper, slithery frequency or words for this. But then, as his father fumbles, the boy hears his decoding head explain:

Even so, it could happen for real, you know. It could happen like a ball whizzing straight for your head.

Suddenly, the boy can see it. He's thinking of how he once watched a walloping line drive—*kapow*, right off the bat, screwing straight for his forehead. *Woof.* Powerless to move, he stupidly watches that widening white ball, knowing no matter which way he ducks it's gonna bean him for sure. And then as he and his dad open the door to the house—the phone rings, and his dad looks at him scared, because, of course, now he sees it, too. That ball's burning for them both, and the kid just stands there, stunned in the doorway, wondering how he should act. Act surprised? Act upset and run wailing into his dad's arms? Act no way because his ears are ringing and he doesn't know how to act yet? But it's too late, because he knows, sure as sin, that whatever he does he'll be wrong—he'll be impure and phony because he wondered. He'll be wrong because he thought and didn't just act.

But, in truth, that ball was heading straight for me as I scribbled down this scene. After twenty-seven years, it was burning in again as my train arrived in Washington and my wife pulled up in our red Toyota.

"Boy, what a marathon day—" I swung my briefcase into the backseat. "Well, how are you?"

There were tears in her eyes. "I feel so bad," she wheezed. "Honey, your father died this afternoon. A heart attack. Your stepmother came home and found him dead on the bathroom floor."

I didn't cry then. I couldn't move. For the next hour, as I spoke to my stepmother on the phone, I fell into that same old ear-buzzing stupor, waiting for the pain to bloom and burn through—waiting in the transfixed way the boy used to hold a slow-burning match in his fingers, seeing how long he could stand it before flicking it away with a teary wince.

But this gray, dumbstruck phase passed soon enough. Once my wife and I got into bed, I cried all right. This time I felt none of the shame and prudishness the boy had felt before his father's red, exposed grief. Up in bed then, in my wife's arms, pressed against her pregnant belly, I learned again how to cry. Like an old song I learned it, with that same witless, eye-burning helplessness the kid had felt late at night, blurting into his pillow with the ends wrapped around his ears so his old man would never know.

In my memory the man asleep in the next room was no longer just affable old "Pop," not the "old man," "Dad," or that more forbidding word, "Father"; in my regressive state of mind he was not even remotely so well formed or sophisticated a concept. Rather, my mind reverted to the more primitive squall of "Daddy," back to the point where you remember only the least and deepest, most lost and buried childish things: back to the "once" of that little creek by your house and him squatting beside you, when his hair was dark and life was still a wondrous, sunny, after-rain thing. Once his upturned shoes in the squishy, and once the echoes you two made in the darkness under the loud bridge, both bombing the water with rocks and whanging your little cap gun because, as you both knew, this was absolutely the wildest, most funnest thing ever.

That sublime coincidence of life was once him and you—actually, it was the both of you, and your mother, once. It was all of you, but the truly astounding thing is to lapse into that deep amnesia of childhood, that glimmering primordial lake when to you "Daddy," like "Mama," meant all in the world that was good. With that, it doesn't matter that you once fought with your father, or that once there were times when you seriously imagined hating him. You see, none of that matters now, because for some time you can't rationally speak of any of this, just as you can't, for the life of you, remember even a single thing bad about him.

OLD NO MORE

It's not immortality scientists are after. They want Americans to age with grace and vitality

In an internist's office, in the year 2020, a young physician writes out several prescriptions for his patient, a slender and energetic man of 75. Although he lifts weights regularly, recently switched careers to become a park ranger and enjoys an active sex life, he is anxious to get the results of his physical. "Well, your hormone profile is holding steady at about the 25-year-old level," the doctor reassures him, "so we'll continue the same therapy. And keep your calories down. Have a nice day."

This is no far-flung fantasy. Scientists determined to overthrow the tyranny of aging are already playing out parts of this scenario in research centers across the country. They're testing a variety of promising strategies—from boosting nutrition to giving hormonal tuneups—and are confident that they'll soon be able to manipulate the body's chemistry to stave off the ravages of old age. Indeed, estrogen replacement and calcium supplements are already widely used to forestall osteoporosis in postmenopausal women, notes Daniel Rudman, who discovered in studies at the Veterans Affairs Medical Center in Milwaukee that restoring human growth hormone to youthful levels turns flab into muscle. "Twenty years from now," says Rudman, "physicians may well be prescribing custom-tailored cocktails that will protect the elderly from degenerative damage, help them stay physically active and generally improve the quality of their lives."

Boomer crisis. Humankind has dreamed of preserving youth since earliest history, but today many researchers aren't so much drawn by the mythical quest for immortality as they are concerned about the modern-day problem of a growing population of frail elderly. "We have no

---

Scientists are confident they'll soon manipulate the body's chemistry to stave off old age

---

more than 15 or 20 years to unravel the secrets of age-related disease and to develop interventions," says Daniel Perry of the Alliance for Aging Research. "If we don't, we'll have a huge population of infirm baby boomers to whom we can offer nothing better than painkillers and nursing homes."

With no time to lose, scientists who study aging are working steadily toward their new goal: extending the number of healthy years of life, or a person's "health span." The best strategy for maintaining youthful function over a lifetime (and, not incidentally, for keeping down health care costs) is to prevent age-related degeneration from occurring in the

first place, many researchers believe. And that's increasingly feasible. As Eugene Roberts of the City of Hope hospital in Duarte, Calif., explains, "Aging is not a natural process but a combination of degenerative diseases, which are not necessarily inevitable."

Over the past decade, researchers have advanced swiftly in their understanding of age-related declines: losses in immunity, memory, cardiac function and basic ability to respond to stress, among others. They know that, in general, aging results because the everyday wear and tear of living causes accumulative damage to tissues. At the same time, the body's ability to defend and repair itself gradually declines with age. While much of the damage occurs randomly, a person's ability to fend off assaults is controlled by genetics. That's why some people are born with the ability to weather a lifetime of harmful habits like smoking and drinking, while others, who are health-conscious, succumb to disease before middle age.

One way to combat aging, scientists believe, is to trap damaging agents before they can do the body harm. At the top of researchers' list of biochemical outlaws is a group of chemicals called free radicals. Some of these extremely reactive compounds hail from environmental sources, such as radiation and smog, but the bulk are generated as byproducts in the body's normal course of converting sugar and oxygen to energy—a job performed in every cell by structures called mitochondria. Thousands of these tiny powerhouses wander through cells' interiors, leaking free radicals that burn holes in membranes and leave hot spots of so-called oxidative damage in their wake, explains John Carney of the University of Kentucky in Lexington. Free radicals mangle not only vital protein enzymes and molecules carrying the genetic code but also the energy-generating mitochondria themselves, half of which may be dysfunctional in old animals.

Researchers are discovering chemical agents that may help prevent cell degeneration

---

Researchers are now discovering chemical agents that sop up free radicals and may be useful in preventing cell and tissue degeneration. For example, Carney has reported that a compound called PBN halts destructive free-radical reactions and that daily administering of PBN in aged gerbils restores the function of oxidized proteins in their brains. Older gerbils treated with PBN, he says, made fewer errors than did untreated agemates when relying on spatial memory to run through a maze. Furthermore, the PBN-treated animals were better protected from stroke-induced brain damage. "Aging is just a slower, smoldering crock-pot version of the oxidation that goes on in a stroke," explains Carney. He and his colleagues are now trying to develop compounds similar to PBN that might be safely used in humans.

Other, more natural free-radical quenchers—vitamins E and C and beta carotene—are looking increasingly promising in warding off degenerative disease. For instance, researchers at Harvard's School of Public Health, in a study that included more than 130,000 healthy middle-aged and older adults, found that consuming at least 100 international units of vitamin E every day

for two or more years reduced the risk of cardiovascular disease. This finding dovetails with evidence that heart disease is sparked when—like butter turning rancid—the blood's "bad" LDL (low-density lipoprotein) cholesterol gets oxidized by free radicals. Other epidemiological studies suggest that beta carotene—a compound related to vitamin A—helps the body thwart cancer, particularly of the lung. Vitamins C and E, says Jeffrey Blumberg of Tufts University in Boston, appear to retard the formation of cataracts. Together these three antioxidant vitamins may complement each other by targeting and protecting a variety of tissues and organs, Blumberg believes.

Researchers suspect that aside from the role of free radicals, many of the stereotypical symptoms of old age may, in fact, be due to poor nutrition. In a recent study of 96 healthy Canadians over age 65, Ranjit Kumar Chandra of the Memorial University of Newfoundland found that those who took a daily vitamin and mineral supplement (closely approximating the current Recommended Daily Allowance, or RDA, but with extra doses of vitamin E and beta carotene) showed signs of boosted immunity and spent half as many days sick with infections as did those taking placebos. Blumberg and his colleagues at Tufts are now aiming to determine RDAs specifically for the elderly based on optimum health and functioning. "Proper nutrition won't abolish the aging process," says Blumberg, "but it could slow the decline and postpone the onset of disease."

One trace nutrient—chromium—may prove to be a particularly potent weapon against aging, according to new research by Gary Evans of Bemidji State University in Bemidji, Minn. When he gave chromium picolinate to rats, he found a dramatic one-third increase in average life span. Chromium is known to be essential for the effectiveness of insulin, and Evans believes the rats lived longer because the chromium reduced their blood sugar levels by

25 percent. Evans and others had previously observed in diabetics that chromium normalizes blood glucose levels and appears to reduce symptoms of "accelerated aging" like atherosclerosis and kidney disease.

Glucose, the body's sugar fuel, is a conspirator in the aging process, scientists believe. As glucose seeps through the blood and tissues, it reacts with proteins and causes them to permanently link together, explains Anthony Cerami, president of the Picower Institute for Medical Research in Manhasset, N.Y., who first proposed this mechanism in 1975. Over time, glucose makes joints stiff, blood vessels inflexible and bones brittle and yellow. While Evans investigates the use of chromium in maintaining insulin's efficiency at keeping glucose levels low, Cerami is testing in diabetics a different anti-aging substance, called aminoguanidine, that actually inhibits the protein-linking reaction.

So far, reducing caloric intake appears to be the most effective way to beat the age game

---

Destructive calories. So far, however, reducing caloric intake appears to be the most effective way to beat the age game. It is well-known that rats live about one-third longer when fed 60 to 70 percent of the calories they would normally consume in an all-you-can-eat situation. Caloric restriction is the only strategy that extends the maximum life span of a variety of mammals—from mice to dogs to monkeys. But more important, these animals (which still get needed nutrients from supplements) act friskier, boast shinier coats and suffer fewer diseases. In rats, for example, tumor growth is reduced by at least 30 percent, and testicular, breast and other hormonally induced cancers are practically eliminated, says Ron Hart of the National

Center for Toxicological Research in Arkansas.

Caloric restriction appears to work not only by keeping down glucose and free radicals but also by fortifying the body's defenses. According to Hart, rats on caloric restriction have enzymes that are three to four times more active in attacking free radicals. The rodents also show increased levels of DNA repair enzymes, he says, and are at least five times better at disabling carcinogens like aflatoxin. Such dramatic improvements have inspired Hart and some of his colleagues to cut down on calories themselves, especially since they've observed that reducing caloric intake even by 12 percent yields some benefits. Researchers are now anxious to determine the optimum caloric intake for healthy, long-lived humans. Says Hart: "The 19th-century diet may not be the proper one for the 21st century."

Another clinical intervention is on the horizon as scientists divine the mysteries of hormones that maintain youth and health. Hormones—the chemical messengers that circulate throughout the body—turn genes on and off to regulate how cells of various tissues and organs grown, function and repair themselves. "We now believe that some of the symptoms we call aging are really due to hormone deficiencies," says S. Mitchell Harman of the National Institute on Aging in Baltimore.

Indeed, researchers have discovered that just as estrogen production drops during female menopause, many other hormones also decline with age. For instance, by age 65 at least 40 percent of men produce such low amounts of testosterone that their health may be compromised, says Fran Kaiser of St. Louis University's Medical School. She found that giving such men an injectable form of testosterone for three months increased their muscle strength and sex drive and countered their anemia.

Scientists are now optimistic that they can restore youthful function in the elderly by replacing the hormones they lose with age. Searching for patterns in the way hormones

Scientists hope to restore youthfulness in the elderly by replacing hormones

and health fade with time, researchers hope to sketch "the youthful hormone profile." To that end, the National Institute on Aging is sponsoring nine clinical trials to investigate various hormone therapies.

Hormones of youth. Many of the studies will focus on human growth hormone, which not only ensures proper growth in children but also influences body composition in adults. When elderly men with low levels of growth hormone were given supplements, their fat shrank by 14 percent, their lean body mass expanded by 9 percent and their skin increased in thickness by 7 percent, Daniel Rudman of the Medical College of Wisconsin reported in 1990. Other research groups have since shown that the hormone improves the functioning of lung and heart muscles in the elderly. Scientists are now attempting to minimize the side effects—primarily inflammation of joints—with adjustments to dosages.

Therapy with a hormone called DHEA shows special promise because the body converts it to a variety of hormones that decline with age, including those governing sexual and immune functions. As a precursor to many compounds, DHEA exhibits a broad array of actions. For example, low doses of DHEA improve memory in mice, according to City of Hope's Roberts, who is testing its effect on people's cognitive function. Other researchers have marshaled evidence that it prevents obesity, diabetes and atherosclerosis in laboratory animals. DHEA—which reaches peak blood levels at about age 25 and drops dramatically by age 70—can be replaced with little fear of serious side effects, says Roberts, because the tissues turn it into active hormones only as needed.

DHEA may first be used to revitalize the ailing immune systems of the

elderly. At the University of Utah Medical Center in Salt Lake City, Raymond Daynes and his colleagues are preparing to restore youthful levels of DHEA in a group of healthy elderly men and women. After one month of hormone therapy, he will vaccinate them for hepatitis B and measure how well their immune systems call up their antibody defenses. While most elderly people respond poorly and are easily overwhelmed by new infectious invaders, Daynes is hopeful that DHEA will give them added protection. He recently showed that old mice fed low doses of DHEA in their water regained youthful immune systems.

Scientists who study aging are gaining new credibility as they integrate the knowledge that has accumulated from all areas of biomedicine over the past decade. "The field has moved from the realm of charlatans to legitimate science—it's not vanity, not science fiction anymore," says the Alliance for Aging Research's Perry. Many of these researchers approach their work with the utmost urgency. "there's a social imperative that we pursue any avenue that keeps people healthy, strong and productive longer," says Harman of the National Institute on Aging.

In truth, no one knows what genetic potential for longevity humans have inherited

In pursuit of the goal of extending the human health span, researchers may also wind up extending the maximum human life span—a more controversial outcome. In truth, no one knows what genetic potential for longevity humans have inherited. The oldest people so far have survived despite lives of relative hardship. As the best-cared-for generation in history, baby boomers may well shatter the ceiling on the so-called maximum life span when the first one turns 121 in the year 2067.

—**Karen F. Schmidt**

The Naturalness of Dying

Jack D. McCue, MD

Evidence that dying occurs as a natural, final event in the wholeness of human life is culturally, artistically, and scientifically persuasive. Very elderly patients eventually undergo a process of functional declines, progressive apathy, and loss of willingness to eat and drink that culminates in death, even in the absence of acute illness or severe chronic disease. Despite clinical resemblances to depression and dementia, aging itself and a loss of will to live are the most probable explanations for natural dying. Acceptance of the naturalness of dying, however, directly conflicts with the medicalization and legalization of death that characterizes modern society's treatment of dying elderly patients. We prefer instead to believe that dying results from disease and injury, which may yield to advances in medical technology. The progressive move of the dying out of the home and into acute and long-term care facilities suggests that medicalization may be an irreversible process. Viewing dying as an independent diagnosis in patients who are obviously undergoing terminal declines from aging and chronic diseases can facilitate communication about spiritual and palliative care needs, which tend to be neglected in the medicalized view of dying. Physicians and nurses may need to assume the role of medical stewardship to help prevent the overtreatment and overtesting of modern medicine's approach to the dying. The emotional burdens of caring for the dying elderly, however, must be addressed openly through collaborative work, institutional policies on limitation of treatment, and support building among physicians and other caregivers.

(*JAMA.* 1995;273:1039-1043)

THERE are now more elderly persons living in the last few years of their lives than at any time in our society's history. Perhaps a reflection of the interests of our aging population, recently published books in the trade press voice growing concern about loss of control over the quality of death, as well as discomfort with modern medicine's tendency to view dying and death as disease-related events—a view that rejects the personal and spiritual dimensions of a milestone event of our human existence.[1-7] Some of the concern may arise from the perception that caregivers lack skills in the art of palliative care for the dying of all ages; most physicians care for dying patients infrequently and, historically, have done so reluctantly.[8,9] The fragmentation and subspecialization of medical care, moreover, may be a special problem for the dying elderly, whose care is left in the hands of strangers with no knowledge of their patients when they were healthy and independently functioning.[10] Inadequate medical education and training are undoubtedly at fault as well;

clinical teaching of students and residents in the hospital is largely the responsibility of young physicians who are unfamiliar with the values of elderly persons and generally uncomfortable with dying and death.[11-14]

There is a more fundamental difficulty at issue, however. Dying, which was once viewed as natural and expected, has become medicalized into an unwelcome part of medical care.[9] It has been distorted from a natural event of great social and cultural significance into the end point of untreatable or inadequately treated disease or injury.[15] Worse, death has become medicine's enemy—a reminder of our limitations of medical diagnosis and management.[4(p198)] After an anticipated death from a known terminal illness, for example, medical colleagues would be expected to make humane efforts to help family and caregivers understand this natural event and assuage their feelings of loss and sadness. Instead, the medical decisions leading up to the death may be defensively reviewed with the family, then scrutinized for mistakes by peers at clinicopathologic conferences, reported to risk management to be certain that liability issues are addressed, or critiqued in mandated quality assurance reviews. It is little wonder that physicians engage in inappropriately heroic battles against dying

and death, even when it may be apparent to physician, patient, and family that a rapid, good death is the best outcome.

Viewing dying and death as merely a failure of medical diagnosis and therapy is antiholistic and trivializes the final event of our lives, stripping it of important nonmedical meaning for patients, family, and society. This narrow view of dying may be a particular concern for the very elderly, for whom death is an expected and sometimes desired event. Respect for the wholeness of life requires that we not debase its final stage; art, literature, and the social sciences teach us that a good death can be a natural, courageous, and thoughtful end to life.[16-19]

IS DEATH OF THE VERY ELDERLY A NATURAL EVENT?

Healthy very elderly persons who do not develop acute or chronic debilitating diseases eventually undergo irreversible fatal declines at about 100 years of age, near the estimated maximum human life span.[20] Neuropsychological and functional status testing indicates that while losses of intellectual capacity and functional ability appear at different ages and progress at different rates in individual persons, these losses increase exponentially with age and occur universally in very advanced age.[21-32] Presumably by virtue of their universality, these so-called terminal declines that precede the deaths of the very elderly, to which we cannot as yet ascribe trauma-related or disease-related causes, are as natural in advanced age as growth and development are in the healthy young person. Whether the inevitable declines and deaths of very elderly persons should be termed "natural" has been disputed, however, because the possibility of an undiscovered disease can never be excluded. Some find objectionable the positive implication of the word "natural," and others object to its use simply on empirical philosophical grounds.[3,19,33,34]

It is possible that the course of dying for many very elderly persons has an important psychological or spiritual dimension—the loss of a will to live. For example, in a study of elderly persons, "enthusiasm for life" correlated better with longevity than some commonly used objective measures of health status, and a recent study demonstrated that all-cause mortality was increased in middle-aged

From the Department of Medicine, University of Massachusetts Medical School, Worcester, and Berkshire Medical Center, Pittsfield, Mass.
Corresponding author: Jack D. McCue, MD, Berkshire Medical Center, 725 North St, Pittsfield, MA 01201.

men who had poor social supports or had sustained stressful life events.[35,36] Physicians may be particularly skeptical that loss of will to live may cause death; an older survey found that 5% to 17% of physicians, in contrast to 34% to 48% of medical students or lawyers and other nonphysicians, believe that psychological factors play an important causative role in the occurrence or timing of death.[37-39]

For some very elderly patients, however, the conclusion that their death is natural, ie, caused by age-related declines in cognition, function, and will to live, is based simply on the apparent absence of any fatal condition that could reasonably explain the declines and death. For example, a recent autopsy study on the causes of death in elderly Japanese persons concluded that "senility," which the authors diagnosed in an aged person who had no identifiable disease to explain death but did have pathologically identifiable changes of advanced age, was the primary cause of death in approximately 7% of autopsied patients older than 70 years of age and was the only identifiable potential cause of death in 1%.[40] Three examples of probable natural death in elderly patients whose deaths were not explainable by acute or chronic diseases follow.

PATIENT EXAMPLES

In 1983 patient 1, an 87-year-old woman, was admitted to a nursing home following hospitalization for pneumonia during which her son, with whom she had lived, died. She was afraid to live alone and was unable to handle her personal finances, but she was angry that she could no longer live independently, as she preferred. She had no known medical problems, had a normal physical examination with a weight of 57.6 kg, had normal routine laboratory tests, and was fully functional on activities of daily living (ADL) evaluation. Two years later, however, she was noted to be confused and intermittently fearful, and her ADL evaluation indicated a decline with at least moderate assistance needed in all activities.

In late 1987 her sister, also a patient at the nursing home, died, and for the remainder of her life, patient 1 asked for and looked for her sister. At that time her weight began to decline steadily, decreasing to 45.9 kg in August 1989, but she did not have a depressed mood and continued to participate in group recreational activities and trips. Empirical trials of imipramine hydrochloride and fluoxetine were poorly tolerated and did not change her lack of interest in eating. In September 1989 she lost interest in caring for herself and began to resist caregivers' attempts to feed her. For the last 2 months of her life she required intravenous fluids—despite being fully alert, conversational, eager to engage in humorous and witty banter, and fully able to eat and drink when willing to do so. Her grandson requested that intravenous fluids be stopped; she agreed and died 2 weeks later. Three days before her

death a careful physical examination indicated no reason for her fatal decline.

Patient 2, an 81-year-old woman, was admitted to a nursing home after an unintended phenobarbital overdose in 1961. She had no known health problems and was capable of continuing to care for herself, but was convinced by family to give up her home. Her functional status remained unimpaired until 1975 when, at the age of 95 years, she began to experience minor falls, occasional confusion, and weakness. During that year her ADL assessment declined from minimal assistance in all activities to complete assistance in all activities. In 1977 she lost the ability to walk with a walker and in 1981 had to be lifted from bed to chair by caregivers. She could feed herself and understand conversation or requests until 1984 when, at the age of 105 years, she became totally confused.

From 1984 to 1989 her weight declined from 58.5 to 45 kg, despite vigorous encouragement by staff to eat, modification of diet to her preferences, and an attentive and involved family. Yearly physical examinations and routine laboratory testing during nearly three decades gave no evidence of acute or chronic diseases. Six months before her death she developed minor pressure ulcers, but was otherwise healthy and had a normal complete blood cell count 1 month before her death. Her family requested that she not receive intravenous fluids or enteral tube feedings, and she died exactly 4 months before her 110th birthday.

In 1979 a 90-year-old woman (patient 3) was admitted to a chronic disease hospital for care after surgical repair of a hip fracture. She was mildly forgetful and confused on admission, but cheerful and socially interactive. She required moderate assistance for most ADLs, but after a rehabilitation program that led to a weight gain of 4.5 kg from her admission weight of 37.4 kg, she could perform all activities with no more than minimal assistance. She continued to gain weight, reaching a maximum of 56.2 kg, which she maintained until 1987.

She remained physically healthy until 1988, experiencing no serious acute medical illnesses and receiving no medications for chronic diseases. In 1984, however, her ADL status began to decline progressively until 1985, when she required complete assistance in all activities despite the absence of deterioration in mental status or a diagnosable disease. In 1988 she became disoriented and confused, although until her death she was attentive when spoken to, smiled generously, and enjoyed all social contact even though her speech was unintelligible to caregivers. In mid 1988 she required more encouragement at meals, and her weight progressively decreased from 53.1 to 34.2 kg at her death 18 months later. Yearly physical examinations and routine laboratory testing in the long-term care facility suggested no medical explanation for her declines. More aggressive evaluation was not desired by physician or family. In early 1989 she began to refuse oral fluids as well; she received intravenous fluids almost continuously for a year and was receiving intravenous fluids at her death 6 days short of her 100th birthday.

COMMENT

These three patients suffered functional and cognitive declines and even-

tually died without an identifiable chronic or acute illness or injury. They appear to have died naturally of old age. Their progressive loss of interest in self-care or in the world outside their immediate environment in their nursing home also resembles what has been called "taking to bed."[41]

Are there other plausible medical explanations for presumed natural dying of patients such as these? Major depression, for example, which is especially common in elderly long-term care residents, is a recognized risk factor for mortality in the elderly and may lead to refusal of life-sustaining therapy.[42-48] Similarly, if brain aging were the underlying cause of natural dying, could it be reliably distinguished from degenerative neurological diseases such as Alzheimer's disease, which is highly variable in its clinical manifestations?[49-53] Unfortunately, attributing the functional and intellectual declines of advanced age to untreatable degenerative neurological disorders does not address the possibility of coexisting natural dying and disease and may distract caregivers' attention from more humane and helpful nonmedically oriented treatment.[51] Additionally, it is often difficult to be certain of the meaning of a diagnosis of depression in the very elderly who may have sustained many real personal and social losses, do not exhibit classical manifestations of major depression, and may respond poorly to antidepressant therapy.[42,54-57]

Caloric intake normally declines with advanced age, and next to age and functional status, weight is the most consistent independent predictor of longevity in the elderly.[58-62] Declines in thirst and the so-called anorexia of aging[63-65] are probably caused by central nervous system changes, whether degenerative disease or brain aging.[66,67] For example, outpatients with dementia had an 11% to 13% lower body weight than controls, although they did not appear to be in poor health.[68] Loss of motivation to eat and drink—whether volitional or a result of neurological or psychiatric changes with aging—may thus be an important component of natural dying and poses an ethically interesting parallel to terminally ill patients who refuse hydration and nutrition to hasten their death.[69,70]

Origins of the Reluctance to Recognize the Naturalness of Dying

The history of dying and death recounted by Aries[9] concludes that our current attitudes and beliefs, which he names "the medicalization of death," result not from reflection on past insights into dying and death, but from social and scientific changes that cannot be considered wholly beneficial. For example, modern medicine increasingly can control the tempo and form of dying and determine with precision the time and place of death, thus making it possible to continue or discontinue life-sustaining technology for ideal timing of organ transplantation, to allow family to be present for a loved one's death, or to delay death for the convenience of court deliberations. Yet this technology also has made death a starkly unnatural event and has intensified debates over distinguishing disease-related death from death hastened by palliative treatment for a terminal illness or physician-assisted death.[69-77]

For many reasons, dying now occurs almost exclusively in hospitals or long-term care facilities, which inevitably leads to a more medicalized approach to the final days of life. It has been estimated that more than 80% of persons in the United States die in institutions, including a substantial number for whom home hospice care was arranged,[78] in dramatic contrast to the less than 50% of persons 50 years ago and nearly none a century ago.[9] This change is probably irreversible—it is unlikely that we will, as a society, decide to take our dying elders back into our homes. We seem to tolerate the sights and smells of dying less well than was the case earlier in this century. Similarly, our concerns for sanitation are greater, and our homes do not seem adequate to meet the needs of dying relatives. The expectation of the use of at least minimal medical technology at the time of death, such as intravenous fluids and oxygen, may or may not be rational, but it can cause families to feel neglectful of elders who might be denied such technology if they die at home.[34,73,74,78-85]

More recently, the medicalization of dying has been encouraged by our hopes that fatal medical problems will all eventually yield to technological innovation—perhaps even aging itself. Gruman[86] traced our determination to continue aggressive treatment for hopelessly ill patients to a historic "heroic positivist" philosophy of medicine, in which there is intrinsic value to action. In other words, it is better to "do something" than to do nothing, even if that action is known to have no benefit. Supporting this assertion, Dozor and Addison[87] noted how biomedical technology derailed physicians' attempts to work toward an openly shared goal of a good death for their dying patients. It may be that the heroic positivist approach has now become integrated into the ethos of modern, technologically oriented medical care and, perhaps in an exaggerated form, into American medicine.[88] The continued diagnostic searches and treatment of obviously dying patients now

seem to have intrinsic value for most family and caregivers, even when they are potentially harmful to dying patients.

Avoidance of acknowledging the inevitability of an elderly patient's death through medicalization may be a coping mechanism that helps medical caregivers deal with the emotional difficulties intrinsic to working with the dying. It has long been recognized that working with the dying is fatiguing and stressful.[81,87,89-92] Krakowski[93,94] reported that deaths of patients can cause stress reactions in physicians that are comparable to reactions to personal or family illnesses. Symptoms in caregivers can reach the intensity of a posttraumatic stress disorder and can lead to caregiver burnout, which makes it difficult for dedicated physicians, nurses, and allied medical staff to continue to provide empathic medical care.[95,96] Sociologists who study death have hypothesized that physicians may fear death more than non-physicians.[95,97-101] Whether true or not, it is intuitively plausible that physicians who have not come to terms with their own feelings about death are more likely to treat a dying patient medically, concentrating on disease processes and laboratory testing rather than addressing the emotional, spiritual, and social implications of their patient's dying.[8,80,95,98-103] Other studies and commentary indicate that communication among elderly patients, family, and physicians about issues such as life support or terminal care is frequently ineffective, delayed, or avoided altogether.[78,98-106] Unfortunately, physicians, perhaps more than other medical professionals, are not skilled at asking for or receiving emotional support as they attempt to deal with these stressful patient care situations or their personal concerns about their own mortality.[107]

What Can Be Done?

The medicalization of dying is a pernicious trend that runs counter to several powerful societal changes and results in wasteful and bad medical care. It deprives the dying of their autonomy, leading to questions such as "Whose death is this?"[108,109]—questions that will be asked with more vigor as the generation that grew up in the culture of narcissism reaches seniority.[110] Although we are only beginning to explore the economics of dying, and it is not clear whether limitation of technology at the end of life will be meaningfully cost beneficial,[111] the aggressive use of technology in very elderly dying patients is intuitively a wasteful use of the limited resources that we are willing to spend on medical care.[112-114] Finally, as our society explores the spiritual dimensions of medical care and the solutions of other cultures to disease and dying, there may be greater impatience with the in-

adequacy of bioscientific medicine's narrow approach to dying.[80,115] Callahan[3] pessimistically concluded, however, that acceptance of the naturalness of the declines and frailty that come with old age is inconsistent with our individualistic and pluralistic culture.

Very elderly patients with clearly declining trajectories in their willingness to eat, willingness to participate in self-care and social activities, and intellectual capability are often readily and precisely identifiable.[27,41,116-119] Like patients receiving hospice care for terminal illness, the naturally dying elderly also benefit from non–disease-oriented care that recognizes their spiritual needs and relieves their symptoms.[2,120] Graham and Lively[106] proposed that when obviously dying patients are identified, making "dying" a diagnosis, pushing medicalization a step farther can give caregivers, patients, and families a focus for planning medical care and weighing the benefits and costs of therapies. Making dying a diagnosis recognizes it as a chronic and incurable condition—an inevitable process that is independent of underlying diseases. As such, it requires acceptance and accommodation, not fruitless attempts at diagnosis and cure.[121] Diagnostic terms—even terms as imprecise as "dying"—can benefit such patients by reducing uncertainty and facilitating communication about treatment issues. Ivan Ilyich's epic search for a name for his fatal illness emphasized his physicians' importance (and in his case their failure as well) in determining his destiny. "The worst torment was the lie, that for some reason was accepted by everyone, that he was only sick, and not dying. ... This lie that was being told on the eve of his death, this lie that degraded the formidable and solemn act of his death."[122]

The personal and professional stresses that lead physicians to medicalize dying must also be dealt with. Mount[96] properly emphasizes the critical importance of a collaborative working environment to diminish the stresses of those who work with the dying. Physicians, other caregivers, and administrative staff of acute and long-term care facilities can together develop humane institutional policies on limitations of treatment that lift from physicians and nurses the unfair burden of making difficult, painful decisions in isolation.[123-125] The exaggerated fears of liability risks that pressure physicians and nurses to withhold palliative treatment or continue futile therapy in patients near the end of life must be addressed in a forthright fashion.[126-128] On a personal level, physicians who reconnect to the powerful spiritual dimensions of the patient-physician relationship that presumably motivated them to enter the health care professions can help convert stressful decision making with dying patients into maturing and fulfilling encounters.[129-132] Caregivers need to acknowledge that caring for the dying is intrinsically stressful, and they must attend to self-care through good health practices, limit setting, and opportunities for distraction, humor, and relaxation.[90,133,134]

To offer more humane medical treatment to our dying patients and to improve communication among patients, families, and physicians, we must reject the narrow biomedical view of dying and relearn some of the palliative and healing skills prevalent before the birth of modern scientific medicine, when less could be done to cure disease. The dying elderly patient who has what Callahan[3] described as a physician steward may be able to avoid the impersonal and fragmented care, overtesting, overtreatment, and unnecessary hospitalization that result from the medicalization of dying. We can unburden from distressed families the responsibility for the consequences of painful decision making and verbalize what patients and families usually already know—that aggressive diagnostic studies and therapy can only slow declines in the very elderly, not reverse them, and at some point become harmful. Often the most effective intervention that we can offer is time spent with patients and family, listening to concerns and acknowledging their value and touching—a physician's role that is hard to teach and harder to learn in medical education dominated by subspecialist- and procedure-oriented medical centers. We can, at a minimum, heed the powerful lessons taught by experiences with illness and death in our colleagues and loved ones.[10,135]

It is hoped that physicians can begin to lead our society to the recognition that declines and dying in the very elderly are not a failure of medical diagnosis or treatment, but part of a natural process that has positive as well as negative dimensions. Death makes way for the birth of children, just as the deaths of others made way for us.[136] Dying bravely is heroic, and a heroic death may be the most intense memory that we can pass to posterity. The spiritual dimension of dying bonds persons together—family, caregivers, and strangers—and can effect dramatic changes in the lives of those touched by the death.[132] On its simplest human level, for many very elderly persons death is an undeniably desirable relief from suffering.

Kathryn McCue and Lewis Cohen, MD, spent many hours in careful review of the manuscript.

References

1. Nuland SB. *How We Die: Reflections on Life's Last Chapter.* New York, NY: Alfred A Knopf Inc; 1994.
2. Callanan M, Kelley P. *Final Gifts.* New York, NY: Poseidon Press; 1992.
3. Callahan D. *Setting Limits: Medical Goals in an Aging Society.* New York, NY: Simon & Schuster; 1987.
4. Callahan D. *The Troubled Dream of Life: Living With Mortality.* New York, NY: Simon & Schuster Inc; 1993.
5. Quill T. *Death and Dignity.* New York, NY: WW Norton & Co Inc; 1994.
6. Glick HR. *The Right to Die.* Irvington-on-Hudson, NY: Columbia University Press; 1992.
7. Macklin R. *Enemies of Patients.* Oxford, England: Oxford University Press; 1993.
8. Tolle SW, Elliot DL, Hickam DH. Physician attitudes and practices at the time of death. *Arch Intern Med.* 1984;143:1447-1449.
9. Aries P. *The Hour of Our Death.* New York, NY: Vintage Books; 1981.
10. Southwick F. Who was caring for Mary? *Ann Intern Med.* 1993;118:146-148.
11. Hull FM. Death, dying and the medical student. *Med Educ.* 1991;25:491-496.
12. Gates MF, Kaul M, Speece MW, Brent SB. The attitudes of beginning nursing and medical students toward care of dying patients: a preliminary study. *Hospice J.* 1992;8:17-32.
13. Kitchen AD. Second-year medical students' experiences with death among their families and friends. *Med Educ.* 1986;61:760-761.
14. Howells K, Gould M, Field D. Fear of death and dying in medical students: effects of clinical experience. *Med Educ.* 1986;20:502-506.
15. Mendez OE. Death in America: a clinician's perspective. *Crit Care Clin.* 1993;9:613-626.
16. Shakespeare W. *As You Like It.* Act II; scene 7.
17. Erikson EH. *The Life Cycle Completed: A Review.* New York, NY: WW Norton & Co Inc; 1982: 60-61.
18. Aurelius M; Long G, trans. *The Meditations of Marcus Aurelius Antonius.* AD 160.
19. de Beauvoir S. *The Coming of Age.* New York, NY: GP Putnam; 1972.
20. Miller RA. The biology of aging and longevity. In: Hazzard WR, Bierman EL, Blass JP, et al, eds. *Principles of Geriatric Medicine and Gerontology.* 3rd ed. New York, NY: McGraw-Hill International Book Co; 1994:3-18.
21. White N, Cunningham WR. Is terminal drop pervasive or specific? *J Gerontol.* 1988;43:141-144.
22. Moehle KA, Long CJ. Models of aging and neuropsychological test performance decline with aging. *J Gerontol.* 1989;44:176-177.
23. Larrabee GT, Levin HS, High WM. Senescent forgetfulness: a quantitative study. *Dev Neuropsychol.* 1986;2:373-385.
24. Reed HBC, Reitan RM. Changes in psychological test performances associated with the normal aging process. *J Gerontol.* 1963;18:271-274.
25. Johansson B, Berg S. The robustness of the terminal decline phenomenon: longitudinal data from the digit-span memory test. *J Gerontol.* 1989;44: 184-186.
26. Jarvik LF. Aging of the brain: how can we prevent it? *Gerontologist.* 1988;28:739-737.
27. Bortz WM. The trajectory of dying: functional status in the last year of life. *J Am Geriatr Soc.* 1990;38:146-150.
28. Branch LG, Katz S, Kniepmann K, et al. A prospective study of functional status among community elders. *Am J Public Health.* 1984;74:266-268.
29. Botwinick J, Weston R, Storandt M. Predicting death from behavioral test performance. *J Gerontol.* 1978;33:755-752.
30. Mortimer JA. Epidemiology of dementia: cross-cultural comparisons. *Adv Neurol.* 1990;51:27-33.
31. Crum RM, Anthony JC, Bassett SS, Folstein MF. Population-based norms for the Mini-Mental State Examination by age and educational level. *JAMA.* 1993;269:2386-2391.
32. Perls TT, Morris JN, Ooi WL, Lipsitz LA. The relationship between age, gender and cognitive performance in the very old: the effect of selective survival. *J Am Geriatr Soc.* 1993;41:1193-1201.
33. Callahan D. On defining a natural death. *Hastings Cent Rep.* 1977;7:32-37.
34. Monmeyer RW. *Confronting Death.* Bloomington: Indiana University Press; 1988.
35. Bocquet H, Grosclaude P, Cayla F, et al. Disabilities, subjective health and mortality after a 3-year follow-up of a rural aged population. *Rev Epidemiol Sante Publique.* 1987;35:151-156.
36. Rosengren A, Orth-Gomer K, Wedel H, Wilhelmsen L. Stressful life events, social support, and mortality in men born in 1933. *BMJ.* 1993;307: 1102-1105.
37. Schneiderman ES. Death: the enemy. *Psychology Today.* 1970;4:67-72.
38. Schneiderman ES. You and death. *Psychology Today.* 1970;5:43-45.
39. Warren WG. *Death Education and Research: Clinical Perspectives.* New York, NY: Haworth Press Inc; 1989.
40. Ueda K, Hasuo Y, Ohmura T, et al. Causes of death in the elderly and their changing pattern in Hisayama, a Japanese community: results from a long-term and autopsy-based study. *J Am Geriatr Soc.* 1990;38:1332-1338.
41. Clark LP, Dion DM, Barker WH. Taking to bed: rapid functional decline in an independently mobile older population living in an intermediate-care facility. *J Am Geriatr Soc.* 1990;38:967-972.
42. Blazer D. Depression in the elderly. *N Engl J Med.* 1989;320:164-166.
43. Murphy E. The prognosis of depression in old age. *Br J Psychiatry.* 1983;142:111-119.
44. Murphy E, Smith R, Lindesay J, et al. Increased mortality rates in late-life depression. *Br J Psychiatry.* 1988;152:347-353.
45. Koenig HG, Shelp F, Goli V, et al. Survival and health care utilization in elderly medical inpatients with major depression. *J Am Geriatr Soc.* 1989;37: 599-606.
46. Lee MA, Ganzini L. Depression in the elderly: effect on patient attitudes toward life-sustaining therapy. *J Am Geriatr Soc.* 1992;40:983-988.
47. Rovner BW, German PS, Brant LJ, Clark R, Burton L, Folstein MF. Depression and mortality in nursing homes. *JAMA.* 1991;265:993-996.
48. Lee MA. Depression and refusal of life support in older people: an ethical dilemma. *J Am Geriatr Soc.* 1990;38:710-714.
49. Friedland RP, Koss E, Haxby JV, et al. Alzheimer disease: clinical and biologic heterogeneity. *Ann Intern Med.* 1988;109:298-311.
50. Stern Y, Gurland B, Tatemichi TK, et al. Influence of education and occupation on the incidence of Alzheimer's disease. *JAMA.* 1994;271:1004-1010.
51. Goodwin JS. Geriatric ideology: the myth of the myth of senility. *J Am Geriatr Soc.* 1991;39:627-631.
52. Von Dras DD, Blumenthal HT. Dementia of the aged: disease or atypical-accelerated aging? biopathological and psychological perspectives. *J Am Geriatr Soc.* 1992;40:285-294.
53. Forbes WF, Hirdes JP. The relationship between aging and disease: geriatric ideology and myths of senility. *J Am Geriatr Soc.* 1993;41:1267-1271.
54. Koenig HC, Goli V, Shelp F, et al. Antidepressant use in elderly medical inpatients: lessons from an attempted clinical trial. *J Gen Intern Med.* 1989; 4:448-450.
55. Koenig HF, Meadow Cohen HJ, Blazer DG. Depression in elderly hospitalized patients with medical illness. *Arch Intern Med.* 1988;148:1929-1936.
56. Koenig HG. Depressed or just sick? *Arch Intern Med.* 1990;150:1349-1350.
57. Kaotona CLE. Depression in old age. *J Med Gerontol.* 1991;1:371-384.
58. Radman D, Mattson DE, Nagraj HS, et al. Antecedents of death in the men of a Veterans Administration nursing home. *J Am Geriatr Soc.* 1987; 35:496-502.
59. Tayback M, Kumanyika S, Chee E. Body weight as a risk factor in the elderly. *Arch Intern Med.* 1990;150:1065-1072.
60. Lee IM, Paffenbarger RS. Change in body weight and longevity. *JAMA.* 1992;268:2045-2049.
61. Klonoff-Cohen H, Barrett-Connor EL, Edelstein SL. Albumin levels as a predictor of mortality in the healthy elderly. *J Clin Epidemiol.* 1992;45: 207-212.

62. Launer LJ, Harris T, Rumpel C, Madans J. Body mass index, weight change, and risk of mobility disability in middle-aged and older women. *JAMA.* 1994;271:1093-1098.

63. Sandman P, Adolfsson R, Nygren C, et al. Nutritional status and dietary intake in institutionalized patients with Alzheimer's disease and multi-infarct dementia. *J Am Geriatr Soc.* 1987;35:31-38.

64. Dwyer JT, Coleman KA, Krall E, et al. Changes in relative weight among institutionalized elderly adults. *J Gerontol.* 1987;42:246-251.

65. Keller HH. Malnutrition in institutionalized elderly. *J Am Geriatr Soc.* 1993;41:1212-1218.

66. Thompson MP, Morris LK. Unexplained weight loss in the ambulatory elderly. *J Am Geriatr Soc.* 1991;39:497-500.

67. Phillips PA, Rolls BJ, Ledingham JGG, et al. Reduced thirst after water deprivation in healthy elderly men. *N Engl J Med.* 1984;311:753-759.

68. Berlinger WG, Potter JF. Low body mass index in demented outpatients. *J Am Geriatr Soc.* 1991;39:973-978.

69. Bernat JL, Gert B, Mogielnicki RP. Patient refusal of hydration and nutrition: an alternative to physician-assisted suicide or voluntary active euthanasia. *Arch Intern Med.* 1993;153:2723-2727.

70. Cook ML. The end of life and the goals of medicine. *Arch Intern Med.* 1993;153:2718-2719.

71. Youngner SJ, Bartlett ET. Human death and high technology: the failure of the whole-brain formulations. *Ann Intern Med.* 1983;99:252-258.

72. Youngner SJ, Landefeld CS, Coulton CJ, et al. 'Brain death' and organ retrieval: a cross-sectional survey of knowledge and concepts among health professionals. *JAMA.* 1989;261:2205-2210.

73. Yarborough M. Continued treatment of the fatally ill for the benefit of others. *J Am Geriatr Soc.* 1988;36:63-67.

74. Smedira NG, Evans BH, Grais LS, et al. Withholding and withdrawing life support from the critically ill. *N Engl J Med.* 1990;322:309-315.

75. Halevy A, Brody B. Brain death: reconciling definitions, criteria, and tests. *Ann Intern Med.* 1993;119:519-525.

76. Phillips DP, Smith DG. Postponement of death until symbolically meaningful occasions. *JAMA.* 1990;263:1947-1951.

77. Burgess MM. The medicalization of dying. *J Med Philos.* 1993;18:269-279.

78. Wanzer SH, Federman DD, Adelstein SJ, et al. The physician's responsibility toward hopelessly ill patients. *N Engl J Med.* 1989;320:844-849.

79. Brurera E, de Stoutz N, Velsco-Leiva A, et al. Effects of oxygen on dyspnoea in hypoxaemic terminal-cancer patients. *Lancet.* 1993;342:13-14.

80. Kubler-Ross E, ed. *Death: The Final Stage of Growth.* New York, NY: Touchstone Books; 1975.

81. Hilfiker D. Allowing the debilitated to die: facing our ethical choices. *N Engl J Med.* 1983;308:716-719.

82. Lo B, Josen AR. Clinical decisions to limit treatment. *Ann Intern Med.* 1980;93:764-768.

83. Emanuel EJ. Should physicians withhold life-sustaining care from patients who are not terminally ill? *Lancet.* 1988;1:106-108.

84. Lynn J, ed. *By No Extraordinary Means: The Choice to Forgo Life-Sustaining Food and Water.* Bloomington: Indiana University Press; 1986.

85. Callahan D. On feeding the dying. *Hastings Cent Rep.* 1983;13:22.

86. Gruman GJ. Ethics of death and dying: historical perspective. *Omega.* 1978-1979;9:203-237.

87. Dozor RB, Addison RB. Toward a good death: an interpretive investigation of family practice residents' practices with dying patients. *Fam Med.* 1992;24:538-543.

88. Payer L. *Medicine and Culture.* New York, NY: Henry Holt & Co; 1988.

89. Artiss KL, Levine AS. Doctor-patient relation in severe illness. *N Engl J Med.* 1974;288:1210-1214.

90. McCue JD. The effects of stress on physicians and their medical practice. *N Engl J Med.* 1982;306:458-463.

91. Garland J. Adaptation skills in the elderly, their supporters and careers. *Br J Psychol.* 1985;58:267-274.

92. Vickio CJ, Cavanaugh JC. Relationships among death anxiety, attitudes toward aging, and experiences with death among nursing home employees. *J Gerontol.* 1985;40:347-349.

93. Krakowski AJ. Stress and the practice of medicine, II: stressors, stresses and strains. *Psychother Psychosom.* 1982;38:11-23.

94. Krakowski AJ. Stress and the practice of medicine, I: the myth and reality. *Br J Psychosom Res.* 1982;26:91-98.

95. Martin CA, Julian RA. Causes of stress and burnout in physicians caring for the chronically and terminally ill. In: Paradis LA, ed. *Stress and Burnout Among Providers Caring for the Terminally Ill and Their Families.* New York, NY: Haworth Press Inc; 1987:121-146.

96. Mount BM. Dealing with our losses. *J Clin Oncol.* 1986;4:1127-1134.

97. Feifel H, Branscomb A. Who's afraid of death? *J Abnorm Psychol.* 1973;49:278-286.

98. Seravalli EP. The dying patient, the physician, and the fear of death. *N Engl J Med.* 1988;319:1728-1730.

99. Schulz R, Aderman D. Physicians' death anxiety and patient outcomes. *Omega.* 1978-1979;9:327-332.

100. Kane AC, Hogan JD. Death anxiety in physicians: defensive style, medical specialty, and exposure to death. *Omega.* 1985-1986;16:11-22.

101. Feifel H, Hanson S, Jones R, et al. Physicians consider death. In: Proceedings of the 75th Annual Convention of the American Psychological Association. 1967;2:201-202.

102. Tolle SW, Girard DE. The physician's role in the events surrounding patient death. *Arch Intern Med.* 1983;143:1447-1449.

103. Kinsella TD, Stocking CB. Failed communication about life-support therapy: silent physicians and mute patients. *Am J Med.* 1989;86:643-644.

104. Finucane TE, Shumway JM, Powers RL, et al. Planning with elderly outpatients for contingencies of severe illness: a survey and clinical trial. *J Gen Intern Med.* 1988;3:322-325.

105. Quill TE. Recognizing and adjusting to barriers in doctor-patient communication. *Ann Intern Med.* 1989;111:51-57.

106. Graham H, Livesley B. Dying as a diagnosis: difficulties of communication and management in elderly patients. *Lancet.* 1983;2:670-672.

107. Martin CA, Julian RA. *Stress and Burnout Among Providers Caring for the Terminally Ill and Their Families.* New York, NY: Haworth Press Inc; 1987.

108. Luddington AV. The 'death control' dilemma: who is to make end-of-life decisions: you and your patient, or 'the system'? *Geriatrics.* 1993;48:72-77.

109. Slomaka J. The negotiation of death: clinical decision making at the end of life. *Soc Sci Med.* 1992;35:251-259.

110. Lasch C. *The Culture of Narcissism: American Life in an Age of Diminishing Expectations.* New York, NY: WW Norton & Co Inc; 1978:207-217.

111. Emanuel EJ, Emanuel LL. The economics of dying: the illusion of cost savings at the end of life. *N Engl J Med.* 1994;330:540-549.

112. Maksoud A, Jahnigen DW, Skibinski CI. Do not resuscitate orders and the cost of death. *Arch Intern Med.* 1993;153:1249-1253.

113. Bayer R, Callahan D, Fletcher J, et al. The care of the terminally ill: morality and economics. *N Engl J Med.* 1983;309:1490-1494.

114. Chambers CV, Diamond JJ, Perkel RL, Lasch LA. Relationship of advance directives to hospital charges in a medicare population. *Arch Intern Med.* 1994;154:541-547.

115. Merman AC. Spiritual aspects of death and dying. *Yale J Biol Med.* 1992;65:137-142.

116. Palmore E, Cleveland W. Aging, terminal decline, and terminal drop. *J Gerontol.* 1976;31:76-81.

117. Guralnik JM, LaCroix AZ, Branch LG, et al. Morbidity and disability in older persons in the years prior to death. *Am J Public Health.* 1991;81:443-447.

118. Dontas AS, Tzonou A, Kasviki-Charvati P, et al. Survival in a residential home: an eleven-year longitudinal study. *J Am Geriatr Soc.* 1991;39:641-649.

119. Reuben DB, Rubenstein LV, Hirsch SH, Hays RD. Value of functional status as a predictor of mortality: results of a prospective study. *Am J Med.* 1992;93:663-669.

120. Schmitz P, Lynn J, Cobbs E. The care of the dying patient. In: Hazzard WR, Bierman EL, Blass JP, et al, eds. *Principles of Geriatric Medicine and Gerontology.* 3rd ed. New York, NY: McGraw-Hill International Book Co; 1994:383-390.

121. Jennings B, Callahan D, Caplan AL. Ethical challenges of chronic illness. *Hastings Cent Rep.* 1988;18(suppl):1-16.

122. Tolstoy L; Solotaroff L, trans. *The Death of Ivan Ilyich.* New York, NY: Bantam Books; 1981.

123. Uhlman RF, Clark H, Pearlman RA, et al. Medical management decisions in nursing home patients: principles and policy recommendations. *Ann Intern Med.* 1987;106:879-885.

124. Braithwaite S, Thomasma DC. New guidelines on forgoing life-sustaining treatment in incompetent patients: an anti-cruelty policy. *Ann Intern Med.* 1986;104:711-715.

125. Miles SH, Singer PA, Siegler M. Conflicts between patients' wishes to forgo treatment and the policies of health care facilities. *N Engl J Med.* 1989;321:48-50.

126. Sager M, Volks S, Drinka P, et al. Do the elderly sue physicians? *Arch Intern Med.* 1990;150:1091-1093.

127. Perkins HS, Bauer RL, Hazuda HP, Schoolfield JD. Impact of legal liability, family wishes, and other 'external factors' on physicians' life-support decisions. *Am J Med.* 1990;89:185-194.

128. Solomon MZ, O'Donnell L, Jennings B, et al. Decisions near the end of life: professional views on life-sustaining treatments. *Am J Public Health.* 1993;83:14-23.

129. Peters AL. Death and medicine: a personal account. *Am J Med.* 1990;89:81-82.

130. Branch WT. Meaningful experiences in medicine. *Am J Med.* 1990;88:56-59.

131. Matthews DA, Suchman AL, Branch WT. Making 'connexions': enhancing the therapeutic potential of patient-clinician relationships. *Ann Intern Med.* 1993;118:973-977.

132. Suchman AL, Matthews DA. What makes the patient-doctor relationship therapeutic? exploring the connexional dimension of medical care. *Ann Intern Med.* 1988;108:125-130.

133. Durand RP, Dickinson GE, Sumner ED. Family physicians' attitudes toward death and the terminally-ill patient. *Fam Pract Res J.* 1990;9:123-129.

134. Quill TE, Williamson PR. Healthy approaches to physician stress. *Arch Intern Med.* 1990;105:1857-1861.

135. Eddy DM. A conversation with my mother. *JAMA.* 1994;272:179-182.

136. Jonas H. The burden and blessing of mortality. *Hastings Center Rep.* 1992;22:34-40.

The Dying Process

Death is the final stage of life. While death comes at various ages and in differing circumstances, for most of us there will be some time to reflect on our lives, our work, our relationships, and what our expectations are for the ending of that life. This is called the process of dying. In the past two decades, a broad range of concerns has arisen about that process and how aging, dying, and death can be confronted in ways that are enlightening, enriching, and supportive of those who are coming to the close of their lives. Efforts have been made to delineate and define various stages in the process of dying so that comfort and acceptance of our inevitable death will be eased. Awareness of the coming of death allows us to come to grips with the profound emotional upheaval to be experienced. The fears of the experience of dying are often more in the imagination than in reality, as the articles in this unit will show. The varied social, religious, and psychological responses that constitute the process of dying and the supports sought can be studied and used to the benefit of all.

Key players in the drama that will unfold are physicians and nurses who attend the dying. While nurses are usually appreciated as supportive and compassionate, physicians, however, are often seen as aloof from dying patients. Indeed, a considerable amount of literature documents the unwillingness or inability of doctors to communicate adequately and meaningfully with their dying patients. For some, death is seen as an enemy that has defeated the healing mission. Others find that concerns about their own deaths interfere with their ability to talk about dying and death in significant ways. Some physicians have thought carefully about our mortality and have written about enlightened approaches to helping the dying. One study shows that there is an increasing number of physicians who are comfortable in discussing dying and death with patients. The process of dying can be profoundly influenced by the compassion and the support of those trained to be with—and for—the dying. Sensitivity to the needs we all have for love and comfort, awareness of the exquisitely personal nature of death, and a willingness to attend to the difficult tasks at hand will greatly enhance and enrich the experience for all.

The care of dying persons has always been difficult and demanding. The relatively recent use of the hospital as the place of death raises concerns about its appropriateness. Many people are seeking to regain control of the process of dying—how, when, and with whom are valid questions to be considered. The high technology of the hospital and the lack of sensitivity of some caregivers to the personal aspects of dying have fanned the demands of many to die at home within their own defined environment. In former times, persons died at home with family and friends in attendance. Now we fear abandonment in our dying in an isolated room down a long corridor in a large hospital. For many, death is accepted for what it is: a time of transition or of ending. It is the thought of dying alone that terrifies many.

One neglected aspect of the care of the dying is the spiritual dimension of life. The intensely personal aspects of spiritual issues and commonly observed ignorance of them can produce uneasiness in caregivers, both professionals and friends. It is important to be informed and alert to this profound support for those who suffer, who are in pain, and for those who are coming to the end of life. Finding sensitive and empathic spiritual guidance can be a dominant support and a cheerful companion for the closing days. Another aspect often ignored is the effect of ethnic and cultural factors on our care and on our understanding of the significance of death on persons from widely disparate traditions.

The development of the hospice movement in the United States over the past 20 years offers an alternative to the impersonal aspects of hospitalization. Hospice offers both home care and institutional care for the dying in a quiet environment with personal attention to the exquisitely intimate process of dying and an assurance of the relief of pain. Though hospice had its conceptual origin in the Middle Ages, the original model is St. Christopher's in London, developed in the late 1960s by Dame Cecily Saunders. "Hospice Care for the 1990s: A Concept Coming of Age" brings the reader up to date on this important movement.

Looking Ahead: Challenge Questions

In an environment of advanced technology that has altered the ways in which we die, how are we to change our understanding of the dying process, enrich our engagement with those who are dying, and find a basis for our own growth toward death?

How are the experiences of some who have been near death to be evaluated as we consider our own religious and philosophical engagement with that awesome time of transition?

With the impressive experiences of the hospice movement to guide us, how can we improve our community witness to good care so that we can help the dying in ways that enrich their journey?

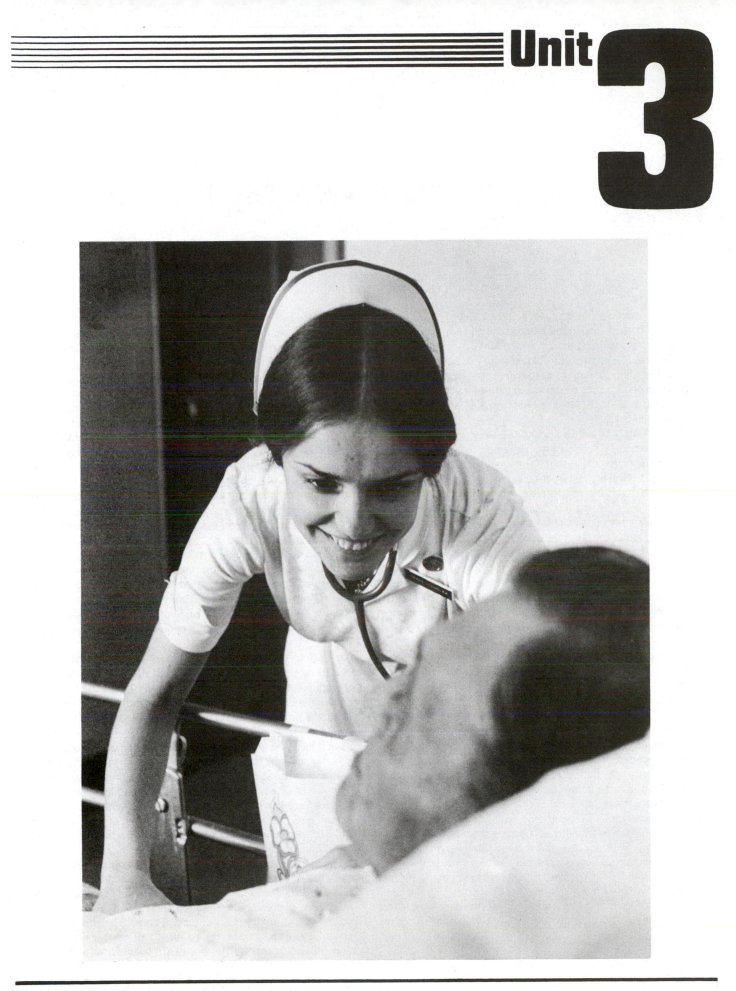

A Conversation With My Mother

You have already met my father.[1] Now meet my mother. She died a few weeks ago. She wanted me to tell you how.

Her name was Virginia. Up until about 6 months ago, at age 84, she was the proverbial "little old lady in sneakers." After my father died of colon cancer several years ago, she lived by herself in one of those grand old Greek revival houses you see on postcards of small New England towns. Hers was in Middlebury, Vermont.

My mother was very independent, very self-sufficient, and very content. My brother and his family lived next door. Although she was quite close to them, she tried hard not to interfere in their lives. She spent most of her time reading large-print books, working word puzzles, and watching the news and professional sports on TV. She liked the house kept full of light. Every day she would take two outings, one in the morning to the small country store across the street to pick up the *Boston Globe*, and one in the afternoon to the Grand Union across town, to pick up some item she purposefully omitted from the previous day's shopping list. She did this in all but the worst weather. On icy days, she would wear golf shoes to keep from slipping and attach spikes to the tip of her cane. I think she was about 5 feet 2 and 120 pounds, but I am not certain. I know she started out at about 5 feet 4, but she seemed to shrink a little bit each year, getting cuter with time as many old people do. Her wrinkles matched her age, emphasizing a permanent thin-lipped smile that extended all the way to her little Kris Kringle eyes. The only thing that embarrassed her was her thinning gray hair, but she covered that up with a rather dashing tweed fedora that matched her Talbots outfits. She loved to tease people by wearing outrageous necklaces. The one made from the front teeth of camels was her favorite.

To be sure, she had had her share of problems in the past: diverticulitis and endometriosis when she was younger, more recently a broken hip, a bout with depression, some hearing loss, and cataracts. But she was a walking tribute to the best things in American medicine. Coming from a family of four generations of physicians, she was fond of bragging that, but for lens implants, hearing aids, hip surgery, and Elavil, she would be blind, deaf, bedridden, and depressed. At age 84, her only problems were a slight rectal prolapse, which she could reduce fairly easily, some urinary incontinence, and a fear that if her eyesight got much worse she would lose her main

pleasures. But those things were easy to deal with and she was, to use her New England expression, "happy as a clam."

"David, I can't tell you how content I am. Except for missing your father, these are the best years of my life."

Yes, all was well with my mother, until about six months ago. That was when she developed acute cholelithiasis. From that point on, her health began to unravel with amazing speed. She recovered from the cholecystectomy on schedule and within a few weeks of leaving the hospital was resuming her walks downtown. But about six weeks after the surgery she was suddenly hit with a case of severe diarrhea, so severe that it extended her rectal prolapse to about 8 inches and dehydrated her to the point that she had to be readmitted. As soon as her physician got her rehydrated, other complications quickly set in. She developed oral thrush, apparently due to the antibiotic treatment for her diarrhea, and her antidepressants got out of balance. For some reason that was never fully determined, she also became anemic, which was treated with iron, which made her nauseated. She could not eat, she got weak, her skin itched, and her body ached. Oh yes, they also found a lump in her breast, the diagnosis of which was postponed, and atrial fibrillation. Needless to say, she was quite depressed.

Her depression was accentuated by the need to deal with her rectal prolapse. On the one hand, she really disliked the thought of more surgery. She especially hated the nasogastric tube and the intense postoperative fatigue. On the other hand, the prolapse was very painful. The least cough or strain would send it out to rub against the sheets, and she could not push it back the way she used to. She knew that she could not possibly walk to the Grand Union again unless it was fixed.

It was at that time that she first began to talk to me about how she could end her life gracefully. As a physician's wife, she was used to thinking about life and death and prided herself on being able to deal maturely with the idea of death. She had signed every living will and advance directive she could find, and carried a card that donated her organs. Even though she knew they would not do anyone much good (*"Can they recycle my artificial hip and lenses?"*), she liked the way the card announced her acceptance of the fact that all things must someday end. She dreaded the thought of being in a nursing home, unable to take care of herself, her body, mind, and interests progressively declining until she was little more than a blank stare, waiting for death to mercifully take her away.

Edited by Roxanne K. Young, Associate Editor.

From *Journal of the American Medical Association*, Vol. 272, July 20, 1994, pp. 179-181. © 1994 by the American Medical Association. Reprinted by permission.

"I know they can keep me alive a long time, but what's the point? If the pleasure is gone and the direction is steadily down, why should I have to draw it out until I'm 'rescued' by cancer, a heart attack, or a stroke? That could take years. I understand that some people want to hang on until all the possible treatments have been tried to squeeze out the last drops of life. That's fine for them. But not for me."

My own philosophy, undoubtedly influenced heavily by my parents, is that choosing the best way to end your life should be the ultimate individual right—a right to be exercised between oneself and one's beliefs, without intrusions from governments or the beliefs of others. On the other hand, I also believe that such decisions should be made only with an accurate understanding of one's prognosis and should never be made in the middle of a correctable depression or a temporary trough. So my brother, sister, and I coaxed her to see a rectal surgeon about having her prolapse repaired and to put off thoughts of suicide until her health problems were stabilized and her antidepressants were back in balance.

With the surgeon's help, we explored the possible outcomes of the available procedures for her prolapse. My mother did not mind the higher mortality rates of the more extensive operations—in fact, she wanted them. Her main concern was to avoid rectal incontinence, which she knew would dampen any hopes of returning to her former lifestyle.

Unfortunately, that was the outcome she got. By the time she had recovered from the rectal surgery, she was totally incontinent "at both ends," to use her words. She was bedridden, anemic, exhausted, nauseated, achy, and itchy. Furthermore, over the period of this illness her eyesight had begun to fail to the point she could no longer read. Because she was too sick to live at home, even with my brother's help, but not sick enough to be hospitalized, we had to move her to an intermediate care facility.

On the positive side, her antidepressants were working again and she had regained her clarity of mind, her spirit, and her humor. But she was very unhappy. She knew instinctively, and her physician confirmed, that after all the insults of the past few months it was very unlikely she would ever be able to take care of herself alone or walk to the Grand Union. That was when she began to press me harder about suicide.

"Let me put this in terms you should understand, David. My 'quality of life'—isn't that what you call it?—has dropped below zero. I know there is nothing fatally wrong with me and that I could live on for many more years. With a colostomy and some luck I might even be able to recover a bit of my former lifestyle, for a while. But do we have to do that just because it's possible? Is the meaning of life defined by its duration? Or does life have a purpose so large that it doesn't have to be prolonged at any cost to preserve its meaning?

"I've lived a wonderful life, but it has to end sometime and this is the right time for me. My decision is not about whether I'm going to die—we will all die sooner or later. My decision is about when and how. I don't want to spoil the wonder of my life by dragging it out in years of decay. I want to go now, while the good memories are still fresh. I have always known that eventually the right time would come, and now I know that this is it. Help me find a way."

I discussed her request with my brother and sister and with her nurses and physician. Although we all had different feelings about her request, we agreed that she satisfied our criteria of being well-informed, stable, and not depressed.

For selfish reasons we wanted her to live as long as possible, but we realized that it was not our desires that mattered. What mattered to us were her wishes. She was totally rational about her conviction that this was "her time." Now she was asking for our help, and it struck us as the height of paternalism (or filialism?) to impose our desires over hers.

I bought *Final Exit*[2] for her, and we read it together. If she were to end her life, she would obviously have to do it with pills. But as anyone who has thought about this knows, accomplishing that is not easy. Patients can rarely get the pills themselves, especially in a controlled setting like a hospital or nursing home. Anyone who provides the pills knowing they will be used for suicide could be arrested. Even if those problems are solved and the pills are available, they can be difficult to take, especially by the frail. Most likely, my mother would fall asleep before she could swallow the full dose. A way around this would be for her to put a bag over her head with a rubber band at her neck to ensure that she would suffocate if she fell asleep before taking all the pills. But my mother did not like that idea because of the depressing picture it would present to those who found her body. She contemplated drawing a happy smile on the bag, but did not think that would give the correct impression either. The picture my mother wanted to leave to the world was that her death was a happy moment, like the end of a wonderful movie, a time for good memories and a peaceful acceptance of whatever the future might hold. She did not like the image of being a quasi-criminal sneaking illegal medicines. The way she really wanted to die was to be given a morphine drip that she could control, to have her family around her holding her hands, and for her to turn up the drip.

As wonderful as that might sound, it is illegal. One problem was that my mother did not have a terminal condition or agonizing pain that might justify a morphine drip. Far from it. Her heart was strong enough to keep her alive for 10 more years, albeit as a frail, bedridden, partially blind, partially deaf, incontinent, and possibly stroked-out woman. But beyond that, no physician would dare give a patient access to a lethal medicine in a way that could be accused of assisting suicide. Legally, physicians can provide lots of comfort care, even if it might hasten a patient's death, but the primary purpose of the medicine must be to relieve suffering, not to cause death. Every now and then my mother would vent her frustration with the law and the arrogance of others who insist that everyone must accept their philosophy of death, but she knew that railing at what she considered to be misguided laws would not undo them. She needed to focus on finding a solution to her problem. She decided that the only realistic way out was for me to get her some drugs and for her to do her best to swallow them. Although I was very nervous at the thought of being turned in by someone who discovered our plan and felt it was their duty to stop it, I was willing to do my part. I respected her decision, and I knew she would do the same for me.

I had no difficulty finding a friend who could write a prescription for restricted drugs and who was willing to help us from a distance. In fact, I have yet to find anybody who agrees with the current laws. (*"So why do they exist?"*) But before I actually had to resolve any lingering conflicts and obtain the drugs, my mother's course took an unexpected and strangely welcomed twist. I received a call that she had developed pneumonia and had to be readmitted to the hospital. By the time I made contact with her, she had already reminded her attendants that she did not want to be resuscitated if she should have a heart attack or stroke.

"Is there anything more I can do?"

Pneumonia, the old folks' friend, I thought to myself. I told her that although advance directives usually apply to refusing treatments for emergencies such as heart attacks, it was always legal for her to refuse any treatment. In particular, she could refuse the antibiotics for the pneumonia. Her physician and nurses would undoubtedly advise her against it, but if she signed enough papers they would have to honor her request.

"What's it like to die of pneumonia? Will they keep me comfortable?"

I knew that without any medicine for comfort, pneumonia was not a pleasant way to die. But I was also confident that her physician was compassionate and would keep her comfortable. So she asked that the antibiotics be stopped. Given the deep gurgling in her throat every time she breathed, we all expected the infection to spread rapidly. She took a perverse pleasure in that week's cover story of *Newsweek*, which described the spread of resistant strains.

"Bring all the resistant strains in this hospital to me. That will be my present to the other patients."

But that did not happen. Against the odds, her pneumonia regressed. This discouraged her greatly—to see the solution so close, just to watch it slip away.

"What else can I do? Can I stop eating?"

I told her she could, but that that approach could take a long time. I then told her that if she was really intent on dying, she could stop drinking. Without water, no one, even the healthiest, can live more than a few days.

"Can they keep me comfortable?"

I talked with her physician. Although it ran against his instincts, he respected the clarity and firmness of my mother's decision and agreed that her quality of life had sunk below what she was willing to bear. He also knew that what she was asking from him was legal. He took out the IV and wrote orders that she should receive adequate medications to control discomfort.

My mother was elated. The next day happened to be her 85th birthday, which we celebrated with a party, balloons and all. She was beaming from ear to ear. She had done it. She had found the way. She relished her last piece of chocolate, and then stopped eating and drinking.

Over the next four days, my mother greeted her visitors with the first smiles she had shown for months. She energetically reminisced about the great times she had had and about things she was proud of. (She especially hoped I would tell you about her traveling alone across Africa at the age of 70, and surviving a capsized raft on Wyoming's Snake River at 82.) She also found a calming self-acceptance in describing things of which she was not proud. She slept between visits but woke up brightly whenever we touched her to share more memories and say a few more things she wanted us to know. On the fifth day it was more difficult to wake her. When we would take her hand she would open her eyes and smile, but she was too drowsy and weak to talk very much. On the sixth day, we could not wake her. Her face was relaxed in her natural smile, she was breathing unevenly, but peacefully. We held her hands for another two hours, until she died.

I had always imagined that when I finally stood in the middle of my parents' empty house, surrounded by the old smells, by hundreds of objects that represent a time forever lost, and by the terminal silence, I would be overwhelmingly saddened. But I wasn't. This death was not a sad death; it was a happy death. It did not come after years of decline, lost vitality, and loneliness; it came at the right time. My mother was not clinging desperately to what no one can have. She knew that death was not a tragedy to be postponed at any cost, but that death is a part of life, to be embraced at the proper time. She had done just what she wanted to do, just the way she wanted to do it. Without hoarding pills, without making me a criminal, without putting a bag over her head, and without huddling in a van with a carbon monoxide machine, she had found a way to bring her life gracefully to a close. Of course we cried. But although we will miss her greatly, her ability to achieve her death at her "right time" and in her "right way" transformed for us what could have been a desolate and crushing loss into a time for joy. Because she was happy, we were happy.

"Write about this, David. Tell others how well this worked for me. I'd like this to be my gift. Whether they are terminally ill, in intractable pain, or, like me, just know that the right time has come for them, more people might want to know that this way exists. And maybe more physicians will help them find it."

Maybe they will. Rest in peace, Mom.

David M. Eddy, MD, PhD
Jackson, Wyo

My mother wants to thank Dr Timothy Cope of Middlebury, Vermont, for his present on her 85th birthday.

1. Eddy DM. Cost-effectiveness analysis: a conversation with my father. *JAMA.* 1992;267:1669-1672, 1674-1675.
2. Humphry D. *Final Exit.* Secaucus, NJ: Carol Publishing Group; 1991.

Planning to Die

Jeanne Guillemin

Jeanne Guillemin is professor of sociology at Boston College. She has published widely on questions of medical technology and is co- author (with Lynda L. Holmstrom) of Mixed Blessings. Intensive Care for Newborns.

Thirty years ago, in *The American Way of Dying,* Jessica Mitford roundly criticized Americans for their obsessive denial of death and their equally obsessive fixation on immortality. To the puritanical American sensibility, a miasma of shame surrounds the event of death. The quicker one died and the less the family and community were troubled, the better. Funeral directors, a uniquely American profession, assumed all responsibility for the corpse, including its embalmed, cosmetic display and its rapid dispatch to the cemetery or to the crematorium. Denial of death was also the theme of Philippe Ariès' work *Western Attitudes Toward Death* (1974). He credits early twentieth-century America with the invention of the modern attitude toward mortality. Death, once so banal a presence that Renaissance markets were held in graveyards and so communal that relatives and friends crowded the bedchambers of the dying, lost its tame aspect. Under the influence of urban industrialization, it became detached from domestic traditions, not the least of which was a religious understanding of the appropriateness and even the banality of the self's demise. In our times, Ariès argues, death became wild and obscene because we cherish an individualism that cannot be relinquished without extreme anguish. As with sex, death was not to be talked about in front of children or in polite company.

Today the American public is confronting mortality in ways that were unthinkable when Mitford was writing and improbable even to Ariès. The emphasis now is on rational planning for one's death that goes far beyond buying a burial plot. Topics such as traversing the emotional stages of dying, how to compose a living will to instruct final medical decisions, and the merits of rational suicide are ordinary fare on television and radio talk shows and in popular magazines. The head of the Hemlock Society, Derek Humphry, has a bestseller in *Final Exit,* a how-to book on "happy death." Jack Kevorkian, another book author, has gained notoriety for his "mercitron" devices, recently used by three women to end their lives. Despite his subsequent indictment for homicide, the public is far from outraged by the idea of physician-assisted suicide. In 1991, the state of Washington gained national attention with a popular referendum on the issue. The voting public there ultimately balked at granting it legal status, but polls had already revealed widespread support for the option of medically supervised suicide. In 1992, the state of New Hampshire initiated the nation's first legislation that would authorize physicians to write prescriptions to hasten the death of terminally ill patients.

This new frankness concerning death is due in part to changing demographics. The population of the United States has aged, with more people than ever living out a seventy-two year life span. Many are surviving decades beyond it. Perhaps aging alone would shift any society's focus to the end of life. Yet death itself has become unexpectedly familiar because of the AIDS epidemic, which has brought grief to hundreds of thousands of young victims, their families, and friends. Add to this the fact that the United States has the highest homicide rate of any industrialized country, with a disproportionate number of casualties among young minority males, and the difficulties of denying death and its repercussions become clear. Old or young, one thinks, "This could be me."

Still, death is far from tamed; it is now newly wild and familiar. The current discussion of how to die gives evidence of terrible fears that those final circumstances are beyond one's control. In a culture that prizes individual autonomy, there is a no more degrading scenario than the gradual diminution of physical and mental powers, the prolonged and painful helplessness, with mental lapses preceding and even obscuring the experience of dying. American anxiety about dying centers on how the individual can avoid dependence. Unfortunately, the two environments where death is likely to happen are poorly prepared to reduce this anxiety and are, in fact, increasing it. Neither the hospital, where 80 percent of Americans die, nor the home, where growing numbers of patients are being cared for, can be counted on to alleviate fears about death as a scenario of degradation.

Hospital Care and Uncare

In pondering the phenomenon of shameful death ("la mort inversée"), Ariès sees the modern hospital as the environment where depersonalized efficiency and order quell the fears of the dying. As a cultural instrument of repression, the hospital guarantees that the graceless, physically repulsive facts of expiration are hidden from view and that the emotional climate at the bedside is restrained. The sheets are clean, the meals regular, and the staff professional. Replacing family and friends is the hospital team, led by the physician. "They are," wrote Ariès, "the masters of death—of the moment as well as of the circumstances. . . ."

In the last two decades, hospital-based medicine has undergone radical changes and Americans have largely lost confidence in its protective guarantees, as chill and repressive as they have been. Hospital organization, once able to guarantee benign order for both birth and death, has been altered not with reference to the social or spiritual needs of patients, but in reaction to market incentives that favor large hospitals selling progressive medicine. The hospitals that survived the fierce competition of the 1980s did so by heavy investment in new and experimental technologies and by the build-up of centralized facilities offering a profitable mixture of specialized and acute care services. Small community hospitals closed by the hundreds. Public hospitals, burdened with welfare patients, are foundering. Private mega-hospital chains, like Humana, thrive because they serve only privately insured patients.

Far from being beneficent institutions, most hospitals today are businesses that serve clients. Linked to proliferating technological options and required to support high-priced professionals, their main incentive is to maximize returns on their investments. They are only unlucky if they do not. Cost control measures to cap procedure charges, such as Diagnostic Related Groups (D.R.G.'s), have merely succeeded in moving patients more quickly out of their hospital beds to make

room for more. Costs for hospital medicine and services continue to rise and inflate health insurance coverage, which growing numbers of Americans cannot afford.

The progressive technologies being marketed through American hospitals fall into two categories. Both affect how we die. One kind addresses the diseases of the growing numbers of patients fortunate enough to survive past youth, at which point they become vulnerable to cardiac disease, cancer, stroke, kidney and liver failure. When Aaron Wildavsky coined the phrase, "doing better and feeling worse," in reference to modern American health care, he aptly summarized its major problem. The important determinants of health and illness—life style, genetics, and the environment—are outside the scope of medicine. Its principal technologies, geared toward an aging clientèle, must be of the patch-and-mend variety, lacking the "magic bullet" efficiency of penicillin and sulfa drugs. Success with these "half-way technologies," as Lewis Thomas called them, is difficult and uncertain. Very sick patients do much more than lose faith in medicine. They take it on, they wrestle with it, and often they feel defeated by it. They are not just disappointed consumers. They engage their bodies and souls in a battle for life.

Hospitals were organized, not for the patients' social and spiritual needs, but in reaction to market conditions.

The role of the physician in treating the very sick patient is problematic, in part because doctors are only apparently disinterested in advising about medical treatment options. Many patients fail to understand that physicians like car dealers, will promote their products, if asked. Not that physicians are necessarily driven by profit motives, but they are integrated into the hospital reward system, now heavily invested in high-technology resources—machines, laboratories, consultants—that must be used to get a return. Perhaps unwittingly, physicians often inform seriously ill patients about therapy in ways that encourages it. The use of statistical odds, for example, is a commonplace, as when a doctor refers to scientific studies to inform a patient about survival rates for cancer, using surgery or drugs or some combination of both. When cancer or any other disease is in an advanced stage, this tactic is little better than offering a lottery ticket to someone who is destitute. What even educated patients often do not know is that many clinical studies are poorly executed—without controls and on small samples—and yield only the most tentative results. Or, if they are well conceived and implemented, the patients researched may share none or few of the characteristics—age, gender, medical history, and so on—of the patient being informed. There is little or nothing in their training that prepares physicians to develop a posture of integrity and more genuine disinterest or new words of counsel for the seriously ill who should perhaps not venture any therapeutic course.

For a very sick patient, surgery, chemotherapy, or organ transplant might work. Then again, it might not. It will certainly be a physical and emotional ordeal, causing pain that is especially alienating because it is impossible to know whether it is part of recuperation or a sign of further degeneration. The patient cannot know, nor can the therapist, until test results come back. Even then, many therapies require years of monitoring, especially in the case of cancer, during which one simply does not know if a true cure has been effected. Starting with Susan Sontag's *Illness As Metaphor* to the essay on resisting chemotherapy by the anthropologist Susan DiGiacomo, the patient-as-survivor literature constitutes a searing criticism of how physicians mishandle patients confronting death.

The really bad news is that medical technology can offer multiple sequential therapeutic options for the same fatal disease. This creates uncertainty and uncertainty in medicine, as Wildavsky and others have noted, is often resolved by doing more. If drugs and surgery fail, other drugs or more surgery are substituted. The more advanced the disease, the more the desperate patient will value inclusion in an experimental trial of some new therapy, whereby she or he is diminished to a statistic and risks more physical devastation. This way of progressing toward death—by hopes raised and dashed, by technological assaults on the body, followed by periods of incomplete and uncertain recuperation—is, of course, not the road traversed by people who are cured. Many people overcome blocked arteries, for example, or cancer because the therapy works. But subjection to experimental medicine is the pathway of everyone's last cure. No matter what the patient's age or how advanced the disease, or even if it is considered incurable, the options for more tests and treatment exist, in refined or experimental form, appropriate or inappropriate, as the physician advises.

The intensive care unit is the other important kind of technology that hospitals market. It has revolution-

ized the way Americans die, but not for the better. The concept of high-technology life support took hold in the early 1970s in response to a perceived need, public and professional, for emergency medical services. The argument for emergency medical units was and is based on the reduction of waste in human lives. Immediate aggressive intervention, not unlike that of a M.A.S.H. unit, would save victims of accidents, of heart attack and stroke, as well as premature infants, and post-operative patients. The key was vigorously sustained intervention with the maximum resources of a large central hospital. Emergency and intensive care facilities, costing billions of dollars, became part of the expansion of central hospitals throughout the 1970s and 1980s. Patients *in extremis* are always in good supply and treating them quickly in high-use beds has often helped hospitals underwrite less profitable services. Such heavy investment in acute care emphatically denied a preventive and more cost-efficient approach to health problems and to the general social problem of death by violence. Nor did emergency care enthusiasts predict that many whose lives were saved would not be able to resume normal lives or even a conscious existence, and would be passed off to chronic care facilities or to their families.

Subjection to experimental medicine is the pathway of everyone's last cure.

Even less concern is being expressed for the I.C.U. patient's experience of having to live attached to machines or dying that way. From the perspective of the conscious patient, experiencing what it means to be "worked on" by teams of strangers, to be coded for resuscitation (or not), to lie among others near death or already dead, to be dependent on and surrounded by wires and machines, intensive care imposes the most feared scenario: prolonged helplessness, often in pain. For years, hospital staff have known about "I.C.U. psychosis," the severe and not uncommon disorientation of patients reacting to the windowless, mechanical environment. For years, the only remedy has been to set a clock where the patient could see it.

The impact of the intensive care unit on the American way of dying has been profound, for it is there that contemporary medicine routinely eliminates the primary actor, the patient, from the ritual of dying. This is done by first selecting uncommonly passive patients in crisis. Medicine then perfected the way of artificially sustaining the clinically (if not legally) dead patient and replacing the old rituals of professional-patient interaction with emergency medical intervention, that is, professional team management of machines and bodies. Dying in this context is not something the individual patient, potentially a living corpse, really does, since it is a matter of the staff's withdrawing life supports. It has also become increasingly unclear what responsibility the once "masters of death" assume in hospital death scenarios. With few exceptions, modern physicians are revolted by death, leaving to nurses the "dirty work" of interacting with grieving families, the actual release of the patient from support machines, and ministering to the dead body.

Dying at Home

Recalling a time, long gone, when people died at home, Michel Foucault describes the family's gaze fixed on the sick person as full of "the vital force of benevolence and the discretion of hope." The contemporary alternative of dying at home guarantees no such comfort. Yet many households, prepared or not, must accept the prospect of such caretaking, even though the patient's death at the last minute takes place in the hospital.

The choice to refuse medication or food may be rational if one truly believes it is time to die.

Since the introduction of D.R.G.'s in 1983, the allowable length of hospital stay for Medicare patients has been sharply decreased. Growing numbers of chronically ill and elderly people are being cared for by relatives. But the family context has its problems: emotional ambivalence, instability, isolation from the larger community, and even violence. Hospice care, once hailed as the humane alternative to dying in the hospital, provides only minor support in terms of supplies and service. Family members, especially women, are left with the daily responsibility for patient care, which now often includes complex regimens of infusion drugs, intravenous feeding, oxygen support, and physical therapy. For most of the elderly, long-term nursing home care is economically not feasible. Hospitals have no room for those who are dying slowly—but then who does?

The toll of rejection may be seen in the increasing rate of suicide among the elderly. Between 1981 and 1986, suicides among people over sixty-five rose sharply, from 12.6 per 100,000 to 21.8. Starvation, refusal of medication, and guns were the principal means. How such private decisions are reached or even if they can count as rational, we do not know, although fear of being a burden is frequently reported in anecdotes. Such a fear itself is not irrational. Government and professional support for home care is minimal. Home-care providers receive scant training for the technical tasks they perform, no provision for relief, and no credit for the round-the-clock time they give. Having little or no reimbursement incentives, physicians generally ignore patients cared for at home. Cost coverage for home care varies with the insurance carrier. Even under private insurance plans, many items must be paid for out-of-pocket. In the last ten years, unregulated commercial agencies have taken over the growing, multi-billion dollar home-care industry and have inflated the retail cost of everything—needles, gauze, plastic tubing, rubber sheets, bed rentals, and drugs—in ways that parallel hospital charges for aspirin and the price of Pentagon coffee pots.

As death re-enters the American household, it is tamed only by the resources a family or perhaps only a single relative or friend can muster. Maybe the community has a free slot in the hospice program, maybe the physician will do more than telephone, maybe a member of the clergy will visit. But there are no guarantees. If the scenario of hospital death is daunting, so too is the vision of a drawn-out, painful expiration, resented and uncomforted by those intimates or the intimate to whom one is a burden. The choice to refuse medication or even food may be rational, if one truly believes it is time to die. But the rationale "I am only a burden" threatens all of us, for we are all at some time in our lives completely dependent on others.

Confronting Death

The present controversy surrounding physician-assisted suicide and rational suicide in general may be all to the good, if it promotes change in our institutions. How many people would be interested in a quick (six minutes), painless death in a parked van (the scenario for Janet Adkins, the first user of Kevorkian's mercitron machine), if hospitals and homes provided a more humane context for dying? Or is it that Americans, Puritans still, ask for nothing more than clean sheets and a morphine drip? This may be true. The rational suicides reported in the media all have a tidy, pain-free aura about them.

Critics, such as Mitford and Ariès, accurately identified our cultural denial of death as a serious aberration.

We want death to never happen, to be a non-experience, or an event that cannot threaten our dignity. Yet, as the philosopher Paul Ramsey used to say, there is nothing at all dignified about dying—one might add, nor happy either. Death must be seen for what it is—cruelly inevitable, a painful rendering, our finitude—if we are to understand the human condition and even begin to ask about the meaning of life. Death is momentous, in the general and in the specific. For the dying person, spirit and body are inescapably involved in a final reckoning. No witness can be untouched, except by a distortion of the most fundamental truth, that we are mortal. The distance between us and the dying person is only an accident of time.

It is this sense of mortality we try to hide from and the reason we have created institutions of denial. Oddly enough, we even deny the extent to which these institutions contribute to our problems. In the innumerable debates and discussions about death, the focus remains on individual strategies, as if, for example, one person's choice of suicide over protracted terminal illness constituted a justification in itself, prompted by psychology, legitimated by one's will, and with no social consequences or meaning. Yet our hospitals are strange and alienating environments to the extent that they obfuscate this truth of mortality by therapeutic experimentalism, intensive care, and also the "harvesting" of organs from living corpses. Our homes are threatening to the extent that people are left in isolation to deal with life as a burden and death as an obscenity. The quick-fix suicide machine or the plastic bag method described in *Final Exit* might relieve the individual of woe and suffering, but what about the rest of us, who will dutifully attend to our living wills and then await the worst? We know that death is not obscene; it cannot by itself deprave us. But it is frightening in its familiarity and cannot be simply planned away. Rather, we should envision institutional reforms. We need physicians educated to say more to the dying patient than "Have a nice trip" (Kevorkian's farewell to Janet Adkins). We need hospitals with staff motivated to give humane attention, not overtreatment, to the dying. We need compensation for families that give home care so that they can afford to be kind and old people can die in relative peace. Death is indeed a wild beast of sorts. These are ways to tame it.

READINGS SUGGESTED BY THE AUTHOR:

Philippe Ariès. *Western Attitudes Toward Death*. Baltimore, Md.: Johns Hopkins University Press, 1974.

Susan DiGiacomo. "Biomedicine in the Cultural System: An Anthropologist in the Kingdom of the Sick," in *Encounters with Biomedicine: Case Studies in Medical Anthropology*, Hans Baer (ed.). New York: Gordon and Breach Science Publishers, 1987.

Susan Sontag. *Illness as Metaphor*. New York: Farrar, Straus, and Giroux, 1988.

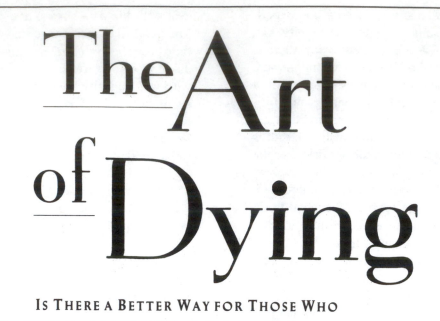

The Art of Dying

IS THERE A BETTER WAY FOR THOSE WHO

WILL NEVER RECOVER?

MARILYN WEBB

Marilyn Webb is the author of the book, The Art of Dying: The New American Way of Death, *scheduled for publication by Bantam Books, fall 1996.*

FIVE YEARS AGO, CYNTHIA O'Neal's friend Archie died of AIDS. "It was the first time I'd ever been with someone who was dying," she says. "He was 32. It totally transformed anything I'd thought before about death."

By the time Archie realized he was dying, he had been hooked up night and day to a machine that dripped nutrients directly into his stomach. This was not a life he wanted, so he asked his friends and his doctor to unhook the machine. "He wanted to make the most of the time he had left," O'Neal says. "Thankfully, the doctor said yes."

Gathering his family and friends, Archie said, "Please put me in a wheelchair and let's go to the Metropolitan Museum." For the next four days he was wheeled around the Met, the Frick, and the Whitney. He lived only on water. Then he got so weak that he had to go back home to bed. He died five days later.

"He was near a coma, in and out," O'Neal says. "But there were times when he became alert. Once he sat up and said he wanted iced coffee, good champagne, and a 3 Musketeers bar. He ate with relish and managed to keep it all down. But he never ate again."

Archie always loved sweet-smelling oils. "A close friend began massaging his back, his feet, his shoulders. And we all held him, and each other, very close. It was extraordinary—like a birthing," O'Neal says. "He would go to sleep—a very deep sleep, like a coma. His breathing would slow, and then he'd come back. I'd say, 'Where were you? Picking out a good room?' And he'd smile and say, 'Boy, I was really far away from my body, and it was a big effort to get back in.' He slept longer and longer, and then, he just died. It was very, very beautiful, like seeing him off on a great journey."

Archie taught O'Neal that, awful as it is to lose someone you love, dying itself isn't something terrifying. And the experience changed her whole life. Today O'Neal is the founding director of Friends in Deed, an organization that provides emotional and spiritual support to people facing life-threatening illnesses. She is part of a movement that's beginning to explore natural dying, much as the Lamaze movement explored natural childbirth several decades ago. This new movement is predicated on a major shift in cultural thinking and a sea change in medical technology and the law.

SOME CALL IT "CONSCIOUS DYing." It is spiritual but not religious. It is not euthanasia, nor is it suicide. It is dying a dignified death when the prognosis is terminal and further treatments are of questionable value. Some of those who work with terminal patients have developed their ideas through the hospice movement or the literature of near-death experience; some are psychiatrists who have developed a new field, psycho-oncology. All seem intent on helping people like Archie die the deaths they choose.

"Like birthing," hospice nurses Maggie Callanan and Patricia Kelley write in their important new book, *Final Gifts* (Poseidon Press), "dying can be an opportunity for the whole family to share positive experiences rather than only sadness, pain, and loss." The key is knowing what to expect when we die, for that knowledge reduces the panic and fear.

"Dying is a unique experience for each patient, yet it is not so unpredictable that you can't provide some guidelines that families find very helpful," says Genevieve Foley, director of nursing practices at Memorial Sloan-Kettering Cancer Center. She works with dying children. "The death of a child," she says, "is one of the most important events in a family's history, and it will have a ripple effect for generations if it isn't handled well."

Handled well, death can be both painless and peaceful. Natural dying rests on new advances in medication, new modes of medication delivery, and new thinking about pain control. Morphine and other narcotics won't necessarily turn the terminally ill into addicts, and will almost always take away pain. But until recently, doctors, who get little training in pain control in medical school, have been reluctant to use narcotics for pain relief.

"We all fear pain. Maybe a third of all cancer patients have pain; two thirds have it in the terminal stages," says Dr. Jimmie C. Holland, chief of psychiatry services at Sloan-Kettering and author of the classic text *Handbook of Psychooncology*. "Virtually all of it is controllable, yet we have an undertreatment of pain and depression. If we can treat both of them, we can make patients more hopeful and improve their quality of life. These are the issues the physician-assisted suicide debate isn't taking into account. So society is moving into a very complex area without understanding that our palliative care is sophisticated, but isn't being used nearly enough."

Targeted pain medications, given regularly or in doses that a patient can control, let most patients remain pain-free till death, while keeping their senses intact. Drugs to counteract debilitating symptoms—nausea, bowel or bladder dysfunction, shortness of breath, or severe depression—can contribute much toward comfort. These new medications give people an unprecedented ability to choose how they die, and where. Taking the pain and fear out of dying provides a major alternative to Dr. Death when a prognosis really is bleak. And this view comes not a moment too soon.

UNFORTUNATELY, DEATH —not just the lingering illnesses of elderly parents but the premature deaths of young people like Archie— has taken on a terrible familiarity in the past ten years. And these days, people who care for the dying face unprecedented ethical dilemmas. Medical science has advanced so far that what many people most fear is a slow death on machinery that prolongs life but makes it a living hell.

In 1976, a New Jersey court decision gave Joseph and Julia Quinlan the legal right to take their comatose, permanently impaired 22-year-old daughter, Karen Anne, off a respirator. In 1990, the Supreme Court ruled that an individual has a constitutionally protected right to refuse medical treatment. When the patient is incompetent, states can require clear and convincing evidence that removing life-sustaining equipment is what the patient would have wanted. That ruling eventually allowed the parents of 33-year-old Nancy Beth Cruzan to have her feeding tube removed. In the years between these landmark cases, other court decisions changed the legal definition of death and tried to clarify the circumstances under which patients or their families could refuse treatment.

In December 1991, the federal government enacted the Patient Self-Determination Act (PSDA). All medical facilities receiving federal funds must now inform patients of their right to prepare advance directives for their care. All states now have legislation on advance directives, including living wills and/or health-care proxies.

New York State has no law on living wills. However, court decisions have recognized that hospitals should honor such documents if they contain clear evidence of the patient's wishes. And almost two years ago, the state's health-care-proxy law went into effect; it requires hospitals and doctors to allow a "proxy," previously designated, to make the medical decisions for an incompetent adult.

Regrettably, says Tracy Miller, executive director of the New York State Task Force on Life and the Law—set up to make recommendations to the governor on issues arising from advances in medical technology—most people don't sign health-care-proxy forms. And if a patient who has lost his capacity to make his own decisions has not designated a proxy or signed a living will that provides specific, clear, and convincing evidence of his treatment wishes, no one has the authority to speak for him.

Studies suggest that only 15 percent of adults will sign a proxy form. (To get a form, send a stamped, self-addressed envelope to Proxy, Box 1634, New York, New York 10116.) For that reason, in January 1993 the Task Force will present a bill to the State Legislature calling for a Treatment Decisions Law. That, Miller says, "will let families or close friends make decisions at people's bedside—whether or not patients have signed a proxy form—rather than in a courtroom."

Such a law would prevent worst-case scenarios like the plight of Murray Elbaum and his wife, Jean. For two years, Murray tried to have his comatose wife's life-sustaining equipment shut off. Since she had not put her wishes about medical treatment in writing, the nursing home caring for her refused to do so. Finally, Murray won his case in court. But another court ruled that he must pay the $100,000 the nursing home charged during the time he had tried to force it to stop the treatment.

UNTIL 1969, WHEN DR. Elisabeth Kübler-Ross brought death out of the closet with her landmark book *On Death and Dying* (Macmillan), the subject wasn't discussed with doctors, with family, or in polite company. A century ago, death occurred at home, in full family view, usually within a religious framework. But modern medicine brought with it a secular ethos of antiseptic death behind hospital doors. Doctors never told patients they were dying. That denial of death took away the deathbed moment—a moment that, at least in medieval times, brought last requests and religious visions.

Dr. Kübler-Ross changed that. Not only did she describe the psychological stages patients go through in accepting death, she argued that it's crucial to tell them the truth and help them cope.

Now there are organizations like Choice in Dying that give legal and medical advice on decisions about life-sustaining equipment. And there is new thinking on death itself. The studies of near-death experiences (NDEs) by medical doctors Raymond Moody Jr., Melvin Morse, and Diane Komp and psychologist Kenneth Ring show that NDEs have a positive impact on the lives of those brought back from death. Dame Cicely Saunders and Sandol Stoddard have publicized the palliative-care approach of hospices. And New Age thinkers Stephen and Ondrea Levine, Marianne Williamson, and even Ram Dass have offered a new spiritual dimension to a primarily secular generation.

Naturally, there are critics. But even if the answers this natural-dying movement is beginning to give are wrong, they still provide solace in times that are, psychologically, deeply difficult. And if these views on death are right, human beings may find in dying more hope than despair.

The new ideas have begun to have an impact on care and support programs, from the old-line—at Sloan-Kettering and Columbia-Presbyterian medical centers— to hospices to newer groups like Gay men's Health Crisis, the Manhattan Center for Living, God's Love We Deliver, and Friends In Deed.

"How do you talk to people about dying?" asks Dr. Holland. "People die as they live. Some want to be a very active part of dying, and talk about it. Others don't want any part of it at all."

Now that death has become a subject of public debate, people have begun to ask— and find answers to—age-old questions: What is dying really like? How can we best handle our own deaths? And how can we help someone we love?

Three years ago, my stepfather died of Alzheimer's, spending most of his final days barely lucid. But one day, a few months before the end, I found him lounging in a chair, looking as he had when he was still a lawyer, saying things he once would have scoffed at.

"Your father was here this morning," he said. "He told me to tell you he loves you very much, although he says you probably don't think so." My father had died 26 years earlier, during an explosive time in our relationship. Had he come back, that's probably what he would have told me—and my stepfather couldn't know that.

Hospice nurses Callanan and Kelley say that many dying patients have experiences similar to my stepfather's. In their book, they call this "nearing death awareness," because these experiences are similar to those described by people who have "died" and returned, people with near-death experiences. People who die suddenly are flooded with certain typical sensations, but those who die slowly, Callanan and Kelley say, experience that process more gradually. For a while before they die, they live in this and that "other" world simultaneously.

The descriptions of people who report near-death experiences are consonant with traditional religious teachings about death and resurrection—and that makes NDEs controversial. According to Dr. Moody, author of the 1975 NDE classic *Life After Life* (Bantam Books), people who have "died" sudden deaths (who have gone into cardiac arrest, for instance) and have been brought back through emergency measures often report similar sensations. Relatives or friends who have died, or beings emanating light and peace, come to greet them; the patient often feels as if he's going through a tunnel; and often his life *does* pass before his eyes. The religious mention seeing Jesus or God instead of just saying that they saw light.

Since Moody published his book, there have been more reports of NDEs, probably because emergency medical care now saves lives that might have been lost before. A 1982 Gallup Poll estimated that 35 percent of adults who have come close to death reported having had NDEs. Now there is an International Association of Near Death Studies, a *Journal of Near-Death Studies,* and a national network of support groups for those who have had these experiences.

Dr. Kübler-Ross has joined this discussion. These days, she is director of the Elisabeth Kübler-Ross Center in Head Waters, Virginia, where she and a large staff run "Life, Death, and Transition" workshops. In 1991, she published *On Life After Death* (Celestial Arts), in which she says that for twenty years she studied NDEs in her patients, concluding that there *is* somewhere we go when we die.

"The dying experience is almost identical to the experience at birth," she says. "It is a birth into a different existence. For me, it is no longer a matter of belief but rather a matter of knowing."

One of the pieces of evidence Dr. Kübler-Ross points to is patients' descriptions of events that took place while they were clinically dead—things they could not have known unless they were actually

watching from somewhere other than inside their bodies. Other researchers—including Dr. Moody; Dr. Ring, professor of psychology at the University of Connecticut in Storrs and author of *Heading Toward Omega* (Quill); and Dr. Morse, also an author and a Seattle pediatrician—report similar things.

Some patients described in detail medical procedures used to revive them even though they otherwise had little medical knowledge. "What we have in the contemporary NDE," writes Dr. Ring, "is a modern version, cloaked in the symbols of our own time, of the ancient mystery teachings concerning life, death, and regeneration.

This is the stuff of tabloids, but the surprise is that NDE descriptions from children match those of adults. And the experience has a tremendous impact on the rest of the lives of both children and adults, for it eliminates the fear of death. And, unlike adults, "children never worry about whether people will believe them when they tell their near-death experiences," says Dr. Komp, a hematologist/oncologist at the Yale University Department of Pediatrics—report similar things.

There are—naturally—many skeptics. Daniel Dennett, Ph.D., director of the Center for Cognitive Studies at Tufts University and author of *Consciousness Explained* (Little, Brown), says the experiences we call NDEs can all be explained by the physical effects of the dying brain—that they are the brain's biochemical way of dealing with traumatic stress. But more frequently, the medical-care community is bypassing explanations.

"Some of my patients see relatives or people who've died before them," says nurse Nessa Coyle, director of the supportive-care program of the pain-service department at Sloan-Kettering. "Who knows if it's an afterlife, or metabolic changes, or lack of oxygen, or toxins, or side effects from medication? It happens. And usually it helps people feel comforted."

It's just this comfort that spawned support groups and programs that use NDE and nearing-death research to help people cope with their own deaths or the deaths of relatives and friends. For a secular world, this is as close to the classic teachings of organized religion as many hip people seem to want to get. And it serves an important similar purpose.

GANGA STONE IS THE founder of God's Love We Deliver, a program that provides meals for homebound people with AIDS. Since January, she has been teaching an ongoing course, "The Conversation," at Friends in Deed.

This past April 7, Eric, who is about 30,

attended a Friends in Deed course for the first time. When Albert, a friend of his, died of AIDS, he had dementia, Eric says. "The nurses thought he was hallucinating, but I thought he was showing the way to another world. Albert kept talking about standing next to Jesus, saying he was walking through other rooms in his apartment [there were none], pointing to blue walls and saying there was white light. When he died, the energy he gave off filled the room for hours afterward. It energized everyone around him." Eric came to the meeting to try to make sense of this.

"I try to remind people that death is a transition and that only the body dies," Stone says. She notes that the spirit, as many religions suggest, disengages and moves on. To understand this, she assigns readings, including the literature of NDE. Using "lucid dreams" and meditation, she also tries to help people explore in a practical way that state of consciousness that exists outside the thinking mind, a consciousness, she says, that is probably similar to what occurs when we die.

It's April 23. At Cabrini Hospice, Audrey Hill, 59, is "actively dying." She has lost 60 pounds and is lying on her bed, as thin as an Appalachian mother in a photograph taken in the Depression. Cheeks caved in. Eyes bulging. Great gaps in her mouth were caps have fallen off. Lips pursed. Clutching a soft stuffed rabbit. Audrey's eyes keep rolling up in her head. Sometimes she stares at nothing. And then she comes back. And smiles. She says that when she's "away," it's "like sleeping."

Today, her breathing stops often, for great lengths of time, making it seem as if there will be no more breaths. Then, casually, she takes another.

When I am introduced, she looks up from her pillow and smiles, with the most incredibly warm eyes. She sticks out her hand and says, quite graciously, "Hello, I'm Audrey." It's easy to fall in love with her. She is grateful for very small things—sips of water from a cup held by more steady hands, a pillow fluffed, someone to hold her hand—so full of compassion and humor.

When she comes "back," she strokes my hand, as if to calm me for what I see, and says: "Tell me about your loves." Audrey somehow spreads love all over the room. I've since learned, spending time with several other people near death, that this is one trait many project.

She is dying of cervical cancer, which, by the time she discovered it, had eaten into her kidneys and liver and moved up her spine. The pain was excruciating. Her chances were small, so she decided she'd rather have help with the pain at a hospice than prolong her agony with tortuous treatments that had minimal chance for success. Audrey is afraid of being abandoned, though, and she's also afraid of being a burden to her children.

Tears slip quietly from the corners of her eyes. "You think about things you could have done, things you might have wanted to do or say, but then, you realize you've run out of time." But for some reason, Audrey has had more time than anyone expected.

She was diagnosed in January 1991; in February, she was told she had only 40 days to live. Her son Jonathan, now 30, who is marketing director for Baltia Airlines, got a larger apartment so she could move in with him and he could care for her. He had hospice to help, as well as his sister, Margaret Hill Andrews, 26, who lives across Central Park from him. Their father had died ten years before.

"She's said that except for the fact that she's dying, this has been the most terrific time of her life," Jonathan says. "She was a workaholic, working eighteen-hour days as the founding president of the Travel Group. She had to stop work in June '91, and then she began cooking, doing needlepoint, learning to play the guitar, and holding late-night salons with her friends—philosophical discussions on dying—just having a good time. But in between she's had a stroke, she's broken her hip, and you never know whether this minute will be her last." Now it's been more than a year on a roller coaster of last breaths and revivals, and the tension has everyone exhausted, including Audrey.

SOMETHING—NO ONE CAN FIGure out what—is making Audrey hang on. Usually, when someone is as sick as Audrey is but doesn't let go, it's because of some unfinished business, says Sister Loretta Palamara, Cabrini Hospice's pastoral-care coordinator. "Sometimes when people are not dying—just hanging around—they have to hear one more thing," she says. Over the past twelve years, Sister Loretta estimates, she's been with at least 1,000 people as they've died. With Jonathan and Margaret, she spent hours trying to figure out what was worrying Audrey.

"I try to find the key that's psychologically keeping people who are ready, as she is, from going on," Loretta says. "Sometimes I'm flabbergasted to discover what it is."

Audrey died this past June. Near the end, she told her children she was waiting for her dead husband to come for her. When he did, she announced his presence to everyone. She was enormously calm for a few days, talking with him as if he were in the room. Then she said good-bye to her family and friends, and went.

"Usually," Sister Loretta says. "if you find the right thing, patients go on the spot. I've been trying to empower families to do this themselves. They have to stay open to find out what that thing is. If you're filled with judgments, you won't find anything. But if your heart is open, you will."

Children, too, have the same kind of need for finishing business and will hang on until they've tied up loose ends, or even until parents give them permission to die. But sometimes they hang on so long that it's sheer torture. "A child," says Penelope Buschman, Columbia-Presbyterian Medical Center's clinical specialist for child and adolescent psychiatric nursing, "needs to have the information on dying that he's asking for so he has time to make the plans he wants to make.

"I had a little 11-year-old girl with a brain tumor who had asked the night nurse at 2 A.M. to call her family. She had made out her will and talked to each member, her siblings and her parents, going over what things she wanted to give each of them," Buschman says. "She died the next day. She had certain work she had to complete, and she knew the time frame involved. Fortunately, she was listened to. I think children do have a sense that they are dying, so their requests are very important."

If the child is having difficulty letting go, Buschman, like Sister Loretta, tries to find the problem. "Another little girl, Elizabeth, who was 11, had become almost mute. She said, 'I want to be able to tell my mother how lonely and scared I am, and I know I'm going to die and to talk about it. She keeps wanting to cheer me up and say I'm not going to die.'

"I told the mother, 'Elizabeth wants you to just listen to her and not respond by covering it over, because she has some very important things to say.' So she did, and she just held her, and Elizabeth died soon afterward."

When children hang on, sometimes it's because they are worried about what will happen to their parents without them. They feel protective, especially children of single parents or those in difficult stepfamilies. They need to be told the parent will be okay, that it's all right for them to go.

Modern psychiatry has come to rely on carefully targeted medications, in addition to all this talk, to help people cope with the emotional pain surrounding dying. But its methods also have critics from the natural-dying movement who say that doctors interpret pre-death restlessness (groaning, tossing) or pre-death visions as a medical problem requiring psychiatric drugs rather than as psychological issues that naturally occur in dying. The restlessness is considered severe anxiety by physicians, and the visions tend to be seen as hallucinations. Sedatives and psychotropic drugs can either quiet the symptoms or take them away.

"We know from one study at Sloan-Kettering that 85 percent of all cancer patients had terminal delirium. Not all had visual hallucinations," says Dr. Jon Levenson, a psychiatrist at Columbia-Presbyterian specializing in the care of AIDS and cancer patients. "But there are times when the family can't tolerate what's happening. And the family members live on, so we try to look at the terminally ill patient as a system that includes the family. How a relative is handling the ongoing illness can dramatically affect how he or she will go on to grieve, because those last moments can be indelibly printed on that family member. So how someone dies is very important."

The psychiatric view is that these are hallucinations caused by the breakdown of body organs or the side effects of drugs. From this medical perspective—that everything is over once the body shuts down—the continuation of the family becomes more important than the journey the dying person is trying to make.

"The patient may develop delirium—which is common in the weeks before death," says Dr. Levenson. "The family may not be recognized; the patient may be hallucinating, restless and agitated. It may be that these visual hallucinations are driven by the medical process. But they can still have meaning for an individual as he attempts to cope with these perceptual disturbances."

One source of confusion is the lack of information families have on just what to expect when someone dies. Genevieve Foley and other staff members at Sloan-Kettering say that it helps to tell patients and families as much as possible about what will happen. Some patients have pre-death restlessness. Should a family opt to have the patient die at home, Foley says, there are many variables on what to expect physically. She lets family members know when to call 911, when not to, and what the legal responsibilities of these help agencies are when someone calls.

But each disease has a slightly different course. "I was talking to a man with advanced head, face, and neck cancer, and he wanted to know 'Well, how am I going to die?' " says Nessa Coyle, of Sloan-Kettering's pain control unit. "Will it be quick or slow?' They have told him he could bleed out, which would be fast if the tumor eats into an artery. I told him I don't know, but one thing I do know is that his pain will be controlled. That was a big relief to him. The days of 'Nothing more can be done' are over. The focus is changed, though. We can help patients with pain, nausea, constipation, anxiety. Low-dose morphine will control shortness of breath. If they want to die sleepy, we will let them slowly go into sleep with medication. If they want to be alert, we can do that too. We talk to them first to find out what they fear most and what their desires are, how they want to die." In terms of choice, medical care has come a long way.

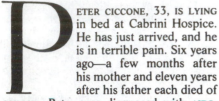

ETER CICCONE, 33, IS LYING in bed at Cabrini Hospice. He has just arrived, and he is in terrible pain. Six years ago—a few months after his mother and eleven years after his father each died of cancer—Peter was diagnosed with AIDS. He had taken care of both of his parents. Just after his mother died he met Ron Burris, 38, and fell completely in love. And there was another heartbreak.

"With Peter, it's like we're married," Ron says. "You wouldn't throw out your husband if he got sick. In all of New York I chose Peter, so why would I want to leave him when he's so sick? I like to make him smile. But you're supposed to have this happen after years of marriage, when you're 94 years old, not when you're 33. Still, you know, it's for better or worse."

In Peter's case, it has gone from worse to worse. He was one of the first AIDS patients to go on AZT after the FDA approved it. He hasn't gotten PCP or cancer—things people with AIDS normally die of—and only recently did he get wasting disease. Instead, he developed neuropathy. Peter is the only survivor of the AIDS support group he belonged to through Gay Men's Health Crisis. In some ways, Peter thinks, the others had better luck. His illness has been slow torture.

"At first, my hand started falling asleep, just out of nowhere," he says. "But after a year, my legs started going numb. The AIDS virus had started to affect the brain and central nervous system, but I didn't know that then. Soon I had pain in my legs, and I had trouble standing."

After very painful tests, the doctors determined that his illness would be progressive. "At first, I needed a cane. Then I had to stop work as a hairdresser and go on disability," he says. "I went from a cane to a walker to a wheelchair, and then I couldn't even move the chair with my hands, I was in so much pain. Nothing would help." For a year, Peter lived in a reclining chair; now he is bedridden.

"One day, I could no longer even use the commode by myself, so I held Ron, and we both broke down and cried. I decided I wanted to go to a hospice; I couldn't stand it anymore.

"I know when it hits my diaphragm, I die," Peter says, "but this pain kills. I don't want any more painful tests. There's no cure, and I'm tired of being a guinea pig. In the hospitals I have painful tests; at home, I'm just always in pain; but here

I'm in a place where I can get all the pain relief I need and I won't be treated like a leper." For this, Peter is eternally grateful.

Ron also has AIDS, but he isn't as sick yet as Peter is. Still, except for help from the gay community and now the hospice, they've had to face caring for Peter almost by themselves. Both their families—what's left of them—have had a hard time coping with their relationship, with the fact that they are both ill, with how young they are, and (for Peter's brother and sister) with so many losses. And it's been hard for Peter and Ron, both because they love and need their families and because they have since also lost many of their close friends.

"AIDS patients are different from cancer patients," says Sloan-Kettering's Nessa Coyle, echoing the sentiment of many in the medical community. "They have seen so many friends die that they have suffered multiple losses. The human spirit can take only so much. Also, they are often alienated from their families, and even though the gay community has been enormously supportive, there is pain in this."

Gay Men's Health Crisis has risen to the occasion—as it has for women, children, even grandmothers with AIDS. It provides a buddy system for shopping, dog walking and other daily needs, legal help, medical advice, a food program, and a vast array of support groups. But the cumulative grief is palpable.

"There's not really enough time to mourn," says Mark Aurigemma, until recently GMHC's spokesman. "It's not like the old view of grief, when someone important dies every five years. Here it's not uncommon for people to lose two people they love in a week and to be HIV positive themselves." They tend to cope with this by giving to others, being a volunteer when their lover has gone or their best friend isn't yet cold in the ground.

"The AIDS community is the fastest-growing spiritual mass on this planet," says Stephen Levine, who, with his wife, Ondrea, has for the past fifteen years run workshops for terminally ill patients or any person suffering from bereavement. They have written an important series of books, most notably *Who Dies?* and *Guided Meditations, Explorations and Healings.*

To help the dying, Levine has some prescriptions: Let patients be at home. These days, there are hospital and hospice programs to give support at home or to take you in quickly if things get too scary or out of hand. Also, help patients learn to use meditation on a regular basis, to keep down the spikes of agony and give the dying person some last sense of control. And even if they're in a coma, touch them and talk to them. Play music they love, perhaps; hearing is usually the last sense to go.

"Every day, things change," Levine says. "Give them the control—of their pain medication, their food, whether they want to talk, and when. Maybe have an ombudsman who protects and guards their space, since at home you can be flooded with relatives you don't want to see. One's deathbed is not the time to have to be polite. And most of all, understand that when they die, it can be very messy. Their emotional state is in flux, and so are their bodies. Just be guided by your heart. If you're with someone who's dying, just love them."

NE DAY, AT CABRINI— the hospice that sheltered both Audrey and Peter—Sister Loretta walked in to sit with a dying patient named Joseph. A young doctor—a new resident—was standing near him.

"Joseph was actively dying, and the young doctor didn't know what to do, since he'd done everything he could do, medically," Sister Loretta says. "Joseph had signed papers requesting no treatment. I pulled up a chair and began stroking his arm and talking to him gently. The doctor saw a pack of cigarettes on the TV and asked if he could take one. They were Joseph's. He wouldn't be needing them anymore, so I told him okay, I didn't think he'd mind.

"The doctor went out into the hall, smoking and pacing. He kept looking back in. Then he came back and sat there as I sang softly to Joseph and told him, 'Look for your parents. They're going to show you new playgrounds.' Boy, was I nervous. I'd never had a doctor watch me before. But I kept on.

"All of a sudden, Joseph smiled, tried to sit up, and held out his arms. 'Sister,' he said, 'I see them.' I asked who. 'My parents,' he told me. 'And they're just as beautiful as you said.' Right after that, he died.''

Just then, Sister Loretta said, the doctor's beeper went off and he started to run out of the room. She asked if he wanted the cigarettes. He called back that he didn't smoke. She sat with Joseph about ten minutes longer, still stroking him. Then she went to find the young doctor.

"I wondered how he was, because he seemed so nervous. 'I know you've seen death before,' I said.

" 'Sister,' he told me, 'I've seen deaths, but only in emergency situations. It's always been so frenetic and violent. Never so peaceful like that. You know, if people have to die, everyone should be able to die like that.' ''

DIMENSIONS OF DYING

Yale doctors are helping their patients talk about death—and are hearing a lot they didn't learn in medical school.

Bruce Fellman

The last time Mary Kathleen Figaro talked to Noel (not her real name), a cancer patient at Yale-New Haven Hospital, the woman was close to death. And yet, said Figaro, who this fall entered her third year at the School of Medicine, although the end was clearly in sight, Noel, an emigrant from Barbados who was in her early 30s, was not brooding about the past. "She kept on talking about going to immigration—she was looking directly at the future," explained Figaro. "It was obvious she wasn't going to make it, and she knew that, I guess, but against all odds, she was dreaming of a future. She taught me that you could have hope even in a hopeless situation."

Noel died only weeks after her first conversation with Figaro, but not before providing the future physician with numerous other insights about the nature of the doctor-patient relationship at the end of, as well as throughout, life. But this "mentorship" was not simply the result of a happenstance meeting in a cancer ward. The women came to know each other because of an innovative and, according to a recent survey of 111 U.S. medical schools that appeared in the journal *Academic Medicine,* a unique approach to the once-taboo topic of death and dying.

The "Seminar on the Seriously Ill Patient," developed in 1986 by Medical School chaplain Alan C. Mermann '79MDiv, is an elective course, usually taken in the first year, that pairs each student in the class with someone who is dying. As a result of frequent conversations between acolyte and mentor—often several times a week over the course of a semester—along with readings, weekly discussions with peers, and plenty of private soul-searching, a doctor-to-be develops an understanding of what to say, what not to say, and when to say nothing at all.

"This is learnable information," says Mermann, who is also a pediatrician. "But first, you have to have some direct, personal experience."

A sizable number of students come to the course having had no experience whatsoever with death. "I'd never even been to a funeral," notes Michael Fischer, who is going into his second year as a medical student.

Fischer's teacher was a women in her mid-30s who was battling recurrent cervical cancer, and he recalls sitting with her while she underwent chemotherapy. "Her treatment was pretty routine and uncomplicated, but for her, it was *everything,*" he explains, adding that he can now see how easy it would be to lose sight of a patient's perspective. "I just tried to be there for her to talk to, and I came away from our conversations with an understanding of what it's like to be dealing with pain, extended disability, the stigma of having cancer, and mortality. I hope I can keep that knowledge on file."

At most medical schools, these lessons in listening are hard to come by because the curriculum generally calls for little more than a few formal lectures on various aspects of end-stage diseases and a talk by a terminally ill patient or two about what it's like to be dying. And while Mermann feels that this modest approach is infinitely better than the way the subject was treated when he was in school in the 1950s—typically, it was ignored— he argues that students and, ultimately, society will be better served by providing physicians-to-be with direct contact with patients whose care can bring out the best—and worst—in the medical establishment. "One hopes this experience will make them better doctors," says Mermann, who is quick to add that he hasn't done any follow-up studies.

Annie Egan '92MD doesn't need statistics to know how crucial the Yale course was for her. Now a senior resident in pediatrics at the Children's Hospital of Pittsburgh, Egan took the seminar in 1988 and was mentored by a woman in her early 30s who was dying of advanced lymphoma. "There's a saying around medicine that you learn the most from the sickest patients, and though her experience as an adult was very different from what I deal with in pediatrics, there was at least one lesson I've carried with me," Egan explains. "I learned that the most important thing in the relationship was honesty."

There was another critical lesson. In telling her life's story, Egan's teacher talked about how her boyfriend had left her as soon as her cancer was diagnosed and how she'd had to move in with her mother. "I'd had a fair amount of experience with death in my own family," says Egan, explaining that in her case, the family came closer together each time one of its own died. In her teacher's case, however, the family disintegrated.

3. THE DYING PROCESS

One night while Egan was on call at the Children's Hospital, an 8-year-old was brought in with blood in his urine. The mother was in tears, the pediatrician recalls, complaining that no one, including her child's doctor, would give her a straight answer about what was wrong. An X-ray showed an ominous mass, probably a bladder tumor, and it fell to Egan to deliver the news.

There are doctors who would do so and then disappear, but Egan faced the family members directly. "I told them, 'Your life has now profoundly changed, and it's time to reach out for help.' My teacher made me acutely aware of the fragility of family structure in a medical crisis, and how you have to treat the family, not just the patient. I wouldn't have thought of that before taking the course."

Too often in what one physician has dubbed the "high-tech wasteland" of modern medicine, the essential twin skills of empathy and listening get lost, says Mermann. There are many reasons.

Chief among them is what professors at the Medical School frequently call the "third-year syndrome." Mermann explains that students, most of whom entered medicine with the altruistic motive of caring for the sick, often "run smack into disillusionment" in the third year of schooling when they begin the clinical portion of their education and have to shift their focus to technique. "They see patients winding up as little more than numbers, even called disparaging names like 'scum bag' and 'dirt ball,' and this leaves students startled and upset," says Mermann.

Of course, a certain amount of detachment is essential, both for sound medical judgment and for psychological survival, but there is an ever-present danger that detachment will become what is technically known as alexithymia, the inability to feel emotion. Worse still, in the ever-faster-paced world of the hospital where most doctors learn the trade, there is, increasingly, too little time to develop any kind of relationship with someone who will eventually be well, let alone someone who is dying.

"A hospital like Yale-New Haven is simply a very difficult place to carry out the care of a terminally ill patient," says Gerard Burrow, dean of the Medical School. "The whole place is set up to run on a 24-hour-a-day, battle-station type arrangement." Still, those doctors who avoid becoming shell-shocked and continue to have the "healer's touch" tend to be lionized by those who are in their care. Horror stories abound about the physician who walks in, looks at the chart, and doesn't even ask a patient's name. "Compare this," says Mermann, "to the doctor who sits down on your bed, takes your hand, and asks, 'How are you this morning?' The amount of time the physician is in the room is exactly the same—you're still getting 37 seconds—but to the patient, the difference between the two doctors is phenomenal."

Never is the difference more noticeable than when someone is dying, and yet at that time, a physician's response is frequently to pull back, even vanish. Medical students, notes Mermann, are understandably anxious about confronting death, but this *timor mortis*—"the fear of death"—often persists among the doctors who are training them. And since, as Dean Burrow notes, students in their clinical training learn primarily by example, it is not surprising that they too come to avoid this painful subject.

Another barrier to dealing with the dying is that many physicians see death as a sign that they've failed. That syndrome is outlined in detail in the recent bestselling book, *How We Die: Reflections on Life's Final Chapter* (Alfred A. Knopf, 1994). Written by Sherwin B. Nuland '55MD, an associate clinical professor of surgery at Yale, it explains that while doctors are exhaustively trained to solve what the author terms "the riddle" of disease, admitting defeat in the face of the inevitable and providing care without cure are rarely part of the modern physician's education—or inclination.

Mermann's popular course, which last year was taken by nearly half of the Medical School's first-year students, is designed to create a cadre of doctors who, having seen the effects of a terminal illness through the eyes of a patient, are less likely to break, however inadvertently, a central tenet of the physician's creed: First, do no harm.

And harm can indeed result from what amounts to a fundamental failure to communicate. Nuland, who has more than 30 years of surgical experience, recounts numerous instances of "heroic" lifesaving interventions, not all of which turned out to be, from the patient's point of view, wise or even desirable. "Doctors really believe in their own beneficence, and they think that whatever recommendation they make is the right one for their patient," notes Nuland. "But that's an enormous obstacle to reality because it means that physicians approach the patient's problem with a whole different set of values than those of the patient."

As an illustration, Nuland relates the case of a 92-year-old woman he calls "Hazel Welch," who arrived at YNHH unconscious, a victim of a perforated digestive tract. Already afflicted with severe arthritis, gangrene, and arteriosclerosis—her leukemia was in remission—Miss Welch, when she regained consciousness after treatment in the hospital's emergency room, refused surgery. "In a broad Yankee inflection, she told me that she had been on this planet 'quite long enough, young man' and didn't wish to go on," Nuland writes.

The doctor heard what the patient was saying, but didn't absorb its importance. "How can you let someone die when you think you can save her? It made no sense," Nuland explains. So, deliberately minimizing the post-operative difficulties his patient would face, he talked her into agreeing to the surgery, which she survived, only to die from a stroke, probably brought on by the procedure, two weeks later.

From his current vantage point as a retired, 63-year-old surgeon, Nuland views his intervention in the case of Hazel Welch as clearly inappropriate. "Had I the chance to relive this episode, or some others like it in my career, I would listen more to the patient and ask her less to listen to me," he says.

Nevertheless, he would have operated. "The accepted code of my specialty demanded it," he says. "My treatment in this case was based not on her goal but on mine. I pursued a form of futility that deprived her of the particular kind of hope she had longed for—the hope that she could leave this world without interference when an opportunity arose.

Doctors who don't know their patients—a common circumstance in the tertiary-care hospitals where most people now come to die—are particularly likely to pursue what ironically is a hopeless path. "We take away their clothes, and, as Eric Cassell, a practicing internist, has said, we take away their personhood—we don't see patients in their setting," Nuland says. "But you make one house call, and your viewpoint of a patient changes so much. You see a crucifix, look at certain kinds of books, hear bits of conversation, walk up three flights of steps, and you understand things you never understood. Only a doctor who knows that house, and knows the person who lived there—and not a doctor who met the patient on the day the kidneys began to fail—can help that person make decisions about life and death."

Nuland, and many others who are embroiled in the debate over the direction of health care in the U.S., argues for the creation of a new breed of family practice doctor: a cradle-to-grave physician who is trained to radiate the empathy embodied in a Norman Rockwell portrait as well as to deal with most health problems in his or her own office, while acting as a broker when there is a need for specialists. However, current trends in medicine—like the push toward health maintenance organizations with their constantly changing cast of care-givers—and the mobility of the American public, make the return of the family doctor more of a fantasy than a realistic prospect. Says gastroenterologist Howard Spiro, professor of medicine and director of the Medical School's Program for Humanities in Medicine: "We're all strangers taking care of strangers. Everyone ought to have some family physician or nurse practitioner out there who does know you, but the notion that you'll always know your doctor is hopelessly romantic."

All of which—the reluctance to confront death, the need to keep fighting it, and the conflict of interests—can conspire to place terminally ill patients and their families in a nightmarish limbo, a lonely place from which the likes of Jack Kevorkian and his suicide machine sometimes seem to offer the only hope of easy escape.

"We don't accept death as a natural phenomenon," says author, retired surgeon, and Yale professor Richard Selzer. "This is wrong."

But some 20 years ago, Morris Wessel, clinical professor of pediatrics, Florence Wald, former dean of the School of Nursing, and a number of colleagues created an alternative when they started the first hospice in this country. Modeled after the nursing-intensive approach to dying that was pioneered in England by Cicely Saunders in the 1960s, the hospice was developed to offer, either in a specially designed facility or, when possible, in the home, a kind of care that was radically different from what existed in hospitals.

There comes a point when nothing more—no additional testing, surgery, or any of the myriad other procedures in the medical arsenal—can be done to reverse the inevitable. "At a hospice, we help patients and families deal with the end," says Robert Donaldson, a Yale professor of medicine and a doctor at Connecticut Hospice, Inc., which is located in Branford. "We provide support, relief from symptoms, particularly pain, and the assurance that we're here, no matter what," says Donaldson. "If you don't do that, you haven't finished your job as physician."

Death can be hideous, cruel, and utterly capricious, but when the pace of life's final journey is somewhat stately, even predictable, the hospice—there are now more than 2,000 in this country—offers what many consider the closest thing to a "good death" on this planet. "The surroundings are pleasant, and the rules are loose—if you want to have a beer, so be it, says Donaldson, noting that right until the end, patients retain their personhood. "And they're so relieved to get out of the stream of diagnostic technology, where they're punctured and invaded all the time.

Less treatment and more caring may be just what the doctor ordered—or should order, says Donaldson. "The patients are grateful, because I can provide what they need. I find that very enriching."

To every thing there is a season.

So notes the Old Testament book of Ecclesiastes, and in the modern debate over how to best care for the dying, that ancient declaration provides worthwhile advice, says Richard Selzer, a retired New Haven surgeon and former Yale professor whose most recent book, *Raising the Dead,* offers an intimate look at the author's own harrowing and near-fatal brush with Legionnaire's disease. "We don't accept death as a natural phenomenon—this is wrong," says Selzer, acknowledging the irony in his statement. For had the 67-year-old physician's doctors been more accepting, he wouldn't be around to tell his tale.

While there is a time to die, says the author of Ecclesiastes, precisely when is now a matter that modern medicine has taken largely out of the hands of God and nature. But just as the women's movement helped reclaim birth from the medical establishment, patients are asserting their formerly God-given right to a decent end. At Yale, doctors-to-be are gradually learning to listen.

Peter Bernstein '86, '91MD, took Mermann's course in 1987 as a kind of test. "I was afraid that I couldn't deal with sick or dying people," says Bernstein, now chief resident in obstetrics and gynecology at YNHH. So he was terrified when he met "Bob," a man in his 40s who was losing his fight with a long-term illness. Over the course of a semester, the student sat with his teacher through CAT scans, transfusions, and the interminable waits for appointments. "Seeing Bob go through all this opened me up to the idea that explaining things and just sitting with a patient is really important," notes Bernstein, recalling his grandfather, a pediatrician who practiced medicine in the days before antibiotics when often the best thing a doctor could do was hold a patient's hand. "I'm still learning as a doctor, but my real education began with Bob."

A DECADE BEYOND MEDICAL SCHOOL: A LONGITUDINAL STUDY OF PHYSICIANS' ATTITUDES TOWARD DEATH AND TERMINALLY-ILL PATIENTS

GEORGE E. DICKINSON and ROBERT E. TOURNIER

Department of Sociology and Anthropology, College of Charleston, Charleston, SC 29424, U.S.A.

Abstract—Physicians were surveyed soon after graduation from medical school in 1976 to determine their attitudes toward death and terminally-ill patients and their families. A follow-up survey of the 1093 respondents was made in 1986 to ascertain if changes had occurred in their attitudes. Eight of the eleven Likert-type items showed statistically significant differences over time and by attitudes toward terminally-ill patients and their families. These data present evidence to suggest that physicians in 1986 were more open in telling dying patients their prognosis than in 1976.

Key words—physicians, attitudes, dying patients

Practicing physicians in nearly every specialty of medicine must from time to time deal with patients who are dying or have a life threatening disease. Many young doctors have difficulty facing their own feelings about death since this can be very stressful [1]. Therefore, Herman Feifel [2] hypothesized that physicians enter medicine because of their own above-average fear of death and try to conquer this fear by entering a profession where dying and death are rather frequent. Medical schools have traditionally not allocated much time and effort to helping students relate to terminally-ill patients and their families, though recent trends are encouraging [3]. Physicians receive limited training in learning to communicate easily with patients, and nowhere are some physicians' difficulties with communication more exposed than when they are dealing with those who are very sick. Death creates problems, not the least of which are the emotional reactions to death and difficulties in acknowledging its inevitability for all. Through their body language and deliberate avoidance of the issue, doctors can send the message that these concerns are not within the medical province.

Young physicians may focus so much on trying to acquire the science of medicine that they ignore the art—the human face—of medicine. In medical training it is necessary for medical students to develop technical skills necessary to deal efficiently with illness. During this period, however, and without appropriate training and acknowledgement of the feelings elicited by medical work, it is likely that responses harmful to both physician and patients will develop [4]. Weston and Lipkin [5] note:

Physicians may have a staggering knowledge of disease but be naive about human suffering; they may know precise drug treatment but stand empty-handed and mute before the patient who desperately needs counsel and support to cope with a terminal illness; they may be masters of medicine's remarkable biotechnical resources but lack power to heal the human spirit.

As Coombs [6] observes, becoming a doctor requires more than learning a body of knowledge and a set of skills; it also requires a significant transformation in the person of the student.

The current study is an effort to note the impact of the passage of time, a decade of having to confront death and increasing personal and professional maturity on the attitudes of physicians toward death and terminally-ill patients and their families.

METHODOLOGY

Graduates of the classes of 1972–1975 from five geographically distributed medical schools (University of Southern California, University of Colorado, Vanderbilt University, Pennsylvania State University and Yale University) were selected to receive a questionnaire to determine attitudes toward dying patients. These schools came from a 1975 survey [7] of curricula in death education in the 113 medical schools in the United States. Of the 107 responding schools, these five were the only programs offering a thanatology course for the previous four years.

Names of the graduates were obtained from the American Medical Association in Chicago. The questionnaire was refined by a panel of judges consisting of fifteen current medical students and recent medical school graduates and mailed to the 1664 physicians in the fall of 1976 with three follow-up mailings to nonrespondents. Using the *American Medical Association Directory* to obtain current addresses, the same survey was mailed again in 1986 to respondents of the first survey to determine if their attitudes toward death and terminally-ill patients and their families had changed in the decade. Both surveys were accompanied by a cover letter and a self-addressed stamped envelope.

Respondents were asked to indicate the degree to which they agree or disagree with each of eleven Likert-type items on a five-point scale ranging from strongly agree to strongly disagree with a neutral choice in the middle (1 = strongly agree and 5 = strongly disagree). Listed below are the statements which concerned attitudes toward death and reactions toward dying patients and their families:

1. When one of my patients dies, I always wonder if something could have been done to save him/her. (Wonder)
2. I feel as comfortable with a dying patient as I do with any other patient. (Comfortable)
3. I do not think about death very much. (Think)
4. Treating a dying patient is one of the most unpleasant aspects of my profession. (Unpleasant)
5. Whenever possible, I avoid a person who is dying from an irreversible condition. (Avoid)
6. I try to avoid telling a patient directly that he/she is dying. (Tell)
7. I find it more difficult to deal with the family of a dying patient than with families of my other patients. (Family)
8. A patient's death does not depress me when I know there was nothing I could do to save him/her. (Depress)
9. Telling a person he/she is going to die is difficult for me. (Difficult)
10. I believe physicians refer terminal patients to other physicians more often than nonterminal patients in order to avoid having to deal with their dying. (Refer)
11. I think it is essential that a dying patient be told of his/her prognosis. (Pt Told)

The mean and standard deviation for each variable was calculated, and a t-test was run for each pair of variables to test the significance of the changes in the Likert-type items over time.

RESULTS

Of the 1540 questionnaires received (124 were returned because of wrong addresses) by the intended respondents in 1976, 1093 usable questionnaires were returned (71% return rate). For the 1986 mailing, respondents from the first mailing were surveyed to determine if changes had occurred in their attitudes toward death and terminally-ill patients and their families. Nonrespondents from 1976 were omitted since possible change over time was our concern. A 55% response rate was achieved from the 1986 mailing. In both surveys 90% of the respondents were male and 10% female. The average age of the respondents in the 1986 survey was 38.74 with a range of 34–55 years.

As can be noted in Table 1, statistically significant differences were noted with 8 of the 11 attitudinal

statements toward death and terminally-ill patients and their families. No significant changes were noted from 1976 to 1986 with three items: "Treating a dying patient is one of the most unpleasant aspects of my profession"; "Whenever possible, I avoid a person who is dying from an irreversible condition"; and "A patient's death does not depress me when I know there was nothing I could do to save him/her". Thus, the unpleasantness of treating a dying patient, the avoidance of a dying patient, and being depressed over the death of a patient seem to have remained unchanged with these physicians over the decade.

Significant shifts in attitudes toward *agreement* occurred between 1976 and 1986 with these two statements. "When one of my patients dies, I always wonder if something could have been done to save him/her" showed more agreement in 1986 than a decade before. This statement likely reflects professional maturity and increased competence by the physicians after ten years of practicing medicine.

The other statement with responses shifting toward agreement between 1976 and 1986 was: "I think it is essential that a dying patient be told of his/her prognosis". Earlier in one's career, a physician might have more of a sense of shielding the patient, whereas with more experience, one is perhaps less protective. In the intervening decade one becomes more accustomed to dealing with death and/or is forced to come to grips wth attitudes toward death. Increased attention to death and dying education could also accelerate this transformation.

Such a change is also not surprising in light of the American Medical Association's shift in policy in 1980 of encouraging physicians to tell the patient his/her prognosis.* Previously, the AMA had left the decision to tell to the discretion of the physician: 'therapeutic privilege' (physician shared what he/she thought was best for the patient—'privilege' of telling what one wished to tell).

Rather than the change being the result of the AMA policy shift, perhaps the AMA's policy was simply confirming what was already taking place. For example, in 1979 Novack, Plumer and Smith [8] repeated a survey earlier conducted by Oken in 1961 and found that 97% of the 264 physicians respond-

---

*The current position of the AMA is "the physician must properly inform the patient of the diagnosis and of the nature and purpose of the treatment undertaken or prescribed. The physician may not refuse to so inform the patient".

Table 1. Physicians' attitudes toward death and terminally-ill patients and their families: 1976–1986

Likert item	1976			1986			
	Mean	SD	N	Mean	SD	N	Significance
1. Wonder	3.864	0.986	1062	2.174	1.004	644	<0.001
2. Comfort	2.489	0.995	1071	3.246	1.083	646	<0.001
3. Think	2.673	1.049	1075	3.233	0.990	651	<0.001
4. Unpleasant	3.436	1.105	1069	3.374	1.109	642	NS
5. Avoid	4.024	0.825	1067	4.056	0.834	648	NS
6. Tell	3.576	1.117	1058	3.799	0.998	638	<0.001
7. Family	3.022	1.150	1068	3.217	1.116	645	0.001
8. Depress	2.879	1.151	1068	2.856	1.127	648	NS
9. Difficult	2.175	0.905	1061	2.300	0.924	641	0.007
10. Refer	2.825	1.024	1063	2.968	1.009	647	0.005
11. Pt Told	3.895	1.012	1062	2.022	0.930	648	<0.001

ing indicated a preference for telling the person the details of the diagnosis, whereas the original study by Oken had indicated that 90% of physicians in the survey did *not* favor telling a cancer patient his/her diagnosis. A similar study published in 1980 by Hardy [9] reported on a survey of 185 practicing Tennessee physicians regarding their communication patterns with cancer patients and found that 98% indicated that they always or usually inform patients that they have cancer. Klenow and Youngs [10] concluded that in the 1980s informing the patient of his or her prognosis became a widespread tendency. A 1991 study by Seale [11] in England suggests a general preference for openness about illness and death, tempered by the consideration that bad news needs to be broken slowly in a context of support, while recognizing that not everyone wishes to know all.

The majority of changes in attitudes over the decade by these physicians was toward *disagreement*. In 1986 these physicians disagreed more with the statement "I feel as comfortable with a dying patient as I do with any other patient". This finding is certainly consistent with the conclusions of a study by Joyce Cochrane [12] of 99 oncologists: the respondents with more years of experience as physicians and more years of experience of caring for dying patients reported feeling less comfortable with dying patients than with other patients.

"I do not think about death very much" was also disagreed to more in 1986 than in 1976. This tends to agree with the finding of increased discomfort with dying patients after more years of practice: these physicians are apparently getting more anxious about death the longer they practice.

"I try to avoid telling a patient directly that he/she is dying" revealed more disagreement by physicians in 1986 than a decade earlier. This is consistent with the finding of more physicians finding it essential to tell the patient in 1986 than in 1976 of his/her prognosis.

"Telling a patient he/she is going to die is difficult for me" was disagreed to more in 1986 than earlier. This is consistent with less avoidance of telling the patient the prognosis.

More physicians disagreed with the statement "I find it more difficult to deal with the family of a dying patient than with families of my other patients" in 1986 than soon after graduating from medical school. Apparently, with more practice the physicians in this survey are feeling better about their relationships with families of terminally-ill patients. Likewise, more disagreement was revealed in 1986 in response to the statement "I believe physicians refer terminal patients to other physicians more often than nonterminal patients in order to avoid having to deal with their dying".

CONCLUSIONS

In comparing physicians' responses to Likert-type items on attitudes toward death and terminally-ill patients and their families between 1976, soon after graduating from medical school, and 1986, signifi-

cant changes occurred. After ten years of practice, physicians felt it more essential that a dying patient be told his/her prognosis, were therefore less likely to avoid telling the patient, and found telling the patient to be less difficult in 1986. These findings support the general trend of the 1980s and 1990s of the consumer's right to know his/her prognosis.

Physicians in 1986 believed that doctors were less likely to refer dying patients to other physicians to avoid dealing with them and found it less difficult to deal with the family of the dying patient than these physicians felt in 1976. Thus, one might suggest that contact makes the physician more familiar, and thus more at ease. However, compared to physicians in 1976, doctors in 1986 felt less comfortable with dying patients, thought about death more and were more likely to wonder if they could have saved the patient.

These findings suggest that differences occurred in doctors' attitudes toward death and terminally-ill patients and their families over a decade. Perhaps the most conclusive finding is that physicians in 1986 tended to show more of an openness toward informing the patient of his/her prognosis than in 1976, a finding in agreement with other recent research. Thus, it appears that the patient is the beneficiary of these changes over time.

REFERENCES

1. Firth C. J. Emotional distress in junior house officers. *Br. Med. J.* **295,** 533–536, 1987.
2. Feifel H. Death. In *Taboo Topics* (Edited by Faberow L.). Atherton Press, New York, 1963.
3. Mermann A. C., Gunn D. B. and Dickinson G. E. Learning to care for the dying: a survey of medical schools and a model course. *Acad. Med.* **66,** 35–38, 1991.
4. Black D., Hardoff D. and Nelki J. Educating medical students about death and dying. *Arch. Dis. Childhood* **64,** 750–753, 1989.
5. Weston W. W. and Lipkin M. Doctors learning communication skills: developmental issues. In *Communicating with Medical Patients* (Edited by Stewart M. and Roter D.). Sage Publications, London, 1989.
6. Coombs R. H. *Mastering Medicine: Professional Socialization in Medical School.* Free Press, New York, 1978.
7. Dickinson G. E. Death education in U.S. medical schools. *J. Med. Educ.* **51,** 134–136, 1976.
8. Novack D. H., Plumer R. and Smith R. L. Changes in physicians' attitudes toward telling the cancer patient. *J. Am. Med. Assoc.* **241,** 897–900, 1979.
9. Hardy R. E., Green D. R., Jordan H. W. and Hardy G. Communication between cancer patients and physicians. *Southern Med. J.* **73,** 755–757, 1980.
10. Klenow D. J. and Youngs G. A. Changes in doctor/patient communication of a terminal prognosis: a selective review and critique. *Death Studies* **11,** 263–277, 1987.
11. Seale C. Communication and awareness about death: a study of a random sample of dying people. *Soc. Sci. Med.* **32,** 943–952, 1991.
12. Cochrane J. B., Levy M. R., Fryer J. E. and Oglesby C. A. Death anxiety, disclosure behaviors, and attitudes of oncologists toward terminal care. *Omega* **22,** 1–12, 1990–1991.

Attitudes to death and bereavement among cultural minority groups

Caroline Walker, SRN, SCM, DipN (Lond.)

Ms Walker wrote this study as part of her JBCNS course. She is a student health visitor at Oxford Polytechnic.

As members of a caring team both in community and hospital nursing, it is helpful to know something of the cultural background of the patients we are to care for. This is especially important when caring for the terminally ill patient and in supporting his family and friends.

In times of great stress a person will lean towards his own culturally acquired ways of coping which may seem strange to people of a different culture. We should try to ensure that the patient is allowed to die his own death[1], not one imposed upon him by someone else. In hospital there can be conflict between the routine of ward work and an individual's expectations which can lead to fear as well as loss of dignity and identity.

Culture and religion

Culture can be described as a way of living of people of a particular group[2]. Therefore, to understand a person's attitude to death and bereavement, one must have an idea of his philosophy of life. In this respect it is difficult to separate cultural influences from religious beliefs; described in *The Concise Oxford Dictionary* as the recognition of a superhuman controlling power of a personal God entitled to obedience, and the effect of such recognition on personal conduct and mental attitude.

The extended family is the centre of all Asian cultures and has a very strong influence on behaviour and outlook

---

It is interesting to note that for the majority of our population, in death more than any other event, religious tradition holds a monopoly. Many infants are not christened, many marriages take place in register offices, but it is very rare for funeral ceremonies not to be accompanied by religious rites. However, under 20% of people appear regularly to practise religious devotions. Orthodox Christianity teaches that the soul continues to exist after death but 25% of the population firmly state that they do not believe in a future life of any kind, 25% are uncertain and only 15% are sure of a future existence[3]. This appears to be a contradiction between what is normal funeral ceremonial practice, usually based on the belief of some form of afterlife and what the majority of people would state and practice as their normal religious beliefs. In effect, the majority of people turn, at times of great stress, towards the religion of their culture despite their usual apathy towards it.

Cultural traditions change far more slowly in respect of social structure and personal relationships than in any other aspect. This is important to remember in health care as failure to allow the individual to exercise traditional and religious responsibilities, perhaps in the form of ritual ceremonies at important family events (such as birth and death), can result in feelings of guilt and failure[2].

Of immigrant residents only 3% form a cultural minority. It is also very significant to note that the majority of these people are in the under 40 age group[4]. As the average life expectancy is 'three score years and ten', in generations to come those involved in health care will undoubtedly have more contact with death among cultural minority groups than they do at present.

Experience of death

Among the minority groups from third world countries (the Asian and African continents in particular, but also the West Indies) natural death has been a much more common experience, particularly for the older generation. The majority of people would not have reached adulthood without experiencing the death of a close relative. Death did not hold the mystery or taboo that it does to many people today, and this seems to enable them to cope with it more easily. There is an expected pattern of behaviour for the bereaved. Rites performed for the dead have important effects for the living[3] resulting in less fear of death for an individual and easier adjustment for the bereaved. This is something that I witnessed many times when working with the Shona people in Zimbabwe where death was more common among all age groups but particularly so in young children and babies than in western societies.

Asian culture

There are 4–5000 Asians living in Oxford, mostly from Pakistan and Bangladesh with a smaller group originating from East Africa. It is important to remember that they have come from very different social, educational and economic backgrounds. While sharing many basic values and attitudes, they have certain differences—a Sikh from the Punjab and a Moslem from Bangladesh may have as little in common as a Protestant from Sweden and a Catholic from Spain but are grouped together as Asian[5].

Most Asians originating from the Indian sub-continent come from rural areas while those from East Africa come from towns and cities, mostly from commercial backgrounds but with great variation in wealth[5].

Extended family system

The extended family is the centre of all Asian cultures and has a very strong influence on behaviour and outlook. Each member considers himself as a part of the extended family group rather than as an independent individual; important decisions cannot be made without consultation with the whole family. This can create problems when the head of the family group is still resident in India.

Illness is traditionally the responsibility of the whole family and the obligation to take part in appropriate celebrations of family events is binding on all members of the group, not just the closest relatives, as in British society. As a result, hospital admission in illness may appear as rejection of the patient by the family, leaving the individual to the mercy of strangers in a strange and often forbidding environment[2].

The attitude to old people is also different. Factors which a British family may find difficult to accept and cope with, such as confusion, incontinence and overcrowded accommodation, are happily contained within the extended Asian family. The elderly are respected, their dependence accepted and rarely would the family consider not caring for them at home. However, it is important to remember that at present there are relatively few old people in the Asian community.

Attitudes to medical care

Many Asians have a fear of hospitals because of the differences in medical care experienced in their country of origin. On the whole, only the very seriously ill are admitted to hospital and the practical care is very different. The idea of bed rest is a good example. Most Asians feel that the sick (including postoperative patients and after childbirth) should stay in bed as long as possible with minimum activity. Therefore they become very distressed when encouraged to mobilise. There is also a great fear of catching a chill when ill, so they do not usually take cold drinks, they wrap up well and do not like to bathe too much.

A sick person is expected to express anxiety and suffering openly, he is not expected to be cheerful or active, so that the idea of active rehabilitation and physiotherapy in illness is considered very odd. In our culture, a very ill person, particularly in the terminal stages, will only expect immediate family or very close

friends to intrude on what is often considered a very private situation. However, in the Asian community the opposite situation prevails, the whole family feeling bound to visit as often as possible.

The family expect to play a major part in supporting the sick person, usually day and night, and like to undertake much of the bedside nursing care[5]. If this is not allowed, the family can be made to feel neglectful and very guilty and it may well make it more difficult later to come to terms with the death of the patient. A sick person should never be left alone.

Many Asian women fear being examined by a male; they should be attended by females whenever possible. Male doctors should always be chaperoned and unnecessary removal of undergarments avoided. In the home, Asian women would prefer examinations to be made in complete privacy and any interpreters should be of the same sex as the patient. A mixed hospital ward would be very distressing for an Asian patient. In some cultures, especially among Moslems, nurses are held in low esteem, because their job involves physical contact with the opposite sex, and this can sometimes account for the attitude of Asian patients towards nursing staff[5].

If we are to care adequately and compassionately for the terminally ill patient, all these feelings must be taken into consideration both on a practical and emotional level. Tact and flexibility will be necessary while taking into consideration the feelings of other patients.

To most Asians, religion is a natural part of life. Most traditions have a religious significance by which people will judge themselves and others[5]. These traditions will become particularly important in stressful times such as serious illness, death and bereavement.

The Moslem community

The majority of the Asians in Oxford belong to the Moslem community whose faith is Islam, founded in the seventh century by the prophet Mohammed. Their philosophy is based on the 'Five Pillars of Islam' with Friday as the holy day when prayer is particularly important. Prayer is always preceded by a ritual cleansing and the head must face towards Mecca (south-east). Everyone is accountable to God for what he does on earth, and when he dies he will be judged and rewarded or punished in the life hereafter. Therefore if a patient is unable to adhere to his religious duties great distress may result, particularly to a person who feels that he is soon to be judged.

It may be necessary to rearrange the furniture so that the patient can face Mecca. Personal hygiene is very important to Moslem people as it is linked with spiritual purity. They prefer to wash in running water, women usually do not undress completely but wear a special petticoat and the left hand is always used for washing after toilet purposes and considered 'unclean'.

A patient's bed-table and food should always be placed in reach of the right hand. Food regulations are strict—all pork and alcohol are prohibited. Moslems are vegetarian outside the home, as meat should be ritually prepared.

When a Moslem is dying, a relative or another person of the same faith recites appropriate verses from the Koran so that these are the last words heard by the person. The custom of undertakers is foreign to most Asian people and it may be difficult to enable the family to attend to their duties while conforming to the legal regulations.

It is usual for the family to wash and prepare the body, so other attendants should, wearing gloves, straighten the body and remove any drainage tubes; the head of the deceased being turned towards the left shoulder, so that the person can be buried facing Mecca[6].

A member of the family of the same sex will wash the body, preferably at home, reciting special passages from the Koran. The body is then clothed in white and buried without a coffin within 24 hours of death. The men take the body to the mosque or graveside for further prayers before burial, the body facing towards Mecca and the grave unmarked.

Moslems are opposed to cremation and also to post-mortem examinations. In Islam a person is not the owner of his body so no part of it should be cut out or harmed, so organ donation is not allowed. It is very difficult to comply with all these customs and consequently very devout Moslems may go to the expense of taking their dead home to be buried[5].

The grave is visited every Friday for 40 days and alms are given to the poor. The whole family comes together to show grief, a period of unconcealed sorrow is considered necessary to allow the grief to heal. A widow is not expected to be brave or to be in control of her feelings and there is an obligation for the family to visit her and share in the mourning.

When a Moslem is dying, a relative or another person of the same faith recites appropriate verses from the Koran so that these are the last words heard by the person

---

The Hindu community

There is a small Hindu group in Oxford and a temple at the home of one of the leaders. The Hindu faith is centred on the transmigration of the soul with indefinite reincarnation. When a person dies, that person is born again as another child in another place on earth. The new body a person gets depends upon what sort of life he has led. If they are good they will have whole bodies in the next life, but if not they will have some defect such as being deaf, dumb or blind. As the soul moves from body to body it hopes to become purer and purer until in the end it reaches God[7].

Again prayer is important, with ritual cleansing, and the left hand is considered 'unclean'. The feelings of loss of dignity, and fear of affecting the quality of one's next life can be very great if religious customs cannot be adhered to. There are strict dietary regulations, both beef and pork are banned and many Hindus are vegetarians.

Hindu women wear a nuptial thread around the neck and sometimes a red mark on the forehead—these should not be removed. A male may have a sacred thread around the arm indicating attainment of adult religious status—it will cause great distress if this is removed. In the case of a dying patient the Hindu priest will tie a thread round the neck or wrist to indicate that a blessing has been given—again this should not be removed. Readings from the *Bhagavad Gita* give great comfort to the dying person. A Hindu person would usually prefer to die at home and may wish to be on the floor, near to mother earth[7].

The eldest son is responsible for the funeral arrangements (in India he sets fire to the funeral pyre) so it is very important to a Hindu to have a surviving son to perform these rites. There is no ritual washing of the body, so this can be performed by nursing staff. Cremation is usual and the ashes are traditionally scattered on water. The Ganges is the Hindu holy river and some devout people may wish the ashes to be sent home to the holy city of Benares for the ashes to be scattered in the Ganges[8].

There is a set pattern of mourning, relatives and friends visiting regularly to comfort the close family and to offer gifts of money, food and clothes. A final service is held on the 11th day called the kriya—the priest recites: 'Death is certain for the born, rebirth is certain for the dead: you should not grieve for what is unavoidable'[8].

Sikh community

There is a small group of Sikhs in Oxford, mostly from the Punjab area

117

of India. Their faith is a combination of elements of both Hindu and Mosem beliefs but tends to be more flexible. It was founded in 1469. They share the Hindu belief in transmigration of the soul and favour cremation for disposal of the dead with the ashes being thrown into water. There is no objection to hospital staff handling the body.

There are five traditional symbolic marks which all practising Sikhs should wear:

1. Kesh—Long, uncut hair and unshaven head.

2. Kanga—a comb to keep the hair in place and symbolise discipline.

3. Kara—A steel bangle worn on the right wrist to symbolise strength and unity.

4. Kirpan—A sword, the symbol of authority and justice, often worn as a brooch.

5. Kachj—A pair of shorts initially to allow freedom of movement in battle, now a symbol of spiritual freedom.

It could cause distress for any of these symbols to be removed from a dying person. Following death, relatives and friends take part in a series of services, either in the deceased's home or in the temple, for a period of 10 days with a final service to mark the end of the official mourning period[8].

Buddhists

Buddhism began in the sixth century BC against a background of Hinduism, Buddha being a former Hindu prince. It has spread to many parts of the world and there is a lot of variation between different geographical areas. However, the underlying principle of all Buddhism is belief in reincarnation of the soul. There is great emphasis on meditation to relax the mind and body in order to see life in its true perspective. Many people belief in meditating on one's death while still in health.

It is important for a patient to be allowed quietness and privacy for meditation. Great importance is also attributed to the state of the mind at death which should be calm and hopeful and as clear as possible. To this end some patients may be reluctant to take drugs, which must be respected. There are no special rituals regarding the body and cremation is common[7].

The Jewish community

For the Orthodox Jew there is a very specific structure with regard to death and a specific pattern of mourning for the bereaved. Comfort is drawn from a confession which acts as a *rite de passage* to another phase of existence and also from readings from the Psalms. The family may wish to be present at death and a Rabbi should visit if one is available.

It is not acceptable for a non-Jewish person to handle the dead body, so gloves should be worn so that there is no direct contact. The family may express a wish to prepare the body themselves or send a member of their community to do so. Burial should take place within 24 hours of death, unless it involves the Sabbath (Saturday) in which case it may be slightly longer. Strict Orthodox Jews may want someone to stay with the body until burial, which can create difficulties in a hospital mortuary.

The chief mourner, usually the spouse, is expected to take full responsibility for the funeral arrangements and during the service is expected and encouraged openly to express grief. The mourners do not leave the graveside until it has been completely filled. There is a period of intense mourning for seven days, during which the mourners do no work, are visited frequently, brought their food and encouraged to talk of the deceased. The tearing of clothes is accepted as a visible symbol of being inwardly torn by grief. There follows a period of 30 days of gradual readjustment and then, at the end of a year, a gravestone is erected and the official period of mourning is completed[3].

Conclusion

It must be remembered that members of any cultural group vary considerably in their observance of that culture. It is important to treat each person as an individual and to consult with the patient and his family as to their specific needs. Every effort must be made to find an interpreter when there is a language problem.

It is interesting to note that in the various groups considered there are many similarities. All appear to have very specific guidelines of behaviour associated with dying, death and bereavement. This is different from the majority of the population who do not have particularly strong religious beliefs and, as a result, no specific guidelines to help them cope with the stress.

On the whole, people are expected to keep their grief under control, carry on as normal and not discuss it as this tends to embarrass others. As a result, they tend to become very isolated in their grief. In the long term this will make it more difficult to cope with. Perhaps we have much to learn from the minority groups in our society whose ways may seem strange.

References

1. Speck, Rev. P. *The chaplain and other cultures*. Extracts from a talk at the Royal Free Hospital, London. *Hospital Chaplain*, 1981,**75**.

2. Read, M. *Culture, Health and Disease*. London, Tavistock Publications, 1966.

3. Gorer, G. *Death, Grief and Mourning*. London. The Cressett Press, 1965.

4. Rathwell, T. Health planning sensitive to the needs of ethnic minorities. *Radical Community Medicine*, 1981, **6**: 3–7.

5. Henley, A. *Asian patients in hospital and at home*. London. King Edward Hospital Fund, 1979.

6. Speck, Rev. P. *Loss and Grief in Medicine*. London. Bailliare Tindall, 1978.

7. Bridger, P. *A Hindu family in Britain*. Religious Education Press, 1979.

8. Owen-Cole, W. *A Sikh family in Britain*. Religious Education Press, 1973.

I would like to thank Canon John Barton, chaplain, John Radcliffe Hospital, for his help and introduction to useful literature and to Mrs Anornita Goswami, health liaison officer, Oxfordshire Council for Community Relations.

The Spiritual Needs
of the Dying*

Kenneth J. Doka

It has become a truism to describe contemporary American culture as secular. To Becker it is that very secularization that has led to the denial of death [1]. Yet the term "secularization" often has very ambiguous, different, and even conflicting meanings [2]. To many, secularization is essentially a social process whereby religious symbols and doctrines lack social significance and societal decisions are made on a rational and pragmatic rather than on a theological or spiritual basis. Such definition does not deny the potency of both religion and spirituality on an individual level. Gallop polls affirm that vast majorities of Americans both believe in God and consider religion and spirituality important in their lives. This is clearly evident when one faces the crisis of dying, a crisis when scientific explanations are largely silent.

Individuals, of course, differ in the extent that religion plays a part in their lives. These differences continue even throughout the dying process. As Pattison noted, dying persons will use belief systems as they have used throughout life—constructively, destructively, or not at all [3]. To some individuals, belief systems can be a source of comfort and support; to others, it will be a cause for anxiety. Pattison even notes that individuals who seem to find religion in terminal illness often show a basic continuity, for these "foxhole" religionists are likely to be individuals who seek out and grasp each new treatment, diet, or drug.

Counselors are increasingly recognizing the value in exploring religious and spiritual themes with the dying; for dying is not only a medical and personal crisis, it is a spiritual one as well. Though individuals may adhere to different religious beliefs and explanations, or even then lack them, dying focuses one on questions such as the meaning of life, the purpose of one's own existence, and the reason for death, that have an inherently spiritual quality. Thus as individuals struggle with dying, spiritual and religious themes are likely to emerge. In fact, often these spiritual interpretations are, to paraphrase Freud "a royal road into the unconscious."

While this chapter will emphasize religious and spiritual themes in the terminal phase of disease, it is important to recognize the presence of these themes throughout the illness. Even at the point of diagnosis, persons may interpret the disease in a spiritual or religious sense. For example, one person may define AIDS as a punishment from God. That interpretation is likely to have very different reverberations throughout the illness than those from someone who sees the disease as a result from an unfortunate exposure to a virus.

It is not unusual for a person's interpretation of the disease to have religious and spiritual dimensions. Every disease has a component of mystery. Why does one smoker get lung cancer and another not? Why does a disease manifest itself at any given time? Why, in fact, do we die? None of these questions yield to totally satisfactory scientific and rational explanations.

Hence in exploring someone's interpretation of disease, it is essential to be sensitive to these religious or spiritual dimensions. Often because religious or spiritual explanations are not socially validated, individuals may be reluctant to share them or even be fully aware of them. There is a need then for counselors to probe for such issues in a permissive and nonjudgmental atmosphere.

Religions of spiritual themes may also be intertwined with affective responses evident in the living-dying interval. Numerous observers have noted that persons with a life-threatening or terminal disease often exhibit emotions such as anger, guilt, bargaining, resignation, hope and anxiety [4, 5]. All of these responses may be tied to spiritual concerns. Anger

*A section of this chapter has been previously published by the author in the *Newsletter of the Forum for Death Education and Counseling,* 6, pp. 2–3.

may not only be directed against significant others but also cosmically—against nature, the universe, fate, or God. And such anger can be combined with both guilt and fear that anger toward the deity or other transcendental power is both wrong and dangerous. One person, for example, as both angry at God for her disease, but also was fearful that God would continue to punish her for that anger. In counseling, the woman has been able to reinterpret her anger as a form of prayer, and with that a reaffirmation of both her relationship to God (e.g., she had the freedom to communicate such anger) and his power. A comment by Easson helped [6]. In describing the anger of a thirteen-year-old boy with leukemia, he noted the child's comment that "if God is God, He will understand my anger, if He does not understand my anger, He is not God" [6, p. 91]. This allowed the woman to see her anger as an aspect of faith.

Similarly bargaining may be directed toward God leading to a sense of hope or resignation if the bargain is perceived as accepted and a sense of anger, guilt and fear is perceived as denied. One man with leukemia gave up hope at the time of his first relapse. In his mind he had made a "bargain" with God at the time of his first hospitalization. At that time he had hoped for the health to participate in a family event. When a relapse soon followed, he now believed that God had fulfilled his part of the deal-the man was now resigned to dying. Such bargains do not have to be theistic in nature. One woman once had made a deal with "the universe" to give something back if she achieved a desired success. In her own intensely spiritual frame of reference, her illness was a manifestation of her selfishness and unwillingness to part with her time or possessions. She had not fulfilled her promise, her illness was the result.

It is important then for counselors to recognize that *any* response to life-threatening illness can be intertwined with religious themes. Throughout the illness, these religious or spiritual interpretations should be explored as they can facilitate or complicate a person's response to illness.

Religious and spiritual values may also influence treatment decisions. Extreme examples of this may be found when adherence to particular beliefs precludes certain medical procedures such as blood transfusions or even causes patients to reject any conventional medical therapies. But even in other cases, religious and philosophical perspectives may certainly be part of treatment decisions. For example, persons may decline treatments because of personal perspectives on quality of life or because they perceive a value to life or an obligation to God or fellow humans. Perspectives in euthanasia may be profoundly influenced by religious and spiritual values.

While religious and spiritual themes are often found throughout the struggle with life-threatening illness, they are often especially critical in the terminal phase. For beyond the medical, social, and psychological needs of dying individuals, there are spiritual needs as well. The terminally ill patient recognizes Becker's paradox that humans are aware of finitude yet have a sense of transcendence [1]. It is this paradox that underlies the three spiritual needs of dying persons: 1) the search for meaning of life, 2) to die appropriately, and 3) to find hope that extends beyond the grave.

1. THE SEARCH FOR MEANING OF LIFE

One major crisis precipitated by dying is a search for the meaning of one's life. Theoreticians of various disciplines have long recognized that we are creatures who create and share meaning. This purposiveness extends to self as well. In the prologue of the play *Ross,* a biography of Lawrence of Arabia, various characters posthumously assess Lawrence's life. As the spotlight descends on one Arab chieftain, he defiantly exclaims "that history will sigh and say 'this was a man!' " It is a statement that in one way or another we wish to make that our life had purpose, significance, and meaning. Developmental psychologists and sociologists, such as Erickson, Butler, and Marshall, assert that the knowledge of impending death creates a crisis in which one reviews life in order to integrate one's goals, values and experience [7–9]. This awareness of finitude can be a consequence of either old age or serious illness. Even very young children, and their families, will review the child's life to find that sense of purpose.

The failure to find meaning can create a deep sense of spiritual pain. Individuals may feel that their lives changed or meant nothing. This has implications for caregivers. One of the most important things that caregivers can do for dying persons is to provide time for that personal reflection. While the caregiver can help dying persons find significance in their lives, things they have done, events they have witnessed, history that they have experienced all provide fruitful areas for exploration. Counselors may use varied techniques to facilitate this process. Reviewing life and family histories, viewing family or period photographs and mementos or sharing family humor and stories can facilitate this process. Films, music, books, or art that evoke earlier periods or phases of life can encourage reminiscence and life review.

Religious beliefs or philosophical and spiritual systems can be very important here. They can give one's life a sense of cosmic significance. And, they can provide a sense of forgiveness—to oneself and to others—for acts of commission and omission and for dreams not accomplished.

2. TO DIE APPROPRIATELY

People not only need assurance that they have lived meaningfully, they must die meaningfully as well. First, people want to die in ways consistent with their own self-identity. For example, a group of elderly women have established a call system to each other. Each woman has a set of multiple keys to each other's apartment. "This," one woman assured, "was so we don't die stinking up the apartment and nobody has to break down any doors." To these old-world women, cleanliness and orderliness are key virtues. The thought of leaving dirt and disorder even at the moment of demise is painful. They wish to die congruent with the ways in which they lived.

Dying appropriately also means dying comprehendingly. It means being able to understand and interpret one's death. If one suffers, it means having a framework to explain suffering. Pope John Paul noted that our secular and comfort-oriented society lacks a theology of pain. This suggests that caregivers need to explore with patients their beliefs about pain and death.

To die appropriately is difficult in a technological world. The fantasy of a quick death surrounded by loving relatives contrasts starkly with the reality of dying by chronic disease, alone, and institutionalized. It is little wonder that people fear not so much the fact of death as the process of dying. Caregivers can be helpful here in a number of ways. First, by empathetic listening, they allow the dying space to interpret their deaths. Second, whatever control can be left to the dying aids in their construction of their deaths. The opportunity to discuss one's death with relatives, either near the time of death or earlier, permits occasion to prepare to die as one lived. This allows specifying modes of treatment, ritual requests, special bequests, or simply educating families in the details that accompany death.

3. TO FIND HOPE THAT EXTENDS BEYOND THE GRAVE

Another spiritual need is transcendental. We seek assurance in some way that our life, or what we left, will continue. Perhaps the popularity of Moody's *Life After Life* [10] is that it recasts traditional images of the afterlife in a quasiscientific framework.

But there are many ways that we can look toward continued existence. Lifton and Olson spoke of five modes of symbolic immortality in our progeny [11]. A second mode is the creative mode in which we see continuance in our creations. This can include the singular accomplishments of the great or the more mundane contributions of the average. The last three modes, theological, eternal nature, and transcendental, relate to conceptualizations of immortality proferred in various belief systems. We might add a sixth—a communal mode where we see our life as part of a larger group. The continued survival of the group gives each life significance and each person lives in the community's memory. Such a theme is often evidence in Jewish thought.

Religion and other belief systems are one way to provide critical reassurance of immortality. Religious rituals may affirm a sense of continuity even beyond death. Yet Lifton and Olson's typology remind that there are other things that help as well. Actions of caregivers are important too. The presence of personal artifacts and dignified treatment of the terminally ill reaffirm personhood and suggest significance. Institutional policies that encourage intergenerational visiting provide subtle reminders of one's biological legacy.

SUMMARY

Yet while there seems some recognition of these spiritual needs, it remains unclear as to how well these needs are being met. Observers have recognized a variety of obstacles to religious or spiritual wholeness [12]. Some of these obstacles may be structural. Lack of access to clergy, a lack of privacy, or a reluctance of caregivers to explore religious and spiritual issues can inhibit any attempt to address there spiritual concerns.

The lack of structure may also be an inhibitor. Within the Christian tradition, there is an absence of recognized ritual that mandates the presence of clergy and focuses on spiritual issues such as reconciliation and closure. Such a ritual has never been particularly significant in Protestant liturgy or theology. In the Roman Catholic tradition, the sacrament of extreme unction, or popularly "last rites," has changed its meaning significantly since 1974. Retitled (or restored to the title of) "anointing of the sick," it now emphasizes a holistic notion of healing that is rooted in a context of prayer and counseling. While much is gained by this change, it ends the notion of a sacramental rite of passage into death. Death becomes simply a medical event where clergy have no defined role. There then is an absence of any structure of ritual that focuses on addressing these spiritual needs.

Other failures may be failures of personnel. Clergy or clinicians may be unable to facilitate this process. There may be a number of reasons for this. Clergy may be intolerant of other beliefs or seek to proselytize. They may fail to be understanding. They may hide behind prayer or ritual. Intellectually or emotionally they may have little to offer dying persons. Other caregivers may not be religious, may not have explored their own spiritual beliefs, or are hesitant to explore beliefs of others.

Finally, dying persons may be unable to meet their own spiritual needs. They may lack conviction in their own beliefs, fail to appreciate or explore their own spiritual needs, or be consumed by dysfunctional elements of their own belief system [12].

Clergy and clinicians can facilitate spiritual wholeness in a number of ways. First, in their own conversations with dying persons, they can provide individuals with opportunities to explore these concerns in a nonthreatening and nonjudgmental atmosphere. These are times to listen and explore the individual's perspective. Should some of these beliefs have dysfunctional elements, counselors can explore the ways that these issues can be addressed within the belief structure. For example, in one case, a man was consumed with religious guilt. Exploration of his own beliefs allowed him to address how that guilt could be expiated.

Varied rituals may facilitate this process. Rituals such as confession or communion can provide a visible sign of forgiveness. As DeArment notes, prayer can be a powerful way to express emotion or approach intimate reflection without the patient feeling exposed or vulnerable [13]. It can also be useful to explore faith stories or "paricopes" with individuals. By asking persons to relate faith stories that they believe speak to their situations, one can assess significant issues and themes in their own spiritual journeys. Sometimes one can help individuals reframe these faith stories to derive additional support. For example, many individuals in the Judaic-Christian tradition interpret Job as fatalistically responding to loss. "The Lord giveth and taketh." Another way to view that story, though, is as a long intense struggle of Job as he experiences loss. The latter is often more helpful to people in struggle and is quite faithful to text. In those cases in which the counselor cannot utilize such rituals or beliefs, they are still able to assist in locating empathic clergy or layperson of the person's own faith. This also reminds one that faith communities—the churches, congregations, and temples—that individuals may belong to can be helpful resources.

In recent years, there has been increasing recognition that dying persons not only have medical needs but psychological and social needs as well. Recognition of spiritual needs, too, will allow individuals to approach death as they have approached life—wholly.

REFERENCES

1. E. Becker, *The Denial of Death,* Free Press, New York, 1973.
2. J. A. Winter, *Continuities in the Sociology of Religion,* Harper and Row, New York, 1977.
3. G. M. Pattison, *Religion, Faith, and Healing, The Experience of Dying,* Prentice Hall, New Jersey, 1977.
4. E. Kubler-Ross, *On Death and Dying,* Macmillan, New York, 1969.
5. T. Rando, Grief, *Dying and Death: Clinical Interventions for Caregivers,* Research Press, Champaign, Illinois, 1984.
6. W. Easson, *The Dying Child: The Management of the Child or Adolescent Who is Dying,* Charles C. Thomas, Springfield, Illinois, 1970.
7. E. Erickson, *Childhood and Society,* Macmillan, New York, 1963.
8. R. Butler, The Life Review: An Interpretation of Reminiscence in the Aged, *Psychiatry, 26,* p. 1, 1963.
9. V. Marshall, *Last Chapters: A Sociology of Aging and Dying,* Brooks/Cole, Monterey, California, 1980.
10. R. Moody, *Life After Life,* Bantam Books, New York, 1975.
11. R. Lifton and E. Olson, *Living and Dying,* Bantam Books, New York, 1974.
12. T. Attig, Respecting the Dying and Bereaved as Believers, *Newsletter of the Forum for Death Education and Counseling, 6,* pp. 10–11, 1983.
13. D. DeArment, Prayer and the Dying Patient: Intimacy Without Exposure, in *Death and Ministry,* J. Bane, Kutcher, Neale and Reeves, Jr. (eds.), Seabury Press, New York, 1975.

Spiritual Aspects of Death and Dying

Alan C. Mermann, M.D., M.Div.

Chaplain, Yale University School of Medicine, New Haven, Connecticut

Received August 28, 1991

Dying is an event beyond our comprehension, an experience that can only be imagined. Patients with cancer have a gift denied many others: some time to prepare for the approaching end of life.

This time can be used to bring old conflicts to a close, to say goodbye and seek forgiveness from others, to express love and gratitude for the gifts of a life. Physicians can help patients by being aware of the spiritual dimensions to life that many patients have. In major religious traditions, death is accepted as the natural end of the gift of life and as a point of transition to another, yet unknown, existence.

For many patients, it is not death that is feared, but abandonment. The physician's awareness of the spiritual needs of patients can make care of the dying more rewarding and fulfilling for all concerned.

Death is an event beyond our comprehension. Although we know all that lives will die, the experience of dying can only be imagined. The consequence of death is quite clear: a life—with all that that word implies—comes to an end. Does dying have any significance for us while we are alive, other than confirmation of our mortality? We have a long, rich, and diverse history of contemplation and reflection on death, and this heritage can enrich the lives of patients who are dying, their families, and the physicians who care for them. I shall comment on several spiritual aspects of dying which are of concern to the seriously ill, consider their import for the physician, and, last, discuss a Christian perspective on death.

THE PATIENT

Persons dying with cancer have been given a gift denied those who die by accident or cardiovascular catastrophe: some time. How that time is used will determine its quality. Doctor Johnson's famous remark is perennially applicable: "Depend upon it, sir, when a man knows he is to be hanged in a fortnight, it concentrates his mind wonderfully" [1]. A compassionate ancillary service of caregivers is helping patients use their remaining time to good purpose. The focus of the patient on the structure and content of the remaining days of life can be enhanced by the physician who appreciates the depth of the feelings engendered by the approach of the end.

Awareness that one is dying can elicit overwhelming sensations of fear and loneliness. Terror of the unknown ahead, both the way of dying, and the dread of the undisclosed after death, can produce guilt and anxiety in us as we look back at our lives. For many, death brings an end to a life of conflict with others, some of whom are closely related, although estranged. The time comes to "tidy up" the life, pulling in the loose ends to fashion a clean break. Despite the ravages of the disease and its therapies, one can die healthy in mind and spirit. In dying, a life can be restored, in the sense that personal relationships with others and with the world are defined and made explicit. There are more diseases than the obvious physical ones. Henry David Thoreau wrote, "The incessant anxiety and strain of some is a well-nigh incurable form of disease. We are made to exaggerate the importance of what work we do; and yet how much is not done by us! or, what if we had been taken sick? How vigilant we are! determined not to live by faith if we can avoid it; . . ." [2].

A difficult and demanding task of the physician is to assist the patient in setting therapeutic priorities: what

Address reprint requests to: Alan C. Mermann, M.D., M.Div., Yale University School of Medicine, 333 Cedar Street, New Haven, CT 06510-8020

From *The Yale Journal of Biology and Medicine*, Vol. 65, 1992, pp. 137-142. © 1992 by The Yale Journal of Biology and Medicine. Reprinted by permission.

can be treated, at what cost, and for what benefit. Current interest in explicit discussion of advance directives correctly addresses this problem. Patients can be helped to discern the responsible actions called for so that conflicts can be resolved as well as possible, and the end approached with dignity and composure. One aspect of a restored life that is often ignored is recognition of a spiritual component to life. For many of us, the demands of everyday living and working effectively limit our spiritual development. Although we may have achieved graduate-level accomplishments in academic, professional, or business careers, the learning and reflection that produce growth in spiritual matters may not have proceeded as far. Many have not pursued the study, introspection, and questioning necessary to develop a mature faith, capable of withstanding the challenges that illness, loss, and death will present. For some physicians, common beliefs about a God active in the world run counter to experience, although religion is viewed as a supporting structure for ethical and moral principles of our past [3]. The abrupt and shocking announcement that suffering and death are a new part of our story may catch us with beliefs and a faith unable to support a challenge of that magnitude. At this point in the story, advice and counsel are needed by patients so that they can be helped to a fuller realization of the spiritual aspects of their lives. This help does not imply a set of doctrinal statements or a formal creed that codifies belief. It does mean finding the resources required to help another formulate and utilize a philosophical or religious world view that can support the stress of the rest of the journey to its end. In other words, when the unexpected and inevitable happens to us, we may need guidance to bring to expression a faith that will sustain us in our plight.

We see our relationships to the created order of our world in varied ways. Disregarding, for the moment, sectarian and religious faith distinctions, many persons hold a sense of timelessness in their understanding of what it means to "be." The mystery of existence, awe and joy before the natural order, a sense of the sublime in all the manifestations of our loves, and a sure confidence in continuity through children create in many a sense of union with the infinite and the immortal. Details of the many faiths which provide this confidence vary widely, yet there is a commonality that permits a broad acceptance of faiths that can inform our lives. Although we may learn about these faiths, understand their defining intellectual characteristics, and observe their evidences in the lives of others, personal commitment and loyalty usually call for a "leap of faith," to use Kierkegaard's famous phrase. Lockhart McGuire, a professor of medicine at Virginia, who had been diagnosed with metastatic cancer, noted in an address to medical students that "By whatever method the leap of faith occurs, it can be orienting during life and in the face of death, possibly transcendent and even redemptive" [4]. These are the three hopes inherent in faith: it holds us on our proper course despite the trials and tribulations of all of life; it leads us to an understanding of self and cosmos that exceeds the mundane; it can make our lives objects of value and respect.

The search for spiritual unity runs like a thread through our history. By many and varied paths, we have searched for answers to our questions about the mysteries of existence that are so magnified and highlighted by the approach of death. The pain and suffering that are often coincident with dying are understood by many as an enlightening part of the journey we make toward a developed concept of God. This construct provides the base and the power for the fruits of faith: mature emotions, competent judgment, and revealing insight. For many, final realization of the self in a way not understandable here and now is the end we seek. To this end, faith is cultivated by study and prayer. One of the goals of a life informed by faith is freedom from fear: both fear of living and fear of dying. A life lived in some depth of religious faith, enriched by gifts of the spirit, and bound to others in mutual love and affection can face the inevitable losses in death graced with hope.

THE PHYSICIAN

One of the signs of sensitivity in those who care for the dying is awareness of the private spiritual needs we all share as persons. A paradox exists in the personal experiences of many physicians who treat the seriously ill. After years of close association with others who are suffering, in pain, and approaching the end of life, some doctors display a lack of insight into the role death plays in life. A surgeon, diagnosed with metastatic lung cancer, describes his "awakening":

> Simply accepting this prognosis was completely intolerable for me. I felt I was not yet ready to be finished. I still had not seen and done and shared with the people I love. . . . I could sit back and let my disease and my treatment take their course, or I could pause and look at my life and ask, What are my priorities? How do I want to spend the time that is left? . . . I began to focus on choosing to do things every day that promote laughter, joy, and satisfaction. . . . I began to make choices to do the things that felt good to me . . . [5].

The poignancy in these words cries out to us. To be in one's fifties, successful in a profession, if not necessarily in personal relationships, and yet only to be opened to the meaning of living by the imminence of one's death, is tragic indeed. While it may be common for this state to occur, it is not necessary and suggests a belated pursuit of things psychological and spiritual, and a failure to learn from professional and personal experiences the values and joys of life. One would expect that years of surgical training and practice would have provided many situations where values, commitments, and questions of beauty, truth, and goodness were made exquisitely relevant by attentive care to the needs of the dying.

Varied reasons are offered for the insensitivity of some doctors to the personal and spiritual needs and concerns of the dying: the medical, sociological, and psychological literature fully considers these issues. Some physicians hesitate to be involved with dying patients other than treating medical problems. Doctors may regard developed and open communication about dying as beyond their role, requiring an emotional commitment that is not possible. Feelings of personal inadequacy and lack of training contribute to the distancing [6–8]. Institutional care and specialty training also contribute to the isolation and dehumanizing of dying patients. Physicians may view the death of a patient as a sign of defeat for a profession dedicated to healing and well-being, with the implication that doctors have nothing to offer patients when clinical skills prove, as they must, ultimately ineffective [9,10]. Physicians may have above-average fears of death; hence their choice of work which allows engagement with it [11]. Direct and ongoing encounters with the dying easily trigger our universal anxiety, as we contemplate the end of any life and its disclosure of mortality. Death remains an experience beyond our comprehension [12]. These comments made by observers of the medical scene are on the professional life of the physician. What is the personal effect of these considerations on the life of a doctor who cares for patients with cancer?

Several fundamental segments of self-understanding and of relationships with patients and their families can be clarified and probably altered by facing the probing and painful questions posed by the approaching death of another.

1. Does life have meaning? The shadow of death sweeps away easy answers and supports the alternative of considering anew the measured thought of the past about this human journey. This question posits a place for the life of the spirit as enricher of the life that is lived until death.
2. The major religions in Western culture stand firm in their faith in a life after death. This conviction is rooted in the experiences and the revelations of believers and has supported and illumined the human encounter with death. Paul aptly called it a mystery, and quoted the prophets Isaiah and Hosea: "Death is swallowed up in victory." "O death, where is thy victory? O death, where is thy sting?" [13].
3. What will it mean to "not be?" Our dying patients can raise those spiritual questions that have called to us for so many centuries. Answers may come from a faith that seems idiosyncratic or simplistic to us. Nevertheless, the roles of religious faith and the life of the spirit in enriching our journey and providing meaning where chaos may seem to reign can open our hearts and minds to different realities. As Thoreau observed, "Be it life or death, we crave only reality" [14].

4. The evolving relationships with seriously ill and dying patients, if reflected upon, call upon the very skills perfected in medical training, although the application is now in the personal and spiritual realms. Listening with true compassion, using thought rigorously trained by education and experience, we become aware that our dying patients are ourselves farther along on a common journey.
5. As life comes to a close, persons require honesty from those who care for them and open communication about what the future holds. Love, in its many forms, is a gift we can offer those who face death. The intimate relations between love and forgiveness suggest a role for the physician as advocate in resolution of conflicts of long duration within families and with others. An examined life may invoke a deep desire for forgiveness by God so that true peace may come at last.

A CHRISTIAN PERSPECTIVE ON DYING AND DEATH

There is no singular Christian understanding of the human experiences of living and dying. Beliefs about details of faith are as diverse and contradictory as other human activities display. There are, however, certain basic convictions about life and its end in death, and the consequences of that death, that inform a Christian about their meanings. This discussion is offered to provide an overview of those convictions and beliefs.

Life is a gift of God to be valued as sacred, although not an ultimate value; that label applies only to God. For this reason, vigorous efforts are made to treat disease and injury, to prevent public health threats, and to perform research that will further our knowledge of medicine. Death is inevitable for all that lives, however, and there are situations in which treatment is not indicated or should be withdrawn. This ethos informs much of the current debate about allowing patients to die by withholding or discontinuing therapy.

Christianity had its beginnings in Judaism and is referred to by Paul as a branch of the tree that has its common root in the faith of Israel [15]. God is accepted as a creative force in history, seeking, through love of the creation and holy laws, to bring fulfillment to life here. The Christian faith has its origin in what is considered a unique event in history: Easter. Jesus, dead on the cross and buried, is subsequently seen, touched, and spoken with by his followers as one risen from the dead. The resurrection of Jesus as the Christ, or Messiah, is the central reality of the faith. For nearly two thousand years, believers have argued the theological interpretations of the gospel stories and the relationships among God, Jesus, and the Church. A basic doctrine is accepted, which proclaims God manifest to us as three persons: (1) Creator of all that is; (2) Jesus who, as both man and God, has redeemed the world; (3) Holy Spirit, who is present to us as counsellor.

Death is the end of life as we know it; it is inevitable and not to be feared but to be accepted as the closing out of one form of being in hope of another, an eternal existence with God. The nature and form of that new life cannot be known, but remain a mystery beyond our understanding. Paul, in his letter to the church at Corinth, states his understanding of the relationship between death to this life and hope in another in his expectation of the total loss of the body as we know it. His simile compares the body to a seed, which must die unto itself in order to become a plant. If it remains a seed, no new life is possible [16]. Similarly, the resurrection of Jesus would lack its power if Jesus had not died. The influences of Greek philosophy are still present in perennial talk of the soul, an elusive part of us, inherently pure and good in comparison to the body, which is inexorably subject to the sins of the flesh and will perish. Christian belief, in contrast, accepts the finality of death and the loss of the body as we know it, in full confidence that, at a time and in a place known to God, a new life will begin.

For the physician, respect for the patient's faith is an important factor in care—not the literal tenets of that faith, but rather the existence of it. Since death is the final act of living, and a time of expectation, it holds no threat. It is, rather, the process of dying which is the time of anxiety and dread. Fear of abandonment in a time of suffering, pain in body from disease or treatment, and pain in mind from personal losses and estrangements: these are the focal points for the physician's support, assistance, and affection. It has been a common observation that, as patients become more sick, the duration of the physician's visit shortens. When the personal needs of the dying patient are greatest, and the need for technical expertise is lessening, the defining attributes of the good physician can be displayed at their finest. The spiritual life of the dying is a concern in their care. The physician sensitive to the varied nuances of the life of the spirit can help to make this hour of transition a time of peace and acceptance.

REFERENCES

1. Hill GB (ed): Boswell's Life of Johnson, Vol 3 The Life (1770–1780). Oxford, UK, Clarendon Press, 1934, p 167
2. Thoreau HD: Walden. In The Portable Thoreau, revised edition. Edited by C Bode. New York, Viking Press, 1964, p 266
3. Mermann AC: Coping strategies of selected physicians. Persp Biol Med 33(2):268–279, 1990
4. McGuire L: Ourselves and patients who are dying. The Pharos of Alpha Omega Alpha 53 (Winter):1, 6–8, 1990
5. Mack RM: Occasional notes: Lessons learned from living with cancer. N Engl J Med 311:16–42, 1984
6. Behnke M, Nackashi JA, Raulerson MD, Schuler PM, Mehta P: The pediatrician and the dying child. S Issues Compr Ped Nurs 8(1):69–83, 1985
7. Schulz R, Aderman D: How the medical staff copes with dying patients: A critical review. Omega 7(1):11–21, 1976
8. Mermann AC, Gunn DB, Dickinson GE: Learning to care for the dying: A survey of medical schools and a model course. Acad Med 66(1):35–38, 1991
9. Morgan JD: The teaching of palliative care within the context of an undergraduate course on death, dying, and bereavement. J Pal Care 1 and 2:32–33, 1988
10. Seeland IB: Death: A natural process. Loss, Grief & Care 2(1–2):49–56, 1988
11. Feifel H: Death. In Taboo Topics. Edited by NL Farberow. New York, Atherton Press, 1963, pp 8–21
12. Freud S: Thoughts for the times on war and death (1915). In Collected Papers, Vol 4. Translated by J Riviere. London, UK, Hogarth Press, 1948, pp 304–305
13. The Bible, I Corinthians 15:54–55
14. [2], p 351
15. The Bible, Romans 11:16b–24
16. Ibid, I Corinthians 15:35–50

Hospice care for the 1990s:

A concept coming of age

In this article the authors present an overview of the history, development, and design of the typical American hospice. Focus is placed on the interdisciplinary team which is the primary implement for the delivery of hospice care. Common clinical and management issues are discussed.

Marian Gentile, RN
Hospice Manager
Forbes Hospice

Maryanne Fello, RN, MEd
Director, Cancer Services
Forbes Health System
Pittsburgh, Pennsylvania

THE ROOTS OF HOSPICE

Even though its roots can be traced to the Middle Ages, the modern hospice program did not take shape until the mid-1960s. At that time, the work of two remarkable physicians, Elisabeth Kubler-Ross, and Dame Cicely Saunders, converged to bring the emotional and physical needs of the dying to the forefront.

In 1970, Kubler-Ross' landmark book, *On Death and Dying*,[1] revolutionized the psychologic approaches to patients with terminal illness. After several years of observation and actual interviews with the dying, Kubler-Ross created a theoretic framework describing the psychologic stages of dying and pointed out to health care workers a sobering fact: as dying patients needed *more* attention and support, they were actually receiving *less*. Indeed, Kubler-Ross brought death and dying "out of the closet," making health care providers and society in general more aware that death is a part of life and a legitimate part of clinical care, and that with sensitivity and understanding it can be faced openly and honestly.

In 1967, while Kubler-Ross was working at the University of Chicago Hospital, a British physician, Cicely Saunders, MD, opened the doors of St Christopher's Hospice in London. Trained as a nurse and social worker, she received her medical degree and set about her life's work to improve the care of the dying—and what better background? Some have called Saunders "a whole hospice team wrapped up in one person"!

Saunders' approach to the dying was first and foremost geared to achieving and maintaining comfort. Her approach to pain management has shaped the development of a pain control philosophy that has become a benchmark of hospice care.

Her model, prescribing an interdisciplinary team, communicating effectively, treating symptoms of terminal disease, including the patient *and* family,[2] has been replicated in concept over 1,400 times in the United States today.

HOSPICE IN THE UNITED STATES

In the early 1970s, as the work of Kubler-Ross and Saunders became known, individuals in the United States became eager to put their concepts into action. The United States programs, however similar in concept to the British world, were very different in design. The first US hospice, Hospice of Connecticut (New Haven) began to deliver care to the dying at home, since funding problems forced delays in the construction of a free-standing facility. After 6 years of delays an inpatient unit was christened in 1980 "but its early years as a home care program left an indelible impression on the purposes and practices of the hospice staff and administrators. It provided the country with a new and different model of care for the dying, care focused primarily on patients at home."[2(p11)]

As the hospice movement spread across the United States, programs took on various shapes and sizes. In most instances the shape of each hospice was determined by its genesis. For example, if a hospital felt that its commitment included the provision of terminal care, its hospice program would probably be a hospital-based hospice; if a group of active lay volunteers began a program, it might be a consortium model hospice. In all, there are at least six common program designs for hospice.

In an effort to more exactly define this concept, the National Hospice Organization (NHO) and the then Joint Commission on Accreditation of Hospitals (JCAH) developed standards of care to which hospice should adhere. Standards were developed in seven areas: (1) the patient and family as the unit of care, (2) interdisciplinary team services, (3) continuity of care, (4) home care services, (5) symptom control, (6) bereavement, and (7) quality assurance.

Most significant in the creation of uniformity of hospice programming was the addi-

Reprinted from *The Journal of Home Health Care Practice*, Vol. 3, No. 1, November 1990, pp. 1-15, with permission of the authors and Aspen Publishers, Inc. © 1990.

tion of hospice to the Federal Medicare Program in 1982. Maintenance of a certification to deliver hospice care calls for rigid adherence to the standards developed. As we look toward the 1990s, many uncertainties still exist, many questions remain unanswered, such as

- What is the best model for delivery of hospice care?
- Will hospice in the United States face a dilemma as larger programs force out small, community programs?
- Will hospice care be assimilated into mainstream health care, or can it only stand alone?
- Will patients be *forced* to participate in hospice?
- What will be the impact of high technology on the dying process?

CRITERIA FOR ADMISSION

Probably the most crucial in the management of a hospice in today's society is the development of the program's admission criteria. Surely the kinds of support the hospice offers might be well received by any patient and family facing a major illness, but just when during that illness does a patient become eligible?

After years of developing a careful decision-making process, the authors' hospice has developed a fairly rigid set of three criteria for admission:

1. completion of all active, curative treatment
2. patient's awareness of diagnosis and prognosis
3. patient and family's clear understanding of the goals of hospice care.

Clearly these criteria bring to mind grey areas for questioning such as, "What if a patient is receiving palliative chemotherapy?" "What if a patient knows the diagnosis but not the prognosis?" "What if the family is divided about how the patient's illness should be treated?" And more recently, "What if the patient wants no life supports, but does want artificial hydration and nutrition?" These so-called grey areas demand that each patient's application for hospice care is reviewed in depth with the *most* important question: "Are the patient and family choosing supportive care for a terminal disease with the care delivered primarily in the home setting?"

WHO WORKS IN A HOSPICE PROGRAM?

In this age of nursing shortages across the country, the opportunity to work in a hospice setting still draws nurses. Why?

Two reasons come to mind. The first is the satisfaction of the work itself. To assist the patient and family during the dying

Fig 1. Behind the scenes discussions during an interdisciplinary team meeting.

process carries many rewards. Becoming involved after a family has been told "there is nothing more to be done" can restore the family's faith that it will not be abandoned even though curative medical treatment has been exhausted. Helping a family know what to expect, putting effective symptom management skills into practice, and supporting with effective counseling skills makes a hero of many nurses in the eyes of grateful families.

The second draw is the role of the nurse within the hospice team itself. Medical intervention takes a back seat to nursing intervention in terminal care. This fact thrusts the nurse into a primary role for both direct care and the coordination of the care provided by other members of the team. More will be said about that role later in the discussion of the interdisciplinary team.

An early study done by Amenta[3] has proven itself true many times: nurses (and others) who are drawn to hospice tend to be religious, realistic revolutionaries and they find in a hospice program a setting that is just short of an ideal medium for fundamental, holistic, independent nursing practice.

THE INTERDISCIPLINARY TEAM

The essence of hospice care is derived from the multifaceted and comprehensive approach of the hospice interdisciplinary team, whose members look for solutions to a patient's medical, psychosocial, and spiritual problems. The diversity of talent, cultural and ethnic backgrounds, life style, and educational background creates a blend

that can sort out various problems to find the approach most suitable for that individual patient and family. A well-coordinated, confident group of hospice professionals can work together with everyone having equal say in most matters only if each team member is comfortable offering information from his or her experience and knowledge as well as listening to and accepting the differing contributions of others (see Fig 1).

The essence of hospice care is derived from the multifaceted and comprehensive approach of the hospice interdisciplinary team, whose members look for solutions to a patient's medical, psychosocial, and spiritual problems.

"Role blurring" (overlapping of duties of various professional disciplines) is acceptable and actually encouraged to some extent within hospice programs. Every team member has an area of expertise accompanied by some primary responsibilities but each also must have some knowledge of other disciplines and be sensitive to problems and needs not directly related to the particular area of expertise. A common example of role blurring is when a hospice nurse spends time with family members advising them on how to approach the children about an impending death. There is no need (and often, no time) to wait until the counselor can be called to talk or meet with the family. A well-trained, experienced, and sensitive hospice nurse can

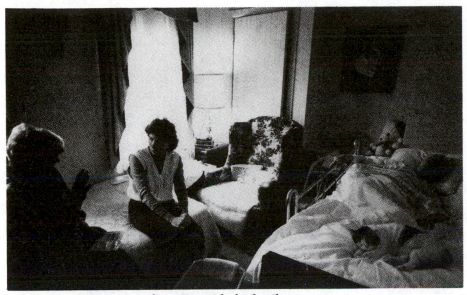

Fig 2. Hospice nurse spending time with the family.

give meaningful and accurate information in this situation. However, the lines must be drawn when the problems require more specific expertise and that team member must defer to another member of the team. Furthermore, sharp distinctions must be made in some areas because of primary responsibility and liabilities (ie, the patient's physician has the final decision in the ordering of medications, treatments, etc). Hospice personnel need to be cognizant of and comfortable with role blurring and to know their boundaries.

THE COMPOSITION OF THE INTERDISCIPLINARY TEAM AND THE MEMBERS' ROLES

The composition of the hospice team may vary from program to program depending on the model and whether the program is Medicare certified to provide hospice care. Typical members are discussed below.

Hospice nurse

Often the nucleus of a hospice team, the nurse may find herself or himself in the role of coordinating the care of most patients. Because the majority of hospice patients need some assistance with symptom management along with accompanying problems related to their physical care, the discipline of nursing is drawn on heavily by hospice care. It is the hospice nurse who is available 24 hours a day as needed by patients and families; it is usually the nurse who has the most day-by-day contact with the families, who visits regularly and calls frequently to give added reassurance and guidance (see Fig 2). Re-

gardless of the setting, the nurses are the principal support to patients and their families.

Clinical competence coupled with sensitivity and kindness seem to be key ingredients in the practice of hospice nursing. Hospice nurses generally have a great deal of autonomy on the job which, in itself, means that they must have good decision-making skills in addition to better than average communication abilities. The ability to communicate is demonstrated most keenly when a patient and family have chosen an avenue of treatment (or more often, nontreatment) that is contrary to the physician's plan. On the other hand, the hospice nurse may need to help a patient understand why no further treatment is advocated by the patient's physicians; the nurse must then employ gentle methods of reinforcing bad news. By staying open to communication from many directions, the hospice nurse can open up meaningful and useful dialogue not only for that patient and family but also for the community at large.

Hospice aide

Working closely with the hospice nurses, the home health aide is one of the most valuable members of the hospice team. Formally the home health aide's role is to help provide personal care and light housekeeping duties in the home. The home health aide is encouraged to provide the care in the way that is most satisfying to the family—either by working with the family member to help provide the care or by doing the care alone to allow the family a much needed rest. (It is important for

some families to feel like they have "done it all" even when it drives them to the point of exhaustion.) By working *with* the family they give the family members some assistance and help lighten the load and still allow them to feel that they really have done it all (see Fig 3).

Light housekeeping duties can be of great importance in some households. At times the primary caregiver is somewhat incapacitated or just plain tired. Having someone clean up last night's supper dishes or vacuum the carpets or launder a few loads of clothes can be supportive to a caregiver and an emotional boost as well.

Without question, however, the home health aide plays an important informal role. The aide's visits are generally longer than those of other members of the team (except the volunteer) and are geared to giving the caregiver a break. This may be the time the family relaxes just a bit more than usual and starts talking. Relationships between families and home health aides often become very intimate. Caregivers may derive their greatest support from the chance to talk over coffee with their friend, the home health aide. There is less professional distance obvious in these relationships. And, even though the relationships are encouraged, the aide must attempt to remain objective and not become enmeshed in family problems.

Counselor

The person looking most closely at families and family dynamics is the hospice counselor. The counselor's educational background is generally in the areas of psychology or social work. This specialized training is brought into practice in the usual ways of seeking out community resources, and finding help with financial, legal, and insurance issues. With hospice patients these problems take on exaggerated proportions because so much is happening at once in their lives. Sorting through these issues can bring about some peace of mind for the patient and caregivers but also permits insight into the more critical areas of the family system. Developing a relationship while working on the more tangible problems is a natural link into the more private (and thus guarded) family relationships. The crux of many of the difficulties for hospice families can be found within the family system. The counselor must employ special skills and sensitivity to help the families work through their issues. Most important, the counselor must sort through the details of the particular difficulty and offer options but allow the family to make the actual decision. This is a formidable task at times because many families have great difficulty making decisions or may be asking the counselor to rescue them. Developing skills that help people adapt to the crisis of terminal illness and all of its ramifications requires much emotional fortitude and keen perceptive talents on the part of the counselor.

Therapists

Physical therapists, occupational therapists, and speech therapists contribute in their own way to the enhancement of each day of life for a hospice patient. Physical therapists usually teach families transfer techniques, proper positioning, and maintenance exercises for the patients. Because rehabilitation is generally not feasible for the terminally ill patient, the emphasis is on maintaining strength and mobility as long as possible. In conjunction with this maintenance plan the occupational therapist evaluates the patient and the home setting for ways to continue a semblance of the patient's former activities of daily living. In both cases the emphasis is on maintaining function as long as possible and conserving energy so that remaining energy can be channeled into the patient's most important activities. Speech therapists emphasize communication and swallowing problems, both of which might be seen in the same patient (such as patients with brain tumor or amyotrophic lateral sclerosis [ALS]). Some hospice programs also include music and art therapists as part of the interdisciplinary team. Each of these therapists, using individual expertise, tries to enable patients to maximize their diminishing physical and communication abilities.

Nutritionist

Specializing in the nutritional aspects of terminal illness, the nutritionist counsels families on the special needs of these patients. The nutritionist focuses on understanding the meaning of food in each individual family system. Recognizing different ethnic and cultural views relating to food, the nutritionist attempts to help families look at these nutritional problems from their own perspective. Families for whom food was the center of life and pleasure need to continue to work on feeding and nourishing their dying family member. For them the emphasis is on getting as much nourishment as possible into every bite while knowing that the patient's food intake will probably continue to decline. At the same time the nutritionist emphasizes that what is most important at this stage of life is to eat and *enjoy*—not just to eat for the sake of eating. Families need to be told that nutritional problems are common-

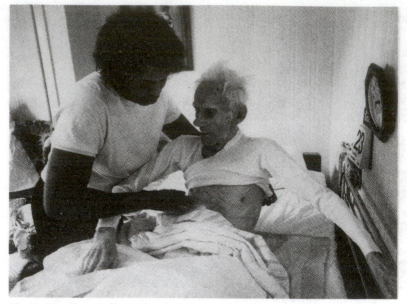

Fig 3. Hospice staff member helping with a patient's personal care at home.

place and that it is not their failing if the patient continues to lose weight and has a poor appetite. No one says that more convincingly than the hospice nutritionist.

Medical director

A major force within the interdisciplinary team is the medical director. The medical director presents the physician's view within the hospice framework and then represents the hospice approach to the medical community whose members often are struggling with decisions related to terminal illness in other settings such as acute care. The medical director must possess expertise in clinical aspects of symptom management in order to help implement effective palliative care. The medical director plays a variety of parts. On one hand, the medical director may actually manage the care of some hospice patients or act as a consultant to the care in other cases. Acting as a teacher, the medical director works with the rest of the hospice staff and interdisciplinary team to under-

---

The hospice medical director can most fully see the patient in the context of prior medical history and will be instrumental in helping the team plan for the patient's medical care in the days ahead.

---

stand the various disease processes and their clinical implications. It is the hospice medical director who can most fully see the patient in the context of prior medical

history and who, because of the physician's knowledge of the natural history of the disease process, will be instrumental in helping the team plan for the patient's medical care in the days ahead. The hospice medical director must display compassion and patience to the other team members while often acting as a stabilizing force within the group framework.

Chaplain

Spiritual care is an integral component of the hospice concept. Clergy serving as hospice chaplains form the most formal aspect of a hospice pastoral care program. All members of a hospice team must be able to attend to the spiritual needs of patients and families as questions and fears arise when death becomes more imminent. But the chaplain is a resource to both the staff, as staff persons address the spiritual concerns of patients and families, and the terminally ill patients and their families who are grappling with those life and death issues.

Chaplains represent faith and a link to God and eternity. They must be careful to help patients explore spiritual dimensions in a broad sense, not within one particular denomination or religious affiliation unless requested by the patient. Many of the patients to which hospice chaplains minister have been alienated from formal religion and now are feeling a need to reestablish themselves with their spiritual roots. Caution and sensitivity, along with a caring and loving nature, enable the chaplain to explore areas sometimes unreachable by anyone else.

Table 1. Equianalgesic comparison of common narcotic analgesics

Drug	Onset (min)	Peak (h)	Duration* (h)	Plasma half life (h)	Equianalgesic doses† (mg) IM	Equianalgesic doses† (mg) PO
Morphine	15–60	.5–1	3–7	2–4	10	60
Levorphanol	30–90	.5–1	4–8	12–16	2	4
Hydromorphone	15–30	.5–1	4–5	2–3	1.5	7.5
Oxymorphone	5–10	.5–1	3–6	nd	1	6
Methadone	30–60	.5–1	4–6‡	15–30	10	20
Meperidine	10–45	.5–1	2–4	3–4	75	300
Fentanyl	7–8	nd	1–2	1.5–6	0.1	nd
Codeine	15–30	.5–1	4–6	3	130	200
Oxycodone (PO)	15–30	1	4–6	nd	nd	30
Propoxyphene (PO)	30–60	2–2.5	4–6	6–12	nd	130
Hydrocodone	nd	nd	4–8	3.3–4.5	nd	nd

IM = intramuscular, PO = oral, nd = No data available.
*After IV administration, peak effects may be more pronounced but duration is shorter. Duration of action may be longer with the oral route.
†Based on acute, short-term use. Chronic administration may alter pharmacokinetics and decrease the oral–parenteral dose ratio.
The morphine oral–parenteral ratio decreases to 1.5–2.5:1 on chronic dosing.
‡Duration and half life increase with repeated use due to cumulative effects.
Adapted with permission from *Drug Facts and Comparisons*. Philadelphia; Pa: J.B. Lippincott; 1990:949.

The hospice chaplain represents the religious community within the context of the interdisciplinary team and, in turn, represents the hospice program in the community. Chaplains not only work directly with patients and families but also may participate in staff and volunteer training and continuing education. Hospice chaplains participate regularly in interdisciplinary team meetings where each patient's medical, social, and spiritual picture is reviewed. And the chaplain's involvement continues into the bereavement period when spiritual care may be the most important ingredient in grief support.

Volunteers

Embracing the spirit of hospice care, the volunteers donate their time to hospice programs and the terminally ill patients the programs serve. It is doubtful that any other area of health care involves volunteers to the extent that hospices do. Many hospice programs could not continue to operate without their volunteer constituency and no program could be considered a full-service hospice without a strong volunteer component.

Volunteers are in a position to provide a tremendous contribution to the hospice program and to individual patients and families. Because expectations of the volunteers are naturally high it is vital that they are carefully selected and trained. Hospice programs gear their selection and training programs to their own needs with training usually comprised of 20 to 40 hours of lectures, group discussion, outside reading, and instruction on physical care including hands-on nursing care. Then the volunteers begin assisting the hospice staff, all the while becoming entrenched in the care of terminally ill patients and their families. At the same time it is important for staff to supervise volunteers and provide them with outlets for emotional support.

Every component of a hospice program might include volunteers from inpatient care to home care and bereavement care, but they also help with office duties, speaker's bureau work, and fundraising. Some serve on hospice boards and help formulate and enact policy changes. Each area has its own needs and calls upon many different kinds of talents.

The most common area of hospice volunteering is the home care setting. Volunteers in the home act in the capacity of a friend—one who knows how to care for a sick person. Most commonly the volunteer provides respite for the caregivers by affording them an opportunity to get out of the home during the volunteer's visit. Even if the caregivers do not choose to leave the home, they have a chance to rest or do other chores without having to be concerned with the patient's care. Other home care volunteer duties include light housekeeping, laundry, grocery shopping, meal preparation, errands, even babysitting to give caregivers more time with the patient.

Volunteers give an added dimension to the families and the programs they serve. Their perspective is one of kindness and caring, along with a belief in maintaining human dignity in the dying process. They give much of themselves and reap only the gratification that comes from helping people in their darkest hour.

THE ROLE OF THE FAMILY IN HOSPICE CARE

In the early days of the hospice programming, many held the view that hospice staff was essential to do *for* the family, to be a substitute for the family in the care of the patient. Hospice, by its very nature, seemed to attract those helpers caught up with the notion of the "rescue fantasy." This, combined with an underestimation of what families are capable of doing, made for much overfunctioning and early warning signs of staff burnout.

As staff members learned together about the nature of family systems and how best to be helpful, they realized that the primary role of the hospice nurse was to be an enabler. When staff members share their competence in caring with families, rather than taking over, families are able to feel as if *they* did everything they could until their loved one died. One of the highest compliments to hospice staff is the thank-you note that says, "You gave us what it took to be able to do it ourselves. . . ."

PAIN MANAGEMENT

Probably the most valuable contribution to the health care system at large has been the development of the body of knowledge by hospice professionals regarding pain management. Even though only approximately 50% of hospice patients have moderate to severe pain problems, pain is often what patients and families fear most. Some of the most important pain management concepts follow.

- Chronic pain management requires regularly scheduled (not prn) delivery of appropriate analgesia *in advance of* the return of pain.
- Patients do *not* exhibit signs of drug addiction (ie, drug-seeking behavior, ever-escalating dosages) when placed on appropriate pain management program.
- Various routes of administration (ie, sublingual, rectal, oral) can be equally effective to the IV route when used in equianalgesic ratios (see Table 1).
- Morphine and its derivatives are by far the most useful drugs in the management of intractable pain.
- Knowledge of combinations of drugs such as narcotics with nonsteroidal antiinflammatory drugs can be very effective for bone pain.
- Careful assessment of pain and all of

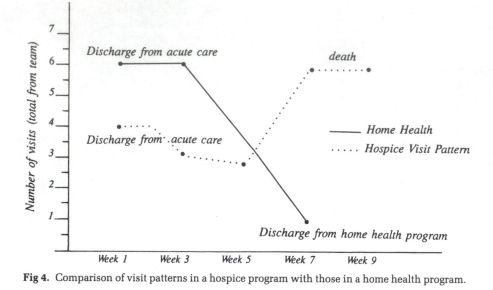

Fig 4. Comparison of visit patterns in a hospice program with those in a home health program.

den and is barely conscious, starting IVs could be considered invasive and will probably not add an iota of quality. In the authors' experience, slow dehydration caused by ingestion of less and less fluids and finally no fluid does not usually create much discomfort. The usual symptoms created by this slow dehydration process are slight elevation of body temperature, which can be counteracted by acetaminophen suppositories, and drying of the mucous membranes like the nose and mouth, which should be kept moistened. Rapid dehydration, on the other hand, which is usually caused by prolonged vomiting, severe diarrhea, or mechanical evacuation of stomach contents, can be significantly more uncomfortable. Without replacement IVs a person will weaken and die quickly. Some patients choose to forego IV therapy knowing full well the eventual outcome.

its components is essential to developing an effective intervention.

Before dealing with some of the more complex psychosocial problems such as loss and grief, the hospice nurse must make a thorough evaluation of all symptoms, particularly pain. As Maslow[4] suggested in his theory of human motivation, basic physiologic needs must be addressed and satisfied before higher order needs can be considered.

NUTRITIONAL PROBLEMS IN THE TERMINALLY ILL

Even more common than pain management, nutritional problems call for much expertise from hospice staff. The fundamental piece of information for staff to gather is the meaning of food during the patient's illness and in the life of that patient and family. It is important for the hospice staff to deal with this issue sensitively because of strong individual and cultural beliefs about the importance of food.

Nutritional deficiencies usually result from nausea, with or without subsequent vomiting; mouth soreness, which may be caused by treatment or vitamin deficiencies; or anorexia. Nausea can generally be at least partially controlled by antiemetics. As with pain management, regular and prophylactic administration of antiemetics is important. Mouth soreness can usually be remedied by healing mouthwashes, topical anesthetics, and vitamin supplements. Anorexia is more complex. Quite commonly, terminally ill cancer patients simply have no appetite. Food is unappealing and may taste different from what they recall, and early satiety is the norm. "Two bites and they can't eat another thing" is an

often heard lament from many a family. Anorexia as a symptom in this situation is not easily remedied. Families should learn not to make nutrition a battleground; they should encourage the patient to eat but not force feed. The nutritional content of food is far less important at this stage in life than being able to eat and to enjoy the experience of eating. Beer and pizza may be just the thing to get a little nourishment into that disease-ravaged body. No amount of nutrition will stop the progress of the disease but attempting to maintain protein stores can help skin integrity and the patient may not weaken quite so quickly.

More critical is the issue of hydration. A person can live quite a while without food (as evidenced by hunger strikers who do not eat but ingest fluids) but a human being cannot live for any length of time without fluids. IV therapy questions are often raised by families and hospice nurses must be prepared to discuss this sensitive issue. An

The nutritional content of food is far less important at this stage in life than being able to eat and to enjoy the experience of eating.

assessment must be made of the patient's performance status, the rapidity of dehydration, level of consciousness with accompanying thirst, and patient and family views concerning hydration and other invasive procedures.

If a patient has been ambulatory but is weakening and is dehydrated, a liter or two of fluid can certainly enhance quality of life temporarily. If, however, the patient is in an extremely debilitated state, is bedrid-

VISIT PATTERNS

Most hospice referrals (75%) are made at the point of a patient's discharge from an acute care facility. Many times, families are asked by the facility to give home care one more try. Often during the hospital stay the patient has been evaluated and "tuned up," providing for a stable medical condition, at least initially. The visit pattern for hospice patients starts moderately at the time of admission to the program with an increase in the frequency of visits as the patient's condition begins to change. This can be contrasted (see Fig 4) with a referral of a nonterminal patient to a home health agency where the patient's needs are the greatest initially and diminish over a period of weeks (eg, a patient with a new colostomy). Generally, the hospice visits increase in number and duration as death approaches. It is vital to be able to increase the number of visits as the patient deteriorates, thus allowing the family to feel the ever-increasing support from the hospice staff.

PREPARATION FOR A HOME DEATH

A person dying at home surrounded by family and the familiar smells, sounds, and sights can be an exceedingly beautiful experience. Almost nothing can make family members feel any better about themselves than caring for someone they love and being able to keep the loved one at home for the duration of the illness. For some a home death is the ultimate gift. For others the very thought of someone dying at home is repugnant. A hospice nurse's greatest challenge may be discerning the choice relating to home death for each patient and family. Some families feel a home death would be wonderful but unmanageable for them, while others may see a home death in much simpler terms than are accurate and are inadequately prepared physically and emotionally. The hospice nurse needs to convey to these families the sense that (1) a home death is manageable for nearly every patient and family if they have proper support; (2) it is important to address needs as they arise, so that a crisis does not occur because of unrealistic or inadequate preparation; 3) not every patient can die at home no matter how much he or she is loved and supported. It is not an indication of failure if an institutional death is necessary or is chosen by the family.

Preparing for a home death is really not too difficult if the professional people supporting the family believe home death is acceptable and are willing to help the family through it. Most patients and families say that they fear not the death but rather the dying. They are concerned about suffering.

First and foremost it must be explained that the physical symptoms will be kept to a minimum, and that the hospice staff and the patient's physician will see to it that enough of the needed medication will be supplied to keep the symptoms at bay. Some families worry about emotional suffering, but most people worry about physical suffering.

The hospice staff must be aware that many families crumble temporarily and need extra visits, telephone calls, and pats on the back to get through that time when they believe they cannot get through it. One of these crises is generally all that is seen, and the sailing is usually much smoother after that. Families may be more intent than ever to achieve a home death because now they know they can.

It is useful to alert the patient's physician and funeral home that a home death is expected. When a patient dies at home, the physician may not always be required to come and pronounce the patient dead. In some states a nurse may do the pronouncement and in other states the family may simply notify the physician and their funeral home. The words "expected home death" can be magic if the funeral home is called and its staff decides to call the local coroner. Regulations differ from state to state and accepted practices differ from municipality to municipality, but notification of the physician and the funeral home can allay many problems and their accompanying heartache. Somehow being forced to have your loved one's body taken to a local emergency department if no physician (or nurse in some locales) is available lacks the dignity that we strive for when people die at home.

ON-CALL SYSTEM

Essential to the success of a hospice program is the development of a nurse on-call system. Terminal care problems have no respect for the usual 9-to-5 Monday through Friday work week. Families need to be assured that they are only a telephone call away from expert advice or a home visit. It is extremely comforting to a family to know that someone who understands the problems can be reached regardless of the time or the day of the week. Problems always seem worse in the middle of the night and it is important to be able to reach someone and discuss them. That, coupled with the option of a home visit if needed, is often a major reason why hospice patients can remain at home until they die.

Staffing an on-call schedule is done many different ways. Most hospices use their own staff on a rotating basis, others hire extra nurses to work on call, and some use their own staff during the week with the extra staff being on call for weekends and holidays. When hospices are using their own nurses for on call they may change the person on call every day, every few days or even weekly. Whatever works best for each individual program is the right way to manage an on-call system because being on call is, perhaps, one of the most stressful parts of hospice nursing. It is difficult to work all day or all week and then be on call that night or for the weekend. On the other hand, each nurse has a slightly different way of doing things and sometimes the nurse prefers to be the person on call for better continuity of care and follow through with his or her patients. Opinions on this aspect of hospice nursing are as diverse as the many models of hospice care.

STAFF BURNOUT

One of the common concerns of outsiders viewing a hospice team in action is the expectation of "burnout" of team members. With the experience of successive losses, there is pervasive fear that the staff will not be able to survive in this working environment for long.

With this in mind, the early hospice team developers created support systems, both formal and informal, to prevent burnout from happening. Much to the surprise of hospice managers, the issue of burnout has not been a problem. Staff members come to hospice with an expectation that they will lose every patient they meet, and so for the most part they gear their involvement accordingly. It is wonderful to watch a well-integrated team taking turns with families; moving toward and away from intimacy with patients, knowing that the hospice team as a whole provides even more than the sum of its parts.

What is apparent about burnout, however, is that staff is susceptible to common work setting problems such as patient workload demands, shrinking continuing education monies, and staff personality differences. Hospice staff members have needs similar to those of any workers in a health care setting: They need to feel support from their managers, to see that their good work is valued by the agency, and to be treated fairly with scheduling, work space, patient load, time-off requests, and compensation.

Staff members leave the hospice setting for all the normal reasons: to pursue education, to change location, to spend more time with children. And, yes, it is sometimes a healthy decision to leave hospice to seek a more varied or diverse health care experience. With each person's coping abilities differing so greatly, there is no standard 2-year or 3-year stint prescribed for hospice. More important, each individual must continually evaluate job satisfaction, self-esteem, and overall personal and career goals.

REFERENCES

1. Kubler-Ross E. *On Death and Dying*. New York, NY: Macmillan; 1970.
2. Torrens PR. *Hospice Programs and Public Policy*. Chicago, Ill: American Hospital Publishing, Inc; 1985.
3. Amenta MO, Bohnet NL. *Nursing Care of the Terminally Ill*. Boston, Mass: Little, Brown, 1986.
4. Maslow AH. *Motivation and Personality*. New York, NY: Harper & Row; 1954.

SUGGESTED READINGS

Lack SA, Buckingham RW III. *First American Hospice Three Years of Home Care*. New Haven, Conn: Hospice, Inc.; 1978.
Mor V, Greer DS, Kastenbaum R. *The Hospice Experiment*. Baltimore, Md: The Johns Hopkins University Press; 1988.
Stoddard S. *The Hospice Movement A Better Way of Caring for the Dying*. New York, NY: Random House; 1978.
Zimmerman J. *Hospice Complete Care for the Terminally Ill*. Baltimore, Md: Urban and Schwartzenberg; 1986.

Ethical Issues of Dying, Death, and Suicide

Unit 4

One of our concerns about dying and death pressing hard upon our consciences is the question of helping the dying to die sooner with the assistance of the physician. Public awareness of the horrors that can be visited upon us by artificial means of ventilation and other support measures in a high-tech hospital setting has produced a literature that debates the issue of euthanasia—a good death. Is it the function of the doctor to assist patients in their dying, to actually kill them at their request? As individuals think through their plans for care when dying, there is a steady increase in the demand for control of that care.

Another controversial issue is physician-assisted suicide. The highly publicized suicides in Michigan and the popularity of the book *Final Exit* make these issues prominent in national—and international—concern. Legislative action has been taken in some states to permit physician-assisted suicide, and it is pending in a number of others. Again, is this the role of individuals called health care providers? The pro and contra positions are presented in several articles in this unit. Although the issue is difficult and personally challenging, as a nation we are in the position of being required to make difficult choices.

The word, suicide, meaning "self" and "to kill," was first used in English in the mid-1600s. Early societies sometimes forced certain members to commit suicide for ritual purposes and occasionally expected such of widows and slaves. There is also a strong inheritance from Hellenic and Roman times of rational suicide when disease, dishonor, or failure were considered unbearable. In the early Middle Ages, attitudes toward suicide changed when St. Augustine laid down rules against it that became basic Christian doctrine for centuries.

In recent years, suicide has attracted increasing interest and scrutiny by sociologists, psychologists, and others in an effort to reduce the incidence. Suicide is a major concern in the United States today. Understanding suicide is important so that warning signs in others can be recognized. Various suicide types, cross-cultural rates, and a history of suicide are presented in the article by Ronald Maris, "Suicide." In "We Have a Problem," Jane Marks presents one mother's view of her child's response to her father's suicide. The role of counseling in allowing feelings to be expressed is examined.

Just what constitutes suicide is not clear today. Risky behavior that leads to death may, or may not, be classified as suicide. We have differing attitudes toward suicide, and these are discussed in this unit. Suicide rates are high in adolescents, the elderly, and males. A person with high vulnerability to suicide is an alcoholic, depressed male between the ages of 75 and 84. Suicidal persons tend to talk about the attempt prior to the act and often display observable signs of potential suicide. Males are more likely to complete suicide than females because they tend to use more lethal weapons. For suicidal individuals, the act appears to be an easy solution to their problems—but it is a permanent answer to an often temporary set of problems.

Looking Ahead: Challenge Questions

The question, "What is a good death?" has been asked for centuries. What would constitute a good death in this time of high-tech medical care? Does the concept of a good death include the taking of a life?

Does the role of the health care provider include taking life or providing the means for others to do so?

What constraints could be implemented to prevent the killing of individuals we do not consider worthwhile contributors to our society?

Should there be limits placed on the length of life as we consider the expenses involved in the care of the elderly and the infirm?

For some individuals, suicide may seem to be the best solution to their situation. How might our society help such individuals trying to "solve" their problems?

Is the concept of "rational suicide" rational? Defend your answer.

Do you believe that high risk-taking persons—such as heavy smokers, race car drivers, overeating or undereating individuals, or persons mixing alcohol and drugs—are suicidal?

Doctor, I Want to Die. Will You Help Me?

Timothy E. Quill, MD

IT HAD been 18 months since a 67-year-old retired man whose main joy in life was his two grandchildren was diagnosed with inoperable lung cancer. An arduous course of chemotherapy helped him experience a relatively good year where he was able to remain independent, babysitting regularly for his grandchildren.

Recent tests revealed multiple new bony metastases. An additional round of chemotherapy and radiation provided little relief. By summer, pain and fatigue became unrelenting. He was no longer able to tolerate, much less care for, his grandchildren. His wife of 45 years devoted herself to his care and support. Nonetheless, his days felt empty and his nights were dominated by despair about the future. Though he was treated with modern pain control methods, his severe bone pain required daily choices between pain and sedation. Death was becoming less frightening than life itself.

See also pp 140 and 141

A particularly severe thigh pain led to the roentgenogram that showed circumferential destruction of his femur. Attempting to preserve his ability to walk, he consented to the placement of a metal plate. Unfortunately, the bone was too brittle to support the plate. He would never walk again.

One evening in the hospital after his wife had just left, his physician sat down to talk. The pain was "about the same," and the new sleep medication "helped a little." He seemed quiet and distracted. When asked what was on his mind, he looked directly at his doctor and said, "Doctor, I want to die. Will you help me?"

Such requests are dreaded by physicians. There is a desperate directness that makes sidestepping the question very difficult, if not impossible. Often, we successfully avoid hearing about the

From the Program for Biopsychosocial Studies, School of Medicine, University of Rochester, and the Department of Medicine, The Genesee Hospital, Rochester, NY.

The views expressed in this article are those of the author and do not necessarily represent those of the University of Rochester or the Department of Medicine.

Reprint requests to the Department of Medicine, The Genesee Hospital, Rochester, NY 14607 (Dr Quill).

inner turmoil faced by our terminally ill patients—what is happening to the person who has the disease. Yet, sometimes requests for help in dying still surface from patients with strong wills, or out of desperation when there is nowhere else to turn. Though comfort care (ie, medical care using a hospice philosophy) provides a humane alternative to traditional medical care of the dying,[1-7] it does not always provide guidance for how to approach those rare patients who continue to suffer terribly in spite of our best efforts.

This article explores what dying patients might be experiencing when they make such requests and offers potential physician responses. Such discussions are by no means easy for clinicians, for they may become exposed to forms and depths of suffering with which they are unfamiliar and to which they do not know how to respond. They may also fear being asked to violate their own moral standards or having to turn down someone in desperate need. Open exploration of requests for physician-assisted death can be fundamental to the humane care of a dying person, because no matter how terrifying and unresolvable their suffering appears, at least they are no longer alone with it. It also frequently opens avenues of "help" that were not anticipated and that do not involve active assistance in dying.

"Doctor, I want to die" and "Will you help me?" constitute both a statement and a query that must each be independently understood and explored. The initial response, rather than a yes or no based on assumptions about the patient's intent and meaning, might be something like: "Of course, I will try to help you, but first I need to understand your wish and your suffering, and then we can explore how I can help." Rather than shying away from the depths of suffering, follow-up questions might include, "What is the worst part?" or "What is your biggest fear?"

THE WISH TO DIE

Transient yearnings for death as an escape from suffering are extremely common among patients with incurable, relentlessly progressive medical illnesses.[8-10] They are not necessarily signs

of a major psychiatric disorder, nor are they likely to be fully considered requests for a physician-assisted death. Let us explore some of their potential meanings through a series of case vignettes.

Tired of Acute Medical Treatment

A 55-year-old woman with very aggressive breast cancer found her tumor to be repeatedly recurring over the last 6 months. The latest instance signaled another failure of chemotherapy. When her doctor was proposing a new round of experimental therapy, she said, "I wish I were dead." By exploring her statement, the physician learned that the patient felt strongly she was not going to get better and that she could not fathom the prospect of more chemotherapy with its attendant side effects. She wanted to spend what time she had left at home. He also learned that she did not want to die at that moment. A discussion about changing the goals of treatment from cure to comfort ensued, and a treatment plan was developed that exchanged chemotherapy for symptom-relieving treatments. The patient was relieved by this change in focus, and she was able to spend her last month at home with her family on a hospice program.

Comfort care can guide a caring and humane approach to the last phase of life by directing its energy to relieving the patients' suffering with the same intensity and creativity that traditional medical care usually devotes to treating the underlying disease.[1-7] When comprehensively applied, in either a hospice program or any other setting, comfort care can help ensure a dignified, individualized death for most patients.

Unrecognized or Undertreated Physical Symptoms

A stoical 85-year-old farmer with widely metastatic prostate cancer was cared for in his home with the help of a hospice program. Everyone marveled at his dry wit and engaging nature as he courageously faced death. He was taking very little medication and always said he was "fine." Everyone loved to visit with him, and his stories about life on the farm were legendary. As he became more withdrawn and caustic, people became concerned, but when he said

From *Journal of the American Medical Association*, Vol. 270, August 18, 1993, pp. 870-875. © 1993 by the American Medical Association. Reprinted by permission.

he wished he were dead, there was a panic. All the guns on the farm were hidden and plans for a psychiatric hospitalization were entertained. When his "wish for death" was fully explored, it turned out that he was living with excruciating pain, but not telling anyone because he feared becoming "addicted" to narcotics. After a long discussion about pain-relieving principles, the patient agreed to try a regular, around-the-clock dosage of a long-acting narcotic with "as needed" doses as requested. In a short time, his pain was under better control, he again began to engage his family and visitors, and he no longer wanted to die. For the remainder of his life, the physical symptoms that developed were addressed in a timely way, and he died a relatively peaceful death surrounded by his family.

Though not all physical symptoms can be relieved by the creative application of comfort care, most can be improved or at least made tolerable. New palliative techniques have been developed that can ameliorate most types of physical pain, provided they are applied without unnecessary restraint. One must be sure that unrelieved symptoms are not the result of ignorance about or inadequate trials of available medical treatments, or the result of exaggerated patient or physician fears about addiction or about indirectly hastening death. Experts who can provide formal or informal consultation in pain control and in palliative care are available in most major cities and extensive literature is available.[11-14]

Emergent Psychosocial Problems

A 70-year-old retired woman with chronic leukemia that had become acute and had not responded to treatment was sent home on a home hospice program. She was prepared to die, and all of her physicians felt that she would "not last more than a few weeks." She had lived alone in the past, but her daughter took a leave of absence from work to care for her mother for her last few days or weeks. Ironically (though not necessarily surprisingly), the mother stabilized at home. Two months later, outwardly comfortable and symptom-free under the supportive watch of her daughter, she began to focus on wanting to die. When asked to elaborate, she initially discussed her fatigue and her lack of a meaningful future. She then confided that she hated being a burden on her daughter—that her daughter had children who needed her and a job that was beginning to cause serious strain. The daughter had done her best to protect her mother from these problems, but she became aware of them anyway. A family meeting where the problems were openly discussed result-

ed in a compromise where the mother was admitted to a nursing facility where comfort care was offered, and the daughter visited every other weekend. Though the mother ideally would have liked to stay at home, she accepted this solution and was transferred to an inpatient unit where she lived for 2 more months before dying with her daughter at her side.

Requests for help in dying can emanate from unrecognized or evolving psychosocial problems.[15] Sometimes these problems can be alleviated by having a family meeting, by arranging a temporary "respite" admission to a health care facility, or by consulting a social worker for some advice about finances and available services. Other psychosocial problems may be more intractable, for example, in a family that was not functioning well prior to the patient's illness or when a dominating family member tries to influence care in a direction that appears contrary to the patient's wishes or best interest. Many patients have no family and no financial resources. The current paucity of inpatient hospices and nursing facilities capable of providing comfort care and the inadequate access to health care in general in the United States often mean that dying patients who need the most help and support are forced to fend for themselves and often die by themselves. The health care reimbursement system is primarily geared toward acute medical care, but not terminal care, so the physician may be the only potential advocate and support that some dying patients have.

Spiritual Crisis

A 42-year-old woman who was living at home with advanced acquired immunodeficiency syndrome (AIDS) began saying that she wished she were dead. She was a fundamentalist Christian who at the time of her diagnosis wondered, "Why would God do this to me?" She eventually found meaning in the possibility that God was testing her strength, and that this was her "cross to bear." Though she continued to regularly participate in church activities over the 5 years after her initial diagnosis, she never confided in her minister or church friends about her diagnosis. Her statements about wishing she were dead frightened her family, and they forced her to visit her doctor. When asked to elaborate on her wish, she raged against her church, her preacher, and her God, stating she found her disease humiliating and did not want to be seen in the end stages of AIDS where everyone would know. She had felt more and more alone with these feelings, until they burst open. Once the feelings were acknowledged and understood, it was clear that they defied simple so-

lution. She was clearly and legitimately angry, but not depressed. She had no real interest in taking her own life. She was eventually able to find a fundamentalist minister from a different church with an open mind about AIDS who helped her find some spiritual consolation.

The importance of the physician's role as witness and support cannot be overemphasized. Sharing feelings of spiritual betrayal and uncertainty with an empathetic listener can be the first step toward healing. At least isolation is taken out of the doubt and despair. The physician must listen and try to fully understand the problem before making any attempt to help the patient achieve spiritual resolution. Medically experienced clergy are available in many communities who can explore spiritual issues with dying patients of many faiths so that isolation can be further lessened and potential for reconnection with one's religious roots enhanced.

Clinical Depression

A 60-year-old man with a recently diagnosed recurrence of his non-Hodgkin's lymphoma became preoccupied with wanting to die. Though he had a long remission after his first course of chemotherapy, he had recently gone through a divorce and felt he could not face more treatment. In exploring his wishes, it was evident he was preoccupied with the death of his father, who experienced an agonizing death filled with severe pain and agitation. He had a strong premonition that the same thing would happen to him, and he was not sleeping because of this preoccupation. He appeared withdrawn and was not able to fully understand and integrate his options and the odds of treatment directed at his lymphoma, the likelihood that comfort care would prevent a death like his father's, or his doctor's promise to work with him to find acceptable solutions. Though he was thinking seriously of suicide, he did not have a plan and therefore was treated intensively as an outpatient by his internist and a psychotherapist. He accepted the idea that he was depressed, but also wanted assurances that all possibilities could be explored after a legitimate trial of treatment for depression. He responded well to a combination of psychotherapy and medication. He eventually underwent acute treatment directed at his lymphoma that unfortunately did not work. He then requested hospice care and seemed comfortable and engaged in his last months. As death was imminent, his symptoms remained relatively well controlled, and he was not overtly depressed. He died alone while his family was out of the house. Since his recently filled prescription bottles were all empty, it may have been a drug overdose (presumably to avoid an end like his father's), though no note or discussion accompanied the act.

Whenever a severely ill person begins to talk about wanting to die and begins to seriously consider taking his or her own life, the question of clinical depression appropriately arises.[16] This can be a complex and delicate determination because most patients who are near death with unrelenting suffering are very sad, if not clinically depressed. The epidemiologic literature associating terminal illness and suicide assumes that all such acts arise from unrecognized and/or untreated psychiatric disorders,[17-19] yet there is a growing clinical literature suggesting that some of these suicides may be rational.[2,16,20-25]

Two fundamental questions must be answered before suicide can be considered rational in such settings: (1) Is the patient able to fully understand his or her disease, prognosis, and treatment alternatives (ie, is the decision rational), and (2) is the patient's depression reversible, given the limitations imposed by his illness, in a way that would substantially alter the circumstances? It is vital not to overnormalize (eg, "anyone would be depressed under such circumstances") or to reflexively define the request as a sign of psychopathology. Each patient's dilemma must be fully explored. Consultation with an experienced psychiatrist can be helpful when there is doubt, as can a trial of grief counseling, crisis intervention, or antidepressant medications if a potentially reversible depression is present and the patient has time and strength to participate.

Unrelenting, Intolerable Suffering

The man with widely metastatic lung cancer described in the introduction felt that his life had become a living hell with no acceptable options. His doctors agreed that all effective medical options to treat his cancer had been exhausted. Physical activity and pride in his body had always been a central part of who he was. Now, with a pathologic fracture in his femur that could not be repaired, he would not even be able to walk independently. He also had to make daily trade-offs between pain, sedation, and other side effects. At the insistence of his doctor, he had several visits with a psychiatrist who found his judgment to be fully rational. Death did not appear imminent, and his condition could only get worse. Even on a hospice program, with experts doing their best to help address his medical, social, personal, and spiritual concerns, he felt trapped, yearning for death. He saw his life savings from 45 years of work rapidly depleting. His family offered additional personal and financial resources. They

wanted him to live, but having witnessed the last months of progressive disability, loss, and pain, with no relief in sight other than death, they respected his wishes and slowly began to advocate on his behalf. "We appreciate your efforts to keep him comfortable, but for him this is not comfortable and it is not living. Will you help him?"

Physicians who have made a commitment to shepherd their patients through the dying process find themselves in a predicament. They can acknowledge that comfort care is sometimes far less than ideal, but it is the best that they can offer, or they can consider making an exception to the prohibition against physician-assisted death, with its inherent personal and professional risks. Compassionate physicians differ widely on their approach to this dilemma,[20-24,26-29] though most would likely agree with an open discussion with a patient who raises the issue and an extensive search for alternatives.

Clinical criteria have been proposed to guide physicians who find assisted suicide a morally acceptable avenue of last resort[25]: (1) the patient must, of his or her own free will and at his or her own initiative, clearly and repeatedly request to die rather than continue suffering; (2) the patient's judgment must not be distorted; (3) the patient must have a condition that is incurable and associated with severe, unrelenting, intolerable suffering; (4) the physician must ensure that the patient's suffering and the request are not the result of inadequate comfort care; (5) physician-assisted suicide should only be carried out in the context of a meaningful doctor-patient relationship[22]; (6) consultation with another physician who is experienced in comfort care is required; and (7) clear documentation to support each condition above should be required (if and when such a process becomes openly sanctioned). It is not the purpose of this article to review the policy implications of formally accepting these criteria or of maintaining current prohibitions.[20-29] Instead, it is to encourage and guide clinicians on both sides of the issue to openly explore the potential meanings of a patient's request for help in dying and to search as broadly as possible for acceptable responses that are tailored to the individual patient.

THE REQUEST FOR HELP IN DYING

Dying patients need more than prescriptions for narcotics or referrals to hospice programs from their physicians. They need a personal guide and counselor through the dying process—someone who will unflinchingly help them face both the medical and the personal aspects of dying, whether it goes smoothly or it

takes the physician into unfamiliar, untested ground. Dying patients do not have the luxury of choosing not to undertake the journey, or of separating their person from their disease. Physicians' commitment not to abandon their patients is of paramount importance.

Requests for assistance in dying only rarely evolve into fully considered requests for physician-assisted suicide or euthanasia. As illustrated in the case vignettes, a thorough exploration and understanding of the patient's experience and the reason the request is occurring at a given moment in time often yield avenues of "help" that are acceptable to almost all physicians and ethicists. These clinical summaries have been oversimplified to illustrate distinct levels of meaning. More often, multiple levels exist simultaneously, yielding several avenues for potential intervention. Rather than making any assumptions about what kind of help is being requested, the physician may ask the patient to help clarify by asking, "How were you hoping I could help?" Exploring a patient's request or wish does not imply an obligation to accede, but rather to seriously listen and to consider with an open mind. Even if the physician cannot directly respond to a rational request for a physician-assisted death because of personal, moral, or legal constraints, exploring, understanding, and expressing empathy can often be therapeutic.[30,31] In addition, the physician and the patient may be able to find some creative middle ground that is acceptable to both.[32,33] Finding common ground that can enhance the patient's comfort, dignity, and personal choice at death without compromising the physician's personal and professional values can be creative, challenging, and satisfying work for physicians.

WHAT DO DYING PERSONS WANT MOST FROM THEIR PHYSICIANS?

Most patients clearly do not want to die, but if they must, they would like to do so while maintaining their physical and personal integrity.[34] When faced with a patient expressing a wish for death, and a request for help, physicians (and others) should consider the following.

Listen and Learn From the Patient Before Responding

Learning as much as possible about the patient's unique suffering and about exactly what is being requested is a vital first step. Physicians tend to be action oriented, yet these problems only infrequently yield simple resolutions. This is not to say they are insoluble, but the patient is the initial guide to defining the problem and the range of acceptable interventions.

Be Compassionate, Caring, and Creative

Comfort care is a far cry from "not doing anything." It is completely analogous to intensive medical care, only in this circumstance the care is directed toward the person and his or her suffering, not the disease. Dying patients need our commitment to creatively problem-solve and support them no matter where their illness may go. The rules and methods are not simple when applied to real persons, but the satisfaction and meaning of helping someone find his or her own path to a dignified death can be immeasurable.

Promise to Be There Until the End

Many people have personally witnessed or in some way encountered "bad deaths," though what this might mean to a specific patient is varied and unpredictable. Patients need our assurance that, if things get horrible, undignified, or intolerable, we will not abandon them, and we will continue to work with them to find acceptable solutions. Usually those solutions do not involve directly assisting death, but they may often involve the aggressive use of symptom-relieving measures that might indirectly hasten death.[3,35] We should be able to reassure all our patients that they will not die racked by physical pain, for it is now accepted practice to give increasing amounts of analgesic medicine until the pain is relieved even if it inadvertently shortens life. Many patients find this promise reassuring, for it both alleviates the fear of pain, and also makes concrete the physician's willingness to find creative, aggressive solutions.

If Asked, Be Honest About Your Openness to the Possibility of Assisted Suicide

Patients who want to explore the physician's willingness to provide a potentially lethal prescription often fear being out of control, physically dependent, or mentally incapacitated, rather than simply fearing physical pain.[36] For many, the possibility of a controlled death if things become intolerable is often more important than the reality. Those who secretly hold lethal prescriptions or who have a physician who will entertain the possibility of such treatment feel a sense of control and possibility that, if things became intolerable, there will be a potential escape. Other patients will be adequately reassured to know that we can acknowledge the problem, talk about death, and actively search for acceptable alternatives, even if we cannot directly assist them.

Try to Approach Intolerable End-of-Life Suffering With an Open Heart and an Open Mind

Though acceptable solutions can almost always be found through the aggressive application of comfort care principles, this is not a time for denial of the problem or for superficial solutions. If there are no good alternatives, what should the patient do? There is often a moment of truth for health care providers and families faced with a patient whom they care about who has no acceptable options. Physicians must not turn their backs, but continue to problem-solve, to be present, to help their patients find dignity in death.

Do Not Forget Your Own Support

Working intensively with dying patients can be both enriching and draining. It forces us to face our own mortality, our abilities, and our limitations. It is vital to have a place where we can openly share our own grief, doubts, and uncertainties, as well as take joy in our small victories.[37] For us to deepen our understanding of the human condition and to help humanize the dying process for our patients and ourselves, we must learn to give voice to and share our own private experience of working closely with dying patients.

The patients with whom we engage at this level often become indelibly imprinted on our identities as professionals. Much like the death of a family member, the process that they go through and our willingness and ability to be there and to be helpful are often replayed and rethought. The intensity of these relationships and our ability to make a difference are often without parallel. Because the road is traveled by us all, but the map is poorly described, it is often an adventure with extraordinary richness and unclear boundaries.

In memory of Arthur Schmale, MD, who taught me how to listen, learn, and take direction from the personal stories of dying patients.

[See Commentary, next page]

References

1. Wanzer SH, Adelstein SJ, Cranford RE, et al. The physician's responsibility toward hopelessly ill patients. *N Engl J Med.* 1984;310:955-959.
2. Wanzer SH, Federman DO, Adelstein SJ, et al. The physician's responsibility toward hopelessly ill patients: a second look. *N Engl J Med.* 1989;320:844-849.
3. Council on Ethical and Judicial Affairs, American Medical Association. Decisions near the end of life. *JAMA.* 1992;267:2229-2233.
4. Rhymes J. Hospice care in America. *JAMA.* 1990; 264:369-372.
5. Hastings Center Report. *Guidelines on the Termination of Life-Sustaining Treatment and the Care of the Dying.* New York, NY: The Hastings Center; 1987.
6. Zimmerman JM. *Hospice: Complete Care for the Terminally Ill.* Baltimore, Md: Urban & Schwarzenberg; 1981.
7. Quill T. *Death and Dignity: Making Choices and Taking Charge.* New York, NY: WW Norton & Co; 1993.
8. Aries P. *The Hour of Our Death.* New York, NY: Vintage Books; 1982.
9. Kubler-Ross E. *On Death and Dying.* New York, NY: Macmillan Publishing Co Inc; 1969.
10. Richman J. A rational approach to rational suicide. *Suicide Life Threat Behav.* 1992;22:130-141.
11. Foley KM. The treatment of cancer pain. *N Engl J Med.* 1989;313:84-95.
12. Kane RL, Bernstein L, Wales J, Rothenberg R. Hospice effectiveness in controlling pain. *JAMA.* 1985;253:2683-2686.
13. Twyeross RG, Lack SA. *Symptom Control in Far Advanced Cancer: Pain Relief.* London, England: Pitman Books Ltd; 1984.
14. Kerr IG, Some M, DeAngelis C, et al. Continuous narcotic infusion with patient-controlled analgesia for chronic cancer outpatients. *Ann Intern Med.* 1988;108:554-557.
15. Garfield C. *Psychosocial Care of the Dying Patient.* New York, NY: McGraw-Hill International Book Co; 1978.
16. Conwell Y, Caine ED. Rational suicide and the right to die: reality and myth. *N Engl J Med.* 1991; 325:1100-1103.
17. Allenbeck P, Bolund C, Ringback G. Increased suicide rate in cancer patients. *J Clin Epidemiol.* 1989;42:611-616.
18. Breitbart W. Suicide in cancer patients. *Oncology.* 1989;:49-55.
19. MacKenzie TB, Popkin MK. Suicide in the medical patient. *Int J Psychiatry Med.* 1987;17:3-22.
20. Cassel CK, Meier DE. Morals and moralism in the debates on euthanasia and assisted suicide. *N Engl J Med.* 1990;323:750-752.
21. Quill TE. Death and dignity: a case of individualized decision making. *N Engl J Med.* 1991;324:691-694.
22. Jecker NS. Giving death a hand: when the dying and the doctor stand in a special relationship. *J Am Geriatr Soc.* 1991;39:831-835.
23. Angell M. Euthanasia. *N Engl J Med.* 1988; 319:1348-1350.
24. Brody H. Assisted death: a compassionate response to a medical failure. *N Engl J Med.* 1992; 327:1384-1388.
25. Quill TE, Cassel CK, Meier DE. Care of the hopelessly ill: potential clinical criteria for physician-assisted suicide. *N Engl J Med.* 1992;327:1380-1384.
26. Singer PA, Siegler M. Euthanasia: a critique. *N Engl J Med.* 1990;322:1881-1883.
27. Orentlicher D. Physician participation in assisted suicide. *JAMA.* 1989;262:1844-1845.
28. Gaylin WL, Kass R, Pellegrino ED, Siegler M. Doctors must not kill. *JAMA.* 1988;259:2139-2140.
29. Gomez CF. *Regulating Death: Euthanasia and the Case of the Netherlands.* New York, NY: Free Press; 1991.
30. Novack DH. Therapeutic aspects of the clinical encounter. *J Gen Intern Med.* 1987;2:346-355.
31. Suchman AL, Matthews DA. What makes the doctor-patient relationship therapeutic: exploring the connexional dimension of medical care. *Ann Intern Med.* 1988;108:125-130.
32. Quill TE. Partnerships in patient care: a contractual approach. *Ann Intern Med.* 1983;98:228-234.
33. Fisher R, Ury W. *Getting to Yes: Negotiating Agreement Without Giving In.* Boston, Mass: Houghton Mifflin Co; 1981.
34. Cassel EJ. The nature of suffering and the goals of medicine. *N Engl J Med.* 1982;306:639-645.
35. Meier DE, Cassel CK. Euthanasia in old age: a case study and ethical analysis. *J Am Geriatr Soc.* 1983;31:294-298.
36. van der Maas PJ, van Delden JJM, Pijnenborg L, Looman CWN. Euthanasia and other medical decisions concerning the end of life. *Lancet.* 1991; 338:669-674.
37. Quill TE, Williams PR. Healthy approaches to physician stress. *Arch Intern Med.* 1990;150:1857-1861.

Commentary

COMPASSION NEEDS REASON TOO

A growing number of physicians today believe that it is morally permissible, perhaps even required, to assist certain of their patients in the act of suicide.[1-4] They take their inspiration from Quill's account of the way he assisted his young patient, Diane, to kill herself.[5] They are impressed by Quill's compassion and respect for his patient. Like him, they would limit the physician's participation in suicide to extreme cases in which suffering is unrelenting, unrelievable, and unbearable. Like him, they follow a flawed line of moral reasoning in which a compassionate response to a request for assisted suicide is deemed sufficient in itself to justify an ethically indefensible act.

In his article[6] in this issue of THE JOURNAL, Quill provides a more formal and systematic outline of what he believes the appropriate response of physicians should be to a request for suicide. He emphasizes that the reasons for the request must be identified and ameliorated (ie, pain and depression should be properly treated and psychosocial and spiritual crises resolved). To do these things properly, physicians themselves must listen and learn; accept their own mortality; be compassionate, honest, and "present" to their patients; and remain "open" to assisted suicide. If this approach fails to relieve suffering, Quill deems the case extreme enough to justify transgressing the ethical proscription against assisted suicide.

Most of Quill's recommendations are consistent with a physician's responsibility to provide comprehensive palliative care.[7] They would be equally binding on those opposed to assisted suicide. What is not acceptable is the faulty line of reasoning that underlies Quill's seemingly reasonable and moderate approach. That reasoning is marred by three ethical assumptions: (1) that compassion in decision making confers moral validity on the act of assisted suicide; (2) that Quill's decision-making process is, itself, morally sound; and (3) that, by itself, close analysis of cases is sufficient to establish the right and good thing to do in "extreme" cases.

To begin with, Quill begs the most important ethical question, namely, whether in certain cases assisted suicide can be ethically justified. This is the heart of a debate that is far from settled.[8] It cannot be settled here. Elsewhere,[9] I have tried to show that, like active euthanasia, assisted suicide is never morally permissible: both are acts of intentional killing; they are violent remedies in the name of beneficence; they seriously distort the healing purposes of medicine; they are based on erroneous notions of compassion, beneficence, and

From the Georgetown University Medical Center, Washington, DC. Reprints not available.

autonomy; and they divert attention from comprehensive palliative care.[10-12] Moreover, euthanasia and assisted suicide are socially disastrous. They are not containable by placing legal limits on their practice. Arguments to the contrary, the "slippery slope" is an inescapable logical, psychological, historical and empirical reality.

Quill's first implicit assumption is that assisted suicide can sometimes be justified, ie, a morally wrong act can be made morally right if the process used in deciding to perform it and the way it is performed are compassionate and beneficently motivated. The moral psychology of an act has a certain weight in assessing an agent's guilt, but not in changing the nature of the act itself.[10] Even a person's consent is insufficient to make suicide morally right. Nor is it justified by a gentle or genteel "approach" to the act. This, for example, is the stance of those who reject Jack Kevorkian's unseemly and peremptory use of his death machine, but commend Quill's modulated approach.[3] To be sure, Kevorkian shows a shocking disregard for the most elementary responsibilities of a physician to a patient who becomes desperate enough to ask for assisted death.[18] But regardless of whether patients use Kevorkian's machine or Quill's compassionate prescription for sedatives, they are dead by premeditated intention. In either case, physicians, who are the necessary instruments of the patient's death, are as much a moral accomplice as if they had administered the dose themselves.

Even if we grant Quill's first assumption, we are left questioning the moral validity of Quill's recommended decision-making process. On the surface, Quill seems to place the initiative in the patient's hands and suggests that the physician merely be "open" to assisted suicide under the right circumstances. But, ultimately, the determination of the right circumstances is in the physician's hands. The physician controls the availability and timing of the means whereby the patient kills himself. Physicians also judge whether the patients are clinically depressed, their suffering really unbearable, and their psychological and spiritual crises resolvable. Finally, the physician's assessment determines whether the patient is in the "extreme" category that, per se, justifies suicide assistance.

The opportunities for conscious or unconscious abuse of this power are easy to obscure, even for the best-intentioned physician. Physicians' valuation of life and its meaning, the value or nonvalue of suffering, the kind of life they would find bearable, and the point at which life becomes unbearable

(box continued on next page)

(box continued from previous page)

cannot fail to influence their decisions. These values will vary widely even among those who take assisted suicide to be morally licit. The physician might follow all of Quill's recommendations (eg, be honest and compassionate and listen to the patient), but find it virtually impossible to separate personal values from interaction with the patient.

Moreover, physicians must face their own frustrations, fatigue, and secret hopes for a way out of the burdens of caring for a suffering, terminally ill patient. The kind of intense emotional involvement Quill describes in Diane's case can induce emotional burnout in which the physician moves imperceptibly from awaiting the patient's decision and readiness, to subtle elicitation of a request for death. "Getting it over with" may not be only the patient's desire, but that of the physician, other health professionals, and family and friends.[14] Each will have his or her own reason for being open to assisting in suicide. Each reason is capable of being imputed to a vulnerable, exhausted, guilty, and alienated patient. When assisted suicide is legitimated, it places the patient at immense risk from the "compassion" of others. Misdirected compassion in the face of human suffering can be as dangerous as indifference.

Wesley's[15] astute analysis of Quill's treatment of his patient Diane[5] suggests that Quill himself was not totally immune to some of these psychodynamic dangers. The decision to respond to a request for assistance in suicide can be as much a danger to, as a safeguard of, the patient's right to self-determination. If it is known to be a viable option at the outset, it cannot fail to influence the patient, the physician, and everyone else involved in the patient's care. If it is not known at the outset, the patient is deprived of the clues needed to interpret her physician's actions. No matter how we examine it, Quill's "approach" is as morally dubious as the act to which it leads.

Finally, Quill's article implies that with an ever greater knowledge of the patient's circumstances, thoughts, and values and a sincere effort to understand them, we can realiably arrive at a point at which we move from the morally unacceptable to the morally acceptable. This is the "line of cases" approach that relies for its moral validity on the recently revived method of casuistry.[15] Casuistry is a useful method of case analysis rooted in legal procedure, but it is a dubious way to establish a moral norm.

Brody[1] recently used the casuistic method in a logically fallacious attempt to wipe out the distinction between killing and letting die. The problem with relying solely on the casuistic method of paradigm cases is that there must be something beyond the case by which to judge the case. This would be true even if we could encompass all the details of any case. We must still explicate why this case is a paradigm case that can be used in locating other cases along a moral spectrum. When we do, we discover that a normative principle has been at work. Behind every paradigm case, there is a moral system. Different moral systems judge paradigm cases differently. In the end, we must decide among moral systems, not cases.

It is important, therefore, to read through Quill's metaphorically elegant and compassionate story of Diane's death to the reasons underlying his actions. Clearly for Quill, the undeniably important affect of compassion takes on the status of an overriding moral principle. But compassion is a virtue, not a principle. Morally weighty as it is, compassion can become maleficent unless it is constrained by principle. In the world's history, too many injustices have been committed in the name of someone's judgment about what was compassionate for his neighbor. Compassion, too, must be subject to moral analysis, must have its reasons, and those reasons must also be cogent.

Edmund D. Pellegrino, MD

1. Brody H. Causing, intending and assisting death, *J Clin Ethics.* 1993;4:112–113.

2. Wanzer SH, Dyders DD, Edelstein SJ, et al. The physician's responsibility toward hopelessly ill patients, *N Engl J Med.* 1989;320:844–849.

3. Cassel CK, Meir DE. Morals and moralism in the debate over euthanasia and assisted suicide. *N Engl J Med.* 1990;923:750–752.

4. Ubel PA. Assisted suicide and the case of Dr Quill and Diane. *Issues Law Med.* 1993;8:487–502.

5. Quill TE. Death and dignity: a case of individualized decision making. *N Engl J Med.* 1991;324:691–694.

6. Quill TE. Doctor, I want to die, will you help me? *J.A.M.A.* 1993;270:870–873.

7. Lynn J. The health care professional's role when active euthanasia is sought. *J Palliat Care.* 1988;4:100–102.

8. Kass L. Neither for love nor money; why doctors must not kill. *Public Interest.* 1989;94:25–46.

9. Pellegrino ED. Doctors must not kill. *J Clin Ethics.* 1992;8:95–102.

10. Kamisar Y. Are laws against assisted suicide unconstitutional? *Hastings Cent Rep.* 1993;23:32–41.

11. Arkes H, Berke M, Doctor M, et al. Always to care, never to kill; a declaration on euthanasia. *First Things.* 1992;20:46.

12. Council on Ethical and Judicial Affairs, American Medical Association. Decisions near the end of life. *J.A.M.A.* 1991;267:2229–2233.

13. Kevorkian J. *Prescription Medicine; The Goodness of Planned Death.* Buffalo, NY: Prometheus Books; 1991.

14. It's over, Debbie. *J.A.M.A.* 1986;259:272. A Piece of My Mind.

15. Wesley P. Dying safety issues. *J Law Med.* 1993;8:467–485.

16. Jonsen AR. Casuistry as a methodology in clinical ethics. *Thsor Med.* 1991;12:295–307.

Medicine's Position Is Both Pivotal and Precarious in Assisted-Suicide Debate

Paul Cotton

PHYSICIAN-ASSISTED suicide may become as contentious an issue as abortion.

The escalating battle pits those who say they are protecting a right to life against those who are demanding a right to choose. Opposing camps are virtually identical to those that war over abortion with one notable exception: organized medicine.

"They are two different issues," says American Medical Association (AMA) board of trustees secretary Thomas R. Reardon, MD, an internist in Portland, Ore. "Not even experts agree when life begins," so the AMA maintains that abortion is a medical matter best left between patient and physician. Assisted suicide involves "actively participating in the killing of a living, breathing, functioning, cognitive human being who has a terminal illness," says Reardon.

"For myself and for the AMA this is not a religious issue, it is an ethical issue. Our purpose as physicians is to heal." The option of assisted suicide would tarnish the trust on which the physician-patient relationship is based, he says. Traditionally, most physicians would agree.

Solidarity Is Wavering

However, medicine's solidarity is wavering, and that may tip the balance in debate.

In fact, one thing attorneys for both the National Right to Life Committee and self-styled assisted-suicide crusader Jack Kevorkian, MD, agree on is that the unusual neutral stance taken by a deeply divided Oregon State Medical Society partly explains why voters there last fall voted for the first time, anywhere in the world, to fully legalize physician-assisted suicide. (The Netherlands has greatly liberalized its assisted-suicide laws, but the practice is still technically illegal there.) The law would allow physicians to prescribe, at the request of patients with a prognosis of 6 months or less to live, an overdose of pills that can be self-administered.

State medical societies were aggressive in successfully opposing similar referendums in California and Washington that would have allowed physicians to administer lethal injections. But no consensus could be achieved in the Oregon medical society.

Reardon noticed a "schism" by age in that physicians under age 50 were more likely to support passage, reflecting what he calls "a yuppie society coming up that wants instant gratification. They're not used to stress, and do not want to face the difficulties of life. People look for an easy way out."

But some physicians who supported the referendum say they detect the odor of mendacity in medical opposition. They contend that the practice of "sedating to death" terminally ill patients, often without their knowledge or consent, with increasing doses of morphine is already an everyday occurrence that needs to be brought out of the closet.

"What we are talking about happens in this country many times a day," says Peter Goodwin, MD, associate professor of family medicine at Oregon Health Sciences University School of Medicine, Portland, and a leading supporter of the measure. Goodwin does not want to imply dishonesty on any physician's part. But he allows, as do many, that "Dying patients are given larger and larger doses of morphine. We talk about the 'double effect,' and know jolly well we are sedating them into oblivion, providing pain relief but also providing permanent relief, and we don't tell them."

Many older physicians do tend to find openness somewhat objectionable, says Susan W. Tolle, MD, director of the Center for Ethics in Health Care at Oregon Health Sciences University. She notes that in the 1950s physicians rarely told patients about cancer diagnoses. Some still feel as though they should "take the burden onto themselves, and not destroy hope" for the patient. "[Physicians] were using high-dose morphine to end patients' lives 50 years ago, but it was not something you ever talked about openly."

Goodwin says the physician-patient relationship is impaired by the status quo because assisted suicide cannot be discussed legally. "Patients often feel, and the families of dying patients in particular say, that their physicians abandon the dying patient because they are uncomfortable. That happens because the patient does not have a bargaining chip. That chip is saying, 'Doctor, I would like you to help me die.' This provides the patient with the power to initiate a discussion that at present does not occur." Those who do choose to end their lives must do so "without the advice of a physician. Because it is illegal, it inhibits discussion of issues that would most affect a dying person who wants to end life," says Goodwin.

Goodwin says assisted suicide is like the abortion issue with one fundamental difference: there is no argument as to whether there is a third-party interest, like that of the fetus. "It's clear," he says.

Constitutional Challenge

For now, the Oregon law is on hold pending a constitutional challenge by the National Right to Life Committee. It contends that the law violates the constitutional guarantees of equal protection and due process, as well as the Americans With Disabilities Act. And the law has insufficient safeguards to protect those suffering from depression or who are under "undue influence," which may be causing them to consent, says the group's attorney, James Bopp.

Even if safeguards were sufficient, the Oregon law would still be unconstitutional because it discriminates against the terminally ill by exempting them from the protection of laws against manslaughter, says Bopp. "A depressed teenager is protected against [assisted] suicide by general law, but a depressed person with a terminal illness is not," he says. "Very few terminally ill people who are not depressed want to kill themselves.

"The historical reason for laws against assisted suicide has been the recognition that when somebody's seeking suicide, they're responding to a psychiatric illness and not making a rational decision," says Bopp.

The right-to-life movement opposes both abortion and assisted suicide, he says, because both involve "taking innocent human life without sufficient justification. Killing somebody because they are depressed and terminally ill is not sufficient justification."

Those arguments were enough to win a preliminary injunction from Michael

From *Journal of the American Medical Association*, Vol. 273, February 1, 1995, pp. 363-364. © 1995 by the American Medical Association. Reprinted by permission.

R. Hogan, a federal district court judge in Salem, Ore, who wrote in his ruling that "surely, the first assisted suicide law in this country deserves a considered, thoughtful analysis."

Earlier last year, another federal district court judge, in Seattle, Wash, was persuaded by a diametrically different argument to strike down a law against assisted suicide in that state. Judge Barbara Rothstein found that the constitutional guarantee of individual liberty includes the right to seek aid in dying. That ruling is now being challenged before the Ninth Circuit Court of Appeals.

Supreme Court Bound

The inevitable appeals of rulings in those cases may be beaten to the US Supreme Court by a challenge to a recent ruling by the Supreme Court of Michigan. It not only stated that the US Constitution does not prohibit criminal penalties for assisting in suicide, but said that even without a specific statute prohibiting it, suicide assistance "may be prosecuted as a common-law felony."

This case could well be the first to reach the US Supreme Court, according to Geoffrey N. Fieger, attorney for Kevorkian, the former pathologist who has made headlines worldwide by assisting 21 people in ending their lives.

"The fundamental issue is whether the state has the right to intrude in the physician-patient relationship," says Fieger. "This is not about a right to commit suicide, it is about the right not to suffer. At the end of life when the disease process has won, death is certain, and pain cannot be controlled, how the state has an interest in prolonging suffering is beyond me. [Saying that] a law which does not make anybody do anything, that gives people the right to decide, and prevents the state from prosecuting you for exercising your freedom not to suffer, violates somebody else's constitutional rights is insane," he says.

Fieger says assisted suicide is like the abortion issue in that it is opposed by what he calls "radical antiabortionists, very committed religious [zealots] who believe they should control our lives." The issues are different in that "abortion involves a third party, a fetus, they say they are protecting babies. But this is mentally competent adults asking for help in dying. These people are trying to protect us from our own selves."

Whether the courts will ultimately rule that assisted suicide is a privacy matter like abortion remains to be seen. David Orentlicher, MD, JD, secretary to the AMA Council on Ethical and Judicial Affairs, notes that there is no traditional right to assisted suicide, and that of late courts are "very reluctant to expand rights to privacy. This Supreme Court is not likely to be looking to create fundamental rights."

But while prohibitions on assisted suicide are not likely to be found inherently unconstitutional, Orentlicher also suspects that the courts will not recognize the discrimination claims raised by the National Right to Life Committee, because the terminally ill have not been viewed historically as a protected class.

"Most courts would say the Constitution does not require us to prohibit it, but the Constitution does require us to have sufficient safeguards. Courts may set down constitutional boundaries, but they will almost certainly allow states to go either way, so long as if they do permit it, they have appropriate safeguards," says Orentlicher. States also may have trouble if they "try to have open season," with overly strict enforcement of an assisted suicide ban, he says.

"States are going to be given leeway. The Constitution will allow Washington [State] to prohibit and Oregon to permit as long as it is a reasonably drawn statute," concludes Orentlicher. The issue is "going to be settled much more by legislatures than courts, or by public referendum as in Oregon," he says, adding that just because laws allowing assisted suicide "may be permitted to pass does not mean they are a good idea."

The public referendum route may be particularly troubling for opponents of assisted suicide, since public opinion polls are suggesting wide support for legalization. Fully 72% of 1796 members of the general public interviewed in a random survey in Michigan by the University of Michigan Institute for Social Research say they support legalization. Of 726 physicians queried, only 17% supported an outright ban; 39% favored legalization with strict safeguards and 39% preferred no law, leaving the matter between patient and physician.

Wake-up Call?

Reardon says that the Oregon referendum was sold to voters as a matter of "patient control, empowering patients to have control over their own lives and any terminal illness. It is a wake-up call, a message to our profession that we are not meeting our patients' needs, a message from the public that we need to be more aggressive. We need to reassure society that we can control most, if not all, [of dying patients'] pain," he says.

Oregon Health Sciences University is taking that message to heart, "no matter what happens in court" with the new law, by creating a multidisciplinary "comfort care team," says Tolle.

"Our hospital has taken seriously the idea that the vote was probably about a lot more than assisted suicide. The people of our state made a serious comment on the care of the dying, and it is something we needed as an institution and a profession to hear," she says.

Tolle says that only a "very small number of people will ever utilize this option if it becomes legal. But a huge percentage want other degrees of control in the dying process. Most went into the voting booth with vivid memories of a spouse, friend, or neighbor whose dying lacked something they felt powerfully about. They had prolonged suffering of one type or another and felt the medical community was not as responsive as it could have been."

Focus on Comfort

The issue is often not so much pain as comfort, such things as shortness of breath, itching, fluid overload, or mouth and skin care, "things that have a major impact on the quality of life but have not received academic stature," says Tolle.

To change that, the comfort care team will try to give hospice-level attention to patients who are not ready for a hospice. Now, only 10% to 15% of dying patients receive hospice care. Most have cancer, and only receive such care in the last 2 months of life because enrollment requires that physician, patient, and family all "essentially give up hope of a cure. That has proven to be a pretty big obstacle," says Tolle. "Large groups of patients don't have a focus on comfort at the end."

The comfort care team, it is hoped, can act as "a bridge so there is not such a wide chasm to jump across between curative care and the hospice," says Tolle. It will go into the intensive care unit, oncology clinic, and other places "where the hospice has traditionally not found a home because hope of a cure was still being pursued. That's a huge change in mind-set."

Better attention to pain and comfort is all well and good, says Fieger. Yet there will still be some patients for whom pain cannot be controlled. "If by pain control you mean doping somebody up so they're unconscious in some kind of coma before death, I don't want that. If you are talking real pain control, it can't be done all the time, for instance with bone cancer."

Fieger says the most illustrative case is Kevorkian's 20th patient, Ali Khalili, MD. He was an associate clinical professor of physical medicine and rehabilitation at Northwestern University School of Medicine, Chicago, Ill. "He was a pain specialist, he could get any kind of pain medication, but he came to Dr Kevorkian. There are times," says Fieger, "when pain medication does not suffice."

ALWAYS TO CARE, NEVER TO KILL
A DECLARATION ON EUTHANASIA
THE RAMSEY COLLOQUIUM

The following declaration was produced by the Ramsey Colloquium of the Institute on Religion and Public Life in New York City. The Colloquium is a group of Jewish and Christian theologians, ethicists, philosophers, and scholars that meets periodically to consider questions of ethics, religion, and public life. It is named after Paul Ramsey (1913–1988), the distinguished Methodist ethicist, who was a pioneer in the field of contemporary medical studies.

We are grateful that the citizens of Washington State have turned back a measure that would have extended the permission to kill, but we know that this is not the end of the matter. The American people must now prepare themselves to meet similar proposals for legally sanctioned euthanasia. Toward that end we offer this explanation of why euthanasia is contrary to our faith as Jews and Christians, is based upon a grave moral error, does violence to our political tradition, and undermines the integrity of the medical profession.

In relating to the sick, the suffering, the incompetent, the disabled, and the dying, we must learn again the wisdom that teaches us *always to care, never to kill*. Although it may sometimes appear to be an act of compassion, killing is never a means of caring.

The well-organized campaign for legalized euthanasia cruelly exploits the fear of suffering and the frustration felt when we cannot restore to health those whom we love. Such fear and frustration is genuine and deeply felt, especially with respect to the aging. But to deal with suffering by eliminating those who suffer is an evasion of moral duty and a great wrong.

Deeply embedded in our moral and medical traditions is the distinction between *allowing to die*, on the one hand, and *killing*, on the other. That distinction is now under attack and must be defended with all the force available to us.

It is permitted to refuse or withhold medical treatment in accepting death while we continue to care for the dying. It is never permitted, it is always prohibited, to take any action that is aimed at the death of ourselves or others.

Medical treatments can be refused or withheld if they are either useless or excessively burdensome. No one should be subjected to useless treatment; no one need accept any and all lifesaving treatments, no matter how burdensome. In making such decisions, the judgment is about the worth of treatments, *not* about the worth of lives. When we ask whether a treatment is useless, the question is: "Will this treatment be useful for this patient, will it benefit the life he or she has?" When we ask whether a treatment is burdensome, the question is: "Is this treatment excessively burdensome to the life of this patient?" The question is *not* whether this life is useless or burdensome. Our decisions, whether for or against a specific treatment, are to be always in the service of life. We can and should allow the dying to die; we must never intend the death of the living. We may reject a treatment; we must never reject a life.

Once we cross the boundary between killing and allowing to die, there will be no turning back. Current proposals would legalize euthanasia only for the terminally ill. But the logic of the argument—and its practical consequences—will inevitably push us further. Arguments for euthanasia usually appeal to our supposed right of self-determination and to the desirability of relieving suffering. If a right to euthanasia is grounded in self-determination, it cannot reasonably be limited to the terminally ill. If people have a right to die, why must they wait until they are actually dying before they are permitted to exercise that right? Similarly, if the warrant for euthanasia is to relieve suffering, why should we be able to relieve the suffering only of those who are self-determin-

SELF-DETERMINATION

From *Current*, May 1992, pp. 22-24. Originally from *First Things*, February 1991, pp. 45-47. *First Things*, a monthly journal published in New York City by the Institute on Religion and Public Life.

ing and competent to give their consent? Why not euthanasia for the suffering who can no longer speak for themselves? To ask such questions is to expose the logical incoherence and the fragile arbitrariness of suggested "limits" in proposals for legalized euthanasia.

We must not delude ourselves. Euthanasia is an extension of the license to kill. Once we have transgressed and blurred the line between killing and allowing to die, it will be exceedingly difficult—in logic, law, and practice—to effectively limit the license to kill. Once the judgment is not about the worth of specific treatments but about the worth of specific lives, our nursing homes and other institutions will present us with countless candidates for elimination who would "be better off dead."

In the face of such mortal danger, we would direct public attention to four interwoven sources of wisdom in our cultural heritage that can teach us again always to care, never to kill.

RELIGIOUS WISDOM

As Christians and Jews, we have learned to think of human life—our own and that of others—as both gift and trust. We have been entrusted to one another and are to care for one another. We have not been authorized to make comparative judgments about the worth of lives or to cut short the years that God gives to us or others. We are to relieve suffering when we can, and to bear with those who suffer, helping them to bear their suffering, when we cannot. We are never to "solve" the problem of suffering by eliminating those who suffer. Euthanasia, once established as an option, will inevitably tempt us to abandon those who suffer. This is especially the case when we permit ourselves to be persuaded that their lives are a burden to us or to them. The biblical tradition compels us to seek and exercise better ways to care. We may think that we care when we kill, but killing is never caring. Whatever good intentions we might invoke to excuse it, killing is the rejection of God's command to care and of his help in caring.

MORAL WISDOM

We may possess many good things in life. Although we benefit from such goods, they do not constitute our very being. We can, if we wish, renounce such goods or give them into the control of another. Life, however, is not simply a "good" that we possess. We *are* living beings. Our life *is* our person. To treat our life as a "thing" that we can authorize another to terminate is profoundly dehumanizing. Euthanasia, even when requested by the competent, can never be a humanitarian act, for it attacks

the distinctiveness and limitations of being human. Persons—ourselves and others—are not things to be discarded when they are no longer deemed useful.

We can give our life *for* another, but we cannot give ultimate authority over our life *to* another. The painfully learned moral wisdom of our heritage is that persons cannot "own" persons. The decision for euthanasia is not an exercise of human freedom but the abandonment of human freedom. To attempt to turn one's life into an object that is at the final disposition of another is to become less than human, while it places the other in a position of being more than human—a lord of life and death, a possessor of the personhood of others.

Human community and the entirety of civilization is premised upon a relationship of moral claims and duties between persons. Personhood has no meaning apart from life. If life is a thing that can be renounced or taken at will, the moral structure of human community, understood as a community of persons, is shattered. Whatever the intentions of their proponents, proposals for legalizing euthanasia must be seen not as a solution to discrete problems but as an assault upon the fundamental ideas undergirding the possibility of moral order. The alternative to that moral order is the lethal disorder of a brave new world in which killing is defined as caring, life is viewed as the enemy, and death is counted as a benefit to be bestowed.

POLITICAL WISDOM

"We hold these truths," the founders of our political community declared, and among the truths that our community has held is that the right to life is "unalienable." All human beings have an equal right to life bestowed by "Nature and Nature's God." Government is to recognize and respect that right; it does not bestow that right.

This unalienable right places a clear limit on the power of the state. Except when government exercises its duty to protect citizens against force and injustice, or when it punishes evildoers, it may not presume for itself an authority over human life. To claim that—apart from these exceptions—the state may authorize the killing even of consenting persons is to give state authority an ultimacy it has never had in our political tradition. Again, legalized euthanasia is an unprecedented extension of the license to kill. In the name of individual rights it undercuts the foundation of individual rights. An unalienable right cannot be alienated, it cannot be given away. Our political tradition has wisely recognized that government cannot authorize the alienation of a right it did not first bestow.

INSTITUTIONAL WISDOM

Legalized euthanasia would inevitably require the complicity of physicians. Members of the healing profession are asked to blur or erase the distinction between healing and killing. In our tradition, medical caregivers have understood this to be their calling: to cure when possible, to care always, never to kill. Legalized euthanasia would require a sweeping transformation of the meaning of medicine.

In a time when the medical profession is subjected to increasing criticism, when many people feel vulnerable before medical technology and practice, it would be foolhardy for our society to authorize physicians to kill. Euthanasia is not the way to respond to legitimate fears about technology and practice. It is unconscionable that the proponents of euthanasia exploit such fears. Such fears can be met and overcome by strongly reaffirming the distinction between killing and allowing to die—by making clear that useless and excessively burdensome treatments *can* be refused, while at the same time leaving no doubt that this society will neither authorize physicians to kill nor look the other way if they do.

CONCLUSION

This fourfold wisdom can be rejected only at our moral peril. By attending to these sources of wisdom, we can find our way back to a firmer understanding of the limits of human responsibility, and of the imperative to embrace compassionately those who suffer from illness and the fears associated with the end of life. Guided by this wisdom, we will not presume to eliminate a fellow human being, nor need we fear being abandoned in our suffering. The compact of rights, duties, and mutual trust that makes human community possible depends upon our continuing adherence to the precept, *Always to care, never to kill.*

HADLEY ARKES, Amherst College
MATTHEW BERKE, *First Things*
MIDGE DECTER, Institute on Religion and Public Life
RABBI MARC GELLMAN, Hebrew Union College
ROBERT GEORGE, Princeton University
PASTOR PAUL HINLICKY, *Lutheran Forum*
RUSSELL HITTINGER, Catholic University of America
THE REV. ROBERT JENSON, St. Olaf College
GILBERT MEILAENDER, Oberlin College
FATHER RICHARD JOHN NEUHAUS, Institute on Religion and Public Life
RABBI DAVID NOVAK, University of Virginia
JAMES NUECHTERLEIN, *First Things*
MAX STACKHOUSE, Andover Newton Theological School

EUTHANASIA

To cease upon the midnight

The putative right of an individual to determine the manner of his own death conflicts with the supreme value that most societies place on the preservation of life. Recently, the individual has been gaining ground

CRIPPLED in a swimming accident in 1968, Ramon Sanpedro can move only his head. He wants someone to help him commit suicide. So far, two Spanish courts have refused their consent.

Tony Bland, a British football fan, suffered terrible brain injuries in a crowd pile-up at a sports stadium in April 1989, and was left in a persistent vegetative state with no hope of recovery. In March 1993 the House of Lords, Britain's highest judicial authority, gave permission for Bland's feeding tubes to be disconnected. He died 20 days later.

Sue Rodriguez, a Canadian, was suffering from amyotrophic lateral sclerosis, an incurable disease which attacks the brain and spinal cord and impairs functions such as walking, speaking and breathing, when she asked in 1992 for someone to be allowed, legally, to help her die. Canada's Supreme Court found against her by five votes to four. She died in February 1994 with the help of an anonymous doctor.

Jack Kevorkian—"Dr Death"—is an American former pathologist whose eccentricities include creating ghoulish paintings using his own blood. He has "assisted" 20 suicides in the state of Michigan; juries have refused to convict him.

Such are the cases that are driving forward a public and legal debate in the West about the right to die and the right to medical assistance in doing so—a debate mainly for the rich West because in poor countries the artificial prolongation of life is at best a rare luxury; in Japan patients are often not told when they are terminally ill. The debate has been intensifying with the development of medical technologies capable of supporting life, in a narrowly defined form, almost indefinitely; and it has been influenced by a growing sense in many western societies that more responsibility for, and control over, medical treatment should be transferred from doctors to patients. Last year, the Dutch parliament voted to permit doc-

tors to kill severely ill patients under certain conditions (see box, final page). This week, Germany's constitutional court ruled that doctors could allow a terminally ill patient to die. Previously, German doctors had been allowed only to withdraw life-support from patients who were actually dying.

In America, many of the terms of the euthanasia debate in its present form were defined in 1976 by the tragedy of a young

woman called Karen Ann Quinlan, who was being kept alive by machines while in a coma that doctors judged to be irreversible. When her parents asked that the machines be disconnected, the hospital refused; the Quinlans won a court judgment establishing the right of a patient or his surrogate to refuse treatment. The right to pull the plug, sometimes referred to as "passive euthanasia", is now well established.

Doctors in most countries now honour the wish of a terminally ill or very old patient not to be revived should he suffer cardiac or respiratory arrest in hospital. The policy of the American Medical Association is that a doctor "has an ethical obligation to honour the resuscitation preferences ex-

pressed by the patient." In Britain, the Royal College of Nursing, and the doctors' professional body, the British Medical Association (BMA), have come to a similar conclusion. They recommend that hospitals try to determine the wishes of such patients.

More recently, ethicists and the medical establishment have reached a consensus on the treatment of pain in the terminally ill. The principle used to be that pain-relievers should not be administered in such a way as to expose a patient to risk of addiction. The absurdity of worrying about addiction in someone with a short time left to live is now acknowledged. Pain relief is recognised as an overriding priority; and it is considered ethical to provide as much pain relief as necessary even if a doctor believes that doing so may hasten death. Even so, according to Mildred Solomon, co-founder of a Massachusetts organisation called Decisions Near the End of Life, which provides training to carers for the terminally ill, four out of five doctors surveyed in 1993 said that under-treatment of pain among the dying was a more serious problem than over-treatment.

Agreement is more elusive on the issue of what constitutes "appropriate care" of the terminally ill and dying. Some ethicists, for example, see significance in the means needed to nourish a patient, arguing that the surgical insertion of feeding tubes may amount to over-treatment. Other authorities, such as the Royal College of Nursing, see feeding a patient as a basic duty just like keeping him clean, and as difficult to disregard. When the House of Lords agreed that Tony Bland's feeding tubes could be disconnected, it said the decision should not be taken as a general mandate and that each such case should go before a court.

Dr Death comes calling

An even more contentious area is "doctor-assisted suicide", in which a doctor helps a patient to take his own life. This has been Mr Kevorkian's speciality. In each of the 20 deaths he facilitated, the patient took the final step in the process—by connecting a hose, say, or pushing a button. Most western countries, and 44 American states, have laws against assisting suicide; in those that do not, such as Switzerland, medical tradition is against it. That record, however, suggests a unanimity absent in practice.

The *Medical Journal of Australia* reported a survey of 354 doctors who had been asked by patients to hasten death* (for foot-

From *The Economist*, September 17, 1994, pp. 21-23. © 1994 by The Economist, Ltd. Distributed by The New York Times Special Features.

notes, see final page). Only 107 had done so, but twice as many thought the law should be changed to allow such a thing in certain circumstances. A more recent poll of British doctors, reported in the *British Medical Journal*, found a similar pattern[†]. Of 273 respondents, 124 had been asked to hasten actively a patient's death; of those, about a third had done so; but almost half of the total sample said they might do so if the practice was legal (see tables).

In America, a widely remarked article in the *New England Journal of Medicine*[‡] in 1991 created something of a turning-point in attitudes. Timothy Quill, a former hospice director, told the story of "Diane", who had been diagnosed as having leukaemia. Diane had previously recovered from vaginal cancer. She did not want to undergo another series of painful and debilitating treatments with only a 25% chance of surviving. She preferred to choose the time of her death, and asked Dr Quill for barbiturates. He gave them to her and advised her of the amount needed to commit suicide—which she later did. Legally, American doctors can provide patients with drugs that might kill them provided that the drug has a legitimate medical purpose other than suicide. To provide drugs knowing that their likely application will be in suicide is frowned on.

Dr Quill was among the first American doctors to declare openly his role in assisting a death, albeit indirectly. The reaction was muted. Not everyone agreed with his conduct, but there was no rush to condemn it. Giving death a gentle push at a patient's behest does not happen often because the urge to live is usually so strong; but most doctors with long experience of critical care know of cases where it has occurred. A grand jury refused to indict Dr Quill, and in 1992 he and two other doctors published an essay suggesting guidelines for doctor-assisted suicide. The medical establishment remained opposed to the practice, but the taboo of talking about it was at last breached by someone who did not carry the baggage of Mr Kevorkian.

A right to choose

A still more difficult question is whether society should approve, tacitly or otherwise, the next step in the logical sequence, namely the practice of active euthanasia—ie, a doctor administering a substance for no reason other than to cause death. Those who favour legalisation of active euthanasia point to anecdotal evidence from surveys of doctors showing that it already happens. Better to have the decisions made after open discussion with some sort of institutional safeguards, it is argued, than to leave them to the conscience of individual doctors.

Campaigners for voluntary euthanasia argue that some ethical distinctions between what is and is not taboo are already untenable. Withdrawing life-support, for

Last rights %

"In the course of your medical practice, has a patient ever asked you to hasten his or her death?"

	GPs	Consultants
Had been asked to hasten death	64	52
Had been asked for:		
Passive euthanasia only	13	16
Active euthanasia only	25	11
Passive and active euthanasia	27	25
Total who had been asked for active euthanasia	51	36
Not asked to hasten death	36	48

"Have you ever taken active steps to bring about the death of patient who asked you to do so?"

	GPs	Consultants
Yes	30	36
No	70	64

"Sometimes I would be prepared to withdraw or withhold a course of treatment from a terminally ill patient, knowing the treatment might prolong the patient's life."

	GPs	Consultants
Strongly agree	34	45
Agree	54	50
Undecided	5	2
Disagree	5	2
Strongly disagree	1	1

"If a terminally ill patient asked me to bring an end to his or her life, I would consider doing so if it were legal."

	GPs	Consultants
Strongly agree	10	10
Agree	41	30
Undecided	21	21
Disagree	19	26
Strongly disagree	9	12

Source: *British Medical Journal* May 21st 1994
Totals may not equal 100 because of rounding

example, is considered a form of passive euthanasia. But it is not really passive. To unplug a machine is a deliberate action.

In the case of Tony Bland, the British football fan, almost three weeks elapsed after the disconnecting of his feeding tubes during which he was left to waste away. It is hard to see why that was more compassionate "treatment" than a lethal injection that would have given him, and his family, an equally sure release from their agony.

Nor is it easy to draw a clear line between injecting a dose of pain-killer that is likely to cause death (as some doctors do), and injecting a drug that is certain to kill (which is a crime in most places). In 1992 a British rheumatologist, Nigel Cox, was convicted of attempted murder for giving a lethal injection of potassium cyanide to a pain-wracked patient who had begged him to end her suffering. If Dr Cox had given her a huge dose of pain-killers he would never have been put in the dock.

The case for euthanasia is gaining a more sympathetic hearing as modern medicine and institutional care make dying a more prolonged, impersonal and often agonising business. To see a loved one shriv-

elled in pain for weeks or months can be a devastating experience for friends and family; but it is one that may become more commonplace as quick and relatively easy cardiac deaths decline as a percentage of deaths in rich countries, and proportionately more people die of cancer and AIDS. Nor may all hospitals be equal to the task of maintaining some measure of decency and comfort for the dying.

Some arguments for euthanasia insist on parallels with abortion, which the American Supreme Court declared to be a legal right on the grounds that the decision to bear a child was a matter of private choice. An American district court made explicit use of this rationale in May when it overturned a statute prohibiting assisted suicide; now under appeal, the case may reach the Supreme Court. This line of argument sees a decision to end one's life as the ultimate act of self-determination. In doing so, it raises legal and philosophical questions about the state of mind of any person taking such a decision; and it probably invites the question of whether such a right, were it to exist, should be restricted to certain classes of person. Could the young, or the healthy, or the clinically depressed, be denied a "right to die" that was conceded to the old or the desperately sick?

A further problem arises in applying this logic of self-determination to cases where the practical issue is not the right to commit suicide, or to be left to die, but to be helped to die by a doctor. A patient does not have a right to demand, say, a voodoo cure from a doctor; it is not obvious that he should have a right to demand death.

The danger of duty

Organised opposition to the cause of voluntary euthanasia comes chiefly from the handicapped, medical associations and some religious groups, including the Roman Catholic church and orthodox Jews. Interest groups for the handicapped are uncomfortable with any form of euthanasia because they fear its use would inevitably be extended to those with long-term disabilities. The underlying fear is that the right to die will become a duty to die, and that society, the principle of euthanasia once established, might tend to categorise some people as expendable. The old, senile, mentally ill and physically helpless could become tempting targets for cost-cutting.

For doctors and nurses, euthanasia is troubling because they are trained to heal and to save life. Doing the opposite, even with the noblest of intentions, runs counter to their oath. Practitioners in hospices that care for the terminally ill have been at the forefront of medical opposition to euthanasia, arguing that techniques for controlling pain are now so far advanced that fewer people need die in agony. They fear that the availability of euthanasia as an easy option

The Dutch way of dying

HOLLAND has the most liberal regime for voluntary euthanasia of any western country. As a case study, its lessons are much disputed. Admirers cite the care with which the Dutch debated the issue until consensus was reached, and the safeguards that they built into their system. Critics say the safeguards are ineffective and that Holland is skidding down a slippery slope towards licensed killing.

The Dutch parliament decided last year to authorise euthanasia under certain conditions—thus recognising officially a practice common there for at least 20 years. No legal right to euthanasia was created, and doctors could still face prosecution if they failed to follow strict guidelines. These were that a patient must be in a state of unbearable suffering; the desire to die must be "lasting"; the decision to die must be given freely; and the patient must have a clear understanding of his condition.

Few would quarrel with such propositions taken in isolation. But there is a worrying drift in the Dutch experience. An official report found that, in addition to 2,300 reported cases of euthanasia in Holland in 1990, a further 1,040 people had had their deaths hastened without making a formal request for intervention. That figure gives pause for thought; so does the case of a physically healthy but severely depressed Dutch woman who in 1991 asked her psychiatrist to help her die. After consulting with seven colleagues the psychiatrist agreed to the request and gave the patient sleeping pills and a toxic potion; she took them and died. In June the Dutch Supreme Court ruled out prosecution. It thus appears that not all of the notional safeguards may be enforced by the courts.

Johan Legemaate, legal counsel of the Royal Dutch Medical Association, defends the way euthanasia is practised in Holland. He notes that in more than two-thirds of the cases where patients request euthanasia, it is denied, and that in most cases where patients had not formally requested euthanasia and yet received it, there had been previous discussion of the subject. (In most such cases in 1990, according to the report cited above, life was shortened only by a few hours or days. All cases went through an extensive process of review and consultation.) "We feel we have succeeded in creating a large amount of openness and accountability," Mr Legemaate says.

Critics counter, however, that the result is a climate of indifference in which most cases of euthanasia go unreported and patients' rights are being eroded. Euthanasia, they say, so far from giving more freedom to patients, is giving more power over them to doctors.

found majority support for allowing assisted suicide and active euthanasia in certain circumstances, but legislators have not judged the trend a sufficiently compelling one for them to make significant changes to existing laws. In the United States, four state legislatures have rejected bills to allow assisted suicide; referendums in California and Washington have found majorities against change. Initiatives in the British and European parliaments have failed. The Canadian parliament, which has defeated four bills on the issue in the past, has formed a Senate committee on euthanasia and assisted suicide to collect opinion.

The result, in many places, is to leave justice in a muddle. Perhaps that is appropriate. Inadvertently, a sensible mean may have been struck. Laws against assisted suicide, it may be said, are there to express society's unease. At the same time, it is very rare for a practising doctor to be charged with helping a terminally ill patient to die.

"The current law is just about right," says George Annas, an ethicist at the Boston University School of Medicine. "Physicians should understand they are at some risk and so should assist suicide only in very extreme circumstances." He points out the difficulty of creating a better law, particularly one that would be proof against malpractice lawyers: "How do you define the circumstances? What kind of procedural mechanisms would there have to be? It would be such a nightmare."

It is, in fact, not surprising that commissions and parliaments and the public at large should have such difficulty delineating the boundaries of death. To do so means coming to grips not only with the mystery of dying, but also with the meaning of life, and with the relationship between the free will of the individual and the interests of society. To decide not to decide, however, is irresponsible. One of the strongest arguments for more liberal (and more honest) legislation on euthanasia is that it would lighten the burden on doctors who must at present make such terribly difficult decisions alone and without knowing what consequences they may face. In the words of Ian Kennedy, professor of medical law and ethics at King's College, London: "It cannot be fair to doctors to present them with a situation in which they have to guess whether people will subsequently endorse what they have done or whether, if they guess wrong, the law will be applied in all its rigour and they will face a charge of murder."

would diminish the incentive to provide compassionate care for those who preferred to let death take its course. Doctors are also worried that practising euthanasia openly would lead some patients to regard them as bringers of death. The BMA thinks it "contrary to the doctor's role deliberately to kill patients, even at their request".

Most medical associations would agree with that as a general statement. In practice, however, things are less clear-cut. On August 16th the Canadian Medical Association voted not to allow doctors any role in active euthanasia or assisted suicide—but by a fairly narrow majority of 93 to 74. In Britain, though Dr Cox was convicted by a criminal court, he was allowed by a regulatory body, the General Medical Council, to retain his practitioner's licence, a sign that his peers did not consider his action monstrous.

For the Christian churches, the issue is equally fraught. Even in western countries where people have lost the habit of going to church on Sundays, Christian values are still influential. One of the central Christian beliefs is that life is a gift from God which individuals guard but do not own; another is that suffering is a wellspring of redemption and, as such, has value in itself.

This idea has proved a source of strength to many sufferers for centuries. But it is possible to respect that belief and yet still to wonder if at some point suffering can become pointless. Must every single possible moment of suffering be extracted as payment for redemption? And should those not attached to this system of belief be subject to its consequences?

The moral muddle

Most people would say no, albeit often hesitantly. But merely coming to that conclusion is not enough to bring societies any closer to defining a new conceptual framework for regulating death and dying. Opinion polls in many western countries have

* MJA 1988; 148: 623-627; † BMJ 1994; 308: 1332-1334; ‡ NEJM 1991; 324: 691-694

SUICIDE

SUICIDE To many, suicide, or intentional self-killing, seems like the ultimate asocial act of an individual. Yet sociology itself grew out of Emile Durkheim's argument that suicide rates are social facts and reflect variation in social regulation and social interaction (Durkheim [1897] 1951). The concept of suicide derives from the Latin *sui* ("of oneself") and *cide* ("a killing"). Edwin Shneidman defines suicide as "currently in the Western world a conscious act of self-induced annihilation best understood as a multidimensional malaise in a needful individual who defines an issue for which suicide is perceived as the best solution" (1985, p. 203). Several conceptual implications follow from this definition.

Although suicidal types vary, there probably are some common traits that most suicides share (Shneidman 1985). People who choose suicide tend to
- seek a solution to their life problems by dying;
- want to cease consciousness;
- try to reduce intolerable psychological pain;
- have frustrated psychological needs;
- feel helpless and hopeless;
- be ambivalent about dying;
- be perceptually constricted and rigid thinkers;
- manifest escape, egression, or fugue behaviors;
- communicate their intent to commit suicide or die;
- have lifelong self-destructive coping responses (sometimes called "suicidal careers").

Completed suicides need to be differentiated from nonfatal suicide attempts, suicide ideation, and suicide talk or gestures. Sometimes one speaks of self-injury, self-mutilation, accident proneness, failure to take needed medications, and the like—where suicide intent cannot be demonstrated—as "parasuicide." The most common of all self-destructive behaviors are indirect, for example, alcoholism, obesity, risky sports, gambling, and so forth. There are also mass suicides (Jonestown, Guyana, 1978, and Masada in Roman-ruled Palestine, 73 A.D.) and murder-suicides. Individual and social growth probably require some partial self-destruction.

Although most suicides have much in common, suicide is emphatically not one type of behavior. Suicidology will never be an exact science until it carefully specifies its dependent variable. The predictors or causes of suicide vary

TABLE 1
Ten Leading Causes of Death in the United States, 1987

Rank	Cause of death	Rate*	No. of deaths[†]
1	Disease of the heart	312.4	760,353
2	Malignant neoplasms	195.9	476,927
3	Cerebrovascular disease	61.6	149,835
4	Accidents	39.0	95,020
5	Chronic obstructive pulmonary disease	32.2	78,380
6	Pneumonia and influenza	28.4	69,225
7	Diabetes mellitus	15.8	38,532
8	Suicide	12.7	30,796
9	Chronic liver disease	10.8	26,201
10	Atherosclerosis	9.2	22,474

*Per 100,000 population.
[†] Total number of deaths (all causes) in 1987: 2,123,323.

SOURCE: Data from National Center for Health Statistics, 1989.

Reprinted with permission of Macmillan Publishing Company from *Encyclopedia of Sociology*, Vol. 4, pp. 2111-2119. Edgar F. Borgatta, Editor in Chief, Marie L. Borgatta, Managing Editor. © 1992 by Edgar F. Borgatta and Marie L. Borgatta.

immensely with the specific type of suicidal outcome. Suicidologists tend to recognize three to six basic types of suicide, each with two or three of their own subtypes (Maris et al. 1991, chap. 4). For example, Durkheim ([1897] 1951) thought all suicides were basically anomic, egoistic, altruistic, or fatalistic. Freud ([1917] 1953) and Menninger (1938) argued that psychoanalytically all suicides were based on hate or revenge (a "wish to kill"); on depression, melancholia, or hopelessness (a "wish to die"); or on guilt or shame (a "wish to be killed"). Finally, Baechler (1979) added "oblative" (i.e., sacrifice or transfiguration) and "ludic" (i.e., engaging in ordeals or risk and games) suicidal types.

EPIDEMIOLOGY, RATES, AND PREDICTORS

Suicide is a relatively rare event, one to three in 10,000 in the general U.S. population per year. In 1987 there were 30,796 suicides (about 1.5 percent of all deaths). This number amounts to an overall suicide rate of 12.7 suicides per 100,000 population. Suicide is now the eighth leading cause of death, ranking just ahead of cirrhosis and other liver

disease deaths and just behind diabetes deaths. Suicide has been moving up the ladder of the leading causes of death in this century.

Suicide rates in the United States vary considerably by sex, age, and race. The highest rates are observed consistently among white males, who constitute roughly 70 percent of all suicides. White females make up about 20 percent of all suicides. American blacks (especially females) rarely commit suicide (except for some young urban males). Some scholars have argued that black suicides tend to be disguised as homicides or accidents. In general, male suicides outnumber female suicides three or four to one. Suicide rates also increase gradually with age and then drop off some at the very oldest ages. Female suicide rates tend to peak earlier than those of males. Note (in Table 3) that from about 1967 to 1977 there was a significant increase in the suicide rate of fifteen- to twenty-four-year-olds and that elderly suicide rates seem to be climbing again.

Typically, marrying and having children protect one against suicide. Usually suicide rates are highest for the widowed, followed by those of the divorced and the never-married or single. Studies of suicide rates by social class

TABLE 2
Rates of Completed U.S. Suicide by Race and Gender for 1987*

Race-gender group	Number of suicides	Percent of suicides	Rate per 100,000
White males	22,188	72.0	22.1
White females	6,029	19.6	5.7
Black males	1,635	5.3	11.6
Black females	328	1.1	2.1
Other males*	449	1.5	11.6
Other females*	167	0.5	2.5
Totals	30,796	100.0	12.7

*Includes American Indian, Chinese, Hawaiian, Japanese, Filipino, Other Asian or Pacific Islander, and Other.

SOURCE: Data from National Center for Health Statistics, 1990.

TABLE 3
Rates of Completed U.S. Suicide per 100,000 population by Year and Age

Age*	Year 1957	1967	1977	1987
5–14	0.2	0.3	0.5	0.7
15–24	4.0	7.0	13.6	12.9
25–34	8.6	12.4	17.7	15.4
35–44	12.8	16.6	16.8	15.0
45–54	18.0	19.5	18.9	15.9
55–64	22.4	22.4	19.4	16.6
65–74	25.0	19.8	20.1	19.4
75–84	26.8	21.0	21.5	25.8
85 and over	26.3	22.7	17.3	22.1
Total	9.8	10.8	13.3	12.7

*No suicide reported for individuals under five years of age.
SOURCE: Data from National Center for Health Statistics, 1990.

have been equivocal. Within each broad census occupational category there are job types with both high and low suicide rates. For example, psychiatrists have high suicide rates, but pediatricians and surgeons have low suicide rates. Operatives usually have low rates, but policemen typically have high suicide rates.

The predominant method of suicide for both males and females in 1987 was firearms. The second most common method among males is hanging and among females is drug and medicine overdoses. Females use a somewhat greater variety of methods than males do. Suicide rates tend to be higher on Mondays and in the springtime (Gabennesch 1988).

Prediction of suicide is a complicated process (Maris et al. 1991). As with other rare events, suicide prediction generates many false positives (i.e., identifying some deaths as suicides when they are in fact not suicides). Correctly identifying true suicides is referred to as "sensitivity," and correctly identifying true nonsuicides is called "specificity." In one celebrated study using common predictors (see Table 5) Porkorny (1983) correctly predicted fifteen of sixty-seven suicides among 4,800 psychiatric patients, but he also got 279 false positives.

Table 5 lists fifteen major predictors of suicide. Single predictor variables seldom if ever correctly identify suicides. Most suicides have "comorbidity" (i.e., several key predictors are involved), and specific predictors vary with the type of suicide and other factors. Depressive disorders and alcoholism are two of the major predictors of suicide. Robins (1981) found that about 72 percent of all completed suicides were either depressed or alcoholic. Roughly 15 percent of all those with depressive illness and 18 percent of all alcoholics

will eventually commit suicide. Repeated depressive illness that leads to hopelessness is especially suicidogenic.

Nonfatal suicide attempts, talk about suicide or dying, and explicit plans or preparations for dying or suicide all increased suicide risk. However, for the paradigmatic suicide (older white males) 85 to 90 percent of them make only one fatal suicide attempt and seldom explicitly communicate their suicidal intent or show up at hospitals and clinics. Social isolation (having no close friends, living alone, being unemployed, unmarried, etc.) and lack of social support is more common among suicides than among controls. Suicide tends to run in families, which suggests both modeling and genetic influences. There are some important biological and sociobiological predictors of suicide emerging, especially low central spinal fluid serotonin in the form of 5-HIAA (Maris et al. 1991).

HISTORY, COMPARATIVE STUDIES, AND SOCIAL SUICIDOLOGISTS

The incidence and study of suicide has a long history and was fundamental to the foundation of sociology. The earliest known visual reference to suicide is Ajax falling on his sword (c. 540 B.C.). Of course, we know that Socrates (about 399 B.C.) drank the hemlock. In the Judeo-Christian scriptures there were eleven men (and no women) who died by suicide (most notably Samson, Judas, and Saul). Common biblical motives for suicide were revenge, shame, or defeat in battle. Other famous suicides in art history include paintings of Lucretia stabbing herself (after a rape), Dido, and work by Edvard Munch and Andy Warhol.

Suicide varies with culture and ethnicity. Most cultures

TABLE 4
Percent of Completed U.S. Suicides (1987) by Method and Gender

Method	Gender	
	Male %	Female %
Firearms (E955.0–955.4)	64.0	39.8
Drugs/Medications (E950.0–950.5)	5.2	25.0
Hanging (E953.0)	13.5	9.4
Carbon monoxide (E952.0–952.1)	9.6	12.6
Jumping from a high place (E957)	1.8	3.0
Drowning (E954)	1.1	2.8
Suffocation by plastic bag (E953.1)	0.4	1.8
Cutting/Piercing instruments (E956)	1.3	1.4
Poisons (E950.6–950.9)	0.6	1.0
Other*	2.5	3.2
TOTALS	100.0	100.0

*Includes gases in domestic use (E951), other specified and unspecified gases and vapors (E952.8–952.9), explosives (E955.5), unspecified firearms and explosives (E955.9), and other specified or unspecified means of hanging, strangulation, or suffocation (E953.8–953.9).
SOURCE: Data from National Center for Health Statistics, 1990.

TABLE 5
Common Single Predictors of Suicide

1. Depressive illness, mental disorder
2. Alcoholism, drug abuse
3. Suicide ideation, talk, preparation, religion
4. Prior suicide attempts
5. Lethal methods
6. Isolation, living alone, loss of support
7. Hopelessness, cognitive rigidity
8. Older white males
9. Modeling, suicide in the family, genetics
10. Work problems, economics, occupation
11. Marital problems, family pathology
12. Stress, life events
13. Anger, aggression, irritability, 5-HIAA
14. Physical illness
15. Repetition and comorbidity of factors 1–14, suicidal careers

SOURCE: Maris et al., 1991, chap. 1.

have at least some suicides. However, suicide is rare or absent among the Tiv of Nigeria, Andaman islanders, and Australian aborigines and relatively infrequent among rural American blacks and Irish Roman Catholics. The highest suicide rates in the world are found in Hungary, the Federal Republic of Germany, Austria, Scandinavia, and Japan (see Table 6). The lowest rates are found in several South American, Pacific Island, and predominantly Roman Catholic countries (including Antigua, Jamaica, New Guinea, the Philippines, Mexico, Italy, and Ireland).

The sociological study of suicide, of course, started with Durkheim ([1897] 1951) and has continued to the present day, primarily by the following sociologists: Henry and Short (1954); Gibbs and Martin (1964); Gibbs (1988); Douglas (1967); Maris (1969; 1981); Phillips (1974; 1991); Stack (1982); Wasserman (1989); and Pescosolido and Georgianna (1989). It is impossible in an encyclopedia to do justice to the full account of the sociological study of suicide. For a more complete review, see Maris (1989). What follows is only a sketch.

Durkheim claimed that the suicide rate varied inversely with social integration and that suicide types were primarily ego-anomic. However, Durkheim did not operationally define "social integration." Gibbs and Martin (1964) created the concept of "status integration" to correct this deficiency in Durkheim. They hypothesized that the less frequently occupied status sets would lead to lower status integration and higher suicide rates. Putting it differently, they expected status integration and suicide rates to be negatively associated. In a large series of tests from 1964 to 1988 Gibbs found his primary hypothesis to be confirmed only for occupational statuses (which Durkheim also had said were of central importance).

Henry and Short (1954) expanded Durkheim's concept of external and constraining social factors to include interaction with social-psychological factors of "internal constraint" (such as strict superego restraint) and frustration-aggression theory. Henry and Short reasoned that suicide rates would be highest when external restraint was low and internal restraint was high (and that homicide rates would be high when internal restraint was low and external restraint was high).

A vastly different sociological perspective on suicide originated with the work of ethnomethodologist Jack Douglas. Douglas (in the tradition of Max Weber's subjective

TABLE 6
Suicide Rates (per 100,000 of Population) in 62 Countries: 1980–1986

Country	Rate	Country	Rate
1. Hungary	45.3	32. Uruguay	9.6
2. Federal Republic of Germany	43.1	33. Northern Ireland	9.3
3. Sri Lanka	29.0	34. Portugal	9.2
4. Austria	28.3	35. England and Wales	8.9
5. Denmark	27.8	36. Trinidad and Tobago	8.6
6. Finland	26.6	37. Guadeloupe	7.9
7. Belgium	23.8	38. Ireland	7.8
8. Switzerland	22.8	39. Italy	7.6
9. France	22.7	40. Thailand	6.6
10. Suriname	21.6	41. Argentina	6.3
11. Japan	21.2	42. Chile	6.2
12. German Democratic Republic	19.0	43. Spain	4.9
13. Czechoslovakia	18.9	44. Venezuela	4.8
14. Sweden	18.5	45. Costa Rica	4.5
15. Cuba	17.7	46. Ecuador	4.3
16. Bulgaria	16.3	47. Greece	4.1
17. Yugoslavia	16.1	48. Martinique	3.7
18. Norway	14.1	49. Colombia	2.9
19. Luxembourg	13.9	50. Mauritius	2.8
20. Iceland	13.3	51. Dominican Republic	2.4
21. Poland	13.0	52. Mexico	1.6
22. Canada	12.9	53. Panama	1.4
23. Singapore	12.7	54. Peru	1.4
24. United States	12.3	55. The Philippines	0.5
25. Hong Kong	12.2	56. Guatemala	0.5
26. Australia	11.6	57. Malta	0.3
27. Scotland	11.6	58. Nicaragua	0.2
28. The Netherlands	11.0	59. Papua New Guinea	0.2
29. El Salvador	10.8	60. Jamaica	0.1
30. New Zealand	10.3	61. Egypt	0.1
31. Puerto Rico	9.8	62. Antigua and Barbuda	—

SOURCE: Diekstra 1990.

meanings) argued that Durkheim's reliance on official statistics (like death certificates) as the data base for studying suicide was fundamentally mistaken (Douglas 1967). What Douglas said we need to do is to observe the accounts or situated meanings of actual individuals who are known to be suicidal, not some third-party official like a coroner or medical examiner who is not a suicide and who may use ad hoc criteria to classify a death as a suicide. There are probably just about as many official statistics as there are officials.

Maris (1981) extended Durkheim's empirical survey of suicidal behaviors, but not just by measuring macrosocial and demographic or structural variables. Instead Maris focused on actual interviews ("psychological autopsies") of the intimate survivors of suicides (usually their spouses) and compared these cases with control or comparison groups of natural deaths and nonfatal suicide attempters. Maris claimed that individuals who committed suicide had long "suicidal careers" involving complex mixes of biological, social, and psychological factors.

Phillips (1974) differed with Durkheim's contention that suicides are not suggestable or contagious. In a pioneering and stage-setting paper in the *American Sociological Review* in 1974, Phillips demonstrated that front-page newspaper coverage of celebrity suicides was associated with a statistically significant rise in the national suicide rate seven to ten days after the publicized suicide. The rise in the suicide rate was greater the longer the front-page coverage, greater in the region where the news account ran, and higher if the stimulus suicide and the person supposedly copying the suicide were similar. In a long series of similar studies Phillips and others expanded and documented the suggestion effect for other types of behavior and for other groups. For example, the contagion effect appears to be especially powerful among teenagers. Nevertheless, contagion accounts for only a 1 to 6 percent increase over normal expected suicide rates in a population.

Phillips's ideas about contagion have dominated the sociological study of suicide in the 1980s. Work by Stack (1982), Wasserman (1989), Kessler and Stripp (1984), and others have produced equivocal support for the role of suggestion in suicide (Diekstra et al. 1989). Wasserman feels the business cycle and unemployment rates must be controlled for. Some have claimed that imitative effects are statistical artifacts. Most problematic is that the theory of imitation in suicide is underdeveloped.

The most recent sociologist to study suicide is medical sociologist Bernice Pescosolido. She has claimed, contrary to Douglas, that the official statistics of suicide are acceptably reliable and (as Gibbs said earlier) that they are the best basis available for the foundation of a science of suicide. Her latest paper (Pescosolido and Georgianna 1989) examined Durkheim's claim that religious involvement protects against suicide. Pescosolido finds that Roman Catholicism and evangelical Protestantism do protect one against suicide (institutional Protestantism does not) and that Judaism has a small, inconsistent protective effect. Pescosolido concludes that

with disintegrating network ties, individuals who were denied both integrative and regulative supports commit suicide more often.

ISSUES AND FUTURE DIRECTIONS

Much of current sociological research on suicide appears myopic and sterile, compared to early work by Durkheim ([1897] 1951), Douglas (1967), and Garfinkel (1967). Not only is the scope of current research limited, there is very little theory and few book-length publications. Almost no research monographs on the sociology of suicide were written in the 1980s. Highly focused scientific journal articles on imitation have predominated. However, none of these papers has been able to establish if suicides ever in fact were exposed to the original media stimulus! Since suicide does not just concern social relations, the study of suicide needs more interdisciplinary syntheses. The dependent variable (suicide) needs to include comparisons with other types of death and violence, as well as more nonsocial predictor variables (Holinger 1987).

A second issue concerns methods for studying suicide (Lann, Mościcki, and Maris 1989). There has never been a truly national sample survey of suicidal behaviors in the United States. Also, most suicide research is retrospective and based on questionable vital statistics. More prospective or longitudinal research designs are needed, of course, with adequate sample sizes and comparison or control groups. Models of suicidal careers should be analyzed with specific and more appropriate statistical techniques (like logistic regression, log-linear procedures, and event or hazard analysis). It should be noted that federal funds to do any major research on suicide are in short supply and that this is probably the single major obstacle to the contemporary scientific study of suicide.

Third, most studies of suicide are cross-sectional and static. Future research will, it is hoped, include more social developmental designs (Blumenthal and Kupfer 1990). We still have very little solid knowledge about the social dynamics or "suicidal careers" of eventual suicides (Maris 1990). For example, it is well known that completed suicides tend to be socially isolated at the time of death, but how they came to be that way is less well understood. Fourth, in passing it must be noted that even after almost a hundred years of research the relationship of suicide to social class, occupation, and socioeconomic status is still not clear.

Finally, a major issue in the study of suicide is rational suicide, active euthanasia, the right to die, and appropriate death. With a rapidly aging and more secular population and the spread of the AIDS virus, the American public is demanding more information about the legal rights for voluntary assisted death (see the case of Nico Speijer in the Netherlands, Diekstra 1986). The right to die and assisted suicide have been the focus of a few recent legal cases (Humphry and Wickett 1986; Battin and Maris 1983). Rosewell Gilbert, an elderly man who was sentenced to life imprisonment in Florida for the mercy killing of his sick wife, was pardoned in 1990 by the governor of Florida. However, in 1990 the U.S. Supreme Court (*Cruzon v. the State of Missouri*) ruled that hospitals have the right to continue to force-feed even brain-dead patients. The Hemlock Society was founded by Derek Humphry to assist those who wish to end their own lives, make living wills, or pass living-will legislation in their states (however, see the *New York Times,* February 8, 1990, A18). Of course, the state must be cautious that the right to die does not become the obligation to die (e.g., for the aged). These issues are further complicated by strong religious and moral persuasions.

REFERENCES

Alcohol, Drug Abuse, and Mental Health Administration 1989 *Report of the Secretary's Task Force on Youth Suicide,* Vols. 1–4. Washington, D.C.: U.S. Government Printing Office.

Baechler, Jean 1979 *Suicides.* New York: Basic Books.

Battin, Margaret P., and Ronald W. Maris (eds.) 1983 *Suicide and Ethics.* New York: Human Sciences Press.

Blumenthal, Susan J., and David J. Kupfer (eds.) 1990 *Suicide over the Life Cycle: Risk Factors, Assessment, and Treatment of Suicidal Patients.* Washington, D.C.: American Psychiatric Press.

——— Diekstra, René F. W., 1986 "The Significance of Nico Speijer's Suicide: How and When Should Suicide Be Prevented?" *Suicide and Life-Threatening Behavior* 16 (1):13–15.

——— 1990 "An International Perspective on the Epidemiology and Prevention of Suicide." In Susan J. Blumenthal and David J. Kupfer, eds., *Suicide of the Life-cycle.* Washington, D.C.: American Psychiatric Press.

———, Ronald W. Maris, Stephen Platt, Armin Schmidtke, and Gernot Sonneck (eds.) 1989 *Suicide and Its Prevention: The Role of Attitude and Imitation.* Leiden: E. J. Brill.

Douglas, Jack D. 1967 *The Social Meanings of Suicide.* Princeton, N.J.: Princeton University Press.

Dunne, Edward J., John L. McIntosh, and Karent Dunne-Maxim (eds.) 1987 *Suicide and Its Aftermath.* New York: W. W. Norton.

Durkheim, Emile (1897) 1951 *Suicide.* New York: Free Press.

Evans, Glen, and Norman L. Farberow (eds.) 1988 *The Encyclopedia of Suicide.* New York: Facts On File.

Freud, Sigmund (1917) 1953 "Mourning and Melancholia." In James Strachey, ed., *Standard Edition of the Complete Works of Sigmund Freud.* London: Hogarth Press.

Gabennesch, Howard 1988 "When Promises Fail: A Theory of Temporal Fluctuations in Suicide." *Social Forces* 67:129–145.

Garfinkel, Harold 1967 *Studies in Ethnomethodology.* Englewood Cliffs, N.J.: Prentice-Hall.

Gibbs, Jack, and Mark C. Stafford 1988 "Change in the Relation Between Marital Integration and Suicide Rates." *Social Forces* 66:1060–1079.

Gibbs, Jack P., and W. T. Martin 1964 *Status Integration and Suicide.* Eugene: University of Oregon Press.

Gibbs, Jewelle Taylor (ed.) 1988 *Young, Black, and Male in America: An Endangered Species.* Dover, Mass.: Auburn House.

Henry, Andrew F., and James F. Short 1954 *Suicide and Homicide.* New York: Free Press.

Holinger, Paul C. 1987 *Violent Deaths in the United States: An Epidemiological Study of Suicide, Homicide, and Accidents.* New York: Guilford.

Humphry, Derek, and Ann Wickett 1986 *The Right to Die: Understanding Euthanasia.* New York: Harper and Row.

Jacobs, Douglas, and Herbert N. Brown (eds.) 1989 *Suicide, Understanding, and Responding: Harvard Medical School Perspectives.* Madison, Conn.: International Universities Press.

Kessler, Ronald C., and H. Stripp 1984 "The Impact of Fictional Television Stories on U.S. Fatalities: A Replication." *American Journal of Sociology* 90: 151–167.

Lann, Irma S., Eve K. Mościcki, and Ronald W. Maris (eds.) 1989 *Strategies for Studying Suicide and Suicidal Behavior.* New York: Guilford.

Maris, Ronald W. 1969 *Social Forces in Urban Suicide.* Chicago: Dorsey Press.

——— 1981 *Pathways to Suicide: A Survey of Self-Destrucive Behaviors.* Baltimore: Johns Hopkins University Press.

——— 1986 *Biology of Suicide.* New York: Guilford.

——— 1989 "The Social Relations of Suicide." In Douglas Jacobs and Herbert N. Brown, eds., *Suicide, Understanding, and Responding: Harvard Medical School Perspectives.* Madison, Conn.: International Universities Press.

——— 1990 "The Developmental Perspective of Suicide." In Antoon Leenaars, ed., *Life Span Perspectives of Suicide.* New York: Plenum.

———, Alan L. Berman, John T. Maltsberger, and Robert I. Yufit, eds. 1991 *Assessment and Prediction of Suicide.* New York: Guilford.

Menninger, Karl 1938 *Man Against Himself.* New York: Harcourt, Brace.

Pescosolido, Bernice A., and Sharon Georgianna 1989 "Durkheim, Suicide, and Religion: Toward a Network Theory of Suicide." *American Sociological Review* 54:33–48.

Pfeffer, Cynthia R., ed. 1989 *Suicide Among Youth: Perspectives on Risk and Prevention.* Washington, D.C.: American Psychiatric Press.

Phillips, David P. 1974 "The Influence of Suggestion on Suicide." *American Sociological Review* 39:340–354.

———, Katherine Lesyna, and Daniel J. Paight 1991 "Suicide and the Media." In Ronald W. Maris et al., eds., *Assessment and Prediction of Suicide.* New York: Guilford.

Porkorny, Alex D. 1983 "Prediction of Suicide in Psychiatric Patients." *Archives of General Psychiatry* 40:249–257.

Robins, Eli 1981 *The Final Months.* New York: Oxford University Press.

Shneidman, Edwin S. 1985 *Definition of Suicide.* New York: Wiley-Interscience.

Stack, Stephen 1982 "Suicide: A Decade Review of the Sociological Literature." *Deviant Behavior* 4:41–66.

Stafford, Mark C., and Jack P. Gibbs 1988 "Change in the Relation between Marital Integration and Suicide Rates." *Social Forces* 66:1060–1079.

Wasserman, Ira M. 1989 "The Effects of War and Alcohol Consumption Patterns on Suicide: United States, 1910–1933." *Social Forces* 67:129–145.

RONALD W. MARIS

ATTITUDES TOWARD SUICIDAL BEHAVIOR: A REVIEW OF THE LITERATURE

Ellen Ingram and Jon B. Ellis

Ellen Ingram, M.A., is a licensed psychological examiner. Jon Ellis, Ph.D., is a licensed clinical psychologist and assistant professor at East Tennessee State University.

The attitudes people in any given culture [hold] regarding death and suicidal behavior may be viewed as a reflection of that culture's values toward life. This article reviews the literature in the area of societal attitudes toward suicidal behavior. Attitudes include not only how society feels about those who kill themselves but the family members who are left behind as well. Although surveys have shown that many Americans see suicidal people as psychologically disturbed, some groups argue that suicide can be seen as a rational behavior. The idea is postulated that the answer to whether suicide is a rational or irrational act may not be as simple as yes or no.

The opinions that members of a society hold regarding suicidal behavior is a reflection of their values toward human life. These values influence how members of a society are taught to think and behave. Societal attitudes regarding the appropriateness of suicide remain confused and contradictory. Death by suicide affects not only the victim but the victim's family, friends, members of the community, and our entire society. Surviving relatives are thought to be more grief stricken because their loved one willfully took his or her own life, and yet they must also deal with more severe and negative attitudes of the people in the community when

suicide is the cause of death (Cain & Fast, 1972; Calhoun, Selby, & Selby, 1982; McGinnis, 1987; Range, McDonald, & Anderson, 1987; Range & Thompson, 1986). Suicidal behavior is now viewed as an illness, but it may be a symptom of many illnesses because it is an overt expression of emotions such as rage, guilt, loneliness, shame, sorrow, agony, fear, and hopelessness (McGinnis, 1987).

Douglas (1967) conjectured that suicide was widely condemned in our society and could be understood only by a study of the meaning the self-destructive individual attached to the behavior. The meaning in turn should be studied within the context of the values of a particular society attaches to suicide. Singh, Williams, and Ryther (1986) asserted that the situation itself largely defines the extent to which suicide will be approved as an acceptable alternative to living. Society evaluates the appropriateness in terms of the individual involved and the specific circumstances surrounding the suicide. Community attitudes may even influence suicide rates (de Catanzaro, 1981; Douglas, 1967; Dublin, 1963). Some clinicians suggested that a hardening of attitudes toward suicidal behavior may result in lessening of such behavior (Koller & Slaghuis, 1978). Alternatively, a growing influence that is promoting the acceptance of suicide is the right-to-die movement, which advocates an individual's right to commit suicide particularly when a terminal illness is involved (Klagsburn, 1981).

HISTORICAL OVERVIEW

Some cultures encouraged suicide among certain members of their society, usually for religious purposes, believing in life after death (Siegel, 1988). In the Fiji Islands, suicide was expected of the wives of a chief when he died. The women rushed to kill themselves believing the first to die would become the chief's favorite wife in the spirit world. In India, widows practiced suttee. They threw themselves on their husband's funeral pyre believing they could atone for their husband's sins.

The Chinese regarded suicide as acceptable and honorable, particularly for defeated generals or deposed rulers. The Japanese ritualized suicide in the form of hara-kiri, a long drawn out process of disembowelment. A samurai warrior or a member of the military was bestowed much honor if he died in such a way. Ancient Greek and Roman cities differed greatly in their views of suicide. In Thebes, suicide was strongly condemned, but in other Greek communities tribunals existed to hear the arguments of people who wanted to commit suicide.

During the Middle Ages into the 19th century in Western cultures, society placed negative social sanctions on people who attempted or committed suicide. The sanctions included assigning disgrace to the reputation of the deceased, mutilation of the corpse, hanging the corpse from public gallows, denial of Christian burial, confiscation of the deceased's estate, and

From *Death Studies*, Vol. 16, 1992, pp. 31-43. © 1992 by Taylor and Francis, 1101 Vermont Ave., NW, Ste. 200, Washington, DC 20005. Reprinted by permission.

excommunication of the deceased from the church.

INFLUENCES ON CURRENT ATTITUDES

The general attitude of the public toward remains confused and often contradictory (Kluge, 1975). Today there are two extreme views, amid more moderate views, on suicide. The extreme views range from total acceptance to total rejection of the right of an individual to commit suicide. At the center of the debate is the question of whether people should be allowed the right to die without interference. In its narrowest sense, the question relates to people who are terminally ill or in great pain. In its broadest sense, it extends to any person who wants to die (Klagsburn, 1981). Others regard the right to die as a right to refuse life-sustaining treatment (Weber, 1988). A small number of individuals insist that all persons have the right to control their own bodies even in matters of suicide. Any interference with this right is a violation of fundamental liberties. Szasz (1974) was among the most vocal advocates for the individual's right to commit suicide. He stated, "While suicide is not necessarily morally desirable, it is nonetheless a fundamental inalienable right" (p. 67). Maris (1986) disagreed with Szasz's radical individual autonomy. He pointed out that Szasz has no appreciation for the loving the unlovable in our society. He foresaw this view as even contributing to self-destructive behavior.

Most right-to-die advocates make a distinction between a healthy or terminally ill person committing suicide. Advocates argue that medical science has now been able to prolong life artificially to the point that life becomes meaningless. Once the assumption is accepted that there are conditions under which it may be preferable not to sustain life, suicide may be viewed as a reasonable option (Klagsburn, 1981).

Suicide as a Rational Act

Several organizations have been established to promote wider acceptance of the right-to-die movement. Humphry (1987) described the Hemlock Society's position on suicide. Suicide is separated into two types. The first is emotional suicide or irrational self-murder. Their thinking on this type of suicide is to prevent it whenever possible. The second type is justifiable suicide described as rational and planned self-deliverance. They advocate what they call autoeuthanasia. They ethically justify suicide only under certain circumstances. One involves a case of an advanced terminal illness that is causing unbearable suffering to the individual. Another involves a grave physical handicap that is so restrictive that the individual cannot, after due consideration and training, tolerate such a limited existence. This group believes that suicide is ethical only when the person is a mature adult and has made a considered decision. A considered decision is one that was not made at the first knowledge of a life-threatening illness and for which the treating physician's response has been taken into account. Also the person has made plans that do not involve others in criminal liability, and he or she leaves a note stating exactly why he or she is committing suicide. Humphrey believed that for many people just knowing how to kill themselves is in itself a great comfort and often extends their lives. They will often renegotiate with themselves the conditions of their dying.

Another group, Concern for the Dying (Sachs, 1987), has furnished thousands of copies of the Living Will document. The Living Will document expresses the desire of an individual to cease medical intervention under certain conditions. The Society for the Right to Die lobbies state legislatures in an effort to protect the right to refuse extraordinary life-preserving measures. Other groups propose schemes for regulating suicidal acts. Collectively, these groups advocate what is called rational suicide. Rational suicide is characterized by a possession of a realistic assessment of the situation by the individual who is faced with the decision to commit suicide. The individual's mental processes are not impaired by psychological illness or distress, and the person's motivation for the decision would be understandable if presented to objective bystanders (Siegel, 1988). The goals of these groups are for the most part humane, advocating the "right to die with dignity" (Quinnett, 1987).

Opposition to Suicide

Among the opponents, some argue that a person does not have the right to commit suicide regardless of the circumstances. Others believe certain circumstances may be so unbearable that it is understandable why a person commits suicide, but this should be an individual act, and society or the legal system should not encourage this type of behavior. Opponents who hold extreme views argue that life should be preserved regardless of circumstances even in the case of a terminal illness. They believe no one has a right to decide at what point life becomes expendable. They believe condoning any kind of suicide condones them all (Klagsburn, 1981). They argue that there is medical and social justification to intervene and prevent someone from taking his or her life. Suicide is seen as an ambivalent act: Every person who wants to die also wants to live. This view postulates that a person is suicidal only for a short period of time, and if intervention is instigated, the suicidal crisis often passes and the person changes his or her mind.

ACCEPTABILITY OF SUICIDAL BEHAVIOR

Feherman (1989) chaired a 12-member committee that made recommendations to physicians about their responsibility toward terminally ill patients. The committee members agreed that it was not immoral for a physician to assist a terminally ill patient in committing suicide by prescribing sleeping pills and advising the patient of the amount of a lethal dose. Five years before to this, the committee had recommended that physicians listen to the final wishes of their dying patients including removal of a feeding tube. Since then, many recommendations of the committee have been adopted by physicians and the court system.

Forty states and the District of Columbia have living will laws that allow people to specify in advance what treatments they would find acceptable in their final days. A New York State Supreme Court Justice ruled in January 1990 that a family did not have to pay 2 years worth of fees ($100,000) to a nursing home for tending a comatose patient after the family had asked to have the feeding tube removed. Less than 6 months later, in June 1990, the U.S. Supreme Court made a ruling by which family members can be barred from ending the lives of long-term comatose relatives who have not made their wishes known conclusively. In the absence of conclusive evidence that a patient does not wish to be sustained by artificial life-saving devices, the states were given broad power to keep such patients on life-saving systems. The court interprets the [C]onstitution that a competent person, as opposed to someone in a coma, is guaranteed the right to refuse medical treatment.

A poll conducted for *Time Magazine*/CNN television network in 1990 found that 80% of those surveyed thought decisions about ending lives of the terminally ill, who cannot decide for themselves, should be made by the patient's family and physician rather than lawmakers. Of the respondents, 81% believed that a physician with an unconscious patient who has left a living will should be allowed to withdraw life-sustaining treatment, and 57% believed physicians should go even further in such cases and [administer] lethal injections or provide a lethal amount of pills (Gibbs, 1990). Public acceptance of the right of an individual with a terminal illness to commit suicide has been growing, and between 1977 and 1983 the percentage of adults in the United States who believe a terminally ill person has a right to commit suicide increased from 39% to almost 50% (Siegel, 1988). Wellman and Wellman (1986) conducted two surveys assessing attitudes toward suicide. In the first survey, over one half

of both men and women believed that no one should be allowed to commit suicide. In the second survey, 70% of both sexes believed no one should be allowed to commit suicide.

Singh (1979) reported that suicide was considered a rational alternative for those who were suffering from an incurable disease by approximately 40% of the respondents in a national survey. Singh et al. (1986) compared four national surveys conducted between 1977 and 1983. The study examined public opinion on suicide in four situations: incurable disease, bankruptcy, family dishonor, and being tired of living. The highest approval rate for suicide was in the situation in which a person had an incurable disease. In each year an increasing percentage approved of suicide in this situation, from approximately 39% in 1977 to nearly 50% in 1983. There was very little support for a person to commit suicide after having dishonored his or her family or after having gone bankrupt. A person who approved of suicide in the incurable-disease situation would most likely be a college-educated white male under the age of 35 who infrequently attended church services and had a high degree of support for freedom of expression. The approval of suicide was highest in the Pacific region and lowest in the southern regions of the United States. Ginsburg (1971) found a generally punitive and rejecting attitude toward suicidal behavior with little sympathy for those who attempted or completed suicide. Of the respondents, 42% of those who had known someone who had committed suicide felt a person had the right to take his or her own life. Kalish, Reynolds, and Farberow (1974) concluded that respondents to their survey found the victim's situation as well as the victim equally responsible. Johnson, Fitch, Alston, and McIntosh (1980) found that public acceptance of both suicide and euthanasia was highly conditional and limited to certain segments of the population. They found that blacks are less likely to approve of suicide when an individual has an incurable disease than are whites. However, both whites and blacks are

equally likely to disapprove of suicide when an individual has dishonored his or her family or because of bankruptcy. Euthanasia is more acceptable to the general white public than is suicide. Men and women are likely to approve of euthanasia with increased education.

Ramsey and Bagley's (1985) findings suggest a more accepting attitude toward suicide than reported in previous studies. Of the respondents, 90% understood the loneliness and depression associated with suicidal behavior.

REACTIONS TO SURVIVORS OF SUICIDE

Survivors who are bereaved because of the death of a loved one by suicide must deal with their personal grief and at the same time deal with community reactions, which have been found to be more severe and negative than when death is by any other cause (Cain & Fast, 1972; Calhoun et al., 1982). Negative community reactions bring about reduced emotional support (Haim, 1970; Hatton & Valente, 1981; Whitis, 1972) and, at the same time, blame toward the family for the death (Calhoun, Selby, & Faulstich, 1980; Gordon, Range, & Edwards, 1987; Rudestam & Imbroll, 1983). People are more curious about the nature of a suicidal death than a natural death (Rudestam & Imbroll, 1983; Range & Calhoun, in press). Survivors are more likely to experience guilt and have a lengthy psychological resolution of the grief experience (Parks & Weiss, 1983; Rudestam, 1977). Calhoun et al. (1982) found that bereaved survivors of suicide victims reported feeling socially isolated, rejected, and stigmatized. Shneidman (1972) observed that, from all the varied modes of death, suicide brings the greatest stigma on the survivors and produces greater expectations of discomfort in those who must interact with family members (Shepherd & Barraclough, 1974). This reflects what has been termed *ambivalent avoidance* (Whitis, 1972). The most entrenched attitude taken toward suicide is to ignore it (Haim, 1970). Danto (1977) and Danto and Fast (1966) found that the absence of emotional support often reflects the stigma attached to the act of committing suicide (Cain & Fast, 1966). Calhoun, Selby, and Abernathy (1984) investigated reactions of persons who had experienced suicidal bereavement versus bereavement of death resulting form an accident or natural causes. Potential comforters thought that suicide was a more difficult life experience than other modes of death and that they would have difficulty expressing sympathy and would be more uncomfortable at the funeral. These findings were not as pronounced if the comforter was a close friend to the bereaved person. Thus, in this situation, the cause of death may play a lesser role in determining reactions to the survivors.

Calhoun et al. (1986) examined the social rules that govern interactions with bereaved persons. Rules are beliefs by members of a group about whether a specific behavior should or should not be performed in particular situations (Argyle, Furnham, & Graham, 1981). The pattern of the results suggests that the rules for suicide are more constraining. Judgments about the existence of social rules tend to be more inclusive and extreme in a "should not" direction when death is by suicide. They suggested that although individuals may feel greater compassion for the survivors of suicide (Calhoun, Selby, & Steelman, 1983), they may still avoid the situation for fear of violating one of the rules.

Range and Thompson (1986) found that students viewed people in the community as providing mixed messages or unhelpful messages to those who were bereaved as a result of suicide or homicide but as providing helpful messages to those bereaved as a result of other modes of death. Students viewed themselves as being equally helpful regardless of the cause of death. Students viewed those people who were bereaved as a result of homicide as having a more severe reaction than from any other cause of death. Students viewed those who were bereaved as a result of suicide as reacting about the same as those bereaved because of

natural or accidental causes. These differences are contrary to the reports of those who have actually been bereaved as a result of suicide (Range & Calhoun, 1985). It was suggested that the students may have overestimated their own helpfulness.

Several researchers found that a child depicted in a scenario as having committed suicide is perceived as having been psychologically unhealthier than if death had occurred in a different way (Calhoun et al., 1980; Ginn, Range, & Hailey, 1988; Kalish, Reynolds, & Farberow, 1974). This [has] also been found to be true of adolescents (Gordon et al., 1987; Range, Goggin, & Cantrell, in press). Range, Bright, and Ginn (1985) found that people in the community thought that suicidal adolescents were more psychologically disturbed than suicidal children. Community members blamed parents of suicidal adolescents less than they blamed parents of suicidal children and expected to like parents of suicidal adolescents more than parents of suicidal children. It seems people react differently depending on the age of the victim. Ginn et al. (1988) reported that subjects did not attribute psychological disturbance to the parents of a child who committed suicide, but Gordon et al. (1987) found that the mother was also viewed as more psychologically disturbed than if the child had died of natural causes. Also more people are opposed to publishing the cause of death in the newspaper when the cause is suicide (Calhoun et al., 1980; Ginn et al., 1988). Gordon et al. (1987) surveyed parents and their children and found that the parents perceived a youth who died of suicide as more psychologically disturbed than did their adolescent children, but parents expected to experience less tension and have less difficulty in expressing sympathy when visiting the survivors than did their adolescent children. It was found that parents may be more supportive to the bereaved than are adolescents.

Bell (1977) found that college students viewed suicidal peers as cowardly, sick, unpleasant, and disreputable and were much more negative in

their attitudes toward peers who attempted suicide and lived than toward those who completed suicide. Linehan (1973) reported that college students ascribed traditional male and female qualities to completed suicide as opposed to attempted suicide. College students perceived completed suicide to be more active and potent, and which may explain why Bell (1977) found that students judged peers who attempted suicide and lived more harshly than those who died.

Wellman and Wellman (1986) conducted two surveys with college students to assess gender differences in attitudes toward suicide. Most men and women recognized that people could be suicidal, did not judge them harshly, and were receptive to and supportive of suicidal people. However, men, more so than women, were likely to have harsher attitudes toward suicidal people and were less likely to discuss the subject with them because of the belief that discussing it would precipitate suicide. Men were more likely to deny that suicidal people showed warning signs, believing it was more an impulsive act, and men were more likely to deny the increase in adolescent suicide, believing the media was exaggerating the incidence. The authors emphasized that most men do not have negative attitudes toward suicide, but men are more likely to have negative attitudes than women.

SUMMARY

Attitudes toward suicide have varied throughout time and across cultures. As this review points out, such widespread assumptions as "life is sacred" are open to interpretation. Even the idea that life should be saved at all costs has been questioned. The issues that are confronted by researchers who investigate society's attitudes toward not only the person who kills her or himself but the parents, family, and friends of that person call for a serious examination. The idea that suicide is a rational or irrational act has been argued. Like most societal problems, suicide is probably not as simple as that. Should the suicide of an individual who is suffering from a terminal illness and whose prognosis calls for a short life with intense pain be labeled a rational, well-thought-out act or the behavior of a psychologically disturbed person?

Opponents of rational suicide equate suicide with psychological disturbance. Thus, they argue that suicide is irrational. Anecdotal clinical evidence, as well as research, examined the demographics and characteristics of suicidal individuals and suggested that suicide is often a well-thought-out plan of action that may not be a result of severe psychological disturbance (Fox & Weissman, 1975: Patsiokas, Clum, & Luscomb, 1979).

Thus, society's view of suicidal behavior appears to be mixed. Current attitudes include maintaining life. However, growing movements that have stressed an individual's right to die in certain situations served to move societal attitudes away from a simplistic dichotomy of good or bad.

REFERENCES

Argyle, M., Furnham, A., & Graham, J. (1981). *Social situations*. Cambridge, England: Cambridge University Press.

Bell, D. (1977). Sex and chronicity as variables affecting attitudes of undergraduates toward peers with suicidal behaviors. *Dissertation Abstracts International, 38*, 3380B.

Cain, A., & Fast, I. (1966). The legacy of suicide: Observations on the pathogenic impact of suicide upon marital partners. *Psychiatry, 29*, 406–441.

Cain, A., & Fast, I. (1972). The legacy of suicide: Observations on the pathogenic impact of suicide upon marital partners. In A. C. Cain (Ed.), *Survivors of suicide*. Springfield, IL: Charles C. Thomas.

Calhoun, L., Abernathy, C., & Selby, J. (1986). The rules of bereavement: Are suicidal deaths different? *Journal of Community Psychology, 14*, 213–218.

Calhoun, L., Selby, J. & Abnernathy, C. (1984). Suicidal death: Social reactions to bereaved survivors. *Journal of Psychology, 116*, 225–261.

Calhoun, L., Slelby, J., & Faulstich, M. (1980). Reactions to the parents of the child's suicide: A study of social impressions. *Journal of Consulting and Clinical Psychology, 48*, 535–536.

Calhoun, L., Selby, J., & Selby, L. (1982). The psychological aftermath of suicide: An analysis of current evidence. *Clinical Psychological Review, 2*, 409–420.

Calhoun, L., Selby, J., & Steelman, J. (1983). *Individual and social elements in acute grief. A collection of funeral directors' impressions of suicidal deaths*. Unpublished manuscript, University of North Carolina, Charlotte.

Danto, B. (1977). Family survivors of suicide. In B. L. Danto & A. H. Kutscher (Eds.) *Suicide and bereavement* (pp. 11–20). New York: MSS Information Corp.

de Catanzaro, D. (1981). *Suicide and self-damaging behavior: A sociobiological perspective*. New York: Academic Press.

Douglas, J. (1967). *The social meaning of suicide*. Princeton: NJ: Princeton University Press.

Dublin L. (1963). *Suicide: A social and statistical study*. New York: Ronald Press.

Feherman, (1989). Ethical recommendations. *New England Journal of Medicine*.

Fox, K., & Weissman, H. (1975). Suicide attempts and drugs: Contradiction between method and intent. *Social Psychiatry, 10*, 31–38.

Gibbs, N. (1990, March 19). Love and let die. *Time*, pp. 62–71.

Ginn, P., Range, L., & Hailey, B. (1988). Community attitudes toward childhood suicide and attempted suicide. *Journal of Community Psychology, 16*, 144–151.

Ginsburg, G. (1971). Public perceptions and attitudes about suicide. *Journal of Health and Social Behavior, 12*, 200–207.

Gordon, R., Range, L., & Edwards, R. (1987). Generational differences in reactions to adolescent suicide. *Journal of Community Psychology, 15*, 268–273.

Haim, A. (1970). *Adolescent suicide*. (A. M. S. Smith, Trans.). New York: International University Press.

Hatton, C. C., & Valente, S. M. (1981). Bereavement group for parents who suffered a suicidal loss of a child. *Suicide and Life-Threatening Behavior, 11*, 141–150.

Humphry, D. (1987). The case for rational suicide [Letter to the editor]. *Suicide and Life-Threatening Behavior, 17*, 335–338.

Johnson, D., Fitch, S., Alston, J., & McIntosh, W. (1980). Acceptance of conditional suicide and euthanasia among adult Americans. *Suicide and Life-Threatening Behavior, 10*, 157–166.

Kalish, R., Reynolds, D., & Farberow, N. (1974). Community attitudes toward suicide. *Community Mental Health Journal, 10*, 301–308.

Klagsburn, F. (1981). *Too young to die—youth and suicide*. New York: Houghton Mifflin.

Kluge, E. (1975). *The practice and death*. New Haven, CT: Yale University Press.

Koller, K., & Slaghuis, W. (1978). Suicide attempts 1973–1977 in urban Hobart: A further five year follow up reporting a decline. *Australian and New Zealand Journal of Psychiatry, 12*, 169–173.

Lampke, R. (1989). AIDS and the allied health care worker: Fears, fantasies, and facts. *Advances in Thanatology, 7*, 92–103.

Linehan, M. (1973). Suicide and attempted suicide: Study of perceived sex differences. *Perceptual and Motor Skills, 37*, 31–34.

Maris, R. (1986). Basic issues in suicide prevention: Resolutions of liberty and love (the Dublin lecture). *Suicide and Life-Threatening Behavior, 16*, 326–334.

McGinnis, J. (1987). Suicide in America—moving up the public agenda. *Suicide and Life-Threatening Behavior, 18*, 18–32.

Parkes, C., & Weiss, R. (1983). *Physical and psychological responses to suicide in the family—recovery from bereavement*. New York: Basic Books.

Patsiokas, A., Blum, G., Luscomb, R. (1983). Cognitive characteristics of suicide attempters. *Journal of Consulting and Clinical Psychology, 47*, 478–484.

Quinnett, P. (1987). *Suicide the forever decision*. New York: Continuum Publishing.

Ramsay, T., & Bagley, C. (1985). The prevalence of suicidal behaviors, attitudes and associated social experiences in an urban population. *Suicide and Life-Threatening Behavior, 15*, 151–167.

Range, L., Bright, Pl, & Ginn, P. (1985). Public reactions to child suicide: Effects of age and method used. *Journal of Community Psychology, 113*, 288–294.

Range, L., & Calhoun, L. (1985, March). The impact of type of death on the bereavement experience. In L. G. Calhoun (Chair), *Bereavement: Clinical and social aspects*. Symposium conducted at the annual meeting of the Southeastern Psychological Association.

Range, L., Goggin, W., & Cantrell, P. (in press). The false consensus bias as applied to psychologically disturbed adolescents. *Adolescence*.

Range, L., McDonald, D., & Anderson, H. (1987). Factor structure of Calhoun's youth suicide scale. *Journal of Personality Assessment, 51*, 262–266.

Range, L., & Thompson, K. (1986). Community responses following suicide, homicide and other deaths: The perspective of potential comforters. *Journal of Psychology, 121*, 193–198.

Rudestam, K. (1977). Physical and psychological responses to suicide in the family. *Journal of Consulting and Clinical Psychology, 45*, 162–170.

Rudestam, K., & Imbroll. D. (1983). Societal reactions to a child's death by suicide. *Journal of Consulting and Clinical Psychology, 51*, 461–462.

Sachs, A. (1990, November 28). To my family, my physician, my lawyer and all others whom it may concern. *Time*, p. 70.

Shepherd, T., & Barraclough, B. (1974). The aftermath of suicide. *British Medical Journal, 2*, 600–603.

Schneidman, E. S. (1972). Forward. In A. C. Cain (Ed.), *Survivors of suicide* (pp. ix–xi). Springfield, IL: Charles C. Thomas.

Siegel, K. (1988). Rational suicide. In S. Lesse (Ed.), *What we know about suicidal behavior and how to treat it* (pp. 85–102). Northvale, NJ: Jason Anderson.

Singh, B. (1979). Correlates of attitudes toward euthanasia. *Social Biology, 26*, 247–254.

Singh, B., Williams, J., & Ryther, B. (1986). Public approval of suicide: A situational analysis. *Suicide and Life-Threatening Behavior, 16*, 409–418.

Szasz,, T. (1974). *The second sin*. London: Routledge and Kegan Paul.

Weber, W. (1988). What right to die? [Letter to the editor]. *Suicide and Life-Threatening Behavior, 18*, 181–188.

Wellman, M., & Wellman, R. J. (1986). Sex differences in peer responsiveness to suicide ideation. *Suicide and Life-Threatening Behavior, 16*, 360–378.

Whitis, P. (1972). The legacy of a child's suicide. In A. C. Cain (Ed.), *Survivors of suicide* (pp. 155–166). Springfield, IL: Charles C. Thomas.

"We Have a Problem"

"My husband Alex's death was a terrible blow, and I'm afraid that Patty, eight, isn't getting over it. Will time and therapy lessen the pain—or is a father's suicide one hurt that never goes away?"

Jane Marks

Jane Marks is the author of three nonfiction books for teenagers, including *Help! My Parents Are Driving Me Crazy* (Ace Books).

Mia's story.

"Right after it happened, I thought we were doing so well," said Mia Browne, 33. "I fell apart—briefly—but Patty didn't. Even at Alex's funeral, she was calm and brave, and I thought, Yes, we'll make it through this!

"We'd already been through a lot in the past three years, watching a wonderful, loving husband and father sink into deep, unrelenting sadness. 'I'm worthless,' he would say. I tried so hard to convince him that it wasn't true. 'You and Patty would be better off without me,' he insisted over and over again.

"Alarmed, I made him go for help, and he was hospitalized. That was when I learned that depression could be traced back three generations in his family. 'It's genetically loaded,' the doctor said. 'Your husband needs to be on medication.'

"Alex did well on the antidepressant, but two months later, as soon as he came home and was feeling better, he threw the rest of his pills away. 'I'm okay now,' he said. 'Can't you believe me?' And for a short time he did seem calmer, but that must have been only because he'd made his decision to die. Several days later, he went to his office—and shot himself with a hunting rifle.

"Telling Patty was so hard—the hardest thing I've ever had to do. I was tempted to pretend it was a heart attack or at least an accident. But then I realized it would only be more traumatic later, when she learned the truth. So I told her, 'Daddy was very, very sad, and so he decided to end his life.' I stressed that it was nobody's fault, and I assured her that I was still here to take care of her—no matter what—and we would be fine.

"Patty was terrific! I had been working part-time as a nurse, but now I had to work full-time, which meant after-school care for Patty. I felt terrible, but I'd always get a big hug from her—with no resentment or complaints.

" 'I'm proud of you,' I told her, and Patty beamed. But in June, once school was over, I noticed that she wasn't seeing her friends. 'I just want to be with you,' she'd say on the weekends. One week, I was home with the flu, and Patty insisted on staying home to heat up my soup. She proudly brought it in on a tray with a pretty doily she had made out of a paper towel.

" 'Mom, are you okay?' she asked anxiously. 'Yes,' I assured her. Seeing the worried look on her face, I said, 'I'm *not* going to die, honey.' " But even after I was well, Patty stuck close by me.

"The time we spent together was precious. But when Patty's birthday came and she didn't want to invite even one friend over, I grew concerned. 'I don't want anybody,' Patty said, in contrast to the year before, when our problem had been limiting the number of friends.

"I said, 'Okay, we'll have a special dinner out—just the two of us.' We went to a Chinese restaurant where the drinks had little umbrellas in them, and ordered a platter of spare-ribs, some shrimp toast, and morsels of chicken in foil we cooked on skewers in a flame right on our table.

"It was fun—until I said, 'Wouldn't Daddy have liked this place?' Patty stiffened. Her face got blotchy and she turned away. 'It's okay to cry,' I said gently, but she shook her head and pushed her chair back. 'I'm done,' she said. 'Can we go home now?'

"Clearly, talking about Alex was still too painful for Patty, and although it would have made *me* feel better to see her let it out instead of holding in her feelings, I didn't see any point in pushing.

"Was she denying what had happened? That was how my sister, Jenny, saw it. 'Children mourn in their own way,' Jenny said when I telephoned her in Florida, where she lived.

"I tried not to worry, even when I overheard Patty lie to a new kid across the street, saying, 'My parents are divorced too. I might visit my dad this summer.' Knowing I'd overheard, Patty explained, 'Mom, I *had* to say that.'

" 'But why? I told you there's nothing to be ashamed of.'

" 'I know that,' Patty said, 'but the kids act weird.' Patty kicked at some stones. 'I know they're sometimes talking about me because they stop when I get near them.'

" 'Honey, are you sure you're not just imagining . . . ?'

" '*No!*' Patty insisted.

" 'I can't you ignore them?'

" 'I do!' Patty said. 'And don't worry. There's lots of things I can do by myself this summer. I don't need that bunch of dweebs.'

" 'She may have outgrown her old friends,' Jenny suggested. 'After all, look at all she's been through—and look at what *their* big concerns are: TV? New toys?'

"Perhaps Jenny was right, but as the weeks passed, I found myself worrying more and more often. I had taken

From *Parents*, October 1990, pp. 54–59. From Jane Marks's book *We Have a Problem: A Parent's Source Book*, 1992, American Psychiatric Press, 1-800-368-5777, Monday–Friday, 9–5 Eastern Standard Time. Fax 1-202-789-2648, $21.95.

time off to be with Patty, but she spent most of the time reading in her room.

" 'I thought you missed me, but when I'm here you ignore me,' I said, only half joking. Patty threw her arms around me. 'I *am* glad you're home,' she said. But later, when we went to the lake for a picnic and a swim, I felt as though she was doing it only to humor me.

" 'I had fun,' she said, slouched down beside me, her face barely visible under one of Alex's old tennis hats. 'Really! I had the best time.' She looked up, and her eyes were pleading: Believe me, believe me! Why did her words sound so hollow? She's *depressed,* I thought chillingly. That's why Patty isn't having any fun or hanging out with her friends.

" 'Don't get hysterical,' Jenny scolded me. 'How could Patty not be depressed in that house where the three of you lived? It's got to be hard for you, too, Mia. You could come to Florida—stay with us until you find a place. Nurses are in such demand down here, you could write your own ticket.'

"It sounded so tempting, and as soon as she said it, I knew she was right. I had been naive to think that we could ever get on with our lives as long as every room, every nook and cranny, held reminders of Alex—not just the funny, lovable, endearing Alex, but the bitter, hopeless stranger he had eventually become.

" 'Guess what?' I told Patty excitedly. 'How would you like to move to Florida? We could stay with Aunt Jenny, and you'd have Uncle George and all your cousins to horse around with—and you could swim every day, all year long. Imagine that!"

"Patty just stared. 'For real?' she asked. 'Yes!' I said, hugging her. 'It would be like being on vacation all the time . . . and no flu season! And another thing,' I said. 'It would be a fresh start with all new friends.'

" 'But do you want to?' Patty asked cautiously.

" 'Of course!'

" 'Then let's. I can't wait!'

"After that, it seemed as if we spent every spare moment fixing up our house to sell it, putting aside unneeded items for a garage sale, and contacting hospitals and nursing homes within commuting distance of Jenny's house about possible jobs.

"We set up the garage sale, and to my delight, it was well attended, with lots of people eagerly buying the furniture and other 'junk' we weren't planning to take with us.

"Patty helped all morning, but by noon she seemed tired and edgy, so I urged her to take a break. She did leave, only to come back a moment later. 'Stop! You *can't* take that!' she cried suddenly, grabbing an old, chipped vase out of an astonished women's hands.

" 'Patty?' I tried to reach her, but she ducked away. And before I could stop her, she threw the vase to the ground, smashing it to pieces.

"Murmuring and shaking their heads, the customers hurried away to their cars. A boy about Patty's age whispered loudly, 'Mom, is *she* crazy too, like her dad?' Patty kicked at pieces of the broken vase and ran into the house.

"I was shocked and scared. Was this a normal part of Patty's mourning—or something more frightening? One thing was certain: My Patty needed help."

The counselor replies.

Elizabeth B. Weller, M.D., is professor of psychiatry and pediatrics at The Ohio State University College of Medicine, in Columbus. She is also head of the Division of Child and Adolescent Psychiatry and a co-author of Psychiatric Disorders in Children and Adolescents *(W. B. Saunders Co.).*

"Mia was very concerned as she was telling me the story. I agreed to see Patty right away. I said, 'We'll see what's going on, but if Patty was in sound emotional health before your husband's death, that's a hopeful sign.'

"Nor was I any less optimistic when I met Patty the following day. She was a pretty, well-groomed, and polite little girl who looked very sad. In my office, she had no trouble separating from her mother. When I mentioned her father, she started to cry. She then stopped herself. I told her it was okay to cry. 'No!' she said. 'I've got to be brave—for Mommy.'

"I assured her that she didn't need to be brave for me, that this was a safe place for her to let go of all the feelings she'd been holding back. She burst into tears again and began to tell me how her dad had died and how ever since it happened she had felt terrible.

"I asked, 'Have you told your mom how sad you are?'

" 'Oh, no!' Patty said, wiping her eyes. 'She has enough problems, and she has to work so hard.' Patty said that sometimes she had a nightmare that her mom was dying. 'If only things could be like they used to,' Patty sighed. Over our next few sessions, she talked more about her fears and memories.

" 'Sometimes,' she said during one session, 'when it's dark at night, I think I really see my dad—and it's so nice.' Patty's face clouded. 'Does that mean I'm crazy?'

" 'Absolutely not,' I assured her. 'That's normal, and it just means you miss him and wish he were here.' Patty looked relieved and smiled.

" 'What do you miss most about your dad?' I asked.

" 'Oh,' she said, smiling, 'the hugs! Daddy had a mustache, and it always tickled when he kissed me. We used to go for walks and bike rides, and on Sunday mornings we always made pancakes together, and Mom said they were the best.'

"Now she looked troubled again. 'Do you think if I really wished hard, he'd come back?' she asked.

" 'When somebody dies, he can't come back, but you can hold on to the good memories,' I offered.

" 'But what if I grow up and forget about him?'

"I said, 'I don't think you will,' and suggested that she keep a diary of memories that she could illustrate with drawings and photographs.

"Patty nodded. Then she said, 'If I had done better in school and kept my room neater, then Daddy wouldn't have been so sad.'

" 'Patty,' I replied, 'there was nothing you could have done to help him.' I explained that her father had a serious illness called depression. 'He was very sick,' I said, 'and when somebody is sick and his brain is involved, he gets confused. That was why your daddy did what he did.'

" 'Did he hate us?' Patty asked.

" 'Oh, no!' I said. 'He didn't die *because* of you. When you're sick, you don't reason right. He made some wrong choices. In fact, he might have decided to end his life much sooner if he hadn't loved you. Your mother told me how much he loved you— how he called you his special, wonderful daughter.'

" 'I know he did love me,' she agreed. 'And I love him! That's why I want to see him. I've even thought about killing myself so we could be together in heaven, but I don't want to die—or leave my mom. But I wish I could see him. I didn't even get to say good-bye to him.'

"Patty had shared a lot of her feelings, and I told Mia what a productive session we'd had. 'I'm so glad—but I'm surprised,' she said. 'She's always reticent with me, and yet she has poured her heart out to a total stranger like you.'

" 'It's *because* I'm a stranger that she feels free to do so,' I explained. 'Patty knows she doesn't have to protect me, because she knows I won't fall apart.'

" 'Does she think I would?'

" 'In a way, yes. Like any child who has lost a parent to suicide, Patty believes she was somehow responsible for her father's death. She's scared that if she isn't careful, she might make *you* feel so sad and overburdened that you would leave her too.'

"I suggested that Patty could now benefit from therapy—to air her feelings. And it would be a way we could keep an eye on her. Mia agreed, and I began seeing Patty weekly.

"During those sessions, Patty talked a lot about her life. She started the diary of memories that I'd suggested, and she found that while many were happy, others were sad and worrisome. Patty remembered her father's erratic moods and how anxious she had often been about him. 'That was hard,' she said, and wondered if now it was 'okay' to feel relieved that she didn't have to worry anymore.

"I said, 'Sure! It's scary even for grown-ups to live with someone whose moods are so unpredictable. *Anyone* in your shoes would feel very sad—but also relieved at the same time.'

"Throughout our sessions, Patty expressed continuing concern for her mother—panicking if Mia was even a little bit late coming home from work, for example. 'What if my mom dies? What will happen to me then?' Patty asked.

"I said, 'I don't think it's going to happen, but let's think, What if . . . ?' In a joint session with Mia, we discussed that worst-case scenario and what would happen to Patty. Would she live with her grandparents? ('No,' Patty said firmly. 'They're too old, and they might die.')

"Patty said, 'If Mommy dies, I'd like to go live with Aunt Jenny—but not *now!* I don't want to move to Florida.' Hearing this, Mia agreed not to move,

at least not in the near future, in order to avoid more stress for Patty.

"Mia said the idea to move had been for Patty's sake. Now she realized that it wouldn't be helpful and agreed to scrap the moving plans.

"This discussion helped Patty regain a sense of control over her own destiny and also showed her that there was a backup system to protect her, as well as people out there who cared about her.

• • • • • • • • • • •

"I've thought about killing myself so we could be together in heaven."

• • • • • • • • • • •

" 'Now I see why just reassuring her that nothing would ever happen to me was not enough,' Mia said.

"By the time school started, Patty felt much more relaxed. Her feeling that she always had to prop up her mother was less overwhelming, and at the same time, she was learning to let go of feeling even partially responsible for her father's death.

"But she was still very isolated from the children who had been her friends. Part of it came from Patty herself, since she felt jealous of kids with two parents, and left out. But she was also aware of the rumors that her father had been 'crazy.'

"I suggested, 'Why don't you pick one friend you used to like and trust and see if you can make contact?' I said that maybe Mia could talk to the other girl's mom.

"Patty tried it with her friend Rebecca, who confessed, 'I've missed you, but I didn't know what to say to you, so I didn't say anything.'

" 'But she's just one,' Patty said sadly. 'I can't explain to everyone; it would take too long.' Patty asked whether I could come and talk to her class. I said, 'Why not?' and with her teacher's permission, I did just that.

"The fourth-grade class was very attentive, and very interested in what I had to say. Every one of them had heard of a suicide other than Patty's father. One boy mentioned an uncle, another a neighbor. 'Don't you have to be crazy to kill yourself?' a girl named Amber asked.

"I said, 'No, it's an illness that affects the brain, but if the person gets into treatment, we can usually help him function normally.'

" 'Is it catching, like AIDS?' another child wondered. I said, 'No, not at all,' and I could see many children breathe a sigh of relief.

" 'I'd like to learn about the brain,' Rebecca ventured. 'Why *do* people like Patty's dad think differently—and how can we help them stop it?'

"Afterward, Patty thanked me. 'I think I'd like to be a psychiatrist too,' she said. 'I'd like to be like you and help kids. I think I'd be good at that.'

"Patty continued to feel better, but one day in December she came in quite distraught. 'Mom had a date,' she complained. It was clear that it had been a very casual date and that Mia had been home by eight o'clock.

" 'But what if she gets married?' Patty asked. 'I don't want her to date! That's unfair to Dad.'

"Once again, I arranged a joint session with Mia and Patty to clarify Mia's intentions. 'I'm not really dating yet,' Mia said. 'Todd's just a friend.'

" 'But what if someone else comes along?' Patty wasn't giving up. Mia said, 'You're right, I might fall in love some day.' Patty's face fell. 'But Patty,' she went on, 'I promise you that anyone I marry would have to be a very good person. . . . And also, I can tell you right now, nobody will ever take the place of your father.'

"By early spring I saw a lot of progress. Patty felt better about herself and shared her feelings more easily with her mother and her friends. 'Perhaps you don't need to come in every week anymore,' I suggested.

" 'You mean not ever see you again?' Patty looked stricken.

" 'No!' I told her. I would still want to see her at special times like her birthday, her dad's birthday, and the anniversary of his death.

" 'And for an even longer time,' I said, 'I'd like to see you at least once a year so I know that you're okay.'

" 'Oh, *good!*' Patty said. 'Then I'll always know you, and I won't have to lose you.'

"I felt that this was a very good outcome. Still, I warned Mia that Patty might experience more difficulties during adolescence. 'Patty's still a child now, and she may need help making sense of her loss in a different, more mature way later on.'

"It probably won't be all smooth sailing for the Brownes. Small losses will remind them of what they've gone through and will feel like big ones. But those shake-ups will show them that they can survive and have a life full of love and meaning."

Funerals and Burial Rites

Decisions relating to the disposition of the body after death often involve feelings of ambivalence—on the one hand, attachments to the deceased might cause one to be reluctant to dispose of the body, but on the other hand, practical considerations make the disposal of the body necessary. Funerals or memorial services provide methods for disposing of a dead body, remembering the deceased, and helping survivors accept the reality of death. They are also public rites of passage that assist the bereaved in returning to routine patterns of social interaction. In contemporary America, 78 percent of deaths involve earth burial, 17 percent involve cremation, and 5 percent will involve entombment. These public behaviors, along with the private process of grieving, comprise the two components of the bereavement process.

This unit on contemporary American funerals begins with three general articles on the nature and functions of public bereavement behavior. The first article, by Michael Leming and George Dickinson, gives an overview of the present practice of funeralization in American society, including traditional and alternative funeral arrangements. It also discusses the functions of funerals relative to the sociological, psychological, and theological needs of adults and children. In "Rituals: [Five] Ways Americans Deal with Death," the New Orleans jazz funeral, a simple funeral, a Blue Ridge Mountain funeral, a Jewish funeral, and urban rituals are examined. The article by Ronald Barrett ("Psychocultural Influences on African-American Attitudes towards Death, Dying, and Funeral Rites") puts death and dying rituals within a pluralistic and multicultural perspective.

William Whalen discusses commonalities and differences among many religious traditions in "How Different Religions Pay Their Final Respects," and the articles by Dawn Gibeau ("She Plans Funerals That Celebrate Life"), Jane Vernon ("It's Your Funeral"), and Thomas Lynch ("Burying the Ungrateful Dead") demonstrate that the rituals performed at the funeral are closely tied to the cultural backgrounds and religious values of the people who perform them.

The remaining two articles, "Burying Tradition, More People Opt for 'Fun' Funerals," by Carrie Dolan, and "Mourners Will Please Pay Respects at Speeds Not Exceeding 15 MPH," by Alison Woods, conclude this unit by discussing futuristic and nontraditional forms of funeral rituals.

Looking Ahead: Challenge Questions

Describe how the funeralization process can assist in coping with grief and facilitate the bereavement process. Distinguish among grief, bereavement, and funeralization.

Discuss the psychological, sociological, and theological-philosophical aspects of the funeralization process. How do each of these aspects facilitate the resolution of grief?

Describe and compare each of the following processes: burial, cremation, entombment, cryonics, and body donation for medical research. What would be your choice of final disposition of your body? Why would you choose this method, and what effects might this choice have upon your survivors (if any)? Would you have the same or different preferences for a close loved one such as a spouse, child, or parent? Why?

THE CONTEMPORARY AMERICAN FUNERAL

Michael R. Leming

St. Olaf College

George E. Dickinson

College of Charleston

Most people use the words *death, grief,* and *bereavement* confusedly, which can lead to difficulty in communication. The words are closely interrelated, but each has a specific content or meaning. . . . [D]eath is that point in time when life ceases to exist. *Death* is an event. It can be attached to a certain day, hour, and minute. *Grief* is an emotion, a very powerful emotion. It is triggered or stimulated by death. Although one can have anticipatory grief prior to the death of a significant other, grief is an emotional response to death. *Bereavement* is the state of having lost a significant other to death. Alternative processes—such as denial, avoidance, and defiance—have been shown by psychologists and psychiatrists to be only aberrations of the grief process and, as such, are not viable means of grief resolution.

The ultimate method of final **disposition** of the body should be determined by the persons in bereavement. Those charged with these decisions will be guided by their personal values and by the norms of the culture in which they live.

With over two-thirds of American deaths occurring in hospitals or institutions for the care of the sick and infirm, the contemporary process of body disposition begins at the time of death when the body is removed from the institutional setting. Most frequently the body is taken to a funeral home. There, the body is bathed, embalmed, and dressed. It is then placed in a casket selected by the family. Typically, arrangements are made for the ceremony, assuming a ceremony is to follow. The funeral director, in consultation with the family, will determine the type, time, place, and day of the ceremony. In most instances, the public rite or ceremony will have a religious content (Pine, 1971). This procedure described above is followed in approximately 75 percent of funerals. Alternatives to this procedure will be examined later in this chapter.

Following this ceremony, final disposition of the body is made by either earth burial (78 percent), cremation (17 percent), or entombment (5 percent). (These percentages are approximate national averages and will vary by geographical region.) The bereavement process will then be followed by a period of postfuneral adjustment for the family.

HOW THE FUNERAL MEETS THE NEEDS OF THE BEREAVED

Paul Irion (1956) has described the following needs of the bereaved: reality, expression of grief, social support, and meaningful context to the death. For Irion, the funeral is an experience of significant personal value insofar as it meets the religious, social, and psychological needs of the mourners. Each of these dimensions is necessary to return bereaved individuals to everyday living and, in the process, resolve their grief.

The *psychological* focus of the funeral is based on the fact that grief is an emotion. Edgar Jackson (1963) has indicated that grief is the other side of the coin of love. He contends that if a person has never loved the deceased—had an emotional investment of some type and degree—he or she will not grieve upon death. Evidence of this can easily be demonstrated by the number of deaths that we hear, see, or read about daily that do not have an impact on us unless we have some kind of emotional involvement with those deceased persons. We can read 78 deaths in a plane crash and not grieve over any of them unless we personally knew one or more of the individuals killed. Exceptions to the above might include the death of a celebrity or public figure, when people experience a sense of grief even though there has never been any personal contact.

Excerpt from *Understanding Dying, Death, and Bereavement,* Third Edition, 1994, by Michael R. Leming and George E. Dickinson, pp. 458-462. © 1994 by Holt, Rinehart & Winston, Inc. Reprinted by permission.

In his original work on the symptomatology of grief, Erich Lindemann (1944) stressed this concept of grief and its importance as a step in the resolution of grief. He defines how the emotion of grief must support the reality and finality of death. As long as the finality of death is avoided, Lindemann (1944) believes grief resolution is impeded. For this reason, he strongly recommends that the bereaved persons view the dead. When the living confront the dead, all of the intellectualization and avoidance techniques break down. When we can say, "He or she is dead, I am alone, and from this day forward my life will be forever different," we have broken through the devices of denial and avoidance and have accepted the reality of death. It is only at this point that we can begin to withdraw the emotional capital that we have invested in the deceased and seek to create new relationships with the living.

On the other hand, viewing the corpse can be very traumatic for some. Most people are not accustomed to seeing a cold body and a significant other stretched out with eyes closed. Indeed, for some this scene may remain in their memories for a lifetime. Thus, they remember the cold corpse, not the warm, responsive person. Whether or not to view the body is not a cut-and-dried issue. Many factors should be taken into account when this decision is made.

Grief resolution is especially important for family members, but others are affected also—the neighbors, the business community in some instances, the religious community in most instances, the health-care community, and the circle of friends and associates (many of whom may be unknown to the family). All of these groups will grieve to some extent the death of their relationship with the deceased. Thus, many people are affected by the death. These affected persons will seek not only a means of expressing their grief over the death but also a network of support to help cope with their grief.

Sociologically, the funeral is a social event that brings the chief mourners and the members of society into a confrontation with death. The funeral becomes a vehicle to bring persons of all walks of life and degrees of relationship to the deceased together in one place for expression and support. It is for this reason that in our contemporary culture the funeral becomes an occasion to which no one is invited but all may come. This was not always the case, and some cultures make the funeral ceremony an "invitation only" experience. It is perhaps for this reason that private funerals (restricted only to the family or a special list of persons) have all but disappeared in our culture. (The possible exception to this statement is the funeral for a celebrity—where participation for the general public is limited to media coverage.)

At a time when emotions are strong, it is important that human interaction and social support become a high priority. A funeral can provide this atmosphere.

To grieve alone can be devastating because it becomes necessary for that lone person to absorb all of the feelings into him- or herself. It has often been said that "joy shared is joy increased"; surely grief shared will be grief diminished. People need each other at times when they have intense emotional experiences.

A funeral is in essence a one-time kind of "support group" to undergird and support those grieving persons. A funeral provides a conducive social environment for mourning. We may either go to the funeral home to visit with the bereaved or for the purpose of working through our own feelings of grief. Most of us have had the experience of finding it difficult for the first time to discuss the death with a member of the family. We seek the proper atmosphere, time, or place. It is during the funeral, the wake, the shiv'ah, or the visitation with the bereaved where we are provided the opportunity to express our condolences and sympathy comfortably.

Anger and guilt are often deeply felt at the time of death and will surface in words and actions. They are permitted within the funeral atmosphere as honest and candid expressions of grief, when at other times, they might bring criticism and reprimand. The funeral atmosphere says in essence "You are okay, I am okay; we have some strong feelings, and now is the time to express and share them for the benefit of all." Silence, talking, touching, feeling, and all means of sharing can be expressed without the fear of it being inappropriate.

The third function of the funeral is to provide a *theological* or *philosophical* perspective to facilitate grieving and provide a context of meaning in which to place one of life's most significant experiences. For the majority of Americans, the funeral is a religious rite or ceremony (Pine, 1971). For those who do not possess a religious creed or orientation, death will find definition or expression in the context of the values that the deceased and the grievers find important. Theologically or philosophically, the funeral functions as an attempt to bring meaning to the death and life of the deceased individual. For the religiously oriented person, it will perhaps contain a belief or understanding of an afterlife. For others, it may be seen only as an end of biological life and the beginning of symbolic immortality caused by the effects of one's life on the lives of others. The funeral should be planned in order to give meaning to whichever value context is significant for the bereaved.

"Why?" is one of the most often asked questions at the moment of death or upon being told that someone we know has died. Though it cannot provide the final answer to this question, the funeral can place death within a context of meaning that is significant to those who mourn. If it is religious in context, the theology, creed, and articles of faith confessed by the mourners will give them comfort and assurance as to the meaning of death. Others who have developed a personally meaningful philosophy of life and death will seek to place the death in that philosophical context.

Cultural expectations require that we typically dispose of the dead with ceremony and dignity. The funeral can also ascribe importance to the remains of the dead.

The Needs of Children and Their Attendance at Funerals

For children, as well as their adult counterparts, the funeral ceremony can be an experience of value and significance. At a very early age, children are interested in any type of family reunion, party, or celebration. To be excluded from the funeral may create questions and doubts in the mind of children as to why they are not permitted to be a part of an important family activity.

Another consideration in denying the child an opportunity to participate in post-death activities is what goes through the child's mind when such participation is denied. Children deal with other difficult situations in life, and when denied this opportunity, many will fantasize. Research suggests that these fantasies may be negative, destructive, and at times more traumatic than the situation from which the child is excluded.

Children also should not be excluded from activities prior to the funeral service. They should be permitted to attend the visitation, wake, or shiv'ah. (In some situations it would be wise to permit children to confront the deceased prior to the public visitation.) It is obvious that children should not be forced into this type of confrontation, but, by the same token, children who are curious and desire to be involved should not be denied the opportunity.

Children will react at their own emotional levels, and the questions they ask will usually be asked at their level of comprehension. Two important rules follow: Never lie to the child, and do not overanswer the child's question.

At the time of the funeral, parents have two concerns about their children's behavior at funerals. The first is that they are worried that the child will have difficulty observing the grief of others—particularly if the child has never seen an adult loved one cry. The second is that parents themselves become confused when the child's emotional reactions may be different from their own. If the child is told of a death and responds by saying "Oh, can I go out and play?" the parent may interpret this as denial or a suppressed negative reaction to the death. Such a reaction can increase emotional concern on the part of the parent. However, if the child's response is viewed as only a first reaction, and the child is provided with loving, caring, and supportive attention, the child will ordinarily progress into an emotional resolution of the death.

The final reasons for involving children in post-death activities are related to the strength and support that they give other grievers. They often provide positive evidence of the fact that life goes on. In other instances, having been an important part of the life of the deceased, their presence is symbolic testimony to the immortality of the deceased. Furthermore, it is not at all unusual for a child to change the atmosphere surrounding bereavement from one of depression and sadness to one of laughter, verbalization, and celebration. Many times the child does this through his or her normal behavior, without any understanding of the kind of contribution being made.

REFERENCES

Irion, Paul E. 1956. *The Funeral: An Experience of Value.* Milwaukee: National Funeral Directors Association.

Jackson, Edgar N. 1963. *For the Living.* Des Moines, IA: Channel Press.

Lindemann, Erich. 1944. "Symptomatology and Management of Acute Grief." *American Journal of Psychiatry,* 101, (September):141–148.

Pine, Vanderlyn R. 1971. *Findings of the Professional Census.* Milwaukee: National Funeral Directors Association (June).

Rituals

[Five] ways Americans deal with death

Cuttin' the body loose

Dancing in defiance of death in New Orleans

They gon cut the body loose!"
One short brother with a big mustache was running up and down the funeral procession explaining that they wasn't going to have to go all the way to the cemetery on account of they was going to cut the body loose. This meant that the hearse would keep on going and the band and the second liners and the rest of the procession was going to dance on back to some tavern not too far away.

"They gon cut the body loose, y'all."

The marshal, out in front of the hearse, was draped in a blue-black suit that was a little too big and too long but was all the better to dance with. He wore yellow socks and brown shoes as a crazy combination of his own. After the body was cut loose, the steps he invented were amazing contortions of knees, shins, and flying feet. He executed those moves with the straightest, most nonchalant, don't-give-a-damn look I have ever seen on anybody's face what was doing as much work as he was doing under this merciless hot sun. He had somebody by him fanning and wiping his face after every series of grief-inspired movements. He looked so sad to be dancing so hard and making so many others of us smile as we watched him. We tried to imitate some of his easier and more obvious moves but couldn't. He was the coolest person in that street marching toward a tavern two or three blocks away under a 2:30 p.m. New Orleans summer sun. The coolest.

So we stood in a line and the second liners were shouting, "open it up, open it up," meaning for the people in front to get out the way so the hearse could pass with the body. After the hearse was gone we turned the corner and danced down to the bar.

Like a sudden urge to regurgitate and with the intensity of an ejaculation, an explosive sound erupted from the crowd under the hot New Orleans sun. People spontaneously answered the traditional call of the second line trumpet.

"Are you still alive?"
"YEAH!"
"Do we like to live?"
"YEAH!"
"Do you want to dance?"
"YEAH!"
"Well damn it, let's go!"

The trumpeter was taunting us now, and the older people were jumping from their front porches as we passed them, and they were answering that blaring hot high taunt with unmistakable fires blazing in their 60-year-old black eyes. They too danced as we passed them. They did the dances of their lives, the dances they used to celebrate how old they had become and what they had seen getting to their whatever number years. The dances they used to defy death.

Nowhere else in this country do people dance in the streets after someone has died. Nowhere else is the warm smell of cold beer on tap a fitting conclusion for the funeral of a friend. Nowhere else is death so pointedly belittled. One of us dying is only a small matter, an occasion for the rest of us to make music and dance. Nothing keeps us contained. With this spirit and this music in us, black people will never die, never die, never.

We were all ecstatic. We could see the bar. We knew it was ending, we knew we were almost there and defiantly we danced harder anyway. We hollered back even that much louder at the trumpeter as he squeezed out the last brassy blasts his lungs could throw forth. The end of the funeral was near, just as the end of life was near for some of us but it did not matter. When we get there, we'll get there.

—*Kalamu ya Salaam*

Excerpted with permission of the author from a book in progress entitled Banana Republic: Black Street Life and Culture in New Orleans.

From *Utne Reader,* September/October 1991, pp. 78-84. Reprinted by permission.

Caring for our own dead

Americans take back death arrangements from the funeral industry

In 1981, after the death of my husband, I handled his burial arrangements without the use of a funeral director. That was considered unusual at the time.

I had initially made the decision for financial reasons. In addition to the grief of a sudden death, as a new widow I faced an immediate need to take over as the sole breadwinner for my children. There was not enough money in the bank for the next grocery shopping, let alone the thousands of dollars a "traditional" funeral would cost.

As it turned out, the experience provided benefits that were more important than just saving money. The need to remain in control of the physical events helped me to avoid falling apart emotionally. Handling and transporting the body, gathering the paperwork, and making all other arrangements gave me control in a way that was therapeutic. It made me feel less helpless. If I had simply turned the body over to strangers, I would have had a much harder time accepting the reality of John's untimely death. There was no bargaining with God to wake up a pink and powdered lifelikeness.

Often, funeral professionals can provide help that is needed and welcome. Not everyone is inclined—or even able—to build a casket, transport a body, or even, at a time of grief, assemble the information needed for a death certificate or an obituary.

Unfortunately, the role of the funeral industry has gone beyond that of providing help, at a fair price, at a time of need. In all too many instances, funeral directors take over all arrangements. One of several standard packages is chosen, and the family writes the check. If the cost is $5,000, then the deceased gets the $5,000 deal. Relationships that are lovingly complex during life become reduced to package deals at a time of death.

As a society, we've lost the knowledge of caring for our own dead. People feel that they are unable to do anything for a departed friend except spend money. So they spend as much money as they can, and then, after the event, feel unfulfilled as well as broke.

It wasn't always that way, of course. In early America, home funerals were the practice everywhere. Each community had a group of women who came in to help "lay out the dead." Last respects were paid in the homes of family members and in church.

Even today in some parts of this country, religious and ethnic groups have maintained the practice of caring for their own. A funeral director is sometimes called in as a helper, but support groups and family are in control. Native Americans, the Amish, and Quakers, for example, often provide emotional support for a grieving family and actively participate in funeral arrangements.

The funeral industry was organized in the late 1800s and began promoting its members as sophisticated professionals. The centerpiece of its promotional efforts was the practice of embalming, which until that time was considered to be an outdated, exotic custom of the ancient Egyptians. Embalming had one advantage—it preserved bodies for later viewings when refrigeration was not available. It was also promoted as a means of "sanitation"—to prevent the spread of disease. That theory has long since been discredited, but the mythology about embalming has persisted in the United States. Unlike any other country in the world, in the United States embalming is still an "expected" part of the majority of funeral arrangements.

Embalming requires expertise and equipment. Once families and support groups were convinced to turn to the professionals for embalming, it was a simple next step to start depending on professionals for all other aspects of funeral arrangements. Generations of Americans lost the knowledge of how to care for their dead and became completely dependent upon professionals.

To some extent, people are willing victims of the funeral industry. The fact is, in 41 states a family (or a support group with the consent of the family) has the right to handle all death arrangements without the use of a funeral director. In all states, families and friends can take on at least some of the duties usually assigned to a funeral home, if they can find a funeral director who is willing to work with them. If they choose not to do so, the decision is theirs.

Now I think that a quiet revolution is beginning, one that may gradually change what Jessica Mitford termed "the American way of death" in her influential book of the same name (Simon & Schuster, 1963). People are beginning to question whether the best way to say good-bye to a person they love is to shell out big bucks for a funeral. Some are reasserting their rights to control the ways they say good-bye.

If a funeral means anything at all, it is an affirmation of our connections with each other. The person who died was, and is, part of our own lives. Handling funeral arrangements for a friend is a deeply emotional experience. It forces us to think about our spiritual relationships, and to put into perspective our physical relationships.

—Lisa Carlson
Woman of Power

Excerpted with permission from the feminist magazine Woman of Power *(Issue 14). Subscriptions: $26/yr. (4 issues) from Woman of Power, Box 827, Cambridge, MA 02238. Back issues: $7 from same address. Carlson is also the author of* Caring For Your Own Dead *(Upper Access Publishers, Hinesburg, Vermont, 1987).*

Decoration day

Celebrating kin in the Blue Ridge Mountains

Deep in the balsam groves of the Blue Ridge Mountains, time moves reluctantly. Old folk customs linger like the thick mists that creep in at twilight and huddle in the coves until the rising sun nudges them over the horizon.

TV dishes may scar the hillsides and unpicturesque mobile homes line up next to the chestnut bark cottages of another generation, but even in the midst of 20th-century clatter some hardy mountain people continue to live their traditions, celebrations, and superstitions in much the same way they always have. Old ways and rituals are still important to the life of family and community. A keen example of this is the survival of the family graveyard decoration day.

There is hardly a summer Sunday in any area that is not some family's decoration day. Perhaps this tradition has its roots in the outdoor communions and field preachings of 17th-century Scotland; no one knows for sure. Whatever its beginnings, decoration day has survived as a time to renew ties of kinship and friendship, share a meal, and honor the dead.

Each festival day falls on its own established Sunday—the first Sunday of June, for instance, or the last Sunday of July—and is referred to by its ancestral name. There is a Houston Decoration Day, a Pitman Decoration Day, and as many decorations as there are descendants of the pioneer families. These are family graveyards and not churchyards, so there may or may not be a church nearby. On decoration day the preacher and singers situate themselves in a visible spot and begin to preach and sing as people arrive with baskets of fresh flowers and food. The graves are soon heaped with a blaze of color, and care is taken that no grave is slighted.

A long row of tables is set up adjacent to the graveyard. Family members, no matter how extended, are expected to come bearing food and flowers. Friends bring flowers but no food. Both friends and family arriving from a distance are greeted so enthusiastically the preacher may have to shout to be heard. Each family has developed its own liturgy over the years, and each decoration day has a personality of its own.

When I was a child, my favorite decoration fell in early September when chinquapins were ripe and the late summer days were fading into harvest. We were always invited to the Woody family decoration. I remember that last decoration of summer as a mournful celebration in which laughter and handshakes were often punctuated by the sudden onset of tears, especially if the conversation moved into the past.

But the Woody decoration had a beautiful ritual built into the day's structure that was unique. Just as the preacher concluded his remarks for the day and just before the women left the graveyard to set out the stacks of fruit pies and platters of chicken, the family patriarch stood to speak.

"Now, dear friends, we are going to have our living decoration. Tell someone you love them, what they mean to you, while they can still hear you. Tell them today!"

The singers started to sing again, and everyone joined in the minor wails of "Give Me My Roses While I Live." Old men, young men, women, and children milled among the tombstones pinning blossoms on one another's lapels and collars. At the singers' discretion the singing stopped. Tears dried as abruptly as they had begun and we all went to lunch. —*Doris Wiseman Boulton*
Festivals

Excerpted with permission from Festivals *(Vol. 7, No. 3).* Festivals *has suspended publication.*

Heightening the holiness

The work of Jewish burial societies

It has always been a Jewish duty to bury our dead properly. Jewish law requires that we show proper respect for a corpse, protect it from desecration, and ritually cleanse and dress the body for burial. A *chevra kaddisha* (burial society) is a loosely structured group of Jewish men and women who see to it that the bodies of Jews are prepared for burial according to these rules.

Some time ago, a friend asked me if I would like to become a member of the *chevra kaddisha* being formed in Atlanta, and I immediately answered yes. I did not think many people would respond to this call; I also thought my background as a surgeon's assistant would eliminate the squeamishness that others might feel.

At the first meeting—to everyone's surprise—there was a tremendous turnout. Rabbi David Epstein outlined the requirements and pointed out that two different groups would be needed: *shmira*, watching the body for protection against desecration; and *tahara*, the ritual purification of the body. Not surprisingly, more people volunteered for *shmira*—a far easier task—but we had enough people for both groups.

Soon after that meeting, we were called to perform this *mitzvah* for the first time. There were nine women that evening: all of us novices. On the way to the funeral home, we had disguised our fears about what would transpire with lively chatter. Once we entered the room where the body lay, however, we were silent. There was death lying on the table—that mysterious, deepest fear of the unknown that reduces us all to a common humanity. The trepidation all of us felt upon entering the room where the body lay, and the complete physicality of the preparations for *tahara*, served as a remarkable contrast to the spirituality of the occasion and the emotions of everyone present.

We formed a silent circle around the covered body, and our preconceived feelings of dread overcame us. Many of us were shaking, some turned white. Still, there was an unmistakable peace here, in this room.

Following the training given by Rabbi Epstein and using a book he had prepared, we ritually washed our hands three times and recited the prayer of *Rachamim*, requesting kindness for the body. Carefully, we began washing the body on the right side first through a sheet wetted down by a hose. We uncovered only the part of the body we were washing and cleansed it lovingly. We cleaned and filed the nails, removed visible dirt, bandages, and other foreign matter. The body must be cleansed of anything that might come between the purifying water and the body itself.

There is a strict order to this cleaning. We started at the head: the eyes, ears, nose, mouth, and continued down the right side, then the left. When we saw the woman's face, much of our tension lightened. This elderly woman looked so peaceful, so relaxed. She seemed to have found an inner quiet that oddly calmed us.

Now she was ready for *tahara*, the actual purification by water. We cranked the table on which the body was strapped so that it was perpendicular to the floor, and placed a pan underneath. Then we poured three large pails of water over the body in immediate succession, taking care that the flow was continuous.

Afterward, we lowered the table to its horizontal position and dried the body with a sheet. With a peculiar maternalism, we clothed the body in pure-white garments, each specially tied. On this table, all wear the same clothing and all are equal: male and female, rich and poor.

The meticulous care with which we performed these acts, and the time we spent with this woman, heightened our feelings of holiness. A funeral home deals with bodies; we were dealing with a person, and we felt the power of this *mitzvah* as we worked. We were calmed, humbled, hallowed.

—*Betsy Kaplan*
Lilith

Excerpted with permission from the Jewish women's magazine Lilith *(No. 22). Subscriptions: $14/yr. (4 issues) from Box 3000, Dept. LIL, Denville, NJ 07834. Back issues: $4.50 from 250 W. 57th St., New York, NY 10107.*

Urban death rituals

Honoring lives that ended on a city street

Until last week there was nothing at all unusual about the corner intersection half a block from our house. But at 4:30 p.m. last Tuesday, an out-of-control Cadillac came speeding down the steep hill east of here. The 91-year-old man at the wheel may have been dead already from a heart attack when his car hit a Peugeot, killing a woman inside and injuring four others, then collided with a Buick that exploded into flames. Suddenly four people, including two children, were dead and one was dying at the intersection.

When my daughter came home, moments later, she saw the old man on the sidewalk, the Cadillac upside down, diapers strewn across the intersection. Firefighters were working desperately to extract victims from the smoldering wreck. About an hour later, when I got home, the last body was just being removed.

That night I went out to walk the dog, choosing a route away from the accident site. The police flares and yellow ribbons were still up, redirecting traffic. As I returned, I saw that a city cleanup truck had arrived and realized that by morning there would be no sign of the tragedy that had occurred. People would pass this corner again, stepping on the concrete where the children, the women, the dead old man lay just hours before. I felt a need to call out to my neighbors, to gather everyone in a circle around this place of violent death.

In another country, another culture, there would be an acknowledgment. Everything would stop for a while. A ceremony would be held. A medicine man might burn cedar, a priest might burn incense to aid these souls in their travels to the other world. But what do you do in a polyglot city where people are killed daily by gunshots, knives, drugs, accidents? We have no common rituals here to help us.

In the morning I cut some flowers in our garden and headed for the corner. A neighbor joined me and suggested we see if others wanted to add to the bouquet. We stopped at the home of a couple who, being gay men, are closely acquainted with death in this city. They grow exceptionally beautiful flowers and gladly picked their loveliest roses, lilies, dahlias. When we arrived at the corner we found a bouquet of asters already there. We tied it, together with our flowers, to the stop sign.

That afternoon, when my daughter returned from class, she saw dozens of bouquets piled around the stop sign. Someone had tied a small teddy bear to the pole with yellow police blockade tape. By evening a votive candle was burning. Then there was a whole row of candles. Looking out the front window, my daughter called out, "Look, it's a shrine!"

The moon was almost full and the street was bathed in blue light. A woman in a long black skirt, with a black shawl, was standing, her hands folded, beside the flickering candles and the mound of flowers. A new picture had superimposed itself on the afterimage of the accident.

—*Rasa Gustaitis*
Pacific News Service

Excerpted with permission from Pacific News Service (Oct. 1, 1990).

Psychocultural Influences on African-American Attitudes towards Death, Dying and Funeral Rites

Ronald K. Barrett

● ● ●

THE AMERICAN FUNERAL RITES

An historical and retrospective look at the American funeralization process over a four-hundred-year period reveals a number of changes and evolving traditions, demonstrating causality and coincidence in the evolution of the contemporary American funeral industry [24]. In the early years of our country the abundance of lumber and land allowed people to build large homes to shelter often large, extended families. Many of their ceremonial occasions were held in the home. The 1880s characterized the undertaker as a tradesman and merchant who supplied materials and funeral paraphernalia (i.e., caskets, carriages, door badges and scarfs, special clothing, memorial cards, chairs, candles, and other ornaments). By the end of the 19th century the undertakers began to assume a much larger role—assisting more with the deposition of the dead. After the Civil War, embalming became increasingly a conventional American custom, and most states required funeral directors and embalmers to be certified by state licensing. In the 1880s the National Funeral Directors Association began to regulate the profession and established minimum standards of service. With the advent of smaller houses and increasing urbanization, the funeral "parlour" became the place for the preparation of the dead, replacing the family parlor. Although the one-room funeral parlor became the substitute ceremonial room as people no longer used their homes, the custom of survivors sitting up in a vigil with the dead until burial, called the "wake," was often held in the family parlor [15].

The contemporary funeralization process is initialized by the authorization of the funeral home, which removes the body from the place of death. Frequently, upon removing the body, the funeral home begins to prepare the body via bathing, embalming, and dressing. Afterwards it is placed in a casket selected by the family. The traditional wake is an opportunity for members of the community to "pay their respects" and visit with the family prior to the formal funeral service. The preference for viewing or having the body present is optional. Similarly, arrangements for the ceremony and the details of the funeral ritual (i.e., time, place, type of service, etc.) vary and often depend upon family preferences, religion, and ethnicity. In most contemporary American funerals a public rite or ceremony with a religious content is typical in 75 percent of funerals [24]. Following the funeral ceremony, the final disposition of the body is made. The survivors must choose between either burial (85%), cremation (10%), or entombment (5%) [9].[1]

THE AFRICAN PERSPECTIVE ON DEATH AND FUNERAL RITES

The African cultural heritage provides enormous resources for understanding of life and death. According to Opuku [25], these resources are the product of many centuries of experienced and mature reflection and represent Africa's own insights into the meaning and significance of life and death.

According to Chief Musamasli Nangol, the traditional African belief is that in the beginning God intended man

---

[1]The percentages are based on national averages and may vary by geographic region.

to live forever [26]. African scholar and writer John B. Mbiti supports this view [27]. According to Mbiti, there are hundreds of myths in Africa concerning ideas about the origin of death—some documented and researched, others are unrecorded and undocumented. According to traditional African beliefs, God gave the first men one or more of the three gifts of immortality, resurrection, and the ability to become young again. But all three gifts were somehow lost and death came into the world. There are many different explanations as to how the loss took place and how death came about [28].

The variation in myths reflects a general belief that death came about by mistake, but has since remained due to some blame laid upon people themselves (especially women), animals, and, in some cases, evil spirits or monsters. Death therefore spoiled the original paradise of men, separating God from men and bringing many associated sorrows and agonies to men. While there are many variations in beliefs about the origin of death there are no myths in Africa about how death might one day be overcome or removed from the world [27].

Death was accepted as one of the rhythms of life, firmly integrated into the totality of life as an unalterable sequence. Life without death was viewed as clearly contrary to our nature as human beings [25]. A traditional Asante myth illustrates this traditional African view. The Asante believe that when the early human beings started experiencing death, they pleaded with God to put a stop to death. Their request was granted and for three years no one died; however, strangely enough, no one gave birth to a child during this time. The people found this situation unbearable and again pleaded with God, this time to grant them the ability to have children even if it meant accepting death also. Consequently, among the Asante, death and birth are complementary—death taking away members from the society, while birth compensates for the losses death inflicts on the community [25].

Therefore, the traditional African attitude towards death is positive and accepting and comprehensively integrated into the totality of life. Life in the African cultural tradition is so whole that death does not destroy its wholeness. Death becomes, therefore, a prolongation of life. And, instead of a break between life and death, there is continuity between the two [29, p. 138]. According to Mbiti, death is regarded as a journey to man's original place as home, and not as an end or an annihilation [30, p. 157]. The deceased goes to join the ancestors, to live in the land of the spirits ("Living dead").

This means that the relationship between the living and the "Living dead," as Mbiti describes them, remains unbroken and that the community of the living and the community of the "living dead" experience a reciprocal permeability characterized by a constant interaction between the two communities. This wholeness of life expresses itself in the fact that the African family as community is made up of the living as well as the dead. Therefore, the belief in a supernatural or extra-human dimension of the family and community is an extension of the traditional African belief system and world view of life and death [25].

The traditional African funeral rites and ritual reflect a view of death as sorrowful and important. Even though death is accepted as part of life, it is regarded as impolite to state bluntly that someone is dead. It reflects good breeding and courteous comportment to refer to the death of someone in euphemistic terms (i.e., "has gone home," "has joined the ancestors," etc.). Throughout the mourning period, which may last up to three moons, the close relatives of the deceased may not do any work. These tasks are eagerly performed by distant relatives and community friends. Women tend to wail, while men sing and dance, often in praise of the departed one. According to African customs, men are not to cry in front of women because they would appear weak before the very group they are to protect. It is therefore reasonable to assume the traditional funeral masks worn by men may have served as a cover of facial affect as well as a funeral ritual ornament. The body of the deceased is displayed either inside the house or outside on a veranda for public view. The body is displayed until all the relatives have gathered and paid their respects. Any relative who fails to show up for the funeral is often accused or suspected of having bewitched the deceased. A failure to acknowledge the dead is a social offense which is punishable in some communities. Traditional African customs require that gifts of money be given to the family of the deceased to help defray funeral expenses [25].

The African funeral rites vary according to the social status and importance of the deceased. The funeral for children and unmarried people is usually simple and often attended by only close relatives, whereas the funeral for a chief or a king could take on the significance of

Cultural Groups	Orientation		Life View		Ritual Priority		Funeral Social Sig.		Investment		Funeral Disposition
	Avoid	Accept	Life-Death	Death-Birth	Primary	Secondary	Low	High	Low	High	
AFRICAN		✓		✓	✓			✓		✓	GROUND BURIAL
AFRICAN-AMERICAN		✓		✓	✓			✓		✓	GROUND BURIAL

Figure 1. Comparative and descriptive model of traditional African and African-American Funeral Rites.

a national affair requiring much preparation, pomp, and expense [27]. African customs vary considerably in terms of the extent and methods used to prepare the body—sometimes ritually and others times without formality. Generally, the disposal of the body takes place the same day or the next day due to the effects of the tropical heat that accelerate decomposition. In most parts of Africa the traditional ground burial is most commonly favored, although there are vast variations in terms of place of burial, position of the grave, the position of the body in the grave, and grave markings [25–27].

Often after the initial shock of a death and the customary funeral rites, the atmosphere of sadness is soon replaced by laughter and the sharing of funny stories about the dead. When the deceased is a person of note, such as a chief or king, the burial often assumes a carnival atmosphere accompanied with music from drums, dancing, and food for the assembled mourners. Often, the funeral festivities may go on for some time until the community agrees that the important person has been properly acknowledged and properly escorted to the next world. According to custom and tradition, a child of the same sex as the deceased will be born into the family and, according to African custom and tradition, given the name of the deceased—honoring the deceased and symbolizing the wholeness of life [25, 26, 31].

THE AFRICAN-AMERICAN PERSPECTIVE ON DEATH AND FUNERAL RITES

The African-American contemporary response to death is intimately connected and deeply rooted in the traditional African tradition, yet tempered by the American sociocultural experience [32]. Much has been written about the traditional African response to death, yet very few people have acknowledged the African-American response. The African-American funeralization practices and customs have evolved over centuries, reflecting a characteristic disposition and tradition rich in cultural symbolism and customs deeply rooted in and resembling the African experience (see Figure 1).

The earliest, most authoritative work on African-American attitudes towards death and dying is contained in a classic cross-cultural study by Kalish and Reynolds [3]. In this largest study of its type, the researchers examine 100 or more persons in four ethnic groups (African-American, Japanese-American, Mexican-American, and Anglo). Inevitably, a number of ethnic differences were found.

To be an African-American in America is to be part of a history told in terms of contact with death and coping with death. For the Black race in the era of slavery, death or other forms of personal loss could come at any time, at any age, randomly, and often at the whim of someone else [3]. According to Chapman, African-American artists reflect this history in artistic expression in music, spirituals, poetry, novels, drama, and visual arts [34]. Kalish

and Reynolds' survey data indicate that contemporary Black Americans also have significantly more contact with homicide, accidents, and war-time deaths than any other group.

The American sociocultural attitudes and behavior in response to death have been termed "death-avoiding" [1] and "death denying" [18, 20]. However, African-Americans tend to be more accepting and less fearful of death than the three other ethnic groups studied [3]. In a study by Myers, Wass, and Murphey, elderly African-Americans showed a higher level of fear towards death than elderly whites [34]. However, researchers [2, 3] argue that devout and true believers can cope with death more effectively than those with vague or ambivalent views. Kalish and Reynolds report findings that African-Americans perceive themselves as more religious than Anglos and tend to rely on their belief systems more in times of crisis and need [3]. This observation lends more support to the perception of Blacks as less fearful of death than Anglos [35].

The various art forms (i.e., music, literature, theatre, and visual arts, etc.) mirror the attitudes of African-Americans towards death [36]. A consistent theme of death is reflected and often connected to a sense of solace in a theology and belief in the afterlife and promise of a better life [33]. Similarly, another study conducted in Detroit showed that African-Americans, substantially more than Anglos, believed that people should live as long as they can, and that helplessness, but not pain and suffering, would justify dying [37]. Kalish and Reynolds report findings that African-Americans are more likely than Anglos to disapprove of allowing people who want to die to do so [3]. The basic premise appears to hold true: whether it is their religiousness or their survival ordeal,

CULTURAL GROUPS	ORIENTATION	
	AVOIDANCE	ACCEPTANCE
AFRICAN		Opuku (1989) Nangol (1986) Mbiti (1975) Parinder (1976)
AFRICAN-AMERICAN	Myers, Wass & Murphy (1980)	Kalish and Reynolds (1981) Martin & Wrightsman (1965) Lewis (1971) Nichols (1989) Fenn (1989) Connor (1989)
AMERICAN	Rando (1984) Kübler-Ross (1969) Leming and Dickinson (1985) Kavanaugh (1972) Feifel (1959) Feifel (1971) Mitford (1963) Kastenbaum and Aisenberg (1972)	

Figure 2. Cultural influences on attitudes towards death.

5. FUNERALS AND BURIAL RITES

African-Americans express a high acceptance of life and death [3].

Elaine Nichols' *The Last Miles of the Way* is the most comprehensive and authoritative documented anthropological study of African-American cultural traditions and funeral rituals in the southeastern United States (i.e. the South Carolina low-lands) [32]. Nichols' work supports and carefully documents the African cultured origin of many African-American beliefs, traditions, and practices in funeral rites. Nichols' efforts also illustrate and detail the intricate symbolism of burials and grave markings. Fenn also supports Nichols' thesis of African cultural roots in grave markings as Fenn documents methods and symbolism rooted in African Kogo traditions [38]. An anthropological analysis of African-American mortuary practices by Conner [39], also supports Elaine Nichols' classic and insightful scholarly work.[2] While a number of aspects of Nichols' findings may be unique to the southeastern region of the United States (i.e., South Carolina), striking similarities in the African-American experience in other regions lend support to the generalizability of similar cultured influences and behaviors in the subculture of the African-American experience.

The available research [3, 39, 40] provides documented support of the thesis that many of the attitudes, beliefs, and traditions regarding funeral rites, death and dying are deeply rooted in African cultural traditions. The African-American attitudes, beliefs, and funeral rites are also significantly influenced by American attitudes, beliefs, and cultural traditions regarding death, dying, and funeral rites. These studies make a significant contribution to our knowledge and understanding of the African-American experience, however, more research and study is needed to understand better death related behaviors and also provide needed documentation of a very important and regarded sacred psychocultural complex tradition.

African-American attitudes toward funeral rites have remained for too long largely undocumented and lacking in systematic study and observation. Halloween Lewis' [41] analysis of the role of the church and religion in the life of southern Blacks suggests that the religious connection took on special meaning in funeral customs. Lewis notes variations occurring according to the community reputation of the deceased, family wishes, and local church practices. As is common among Protestants, most African-American Protestant churches have no formally prescribed funeral ritual dictated by church hierarchy. Local church custom is followed [42]. According to the denominational procedure outlined in Habenstein and

---

[2] Elaine Nichols' unprecedented anthropological work involved the procurement and analysis of physical evidence and cultural artifacts obtained from both library research and private individual collectors that are a part of a special exhibit in the South Carolina State Museum scheduled for a national tour.

CULTURAL GROUPS	LIFE VIEW	
	LIFE-DEATH	DEATH-BIRTH
AFRICAN		Opuku (1989) Mbiti (1969) Methuh (1982) Mulago (1969)
AFRICAN-AMERICAN		Lomax (1970) Chapman (1968) Nichols (1989) Fenn (1989) Conner (1989)
AMERICAN	Rando (1984) Leming and Dickinson (1985) Kastenbaum and Aisenberg (1972) Kearl (1989) Ranum (1974)	

Figure 3. Cultural influences on attitudes towards death.

CULTURAL GROUPS	RITUAL PRIORITY		FUNERAL SOCIAL SIG.	
	PRIMARY	SECONDARY	LOW	HIGH
AMERICAN	Opuku (1969) Mbiti (1969) Nangol (1969)			Opuku (1989) Mbiti (1969) Nangol (1969)
AFRICAN-AMERICAN	Kalish and Reynolds (1981) Chapman (1968) Nelson (1971) Carter (1971) Nichols (1989) Fielding (1989) Fenn (1989) Conner (1989)			Kalish and Reynolds (1981) Chapman (1968) Nelson (1971) Carter (1971) Nichols (1989) Fielding (1989) Fenn (1989) Conner (1989)
AMERICAN	Mitford (1963)	Reather (1971) Kübler-Ross (1955) Gorer (1955)	Reather (1971) Gorer (1955) Harmer (1971)	Mitford (1963) Fulton (1965)

Figure 4. Cultural influences on attitudes towards death.

CULTURAL GROUPS	INVESTMENT		FUNERAL DISPOSITION
	LOW	HIGH	
AFRICAN		Opuku (1989) Nangol (1986) Mbiti (1975)	Ground Burial Opuku (1989) Nangol (1986) Mbiti (1975) Fenn (1989) Nichols (1989)
AFRICAN-AMERICAN		Kalish and Reynolds (1981) Nichols (1989) Fenn (1989) Conner (1989) Fielding (1989)	Ground Burial Kalish and Reynolds (1981) Nichols (1989) Fenn (1989) Conner (1989) Fielding (1989)
AMERICAN		Mitford (1963) Raether (1971) De Spelder and Strickland (1987) Tegg (1876)	Ground Burial Cremation (10%) Emtombment (5%) Leming and Dickinson (1985)

Figure 5. Cultural influences on attitudes towards death.

176

Lamers [8], the only generalizations that can really be made are: 1) that family members can select the equipment, music, participants, and place of service without dogmatic restriction, and 2) that the minister leads the procession from church to the funeral coach and from the coach to grave site, positioning himself at the head of the grave. This leaves room for considerable variation [3].

While regional and denominational backgrounds influencing the African-American funeral rites vary, there are some striking similarities linked to traditional African-American beliefs and traditions. In a social context where people are treated like objects and with minimal respect, and the channels by which respect can be achieved are blocked, it is understandable for victims to desperately seek a way to affirm themselves and confirm some sense of self-worth and positive self-identity [3]. African-American funerals in the African-American subculture represent a posthumous attempt for dignity and esteem denied and limited by the dominant culture [32, 40]. Funerals in the African-American experience historically are "primary rituals" of symbolic importance. Kalish and Reynolds'[3] survey reveals that African-Americans were more likely to have taken out life and burial insurance than any other group surveyed [3]. It appears that funeral pre-arrangements, wills, and insurance represent psychological readiness, as these are the most practical arrangements that people can make for death. As expected, Kalish and Reynolds report that older African-Americans are more likely to have made death arrangements than middle-aged or younger adults [3].

The African-American mourners, like the African mourners, were more likely to depend upon the church and the community (extended family) for support during bereavement and mourning [40]. Unlike the other ethnic groups surveyed, African-Americans were more likely to rely on friends, church members, neighbors, and non-relatives for practical assistance consistent with the finding that devout believers had less death anxiety, those active in churches had more tradition sources of spiritual and social support [3].

The social support of family and friends is important to those in mourning. Since a death is a significant event and the funeral is an important social occasion, social expectations require participation and some expression of condolence. It is a standard custom that if one cannot attend the funeral, flowers or other expressions of condolences should be sent. The African-American funeral is indeed a primary ritual and a focal occasion with a big social gathering after the funeral and the closest thing to a family union that might ever take place [32, 40, 43].

Kalish and Reynolds [3] report that the great majority of African-American respondents expressed opposition

to elaborate funerals; did not expect friends to participate in covering funeral costs; preferred a funeral with only close friends and relatives; desired African-American clergymen and funeral directors; did not want a wake; wanted the funeral in the church; did not oppose an autopsy; and wanted to be buried. Overall, the African-American funeral is an important event characterized by a programmed atmosphere that is official, ritualistic, serious, and dignified.

ACKNOWLEDGMENTS

The author wishes to acknowledge Luvenia Morant Addison; Dorothy Addison Barrett; Deborah Freathy, Graduate Research Assistant, Loyola Marymount University; Elaine Nichols, Curator, South Carolina State Museum; Harri Close, President, National Funeral Directors & Morticians Association, Inc.; John Hill, III, Chief Administrator, Angelus Funeral Home; Chief Medical Examiner and Staff, Los Angeles County Coroners Office.

REFERENCES

1. R. Kastenbaum and B. R. Aisenberg, The *Psychology of Death*, Springer, New York, 1972.
2. E. Kübler-Ross, *On Death and Dying*, Macmillan, New York, 1969.
3. R. Kalish and D. Reynolds, *Death and Ethnicity: A Psychocultural Study*, Baywood, Amityville, New York, 1981.
4. J. Choron, *Death and Western Thought*, The Macmillan Company, New York, 1963.
5. R. Huntington and P. Metcalf, *Celebration of Death: The Anthropology of Mortuary Ritual*, Cambridge, Cambridge, 1979.
6. D. C. Rosenblatt, Grief in Cross-Cultural and Historical Perspective, in *Death and Dying*, P. F. Pegg and E. Metza (eds.), Pitman Press, London, 1981.
7. M. McGoldrick, P. Hines, E. Lee, and G. H. Preto, Mourning Rituals: How Culture Shapes the Experience of Loss, *Networker*, 1986.
8. W. R. Habenstein and M. W. Lamers, *Funeral Customs the World Over*, Bulfin, Milwaukee, 1963.
9. R. M. Leming and E. G. Dickinson, *Understanding Dying, Death, and Bereavement*, Holt, Rinehart and Winston, New York, 1985.
10. R. P. Cuzzort and W. E. King, *Twentieth Century Social Thought*, Holt, Rinehart and Winston, New York, 1980.
11. J. R. Averill, Grief: Its Nature and Significance, *Psychological Bulletin*, 70:61, 1968.
12. E. Durkheim, *The Elementary Forms of Religious Life*, Macmillan, New York, 1915.
13. M. C. Kearl, *Endings—A Sociology of Death and Dying*, Oxford, New York, 1989.
14. C. Geerty, *The Interpretations of Cultures: Selected Essays*, Basic Books, New York, 1973.
15. L. A. DeSpelder and L. A. Strickland, *The Last Dance: Encountering Death and Dying*, Mayfield, Mountain View, California, 1987.
16. A. M. Hocart, Death Customs, in *Encyclopedia of the Social Sciences 5*, E. R. A. Seligman and A. Johnson (eds.), Macmillan, New York, 1937.
17. P. G. Mandelbaum, Social Issues of Funeral Rites, in *The Meaning of Death*, H. Feifel (ed.), McGraw-Hill, New York, 1959.
18. T. A. Rando, *Grief, Dying and Death*, Research Press Co., Champaign, Illinois, 1984.
19. R. E. Kavanaugh, *Facing Death*, Penguin, Baltimore, Maryland, 1971.
20. H. Feiffel, The Meaning of Death in American Society: Implications for Education, 1971.
21. G. Gorer, *Death, Grief & Mourning*, Crescent Press, London, 1965.

---

[3]The term "primary ritual" is used in this context to refer to an event of primary, major importance in that social context. (Contrastingly, a "secondary ritual" is an event of lesser social priority or significance—informal gatherings, family meetings, local holidays, etc.)

22. H. Feifel, *The Meaning of Death*, McGraw-Hill, New York, 1959.
23. J. Mifford, *The American Way of Death*, Simon and Schuster, New York, 1963.
24. H. C. Raether, The Place of the Funeral: The Role of the Funeral Director in Contemporary America, *Omega, 2*, pp. 136–149, 1971.
25. K. A. Opuku, African Perspectives on Death and Dying, in *Perspectives on Death and Dying*, A. Berger, P. Badham, J. Berger, V. Cerry, and J. Beloff (eds.) The Charles Press, Philadelphia, 1989.
26. C. M. Nangoli, *No More Lies About Africa*, African Heritage, East Orange, New Jersey, 1988.
27. J. S. Mbiti, *Introduction to African Religion*, Heinemann, London, 1975.
28. E. G. Parinder, *African Mythology*, Paul Hamlyn, London, 1967.
29. V. Mulago, Vital Participation: The Cohesive Principle of the Bantu Community, in *Biblical Revelation and African Beliefs*, K. Dickson and P. Ellingworth (eds.), Butterworth, London, 1979.
30. J. S. Mbiti, *African Religions and Philosophy*, Heinemann, London, 1969.
31. I. E. Metuh, *God and Man in African Religion: A Case of the Igbo of Nigeria*, G. Chapman, London, 1982.
32. E. Nichols (ed.), *The Last Miles of the Way: African American Homegoing Traditions 1890–Present*, Dependable, Columbia, South Carolina, 1989.
33. A. Chapman (ed.), *Black Voices: An Anthology of Afro-American Literature*, New American Library, New York, 1968.
34. J. E. Myers, H. Wass, and M. Murphey, Ethnic Differences in Death Anxiety among the Elderly, *Death Education, 4*, pp. 237–244, 1980.
35. D. S. Martin and L. Wrightsman, The Relationship between Religious Behaviour and Concern about Death, *Journal of Social Psychology, 65*, pp. 317–323, 1965.
36. A. Lomax, The Homogeneity of African-Afro-American Musical Style, in *Afro-American Anthropology*, N. E. Whitten and J. F. Szwed (eds.), Free Press, New York, 1970.
37. R. Koenig, N. S. Goldner, R. Kresojevich, and G. Lockwood, Ideas About Illness of Elderly Black and White in an Urban Hospital, *Aging and Human Development, 2*, pp. 217–225, 1971.
38. E. A. Fenn, Honouring the Ancestors: Kongo-American Graves in the American South, in *The Last Miles of the Way*, E. Nichols (ed.), Dependable, Columbia, South Carolina, 1989.
39. C. Connor, Archaeological Analysis of African-American Mortuary Behaviour, in *The Last Miles of the Way*, Dependable, Columbia, South Carolina, 1989.
40. H. U. Fielding, Mourning and Burying the Dead: Experiences of a Lawcountry Funeral Director, in *The Last Miles of the Way*, Dependable, Columbia, South Carolina, 1989.
41. H. Lewis, Blackways of Kent: Religion and Salvation, in *The Black Church in America*, H. M. Nelson, et al. (eds.), Basic Books, New York, 1971.
42. H. M. Nelson, et al. (eds.), *The Black Church in America*, Basic Books, New York, 1971.
43. W. B. Carter, Suicide, Death, and Ghetto Life, *Life-Threatening Behaviour*, L, 1971.

BIBLIOGRAPHY

Abrahamson, H., *The Origin of Death: Studies in African Mythology*, Almgvist, Uppsala, 1951.

Balandier, G. and Maguet, J., *Dictionary of Black African Civilization*, Leon Amiel, New York, 1974.

Boulby, J., Process of Mourning, *International Journal of Psycho-Analysis, 43*, pp. 314–340, Grune and Statton, New York. (Reprinted in G. E. Daniels (ed.), 1965, *New Perspectives in Psychoanalysis*, 1961.

Feifel, H., The Taboo on Death, *The American Behavioral Scientist, 6*, 1963.

Fulton, R., The Sacred and the Secular: Attitudes of the American Public toward Death, Funerals, and Funeral Directors, in *Death and Identity*, R. Fulton (ed.), Wiley, New York, 1965.

Goody, J., *Death, Property, and the Ancestors: A Study of the Mortuary Customs of the LoDagaa of West Africa*, Stock, London, 1962.

Harmer, R., Funerals, Fantasy, and Flight, *Omega, 2*, pp. 127–135, 1971.

Idowu, E. B., *African Traditional Religion*, SCM Press, London, 1973.

Jackson, M., The Black Experience with Death: A Brief Analysis through Black Writings, *Omega, 3*, pp. 203–209, 1972.

Kopytoff, E., Ancestors as Elders in Africa, *Africa, 41*, 1971.

Kutscher, A. H., *Death and Bereavement*, Charles C. Thomas, Springfield, Illinois, 1969.

Lindemann, E., Symptomatology and Management of Acute Grief, *American Journal of Psychiatry, 101*. Reprinted in R. Fulton (ed.) (1965) *Death and Identity*, Wiley, New York, 1944.

Lend, F. H., Why Do We Weep? *Journal of Social Psychology, 1*, 1930.

Opuku, K. A., Death and Immortality in the African Religious Heritage, in *Death and Immortality in the Religious of the World*, P. Badham and L. Badham (eds.), Paragon, New York, 1987.

Parinder, E. G., *African Traditional Religion*, SPCK, London, 1962.

Pinkney, A., *Black Americans*, Prentice Hall, Englewood Cliffs, New Jersey, 1969.

Ranum, P. M., *Western Attitudes toward Death: From the Middle Ages to the Present*, Johns Hopkins University Press, Baltimore, 1974.

Tegg, W., *The Last Act Being the Funeral Rites of Nations and Individuals*, William Tegg & Co., London, 1876.

Thomas, L. R., Litany of Home—Going—Going Forth: The African Concept of Time, Eternity and Social Ontology, in *The Last Miles of the Way*, E. Nichols, Dependable, Columbia, South Carolina, 1989.

Zahan, D., The *Religion, Spirituality, and Thought of Traditional Africa*, E. Martin and L. M. Martin (trans.), University of Chicago, Chicago, 1979.

How different religions pay their final respects

From mummies to cremation to drive-up wakes, funeral rituals reflect religious traditions going back thousands of years as well as up-to-the-minute fads.

William J. Whalen

Most people in the United States identify themselves as Protestants; thus, most funerals follow a similar form. Family and friends gather at the funeral home to console one another and pay their last respects. The next day a minister conducts the funeral service at the church or mortuary; typically the service includes hymns, prayers, a eulogy, and readings from the Bible. In 85 percent of the cases today, the body is buried after a short grave-side ceremony. Otherwise the body is cremated or donated to a medical school.

But what could be called the standard U.S. funeral turns out to be the funeral of choice for only a minority of the rest of the human race. Other people, even other Christians, bury their dead with more elaborate and, to outsiders, even exotic rites.

How your survivors will dispose of your body will in all likelihood be determined by the religious faith you practiced during your life because funeral customs reflect the theological beliefs of a particular faith community.

For example, the Parsi people of India neither bury nor cremate their dead. Parsis, most of whom live in or near Bombay, follow the ancient religion of Zoroastrianism. Outside Bombay, Parsis erected seven Towers of Silence in which they perform their burial rites. When someone dies, six bearers dressed in white bring the corpse to one of the towers. The Towers of Silence have no roofs; within an hour, waiting vultures pick the body clean. A few days later the bearers return and cast the remaining bones into a pit. Parsis believe that their method of disposal avoids contaminating the soil, the water, and the air.

Out of the ashes

The Parsis' millions of Hindu neighbors choose cremation as their usual burial practice. Hindus believe that as long as the physical body exists, the essence of the person will remain nearby; cremation allows the essence, or soul, of the person to continue its journey into another incarnation.

Hindus wash the body of the deceased and clothe it in a shroud decorated with flowers. They carry the body to a funeral pyre, where the nearest male relative lights the fire and walks around the burning body three times while reciting verses from Hindu sacred writings. Three days later someone collects and temporarily buries the ashes.

On the tenth day after the cremation, relatives deposit the ashes in the Ganges or some other sacred river. The funeral ceremony, called the *Shraddha*, is then held within 31 days of the cremation. Usually the deceased's son recites the prayers and the invocation of ancestors; that is one reason why every Hindu wants at least one son.

Prior to British rule in India, the practice of suttee was also common. Suttee is the act of a Hindu widow willingly being cremated on her husband's funeral pyre. Suttee was outlawed by the British in 1829, but occasionally widows still throw themselves into the flames.

Like the Hindus, the world's Buddhists, who live primarily in China, Japan, Sri Lanka, Myanmar, Vietnam, and Cambodia, usually choose cremation for disposing a corpse. They believe cremation was favored by Buddha. A religious teacher may pray or recite mantras at the bedside of the dying person. These actions are believed to exert a wholesome effect on the next rebirth. Buddhists generally believe that the essence of a person remains in an intermediate state for no more than 49 days between death and rebirth.

While Hindus and Buddhists prescribe cremation, the world's 900 million Muslims forbid cremation. According to the Qu'ran, Muhammad taught that only Allah will use fire to punish the wicked.

If a Muslim is near death, someone is called in to read verses from

From *U.S. Catholic*, September 1990, pp. 29–35. Reprinted with permission of *U.S. Catholic*, 205 West Monroe Street, Chicago, IL 60606.

the Qu'ran. After death, the body is ceremonially washed, clothed in three pieces of white cloth, and placed in a simple wooden coffin. Unless required by law, Muslims will not allow embalming. The body must be buried as soon as possible after death—usually within 24 hours. After a funeral service at a mosque or at the grave side, the body is removed from the coffin and buried with the head of the deceased turned toward Mecca. In some Muslim countries the women engage in loud wailing and lamentations during the burial.

Some Islamic grave sites are quite elaborate. The Mogul emperor Shah Jahan built the world-famous Taj Mahal as a mausoleum for his wife and himself. The Taj Mahal, which is one of the finest examples of Islamic architecture, was finished in 1654. It took 20,000 workers about 22 years to complete the project.

The Baha'i faith, which originated in Persia in the nineteenth century as an outgrowth of the Shi'ite branch of Islam, also forbids cremation and embalming and requires that the body not be transported more than an hour's journey from the place of death. Because Bahaism has no ordained clergy, the funeral may be conducted by any member of the family or the local assembly. All present at the funeral must stand during the recitation of the Prayer for the Dead composed by Baha-'u'llah. Several million Baha'is live in Iran, India, the Middle East, and Africa; and an estimated 100,000 Baha'is live in the United States.

In Judaism, the faith of some 18 million people, the Old Testament only hints at belief in an afterlife; but later Jewish thought embraced beliefs in heaven, hell, resurrection, and final judgment. In general, Orthodox Jews accept the concept of a resurrection of the soul and the body while Conservative and Reform Jews prefer to speak only of the immortality of the soul.

Orthodox Judaism prescribes some of the most detailed funeral rites of any religion. As death approaches, family and friends must attend the dying person at all times. When death finally arrives, a son or the nearest relative closes the eyes and mouth of the deceased and binds the lower jaw before rigor mortis sets in. Relatives place the body on the floor and cover it with a sheet; they place a lighted candle near the head.

Judaism in its traditional form forbids embalming except where required by law. After a ritual washing, the body is covered with a white shroud and placed in a wooden coffin. At the funeral, mourners symbolize their grief by tearing a portion of an outer garment or wearing a torn black ribbon. The Orthodox discourage flowers and ostentation at the funeral.

The Jewish funeral service includes a reading of prayers and psalms, a eulogy, and the recitation of the Kaddish prayer for the dead in an Aramaic dialect. Like other Semitic people, Jews forbid cremation. Orthodox Jews observe a primary mourning period of seven days; Reform Jews reduce this period to three days. During the secondary yearlong mourning period, the Kaddish prayer is recited at every service in the synagogue.

Dearly beloved

Christianity, the world's largest religion, carries over Judaism's respect for the body and firmly acknowledges resurrection, judgment, and eternal reward or punishment.

These Christian beliefs permeate the liturgy of a Catholic funeral. Older Catholics remember the typical funeral of the 1940s and '50s: the recitation of the rosary at the wake, the black vestments, the Latin prayers. They probably recall the "Dies Irae," a thirteenth-century dirge and standard musical piece at Catholic funerals prior to the liturgical changes of the Second Vatican Council in the 1960s.

Nowadays, those attending a Catholic wake may still say the rosary, but often there is a scripture service instead. The priest's vestments are likely to be white or violet rather than black. Prayers tend to emphasize the hope of resurrection rather than the terrors of the final judgment.

As death approaches, the dying person or the family may request the sacrament of the Anointing of the Sick. Once called Last Rites or Extreme Unction, this sacrament is no longer restricted to those in imminent danger of death; it is regularly administered to the sick and the elderly as an instrument of healing as well as a preparation for death.

Sacred remains

The Catholic Church raises no objections to embalming, flowers, or an open casket at a wake. At one time Catholics who wished to have a church funeral could not request cremation. In 1886 the Holy Office in Rome declared that "to introduce the practice (of cremation) into Christian society was un-Christian and Masonic in motivation." Today Catholics may choose the option of cremation over burial "unless," according to canon law, "it has been chosen for reasons that are contrary to Christian teaching."

The church used to deny an ecclesiastical burial to suicides, those killed in duels, Freemasons, and members of the ladies' auxiliaries of Masonic lodges. Today the church refuses burial only to "notorious apostates, heretics, and schismatics" and to "sinners whose funerals in church would scandalize the faithful." Catholics who join Masonic lodges no longer incur excommunication, although they still may not receive Communion.

The church has also softened its position on denying funeral rites to suicides. Modern pastoral practice is based on the understanding that anyone finding life so unbearable as to end it voluntarily probably was acting with a greatly diminished free will.

For Roman Catholics, the Mass is the principal celebration of the Christian funeral; and mourners are invited to receive the Eucharist. Most Protestant denominations, except for some Lutherans and Episcopalians, do not incorporate a communion service into their funeral liturgies. The Catholic ritual employs candles, holy water, and incense but does not allow non-Christian symbols, such as national flags or lodge emblems, to rest on or near the coffin during the funeral. In many parishes the pastor encourages the family members to participate where appropriate as eucharistic ministers, lectors, and singers. In the absence of a priest, a deacon can conduct the funeral service but cannot preside at a Mass of Christian burial.

The revised funeral liturgy of the Catholic Church is meant to stress God's faithfulness to people rather than God's wrath toward sinners. The Catholic Church declares that certain men and women who have lived lives of such heroic virtue that they are indeed in heaven are to be known as saints. The church also teaches that hell is a reality but has never declared that anyone, even Judas, has actually been condemned to eternal punishment.

Unlike Protestant churches, Catholicism also teaches the existence of a temporary state of purification, known as purgatory, for those destined for heaven but not yet totally free from the effects of sin and selfishness. At one time some theologians suggested that unbaptized babies spent eternity in a place of natural happiness known as limbo, but this was never church doctrine and is taught by few theologians today.

At the committal service at the grave site, the priest blesses the grave and leads the mourners in the Our Father and other prayers for the repose of the soul of the departed and the comfort of the survivors. Catholics are usually buried in Catholic cemeteries or in separate sections of other cemeteries.

Dressed for the occasion

The funeral rite in the Church of Jesus Christ of Latter-day Saints, which is the fastest growing church in the United States, resembles the standard Protestant funeral in some ways; but one significant difference is in the attire of the deceased. Devout Mormons receive the garments of the holy priesthood during their endowment ceremonies when they are teens. These sacred undergarments are to be worn day and night throughout a Mormon's life. When a Mormon dies, his or her body is then attired in these garments in the casket. At one time Mormon sacred garments resembled long johns, but they now have short sleeves and are cut off at the knees. The garments are embroidered with symbols on the right and left breasts, the navel, and the right knee, which remind the wearer of the oaths taken in the secret temple rites.

Mormons who reached their endowments are also clothed in their temple garb at death. For the men, this includes white pants, white shirt, tie, belt, socks, slippers, and an apron. Just before the casket is closed for the last time, a fellow Mormon puts a white temple cap on the corpse. If the deceased is a woman, a high priest puts a temple veil over her face; Mormons believe the veil will remain there until her husband calls her from the grave to resurrection. Mormons forbid cremation.

Freemasons conduct their own funeral rites for a deceased brother, and they insist that their ceremony be the last one before burial or cremation. Thus, a separate religious ceremony often precedes the Masonic rites. Lodge members will bury a fellow Mason only if he is a member in good standing and he or his family has requested the service.

All the pallbearers at the Masonic services must be Masons, and each wears a white apron, white gloves, a black band around his left arm, and a sprig of evergreen or acacia in his left lapel. The corpse is clothed in a white apron and other lodge regalia.

Masonry accepts the idea of the immortality of the soul but makes no reference to the Christian understanding of the resurrection of the soul and the body. The Masonic service speaks of the soul's translation from this life to that "perfect, glorious, and celestial lodge above" presided over by the Grand Architect of the Universe.

In memorium

Other small religious groups have much less elaborate and formalized funeral services. Christian Scientists, for example, have no set funeral rite because their founder, Mary Baker Eddy, denied the reality of death. The family of a deceased Christian Scientist often invites a Christian Science reader to present a brief service at the funeral home.

Unitarian-Universalists enroll many members who would identify themselves as agnostics or atheists. Therefore, in a typical Unitarian-Universalist funeral service, the minister and loved ones say little about any afterlife but extol the virtues and good works of the deceased.

Salvation Army officers are buried in their military uniforms, and a Salvationist blows taps at the grave side. In contrast, the Church of Christ, which allows no instrumental music during Sunday worship, allows no organs, pianos, or other musical instruments at its funerals.

The great variety of funeral customs through the ages and around the world would be hard to catalog. The Egyptians mummified the bodies of royalty and erected pyramids as colossal monuments. Viking kings were set adrift on blazing boats. The Soviets mummified the body of Lenin, and his tomb and corpse have become major icons in the U.S.S.R.

In a funeral home in California, a drive-up window is provided for mourners so that they can view the remains and sign the book without leaving their cars. In Japan, where land is scarce, one enterprising cemetery owner offers a time-share plan whereby corpses are displaced after brief burial to make room for the next occupant. Complying with the wishes of the deceased, one U.S. undertaker once dressed a corpse in pajamas and positioned it under the blankets in a bedroom for viewing.

The reverence and rituals surrounding the disposal of the body reflect religious traditions going back thousands of years as well as up-to-the-minute fads. All of the elements of the burial—the preparation of the body, the garments or shroud, the prayers, the method of disposal, the place and time of burial—become sacred acts by which a particular community of believers bids at least a temporary farewell to one of its own.

She plans funerals that celebrate life

Dawn Gibeau

NCR Staff

Sr. Mary Beth Stearns is a funeral consultant. On the way to becoming one, she worked in a hospital oncology department, with cystic fibrosis patients with mentally retarded people.

She was a wedding consultant, too, even after she became a nun in 1983. She discovered that weddings often upstage marriage and pit the bride's mother against the groom's mother with the consultant in the middle. "I'd rather do a thousand funerals than one wedding," she said. "Dead people don't talk back."

More than a year ago, Stearns became a licensed funeral director with a degree in mortuary science. As long ago as 1978, when her mother died, she sensed something too rote, too impersonal about standard funeral practice. But for many years she resisted her inclination to enter the field. She eventually succumbed to the prompting of a psychological test that diagnosed her remarkable aptitude for the work.

She had to convince her congregation, the Sisters of St. Joseph of Carondelet, as well, first to become a funeral director and again in 1994 when she created her funeral-planning education and consulting business.

Sisters see themselves as ministering to the living, she said, and she sees her work that way, too. "The funeral is meant for the survivors," she said. "The dead are already taken care of."

Stearns contends that most survivors are unprepared for the dozens of decisions they must make within a few days. "You wouldn't ride by a car lot, see a red car and walk in and write a check for it without checking it out," she said. "Why would you do any less for a person you love who has died?"

People who plan for babies and weddings need also to make plans for burying those they love. "I don't care if you pay $10,000 for a casket, but I want you to know why you're paying $10,000," she said. Making amends to the dead person or fulfilling an unpaid debt "aren't good enough reasons as far as I'm concerned," she said.

She advises people which funeral expenses are required and which are optional. For instance, Minnesota cemeteries require grave liners—cement containers for caskets—but not hermetically sealed vaults. Embalming is required only if the person had a communicable disease, is to be transported across state lines or will not be buried within 72 hours. Stearns recommends visiting funeral homes to compare prices and merchandise. Corporately owned mortuaries, she said, often are the most expensive.

She suggested saving money by passing up the funeral home's thank-you cards and register books, substituting thank-you cards imprinted at a local quick-printing shop and a "nothing" book with blank pages in which visitors at a wake—or before death at a hospital, hospice or home—can write notes, not just names and addresses. The notes can comfort survivors as they discover, "I didn't know Tom Smith lived next to Joe for 27 years"; or "Look at this: Susie's college roommate came, and she remembered . . ."

Stearns recommends buying plenty of death notices initially, because the first copy costs more than additional copies ordered at the same time.

As a consultant, she meets with family groups, charging an hourly fee for her time. She does not anticipate repeat business, and she tells people not to fear they will forget what they've learned from her, even if death in the family is years or decades away. When it occurs and they must make decisions, she said, "bells will ring and red flags go off," reminding survivors what they need to ask about.

She strongly believes in preplanning but not in prepaying because inflation and changes in availability of merchandise erode the ballyhooed benefits of prepayment. It only works, she said, "if you prepay on Tuesday, then die on Tuesday."

As an educator, Stearns has spoken at community education classes, in several parishes and, more often, to women's groups. References from

From *National Catholic Reporter*, January 20, 1995, pp. 21, 22. Reprinted with permission of the National Catholic Reporter, Kansas City, MO.

these talks have compounded, providing most of her clients.

She may be the only U.S. nun engaged in funeral education, although she knows of one other in Albany, N.Y., who is trained as a funeral director. Stearns said she was willing to travel to other states for talks as part of her ministry. Among her recommendations, Stearns is adamant that all survivors who were close to the deceased view the body, no matter how disfigured in death. She said viewing, even if only at the hospital or where the person died, convinces the survivor "the person is really, really, dead" and is important as a final good-bye, "to put some closure on what was and begin the grieving of what is."

Most of all, Stearns sees her ministry as helping people celebrate death as a part of life. In all the world, only the Western culture avoids celebration, she said. "We want to get people in the ground or get them burned as fast as we can so we can get on with our lives. We miss the whole piece of honoring and celebrating that person's life."

Among her suggestions: Surround the casket with pictures and artifacts pertinent to the person, and select songs or scriptural readings in advance, then change the selection as preferences change.

Her ministry is ecumenical, and she prefers working with non-churched people and others who create their own celebrations rather than going along with packaged rituals. For instance, she asks why a person should have a church funeral if he or she never went to church, and she walks out of churches when a priest begins a generic homily by saying, "I really didn't know this person."

As an intern and apprentice in funeral homes, Stearns learned that Protestant ministers more universally have a personal relationship with the dead person, or at least with his or her family, than do Catholic clergy, some of whom delegate mortuary personnel to lead droning "Hailmaryfullofgrace" prayers at the wake or before processing to the church.

Stearns far prefers consulting and educating to funeral directing, although she has cared for the bodies of some of her religious sisters who have asked her to do so. As a mortuary science intern and apprentice in a funeral home, she especially disliked having to offer vulnerable survivors a limited selection of merchandise and being unable to suggest alternatives.

"There are options; we can do what fits for the person," she said. "We can celebrate however that person affected (the survivors)."

Religious congregations may be among the last to change their approach to funerals, she speculated. Nevertheless, a first occurred in her community when a Sister of St. Joseph of Carondelet was cremated in September.

Stearns works with the bereaved, to help them deal with their grief. "First of all, you don't get over grief, you walk through it," she said.

Stearns is trying to persuade her sisters to embrace more of the Jewish tradition, as when, instead of rushing the body to a funeral home for embalming, survivors wash and anoint the body with oils. That "is so beautiful and so sacred, and they dress the body in kind of an off-white garment. It's like baptism.

Everybody goes the same. When I talk to our sisters, I ask them to think how beautiful that would be, because they have spent their entire life with this group of women."

That would be preferable to a funeral home, especially for old sisters, she said. "If the person is 104 years old, you can bet none of her family is living," she said. "That funeral is going to be very small. With the sisters, we can do that any way we want to do it."

Stearns also suggests that Catholics and other Christians consider forgoing the reception-line, wake-in-a-funeral-home and instead adapt the Jewish practice of shiva, in which friends visit the grieving family's home. The survivors "just kind of veg out while people come," she said. "They talk to whom they want to, and they don't talk to whom they don't want to. People bring them food so they don't have to think about making that. It's others doing for them."

Sometimes Stearns works with the bereaved, to help them deal with their grief. "First of all, you don't get over grief, you walk through it," she said. Anniversaries, birthdays, "every first of this and first of that, every time you realize that person is no longer in your life, you have to readjust to make your life work without that person. That's a new loss."

But eventually, "when you have walked through it, you will know that your life has changed and that you can begin again without the physical presence of that person in your life."

Stearns has discovered that her ministry meets a significant need. She wants to convince more and more people that death need not be taboo or scary or morbid. It can and should be a celebration of life, she said. "It can be all of the things it was meant to be."

It's Your Funeral

Taking control of the final celebration of her husband's life, Jane Vernon writes, brought them both strength and understanding

Jane Vernon

My husband announced: "I'd definitely want some e e cummings, and some Dylan. What do you think?"

"I don't think I'd be there, so it doesn't really matter. Whatever you choose will be so personal, so full of significance for us that I can't imagine being able to listen to it in front of other people. It would be far too painful. I don't think I'll be able to go to your funeral."

That was how I felt when my husband, Mike, first began to make suggestions about his own funeral. Nothing could be further from how I felt by the time the funeral was held.

Mile became ill with leukaemia 18 months after we were married, and from the outset we faced our problems together and with total honesty. He was given a good chance of achieving remission, which he did, and in spite of the fairly arduous treatment during the next year, began to feel better. Then about ten months later, he suffered a relapse. At about this time we attended the funeral of a friend. It was a traditional Christian funeral and as we came away Mike and I began to discuss our reactions. It was clear to both of us that, Mike being an agnostic and myself an atheist, such a funeral service would be irrelevant for either of us. What did people do?

What we did was begin to think about funerals. It hurt. To think about a funeral, one has to acknowledge the possibility of death. I'm sure many people thought we were trying to avoid this, but although we were optimistic and usually cheerful, we were realistic. It was an important part of that realism that Mike began to plan his own funeral. We also discussed the possibility, admittedly more remote, of my death occurring first, and what type of funeral I would want. We believed, and

experience has borne this out, that we would feel the pain whenever we planned the funeral—years, months or weeks before our deaths—and that the pain would be no worse because we were thinking ahead. So in a few weeks we had thought, talked and cried ourselves through the concept of our own funerals—whenever they might be. There would be tears again, but never about this. I knew now that not only would I be able to attend my husband's funeral, but I would want to play a major part in its organisation.

So Mike began his list, with the heading "A Celebration Selection". It grew as he discovered more poems, prose and music that he felt had something important to say. Some entries were specific, others simply read "some Shakespeare". One evening, we were sitting down to a candlelit meal and he asked me to listen again to a song he had been playing. "I must have this one. Isn't it wonderful?" It was a song we knew quite well, but it took on so much more meaning in this new context. The song is called "When I'm Gone", by Phil Ochs, and is a wonderful testament of how to live life according to one's beliefs. That evening remains one of my happiest memories of Mike's last six months. It was a remarkably strengthening experience, to submerge ourselves in the intimacy of the occasion, while facing with true acceptance that our life together would have to end, whether in a few months or some years. The choice of that one song seemed to set a theme for the whole occasion—to celebrate life as well as to sorrow for death.

I think this is the focus of a non-religious funeral, to reflect the life and personality of the deceased, and it can be a very positive occasion. People tend to think that only a religious ceremony, with the hope of life after death, can be positive and hopeful, but this was not our

experience. Although Mike's illness and the prospect of his death brought us so much hurt, nevertheless we both recognised the richness of life as we had lived it, and wanted to convey this at his funeral.

Five months after his first relapse, Mike suffered another one. Possible treatment was now limited; he might have only a few weeks left. As his condition deteriorated, we talked in more detail about the funeral. We had obtained a copy of the British Humanist Association booklet *Funerals Without God* (from BHA, 14 Lamb's Conduit Passage, London WC1R 4RH), and this had reassured us that we were allowed to do whatever we wanted. We had had, as I suspect most people have, an underlying feeling that there were certain things one could or could not do at a funeral. We hadn't known how to set about having anything different but *Funerals Without God* gave us the confidence to go ahead.

One feature of a funeral that we had overlooked until now was the tribute. So often this is made by a vicar who never actually knew the person he is talking about. If the person who has died was not a regular churchgoer, what is the alternative? The BHA has a number of "officiants" who can be called upon to conduct a funeral ceremony and who will make a tribute, after close consultation with relatives and friends. This sounded like a good idea, but first Mike wanted to ask his closest friend, Marcus, if he would make the tribute. It was a mark of their deep friendship that Marcus said he would count it a great honour. Many people would not be able to make a public statement at the funeral of a close friend or relative, and we were immensely lucky that we had a friend who, we knew, could do it so well.

Mike wanted to be buried rather than cremated—unusual in an agnostic, ap-

---

The final "Celebration Selection"

Organ Concerto by Poulenc
Excerpt from *The Tempest*
"When I'm Gone" by Phil Ochs,
sung by Dick Gaughan
Poem by e e cummings
Excerpt from *Waiting for Godot*
by Samuel Beckett
"Dueling Banjos"

Tribute:

Part of "And death shall have no
dominion" by Dylan Thomas
"Mr Tambourine Man"
by Bob Dylan
"Songs of Gloucestershire"
by Johnny Coppin

At the Burial:

Poem from *Cymbeline*
Excerpt from *The Prophet*
by Kahlil Gibran

---

parently. *Funerals Without God* assumes that any ceremony will be held in a crematorium, and we realised that finding a suitable room could be a problem. Our local Humanist representative, who is also the BHA funerals coordinator, was able to suggest a firm of local undertakers used to dealing with Humanist funerals. They were extremely helpful, and told me that our local vicar was very approachable. This was true—his welcoming and open-minded attitude meant we would be able to hold our non-religious ceremony in a lovely airy church hall close to our home, to the cemetery and to the local hospital where Mike had by now moved for the last few days of his life. The last instruction he gave about his funeral was that I should use a really good sound system, or he did not want any music played at all. He was right about this. If you want people to listen to carefully chosen music, they must be able to hear it properly.

After 18 months of illness, Mike died. I allowed a week between his death and the funeral. Though I made all the decisions, our friend Marcus shared the organisation with me. Other friends helped by providing and operating the sound system, setting up the room, handing out pamphlets and so on.

We had planned that I should arrive only shortly before the beginning of the ceremony. Afterwards, though it had been our intention that people should mill around and leave as they felt like it, people clearly felt it was up to me to leave first. This meant that, although I asked the funeral directors to make a list of everyone who had attended the ceremony, I was unable to speak to many of them, which I regretted. Perhaps this was a detail we didn't plan for sufficiently in advance.

Making the final selection of music and readings, and typing out the words for the pamphlet, gave me much satisfaction. I wanted all the words of the songs and readings printed so that people could follow what they were listening to, and re-read them later, thereby appreciating them as fully as possible. I also wrote a short introduction to explain how the ceremony had come about and to make sure that people knew nothing was expected of them but to sit and listen. At the end were printed the extracts that were to be read at the cemetery, so people who did not go still had an opportunity to read the words; it also informed people what was happening so they could attend if they wanted to. There were quite a few pamphlets left, so I was later able to send copies to friends who could not attend the ceremony to make sure, as much as I could, that everyone who needed to had an opportunity to share in the grieving.

The whole day of the funeral was very special. Those items not pre-recorded were read by friends, and Marcus gave a tremendously moving address, reaching the Mike each mourner knew. Many were in tears by the end of the ceremony, but this seemed to me to be a good thing: we are often told that grieving is a necessary part of recovery. It also lent a closeness, a feeling of shared experience often absent from funerals where people congratulate each other on being "in control". We drove the short distance from the hall to the cemetery and said our last goodbyes.

I had invited some people to lunch and put up large notices at the hall informing everyone that there was "open house" during the afternoon. Many friends arrived, filling the house and garden with memories, love and joy at having known Mike. So many of them said—and I had to stop them apologising for the phrase—it was "the best funeral" they had been to that I knew we had achieved what Mike and I had hoped for.

We had started out knowing only what would be wrong for us, but not what we could do about it. I knew that, by following our innermost feelings, we had got it right.

BURYING THE UNGRATEFUL DEAD

Thomas Lynch

Thomas Lynch is an undertaker in Milford, Michigan, and is the author of Grimalkin & Other Poems, *published in England by Random House.*

Every year I bury one hundred and fifty of my townspeople. Another dozen or two I take to the crematory to be burned. I sell caskets, burial vaults, and urns for the ashes. I have a sideline in headstones and monuments. I do flowers on commission. I rent my building: eleven thousand square feet, furnished and fixtured with an abundance of pastel and chair rail and crown moldings. The whole mess is mortgaged and remortgaged well into the next century. My modes of transport include a hearse, a limo, two Fleetwoods, and a minivan with darkened windows, which our price list calls a service vehicle and which everyone in town calls the Dead Wagon.

They die around the clock here, without apparent preference for a day of the week or month of the year; there is no clear favorite among the seasons. Nor does the alignment of the stars, the fullness of the moon, or the liturgical calendar have very much to do with it. They go off upright or horizontally, in Chevrolets and nursing homes, in bathtubs, on the interstates, in ERs, ORs, BMWs. And while it may be that we assign more equipment and more importance to deaths that occur in places marked by initials—ICU being somehow better than Greenbriar Convalescent Home—it is also true that the dead don't care. In this way, the dead I bury and burn are like the dead before them, for whom time and space have become mortally unimportant. This loss of interest among the dying is one of the first sure signs that something serious is about to happen. The next thing is they quit breathing.

Nor does *who* matter much either. To say, "I'm okay, you're okay, but him, he's dead!" is, for the living, a kind of comfort. It is why we drag rivers and comb plane wrecks. It is why MIA is more painful than DOA. It is why we have open caskets and classified obits. Knowing is better than not knowing, and knowing it is you is terrifically better than knowing it is me. Once I'm the dead guy, whether you're okay or he's okay won't interest me, because the dead don't care.

Of course, the living, bound by their adverbs and their actuarials, still do. That's the reason I'm in business. The living are careful and often caring. The dead are careless, or maybe it's care-less. Either way, they don't care. These are unremarkable and verifiable truths.

My former mother-in-law, herself an unremarkable and verifiable truth, was always fond of holding forth with Cagneyesque bravado—to wit: "When I'm dead, just put me in a box and throw me in a hole." But whenever I reminded her that we did, in effect, do that with everyone, the woman grew sullen and a little cranky. Later, over meatloaf and green beans, she would invariably burst forth with: "When I'm dead, just cremate me and scatter the ashes."

My former mother-in-law was trying to make carelessness sound like fearlessness. My kids would stop eating and look at each other. The kids' mother would whine: "Oh, Mom, don't talk like that." I'd take out my lighter and begin to play with it.

In the same way, the priest that married me to this woman's daughter—a man who loved golf and gold chalices and vestments made of Irish linen; a man who drove a great black car with a wine-red interior—this same fellow, leaving the cemetery one day, felt called upon to instruct me thus: "No bronze coffin for me. No sir! No orchids or roses or limousines. The plain pine box is the one I want, a quiet Low Mass, and the pauper's grave. No pomp and circumstance."

He wanted to be an example of simplicity, of prudence, of piety and austerity. When I told him that he needn't wait, that he could begin his ministry of good example even today, that he could quit the country club and trade his luxury sedan for a used Chevette, that free of his Florsheims and cashmeres and prime ribs he could become the very incarnation of Saint Francis himself or Anthony of Padua—when I told the priest who had married me these things, he said nothing at all, but turned his wild eye on me in the way that the cleric must have looked on Sweeney years ago, before he cursed him, irreversibly, into a bird.

What I was trying to tell the fellow was, of course, that being a dead saint is no more worthwhile than being a dead philodendron.

Living is the rub, and always has been. Living saints still feel the flames and stigmata, the ache of chastity and the pangs of conscience. Once dead, they let their relics do the legwork, because, as I was trying to tell this priest, the dead don't care.

And that is the truth, abundantly self-evident, that seems, now that I think of it, the one most elusive to my old in-laws, to the parish priest, and to perfect strangers who are forever accosting me in barbershops and in cocktail bars and at parent-teacher conferences, hell-bent or duty-bound on telling me what it is they want done with them when they are dead.

I say, Give it a rest. Once you are dead, call it a day, and let the old man or the missus or the thankless kids decide whether you are to be buried or burned or blown out of a cannon or left to dry out in a ditch. It's not your day to watch.

● ● ●

Burying Tradition, More People Opt for 'Fun' Funerals

For Some, New Rites of Passage Include Parties, Boat Rides and Psychedelic Caskets

Carrie Dolan

Staff Reporter of The Wall Street Journal

SACRAMENTO, Calif.—In a hotel ballroom here, about 3,000 revelers float among bouquets of balloons and mingle around a trio of bars. An ice sculpture drips over the buffet. A seven-piece band, led by a vocalist in a black lace dress, blares out James Brown's "I Feel Good." In the midst of the action is the party's host—lying in a flag-draped coffin.

He was B. T. Collins, a popular California state legislator, who died of a heart attack in March at age 52. A former Green Beret who lost an arm and a leg in the Vietnam War, he was fond of unconventional tributes. He marked his 50th birthday with a parachute jump and once donated a urinal to Santa Clara University's school of law, his alma mater. Known for his disdain for protocol and his love of a good time, he had set aside funds to celebrate his passing. As for his attendance at the festivities, Nora Romero, his longtime administrative assistant, asks: "You don't think B. T. would miss his own party, do you?"

GOING IN STYLE

These days, a small but growing number of people are choosing to be remembered in an upbeat—and sometimes bizarre—fashion. By planning their own send-offs, these forward-looking folks ensure a memorable goodbye to loved ones. "It's a way of saying, 'Hey world, I may be dead, but I'm not gone,' " says Steve Skiles, who has been a funeral director in Belmont, Calif., for three years.

A fun funeral is "a very healthy idea," says Richard Steffen, a friend who helped plan the final party for Mr. Collins, who had a history of coronary trouble. "I was raised Polish Catholic and [services] would always end with a blowout party with a polka band, kielbasa and vodka . . . Everyone would cry in the morning, but by midnight there was no pain."

"There's definitely a trend," toward people planning creative funerals, says Bill Vlcek of the California Funeral Directors Association, which represents about 560 members. Many funerals "still have a somewhat traditional format, but with a personalized spin on it," he says. About 40,000 people have prearranged and prepaid for their services since California's funeral homes began a special program in 1985. Mr. Vlcek estimates that in the San Francisco Bay and Los Angeles areas as many as 20% of funerals are nontraditional. "Less than a half percent" of services are unconventional elsewhere in the state, he says.

GIVING MEANING

"Whatever has meaning to the family and friends is appropriate, even if it may seem outrageous to others," says a spokesman for the Frank E. Campbell Funeral Chapel in New York, which has a "very religious clientele."

Nationally, too, there has been an increase in "preneed" funeral planning, and in efforts to "put more of the personality of the deceased into the funeral," says a spokeswoman for the National Funeral Directors Association in Milwaukee.

Some take a serious interest in their future funerals to leave less work—and a message—for their survivors. Phillip Quattrociocchi, who is dying of AIDS, has planned two services. One, to be held in Sacramento, Calif., where he grew up, will be a traditional, religious service. The other, in San Francisco, where he now lives, will feature a video of himself urging others "to do some volunteer work."

He says he has "picked some excellent speakers" for the obsequies, handled the catering arrangements and hired a graphic artist to design the invitations. "I wanted to get on with living, and not keep worrying about dying," he says.

Jack Smith, 55, a popular San Francisco bar owner, planned a less sober service. After learning that he had terminal cancer, he planned a yacht cruise for 100 friends, set to sail the Saturday after his death. Dave Rose, a friend, recalls that Mr. Smith "handed me an invitation, and said, 'I'm having a party. I just don't have a date on it yet.' "

The cruise featured a jazz band and a blues group, plenty of refreshments and a scattering of the deceased's ashes to the playing of "I'll Be Seeing You." Friends have been talking about it ever since.

POST-GAME GATHERING

When Connie Scramlin, 58, a fan of baseball's Detroit Tigers, learned she had cancer, she arranged to be buried in a club uniform, in a coffin with the team's colors of orange, navy blue and white. "Take Me Out to the Ballgame" was played at her service last June.

"I knew that some people might think it was almost sacrilegious," says Mrs. Scramlin's daughter Debbie Pillsbury, "but most [guests] were really moved."

5. FUNERALS AND BURIAL RITES

Not everyone approves of excessive merrymaking. Deacon Bill Mitchell, of the Catholic Archdiocese of San Francisco, says the emphasis "should be on prayer for the dead, and on . . . consolation for those going through the mourning process. I'm not sure if a great big party does a lot to really help."

Ron Roy, of Woods Glendale Mortuary in Glendale, Calif., with more than 30 years in the funeral business, has met many creative requests, including one from a woman who asked to be interred with a portable TV tuned to her favorite soap operas. Friends of a Hell's Angel placed switchblade knives, brass knuckles and marijuana cigarettes beside the biker's body, which was to be cremated. One couple brought in a parakeet for Mr. Roy to embalm, stipulating that the bird be entombed with the spouse who died first. "That was about 12 years ago, and we're still diligently holding on to Tweety Bird," he says.

Some requests require special effort. Last summer, Mr. Skiles, the Belmont mortician, fulfilled a woman's wish to be buried at sea in a hand-carved canoe.

Full-body burial isn't legal off California's coast, so he and a colleague "put her in the back of a U-Haul truck and drove to Oregon," he says. They rented a fishing boat, went 15 miles offshore, and pushed the canoe overboard.

HAUNTS FOR HOBBYISTS

The price? About $4,000. That can be considerably less than the cost of a traditional funeral-parlor service and burial in certain areas of the country.

Those with more conventional tastes for funerals can still request a bit of flair. San Francisco's Ghia Gallery, for instance, has decorated caskets with graffiti and psychedelic art, and it is developing a line of coffins, each carved from an individual tree. Loretto Casket Co. in Tennessee sells coffins emblazoned with the logos of major universities. At a columbarium in San Francisco, people have found their final resting places in tobacco humidors, cameras and cookie jars, while patrons of other vaults have asked to be stored in a favorite hunting decoy or

bowling pin. Hunters can arrange to have Iowa-based Canuck's Sportsman's Memorials Inc. place their ashes into shotgun shells and fire them into the woods.

A venture once proposed by a Florida group to launch cremated remains into space never got off the ground, however.

And some wishes just can't be honored. Kevin Minke, a counselor at the Telophase Society, a San Diego cremation concern, says he has had customers who "say they want their ashes thrown out with the garbage or flushed down the toilet." Both methods are illegal.

Still, those in the industry appreciate the importance of making a special exit. Mr. Roy arranged to be buried off Canada's coast in fishing gear. "I love to fish and I want them to put me out there with the fish," he says. Mr. Skiles, a self-described "big-breakfast man," has planned a morning cruise for his friends with a menu of pork chops and eggs to accompany a scattering of his ashes.

His wife wants her ashes tossed from a hot-air balloon. "She's always wanted to take one of those balloon trips," he says, "but she's afraid of heights."

Mourners Will Please Pay Respects at Speeds Not Exceeding 15 MPH

Alison Woods

Staff Reporter of The Wall Street Journal

PENSACOLA, Fla.—Willie J. Junior needed something to distinguish himself from more-established competitors when he opened for business. "As the new kid on the block, I had to have something the other funeral parlors weren't offering," says Mr. Junior, whose own funeral parlor opened in 1986.

His answer: A drive-by window affording mourners a view of the deceased.

Junior Funeral Home's viewing window works about the same as those at other drive-through operations. It is set into a cubicle adjoining the funeral home; when it's in use, an open casket and floral arrangement lie behind the glass, under a bank of colored lights designed to show off the deceased to fullest advantage. Drivers follow neatly painted directions through the parking lot to the window, from which—without ever leaving the car—they can view the remains, sign a guest book and be on their way.

"There's nothing spooky about the window—it's very serene," says Mr. Junior. He says it simply meets the needs of the elderly and the disabled, who may have trouble getting in and out of cars, as well as people with unconventional work schedules. It also appeals to those who want to pay their respects without having to dress up and meet the whole family, he says.

Alice S. Johnson says some relatives who went to her father's wake at Junior Funeral Home returned after the service to see him in the viewing window. "A lot of people came by," Mrs. Johnson says. "They thought it was wonderful."

Certainly, the viewing window has been a boon to business for Mr. Junior. Since he opened his doors, he estimates, he has gone from the No. 4 position to No. 2 among Pensacola's black-owned funeral homes in terms of revenue.

Mr. Junior doubts drive-through viewing windows are the wave of the future. The National Association of Funeral Directors estimates that there are only about half a dozen of them in the U.S., and Mr. Junior says only one in 25 families uses his company's window.

Still, Junior Funeral Home has become something of an attraction in Pensacola—and beyond. It twice was the answer to a question posed on the "Hollywood Squares" TV game show and recently was used as a location in a film featuring Phyllis Diller and Tina Louise.

Bereavement

In American society, many act as if the process of bereavement is completed with the culmination of public mourning related to the funeral or memorial service and the final disposition of the dead. For those in the process of grieving, the end of public mourning only serves to make the bereavement process a more individualized, subjective, and private experience. Private mourning of loss for most individuals, while more intense at its beginning, continues throughout their lifetime. The nature and intensity of this experience is influenced by the relationship of the mourner to the deceased, the age of the mourner, and the social context in which bereavement takes place.

This unit on bereavement begins with a general article on the bereavement process. Michael Leming and George Dickinson describe and discuss the active coping strategies related to the bereavement process, disenfranchised grief, and the four tasks of bereavement. In "Coping with Bereavement," A. Scott Henderson encourages health care professionals to be aware that physical symptoms in the recently bereaved may be due to emotional reactions. The next article, "Disenfranchised Grief," provides assistance for caregivers in dealing with the needs of bereaved survivors. Then, Therese Rando, in "The Increasing Prevalence of Complicated Mourning: The Onslaught Is Just Beginning," illustrates the principles described by Leming and Dickinson by providing a critique of America's health care industry and its lack of involvement in the post-death grieving experience. This article discusses many different types of death and the respective influences upon the bereaved, while it also suggests strategies for active coping with grief.

The article "The Spiritual Crisis of Bereavement," by Kenneth Doka, explores the ways in which religious beliefs and the death rituals that accompany them can both facilitate and complicate bereavement. Doka offers suggestions to clinicians on ways that they can assist clients to effectively utilize their belief systems in resolving grief.

The needs of the bereaved, children and adults, and how to assist them with their grieving are addressed in the rest of the unit's articles. "Adolescent Mourning: The Sudden Death of a Peer" examines the experience of adolescent mourning for those suffering the tragic loss of a school friend.

The death of a child is typically regarded as the most difficult of all deaths. The death of a child violates what most believe is the natural order—parents are supposed to die before their children. Furthermore, the death of a child symbolically threatens the family's hope for a future. "Solace and Immortality: Bereaved Parents' Continuing Bond with Their Children" discusses how parents learn to deal with their grief and pain. The final article, "Effects of a Child's Death on the Marital Relationship: A Preliminary Study" by Reiko Schwab, examines the effects of a child's death on the parents' marital relationship. Twenty couples were interviewed and several common themes were discovered. It was discovered that husbands were frustrated with the intensity of their wives' expressions of grief. On the other hand, wives could not understand why their husbands concealed their own expressions of grief. Out of the pain of this mutual misunderstanding an inability to communicate arose in every aspect of the couples' relationships.

Looking Ahead: Challenge Questions

Discuss how the seven stages of grieving over someone's death can also be applied to losses such as divorce, moving from one place to another, or the amputation of a limb (arm or leg). What is the relationship between time and the feelings of grief experienced within the bereavement process?

Describe the four necessary tasks of mourning. What are some of the practical steps one can take in accomplishing each of these tasks? How can one assist friends in bereavement?

What are the special problems encountered in the death of a child and in a perinatal death? How could someone assist friends in this special type of bereavement?

How would you know if someone is experiencing a "normal" bereavement or an "abnormal bereavement"? What are some of the signs of aberrant bereavement? What could you do to assist people experiencing abnormal grief symptoms?

THE GRIEVING PROCESS

Michael R. Leming

St. Olaf College

George E. Dickinson

College of Charleston

Grief is a very powerful emotion that is often triggered or stimulated by death. Thomas Attig (1991) makes an important distinction between grief and the grieving process. While grief is an emotion that engenders feelings of helplessness and passivity, the process of *grieving* is a more complex coping process that presents challenges and opportunities for the griever and requires energy to be invested, tasks to be undertaken, and choices to be made (Attig: 1991:387).

Most people believe that the grieving is a disease-like and debilitating process that renders the individual passive and helpless. According to Attig (1991:389):

> It is misleading and dangerous to mistake grief for the whole of the experience of the bereaved. It is misleading because the experience is far more complex, entailing diverse emotional, physical, intellectual, spiritual, and social impacts. It is dangerous because it is precisely this aspect of the experience of the bereaved that is potentially the most frustrating and debilitating.

Death ascribes to the griever a passive social position in the bereavement role. Grief is an emotion over which the individual has no control. However, understanding that the grieving is an active coping process can restore to the griever a sense of autonomy where the process is permeated with choice and where there are many areas over which the griever does have some control. Thomas Attig (1991:391) helps us to understand the active nature of the grieving process by emphasizing some of the choices that confront those who grieve.

COPING WITH GRIEF

The grieving process, like the dying process, is essentially a series of behaviors and attitudes related to coping with the stressful situation of changing the status of a relationship. Many have attempted to understand coping with dying as a series of universal, mutually exclusive and linear stages. However, since most will acknowledge that not all people will progress through the stages in the same manner, we will list a number of coping strategies used as people attempt to resolve the pain caused by the loss of a personally significant relationship.

Robert Kavanaugh (1972) identifies the following seven behaviors and feelings as part of the coping process: shock and denial, disorganization, volatile emotions, guilt, loss and loneliness, relief, and reestablishment. It is not difficult to see similarities between these behaviors and Kubler-Ross's five stages (denial, anger, bargaining, depression, and acceptance) of the dying process. According to Kavanaugh (1972:123), "these seven stages do not subscribe to the logic of the head as much as to the irrational tugs of the heart—the logic of need and permission."

Shock and Denial

Even when a significant other is expected to die, at the time of death there is often a sense in which the death is not real. For most of us our first response is "no, this can't be true." With time our experience of shock diminishes but we find new ways to deny the reality of death.

Some believe that denial is dysfunctional behavior for those in bereavement. However, denial is not only a common experience among the newly bereaved, but also serves positive functions in the process of adaptation. The main function of denial is to provide the bereaved with a "temporary safe place" from the ugly realities of a social world that only offers loneliness and pain.

With time the meaning of loss tends to expand, and it may be impossible for one to deal with all of the social meanings of death at once. For example, if my wife dies, not only do I lose my spouse, I lose my best friend, my sexual partner, the mother of my children, a source of income, the person who writes the Christmas

MAKING CHOICES IS PART OF THE ACTIVE GRIEVING PROCESS

Thomas Attig

The bereaved can choose whether to indulge in the paralyzing grief emotion or to struggle against what tempts them in it. This fundamental choice may require a kind of hope beyond hope or a faith rooted in convictions that support and sustain the very capacity to affirm life and its meaningfulness. The bereaved can choose their own timing and pacing in undertaking the [bereavement] tasks and define their own styles in addressing them. They can choose to attack the tasks and challenges vigorously, investing much time and energy in their grief work, or they can choose to go slowly, allowing themselves frequent respite from the rigors of the process.

They can choose the focus of their attention. They can choose whether and how to interact with the body of the deceased. They can choose which of their physical surroundings now permeated with new significance they are willing to encounter, what they have need to witness or interest in witnessing, and the like. They can choose to visit or to stay away from places of significance. They can choose to keep, discard, or postpone until later decisions about what is to be done with physical effects, pictures, mementos, and other objects that have significant relation to the deceased. They can choose alternative means of effectively expressing the emotions they experience of the new meanings they discern. They can choose to actively participate in social responses to the death such as the funeral or merely to witness the participations of others. They can choose to do or say what is meaningful to them either in private or together with others. They can choose at times to withdraw from others and at others to reach out for support or comfort. They can choose to find means to building a new and dynamic relation with the deceased, giving shape to their lives in part through continuing, albeit transformed, interaction with the story of the life now ended.

Viewing grieving as an active coping process offers the bereaved some understanding of the possible objectives of and even fruits of their labors. Beyond restored emotional equilibrium, renewed motivation for engaging in everyday life, and revived hope for the future, the bereaved can experience their grieving as life enhancing in yielding increased feelings of strength and security in their own person, deepened self-understanding and self-esteem, enhanced capacities to understand and respond sensitively to others, improved critical perspective on personal relationships, and enriched perspectives of reality and the human condition. Emphasizing the active and potentially life-enhancing character of the coping process motivates the bereaved to invest the energy required for change and life transformation.

Thomas Attig. 1991. "The Importance of Conceiving of Grief as an Active Process." *Death Studies,* Volume 15, pp. 390–392.

---

cards, and so on. Denial can protect me from some of the magnitude of this social loss, which may be unbearable at one point in time. With denial, I can work through different aspects of my loss over time.

Disorganization

Disorganization is that stage in the bereavement process in which one may feel totally out of touch with the reality of everyday life. Some go through the three-day time period just prior to the funeral as if on "automatic pilot" or "in a daze." Nothing normal "makes sense," and an individual may feel that life has no inherent meaning. For some, death is perceived as preferable to life, which appears to be devoid of meaning.

This emotional response is also a normal experience for the newly bereaved. Confusion is normal for those whose social world has been disorganized through death. When my father died, my mother not only lost all those things one loses with a death of a spouse, but she also lost her care-giving role—a social role and master status that had defined her identity in the five years my father lived with cancer. It is only natural to experience confusion and social disorganization when one's social identity has been destroyed.

Volatile Reactions

Whenever one's identity and social order face the possibility of destruction, there is a natural tendency to feel angry, frustrated, helpless, and/or hurt. The volatile reactions of terror, hatred, resentment, and jealousy are often experienced as emotional manifestations of these feelings. Grieving humans are sometimes more successful at masking their feelings in socially acceptable behaviors than other animals, whose instincts cause them to go into a fit of rage when their order is threatened by external forces. However apparently dissimilar, the internal emotional experience *is* similar.

In working with bereaved persons over the past 15 years, I have observed that the following become objects of volatile grief reactions: God, medical personnel, funeral directors, other family members, in-laws, friends who have not experienced death in their families, and/or even the person who has died. I have always found it interesting to watch mild-mannered individuals transformed into raging and resentful persons when grieving. Some of these people have experienced physical symptoms such as migraine headaches, ulcers, neuropathy, and colitis as a result of repressing these intense emotions.

Guilt

Guilt is similar to the emotional reactions discussed above. Guilt is anger and resentment turned in on oneself, and often results in self-deprecation and depression. Typically manifested in statements like "If only...," "I should have...," "I could have...," and "Maybe I did the wrong thing," guilt is a normal part of the bereavement process.

From a sociological perspective, guilt can become a social mechanism to resolve the **dissonance** others feel when unable to explain why someone else's loved one has died. Rather than view death as something that can happen at any time to any one, friends can **blame the victim** of bereavement, and believe that the survivor was in some way responsible for the death—"if he had been a better parent, the child might not have been hit by the car," or "if I had been married to him I might also have committed suicide," or "no wonder he died of a heart attack, her cooking would give anyone high cholesterol." Therefore, bereaved persons are sometimes encouraged to feel guilt because they are subtly sanctioned by others' reactions.

Loss and Loneliness

As we discussed earlier, loss and loneliness are the other side of denial. Their full sense never becomes obvious at once; rather each day without the deceased helps us to recognize how much we needed and depended upon that person. Social situations in which we expected them always to be present seem different now that they are gone. Holiday celebrations are also diminished by their absence. In fact for some, most of life takes on a "something's missing" feeling. This feeling was captured in the 1960s love song "End of the World."

Why does the world go on turning?
Why must the sea rush to shore?
Don't they know it's the end of the world
'Cause you don't love me anymore?

Loss and loneliness are often transformed into depression and sadness fed by feelings of self-pity. According to Kavanaugh (1972:118), this effect is magnified by the fact that the dead loved-one grows out of focus in memory—"an elf becomes a giant, a sinner becomes a saint because the grieving heart needs giants and saints to fill an expanding void." Even a formerly undesirable spouse, such as an alcoholic, is missed in a way that few can understand unless his or her own heart is involved. This is a time in the grieving process when anybody is better than nobody, and being alone only adds to the curse of loss and loneliness (Kavanaugh, 1972:118).

Those who try to escape this experience will either turn to denial in an attempt to reject their feelings of loss or they will try to find surrogates—new friends at a bar, a quick remarriage, or a new pet. This escape can never be permanent, however, because loss and loneliness are a necessary part of the bereavement experience. According to Kavanaugh (1972:119), the "ultimate goal in conquering loneliness" is to build a new independence or to find a new and equally viable relationship.

Relief

The experience of relief in the midst of the bereavement process may seem odd for some and add to their feelings of guilt. My mother found relief in the fact that my father's battle with cancer had ended, even though this end provided her with new problems. I have observed a friend's relief six months after her husband died. This older friend of mine was the wife of a minister, and her whole life before he died was his ministry. With time, as she built a new world of social involvements and relationships of which he was not a part, she discovered a new independent person in herself that she perceived was a better person than she had ever been.

While relief can give rise to feelings of guilt, like denial, it can also be experienced as a "safe place" from the pain, loss, and loneliness that are endured when one is grieving. According to Kavanaugh (1972:121),

The feeling of relief does not imply any criticism for the love we lost. Instead, it is a reflection of our need for ever deeper love, our quest for someone or something always better, our search for the infinite, that best and perfect love religious people name as God.

Reestablishment

As one moves toward reestablishment of a life without the deceased, it is obvious that the process involves extensive adjustment and time, especially if the relationship was meaningful. It is likely that one may have feelings of loneliness, guilt, and disorganization at the same time, and that just when one may experience a sense of relief, something will happen to trigger a denial of the death. What facilitates bereavement and adjustment is to fully experience each of these feelings as normal and realize that it is hope (holding the person together in fantasy at first) that will provide the survivor with the promise of a new life filled with order, purpose, and meaning.

Reestablishment never arrives all at once. Rather, it is a goal that one realizes has been achieved long after it has occurred. In some ways it is similar to Dorothy's realization at the end of "The Wizard of Oz"—she had always possessed the magic that could return her to Kansas. And, like Dorothy, we have to experience our loss before we really appreciate the joy of investing our lives again in new relationships.

DISENFRANCHISED GRIEF

Like other aspects of death-related behavior, grief is socially constructed—people grieve only when they feel that it is appropriate to grieve. In the bereavement role social scripts are provided for grievers and social support is given to those who are recognized as having experienced loss and act in accordance to the norms. However, not all loss is openly acknowledged, socially sanctioned, and publicly shared. Kenneth Doka (1989) uses the term **disenfranchised grief** when referring to phenomena of this type.

According to Doka (1989) there are four types of situations that lead to disenfranchised grief. The first situation is where the *relationship to the deceased is not socially recognized*. Examples of this type of disenfranchised grief would include nontraditional relationships—such as extramarital affairs, heterosexual cohabitations, and homosexual relationships (Doke, 1987 and Thornton, et al., 1991:356). If outsiders are unaware that a relationship exists and the bereaved are unable to publicly acknowledge their loss, they will not receive social support for their grief and their bereavement will be problematic.

A second type of disenfranchised grief will occur when *the loss is not acknowledged by others* as being genuine loss. An abortion or miscarriage is often deemed to be of lesser significance because the mother never had the opportunity to develop a face-to-face relationship with the child (Thornton, et al., 1991). In the case of abortion, it is assumed that since the pregnancy was unwanted, grieving is unnecessary. According to Idell Kesselman (1990:241) whatever one's position on abortion, "we must acknowledge that at least one death occurs—in addition to the fetus, there is often the death of youth, of innocence, of dreams, and of illusion." Kesselman (1990:241) maintains that women who have had an abortion need to express "unresolved feelings of loss" and deal with "issues of death, loss and separation," Kesselman concludes that grief therapy must be a necessary part of abortion counseling.

Two different examples of unacknowledged losses are the death of a companion pet and the death of a former spouse. According to Avery Weisman (1990–1991:241) the loss of a companion animal is often accompanied by intense grief and mourning but is seldom recognized by others as being important and an authentic occasion for bereavement. Likewise, the death of a former spouse is rarely thought of as a legitimate loss because most people believe that grief work should be completed shortly after the divorce.

Related to the unacknowledged loss is the third type of disenfranchised grief where *the grievers are unrecognized*. The death of an adolescent peer or friend is rarely openly acknowledged and socially sanctioned. One of the reasons why wakes and visitation services often attract larger audiences than do funerals is that employers are increasingly unwilling to provide employees with released time from work to attend a funeral of a person who is not family member (Sklar and Hartley, 1990). Other unrecognized grievers are young children, the mentally incompetent and/or retarded, and elderly adults. In each of these cases the bereavement needs of individuals are also often ignored by most social audiences (Sklar and Hartley, 1990; and Kloeppel and Hollins, 1989).

The final type of disenfranchised grief occurs when *the death is not socially sanctioned* as in the case of a death occurring in the act of a crime, or when death is caused by suicide, AIDS, or autoerotic asphyxia (Thornton, et al., 1989; Ness and Pheffer, 1990, and Murphy and Perry, 1988). When people feel ambivalent, awkward, and/or uncomfortable about the cause of the death, they are generally unable or unwilling to provide the social support needed by the bereaved.

According to Kenneth Doka (1989), whenever disenfranchised grief occurs the experience of grief is intensified while the normal sources of social support are lacking. Disenfranchised grievers are usually barred from contact with the deceased during the dying process. They are also frequently excluded from funeral rituals as well as care and support systems that may assist them in their bereavement. Finally, they may often experience many practical and legal difficulties after the death of their loved one. All of these circumstances intensify the problematic nature of bereavement for disenfranchised grievers.

THE FOUR TASKS OF MOURNING

In 1982 J. William Worden published *Grief Counseling and Grief Therapy,* which summarized the research conclusions of a National Institutes of Health study called the Omega Project (occasionally referred to as the Harvard Bereavement Study). Two of the more significant findings of this research, displaying the active nature of the grieving process, are that mourning is necessary for all persons who have experienced a loss through death, and that four tasks of mourning must be accomplished before mourning can be completed and reestablishment can take place.

According to Worden (1982:10), uncompleted grief tasks can impair further growth and development of the individual. Furthermore, the necessity of these tasks suggests that those in bereavement *must* attend to "grief work" because successful grief resolution is not automatic, as Kavanaugh's (1972) stages might imply. Each bereaved person must accomplish four necessary tasks: (1) accept the reality of the loss, (2) experience the pain of grief, (3) adjust to an environment in which the deceased is missing, and (4) withdraw emotional energy and reinvest it in another relationship (Worden, 1982).

Accept the Reality of the Loss

Especially in situations where death is unexpected and/or the deceased lived far away, it is difficult to conceptualize the reality of the loss. The first task of mourning is to overcome the natural denial response, realize that the person is dead and will not return.

There are many ways in which bereaved persons can facilitate the actualization of death. The traditional methods are to view the body, attend the funeral and committal services, and visit the final place of disposition. The following is a partial list of additional activities that can assist in making death real for grieving persons.

1. View the body at the place of death before preparation by the funeral director.
2. Talk about the deceased and the circumstances surrounding the death.
3. View photographs and personal effects associated with the deceased.
4. Distribute the possessions of the deceased among relatives and friends.

Experience the Pain of Grief

Part of coming to grips with the reality of death is experiencing the emotional and physical pain caused by the loss. Many people in the denial stage of grieving attempt to avoid pain by choosing to reject the emotions and feelings they are experiencing. Some do this by avoiding places and circumstances that remind them of the deceased. I know of one widow who quit playing golf and stopped eating at a particular restaurant because these were activities that she had enjoyed with her husband. Another widow found it extremely painful to be with her dead husband's twin, even though he and her sister-in-law were her most supportive friends.

J. William Worden (1982:13–14) cites the following case study to illustrate the performance of this task of mourning:

One young woman minimized her loss by believing her brother was out of his dark place and into a better place after his suicide. This might have been true, but it kept her from feeling her intense anger at him for leaving her. In treatment, when she first allowed herself to feel anger, she said, "I'm angry with his behavior and not him!" Finally she was able to acknowledge this anger directly.

The problem with the avoidance strategy is that it is impossible to escape the pain associated with mourning. According to Bowlby (cited by Worden, 1982:14), "Sooner or later, some of those who avoid all conscious grieving, break down—usually with some form of depression." Tears can afford cleansing for wounds created by loss, and fully experiencing the pain ultimately provides wonderful relief to those who suffer, while eliminating long-term chronic grief.

Adjust to an Environment in Which the Deceased is Missing

The third task, practical in nature, requires the griever to take on some of the social roles performed by the deceased, or find others who will. According to Worden (1982:15), the aborting of this task is to become helpless by refusing to develop the skills necessary in daily living and ultimately withdrawing from life.

I knew a woman who refused to adjust to the social environment in which she found herself after the death of her husband. He was her business partner, as well as her best and only friend. After 30 years of marriage, they had no children, and she had no close relatives. She had never learned to drive a car. Her entire social world had been controlled by her former husband. Three weeks after his funeral she went into the basement and committed suicide.

The alternative to social withdrawal is to assume new social roles by taking on additional responsibilities. Extended families who always gathered at Grandma's house for Thanksgiving will be tempted to have a number of small Thanksgiving dinners after her death. The members of this family may believe that "no one can take Grandma's place." While this may be true, members of the extended family will grieve better if someone else is willing to do Grandma's work enabling the entire family to come together for Thanksgiving. Not to do so will cause double pain—the family will not gather and Grandma will still be missed.

Withdraw Emotional Energy and Reinvest It in Another Relationship

The final task of mourning is a difficult one for many because they feel disloyal or unfaithful in withdrawing emotional energy from their dead loved one. One of my family members once said that she could never love another man after her husband died. My twice-widowed aunt responded, "I once felt like that, but I now consider myself to be fortunate to have been married to two of the best men in the world."

Other people find themselves unable to reinvest in new relationships because they are unwilling to experience again the pain caused by loss. The quotation from John Brantner at the beginning of this chapter provides perspective on this problem: "Only people who avoid love can avoid grief. The point is to learn from it and remain vulnerable to love."

However, those who are able to withdraw emotional energy and reinvest it in other relationships find the possibility of a newly established social life. Kavanaugh (1972:122–123) depicts this situation well with the following description.

At this point fantasies fade into constructive efforts to reach out and build anew. The phone is answered more quickly, the door as well, and meetings seem important, invitations are treasured and any social gathering becomes an opportunity rather than a curse. Mementos of the past are put away for occasional family gatherings. New clothes and new places promise dreams instead of only fears. Old friends are important for encouragement and permission to rebuild one's life. New friends can offer realistic opportunities for coming out from under the grieving mantle. With newly acquired friends, one is not a widow, widower, or survivor—just a person. Life begins again at the point of new friendships. All the rest is of yesterday, buried, unimportant to the now and tomorrow.

REFERENCES

Attig, Thomas. 1991. "The Importance of Conceiving of Grief as an Active Process." *Death Studies, 15*:385–393.

Doka, Kenneth J. 1987. "Silent Sorrow: Grief and the Loss of Significant Others." *Death Studies, 11*:441–449.

Doka, Kenneth J. 1989. *Disenfranchised Grief.* Lexington, MA: Lexington Books.

Kavanaugh, Robert E. 1972. *Facing Death.* Baltimore: Penguin Books.

Kesselman, Idell. 1990. "Grief and Loss: Issues for Abortion." *Omega, 21, (3)*:241–247.

Kloeppel, D. A., and S. Hollins. 1989. "Double Handicap: Mental Retardation and Death in the Family." *Death Studies, 13*:31–38.

Murphy, Sister Patrice, and Kathleen Pery. 1988. "Hidden Grievers." *Death Studies, 12*:451–462.

Ness, David E., and Cynthia R. Pheffer. 1990. "Sequelae of Bereavement Resulting From Suicide." *American Journal of Psychiatry, 147, 3,* (March):279–285.

Sklar, Fred and Shirley F. Hartley. 1990. "Close Friends and Survivors: Bereavement Patterns in a 'Hidden' Population.' *Omega, 21, (2)*:103–112.

Thorton, Gordon, Katherine D. Wittemore, and Donald U. Robertson. 1989. "Evaluation of People Bereaved by Suicide." *Death Studies, 13*:119–126.

Thorton, Gordon, Donald U. Robertson, and Mary Lou Mlecko. 1991. "Disenfranchised Grief and Evaluations of Social Support by College Students." *Death Studies, 15*:355–362.

Weisman, Avery D. 1990–1991. "Bereavement and Companion Animals." *Omega, 22, (4)*:241–248.

Worden, J. William. 1982. *Grief Counseling and Grief Therapy: A Handbook for the Mental Health Practitioner.* New York: Springer Publishing Company.

Coping with bereavement

A. Scott Henderson

Professor A. Scott Henderson is Director of the National Health and Medical Research Council, Social Psychiatry Research Unit, the Australian National University, Canberra A.C.T. 0200, Australia.

Health professionals need to be aware that physical symptoms in the recently bereaved may be due to emotional reactions and they should invoke appropriate support as well as counselling according to local cultural practices.

The consequences of bereavement can by physical as well as emotional.

The loss of someone close is a painful experience. Most people are likely to be bereaved several times in their lives, and to face the task of coming to terms with the loss. Bereavement brings more than distress and sadness: the loss can induce other painful feelings, such as guilt over things said or done in the past. There may also be anger or resentment directed towards the deceased person or to others, including family members and health professionals. Not uncommonly, people who have been bereaved need to unburden their painful thoughts by talking about them with their family and friends. This is part of the grief process, whereby the individual gradually adjusts to life without the deceased person. Occasionally, there may be a need for professional counselling. In some instances, the bereavement may precipitate a depressive disorder.

In addition to the emotional consequences of bereavement, there are often physical symptoms. This is thought to be likely if the process of grieving is blocked for some reason, so that there is incomplete expression of emotional distress. Physicians of the pre-scientific era knew about this when they wrote: "The sorrow that has no vent in tears may make other organs weep."

There is great variation across cultures in people's response to bereavement. Among some Caucasians, concealment or suppression of grief is admired. People may say of a recently bereaved widow, "She is being very brave", meaning that she has given no public display of her distress, and that this is to her credit. This is in marked contrast to many other cultures, where emotional outpouring is expected and encouraged. This seems to help the process of mourning to advance towards a healthy resolution.

Some health problems that may be associated with bereavement are insomnia, headaches, impaired appetite, weight loss, lack of energy, palpitations and indigestion. These symptoms are probably induced by the emotional disturbances of bereavement. What is striking is that, in many countries, there is an increase in smoking and in the use of alcohol and tranquillizers. Another finding has been that young widows and widowers are more likely to develop both psychological and physical symptoms than the elderly bereaved. In general, women cope better with bereavement than men, and the elderly cope better than younger adults.

Reprinted from *World Health*, March/April 1994, pp. 25-27.

Not just folk wisdom

Among the elderly, it has been observed that where one partner in a marriage dies, the surviving partner is more than likely to die soon afterwards. This is not just folk wisdom; it has been shown to be true by statistical analyses of large populations. Indeed, death of a spouse shortens the survivor's life more than if the latter had been diagnosed with cancer. The causes of subsequent death among survivors are not clearly related to psychological causes, such as suicide, or to whatever led to the original death, such as an infection.

It is not known what causes the increase in mortality after bereavement. Possibilities are that people tend to marry others with similar characteristics, perhaps including poor health; or that both spouses have had a similar lifestyle with the same exposure to risk factors; or that the widowed one receives less care, with poorer nutrition and hygiene, leading to decreased resistance to disease; or finally a "desolation effect", in which grief leads to changes in body functions, such as in the immune and endocrine systems. The evidence favours the last two mechanisms, showing that human health depends on the interplay of biological, emotional and social factors, and that only one of these is rarely a sufficient explanation.

The great majority of people go through bereavement without developing a mental or physical disorder, although they will experience emotional distress and a profound sense of loss. The process of grief can take many months to run its normal course, at the end of which the deceased person is still missed, but thinking of her or him does not evoke unduly painful feelings. Such a course of events is likely where the surviving person has previously had good mental adjustment, with few health problems, and where she or he is supported by family and friends. During the period of grief, it is important that the bereaved should think about the deceased person, and above all talk to others about the past, the death itself, and the feelings being experienced. Going over these issues, possibly time and again and with free expression of emotion, is likely to help the person

Loneliness – an aggravating factor of bereavement.

work towards acceptance of the loss. Human beings are remarkably adaptive and resilient, and it is important to remember that bereavement has been part of human experience throughout history. It is therefore not surprising that the majority of people adapt to the loss and, in time, function again normally.

Distressing events

It is indisputable that bereavement is one of the most severe stresses that life brings, particularly when it involves the loss of a parent, spouse or child. Furthermore, the circumstances of the death itself can be deeply distressing, as in an unexpected accident, sudden illness, suicide, natural disaster such as an earthquake or flood, or war. Where there has been torture before the death itself, the grief will clearly be greater, with the added emotions of hatred, anger and revenge.

In normal civilian life, it is known that the recently bereaved are

Strong ties with the social milieu helps survivors to adjust to life without their loved ones.

But what will become of me when I lose my life-long companion?

The bereaved may fall into the dangerous trap of alcohol abuse.

more likely than others to go to a primary health care centre or their general practitioner. For this reason, it is important that health professionals be aware that physical symptoms in the recently bereaved may be due to emotional reactions, and that they invoke appropriate support as well as counselling according to local cultural practices. Religious leaders and support groups can play a major role in helping the bereaved.

Where the grief itself or some unexplained physical symptoms persist for many months afterwards, the possibility of a depressive disorder has to be considered. Here, the practitioner may be helped in the diagnosis by using the "flip-cards" for depression, anxiety, or unexplained physical symptoms which have recently been developed by WHO's Division of Mental Health in Geneva. These single-page outlines not only make it easy to

diagnose a mental disorder where this is suspected, but they also provide a simple treatment plan. For the bereaved, counselling will be the most important part of such care. The fact is that a bereaved person is likely to suffer both physically and mentally. The health worker should therefore not be blind to the possibility that the symptoms experienced during bereavement may be due to serious physical illness.

Disenfranchised Grief

KENNETH J. DOKA

KEN DOKA, PH.D., is a professor of gerontology at the College of New Rochelle in New York. He became interested in the study of death and dying quite inadvertently. Scheduled to do a practicum in a facility that housed juvenile delinquents, he discovered that his supervisor had changed the assignment. Instead, Doka found himself counseling dying children and their families at Sloan-Kettering, a major cancer hospital in New York. This experience became the basis of two graduate theses, one in sociology entitled "The Social Organization of Terminal Care in Two Pediatric Hospitals," and the other in religious studies entitled "Pastoral Counseling to Dying Children and Their Families." (Both were later published.) His doctoral program pursued another longstanding interest: the sociology of aging. In 1983, Dr. Doka accepted his present position at the College of New Rochelle where he specializes in thanatology and gerontology.

Active in the Association for Death Education and Counseling since its beginnings, Dr. Doka was elected its president in 1993. In addition to articles in scholarly journals, he is the author of *Death and Spirituality* (with John Morgan, 1993), *Living with Life-Threatening Illness* (1993), and *Disenfranchised Grief: Recognizing Hidden Sorrow* (1989), from which the following selection is excerpted. His work on disenfranchised grief began in the classroom when a graduate student commented, "If you think widows have it rough, you ought to see what happens when your ex-spouse dies."

Introduction

Ever since the publication of Lindemann's classic article, "Symptomatology and Management of Acute Grief," the literature on the nature of grief and bereavement has been growing.[1] In the few decades following this seminal study, there have been comprehensive studies of grief reactions,[2] detailed descriptions of atypical manifestations of grief,[3] theoretical and clinical treatments of grief reactions,[4] and considerable research considering the myriad variables that affect grief.[5] But most of this literature has concentrated on grief reactions in socially recognized and sanctioned roles: those of the parent, spouse, or child.

There are circumstances, however, in which a person experiences a sense of loss but does not have a socially recognized right, role, or capacity to grieve. In these cases, the grief is disenfranchised.[6] The person suffers a loss but has little or no opportunity to mourn publicly.

Up until now, there has been little research touching directly on the phenomenon of disenfranchised grief. In her comprehensive review of grief reactions, Raphael notes the phenomenon:

> There may be other dyadic partnership relationships in adult life that show patterns similar to the conjugal ones, among them, the young couple intensely, even secretly, in love; the defacto relationships; the extramarital relationship; and the homosexual couple. . . . Less intimate partnerships of close friends, working mates, and business associates, may have similar patterns of grief and mourning.[7]

Focusing on the issues, reactions, and problems in particular populations, a number of studies have noted special difficulties that these populations have in grieving. For example, Kelly and Kimmel, in studies of aging homosexuals, have discussed the unique problems of grief in such relationships.[8] Similarly, studies of the reactions of significant others of AIDS victims have considered bereavement.[9] Other studies have considered the special problems of unacknowledged grief in prenatal death,[10] [the death of] ex-spouses,[11] therapists' reactions to a client's suicide, and pet loss.[12] Finally, studies of families of Alzheimer's victims and mentally retarded adults[13] also have noted distinct difficulties of these populations in encountering varied losses which are often unrecognized by others.

Others have tried to draw parallels between related unacknowledged losses. For example, in a personal account, Horn compared her loss of a heterosexual lover with a friend's loss of a homosexual partner.[14] Doka discussed the particular problems of loss in nontraditional relationships, such as extramarital affairs, homosexual relationships, and cohabiting couples.[15]

This article attempts to integrate the literature on such losses in order to explore the phenomenon of disenfranchised grief. It will consider both the nature of disenfranchised grief and its central paradoxical problem: the very nature of this type of grief exacerbates the problems of grief, but the usual sources of support may not be available or helpful.

The Nature of Disenfranchised Grief

Disenfranchised grief can be defined as the grief that persons experience when they incur a loss that is not or cannot be openly acknowledged, publicly mourned, or socially supported. The concept of disenfranchised grief recognizes that societies have sets of norms—in effect, "grieving rules"—that attempt to specify who, when, where, how, how long, and for whom people should grieve. These grieving rules may be codified in personnel policies. For example, a worker may be allowed a week off for the death of a spouse or child, three days for the loss of a parent or sibling. Such policies reflect the fact that each society defines who has a legitimate right to grieve, and these definitions of right correspond to relationships, primarily familial, that are socially recognized and sanctioned. In any given society these grieving rules may not correspond to the nature of attachments, the sense of loss, or the feelings of survivors. Hence the grief of these survivors is disenfranchised. In our society, this may occur for three reasons.

1. The Relationship Is Not Recognized

In our society, most attention is placed on kin-based relationships and roles. Grief may be disenfranchised in those situations in which the relationship between the bereaved and deceased is not based on recognizable kin ties. Here the closeness of other non-kin relationships may simply not be understood or appreciated. For example, Folta and Deck noted, "While all of these studies tell us that grief is a normal phenomenon, the intensity of which corresponds to the closeness of the relationship, they fail to take this (i.e., friendship) into account. The underlying assumption is that closeness of relationship exists only among spouses and/or immediate kin."[16] The roles of lovers, friends, neighbors, foster parents, colleagues, in-laws, stepparents and stepchildren, caregivers, counselors, co-workers, and roommates (for example, in nursing homes) may be long-lasting and intensely interactive, but even though these relationships are recognized, mourners may not have full opportunity to publicly grieve a loss. At most, they might be expected to support and assist family members.

Then there are relationships that may not be publicly recognized or socially sanctioned. For example, nontraditional relationships, such as extramarital affairs, cohabitation, and homosexual relationships have tenuous public acceptance and limited legal standing, and they face negative sanctions within the larger community. Those involved in such relationships are touched by grief when the relationship is terminated by the death of the partner, but others in their world, such as children, may also experience grief that cannot be acknowledged or socially supported.

Even those whose relationships existed primarily in the past may experience grief. Ex-spouses, past lovers, or former friends may have limited contact, or they may not even engage in interaction in the present. Yet the death of that significant other can still cause a grief reaction because it brings finality to that earlier loss, ending any remaining contact or fantasy of reconciliation or reinvolvement. And again these grief feelings may be shared by others in their world such as parents and children. They too may mourn the loss of "what once was" and "what might have been." For example, in one case a twelve-year-old child of an unwed mother, never even acknowledged or seen by the father, still mourned the death of his father since it ended any possibility of a future liaison. But though loss is experienced, society as a whole may not perceive that the loss of a past relationship could or should cause any reaction.

2. The Loss Is Not Recognized

In other cases, the loss itself is not socially defined as significant. Perinatal deaths lead to strong grief reactions, yet research indicates that many significant others still perceive the loss to be relatively minor.[17] Abortions too can constitute a serious loss,[18] but the abortion can take place without the knowledge or sanctions of others, or even the recognition that a loss has occurred. It may very well be that the very ideologies of the abortion controversy can put the bereaved in a difficult position. Many who affirm a loss may not sanction the act of abortion, while some who sanction the act may minimize any sense of loss. Similarly, we are just becoming aware of the sense of loss that people experience in giving children up for adoption or foster care,[19] and we have yet to be aware of the grief-related implications of surrogate motherhood.

Another loss that may not be perceived as significant is the loss of a pet. Nevertheless, the research shows strong ties between pets and humans, and profound reactions to loss.[20]

Then there are cases in which the reality of the loss itself is not socially validated. Thanatologists have long recognized that significant losses can occur even when the object of the loss remains physically alive. Sudnow for example, discusses "social death," in which the person is alive but is treated as if dead.[21] Examples may include those who are institutionalized or comatose. Similarly, "psychological death" has been defined as conditions in which the person lacks a consciousness of existence, such as someone who is "brain dead."[22] One can also speak of "psychosocial death" in which the persona of someone has changed so significantly, through mental illness, organic brain syndromes, or even significant personal transformation (such as through addiction, conversion, and so forth), that significant others perceive the person as he or she previously existed as dead.[23] In all of these cases, spouses and others may experience a profound sense of loss, but that loss cannot be publicly acknowledged for the person is still biologically alive.

3. The Griever Is Not Recognized

Finally, there are situations in which the characteristics of the bereaved in effect disenfranchise their grief. Here the person is not socially defined as capable of grief; therefore, there is little or no social recognition of his or her sense of loss or need to mourn. Despite evidence to the contrary, both the very old and the very young are typically perceived by others as having little comprehension of or reaction to the death of a significant other. Often, then, both young children and aged adults are excluded from both discussions and rituals.[24]

Similarly, mentally disabled persons may also be disenfranchised in grief. Although studies affirm that the mentally retarded are able to understand the concept of death[25] and, in fact,

experience grief,[26] these reactions may not be perceived by others. Because the person is retarded or otherwise mentally disabled, others in the family may ignore his or her need to grieve. Here a teacher of the mentally disabled describes two illustrative incidences:

> In the first situation, Susie was 17 years old and away at summer camp when her father died. The family felt she wouldn't understand and that it would be better for her not to come home for the funeral. In the other situation, Francine was with her mother when she got sick. The mother was taken away by ambulance. Nobody answered her questions or told her what happened. "After all," they responded, "she's retarded."[27]

The Special Problems of Disenfranchised Grief

Though each of the types of grief mentioned earlier may create particular difficulties and different reactions, one can legitimately speak of the special problem shared in disenfranchised grief.

The problem of disenfranchised grief can be expressed in a paradox. The very nature of disenfranchised grief creates additional problems for grief, while removing or minimizing sources of support.

Disenfranchising grief may exacerbate the problem of bereavement in a number of ways. First, the situations mentioned tend to intensify emotional reactions. Many emotions are associated with normal grief. Bereaved persons frequently experience feelings of anger, guilt, sadness and depression, loneliness, hopelessness, and numbness.[28] These emotional reactions can be complicated when grief is disenfranchised. Although each of the situations described is in its own way unique, the literature uniformly reports how each of these disenfranchising circumstances can intensify feelings of anger, guilt, or powerlessness.[29]

Second, both ambivalent relationships and concurrent crises have been identified in the literature as conditions that complicate grief.[30] These conditions can often exist in many types of disenfranchised grief. For example, studies have indicated the ambivalence that can exist in cases of abortion,[31] among ex-spouses,[32] significant others in nontraditional roles,[33] and among families of Alzheimer's disease victims.[34] Similarly, the literature documents the many kinds of concurrent crises that can trouble the disenfranchised griever. For example, in cases of cohabiting couples, either heterosexual or homosexual, studies have often found that survivors experience legal and financial problems regarding inheritance, ownership, credit, or leases.[35] Likewise, the death of a parent may leave a mentally disabled person not only bereaved but also bereft of a viable support system.[36]

Although grief is complicated, many of the factors that facilitate mourning are not present. The bereaved may be excluded from an active role in caring for the dying. Funeral rituals, normally helpful in resolving grief, may not help here. In some cases the bereaved may be excluded from attendance. In other cases they may have no role in planning those rituals or in deciding whether even to have them. Or in cases of divorce, separation, or psychosocial death, rituals may be lacking altogether.

In addition, the very nature of the disenfranchised grief precludes social support. Often there is no recognized role in which mourners can assert the right to mourn and thus receive such support. Grief may have to remain private. Though they may have experienced an intense loss, they may not be given time off from work, have the opportunity to verbalize the loss, or receive the expressions of sympathy and support characteristic in a death. Even traditional sources of solace, such as religion, are unavailable to those whose relationships (for example, extramarital, cohabiting, homosexual, divorced) or acts (such as abortion) are condemned within that tradition.

Naturally, there are many variables that will affect both the intensity of the reaction and the availability of support. All the variables—interpersonal, psychological, social, physiological—that normally influence grief will have an impact here as well. And while there are problems common to cases of disenfranchised grief, each relationship has to be individually considered in light of the unique combinations of factors that may facilitate or impair grief resolution.

Implications

Despite the shortage of research on and attention given to the issue of disenfranchised grief, it remains a significant issue. Millions of Americans are involved in losses in which grief is effectively disenfranchised. For example, there are more than 1 million couples presently cohabiting.[37] There are estimates that 3 percent of males and 2–3 percent of females are exclusively homosexual, with similar percentages having mixed homosexual and heterosexual encounters.[38] There are about a million abortions a year; even though many of the women involved may not experience grief reactions, some are clearly "at risk."

Disenfranchised grief is also a growing issue. There are higher percentages of divorced people in the cohorts now aging. The AIDS crisis means that more homosexuals will experience losses in significant relationships. Even as the disease spreads within the population of intravenous drug users, it is likely to create a new class of both potential victims and disenfranchised grievers among the victims' informal liaisons and nontraditional relationships.[39] And as Americans continue to live longer, more will suffer from severe forms of chronic brain dysfunctions.[40] As the developmentally disabled live longer, they too will experience the grief of parental and sibling loss. In short, the proportion of disenfranchised grievers in the general population will rise rapidly in the future.

It is likely that bereavement counselors will have increased exposure to cases of disenfranchised grief. In fact, the very nature of disenfranchised grief and the unavailability of informal support make it likely that those who experience such losses will seek formal supports. Thus there is a pressing need for research that will describe the particular and unique reactions of each of the different types of losses; compare reactions and problems associated with these losses; describe the important variables affecting disenfranchised grief reactions;[41] assess possible interventions; and discover the atypical grief reactions, such as masked or delayed grief, that might be manifested in such cases. Also needed is education sensitizing students to the many kinds of relationships and subsequent losses that people can experience and affirming that where there is loss there is grief.

THE INCREASING PREVALENCE OF COMPLICATED MOURNING: THE ONSLAUGHT IS JUST BEGINNING*

Therese A. Rando, Ph.D.

Warwick, Rhode Island

ABSTRACT

In this article, complicated mourning is operationalized in relation to the six "R" processes of mourning and its seven high-risk factors are identified. The main thesis is that the prevalence of complicated mourning is increasing today due to a number of contemporary sociocultural and technological trends which have influenced 1) today's types of death; 2) the characteristics of personal relationships severed by today's deaths; and 3) the personality and resources of today's mourner. Additionally, specific problems in both the mental health profession and the field of thanatology further escalate complicated mourning by preventing or interfering with requisite treatment. Thus, complicated mourning is on the rise at the precise time when caregivers are unprepared and limited in their abilities to respond. New treatment policies and models are mandated as a consequence.

In the 1990s, the mental health profession (a term herein broadly used to encompass any caregiver whose work places him/her in the position of ministering to the mental health needs of another) and the thanatological community are at a crucial crossroads. Current sociocultural and technological trends in American society are directly increasing the prevalence of complicated mourning at the precise point in time at which the mental health profession is particularly both unprepared and limited in its abilities to respond to the needs created. Thanatology has a pivotal role to play in identifying this crisis, delineating the problems to be addressed, and advocating for the development of new policies, models, approaches, and treatments appropriate to today's grim realities. Failure of either profession to recognize these realities is bound to result not only in inadequate care for those who require it, but to place our society at greater risk for the serious sequelae known to emanate from untreated complicated mourning [1].

After a brief review of complicated mourning, this article will: 1) identify the high-risk factors for complicated mourning; 2) delineate the sociocultural and technological trends exacerbating these factors, which in turn increase the prevalence of complicated mourning; 3) indicate the problems inherent in the mental health profession that interfere with proper response to complicated mourning and to its escalation; and 4) point out the pitfalls for addressing complicated mourning that reside in the field of thanatology today. The focus of this article is restricted to raising awareness of the problem and discussing its determinants.

COMPLICATED MOURNING

Historically, there have been three main difficulties in defining complicated mourning. The first stems from the imprecise and inconsistent terminology employed. The very same grief and mourning phenomena have been described at various times and by various authors as "pathological," "neurotic," "maladaptive," "unresolved," "abnormal," "dysfunctional," or "deviant," just to name some of the designations used. Communication has been hampered by a lack of semantic agreement and consensual validation. This author's preference is for the term "complicated mourning." Such a term suggests that mourning is a series of processes which in some way has become complicated, with the implication being that what has become complicated can be uncomplicated. It avoids the pejorative tone of many of the other terms. Additionally, there is no insinuation of pathology in the mourner. Heretofore, complica-

---

*This article is adapted from a keynote address of the same name presented at the 13th Annual Conference of the Association for Death Education and Counseling, Duluth, Minnesota, April 26–28, 1991 and from the author's book, *Treatment of Complicated Mourning*, Research press, Champaign, Illinois, 1993.

tions typically have been construed to arise from the deficits of the person experiencing the bereavement. The term "complicated" avoids the assumption that the complications necessarily stem from the mourner him or herself. This is quite crucial because it is now well-documented that there are some circumstances of death and some postdeath variables that in and of themselves complicate mourning regardless of the premorbid psychological health of the mourner.

A second difficulty stems from the lack of objective criteria for what constitutes complicated mourning. Unlike the analogous medical situation in which the determination of pathology is more readily discerned and defined (e.g., the diagnosis of a broken bone usually can be easily agreed upon by several physicians following viewing of an x-ray), the phenomena in mourning tend not to be so concrete or unarguable. For instance, a woman hearing her deceased husband's voice in some circumstances is quite appropriate, whereas in others it reflects gross pathology.

The third and related difficulty is found because mourning is so highly idiosyncratic. It is determined by a constellation of thirty-three sets of factors circumscribing the loss and its circumstances, the mourner, and the social support received. No determination of abnormality technically ever can be made without taking into consideration the sets of factors known to influence any response to loss [2]. What may be an appropriate response in one circumstance for an individual mourner may be a highly pathological response for a different mourner in other circumstances. For this reason, it appears most helpful to look at complications in the mourning processes themselves rather than at particular symptomatology.

With this as a premise, complicated mourning can be said to be present when, taking into consideration the amount of time since the death, there is a compromise, distortion, or failure of one or more of the six "R" processes of mourning [1]. The six "R" processes of mourning necessary for healthy accommodation of any loss are:

1. Recognize the loss
   - Acknowledge the death
   - Understand the death

2. React to the separation
   - Experience the pain
   - Feel, identify, accept, and give some form of expression to all the psychological reactions to the loss
   - Identify and mourn secondary losses

3. Recollect and reexperience the deceased and the relationship
   - Review and remember realistically
   - Revive and reexperience the feelings

4. Relinquish the old attachments to the deceased and the old assumptive world

5. Readjust to move adaptively into the new world without forgetting the old
   - Revise the old assumptive world
   - Develop a new relationship with the deceased

- Adopt new ways of being in the world
- Form a new identity

6. Reinvest

In all forms of complicated mourning, there are attempts to do two things: 1) to deny, repress, or avoid aspects of the loss, its pain, and the full realization of its implications for the mourner; and 2) to hold onto, and avoid relinquishing, the lost loved one. These attempts, or some variation thereof, are what cause the complications in the "R" processes of mourning.

Complicated mourning may take any one or combination of four forms: symptoms, syndromes, mental or physical disorder, or death [1].

Complicated mourning symptoms refer to any psychological, behavioral, social, or physical symptom—alone or in combination—which in context reveals some dimension of compromise, distortion, or failure of one or more of the six "R" processes of mourning. They are of insufficient number, intensity, and duration, or of different type, than are required to meet the criteria for any of the other three forms of complicated mourning discussed below.

There are seven *complicated mourning syndromes* into which a constellation of complicated mourning symptoms may coalesce. They may occur independently or concurrently with one another. Only if the symptoms comprising them meet the criteria for the specific syndrome is there said to be a complicated mourning syndrome present. If only some of the symptoms are present, or there is a combination of symptoms from several of the syndromes but they fail to meet the criteria for a particular complicated mourning syndrome, then they are considered complicated mourning symptoms. The reader should be advised that a syndrome is not necessarily more pathological than a group of symptoms which clusters together but does not fit the description of one of the complicated mourning syndromes. Sometimes just a few complicated mourning symptoms—depending upon which they are—can be far more serious than the complicated mourning syndromes. With the exception of death, severity is not determined by the form of complicated mourning.

The seven syndromes of complicated mourning include three syndromes with problems in expression (i.e., absent mourning, delayed mourning, and inhibited mourning); three syndromes with skewed aspects (i.e., distorted mourning of the extremely angry or guilty types, conflicted mourning, and unanticipated mourning); and the syndrome with a problem in ending (i.e., chronic mourning).

The third form that complicated mourning may take is of a *diagnosable mental or physical disorder.* This would include any DSM-III-R [3] diagnosis of a mental disorder or any recognized physical disorder that results from or is associated with a compromise, distortion, or failure of one or more of the six "R" processes of mourning. *Death* is the fourth form which complicated mourning may take. The death may be consciously chosen (i.e., suicide) or it may stem from the immediate results of a complicated mourning reaction (e.g., an automobile crash resulting from the complicated mourning symptom of driving at excessive speed) or the long-term results of a complicated mourning reaction (e.g., cirrhosis of the liver secondary to mourning-related alcoholism). The latter two types of death may or may not be subintentioned on the part of the mourner.

GENERIC HIGH-RISK FACTORS FOR COMPLICATED MOURNING

Clinical and empirical evidence reveals that there are seven generic high-risk factors which can predispose any individual to have complications in mourning [1]. These can be divided into two categories: factors associated with the specific death and factors associated with antecedent and subsequent variables.

Factors associated with the death which are known especially to complicate mourning include: 1) a sudden and unanticipated death, especially when it is traumatic, violent, mutilating, or random; 2) death from an overly-lengthy illness; 3) loss of a child; and 4) the mourner's perception of preventability. Antecedent and subsequent variables that tend to complicate mourning include: 1) a premorbid relationship with the deceased which has been markedly angry or ambivalent or markedly dependent; 2) the mourner's prior or concurrent mental health problems and/or unaccommodated losses and stresses; and 3) the mourner's perceived lack of social support.

To the extent that any bereaved individual is characterized by one or more of these factors, that individual can be said to be at risk for the development of complications in one or more of the six "R" processes of mourning, and hence at risk for complicated mourning.

SOCIOCULTURAL AND TECHNOLOGICAL TRENDS EXACERBATING THE HIGH-RISK FACTORS AND INCREASING THE PREVALENCE OF COMPLICATED MOURNING

Social change, medical advances, and shifting political realities have spawned the recent trends that have complicated healthy grief and mourning.

Social change, occurring at an increasingly rapid rate, encompasses such processes as urbanization; industrialization; increasing technicalization; secularization and deritualization (particularly the trend to omit funeral or memorial services and not to view the body); greater social mobility; social reorganization (specifically a decline in—if not a breakdown of—the nuclear family, increases in single parent and blended families, and the relative exclusion of the aged and dying); rising societal, interpersonal, and institutional violence (physical, sexual, and psychological); and unemployment, poverty, and economic problems. Consequences include social alienation; senses of personal helplessness and hopelessness; parental absence and neglect of children; larger societal discrepancies between the "haves" and the "have nots"; and epidemic drug and alcohol abuse, physical and sexual abuse of children and those without power (e.g., women and the elderly), and availability of guns. All of these sequelae have tended to increase violence even

more, to sever or severely damage the links between children and adults, and to expose individuals to more traumatic and unnatural deaths.

Medical advances have culminated in lengthier chronic illnesses, and increased age spans, altered mortality rates, and intensified bioethical dilemmas. These trends, plus those involving social change, accompany contemporary political realities of increasing incidence of terrorism, assassination, political torture, and genocide, which get played out against the ever-present possibility of ecological disaster, nuclear holocaust, and megadeath to impact dramatically and undeniably on today's mourner [4–6].

VIOLENCE: A PARTICULARLY MALIGNANT TREND

Any commentary on present-day trends would be negligent if it did not elaborate somewhat upon the phenomenon of violence in today's society. Violence contributes significantly to the increasing prevalence of complicated mourning, and is associated with most of its generic high-risk factors. One crime index offense occurs every two seconds in the United States, with one violent crime occurring every nineteen seconds [7]. Violent crime has risen to the extent that in April 1991 Attorney General Richard Thornburgh issued the statement that "a citizen of this country is today more likely to be the victim of a violent crime than of an automobile accident" [8]. The U.S. Department of Justice estimates that five out of six of today's twelve-year-olds will become victims of violent crime during their lifetimes [9], with estimates for the lifetime chance of becoming a victim of homicide in the United States ranging from one out of 133 to one out of 153 depending upon the source of the statistics [10]. One category of homicide—murder by juvenile—is increasing so rapidly that it is now being termed "epidemic" by psychologist and attorney Charles Ewing [11], an authority on child perpetrators of homicide.

Other types of crime and victimization are on the rise in the United States. The National Victim Center Overview of Crime and Victimization in America [12] provides some of the horrifying statistics:

- Wife-beating results in more injuries that require medical treatment than rape, auto accidents, and muggings combined.
- More than one out of every 200 senior citizens is the victim of a violent crime each year, making a total of 155,000 elderly Americans who are attacked, robbed, assaulted, and murdered every year—435 each day.
- New York City has reported an eighty percent increase in hate-motivated crimes since 1986, with seventy percent of them perpetrated by those under age nineteen.
- One in three women will be sexually assaulted during her lifetime.
- Every forty-seven seconds a child is abused or neglected.

Certainly, society not only condones, but escalates, violence. Books, movies, music videos, and songs perpetuate the belief that violence is not merely acceptable, but exciting. Books focusing on real-life serial killers; escalating movie violence associated with anatomically precise and sexually explicit images; and music portraying hostility against women, murder, and necrophilia are routine. According to Thomas Radecki, Research Director for the National Coalition on Television Violence, by the age of 18 the average American child will have seen 200,000 violent acts on television, including 40,000 murders [13]. Children's programming now averages twenty-five violent acts per hour, which is up fifty percent from that in the early 1980s [14]. The recently popular children's movie, *Teenage Mutant Ninja Turtles*, had a total of 194 acts of violence primarily committed by the "heroes" of the film, which was the most violent film ever to be given a "PG" rating [15]. In the week of March 11, 1990, *America's Funniest Home Videos* became the highest-rated series on television. Some of the stories on that program that viewers found particularly amusing included a child getting hit in the face with a shovel, seven women falling off a bench, a man getting hit by a glider, and a child bicycling into a tree [15]. All of this provides serious concerns given the twenty-year research of Leonard Eron and L. Rowell Huesmann, who found that children who watch significant amounts of TV violence at the age of eight were consistently more likely to commit violent crimes or engage in spouse abuse at age thirty [13]. These researchers determined that heavy exposure to media violence is one of the major causes of aggressive behavior, crime, and violence in society.

Other forms of violence are increasing as well. Reports of abused and neglected children continue to rise. They reached 2.5 million in 1990, an increase of 30.7 percent since 1986, and 117 percent in the past decade [16]. One out of three girls, and one out of seven boys, are sexually abused by the time they reach eighteen [17]. In the United States, when random studies are conducted without the inclusion of high-risk groups, one in eight husbands has been physically aggressive with his wife in the preceding twelve months [18]. At least 2,000,000 women are severely and aggressively assaulted by their partners in any twelve-month period [18]. It is a myth that what has been termed "intimate violence" is confined to mentally disturbed individuals. While ten percent of offenders do sustain some form of psychopathology, ninety percent of offenders do not look any different than the "normal" individual [19].

SEQUELAE OF THE TRENDS PREDISPOSING TO COMPLICATED MOURNING

As a result of all the aforementioned sociocultural and technological trends, there have been changes in three main areas which have significantly increased the prevalence of complicated mourning:

1. the types of death occurring today
2. the characteristics of personal relationships that are severed by today's deaths
3. the personality and resources of today's mourner.

Each of these adversely impacts in one or more ways upon one or more of the high-risk factors for complicated mourning, thereby increasing its prevalence.

TYPES OF DEATH OCCURRING TODAY

Contemporary American society is witnessing the increase in three types of death known to be at high risk for complicated mourning: 1) sudden and unanticipated deaths, especially if they are traumatic (i.e., characterized not only by suddenness and lack of anticipation, but violence, mutilation, and destruction; preventability and/or randomness; multiple death; or the mourner's personal encounter with death [20]; 2) deaths that result from excessively lengthy chronic illnesses; and 3) deaths of children. Each of these deaths presents the survivors with issues known to compromise the "R" processes of mourning, hence each circumstance is a high-risk factor for complicated mourning.

Sudden and Unanticipated Traumatic Deaths

Sudden and unanticipated traumatic deaths stem primarily from four main causes: 1) accidents; 2) technological advances; 3) increasing rates of homicide and the escalating violence and pathology of perpetrators; and 4) higher suicide rates. Although mortality rates for children and youth in the United States have decreased since 1900, the large proportion of deaths from external causes—injuries, homicide, and suicide—distinguishes mortality at ages one to nineteen from that at other ages; with external causes of death accounting for about ten percent of the deaths of children and youth in 1900 and rising to 64 percent in 1985 [21].

Current trends reveal that "accidents"—a term covering most deaths from motor vehicle crashes, falls, poisoning, drowning, fire, suffocation, and firearms—are the leading cause of death among all persons aged one to thirty-seven and represent the fourth leading cause of death among persons of all ages [22]. On the average, there are eleven accidental deaths and approximately 1,030 disabling injuries every hour during the year [22]. Accidents are the single most common type of horrendous death for persons of any age, bringing deaths which are "premature, torturous, and without redeeming value" [23].

Technological advances simultaneously have both decreased the proportion of natural deaths that occur and increased the proportion of sudden and unanticipated traumatic deaths. For instance, substantial improvements in biomedical technology have culminated in higher survival rates from illnesses which previously would have been fatal. This leaves individuals alive longer to be susceptible to unnatural death. Additionally, the increase in unnatural death is due to greater current exposure to technology, machinery, motor vehicles, airplanes, chemicals, firearms, weapon systems, and so forth that put human beings at greater risk for unnatural death. For example, prior to the advent of the airplane, a crash of a horse and buggy could claim far fewer lives and be less mutilating to the bodies than the crash of a DC-10.

The third reason for the increase in sudden and unanticipated traumatic deaths stems from the increasing rates of homicide and the escalating violence and pathology of those who perpetrate these crimes upon others. The increase in actual homicide incidence; the rising percentage of serial killers; and the types of violence perpetrated before, during, and after the final homicidal act suggest that there are sicker individuals doing sicker things. More than ever before, homicide may be marked by cult or ritual killing, thrill killing, random killing, drive-by shootings, and accompanied by predeath torture and postdeath defilement. The increasing pathology of those who commit violent crimes may be seen as the result of the previously mentioned sociocultural trends, especially but not exclusively the individual's decreasing social connections and sense of power; fewer social prohibitions, and increasing societal violence. It reflects the increasing number of individuals with impaired psychological development, characterized often by an absent conscience, low frustration tolerance, poor impulse control, inability to delay gratification or modulate aggression, a sense of deprivation and entitlement, and notably poor attachment bonds and pathological patterns of relationships.

The fourth reason for the increase in sudden and unanticipated traumatic deaths follows from the higher suicide rates currently found in Western society. As above, these types of death appear to derive from all of the aforementioned trends contributing to complicated mourning in general.

The reader will note that most of the sudden and unanticipated traumatic deaths in this category also are preventable. Given that the perception of preventability is a high-risk factor predisposing to complicated mourning, to the extent that a mourner maintains this perception as an element in his or her mourning of the death that individual sustains a greater chance for experiencing complications in the process.

Long-Term Chronic Illness Death

This type of death is increasing in frequency because of biomedical and technological advances that can combat disease and forestall cessation of life. Consequently, today's illnesses are longer in duration than ever before. However, it has been well-documented that there are significant problems for survivors when a loved one's terminal illness persists for too long [24]. These illnesses often present loved ones with inherent difficulties that eventually complicate their postdeath bereavement and expose them to situations and dilemmas previously unheard of when patients died sooner and/or without becoming the focus for bioethical debates around the use of machinery and the prolongation of life without quality. With the increase in the Human Immunodeficiency Virus (HIV) and Acquired Immunodeficiency Syndrome (AIDS), significant multidimensional stresses arise which engender those known to complicate mourning in anyone (e.g., anger, ambivalence, guilt, stigmatization, social disenfranchisement, problems obtaining required health care, and so forth). The fact that an individual may be positive for the HIV virus for an exceptionally long period of time prior to developing the often long-term, multiproblemic, and idiosyncratic course of their particular version of AIDS, with all of its vicissitudes, gives new meaning these days to the stresses of long-term chronic illness.

Parental Loss of a Child

In earlier years, by the time an adult child died, his or her parents would have been long deceased. Today, with increases in lifespan and advances in medical technology, parents are permitted to survive long enough to witness the deaths of the adult children they used to predecease. Clinically and empirically, it is well-known that significant problematic issues are associated with the parental loss of a child—issues which when compared to those generated by other losses appear to make this loss the most difficult with which to cope [25]. These problematic issues and complicated mourning are now visited upon older parents who remain alive to experience the death of their adult child. There is even some suggestion that additional stresses are added to the normal burdens of parental bereavement when the child is an adult in his or her own right [26]. It is a uniquely contemporary trend, therefore, that associated with all of today's deaths are a greater percentage of parents who, because of medical advancements, are alive to be placed in the high-risk situation for complicated mourning upon the death of their adult child. This is a population that can be expected to increase, and consequently swell the numbers of complicated mourners as well.

CHARACTERISTICS OF PERSONAL RELATIONSHIPS SEVERED BY TODAY'S DEATHS

As a consequence of societal trends, there has been an increase in conflicted and dependent relationships in our society. Both types are high-risk factors when they characterize the mourner's premorbid relationship with the deceased [1]. With more of these types of relationships than ever before, there is a relative increase in the prevalence of complicated mourning, which is predisposed to develop after the death of one with whom the mourner has had this type of bond.

In 1957, Edmond Volkart offered a classic discussion of why death in the American family tends to cause greater psychological impact than in other cultures, specifically causing the family to be uniquely vulnerable to bereavement [6]. The reasons he delineated are even more salient today, and are part of the trends already cited above. Among other trends, he noted that the limited range of interaction in the American family fosters unusually intense emotional involvement as compared to other societies, and that there is an exclusivity of relationships in the American family. Both trends breed overidentification and overdependence among family members, which in turn engender ambivalence, repressed hostility, and guilt that create greater potential for complications after the death. Adding fuel to this fire is the societal expectation that grief expression concentrates on feelings and expression of loss. There is a failure both to recognize and to provide channels for hostility, guilt, and ambivalence.

Problematic relationships are on the rise in our society for other reasons as well. Quite importantly, there is an overall increase in sexual and physical abuse of children, as well as other adults. Research repeatedly documents the malignant intrapsychic and interpersonal sequelae of abuse and victimization [27, 28]. This leaves the victim susceptible to complications in mourning not only because of the myriad symptomatology and biopsychosocial issues they caused, but typically with significant amounts of the anger, ambivalence, and/or dependence known to complicate any individual's mourning. In addition, the victimization may interfere with the mourner permitting him or herself to mourn the death of the perpetrator—an often necessary task that many victims resist because of inaccurate beliefs about mourning in general and/or misconstruals of what their specifically mourning the perpetrator's death may mean [1]. This only further victimizes the person through the consequences of incomplete mourning.

These forms of victimization are not the only experiences which give rise to the conflicted and dependent relationships identified as predisposing to complicated mourning. Individuals raised in families with one or more alcoholic parents or a parent who is an adult child of an alcoholic (ACOA), or with one or more parents who are psychologically impaired, rigid in beliefs, compulsive in behaviors, codependent, absent, neglectful, or chronically ill are vulnerable too. As sociocultural trends escalate these scenarios, relationships characterized by anger, ambivalence, and dependency will become prevalent, and complicated mourning will, in turn, become more frequent.

THE PERSONALITY AND RESOURCES OF TODAY'S MOURNER

Current trends suggest that the personality and resources of today's mourner leave that individual compromised in mourning for three reasons. First, given the trends previously discussed, the personalities and mental health of today's mourners are often more impaired. These impaired persons—who themselves frequently sustain poor attachment bonds with their own parents because of these trends—typically effect intergenerational transmission of these deficits via the inadequate parenting provided to their own children and the unhealthy experiences those children undergo. Clinically, one sees more often these days impaired superego development, lower level personality organization, narcissistic behavior, character disorder, and poor impulse control. Given that one's personality and previous and current states of mental health are critical factors influencing any mourner's ability to address mourning successfully, a trend towards relatively more impairment in this area has implications for greater numbers of people being added to the rolls of complicated mourners.

Another liability for a mourner is the existence of unaccommodated prior or concurrent losses or stresses. In this regard, a second reason for the increased prevalence of complicated mourning comes from the presence of more loss and stress in the life of today's mourner as compared to times in the past. To the extent that contemporary sociocultural trends bring relatively more losses and stresses for a person, both prior to a given death (e.g., parents' divorce) and concomitant with it (e.g., unemployment), today's mourner is relatively more disadvantaged given his or her increased exposure to these high-risk factors.

The third reason for increased complications in mourning arises from the compromise of the mourner's resources. Disenfranchised mourning [29] is on the rise, and the consequent perceived lack of social support it stimulates is a high-risk factor for complicated mourning. It is quite evident that conditions in contemporary American society promote all three of the main reasons for social disenfranchisement during mourning, i.e., invalidation of the loss, the lost relationship, or the mourner [29]. Examples of unrecognized losses that are increasing in today's society include abortions, adoptions, the deaths of pets, and the inherent losses of those with Alzheimer's disease. Cases of the second type of disenfranchised loss that are on the increase include relationships that are not based on kin ties, or are not socially sanctioned (e.g., gay or lesbian relationships, extramarital affairs), or those that existed primarily in the past (e.g., former spouses or in-laws). Increasingly prevalent situations where the mourner is unrecognized can be found when that mourner is elderly, mentally handicapped, or a child. The more society creates, maintains, or permits individuals to be disenfranchised in their mourning, the more those individuals are at risk for complicated mourning given that disenfranchisement is so intimately linked with the high-risk factor of the mourner's perception of lack of social support.

PROBLEMS INHERENT IN THE MENTAL HEALTH PROFESSION WHICH INTERFERE WITH PROPER RESPONSE TO COMPLICATED MOURNING AND TO ITS ESCALATION

There are three serious problems inherent in mental health today that interfere with the profession's response to complicated mourning and its escalation. Each one contributes to increasing the prevalence of complicated mourning either by facilitating misdiagnosis and/or hampering requisite treatment. The three problems are: 1) lack of an appropriate diagnostic category in the DSM-III-R; 2) insufficient knowledge about grief, mourning, and bereavement in general; and 3) decreased funds for and increased restrictions upon contemporary mental health services.

In the DSM-III-R, there is the lack of a diagnostic category for anything but the most basic uncomplicated grief, with the criteria even for this being significantly unrealistic for duration and symptomatology in light of today's data on uncomplicated grief and mourning. If they want to treat a mourning individual, mental health clinicians are often forced to utilize other diagnoses, many of which have clinical implications that are unacceptable. Other diagnoses that clinicians employ to justify treatment and to incorporate more fully the symptomatology of the bereaved individual frequently include one of the depressive, anxiety, or adjustment disorders; brief reactive psychosis; or one of the V code diagnoses.

The second area of problems in the mental health profession is the shocking insufficiency of knowledge about grief and bereavement in general. Mental health professionals tend, as does the general public, to have inappropriate expectations and unrealistic attitudes about grief and mourning, and to believe in and promote the myths and stereotypes known to pervade society at large. These not only do not help, but actually harm bereaved individuals given that they are used to (a) set the standards against which the bereaved individual is evaluated, (b) determine the assistance and support provided and/or judged to be needed, and (c) support unwarranted diagnoses of failure and pathology [30]. Yet, the problem is not all in *mis*information. Too many clinicians actually do not even know that they lack the requisite information they must possess if they want to treat a bereaved person successfully. Without a doubt, the majority of clinicians know an insufficient amount about uncomplicated grief and mourning; and of those who do know an adequate amount, only a fraction of them know enough about complicated mourning. Clinician lack of information and misinformation is the major cause of iatrogenesis in the treatment of grief and mourning.

An overall decrease in funds permitted and an increase in third-party payer insurance restrictions mark contemporary mental health services and constitute the third problem in the field adding to the prevalence of complicated mourning. These changes occur at a time when it not only is becoming more clearly documented that uncomplicated grief and mourning is more associated with psychiatric distress than previously recognized [31] and that it persists for longer duration [32], but precisely when the incidence of complicated mourning is increasing and demanding more extensive treatment for higher proportions of the bereaved. Consequently, at the exact point in time that the mental health community will have more bereaved individuals with greater complicated mourning requiring treatment for longer periods of time, mental health services will be increasingly subjected to limitations, preapprovals, third-party reviews by persons ignorant of the area, short-term models, and forced usage of inappropriate diagnostic classification. This scenario demands that the mental health professional working with the bereaved find new policies models, approaches, and treatments which are appropriate to these serious realities. Failing to do so, the future is frightening as the current system simply is not equipped to respond to the coming onslaught of complicated mourners.

THE PITFALLS FOR ADDRESSING COMPLICATED MOURNING RESIDING IN THE FIELD OF THANATOLOGY TODAY

It is unfortunate, but true: Thanatologists are contributing to the rising prevalence of complicated mourning as are contemporary sociocultural and technological trends and the mental health profession. While it is not in the purview of this article to discuss at length the myriad problems inherent in our own field of thanatology that contribute to complicated mourning, it must be noted:

- A significant amount of caregivers lack adequate clinical information about uncomplicated grief and mourning, e.g., the "normal" psychiatric complications of uncomplicated grief and mourning.
- Many thanatologists, in their effort to promote the naturalness of grief and mourning and to depathologize the way they construe it to have been medicalized, maintain an insufficient understanding of complicated grief and mourning.

- There is nonexistent, or at the very least woefully insufficient, assessment conducted by caregivers who assume that the grief and mourning they observe must be related exclusively to the particular death closest in time and who do not place the individual's responses within the context of his or her entire life prior to evaluating them.
- The phenomenon of "throwing the baby out with the bathwater" has occurred regarding medication in bereavement. Out of a concern that a mourner not be inappropriately medicated as had been done so often in the past, caregivers today often fail to send mourners for medication evaluations that are desperately needed, e.g., antianxiety medication following traumatic deaths.
- The research in the field has not been sufficiently longitudinal and has overfocused on certain populations (e.g., widows), leaving findings that are not generalizable over time for many types of mourners, especially complicated mourners.
- Caregivers do not always recognize that any work as a grief or mourning counselor or therapist must overlay a basic foundation of training in mental health intervention in general. While education in thanatology, good intentions, and/or previous experience with loss may be appropriate credentials for the individual facilitating uncomplicated grief and mourning (e.g., a facilitator of a mutual help group for the bereaved), this is not sufficient for that person offering counseling or therapy.
- Given that thanatology itself is a "specialty area," thanatologists often fail to recognize that the field encompasses a number of "subspecialty areas," each of which has its own data base and treatment requirements, i.e., all mourners are not alike and caregivers must recognize and respond to the differences inherent in different loss situations (e.g., loss of a child versus loss of a spouse or sudden and unanticipated death versus an expected chronic illness death).
- Clinicians working with the dying and the bereaved are subject to countertransference phenomena, stress reactions, codependency, "vicarious traumatization" [33], and burnout.

This constitutes a brief, and by no means exhaustive, listing of the types of pitfalls into which a thanatologist may fall. Each "fall" has the potential for compromising the mourning of the bereaved individual and in that regard has the potential for increasing the prevalence of complicated mourning today.

CONCLUSION

This article has discussed the causes and forms of complicated mourning, and has delineated the seven high-risk factors known to predispose to it. The purpose has been to illustrate how current sociocultural and technological trends are exacerbating these factors, thereby significantly increasing the prevalence of complicated mourning today. Problems both in the mental health profession and in the field of thanatology further contribute by preventing or interfering with requisite intervention. It is imperative that these grim realities be recognized in order that appropriate policies, models, approaches, and treatments be developed to respond to the individual and societal needs created by complicated mourning and its sequelae.

REFERENCES

1. T. Rando, *Treatment of Complicated Mourning,* Research Press, Champaign, Illinois, 1993.

2. T. Rando, *Grief, Dying, and Death: Clinical Interventions for Caregivers,* Research Press, Champaign, Illinois, 1984.

3. American Psychiatric Association, *Diagnostic and Statistical Manual of Mental Disorders,* (3rd ed. rev.), Washington, D.C., 1987.

4. H. Feifel, The Meaning of Death in American Society: Implications for Education, in *Death Education: Preparation for Living,* B. Green and D. Irish (eds.), Schenkman, Cambridge, Massachusetts, 1971.

5. R. Lifton, *Death in Life: Survivors of Hiroshima,* Random House, New York, 1968.

6. E. Volkart (with collaboration of S. Michael), Bereavement and Mental Health, in *Explorations in Social Psychiatry,* A. Leighton, J. Clausen, and R. Wilson (eds.), Basic Books, New York, 1957.

7. Federal Bureau of Investigation, U.S. Department of Justice, *Uniform Crime Reports for the United States,* U.S. Government Printing Office, Washington, D.C., 1990.

8. Violent Crimes up 10%, *Providence Journal,* pp. A1 and A6, April 29, 1991.

9. National Victim Center, *America Speaks Out: Citizens' Attitudes about Victims' Rights and Violence,* (Executive Summary), Fort Worth, Texas, 1991.

10. Bureau of Justice Statistics Special Report, *The Risk of Violent Crime,* (NCJ-97119), U.S. Department of Justice, Washington, D.C., May 1985.

11. Killing by Kids "Epidemic" Forecast, *APA Monitor,* pp. 1 and 31, April, 1991.

12. National Victim Center, *National Victim Center Overview of Crime and Victimization in America,* Fort Worth, Texas, 1991.

13. Violence in Our Culture, *Newsweek,* pp. 46–52, April 1, 1991.

14. J. Patterson and P. Kim, *The Day America Told the Truth,* Prentice Hall Press, New York, 1991.

15. National Victim Center, *Crime, Safety and You!, 1*:3, 1990.

16. Children's Defense Fund Memo on the Family Preservation Act, Washington, D.C., July 2, 1991.

17. E. Bass and L. Davis, *The Courage to Heal: A Guide for Women Survivors of Child Sexual Abuse,* Harper and Row Publishers, New York, 1988.

18. A. Brown, *"Women's Roles" and Responses to Violence by Intimates: Hard Choices for Women Living in a Violent Society,* paper presented at the conference on "Trauma and Victimization: Understanding and Healing Survivors" sponsored by the University of Connecticut Center for Professional Development, Vernon, Connecticut, September 27–28, 1991.

19. R. Gelles, *The Roots, Context, and Causes of Family Violence,* paper presented at the conference on "Trauma and Victimization: Understanding and Healing Survivors" sponsored by the University of Connecticut Center for Professional Development, Vernon, Connecticut, September 27–28, 1991.

20. T. Rando, Complications in Mourning Traumatic Death, in *Death, Dying and Bereavement,* I. Corless, B. Germino, and M. Pittman-Lindeman (eds.), Jones and Bartlett Publishers, Inc., Boston, (in press).

21. L. Fingerhut and J. Kleinman, Mortality Among Children and Youth, *American Journal of Public Health, 79,* pp. 899–901, 1989.

22. National Safety Council, *Accident Facts, 1991 Edition,* Chicago, 1991.

23. M. Dixon and H. Clearwater, Accidents, in *Horrendous Death, Health, and Well-Being,* D. Leviton (ed.), Hemisphere Publishing Corporation, New York, 1991.

24. T. Rando (ed.) *Loss and Anticipatory Grief,* Lexington Books, Lexington, Massachusetts, 1986.

25. T. Rando (ed.), *Parental Loss of a Child,* Research Press, Champaign, Illinois, 1986.

26. T. Rando, Death of an Adult Child, in *Parental Loss of a Child,* T. Rando, (ed.), Research Press, Champaign, Illinois, 1986.

27. C. Courtois, *Healing the Incest Wound: Adult Survivors in Therapy,* Norton, New York, 1988.

28. F. Ochberg (ed.), *Post-Traumatic Therapy and Victims of Violence,* Brunner/Mazel, New York, 1988.

29. K. Doka (ed.), *Disenfranchised Grief: Recognizing Hidden Sorrow,* Lexington Books, Lexington, Massachusetts, 1989.

30. T. Rando, *Grieving: How To Go On Living When Someone You Love Dies,* Lexington Books, Lexington, Massachusetts, 1988.

31. S. Jacobs and K. Kim, Psychiatric Complications of Bereavement, *Psychiatric Annals, 20,* pp. 314–317, 1990.

32. S. Zisook and S. Shuchter, Time Course of Spousal Bereavement, *General Hospital Psychiatry, 7,* pp. 95–100, 1985.

33. I. McCann and L. Pearlman, Vicarious Traumatization: A Framework for Understanding the Psychological Effects of Working with Victims, *Journal of Traumatic Stress, 3,* pp. 131–149, 1990.

The Spiritual Crisis
of Bereavement

Kenneth J. Doka

INTRODUCTION

Loss can be exceedingly painful. Both clinicians and novelists have explored the extraordinary pain that bereavement can bring. They have described in vivid detail the psychological trauma, the social loss, and the existential ache that can accompany significant loss.

Faith, with its rituals and beliefs, can be a powerful elixir at times of loss. Its ritual can provide structure and succor. Its beliefs may offer comfort and conciliation.

Yet like many powerful tools, faith can have both constructive and destructive aspects. It may promise reunion and resurrection, yet also haunt the bereaved with fears of retribution and damnation. To some it may offer forgiveness, while in others it exacerbates guilt. Its rituals may comfort some and trouble others.

But faith, whether in a theistic religious system or a philosophical system is likely to be part of the bereavement process. Just as dying has a spiritual dimension, so does death and bereavement. Questions about the value of the deceased's life, the meaningfulness of the survivor's existence in the face of loss, and the reason for death are common concerns in times of loss and have an inherently spiritual character.

This chapter seeks to explore the ways that beliefs and the rituals that accompany them can both facilitate and complicate bereavement. And it offers suggestions to clinicians on ways that they may assist clients in effectively utilizing their belief systems in resolving grief.

RITUAL AND LOSS

Rituals may be defined as "prescribed symbolic acts that must be performed in a certain way and in a certain order, and may or may not be accompanied by verbal formulas" [1, p. 8]. Often rituals are rooted in a belief system. This is particularly true of rituals that mark significant life events such as birth, puberty, marriage and death. Here historically religious rituals are the commonly accepted "rite of passage" even to those who only nominally adhere to the underlying religious beliefs. Even when those religious beliefs are decisively rejected, persons may still adhere to the rituals or seek alternate rituals more compatible to their own belief system. For example, the British Humanist Society conducts funerals for members who have rejected any religious tradition. For, in any case, there seems a need to mark the transition from life.

Rituals, then, can be a powerful tool for facilitating bereavement. Clinicians and theorists such as Irion, Rando, and Hart have all emphasized the psychological, social, and spiritual benefits of the funeral ritual [1–4]. The funeral can provide an opportunity to reintegrate and reaffirm the group, allow the expression and expiation of emotion, affirm the value of the deceased's life, stimulate remembrance, provide support and structure, offer hope and comfort, and perhaps even teleologically justify loss. This value has also been supported by research that has emphasized the role of the funeral in facilitating grief adjustment [5–14].

Yet there is also evidence that funeral rituals may have dysfunctional elements as well. Anecdotal and newspaper accounts have described funeral rituals that would seem highly troubling to survivors. For example, a priest in a New York City funeral for a young boy mauled by a caged bear suggested in his funeral homily that this early and awful death might be God's way of preserving this child's soul from the peril of future deviance. Similarly it has been reported that some clergy have used funerals of persons who have died from AIDS as a forum to condemn homosexuality or drug abuse. And research has indicated that those who experience complicated bereavement often report troubling funerals [15].

While such dysfunctional funerals may be rare, it does seem that the power of funeral rituals often lies untapped. The increasing bureaucratization of death has resulted in families delegating the planning of rituals to professionals. Secularism and pluralism have narrowed the collective utility of religious language and rituals. It is little wonder, then, that only the mourners closest to the bereaved benefit from the ritual [12].

Funeral rituals remain, then, a powerful tool for resolving grief, yet one that is sometimes destructively used and more often untapped. But there are ways that the power of ritual can be enhanced.

The first is to personalize and individualize such rituals. Rituals that are individualized are both preferred by bereaved and much more likely to facilitate grief adjustment. There are many ways that this can be accomplished. Funeral eulogies or homilies can review the life of the deceased. Prayers, readings, or music can be selected for their special relevance to the deceased. Opportunities can be developed that will allow mourners acts that will express remembrance or affection. For example, in a child's funeral, mourners were invited to place items in the child's casket that represented aspects of that child's life. Montages of photographs, displays of awards, 'creations,' or trophies can all be ways that a funeral ritual is personalized.

Along with personalization, participation has also been identified as a factor in rituals that facilitate grief adjustment [7]. Participation allows symbolic mastery, often so important in the chaos that loss brings. Participation in planning is encouraged when rituals are personalized. But other types of participation can also be encouraged. Participants in rituals may select to read, speak, play music or even sing. They may serve as casket bearers or in other roles. Even children can participate. One widow shared that the most significant part of the funeral to her was when she saw her great-grandson handing out flowers at graveside. This act gave her a comforting sense of continuity.

Participation and personalization not only can enhance funeral rituals but other death rituals as well. Post-funeral rituals have largely disappeared from many religious traditions. This is problematic for three reasons. First, they can be critical in educating both the bereaved and others that grief is a long, time consuming process. For example, in the Orthodox Jewish tradition there are a series of rituals, occurring over a year, that symbolically mark phases in mourning. . . . Underlying such rituals, is an expectation that healing is a slow process and that communal support is essential. In other traditions though, the absence of ritual beyond the funeral may suggest to the bereaved and their community that they should quietly resume their lives and resolve loss.

Secondly, post death rituals allow the bereaved continued public opportunity to express grief. The problem with funeral rituals is that they offer no opportunity beyond the initial time after the death to publicly express emotion, receive support, and act out therapeutically. Post-death rituals provide such opportunity.

Finally, the little research available suggests that post-death rituals can have a significant role in facilitating grief adjustments. Yoder, for example, emphasized the significance of the funeral meal [14]. Bolton and Camp [16] found that post-funeral rituals such as sending acknowledgments, disposing of personal effects, and visits to the grave site, had even more effect on grief adjustment than funeral rites.

Most religious traditions have opportunities to structure such rituals. Masses of remembrance, services on Memorial Day or All Saints Day can provide bereaved with special times to commemorate the deceased.

Clinicians should also utilize the religious traditions and rituals in designing therapeutic rituals. Therapeutic rituals are individually-designed interventions that seek to assist the bereaved in resolving grief. Often religious ceremonies and acts can be well utilized in designing such interventions. For example, an eight-year-old boy had considerable guilt over the fact that he never told a deceased uncle how much he loved him. The counselor decided that the child needed some kind of formal, ritualized, public way to express that emotion. Both the counselor and the child designed a ritual where the child saved money and dedicated flowers in church in loving memory of his uncle. After the service he laid the flowers on his uncle's grave, expressing his love.

In summary then, ritual can be therapeutic interventions in resolving grief. But that role can be enhanced when they are participatory, personalized, and allow bereaved continued opportunity to mark phases in their own grief journeys.

BELIEFS AND BEREAVEMENT

Spiritual and religious beliefs may also have significant influence on the course of bereavement. To Worden the process of bereavement involves the completion of four basic tasks [16]:

1. To accept the reality of death;
2. To experience the pain of grief;
3. To adjust to an environment in which the deceased is missing;
4. To emotionally relocate the deceased and move on with life.

Rituals, of course, can facilitate the completion of these tasks. Rituals often provide opportunity both to encounter the reality of death and express and expiate emotion.

But spiritual belief systems may also influence the resolution of these tasks. This is particularly true of the second and fourth tasks. "Experiencing the pain of grief" means that survivors need to express and work through varied emotions that accompany grief. Often these may have spiritual overtones and/or perhaps spiritual solutions.

For example, one common emotion that survivors often experience is guilt. And guilt often may have a religious or spiritual component. Miles and Demi speak of moral guilt as one manifestation of guilt experience in bereavement [17]. In moral guilt, survivors often feel morally responsible for the death. Some bereaved parents, for instance, may believe that they are morally responsible for their child's death, that their child's death is a result of their own inadequacies or sins.

While such spiritual themes may be a factor in varied emotional responses to loss, spiritual beliefs may also provide effective ways to resolve such emotions. Survivors, for example, may often feel guilty over aspects of their relationship with the deceased. Every religious or philosophical tradition deals with themes of forgiveness. Clinicians then can draw upon these beliefs and acts in assisting clients in working through their guilt.

There may also be cases in which the bereaved's religious and spiritual views may impede emotional expression. Here bereaved persons may feel constrained by their beliefs in expressing certain emotions or in expressing emotion at all. In the former case, the bereaved may feel that certain emotions are unacceptable. For example, in one case, a bereaved mother felt considerable relief over the loss of her child after a long terminal illness. She had a difficult time acknowledging such emotion since she felt guilty over the feeling and fearful that its expression might result in further divine retribution. In the latter case, the experience of grief itself may be denied. In such cases the bereaved may feel that the very expression of grief denies the validity of their faith. The bereaved may believe that any expression of sadness belies belief in the promises of their beliefs, such as the belief in an afterlife. In both situations, counselors must be careful not to challenge that faith but to assist the bereaved in exploring ways that they can express feelings within the context of their own religious tradition.

Religious and spiritual themes may also intertwine with the fourth task, "emotionally relocating the deceased and moving on with life." This task really involves a series of complex acts, for it entails both that the bereaved determine how they wish to remember the deceased as well as how they will resume their own lives. Much as the dying person has needs to die an appropriate death, find meaning in life, and find hope beyond the grave, the bereaved survivors have to struggle with these issues as well. They may need to interpret the death, validate the deceased's life and their role in that life, and maintain a perspective that allows them a sense of the continuance of the deceased, perhaps in an afterlife, alternate mode of existence, memory, or in the life of the community.

Here, too, spiritual beliefs and rituals may have a role in resolving this task. Often rituals, particularly post-death rituals, can provide excellent vehicles for both saying goodbye and sustaining memories. Belief systems may also provide interpretations of the deceased's presence. For example, beliefs about an afterlife can offer reassurance to survivors that the deceased is cared for, allowing survivors a sense of freedom to continue their own lives. There may be another side to this too. Fears related to an afterlife may inhibit a survivor's ability to withdraw emotional energy from the deceased. Here concerns about the ultimate fate of the deceased may inhibit the resolution of grief. Other belief systems may provide different, perhaps equally reassuring and problematic interpretations. For example, beliefs that a person may live on in memory may be very reassuring to some. Others, however, may view this as very fragile. Thus, although one father started a scholarship fund for his late son, he often expressed the fear that in the future his son would simply be "a meaningless name on some award."

Relocating the deceased may mean that survivors find ways to *creatively retain a relationship with the deceased.* It is neither unusual nor problematic that one way of resolving loss can be a form of creative retention. In creative retention, the bereaved decides, in some way or another, to keep the memory of the deceased alive, and to organize at least part of his or her life in such a way to retain that memory and relationship. This need not be unhealthy, provided it recognizes the reality of the loss, allows for continued individual growth, and does not inhibit the development of new relationships. Examples of creative retention may be found in bereaved parents who spend significant time in organizations such as Compassionate Friends. In these cases, these parents often dedicate themselves in assisting other newly bereaved parents resolve loss. Coretta King, who dedicated her life to preserving both the memory and ideals of her late husband, would be another example of creative retention. Often in this response, religious and spiritual beliefs may play a large role. For the very act of creative retention has a transcendental and sacrificial quality that the bereaved need both to explore and understand.

One may also speak of a fifth task in bereavement. This would be *to rebuild faith and philosophical systems that are challenged by loss.* Often significant losses bring on a crisis of faith. All one's beliefs about the nature and fairness of the universe, the existence of a higher power, or even the very nature of God, may be challenged by that loss. C. S. Lewis, in *A Grief Observed* captures this spiritual crisis well [18, pp. 4–5]:

> Meanwhile, where is God? . . . But go to Him when your help is desperate, when all other help is vain, and what do you find? A door slammed in your face. . . .
> Not that I am (I think) in much danger of ceasing to believe in God. The real danger is of coming to believe such dreadful things about him.

Thus, bereaved persons may simultaneously struggle with two losses—the loss of the deceased and the loss of their own beliefs. In resolving grief then, both will have to be addressed.

These struggles of faith can be problematic on a number of levels. Not only can they remove a potentially significant source of comfort, these struggles can also displace energy from the resolution of grief. And they may separate the bereaved from both rituals and community of faith that can possibly provide solace and support.

Counselors, in taking a history of a bereaved person, may wish to ascertain any changes in religious beliefs and behaviors since the illness and death, and explore any faith struggles, Works such as C. S. Lewis *A Grief Observed* [18] or Kushner's *When Bad Things Happen to Good People* [19] can be valued resources, as are empathic clergy.

CONCLUSION

It is clear that persons counseling the bereaved will need to be well aware of both the spiritual issues that arise in the bereavement process as well as rituals and beliefs that may influence the process. In taking histories of the bereaved, counselors should ask about client's religious and spiritual affiliations, beliefs, practices, and rituals. In addition to providing counselors with useful information that may later be explored, such questions also communicate to the bereaved the counselor's openness to discuss such concerns. Naturally, in every action, the counselor needs to communicate respect for those values and traditions.

In exploring a client's religious and spiritual system, counselors need to be aware that there is often a discrepancy between the theologies and practices of denominations and their members [20]. Perhaps even more important than the actual beliefs, or even religiosity of a given individual, is the certainty of their belief and the faith themes around which people organize beliefs. While the latter is unresearched, it is well worthwhile to explore the underlying themes of a client's belief system. For example, one client may emphasize themes of human imperfection and forgiveness while others organize beliefs around themes such as righteous behavior or judgment.

6. BEREAVEMENT

Throughout this exploration, counselors can assess with clients both the importance of their belief system and its role in the bereavement process; that is, in what ways it facilitates and in what ways it impedes grief. This latter question has to be handled respectfully and sensitively. For example, dysfunctional beliefs should not be belittled or dismissed; rather, clients should be encouraged to find alternate interpretations within their tradition. Supportive clergy, religiously-oriented books or other resources may be very helpful here. In one illustrative case, a woman was troubled that her brother's suicide damned him—a basic belief in her fundamentalist faith. Yet a sympathetic clergyman helped her recognize that even within her tradition there were opportunities for continued hope.

The client's religious resources, then, can be utilized to support the bereavement process. Beliefs may be drawn upon to facilitate grief resolution. Rituals may offer powerful, symbolic therapeutic interventions. Clergy may provide additional counsel. Congregations can offer assistance and community. The goal of counseling is first to empower clients to utilize their strengths and resources. In the intensely spiritual crisis of bereavement, neither counselors nor clients can ignore the strength of those spiritual resources.

REFERENCES

1. O. Hart, *Rituals in Psychotherapy: Transitions and Continuity,* Irvington Press, New York, 1978.
2. P. Irion, The Funeral and the Bereaved in *Acute Grief and the Funeral,* V. Pine et al. (eds.), Charles C. Thomas, Springfield, Illinois, 1976.
3. T. Rando, *Dying and Death: Clinical Interventions for Caregivers,* Research Press, Champagne, Illinois, 1984.
4. O. Hart, *Coping with Loss: The Therapeutic Use of Leave-Taking Rituals,* Irvington Press, New York, 1988.
5. C. Bolton and D. Comp, Funeral Rituals and the Facilitation of Grief Work, *Omega, 17,* pp. 343–348, 1987.
6. J. Cook, Children's Funerals and Their Effect on Familial Grief Adjustment, *National Reporter, 4*:10, 11, 1981.
7. K. J. Doka, Expectation of Death, Participation in Funeral Arrangements, and Grief Adjustment, *Omega, 15,* pp. 119–130, 1984.
8. R. Duvall, The Effect of the Presence or the Absence of a Physical Memorial Site and Other Variables Upon the Intensity of a Widow's Grief, *National Reporter, 6*:5, 6, 1983.
9. D. Ferrell, Implications of Cremation for Grief Adjustment, *National Reporter, 6*:7, 1983.
10. D. Huan, Perceptions of the Bereaved, Clergy and Funeral Directors Concerning Bereavement, *National Reporter, 3*:7, 8, 1980.
11. M. Lieberman and L. Borman, Widows View the Helpfulness of the Funeral Service, *National Reporter, 5*:2, 1982.
12. E. Swanson and T. Bennett, Degree of Closeness: Does It Affect the Bereaved's Attitudes Toward Selected Funeral Practices?, *Omega, 13,* pp. 43–50, 1982.
13. R. Winn, Perceptions of the Funeral Service and Post Bereavement Adjustment in Widowed Individuals, *National Reporter, 5*:1, 1982.
14. L. Yoder, The Funeral Meal: A Significant Funerary Ritual, *Journal of Religion and Health, 25,* pp. 149–160, 1986.
15. M. S. Johnson-Arbor, The Effect of Bereavement on the Elderly, *National Reporter, 4*:1, 1981.
16. W. Worden, *Grief Counseling and Grief Therapy* 2nd Edition, Springer, New York, 1991.
17. M. Miles and A. Demi, Toward the Development of a Theory of Bereavement Guilt: Sources of Guilt in Bereaved Parents, *Omega, 14,* pp. 299–314, 1984.
18. C. S. Lewis, *A Grief Observed,* Seabury Press, New York, 1961.
19. H. Kushner, *When Bad Things Happen to Good People,* Avon, New York, 1981.
20. M. Strommen, M. Brekka, R. Underwager, and A. Johnson, *A Study of Generations,* Aubsberg, Minneapolis, Minnesota, 1972.
21. R. Fulton and G. Geis, Death and Social Values, in *Death and Identity,* R. Fulton (ed.), Wiley, New York, 1976.

Adolescent Mourning: The Sudden Death of a Peer

Craig Podell CSW

ABSTRACT: This paper examines adolescents who are mourning the traumatic death of peers. A psychodynamic model is employed in offering crisis intervention to individuals and groups of grieving adolescents within a school setting. Case vignettes highlight the psychological impact of the death of a peer on an adolescent's functioning and ego development.

INTRODUCTION

With the rate of adolescent mortality through suicide, motor vehicle accidents, drug overdoses and other forms of violent death increasing in recent years, many adolescents are being painfully affected by the loss of peers. The grief of these bereaved adolescents has often gone unnoticed as the mourning of family members of the deceased youth is given primary focus and consideration. Moreover, the adolescent's grief is often times neither presented nor observed clearly as a mourning response; rather, it is seen as an expression of developmental conflicts or as acting out in response to family dynamics. The grieving youth remains in need of support and may experience the loss of his friend as traumatically as the loss of a sibling or parent. The study of grief and mourning among adolescents who lose a peer through death has received scarce attention. Those studies which have considered the impact of loss during adolescence have focused primarily on the effects of parental or sibling death upon the adolescent's functioning and development (Aubrey, 1977; Balk, 1983; Bowlby, 1980; Laufer, 1966; Miller, 1983). Gordon (1986), Miller (1983), and Raphael (1983) have given brief mention to the deep impact a friend's death has upon the adolescent's emotional life and development, but otherwise there is little in the psychiatric literature on the topic.

Relationships with peers allow the adolescent to establish a basic sense of security. The adolescent's self-esteem and identity are greatly affected by the quality and nature of the attachment to peers. As Blos (1968) points out, the identifications formed with friends and peer group members during this period establish superego functions which the adolescent relies upon for control and security. "The adolescent's emotional and physical withdrawal from, or opposition to, his world of childhood dependencies and security measures makes him, for some time, seek a protective cover in passionate, but usually transient, peer associations" (p. 253).

The traumatic loss of a peer cannot be taken at its face value but needs to be comprehended in light of the specific meaning of the loss for each adolescent. The difference in responses to the loss is observed in this study to be determined by an interplay of factors. These factors include: 1) the importance of the lost peer to the maintenance of the adolescent's self-esteem; 2) the nature of the relationship in terms of how the lost peer was used in structuring and consolidating the adolescent's identity formation; and 3) the associations and patterns of identification with the lost peer and how they relate to earlier forms of interaction and relationships to the adolescent's parents during childhood. The influence of these factors combines with the adolescent's beliefs and with his experiences with loss and crisis to shape the associative matrix of the meaning of the current loss and his unique grief response. Two case vignettes will be used in this paper to highlight the individual responses and meanings which an adolescent may attach to the death of a peer.

THE GREAT ADVENTURE FIRE

On the evening of Friday, May 11, 1984, five male students from Franklin K. Lane High School in Brooklyn, New York, were burned to death when they were trapped inside the Haunted House at the Great Adventure Amusement Park in New Jersey. Eight hundred other students from the same school had traveled with the victims to the park and were enjoying various activities when the fire broke out. A few of these survivors had left the Haunted House shortly before the flames erupted, while a few others were in the structure and narrowly escaped. However, it was only on Monday morning, with the opening of school, that most of the students learned the shocking reality of their classmates' deaths.

Widespread news coverage was given to this disaster. A great amount of media focus presented the horror of the events, grief of the surviving families, and questions of who was legally responsible for this disaster. What remained hidden was the fact that the sudden and catastrophic loss of these five adolescents triggered a reaction of mass shock and acute grief for hundreds of students and faculty at the victims' school. Most of these grief-stricken students had never before experienced the emotional impact of losing a friend through death, let alone such a violent death. For some students, the death of their fellow students was their first experience with traumatic loss. For others, the deaths elicited memories of the loss of significant persons at an earlier stage of their development.

The therapeutic intervention and study presented in this paper were initiated after several concerned guidance counselors from the victims' school requested help from the Jewish Board of Family and Children's Services in New York City to deal with the many painful reactions of both students and faculty. In spite of the extensive media coverage, no formal offer of support or action was made by the organizational leadership within the school district which was responsible for providing mental health services to the school. Such organizational denial of the psychological needs of children affected by a disaster has been previously documented by Terr (1979) in her work with children involved in the school bus kidnapping in Chowchilla, California, as well as by Lindy, Grace and Green (1983), who reached out to the numerous adolescent survivors of the Beverly Hills Supper Club Fire.

The agency's response to the school's request for outside assistance was immediate. A mobile team of three social workers, who were trained to work with adolescents in crises, entered the school the day following the request for help. The team of social workers was overseen by a supervisor in the school. In addition, a psychiatrist was available to the team in the clinic setting. The initial interventions in the school were: 1) to provide crisis intervention and bereavement counseling to individuals and groups of bereaved students, and 2) to offer consultation to the administrators and guidance staff so that they could cope with their own feelings in reaction to the tragedy. Educational workshops on crisis intervention and bereavement counseling were also offered to the guidance staff to help them offer supports to the students and to identify individuals who would be in need of longer-term individual interventions due to complicated grief reactions. Individual bereaved students, who were referred by teachers and counselors, were seen by one social worker for one to three sessions. Longer-term individual follow-up was provided through the following academic year for 22 students who were presenting complicated and prolonged mourning. Those students who were in need of continued mental health care during the summer months were referred to local mental health clinics.

Social workers went to five classes, totaling 120 students, to assist students in talking about their feelings of grief and to provide education about the nature and course of grief and mourning. Each of these classes was chosen for intervention because one or more of the victims had been a member of the class and at least two students had indicated to their teachers a desire to discuss their grief in class.

The five victims, all Hispanic, were reported to have been model students who had assumed leadership positions in the school. Each victim maintained a wide network of friends. Approximately 35% of the student population of the school was Hispanic. The majority of students who sought individual intervention were of Hispanic background. Membership in this particular ethnic group appears to have affected the strength of the peer bonds to the victims as well as the impact of the deaths on the surviving students.

GROUP RESPONSES TO THE DEATH OF A PEER

The students in the group sessions were initially guarded and tended to suppress their emotional responses to the traumatic loss. Only a few students reported that they had talked with their peers about their reactions. Female students were more willing to talk about their losses than were male students. Almost all of the students had little experience with grief reactions and experienced a sense of isolation and confusion in their state of mourning. Some indicated that they felt their peers would think of them as "crazy."

To lessen the students' fears and anxieties about verbalizing their grief, the group leaders assumed an active and direct role in acknowledging how frightening the reality of death is. Once an empathic connection was established with the fright and pain the students were experiencing, the leaders offered educational information on grief and trauma. The leaders focused on the common reactions of shock, denial, guilt, anger, somatic symptoms and repetitive dreams and images of the deceased. Several students began to relate their own grief experiences to the presented material. Other students then identified with their peers' grief experiences and shared their reactions. When the leaders asked what made the students reluctant to expose their grief in front of their peers, several students expressed the fear of being criticized. Other students indicated that they had been criticized by their parents for expressing their grief at home. Two students who had been at Great Adventure during the fire reported that their parents firmly encouraged them to "forget" and "stop thinking" about the fire when these youngsters spoke of having repetitive thoughts of "seeing all the smoke" and imagining their classmates perishing in the blaze. Their feelings of fright and terror at the prospect of their own children falling victim to the fire led many of the parents of the survivors to use denial as a means of coping with the disaster. By denying, the parents, busy with their own concerns, safeguarded their own energies and attempted to protect their children from the invading post-traumatic experience and accompanying psychic sequelae and pain. Lindy (1985), in his work with survivors of natural disasters, similarly observed how parents, community leaders, and close friends guard the survivor from the "noxious stimuli" (p. 155) of the traumatic event. Lindy feels that it is only with the sanction of these significant individuals that mental health efforts at reparative work can have access to the inner emotional experiences of the survivor.

After some group discussion of their denial and their fears of being denounced for their reactions to the loss of their classmates, the students began to voice their sense of disbelief and preoccupation with the grotesque manner in which their classmates died. Several students presented anxiety about what they considered to be their uncanny and morbid repetitive dreams of the victims burning in the blaze. They feared that the same fateful event which their peers experienced was going to happen to them. Magical associations and identification with the victim were a common theme in these students' dream images. The students felt anxious and out of control of their dreams. They wished for their dreams to stop. One female student reported, "I thought I was going crazy when I awoke yesterday from my dream. In the dream, I saw my friend burning. I reached out to help him and fire began crawling up my arm. I thought I was going to burn with him. After the dream it took me a long time [several hours] to feel that I wasn't going to die too. I had another fire dream last night. I really thought I was flipping out until now. It is good to hear other people are having fire dreams too."

Some students revealed physical symptoms including sleep disturbances, abdominal pain and a feeling of intense subjective stress that was experienced as a general tightening and tension of the muscles. A few individuals revealed that they had used marijuana and tranquilizers as a means of warding off the invasion of disruptive physical and mental pain. Most students stated that prior to the group discussion, they had thought themselves to be alone, crazy, and isolated in experiencing their frightening and distressing psychic images. As a result of feeling reassured, through the social workers' explanations of commonly experienced symptoms of grief, the students were observed to become less guarded and more open in verbalizing their distress and grief.

Particularly upsetting to the group was their shared feeling of being vulnerable and unprotected from death. Statements such as "I never thought about dying until now" and "What's the point of getting good grades and going to college when you can be killed tomorrow?" reflected the common sense of being shocked by the reality of their own mortality and disillusioned with their own aspirations for the future. The traumatic loss destabilized the students' psychic poise and turned their emotional worlds upside down. There was a feeling of having little control over one's direction in life. The adolescents' idealism and aspirations for the future were suddenly placed on hold by the unanticipated calamity. A male student reported that he had been offered a baseball scholarship one week before the fire. In an angry voice he stated, "Life is a bitch, good things happen and then they are quickly taken away." He explained how one of the victims had been offered a scholarship to attend a state university and asked, "Now what is he going to do with the money?" Expressing his loss or belief in a safe and protected world, the student stated, "Life stinks, it doesn't matter what you get for yourself, everything can be taken away just like that." One student said, "I was so excited about becoming a professional model, but now I can't think about anything else but something bad happening and dying."

Feeling unprotected and vulnerable, the students expressed pessimism and mistrust of those who were available to help. Within the group discussion several individuals angrily asked, "What's the point of talking about the fire? No one can bring our friends back. No one can ever guarantee we won't be struck down tomorrow." The students' identification with the victims was pervasive. In many respects they felt themselves to be dead, with no future world to grasp onto for security and life.

Although the group discussions were painful and frightening for the students, the verbal reenactment and abreaction of their imagery and induced feelings helped them move from a passive position to active coping through acknowledgment and intellectual mastery of their grief. Several students approached their teachers after the group discussions seeking referral to a counselor so they could continue to discuss their feelings of grief and anxiety.

INDIVIDUAL ADOLESCENT RESPONSES TO THE DEATH OF A PEER

While the death of a peer does not ordinarily lead to pathology, the impact of the event on the adolescent is greatly determined by the developmental history of adaptation to past losses and by the specific nature and meaning of the current lost peer relationship. The mental health professional working with bereaved youngsters may have difficulty perceiving their grief because the process of mourning is often kept private. These adolescents will frequently express their need for support and assistance through symptomatic behavior such as social withdrawal, suicidal gestures, antisocial behavior, academic decline and accident-proneness. Raphael (1983) observes the presence of psychiatric disorders such as depression, phobias and, at times, severe obsessional neurotic patterns in bereaved adolescents. (pp. 172–173) Adolescents often experience extreme anger over their sense of desertion and their helplessness at not having control over the loss of their peer. Identification with the dead peer often results in paralyzing fear of their own death. In this context Raphael (1983) has observed that the adolescent "rages at the world in angry protest to demonstrate power, to protect against further loss, and even to covertly call back the dead." (p. 172) For these adolescents, their mourning, anger, and sense of abandonment will continue unabated.

The adolescent's capacity for cognitive understanding of the loss of a peer is much more developed than that of the child. However, adolescents who have not experienced the reality of a loss through death are frequently subject to a greater amount of cognitive distortion than individuals who have had this experience. In her study of adolescents' cognitive concepts of death, Turnbull (1980) reported that the prior experience of bereavement aided in the adolescent's eventual acceptance and integration of the concept of death. Therefore, in order to evaluate his comprehension of the event, the clinician needs to elicit the adolescent's fantasies about death.

Many of the adolescents who survived the Great Adventure fire reported being frightened by thoughts that their dead friends were returning to haunt them. Their current reality was invaded by a repetition of the traumatic events. Flashbacks and daydreams months after the fire were common. Several adolescents complained that intrusive daytime visions of the exact scenes of the fire were blocking their ability to concentrate on schoolwork and to sustain conversations with friends. The invasion of traumatic memories of the events surrounding the deaths of their peers suggests the occurrence of a traumatic stress syndrome which has been documented by Horowitz (1976). The traumatic stress of the event overwhelmed the students' egos and complicated their individual responses and mourning. Others reported that they were "spooked" by their thoughts. One student said, "It is like watching a horror movie inside your head with no ending." Terr (1985) similarly observed with the survivors of the Chowchilla kidnapping that when the child's ego is suddenly overwhelmed by external events, he may view the world as "spooky" and "eerie." She postulates, "Much of this supernatural effect may be due to the traumatized individual's restitutive efforts at finding explanations for the unexplainable, trying to think through the unthinkable, and in planning for the unanticipatable." (p. 596)

Nancy, 17 years old, was interviewed as part of a follow-up of the survivors of the fire who were experiencing problems five months after the tragedy. Nancy complained that she was having difficulty concentrating on her studies, her academic performance was deteriorating, and she found it difficult to sleep at night. These symptoms began immediately following the death of two of her friends, Steve and Carl, who were killed in the fire. In the initial interview I asked Nancy what she found most painful about the death of her friends. Her eyes filled with tears and she stated that she could not stop thinking about the tragedy. She was beset with pervasive guilt and rescue fantasies, feeling herself to be responsible for her friends' deaths. She repeated, "If only I was with them in the fire, I could have shown them the way out." In an empathic manner, I pointed out to Nancy that she appeared to be in great pain over feeling so responsible for her friends. I asked her to recall her memories of the relationship she had with her friends. Giving particular attention to Carl, she remembered his being a friendly person who was frightened of dark places. One month prior to the fire, she had helped him find his way out of a school storage room when he became frightened of the dark. She related being at the amusement park during the fire but was in a different section of the park. She first suspected that Carl may have been hurt when she returned to the school bus and her friends did not respond to their names being called out during the teacher's attendance check. Appearing both anxious and vigilant, Nancy stated that after the fire she spoke to no one about her concerns. Her dreams and thoughts of her friends perishing in the blaze made her worried that she was "flipping out" and going crazy. Affirming how frightened she must have been, I commented that her experience of having scary and horrifying dreams and thoughts was part of the painful work of grieving for her friends. Relaxing in her chair she recalled having a dream the evening of the fire that "something bad had happened to Carl." "I woke up screaming, 'he's dead. He was in the fire'." The entire weekend following the Friday evening fire Nancy prayed to God for her friends to be alive. Only upon going to school Monday did she learn the reality of her friends' deaths by seeing their pictures on the front page of the newspapers. Nancy did not return to school for the rest of the term.

During the second interview Nancy reflected back upon her summer months, saying, "Now that I know I wasn't crazy, I should tell you that I thought about killing myself for two months following the fire." Reporting her experience of derealization, she stated, "The whole world was a fog, I no longer knew who I was or where I was going." Returning to school in September was very painful. Nancy described feeling afraid to touch the school steps and handrail, thinking that Steve and Carl must have touched these same objects. She anxiously related that her friends were still alive inside her and questioned whether she was possessed by bad spirits. I nodded and told Nancy that while it was true that Steve and Carl had died, her friendship with them was strong and that it takes time to let go inside of friends to whom she was so attached. She wept while maintaining enough composure to talk about how relieved she felt to no longer feel so crazy and alone in her grief.

In the case described above, we see how Nancy had difficulty mourning her loss. While she was aware of the reality of her friends' deaths, she could not internally detach herself from the lost peers. Her inner and outer world was fixed and "glued" to her lost friends. Her behavior can be viewed in terms of Wolfenstein's findings (1966) that adolescents tend to develop a hypercathexis to the lost object and hide feelings of sadness and despair from others.

Another student deeply affected by the tragedy was Bob. He had a long history of oppositional behavior which had intensified since his return to school in the fall, four months after the fire. His counselor referred him to the school consultant for assessment due to his increased agitation and physical fights with peers and teachers. The referring counselor indicated that Bob had been spending a great amount of time walking in and out of the counseling office during class. He usually walked into the office wearing a white tux shirt and dress jacket which drew the attention of his peers and school staff. When I asked him what was going on in his life, Bob's affect saddened. He took out a picture of his friend Carl and gazed at it. Bob explained that his friend was killed in the fire. He was preoccupied by Carl's death and could find no one who wanted to listen to his grief. "Even my girlfriend tells me to stop talking about Carl. Let him rest in peace." I commented that it was very understandable that he thought a lot about Carl. Bob repeatedly sought my reassurance that it was all right to talk about his grief. Crying as he spoke, Bob related how his whole body tightens up when he thinks about his lost friend. He recalled that the day before the fire Carl had urged him to go to the amusement park. Bob had decided against going and felt that if he had been at the amusement park the outcome would have been different. "Either Carl would be alive, or I would be dead." I pointed out to Bob that of course he wanted to have some control over what happened to Carl but the tough truth is that there is nothing he could have done to change the outcome. When Bob first heard about his friend's death he thought about dying. He related that his suicidal feelings did not last long and that he found comfort in frequently going to Carl's home and visiting with his mother.

As demonstrated above, a common characteristic present in a majority of students who presented complicated and prolonged grief reactions to the loss of their friends was survivor guilt. Survivor guilt has been well documented by such researchers as Lindemann (1944) in his work with survivors of the Coconut Grove Fire in 1943, and by Lifton (1967), who investigated the long-term psychological impact on survivors of the atomic bomb at Hiroshima. Individuals who suffer from survivor guilt scrutinize how they acted before the disaster and death for evidence of their own failure to do right by the lost one. They accuse themselves of negligence and exaggerate the possible importance of minor omissions. The guilt is employed by the survivor to turn the passive experience of helplessness into an active experience of excessive responsibility. Survivor guilt in adolescents is unique because of the specific phase of super-ego development which they are going through.

Some adolescents who are experiencing the influence of a powerful and idealistic superego are likely to experience excessive guilt. Sudden violent deaths frequently elicit guilt due to the adolescent's own destructive fantasies of violent aggressive behavior. In addition, the adolescent's guilt covers possible underlying anger about feeling abandoned by the peer. As was described in the cases of Nancy and Bob, the anger is often turned inward, transformed into guilt with accompanying self-destructive behavior and depressive episodes. This is particularly the case when the youngster's verbal expression of grief is discouraged or unrecognized by others. The guilt and anger then is acted out. Bob's angry protest and self-destructive acting out behavior was partly his desire for recognition of his distress and partly punishment of self and others for the disastrous death of his friend.

As the adolescent's guilt represents an expression of anger about the loss of a peer, it also is a manifestation of the tendency toward magical thinking. The thought is, "If only I had been at one place rather than the other place, all this would not have happened." Just as the small child who has lost a parent feels that he may have caused his parent's distress, illness, and ultimate abandonment, the adolescent feels that he was magically responsible for the death of his friend. Such magical thinking may represent a manifestation of the grieving youngster's regression to an earlier developmental state of organization around prior childhood

losses of significant objects. Earlier losses of significant objects can result in a high degree of ambivalence and aggressive ideation in the adolescent's relations to peers and may increase the guilt suffered over the death of a friend. As Lindy (1985) has noted in his paper on survivors of natural disasters, "the match between repressed unconscious conflict arising from childhood and the specific conflict mobilized in the trauma, exists in survivors of disaster. . . . Such neurotic guilt unfolds spontaneously after the first levels of guilt are acknowledged." (p. 160) Making the connection between the adolescent's current loss and disturbance and his earlier losses and residual conflicts can be a very helpful therapeutic focus for youngsters who are able to use an insight-oriented intervention.

While the loss of a peer may not in and of itself be pathogenic, such a loss can become the core around which earlier conflicts and latent pathogenic elements are reawakened and mobilized. This process may impede the adolescent's developmental thrust toward consolidating ego and regulating self-esteem. Of significance is Phyliss Greenacre's (1962) observation that no early traumatic event is ever wholly digested; rather, increased vulnerability inevitably remains, with the affected individual breaking down at some later date, even if this breakdown is restricted to those occasions where he is faced with a repetition or near repetition of the original injury. The specific pathological impact on the adolescent's developing ego by the current loss of a peer is determined both by the individual's history of loss and by the manner in which the youngster adapted to the loss.

The adolescent who breaks down in a more or less pathogenic manner due to the death of a peer has what Blos (1962) refers to as a "second chance" for reworking earlier losses and conflicts more successfully. Some adolescents who have suffered early traumatic loss may not have had the ego resources and environmental supports to mourn losses suffered in early childhood. For some of these individuals, the adolescent period of development offers greater resources to grieve and mourn than they had as children. The adolescent has a clearer conception of death and has more expanded supports through his relations to peers and adults, than does the child. The combination of expanded environmental supports and developmental maturity may allow the grieving adolescent a better opportunity to work through and master his unresolved childhood losses.

Those adolescent survivors of the Great Adventure fire who experienced prolonged and complicated mourning often appeared to be struggling in belated attempts to master earlier losses and traumas reactivated by the deaths of their peers. Although the adolescents shared the same traumatic experience of losing a friend, the particular ego vulnerability and meaning attached to the loss was unique for each individual.

6. BEREAVEMENT

Having vented her grief and associated guilt during our initial session, Nancy returned for five subsequent sessions in which she revealed how her current grief and fragile ego state were significantly affected by the earlier loss of her biological father. In the second session Nancy's revelation of earlier traumatic loss came out as we talked about how her friends' deaths brought up memories and sad feelings of the death of her cat three weeks prior to the fire. Nancy spoke of feeling helpless and sad when she saw her cat being run over by a car. Since she was speaking of her earlier memories of her lost cat, I asked if she recalled ever losing anyone else that made her sad and helpless. Staring blankly, she remarked that she had been looking at a picture album the night before and thought about how she had not only lost her friend and cat but her father as well. She reported that her biological father had abandoned her mother and herself when she was four years old. Nancy remarked that looking at the photos reminded her of the constant sense of having her father, pet, and deceased friends present in her life despite their real absence. "I don't know if they are really gone or not."

Nancy's focus gradually shifted from talking about the death of her friends and pet to examining the emotional impact of the loss of her father. She described her early history as marked by her father's alcoholism and abandonment when she was four years old. She recalled being informed by her mother around the time she entered primary school that her father began drinking after she was born. Asking Nancy what it was that she thought about most in relation to losing her father, she described feeling responsible and guilty for her father's drinking and abandonment of the family. She said, "Because I was born he started drinking and left us." She reported having no contact with her father after he left. Her mother remarried when she was six years old. She described her stepfather as a caring and effectual person, but the marriage was beset with tension and strife. She assumed the position of mediator between her mother and stepfather, fearing that the marital strife would lead to another separation and loss. I commented to her that she has certainly spent her entire life feeling responsible for all her losses. I asked her how she had been able to endure the emotional burden of such responsibility. She responded by crying and saying, "Well, it all got to me a year ago, everything was pressing in on me because I couldn't stop my parents from threatening each other with separation." The guilt she experienced for feeling so powerless, angry, and responsible over her parents' separation threats led her to attempt suicide through ingesting pills. I pointed out to her that her current feelings of helplessness and guilt over the loss of her friends sounded similar to all the responsibility she had assumed for the loss of her father and the problems in her mother's current marriage. She sighed and said, "I try my best to hold on to people I love but they keep on disappearing anyways." During the course of her brief therapy at the school Nancy and I worked together to help her accept the reality that none of her thoughts or actions could have changed the sequence of events which resulted in her past and present losses. The many connections between her current traumatic loss and earlier repressed fears and feelings of loss were explored. She was able to become more aware of how her earlier guilty ruminations and feelings of excessive responsibility with her parents played a major role in shaping the pattern of relationships to her peers as well as in influencing her own self-concept and identity.

In the case described above, we observe that Nancy's identity was strongly rooted in an early pathological environment which left her feeling guilty over the loss of her father and responsible for holding on to and preventing the loss of other objects. Therefore, her inability to prevent the death of her friend left her especially shaken and vulnerable. Through the therapeutic intervention in the school, Nancy was able to examine her grief in the context of both her past and current relationships and her self-concept. Such examination allowed Nancy a new opportunity to modify her vulnerable sense of identity and her low self-esteem. In this manner the mental health practitioner provides the grief-stricken youngster the opportunity to understand the vulnerability in relation to past traumatic losses and to re-structure the nature both of current object ties and of self-concept and identity formation.

The issue of bereavement for the adolescent concerns less the actual specific nature of how the death of a peer occurred and more the functional meaning and subsequent impact on the youngster's ego. The direct witnessing of a sudden and violent death can intensify short-term grief reactions. However, in the longer-term working-through process, the adolescent must cope with the impact of the loss on his ego functioning rather than simply mourn for the physical absence of the peer. In discussing the impact of trauma on children, Anna Freud (1965) points out that the "traumatic events should not be regarded at their face value but should be translated into their specific meaning for the given child." (p. 139) In this sense, understanding the process of mourning involves a determination of how the deceased peer influenced and strengthened specific ego functions of the bereaved adolescent. In terms of object relations theory, the lost peer served as a self-object, an extension and regulator of the adolescent's ego. Just as the infant's ego is assisted in regulating and coping with environmental stress by the mother's availability and protection, the adolescent's ego and self-esteem are influenced by the identifications and protection derived from bonds with peers. A breech in this bond results in increased ego vulnerability. The process of mourning the loss of a peer who provided needed psychological functions to the adolescent is equivalent to the process of grieving for the self object functions which the peer and earlier parental object served for the youngster.

By understanding the manner in which the deceased peer served to strengthen and consolidate the bereaved adolescent's ego functioning, one will comprehend the basis for empathic intervention with the feelings of loss and ego damage experienced by the youngster. This point can be illustrated by Bob's description of what he lost when his friend Carl died in the fire:

Bob's grief over Carl's death was shattering. During the course of the nine sessions that we met, Bob and I talked about what he felt was missing in his life since Carl's death and what his friend did for him while he was living. Bob idealized Carl, describing him as his best friend and his

source of in...
learned of ...
didn't knov...
described r...
spent talki...
to do toge...
bered tim...
tense and...
him as th...
do no rig...
he was ...
terms a...
mother ...
track" ...
asked ...
respor...
descri...
suppc...
about...
reser...
men...
both...
who...
ing...
pai...
of ...
Re...
C...
d...

a...

father and the ...

Bob's expression of grief was ... ping him
describe what it was that he missed most of all now that Carl
was gone. Bob described his sense of losing part of himself.
"Carl was part of my soul, he was my right hand. He kept
things going for me when I started getting into trouble.
Nobody was ever there to keep me in line as much as Carl."
Over the course of the three months we worked together, Bob
became embroiled in several verbal and physical fights with
peers and teachers. After each incident I directed the focus of
the session to helping him connect his aggressive behavior to
his anger and to his wish for Carl to be there for him to
control his actions. In one session Bob responded to my
comment by saying, "It's so hard to really believe he's dead
and that he will not be there to keep everything together and
going for me. I guess I'll have to deal with keeping things in
line by seeing you and all the other shrinks in this place."
Bob's aggressive behavior in school subsided as he came more
fully to acknowledge the fact of Carl's death and his loss of
the control and protection his friend offered.

In our final session Bob spoke warmly of the joint plans
Carl and he had made together to join the Army and eventually become police officers after graduating from high school.
Reflecting over the loss of his future plans with his friend,
Bob remarked, "Well, I still feel at times like joining the
Army and becoming a cop. That is what Carl would have
wanted." When I asked him what he does now when he sees
himself losing control and heading for trouble, he responded,
"It's much harder for me without Carl, but sometimes I go
over to Carl's house and sit and talk to with his mother. Being
with his mother makes me feel better."

The problems Bob encountered were related to his loss of
the ego functions his friend performed in controlling his

destructive, aggressive impulses, as well as in lending him a
sense of protection and structure for his future aspirations
and goals. Bob's need to rely on his friend as a self-object and
auxiliary ego was reinforced by the earlier loss of a father
figure from whom he could not obtain adequate protection
and security. His mourning and reactive acting out were
connected to his struggle to accept the painful loss of a friend
who compensated for ego deficits resulting from his earlier
loss. Bob's visits to his deceased friend's mother were his
active attempts to restore the external supports and functions he had lost. Visits with Carl's mother and with the
school counselor facilitated Bob's further internalization and
consolidation of the self-object and ego functions his lost
friend had extended to him.

CONCLUSION

Those of us who work with adolescents need to be
especially sensitive to the impact of loss, whether it be
a family member or friend. Not only is death frightening, but the adolescent's inner and outer world is
shaken and changed in some form. The particular way
in which each youngster's psychic life is changed by the
loss is in need of thoughtful and careful assessment to
determine its unique features. Each adolescent cannot
be assumed to have a uniform and identical response to
death. As Joseph Palombo (1981) notes, "We have to
specify the antecedent conditions in the child's ego and
the dynamics within the ego at the time of the occurrence of the event. By doing so, we take into account
constitutional factors, predisposing factors, and factors
relating to the specific manner in which the child
responded to the event." (p. 23).

The death of a peer places the adolescent in a fragile
psychic state. The adolescent's ego is confronted with
its identification with the deceased peer. The ego is
most vulnerable, most open to doubt, and least protected when exposed to the death of a peer. The adolescent questions the meaning of existence, and the
consolidation process which reinforces ego identity and
maturity is left directionless. The adolescent, who
found a protective cover in attachment to peers, becomes frightened and unsure of whom he can trust to
share his distress when a friend dies. Under these
conditions, the adolescent may very well act out his
grief, become depressed and further withdraw from
relationships to other peers and family. The question of
whether a particular adolescent's ego development will
be damaged or eventually strengthened by the traumatic loss is very much determined by the availability of
caring adults who are sensitive to the hidden grief and
pain and able to extend themselves in a manner which
respects the youngster's integrity and autonomy. Some
adolescents may not be able to respond to our offers of
assistance. In such cases, it is important that we
respect the defenses and self-determination of these
individuals. The fact that these youngsters are aware
that emotional support and understanding are avail-

able to them may, in and of itself, strengthen their ability to cope with their loss and lead to a sense of being less alone and unprotected in their pain and mourning.

REFERENCES

Aubrey, R. (1977). Adolescents and death. In E. R. Prichard (ed.), *Social Work with the Dying Patient*. New York: Columbia University Press.

Balk, D. (1983). Effects of Sibling Death on Teenagers. *The Journal of School Health*, 14–18.

Blos, P. (1962). *On Adolescence: A Psychoanalytic Interpretation*. New York: Free Press.

Blos, P. (1968). Character formation in adolescence. *Psychoanalytic Study of the Child*, 23, 245–263.

Bowlby, J. (1980). *Loss, Sadness and Depression*. New York: Basic Books.

Freud, A. (1965). *Normality and Pathology in Childhood*. New York: International University Press.

Gordon. A. K. (1986). The tattered cloak of immortality. In C. A. Corr, J. N. McNeil (eds.), *Adolescence and Death*. New York: Springer Pub. Co. 16–31.

Greenacre, P. (1962). The influence of infantile trauma on genetic patterns. In S. Furst (ed.), *Psychic Trauma*. New York: Basic Books.

Horowitz, M. J. (1976). *Stress Response Syndromes*. New York: Jason Aronson.

Laufer, M. (1966). Object loss and mourning during adolescence. *Psychoanalytic Study of the Child*, 21, 269–293.

Lifton, R. J. (1967). *Death in Life: Survivors in Hiroshima*. New York: Random House.

Lindemann, E. (1944). Symptomatology and management of acute grief. *American Journal of Psychiatry*, 101, 141–148.

Lindy, J. D. (1985). The trauma membrane and other clinical concepts derived from psychotherapeutic work with survivors of natural disasters. *Psychiatric Annals*, 15:3, 153–160.

Lindy, J. D., Grace, M. C., Green, B. L., et al. (1983). Psychotherapy with survivors of the Beverly Hills Supper Club fire. *American Journal of Psychotherapy*, 37, 469–477.

Miller, D. (1983). *The Age Between: Adolescence and Therapy*. New York: Jason Aronson, Inc.

Palombo, J. (1981). Parent loss and childhood bereavement: some theoretical considerations. *Clinical Social Work Journal*, 9, 3–33.

Raphael, B. (1983). *The Anatomy of Bereavement*. New York: Basic Books.

Terr, L. C. (1985). Remembered images and trauma: a psychology of the supernatural. *Psychoanalytic Study of the Child*, 40, 493–533.

Terr, L. C. (1979). Children of Chowchilla. *Psychoanalytic Study of the Child*, 34, 547–623.

Turnbull, H. (1980). The Concept of Death in Bereaved and Non-bereaved Latent and Adolescent Children Related to Attributic and School Performance. Master's Thesis. University of Newcastle, NSW Australia.

Wolfenstein, M. (1966). How is mourning possible. *Psychoanalytic Study of the Child*, 21, 93–123.

Solace and Immortality: Bereaved Parents' Continuing Bond With Their Children

Dennis Klass

Webster University, St. Louis, Missouri

How do bereaved parents find solace in the face of irreparable loss? The essay grows out of a 10-year ethnographic study of a chapter of the Compassionate Friends, a self-help group. A recurring pattern is that long-term solace is intertwined with parents' continuing interaction with the inner representation of their dead child. The essay examines the nature of solace, reviews literature on inner representations of the dead, examines ways parents find solace connected with interaction with the inner representation, explores the shared inner representation as a significant element in social support, discusses solace in terms of the psychosocial meaning of immortality, and draws implications for clinicians.

In the sorrow of grief humans need to be consoled. The defining characteristic of solace is the sense of soothing. To console means to alleviate sorrow or distress. Solace is that which brings pleasure, enjoyment, or delight in the face of hopelessness, despair, sadness, and devastation.

This essay looks at consolation within the resolution of the grief of parents whose children have died. It grows out of a long-term ethnographic study of a local chapter of the Compassionate Friends, a self-help group of bereaved parents (Klass, 1988). The 10-year study has resulted in a large body of materials by which to understand parental grief and the interactions within the Compassionate Friends chapter. Materials include: interviews with bereaved parents, writings by members in chapter newsletters, and notes from meetings.

When a child dies, the parent experiences an irreparable loss, for the child is an extension of the parent's self (Benedek, 1959, 1975). While one of the psychological tasks of parenting in modernity is to separate the child from the self so the child can be experienced as a separate being (Elson, 1984), such separation is seldom complete. When a child dies, a part of the self is cut off. Many parents find the metaphor of amputation useful. In a meeting a father said, "It is like I lost my right arm, but I'm

learning to live as a one-armed man." A parent who seems to have had experience with amputees wrote in a newsletter article:

> For the amputee, the raw bleeding stump heals and the physical pain does go away. But he lives with the pain in his heart knowing his limb will not grow back. He has to learn to live without it. He rebuilds his life around his loss. We bereaved parents must do the same.

Like amputation, parental bereavement is a permanent condition. The hopes, dreams, and expectations incarnate in the child are now gone.

Bereaved parents do find resolution to their grief in the sense that they learn to live in their new world. They "re-solve" the matters of how to be themselves in a family and community in a way that makes life meaningful. They learn to grow in those parts of themselves which did not die with the child. They learn to invest themselves in other tasks and other relationships. But somewhere inside themselves, they report, there is a sense of loss that cannot be healed. A bereaved father wrote in a newsletter:

> If grief is resolved, why do we still feel a sense of loss on anniversaries and holidays and even when we least expect it? Why do we feel a lump in the throat even 6 years after the loss? It is because healing does not mean forgetting and because moving on with life does not mean that we don't take a part of our lost love with us.

A part of them is missing and their world is forever diminished. It is that part of the self which seeks consolation. How do parents find consolation for their irreparable loss?

THE NATURE OF SOLACE

Horton (1981) finds that the majority of people have a history of solace that they nurture. Most adults can easily identify a solace filled object to which they repair when they need soothing: a memory of a special place or person, a piece of music or art, an imagined more perfect world, a sense of divine presence. Horton finds that solace is necessary for the individual who can live in a society. Psychopathic criminals, he says, have no solace

Address correspondence to the author at Webster University, St. Louis, MO 63119.

in their lives. Horton finds that the earliest solace is the transitional object (Winnicott, 1953, 1971) such as a child's security blanket, which helps the child explore new situations and adjust to unfamiliar environments (Passman, 1976; Passman & Weisberg, 1975). Horton says that in adults these objects are no longer transitional, for they are important in the adult's on-going life. Solace is experienced as blended inner and outer reality. There is a noetic quality in this reality that is self-validating. While the content of solace may have rational characteristics, the truth and comfort of solace are neither provable nor challengeable.

A recurring pattern in Compassionate Friends is that parents find long-term solace in continuing interaction with the inner representation of their dead child. Inner representation can be defined following Fairbairn (1952), as: 1) those aspects of the self that are actualized in interaction with the deceased person, 2) characterizations or thematic memories of the deceased, and 3) emotional states connected with those parts of the self and with those characterizations and memories. Phenomena that indicate interaction with the inner representation of a deceased person are a sense of presence, hallucinations in any of the senses, belief in the person's continuing active influence on thoughts or events, or a conscious incorporation of the characteristics or virtues of the dead into the self.

These phenomena may be experienced in altered states of consciousness. Parents often use phrases like: "It was in a dream, but it was different than other dreams." The phenomena may also be experienced in ordinary states of consciousness and accepted as part of the everyday world. Interaction may be consciously sought or it may seem to come unbidden. Interaction with the inner representation of the dead may be continuous with the self as the characteristics or virtues of the dead are incorporated into the self representation. Or the interaction may seem apart from the self representation as the parent says that having such thoughts and feelings is "just not like me."

The inner representation of the dead child has the character of both outer and inner reality. It is not simply an objective presence, for the meaning of the experience is strongly personal. Neither can it be said to be simply subjective. Many parents in the study argue strongly against reducing the experience to a psychic reality, or as one person said, "Don't tell me that this is just in my head?" Yet, at the same time they are usually able to grant that the meaning of the child's presence is very personal and not generalizable to other people's lives.

The message and meaning of the interaction with the inner representations of dead children are self-evident to the bereaved parent. It does not matter to the parents in the study whether, with the help of the spirits of the dead, parapsychologists can bend spoons. Their children appear, act, speak, and influence. The intense meanings they feel within the bond with their child are quite apart from rational proof or disproof.

Inner representations of the dead are not simply individual phenomena, but they are maintained and reinforced within families and other social systems. The dead child is often a part of the bond within the continuing family and is an integral element of the bond between members of the Compassionate Friends. Parents consciously work to maintain the inner repre-

sentation of the child. Several families do this by including the picture of the dead child on family portraits made after the child's death. Others do it by consciously evoking the memory of the child in significant situations. In the Compassionate Friends (1983), the sense of oneness with other bereaved parents and the sense of oneness within the bonds to the dead child can be seen in the "TCF Credo," which has been adopted by the National Board of TCF and which is recited on special occasions such as holiday memorial services, national, and regional meetings.

> We reach out to each other with love, with understanding and with hope. Our children have died at all ages and from many different causes, but our love for our children unites us. . . . Whatever pain we bring to this gathering of The Compassionate Friends, it is pain we will share just as we share with each other our love for our children.

LITERATURE ON INNER REPRESENTATIONS OF THE DEAD

Extent of the Phenomena

There is ample evidence from research on Western cultures that the inner representation of the deceased continues as an active part of the life of the survivor, even though it has little sanction within the dominant scientific worldview. At present, the inner representation of Elvis Presley plays an active part in many people's lives and within some social systems (Moody, 1987). Lehman, Wortman, and Williams (1987) found that 4 to 7 years after an accidental death 90% of widow(er)s and 96% of bereaved parents said that during the past month memories, thoughts, or mental pictures of the deceased had come to their mind. Kalish and Reynolds (1981) found that 44% of a random sample said they had experienced or felt the presence of someone who had died. The dead appeared and spoke in 73.6% of the experiences, the dead were psychologically felt in 20.3%, and in 6%, there was a sense of touch. Rees (1975) found that 46.7% of the Welsh widows he interviewed had occasional hallucinations for several years. Most common was the sense of the presence (39.2%), followed by visual (14%), auditory (13.3%), and tactile senses (2.7%). Glick, Weiss, and Parkes (1974) found among widows a persistent continuing relationship with the inner representation of the dead husband. They report

> In contrast to most other aspects of the reaction to bereavement, the sense of the persisting presence of the husband did not diminish with time. It seemed to take a few weeks to become established, but thereafter seemed as likely to be reported late in the bereavement as early. (p. 147)

Cross Cultural Differences and Continuities

There are wide cultural variations in what is considered to be the appropriate place of the inner representation of the dead in the family and other social systems. Yamamoto and his colleagues (1969) claim that because Japanese religion (both Shinto and Buddhist) involves ancestor worship, which encourages the mourner to maintain contact to the deceased, mourning is different in Japan than in the West.

There are also some obvious continuities across cultures in the phenomena by which inner representations of the dead are manifest. Matchett (1972) reports three instances of Hopi women having visions of recently deceased people. The mental state he describes is not different from that in bereaved parents.

> The experience to be described is neither truly seance nor truly dream, but appears to represent a mental state with some similarities to both. The apparition is real enough to the beholder to be conversed with, to be described in great visual detail, and even at times to be struggled with physically. However, it is clear to the beholder, even during the experience, that this presence with which he argues and struggles as if it were "real" occurs somewhere outside the usual definition of reality. (p. 185)

Functions of the Inner Representation of the Dead

There have been some studies of how inner representations function in the lives of survivors, though often this aspect is not central to the investigation, or the sample has been very small. Among widows, Silverman (1986) argues that maintaining a changed relationship with the inner representations of the deceased spouses allows the widows to find stability in time. Lopata (1973, 1979) finds what she calls "husband sanctification," which allows the widow to "continue her obligation to the husband to remember him, yet break her ties and re-create herself into a person without a partner" (1979, p. 126). Moss and Moss (1980) claim that the sanctified inner representation of the dead spouse is a factor in the relationship between elderly widows and widowers when they remarry. Goin, Burgoyne, and Goin (1979) find widows, even after remarriage, renew the bond with their dead husband as they decide to have a face-lift operation. Among children whose parent has died, Tessman (1978) finds that children "preserve the relationship psychically and continue to make use of whatever mixture of affection and guidance emanated from the parent" (p. 42). Bushbaum (1987) finds that the inner representation of the dead parent is essential to the child's development. College women, Silverman (1987) finds, reintegrate the dead parent into each new developmental stage.

Inner Representations of the Dead in Contemporary Grief Theory

These experiences of bereaved parents run contrary to most contemporary understandings of the healthy resolution of grief, which hold that the inner representation plays no or only a slight role in the survivor's life after the resolution of grief. The two classic models of grief come from Bowlby and his followers and from the psychoanalytic group. The Bowlby model (Bowlby, 1969, 1973, 1980; Parkes, 1972; Parkes & Weiss, 1983; Raphael, 1983; Worden, 1982) expects that after a period of emotionally searching for the deceased, survivors should let go of the inner representation, and resume normal functioning, albeit in changed social roles. The psychoanalytic model (Volkan, 1981, 1985a, 1985b; Tahka, 1984; Dietrich & Shabad, 1989; Furman, 1974; Jackson, 1957) expects that mourning should detach the ego from the affective bond with the deceased and that the inner representation is transformed into an identification which enriches the ego or self representation.

Models of grief that try to go beyond the Bowlby and psychodynamic models do not find a positive place for the inner representation in the resolution. Brice (1991) in his paradoxical model of parental grief finds that his subjects

> painfully came to see that, while they retained a psychical representation of their child, they had irretrievably lost their child's external presence—something of which their mental images were, alas, a poor copy. (p. 2)

Brice says one of the difficulties that parents have with the experience of presence is that they fear insanity. Although Brice mentions his contact with the Compassionate Friends, he does not seem to have seen that with social validation bereaved parents no longer accept the label of insanity. Sanders (1989) notes that sensing the presence or actually seeing the dead person "brought a sense of comfort," but she understands the experiences to be the "cognitive counterpart of yearning" (p. 70). Thus she is saying that interaction with the inner representation of the dead child is wish fulfillment rather than a positive element in resolution.

The contemporary theoretical difficulties are seen in Rando's (1984) attempt to synthesize the literature for clinicians. She says:

> The single most crucial task in grief is "untying the ties that bind" the griever to the deceased individual. This does not mean that the deceased is forgotten or not loved; rather, it means that the emotional energy that the mourner had invested in the deceased is modified to allow the mourner to turn it towards others for emotional satisfaction. (p. 19)

"Emotional energy" is a problematic concept at best, so the idea of "modified" energy explains very little. Rando gives no way the dead can remain loved and remembered, yet have the emotional energy modified except as "rituals, anniversary celebrations, prayers, commemorations, memorializations, and healthy identification" (p. 78). She does not show the mechanisms by which energy modification takes place. Further, she does not say how rituals, etc. function in the resolution of grief, nor does she give any definition or examples of "healthy identification."

There is a minority voice in the literature that is more congruent with this study. Rubin (1985) finds that breaking bonds with the dead is not the function or measure of successful grief.

> It is in the nature of the relationship of the bereaved to the deceased that is the best determination of whether the mourning has been resolved. . . . The greater the comfort and fluidity with which one can relate to the representations (memories, fantasies, feelings) of the deceased—the more one can refer to "resolution" of the loss. (pp. 231–232)

The Question of Pathology

In many contemporary theories of grief, the widespread continued interaction with the inner representations of dead children seem to be pathological, for beginning with Freud, theorists have understood the purpose of grief as relinquishing the lost object so that new attachments in the present can be formed. Failure to sever the bond has been defined as pathological grief. This is not the venue for a full discussion of the unexamined assumptions and lack of data upon which this definition of pathology is based. The author has discussed the issue previously, especially with regard to Bowlby and his followers

(Klass, 1987), but a few comments can indicate the problems with this view of pathology. The most powerful clinical argument for this definition of pathological grief is the link some researchers have established between depression and the unresolved grief of children for deceased parents. Tennant (1988), however, in a detailed review of this body of research concludes:

> Parental loss has all too readily been accepted as a significant risk factor in adult psychopathology. However a reasonable scrutiny of the empirical findings reveals their fragility. . . . there is no evidence that parental death is a significant risk factor for depression. (p. 1049)

The definition of the healthy resolution of grief as severing bonds with the dead does not stand the test of cross-cultural nor of comparative historical analysis. Stroebe, Gergen, Gergen, and Stroebe (1992) in a historical study show that the definition is an artifact of modernism which values goal directedness, efficiency, and rationality.

> In psychology, modernism has given rise to the machine metaphor of human functionality. When applied to grief, this view suggests that people need to recover from their state of intense emotionality and return to normal functioning and effectiveness as quickly and efficiently as possible. (p. 1206)

Modernism, they note, is a reaction against romanticism in which continuing bonds to the dead were valued and nurtured.

That is not to say that inner representations of dead children, like any significant attachment, do not on occasion become twisted in psychopathology. To understand the etiology of pathology in grief, it is useful to look again at the classic work of Lindemann and Cobb (1979). They do not find causal factors in the processes the bereaved undertake to resolve grief. Rather, Lindemann and Cobb find that persons with a prior history of psychopathology or with a social support system loaded with guilt and conflict are likely to exhibit pathology in their grief. Thus pathology in grief is a function of other pathology.

There have been studies of the destructive possibilities of socially maintained inner representations, though less study of the constructive possibilities. Maintaining the inner representation in the form of "replacement children" can be a heavy burden on the child who is expected to live someone else's life (Cain & Cain, 1964; Johnson, 1984; Legg & Sherick, 1976; Poznanski, 1972). Family systems therapists have focused on the ways in which families can get "stuck" by not publicly mourning losses so the family can reorganize without a "ghost" in the family (Walsh & McGoldrick, 1991). On a more positive note, though on a smaller scale, Rynearson (1987) shows how making the inner representation a party to the social system of psychotherapist and client helps the survivor resolve grief in a healthy way.

> While more investigation should be undertaken, it may be that maintaining the bond with the dead prevents pathology. When relationships to the dead are maintained it makes it less likely that their images will be reincarnated in the form of projections which distort our relationships to other people. . . . A heart that grieves, a heart that communes with the dead in reverie, is immune to falling in love on the rebound. By welcoming the ghosts the bereaved may find themselves to be no longer haunted by them. (Mogenson, 1992, p. 20)

INNER REPRESENTATION AS SOLACE

What forms of relationship to their dead child do parents maintain as solace in their lives? Following, are three common ways among members of the Compassionate Friends: linking objects, religious ideas and devotion, and memory. In the descriptions, both the solace that individuals find and how shared solace-bearing inner representations are a part of the bonds within families and communities will be considered.

Linking Objects

Linking objects are objects connected with the child's life that link the bereaved to the dead; in so doing, they evoke the presence of the dead (Volkan, 1981). Six years after his child's death, a father wrote a birthday letter to him:

> I haven't been able to part with the bicycle cart that I bought for you and your sister a few weeks before you died. It's never used anymore but I keep it in my study at home. . . . I still see your smile as you sat there holding our puppy. . . . Your little wind-up toy, the one of Donald Duck sitting in a shoe, sits on top of the file cabinet in my study. I feel close to you when I'm close to your favorite things.

The sense of smell is particularly intimate. Parents often report that they hold their children's clothes which still have the scent of the child. One mother who miscarried wrote that it is not the usual newborn scent that links her to her child.

> So the flowers I place upon his grave
> Are the only scent I know.
> So when I smell a flower
> My son always comes to mind.

The linking object need not be small toys or fast-fading flowers. A father whose daughter had died five years earlier said:

> It's that old pick-up truck. She used to ride around in it with me. She would lean against me on the seat. It has almost 200,000 miles on it, but I am not going to sell it. By now I probably couldn't get anything for it anyway. I told the boys they could work on it and use it if they got it going. But I'll never sell the truck because I can sit in there and feel my daughter. It's great.

The linking object is a self-validating truth to the parent that, though the child be dead, yet the child lives. One parent had many memories of being at the beach with her child. They would look for sand dollars, which the boy saved. Her memory of those times also include natural mystical experiences (see Hood, 1977) in which her bond with nature and with the child are intertwined. In a newsletter article she wrote that the child "was especially awed by the setting sun and as we walked the beaches, always he would stop and watch the sun go down—I did too! I was so happy with him."

> In February I went to Padre Island and one lonely evening I walked the beach alone—just the sand, the sea, a beautiful setting sun, the screeching gulls, God and me. It was there I begged Him to show me a sign that E. lives—to "please send me a sand dollar." I knew that it was not the season for sand dollars. Even the local people had told me that they had not seen sand dollars since last summer. But I only wanted just one sand dollar—just one! Watching the fading sunset and listening to the roar of the waves, darkness began to fall, so I turned to go back when there by my feet, the waves pushed up one lone sand dollar—a small but perfect sand dollar!
> That is exactly the way it happened and I cannot begin to tell you the feelings I had. My prayer had been answered.

The answer to her prayer for a sign that the child still lives is the linking object of the sand dollar. Now that she has had the intense experience of finding the sand dollar, the memory of this experience can be evoked and the memory itself can serve as a linking object.

If the linking object is rich enough, it can serve as an enduring, communally shared symbol. For this to happen, the object must have a cultural meaning by which the parent can connect personal solace to that provided within the social reality. One family in the study found the child's presence at a place in a national park the child had spontaneously called "just like heaven." One couple shared a linking object that has an often unrecognized cultural symbolism. Asked, "Do you ever sense that C. is still around?" the mother answered:

> Every time I see a mourning dove. Mourning doves are magnificent. The day after C. died, Cliff and I were sitting in the den looking out the window and there was a mourning dove on the porch. I didn't know what it was at the time, so I got out my bird book and looked it up. It is m-o-u-r-n-i-n-g dove, not m-o-r-n-i-n-g. It was so ironic because here I'd just lost a daughter and I'm getting out my bird book to look for mourning doves. It was phenomenal that we would see a mourning dove when we were mourning. It's got to mean something, right? So the two of us took this as, "This is C. C. is with the dove." Then, a few days later, there were two doves there. Cliff decided that it was C. telling him that she had a friend with her. It's really fascinating because I'll find myself thinking about her and I'll look around and see the mourning dove. That has become a symbol of C. It was on the year anniversary when we were going to the cemetery and Cliff said, "I wish I could see a mourning dove." So I said, "Come over here, there is usually a mourning dove over here." And I'll be damned if there wasn't a mourning dove on the wire. He said, "That's a sign. Now I can go to the cemetery."

Religious Devotion

Linking objects can have a numinous sense (Otto, 1923) about them, for they function like relics of the saints in which "any personal possession or part of a person's body. . . . can carry the power or saintliness of the person with whom they were once associated and make him or her 'present' once again" (Sullivan, 1987, p. 51). The numinous feeling is clearer in the many people who sense the presence of the child in their religious experience of prayer, ritual, and religious ideation. Religion as used here is the individual's sense of connectedness to that which transcends death (Chidester, 1990). The inner representation of the child is merged with something bigger, but something of which, in the deeper reaches of the psyche, the parent feels a part. Religion can be that provided within an institutionalized framework. One mother wrote a letter to her dead daughters describing the sense of presence at Catholic Mass.

> Every time I attend the sacrifice of the Mass, at the part where our Blessed Lord comes into our hearts, I feel so close to your angelic presence. What a divine experience! The only problem is that it doesn't last long enough. If only the others could share these feelings.

Religion can also be that which is outside of churches or theological doctrine. Parents feel the presence of the child within their bonds with the whole world. On her child's birthday, one mother wrote a letter as if from the child.

> I would have been twenty today, bound by earthly constraints. Do not cry, Mom. I am forever, I am eternal, I am ageless. I am in the blowing wind, the first blades of grass in the spring, the haunting cry of the owl, the shriek of the hawk, the silent soaring of the turkey vulture. I am in the tears of those in mourning, the laughter of little children, the pain of the dying, the hopelessness of the homeless. I am the weightless, floating feeling when you close your eyes at night; I am the heaviness of a broken heart. . . . Like an invisible cocoon I surround you. I am in the moonlight, the sunbeams, the dew at dawn. . . . Do not cry. Remember me with love and laughter and yes, with pain. For I was, I am, and I will always be. Once T., now nameless and free.

The child's presence comes within a sense of the uncanny, a feeling often associated with religious belief and practice (see Dawson, 1989). In a newsletter account, the uncanny appears twice, first as a dream that seems a premonition, and second as an unaccounted-for physical event. A few months before she was murdered, the daughter told her mother of a dream in which she was looking in the window at the family gathered for Christmas.

> On Christmas morning, while we were opening the gifts (which the daughter had made) my husband told me to look out the window. There are two rocking chairs on the porch and one was rocking back and forth. My husband reached over and held my hand, and it was at that moment I remembered what M. had told us about her dream, and I realized then that her dream had become a reality. M. was still with all of us and was indeed content at watching the family she loved so much sharing the joy of Christmas together.

Almost all the parents in the study feel that the child is in heaven. The inner representation of the child as in heaven is held tightly by some parents in the initial shock and disbelief of grief, even before they can develop a sense that they have an active interaction with the child. The separation from the child seems too much to bear for many parents, so even as they feel that their child is nowhere to be found in this world, they retain hope that they will join their child after death. A mother wrote in a newsletter early in her grief, before she had put together an integrated inner representation of the child:

> There's a hole in me. You see, as part of me is missing. I keep looking for my son, and all I find are bits and pieces of him— something he wrote, a picture he took, a book he read, a tape he made, something he drew—but there is an emptiness in me that these bits and pieces cannot fill, that nothing will ever fill. . . . My son is gone and he is not coming back. I will have to go to him and someday I will.

Such a feeling early in the grief often gives way to a more immediate interaction with the inner representation in a way that, while the hope of reunion after the parent's death is retained, there is a sense of a bond with the child in heaven, which is consoling. This is true even with those for whom heaven is not part of their theology. Knapp (1986) found that bereaved parents could not sustain a belief that there is no afterlife for their child. Several people in the study felt the child to be with another significant person who had died. One woman whose father had died 4 years before her child reported:

> It was hard after my father died because I always had this sense that I didn't know where he was. But I was busy with L. because she was so sick all the time. After L. died I was really bothered that I didn't know where she was and that somehow that meant that I didn't know she was safe. That lasted two years. One day I

started crying and I realized I wasn't just crying for L. I was missing my father. And suddenly I just thought, "Daddy is taking care of L. She is OK because she is with him and that's where he is. It is like they are together." That sounds so simple-minded. I don't believe in heaven or afterlife, I think we just live on in memory. But it just feels like I don't have that worry about either of them any more. I know they are together.

Within a social system, sharing a religious sense in the bond with the inner representation of a dead child has a quite common form. Ethnic, racial, or political membership is often infused with religious feelings. Indeed, for many people, God and country feel as one. All peoples encourage a strong bond with the dead hero or martyr. Among the symbols that bind a nation together are the internalized representations of its young who died that the nation could have its land, its freedom, its king, its religion, its form of government, or its economic power. Lincoln's address at Gettysburg offers solace to the parents of those buried there, and at the same time it bonds the citizens to the war dead and to the abstract ideals on which the nation was founded. Such solace can, of course, be used destructively. In some pathological cultural systems or in historical situations in which there has been a regression to what Wilber (1981) calls mythic/membership, blood must be answered by blood. In the name of those fallen for the cause, other people's children may be killed with impunity (Jacoby, 1983). It is difficult to stop a cycle of violence when each side merges the solace of the inner representations of the dead children with a religious feeling of peoplehood and with a drive for revenge which feels as if it has divine sanction.

Memories

Bereaved parents can find solace in memory. Unconflicted and peaceful memory is often at the end of a difficult process of separating self-representation from the inner representation of the child. Memories are at first very painful, for they are reminders of the loss. One mother reflected on the discovery that letting go of the pain did not also mean letting go of the child.

You know, I remember being afraid that someday I would wake up and my feeling of being bonded to K. wouldn't be there. I thought that when the pain left, she would be gone too. But now I find that I hope the memories will come. The times in the hospital are not what I remember. I remember the good times, when she was well. Sometimes I just look at her pictures and remember when we took them. I never know when I will look at the pictures, but I feel better afterwards.

This use of memory as solace seems similar to what Tahka (1984) calls "remembrance formations." He says once the remembrance formation

has been established, its later calling back to mind, reminiscing about it and dismissing it again from the mind, are invariably experienced as activities of the self taking place exclusively on the subject's own conditions. Although it is experienced as a fully differentiated object representation, no illusions of its separate and autonomous existence are involved. In contrast to fantasy objects possessing various wish-fulfilling functions, it includes the awareness that nothing more can be expected from it and therefore, in its fully established forms it has chances for becoming the most realistic of all existing object representations. (p. 18)

A poem in a newsletter makes the point more gracefully.

Memories are the
perennials that
bloom again
after the hard winter grief
begins to
yield to hope.

Memory can be a part of everyday life. The quiet times remembering the dead child have about them a somewhat forbidden quality, but the memory time becomes a personal ritual around which to build a day.

Sometimes I pretend, when no one's around,
that you are still home,
creating your own special sound—
the car, the stereo, singing in the shower.

Such thematic memories, that is memories that catch the essence of the individual child, take the parent out of the present and to a time when the world was better.

I can still envision the surprised, happy look on his face that Christmas when he opened a gift and found a silver vest and pants to wear when he played his bass guitar with his beloved band. . . . I remember when he took me out to eat one Mother's Day, just he and I. . . . how handsome he was in his tux and top hat and how he introduced his date for the prom . . . how proud we all were at his graduation when he gave the welcome address. . . . Wonderful memories are something that no one can take away. Some memories just won't die.

Often it is the emotional states attached to the thematic memories that carry the quality of solace. Writing nearly 20 years after the death of her daughter, a mother reflected on her memory of a beginners' ballet recital.

I can't remember the details of that afternoon. . . . But I remember the feeling, somewhere between laughter and tears. I remember loving that small, beautiful person, my child. I remember my sense of admiration for her, and a fittingly stifled flood of pride. . . . I have forgotten so many things, but I remember the feeling. Always the feeling.

Memory binds family and communities together. In the Compassionate Friends, the members do not remember each other's children as living, for it was the death of the children which brought members to the group. But the solace of memory is important in the group's bond. The group has developed rituals that express the bond with the child as part of the bonds within the community. Such rituals give permission to each parent to hold the inner representation without conflict. A significant portion of national and regional meetings are devoted to ritual activity, such as boards with pictures of the dead children. The holiday candlelight memorial service is the largest gathering of the local chapter. Many of the members, including "alumnae" who no longer attend meetings, bring the child's siblings, grandparents, uncles, aunts, or family friends. The memory of the child is thus included in the holiday and in the family circle. As the children's names are read the parents and those who have come with them rise and light a candle. A liturgy adopted from *Gates of Prayer* (1975), a Jewish prayer book, is a central part of the memorial service.

In the rising of the sun and in its going down,
We remember them;

In the blowing of the wind and in the chill of winter,
  We remember them;
In the opening of buds and in the warmth of summer,
  We remember them;
In the rustling of leaves and the beauty of autumn,
  We remember them;
In the beginning of the year and when it ends,
  We remember them;
When we are weary and in need of strength,
  We remember them;
When we are lost and sick at heart,
  We remember them;
When we have joys we yearn to share,
  We remember them;
So long as we live, they too shall live, for they are now a part of us as
  We remember them.

SOLACE AND IMMORTALITY

This essay has looked at three ways in which the inner representation of the child is a solace-giving, ongoing part of the parent's inner world and social world: linking objects, religious devotion, and memories. In each of those ways, the child remains immortal, in the sense that the inner representation of the child remains a real, living presence in the parent's inner and social world.

Most psychosocial thinking about immortality is from the self's point of view. Individuals fear annihilation of the self and compensate, as one psychoanalytic scholar finds, by a "regression to the union of the archaic idealized omnipotent figure in the death-transformation passage to the 'new existence' . . . based on symbiosis with the undifferentiated god" (Pollock, 1975, p. 341). The death of a child brings a most difficult grief in this culture because the sense of selfhood involved in parenting is a central part of the being. The bond reaches back to the parent's own infancy and the bond with the parent's own parents and it reaches forward to the hopes for the completion of the self which children represent. The death of the child is the death of a part of the self. But the child is also not the self. The parents must still live in a poorer world. The child's immortality need not be so regressive.

The continuing interaction with the inner representation of the dead child in bereaved parents seems to support Lifton's (1974) idea that the sense of immortality is not compensation or denial and therefore not pathological. Lifton finds that the sense of immortality is "man's symbolization of his ties with both his biological fellows and his history, past and future" (p. 685). The parents' bond with the child already symbolizes the parents' ties to their biological, personal, and cultural history. Bereaved parents often remind each other, "When your parent dies, you lose your past. When your child dies, you lose your future." Solace is for living in that poorer world. The immortal inner representation of the child maintains the bonds to history and future, to biology and culture symbolized by the living child.

Winnicott (1953, 1971) notes that art and religion seem to grow out of the blended inner and outer reality first seen in the child's transitional object. The language of one mother writing in the newsletter shows that she already knew the part of herself where she now feels connected to her child.

I cannot open my eyes to see his smile. I close my eyes and listen to my heart, for it is there that he lives. I must dig deeper inside myself to a place that I ever knew existed to feel the joy this child brought.

In many of his sonnets Shakespeare asks how a dead friend or lover can live on. He seems finally to settle upon the immortality of his own art, for if he can join the reality of the deceased to the "eternal lines" of the poem, the dead person is made immortal (see Hubler, 1952). Thus Shakespeare locates the immortality of the dead in his art much the way bereaved parents locate their dead children in their experience of solace.

And every fair from fair sometime declines,
By chance or nature's changing course untrimm'd;
But thy eternal summer shall not fade
Nor lose possession of that fair thou owest;
Nor shall Death brag thou wander'st in his shade,
When in eternal lines to time thou growest:
So long as men can breath or eyes can see,
So long lives this and this gives life to thee. (Sonnet 18)

For their parents, dead children do not lose possession of that fairness they embodied, nor do they wander only in Death's shade. They have lived just the summer, but their summer does not fade; it remains eternal in a part of the parent's psyche and in the social system where the parent feels most at home. The parents find solace in linking objects that evoke the presence of the dead, in religious ideas and devotion which merge the child with other death-transcending connections of the parent's life, and in memories by which time can drop away and the parent can return to the world when it was a better place. So long lives this in the inner and social world of bereaved parents, this gives life to their children who have died.

Such immortality is not the only immortality available after a child dies. For example, passing of genetic material is a universal form of immortality. Shakespeare recognizes:

But were some child of yours alive at time,
You should live twice; in it and in my rhyme. (Sonnet 17)

Human efforts to create external symbols of immortality feel less sure, and in the end less meaningful, than the immortality bereaved parents find in the solace-filled bond with their child.

Not marble, nor the gilded monuments
Of princes, shall outlive this powerful rhyme;
But you shall shine more bright in these contents
Than unswept stone, besmeared with sluttish time. . . .
So, til the judgement that yourself arise,
You live in this, and dwell in lover's eyes. (Sonnet 60)

The immortal children are present in the same world in which the parent lives, not in another world. Harper (1991) says:

There are persons whom we cannot think of except as being alive. They seem to resist destruction, even when dead. . . . Around them, even remembering them, whether away for a while or permanently, we feel the whole world a more vibrant as well as more interesting place. (p. 89)

In a new life which sometimes feels neither sure nor safe, the immortal child provides a solace-filled reality which feels both inside and outside the self, that does not change, and the truth of which cannot be challenged.

CLINICAL IMPLICATIONS

The resolution of parental grief is adaptation, growth, and change, not recovery of the way they were before the death. Parents now live in a different world with a self that has been changed. The change in the world is that a child, their child, has died. Among the changes in the self is the transformed inner representation of the now-dead child. What, then, is the role of the clinician in grief support groups or counseling? Clinical issues may be 1) stress in everyday life after the death of the child, 2) difficulties in transforming the inner representation of the child, or 3) ensuring that the inner representation of the child is held in as healthy a way as possible.

With parents whom Compassionate Friends describe as "well along in their grief," the nature and mode of the inner representation can be determined with questions like: "Who is C. to you right now?" "How are you still in touch with C.?" "Where is C. for you now?" "What role does C. still play in your life?" Most parents whose grief is well toward resolution can give a rather full answer to these questions and often can discuss problems they are having in managing the relationship with the inner representation of the child. This information enables the clinician to share the client's world in order to deal with whatever issues are at hand. Because some phenomena in the interaction with dead children fall outside socially accepted reality, parents may monitor their answer in terms of the perceived attitude of the questioner.

Bereaved parents who are, as Compassionate Friends describe it, "new in their grief" or "early in their grief," will usually not be able to answer the questions to their own satisfaction; and indeed, many answer the question in terms of absence or of the lack of connection. In this case, the clinician makes the inner representation part of the bond with the client. The clinician gets to know the child through photographs, art work, or stories of the child. It is not unusual for parents to bring linking objects into the consulting room. After the child is established as a social reality and the early issues of grief are navigated, parents begin to discuss the problems of living, the meanings of life, and the meanings of the death partly in terms of the meaning of the child now. Often at this time, the clinician will hear reports of visitations or interchanges with the child, and will begin to hear reports of the solace those interactions bring.

There are two especially difficult clinical situations involving the inner representation of the child. The first is when the inner representation is not shared in the client's natural support networks. There are a variety of reasons the inner representation may not be shared. After miscarriage often family and friends do not regard the fetus as a child, while the parent has already bonded with a whole set of hopes and expectations. When a married couple is a birth-parent and a step-parent, conflict may ensue if the step-parent has not deeply bonded to the child and, thus, does not share the birth-parent's inner representation of the dead child. There are also parents who are unusually isolated from social networks, and parents whose child died in such a socially unacceptable way that the parent is cut off from social support. When the inner representation is not a social reality, it is difficult to use it for solace. In these cases, referral to the Compassionate Friends or other grief support groups is often effective. When referral does not work, the therapist and the client can form the community in which the inner representation can become real.

The second difficult situation is when the inner representation

becomes intertwined in individual or family pathology. In these cases, clinicians can work with individual and family using the same theories and techniques they would use if the bond were with the living child. When the child is maintained as a frozen entity in the family system, the issue is flexibility. As the family can be helped to be more flexible, the inner representation will take a healthier place in the new dynamics. If a parent has so identified with the child that the whole selfhood was dependent on the child, the therapeutic issue is differentiation. When differentiation is achieved, the inner representation will provide solace rather than being a reminder of the parent's unfulfilled narcissistic bond.

In the easiest clinical situation, the clinician is called upon to validate the parents, experiences of interaction with the inner representation of their dead child. The clinician's authority can be used to normalize the experience. Learning that such experiences are normal and common often relieves a great deal of stress and thereby allows the parent to accept the solace being offered by the inner representation of the child.

Bereaved parents in the Compassionate Friends remain in active interaction with the inner representations of their dead children. As clinicians learn to understand how these immortal children take their place in the parents' lives, and how the inner representations give solace in the face of irreparable loss, the clinician can more effectively help parents deal with the stresses in their lives and untangle whatever pathologies present themselves.

REFERENCES

Benedek, T. (1959). Parenthood as a developmental phase. *American Psychoanalytic Association Journal, 7,* 389–417.

Benedek, T. (1975). Discussion of parenthood as a developmental phase. *Journal of the American Psychoanalytic Association, 23,* 154–165.

Bowlby, J. (1969–1980). *Attachment and loss (Vols. 1–3).* New York: Basic Books.

Brice, C. W. (1991). Paradoxes of maternal mourning. *Psychiatry, 54,* 1–12.

Bushbaum, B. C. (1987). Remembering a parent who has died: A developmental perspective. *The Annual of Psychoanalysis, Vol. XV.* Madison: International Universities Press, pp. 99–112.

Cain, A. C., & Cain, B. S. (1964). On replacing a child. *Journal of the American Academy of Child Psychiatry, 3,* 443–456.

Chidester, D. (1990). *Patterns of transcendence: Religion, death, and dying.* Belmont, CA: Wadsworth.

Compassionate Friends, The, (1983). Oakbrook, IL: Author.

Dietrich, D. R. & Shabad, P. C. (Eds.). (1989). *The problem of loss and mourning: Psychoanalytic perspectives.* Madison: International Universities Press.

Dawson, L. (1989). Otto and Freud on the uncanny and beyond. *Journal of the American Academy of Religion, 58*(2), 283–311.

Elson, M. (1984). Parenthood and the transformations of narcissism. In R. S. Cohen, B. J. Cohler, & S. H. Weissman (Eds.), *Parenthood: A psychodynamic perspective* (pp. 297–314). New York: Guilford.

Fairbairn, W. D. (1952). *An object-relations theory of the personality.* New York: Basic Books.

Furman, E. (1974). *A child's parent dies: Studies in childhood bereavement.* New Haven: Yale University Press.

Gates of prayer: The new union prayer book (1975). New York: Central Conference of American Rabbis; London: Union of Liberal and Progressive Synagogues.

Glick, I. O., Weiss, R. S., & Parkes, C. M. (1974). *The first year of bereavement.* New York: John Wiley & Sons.

Goin, M. K., Burgoyne, R. W., & Goin, J. M. (1979). Timeless attachment to a dead relative. *American Journal of Psychiatry, 136*(7), 988–989.

Harper. R. (1991). *On presence: Variations and reflections.* Philadelphia: Trinity Press International.

Hood, R. (1977). Eliciting mystical states of consciousness in semistructured nature experiences. *Journal for the Scientific Study of Religion, 16*(2), 155–163.

Horton, P. C. (1981). *Solace, the missing dimension in psychiatry.* Chicago: University of Chicago Press.

Hubler, E. (1952). *The sense of Shakespeare's sonnets.* Princeton, NJ: Princeton University Press.

Jackson, E. N. (1957). *Understanding grief: Its roots, dynamics, and treatment.* New York: Abingdon Press.

Jacoby, S. (1983). *Wild justice, the evolution of revenge.* New York: Harper & Row.

Johnson, S. (1984). Sexual intimacy and replacement children after the death of a child. *Omega: Journal of Death and Dying, 15,* 109–118.

Kalish, R. A. & Reynolds, D. K. (1981). *Death and ethnicity: A psychocultural study.* Farmingdale, NY: Baywood Publishing Company.

Klass, D. (1987). John Bowlby's model of grief and the problem of identification. *Omega: Journal of Death and Dying, 18,* 13–32.

Klass, D. (1988). *Parental grief: Resolution and solace.* New York: Springer.

Knapp, R. (1986). *Beyond endurance: When a child dies.* New York: Schocken.

Legg, C., & Sherick, I. (1976). The replacement child—A developmental tragedy: Some preliminary comments. *Child Psychiatry and Human Development, 70,* 113–126.

Lehman, D. R., Wortman, C. B., & Williams, A. F. (1987). Long-term effects of losing a spouse or child in a motor vehicle crash. *Journal of Personality and Social Psychology, 52,* 218–231.

Lifton, R. J. (1974). On death and the continuity of life: A "new" paradigm. *History of Childhood Quarterly, 1*(4), 681–696.

Lindemann, E., & Cobb, S. (1979). Neuropsychiatric observations after the Coconut Grove fire. In E. Lindemann and E. Lindemann (Eds.), *Beyond grief: Studies in crisis intervention.* New York: Aronson.

Lopata, H. Z. (1973). *Widowhood in an American city.* Cambridge, MA: Schenkman.

Lopata, H. Z. (1979). *Women as widows, support systems.* New York: Elsevier.

Matchett, W. F. (1972). Repeated hallucinatory experiences as a part of the mourning process among Hopi Indian women. *Psychiatry, 35,* 185–194.

Mogenson, G. (1992). *Greeting the angels: An imaginal view of the mourning process.* Amityville, NY: Baywood Publishing Company.

Moody, R. A. (1987). *Elvis after life: Unusual psychic experiences surrounding the death of a superstar.* Atlanta: Peachtree Publishers.

Moss, M. S., & Moss, S. Z. (1980). The image of the deceased spouse in remarriage of elderly widow(er)s. *Journal of Gerontological Social Work, 3*(2), 59–70.

Otto, R. (1923). *The idea of the holy.* Trans. by John W. Harvey. New York: Oxford University Press.

Parkes, C. M. (1972). *Bereavement: Studies in grief in adult life.* New York: International Universities Press.

Parkes, C. M., & Weiss, R. S. (1983). *Recovery from bereavement.* New York: Basic Books.

Passman, R. H. (1976). Arousal reducing properties of attachment objects: Testing the functional limits of the security blanket relative to the mother. *Developmental Psychology, 12,* 468–469.

Passman, R. H., & Weisberg, P. (1975). Mothers and blankets as agents for promoting play and exploration by young children in a novel environment: The effects of social and nonsocial attachment objects. *Developmental Psychology, 11,* 170–177.

Pollock, G. H. (1975). On mourning, immortality, and utopia. *Journal of the American Psychoanalytic Association, 23*(2), 334–362.

Poznanski, E. O. (1972). The 'replacement child': A saga of unresolved parental grief. *Journal of Pediatrics, 81*(6), 1190–1193.

Rando, T. A. (1984). *Grief, dying, and death: Clinical interventions for caregivers.* Champaign, IL: Research Press Company.

Raphael, B. (1983). *The anatomy of bereavement.* New York: Basic Books.

Rees, W. D. (1975). The bereaved and their hallucinations. In Bernard Schoenberg et al. (Eds.), *Bereavement: Its psychosocial aspects.* New York: Columbia University Press, pp. 66–71.

Rubin, S. S. (1985). The resolution of bereavement: A clinical focus on the relationship to the deceased. *Psychotherapy, 22*(2), 231–235.

Rynearson, E. K. (1987). Psychotherapy of pathologic grief: Revisions and limitations. *Psychiatric Clinics of North America, 10*(3), 487–499.

Sanders, C. M. (1989). *Grief: The mourning after.* New York: John Wiley and Sons.

Silverman, P. R. (1986). *Widow-to-Widow.* New York: Springer Publishing Company.

Silverman, P. R. (1987). The impact of parental death on college-age women. *Psychiatric Clinics of North America, 10*(3), 387–404.

Stroebe, M., Gergen, M. M., Gergen, K. J., & Stroebe, W. (1992). Broken hearts or broken bonds: Love and death in historical perspective. *American Psychologist, 47*(10), 1205–1212.

Sullivan, L. E. (1987). Death, afterlife, and the soul. *Selections from the encyclopedia of religion,* Mircea Eliade, Editor in Chief. New York: Macmillan.

Tahka, V. (1984). Dealing with object loss. *Scandinavian Psychoanalytic Review, 7,* 13–33.

Tennant, C. (1988). Parental loss in childhood: Its effect in adult life. *Archives of General Psychiatry, 45,* 1045–1049.

Tessman, L. H. (1978). *Children of parting parents.* New York: Jason Aronson.

Volkan, V. D. (1981). *Linking objects and linking phenomena.* New York: International Universities Press.

Volkan, V. D. (1985a). The scope of depressive states. In V. D. Volkan (Ed.), *Depressive states and their treatment* (pp. 1–17). Northvale, NJ: Jason Aronson.

Volkan, V. D. (1985b). Psychotherapy of complicated mourning. In V. D. Volkan (Ed.), *Depressive states and their treatment* (pp. 271–295). Northvale, NJ: Jason Aronson.

Walsh, F. & McGoldrick, M. (Eds.). (1991). *Living beyond loss: Death in the family.* New York: W. W. Norton & Company.

Wilber, K. (1981). *Up from Eden.* Boulder: Shambhala.

Winnicott, D. W. (1953). Transitional objects and transitional phenomena. *International Journal of Psychoanalysis, 34,* 89–97.

Winnicott, D. W. (1971). *Playing and reality.* New York: Basic Books.

Worden, J. W. (1982). *Grief counseling and grief therapy, a handbook for the mental health practitioner.* New York: Springer Publishing Company.

Yamamoto, J., Okonogi, K., Iwasaki, T., & Yoshimura, S. (1969). Mourning in Japan. *American Journal of Psychiatry, 125,* 1661–1665.

EFFECTS OF A CHILD'S DEATH ON THE MARITAL RELATIONSHIP: A PRELIMINARY STUDY

Reiko Schwab

Old Dominion University, Norfolk, Virginia

This study examined the effects of a child's death on the parents' marital relationship. The participants were 20 couples who lost children in a variety of ways. The data collected through interviews were analyzed to determine common experiences among parents. Five themes were identified and discussed. They were fathers' concern and frustration about their wives' grief, wives' anger over husbands' not sharing their grief, temporary halt in communication, loss of sexual intimacy, and general irritability between spouses. Implications for mental health professionals are discussed.

When a child dies, parents lose part of themselves and some of their hope for the future. Their loss is immense. How does such a loss affect the parents' marital relationship? Studies specifically devoted to this question appear limited. Available literature based on research and clinical observations indicates that the death of a child strains the parents' marital relationship, sometimes resulting in separation and divorce. A study by Nixon and Pearn (1977) indicated that 7 of 29 parent-dyads had separated following the drowning of their children. In contrast, none of the 54 parent-dyads who had a child survive a near drowning had separated. However, some of the bereaved parent-dyads were resilient in response to the loss; 5 actually reported that the tragedy of loss had brought them closer together. Shanfield and Swain (1984) found that many of the 40 parents in their study who had lost adult children in traffic accidents considered their marital relationships improved after bereavement. Based on his study, Klass (1986–87) concluded that marriages did not end because of a child's death but because after the child's death parents felt it was no longer worth struggling with marital problems that had existed before the loss.

Helmrath and Steinitz (1978) interviewed seven couples who had lost an infant and found that the men felt that they had to be "strong" for their spouses and could not break down and cry. They were frustrated over their inability to help their wives resolve their grief and at the little support they received from their wives for their own feelings. On the other hand, the women found it hard to understand why their husbands were not grieving as intensely as they were. Cook (1983), who studied 145 bereaved parents, found that fathers felt responsible for managing and controlling the grief of other family members, especially the grief of their wives. Fathers also found it difficult to grieve openly, and keeping their grief to themselves created a barrier to their wives' attempts to talk about the loss.

In another article, Cook (1988) discussed men's bereavement from a men's studies perspective and pointed out the double binds bereaved fathers face as they struggle to cope with their child's death. On the one hand, men are given little comfort and support in bereavement and are expected to be strong and provide a source of support for their wives and other family members. On the other hand, their nonexpressiveness comes into conflict with their wives' needs for expression. In addition, men face the conflict between the health professionals' notion that expressing feelings is the healthiest way to cope with loss and their personal and social expectations of being manly, which discourage men from openly expressing feelings. Cook's own interview data on mourning strategies reported by 55 bereaved fathers showed that fathers exerted great effort to control their own emotional distress. Typically, they would express it only when alone in order to shield others, particularly their wives. Paradoxically, their wives complained about their husbands' unwillingness to share their thoughts and feelings.

The loss of sexual desire on the part of bereaved parents was reported by Johnson (1984–85). The 14 bereaved parents she interviewed indicated that they did not have the desire or energy for sex soon after losing their children because they were overwhelmed by grief. Parents of a child who died after a brief period of illness tended to abstain from sexual intercourse longer than those who anticipated a child's death for a longer period of time. The abstinence was reported to last from several weeks to a year. However, there was a desire to be held and to be close to each other. Both the men and women in the study agreed that this was out of the ordinary for the men in view of the fact that before their bereavement they could not be physically close without having sex. Cook (1984), who studied parents of fatally ill children, also reported that the couples' sex lives suffered to some degree and that wives grew angry at their husbands' seeking sexual

The author thanks Old Dominion University Research Foundation for its support of the study from which this article evolved.

I gratefully acknowledge the contributions of all the parents involved in the study and Edward Schwab, Jr., who assisted with the interviews of parents.

From *Death Studies*, Vol. 16, No. 2, March/April 1992, pp. 141-154. © 1992 by Taylor and Francis, 1101 Vermont Ave., NW, Ste. 200, Washington, DC 20005. Reprinted by permission.

pleasure when the child's condition was particularly bad.

The paucity of studies focusing specifically on the effects of a child's death on a marital relationship led the present investigator to explore the topic as part of a study on bereaved parents. This article reports the findings based on interviews of bereaved couples.

METHODS

Participants

The group of participants consisted of 20 bereaved marital couples, a total of 40 participants. Initially, 33 couples were contacted personally to solicit their cooperation for the study. Eight of the couples, however, did not participate in the study. In all but one of these eight cases, only the wife was willing to take part in the study, and therefore those couples were not included. In only one instance was neither partner willing to participate. The remaining 25 couples were interviewed. However, for this part of the study, only the data obtained from 20 couples whose child died within the past four years were included. All the couples except one were associated with a support group for parents who had lost a child or who had a terminally ill child; the investigator—a counselor educator and licensed professional counselor—had been involved as an organizer and facilitator with this group for a number of years. One couple was introduced to the investigator by a professional in the community. The sample was heterogeneous, with parents' ages ranging from 27 to 60, with a median of 39. The husbands' occupations varied from semiskilled to professional work; 14 of the wives were homemakers and the others were semiskilled, skilled, or professional workers. Eighteen couples were white and two were black. The deceased children's ages ranged from 0 (stillbirth) to 30 years with a median of 9 years. The children died from a variety of causes such as illness, accident, murder, and stillbirth. The time elapsed since the child's death to the time of the interview ranged from one month to four years, the median being 22 months.

Procedures

The participating couples were interviewed individually and separately by the investigator and another professional who was trained in behavioral sciences. Both had been involved as organizers and facilitators with the support group for bereaved parents referred to earlier. The interviews took place either at the couples' own homes or the home of the investigator, depending on the couples' preference. Most couples were interviewed on the same day; a few interviews took place on separate days.

The interviews, which lasted from one to three hours, were semistructured, with a set of open-ended questions presented in a predetermined order. These questions addressed what each couple found to be the hardest things to deal with after their child's death, recurring thoughts and feelings, methods of coping with their grief, ways in which the child's death affected their marital relationship, other major losses they experienced, and changes they experienced in their attitude toward life as a result of their loss. Aside from the information obtained in response to the question as to how their child's death affected their marriage, each couple's responses to other questions indicated above provided additional data concerning the effects of a child's death on the marital relationship. All interviews were tape-recorded with the permission of the participants.

The interviews were transcribed verbatim, and statements made by the parents about their spouses and their marital relationships were first reviewed and recorded in order to identify appropriate categories. Transcripts were then reviewed again, and comments were recorded in the categories by identification numbers. The recording of data with ID numbers made it possible to determine the frequency with which similar comments were made and to refer back to the transcripts with ease whenever necessary.

RESULTS

Even though the parents' responses to the open-ended questions were diverse, certain themes were identifiable based on the interview data. The themes discussed below were derived from those statements made by one third (seven participants) or more of either the fathers or mothers or both combined. Differences between sexes were evident in the themes that were identified. No one theme stood out as being more prominent than the others. Therefore, the order in which they are discussed is no indication of their relative prominence. The names of individuals used in this section are fictitious in order to conceal their identity.

Fathers' Concern and Frustration About Their Wives' Grief

Fathers' responses revealed a theme involving their concern and sense of frustration and helplessness that there was nothing they could do to ease their wives' grief. In response to the question about the hardest thing they had to deal with after a child's death, some husbands stated that their wives' grief was one of them. They felt responsible for doing something to help their wives but did not know what to do. Having to go back to work, one husband indicated that he intellectualized his grief, while his wife "felt it, grieved, moped, and did not do anything for a long time to the point of it becoming irritating to me. At the same time I felt helpless as to how to get her out of that." Another husband discussed his struggle with his wife's grief, which produced much tension and strain in their marriage:

She tried to kill herself once. . . . It's hard for me. At times, I really wish Jane would go away, either die or just leave me to end the whole thing. Then I have to tell myself that's not the way life is either. . . . We just have to work through this. The more I disengage myself from her, not from the love part but from trying to control her, worry about what she does, or take responsibility for her actions, the better I feel. . . . She has to find her own path.

Some husbands indicated that their wives were so preoccupied with their grief that it was difficult for them to cope with their own grief and the chores of daily living that had to be maintained. They felt that they had to be the strong one in the family at least for a while, although they were deeply shaken themselves. One husband said, "I wanted to be strong for Brenda. . . . When Brenda got herself together I found myself depressed." Another husband spoke of his wife not being able to take care of the bills or household chores and the family being "on the verge of falling apart." Recalling his loneliness; problems with children, work, and money; and frustration with his wife, another husband stated:

I think for the first nine months, she literally ceased to function as a mother to the other children. I mean she put the entire burden of caring for them on me. . . . I thought I was in rather serious depression myself, but I went to your group and also went for individual therapy and never gave up the concept of will-power and doing what you have to do for the rest of the family to function.

Wives' Anger Over Husbands' Not Sharing Their Grief

A second theme indicated the wives' perspectives of what was occurring in their marital relationships, showing the differences in coping between husbands and wives. Many wives expressed their distress, anger, and disappointment about their husbands' unwillingness to share their grief. According to reports by a number of wives and by some husbands themselves, a number of husbands continued to avoid talking about their grief by keeping themselves occupied, drinking, remaining unresponsive, or other measures. Wives initially interpreted such behavior as a sign of not caring enough about the deceased child or as an act of rejection or abandonment of them as spouses; this compounded their sense of loss and strained their marital relationship.

One mother who lost her teenage daughter said, "We avoided the topic but I was so wrapped up [in my grief] and wanted to talk about her. The avoidance of the topic was very, very hard on me. It was like, I remember her; you don't." Another mother said, "Not much communication. I am angry. . . . He is nervous, smokes. I wish Andy was closer to me. He is cold." "When John hurts, he wants to be alone; when I hurt, I need him there with me. . . . So I was hurt because he had left [the hospital soon after she had a stillbirth]; at the same time I was trying to understand [his need to be alone]. . . ." said a young mother.

Reflecting on the way she and her husband coped with their daughter's death, one mother recalled: " . . . he started drinking. Then I felt a second loss. Then I felt more alone. We were pushed apart. There was no chance of relating. . . ." " . . . Cecil totally stopped communicating with me. He wore earphones and a radio when he was home and basically didn't talk. . . . He laid around with earphones and the radio when he was home and went off by himself," said a mother describing the way her marital relationship started to crumble after her child's death, ending

in divorce. A mother who lost a child after a long illness stated:

We were just . . . he was going this way and I was going that way, and we were grieving over the same thing, but we were not able to communicate that for a long time and so . . . he was into drinking and I became very angry over that. . . . I was not very tolerant of what he was going through because all I saw was that it was hurting me. I didn't perceive his drinking as a pain-killing mechanism. I just saw it as an abandonment of me when I needed him.

A number of wives and some husbands indicated that they realized that their spouses' behavior was their way of coping with grief, which was different from their own. The following statements made by a mother represent their insight, which was expressed by other parents as well.

In the beginning I was very, very mad, not in the sense I was blaming him for Teresa's death or anything he did in the past, but just mad at his silence. I took a lot of resentment in that. I was bitter about it. I felt he wasn't there when I needed him, because he didn't talk about it. But in time, in the course of two or three months, I just came to the realization that everybody grieves differently, and George has never been expressive. George does not waste words. He was handling Teresa's death like he did every other situation. . . . So I said to myself that George was there in feelings . . . but he just was unable to express them.

The acceptance of such differences, parents reported, eased tension and contributed to the resolution of conflict in their relationship.

Temporary Halt in Communication

A third theme involved the effects of differing grief reactions on a couple's relationship and, to some extent, overlapped the theme of wives' complaint about husbands' not sharing their grief. The interview data showed that the intensity, complexity, and expression of grief differed between the two parents to varying degrees, ranging from "normal" grief to serious depression (two were hospitalized) and highly controlled expressions of grief. Many parents reported that soon after experiencing the death of a child, their pain was so great that they shut themselves in their own worlds and were unable to relate to any-

one outside themselves. A father said, "Nothing is the same. All of a sudden, the whole world is upside down. At times you are hardly aware that the other exists."

In addition, when one spouse tried to talk with the other, it often triggered crying, which culminated in an uneasy silence. Knowing that it gave pain to their spouses, they either hesitated to talk about the child's death or kept their feelings and thoughts to themselves for some time. "We were so worried about each other's feelings that we were afraid if we grieved openly we would start the other up," said one mother. To use one husband's expression, some couples felt as though they were "walking on eggshells" in their efforts not to say a wrong word.

The highly private nature of grief, its intensity, and the desire not to stir up their spouse's emotions resulted in a virtual cutoff of communication; this appeared to continue for a few days to a few months and in a few cases, even longer. "It was as though we were living in two different worlds," one mother said. The experience of the first few months and how they broke the silence was described by a father who lost his daughter:

For the first two to three months . . . we didn't want to talk. There was basically a cutoff of our relationship. . . . [Yet] we were both doing things together. After the first couple of months we were able to talk. One of the nights we stayed up, we cried, we just held each other for two, three hours. Just cried. That was the beginning of getting back together.

Loss of Sexual Intimacy

Effects of loss on the couple's sexual relationship was a fourth theme. Although not all parents were willing to talk about what they considered to be a highly private affair between husband and wife, a number of parents reported that they or their spouses lost interest in sexual activity for a period of time. A father mentioned that his daughter's death "destroyed sexuality completely for a while, took the interest out of anything joyful," and made him feel "like packing up and leaving." A young woman who had a stillbirth tearfully disclosed, " . . . the very first time we tried to . . . I just broke down and cried. I guess it's because it was sacred, you know, that's where Jane had lived. I just didn't want anything interfering with that." Recalling the night a day or two after her son's sudden death, another mother said, "Sam was just passionately wanting to make love. That just devastated me. . . . I just couldn't believe that this was what he wanted and needed at this time. . . . I resented him terribly."

From husbands' perspectives, their wives' distancing and nonresponsiveness as sexual partners denied them a source of comfort in a period of crisis. A husband expressed his frustration as he said, "We had virtually no sexual relationship. There was a period where I did want a sexual relationship because I always find it comforting and wanted to hold her, but she withdrew from all that. Ultimately, we got back. It took about a year." Another husband said, "At first, I wanted to reach out to Joan. Getting into bed, I wanted to wrap my arms around her, hold another live body close to me. She didn't seem to want to do that. I wanted to have sex right away; she didn't want to. She lost all interest. . . . I had a fear of losing Joan."

A mother shared her view on the basis of her own experience and that of other bereaved mothers with whom she talked: "In observing and talking to other women, [I have found] physical intimacy is the last thing on their mind. Part of it is abhorrent. But to their husbands, they need it in terms of comfort. So it's really a burden to women; it's really repugnant, or repulsive is a better description." This difference no doubt could result in misunderstanding, create distance between spouses, and become an additional source of strain in the process of mourning.

General Irritability Between Spouses
Often bereaved parents were mad at the world, at God, at themselves, or at those people whom they perceived as having had something to do with the death of their child. Their tempers were often short with their spouses; this is another theme heard from bereaved parents. A father who lost his daughter after many years of illness said of his wife: " . . . she was despondent and actually evil and irritable . . . when one feels bad, the other one feels not so good. We would put pressure on the other one to relieve ourselves." "Home life is—we are both irritable; we snap; get into arguments. She does things that irritate me and I do things that irritate her. And we seem to

notice it more now," said another father. Mothers were also aware of their irritability and anger. "The least little thing would end up in arguments; very trivial things. Maybe if he didn't polish the furniture right; he left a spot on the furniture . . ." said a mother. Another mother, who lost her daughter in an accident, said of her psychological state: "For the first six months . . . I was getting mental and was hard on him and angry with him. . . . It's like it was my own personal grief because [I felt] I loved her more than he did."

In addition to husbands' unwillingness to deal openly with grief and wives' lack of interest in sex, couples' anger, resentment, and irritation were expressed about those issues that had existed before their bereavement and those circumstances surrounding the death and bereavement. Such sources of anger and irritation included the mother's belief that the father's relationship with the deceased child was less than what a father-child relationship should have been, father not helping care for the deceased child while the child was ill, husband's drinking, wife's neglect or inability to take care of household chores after the loss, husband not having stayed at the hospital the night before the child died, husband not remembering the deceased child's birthday or anniversary of the child's death, and others. The mother's resentment toward the father who did not remember important dates appeared strong. A father expressed his anxiety and apprehension as he said, "I don't even remember what day Meg died on. . . . My wife—these dates [birthdays, anniversaries, etc.] are locked in her head, so consequently when I don't automatically remember these dates, she gets extremely upset with me." "It was very devastating to me that he had forgotten Jane's birthday. I think that was the beginning of my deep depression. . . ." a mother said, referring to an episode that occurred shortly before her suicide attempt. Even what appear to be relatively minor events and matters that might have been overlooked or quickly forgiven and forgotten had the child lived seemed to become major sources of tension between spouses.

DISCUSSION AND CONCLUSION

The interview data illustrated ways in which the crisis resulting from a child's

death affected the parents' marriage. The themes identified were fathers' concern and frustration about their wives' grief, wives' anger over husbands' not sharing their grief, temporary halt in communication, loss of sexual intimacy, and general irritability between spouses. The death of a child, parents repeatedly stated, was the most devastating thing they had experienced, leaving them feeling mortally wounded. Pain was likened to having an arm amputated without anesthesia or disembowelment or described as "my heart is breaking." While parents were coping with their own acute pain, all that they could do was try to get through each moment, each hour, each day in whatever manner they could. Consequently, the marital relationship suffered.

Couples withdrew from each other at various points in their bereavement, sometimes because of their own intense anguish and at other times out of a desire to avoid increasing their spouses' pain. Fathers were concerned and frustrated over their wives' grief and inability to function in their usual capacity as wives and mothers, while wives were angry and hurt because their husbands were not showing and sharing their grief as much as they were. These findings are in agreement with those reported by Helmrath and Steinitz (1978) as well as Cook (1983, 1988). In addition to men's tendency to control their emotional expressions, their culturally derived notion that they had to remain strong to protect the family coupled with their work responsibilities may have necessitated husbands keeping their emotions under control. Unfortunately, their behavior came into conflict with their wives' need for emotional sharing, which is one of the double binds men face mentioned by Cook (1988). It is also interesting to note that there is some evidence to indicate that marital partners do not always perceive accurately how their spouses are coping with their grief. In one study, it was found that wives perceived that their husbands were neither crying nor talking about their loss as much as husbands considered themselves to be doing (Schwab, 1986), perhaps largely because husbands cried when alone and talked about their loss with people outside the family.

On the basis of what was shared by participants (subsequently corroborated by other bereaved parents with whom the investigator has come into contact), it appears reasonable to conclude that women are more likely to lose interest in sex as a result of bereavement, while men maintain sexual desire or experience only a brief disruption in their sexual interest. Men appeared to seek emotional release or comfort through sexual intercourse, felt personally rejected when their wives refused their sexual advances, and worried about the future of the marriage. On the other hand, women tended to respond to their spouses' sexual desire with disbelief and distress, and some were even repulsed by it. What would comfort men appeared to have a contrary effect on women. The findings are similar to those of Johnson (1984–85) and Cook (1984) discussed earlier.

Couples appeared generally irritable and less tolerant of their spouses. Past conflicts resurfaced and minor events tended to be magnified as they were thrust into the emotional turmoil resulting from the worst tragedy in the parents' lives. However, in the majority of cases the relationships had survived up to the time of the interview. Judging from the interview data, a couple who had a good marital relationship prior to a child's death appear to have come closer together through the tragedy that shattered their lives. They had their share of difficulties including a period of withdrawal from one another and outbursts of anger, but they successfully restored equilibrium in their relationship. As some parents stated, when one was feeling down, the other helped, and by doing so, their relationship was strengthened.

The study had its limitations. The sample was small. Data for the study were retrospective, even though parents' memory of the catastrophic event was fresh and its effects on most of the parents were still acute. The interpretation of the data was subjective. How the experiences of those couples who do not become involved in a support group differ from those who do is not known. Factors such as the cause of the child's death and the age of the child at the time of death may differentially influence the marital relationship. In addition, preexisting marital relationships may have a great deal to do with the ways in which couples handle the crises in their lives. In

this study, no systematic attempt was made to gain information about the parents' marital relationships before the tragedies occurred. Similar studies with larger samples and with better control over variables, such as those discussed above, would be worthwhile.

The findings of the study have implications for counselors working with bereaved parents. Counselors need to be aware of the myriad ways the death of a child affects parents and their marital relationship. Shared tragedy does not necessarily bring the marital partners closer together. When they need one another most, they often find themselves unable to come together or withdrawing into their own private worlds of grief. As is evident in this study and in past studies (Cook, 1983, 1988; Helmrath & Steinitz, 1978; Schwab, 1990), the two sexes deal with the experience of loss in different ways, which can be easily misunderstood and which in turn can lead to conflict between spouses.

From the experiences of working with bereaved parents over the years through a support group, the investigator is well aware that there is little others can do to ease parents' pain or grief itself except for being there for them, to listen and provide support. The complexity and intensity of grief, however, may be confusing as well as anxiety-provoking to many and may result in their seeking assistance from professionals. Professionals can not only help bereaved parents realize what they are experiencing in their relationships or understand how much of it is part of the normal bereavement process but can also help them clarify issues and deal with their differences constructively. For example, the findings of this study suggest that parents will benefit from learning about the loss of sexual interest, which appears to be relatively widely shared among women. It will help parents to know that the lack of desire for intimacy on the part of one spouse or both after their child's death is likely temporary, requires understanding rather than alarm, and need not be interpreted as rejection of one partner by another. Becoming aware of the ways their experience of loss affects spouses differently can prevent or minimize its long-term

negative impact on their relationship. Although their awareness does not automatically resolve conflicts, learning to appreciate their experiences a little more objectively and to be tolerant of one another's ways of coping with grief can help to improve their relationship.

Parents' lives will never be the same again after a child's death. It usually takes several years for parents to restore the semblance of normal living. It is necessary for mental health professionals to realize the immensity of the parents' loss and its impact on their lives while maintaining faith in their eventual healing, which comes only very slowly.

REFERENCES

Cook, J. A. (1983). A death in the family: Parental bereavement in the first year. *Suicide and Life-Threatening Behavior 13*, 42–61.

Cook, J. A. (1984). Influence of gender on the problems of parents of fatally ill children. *Journal of Psychosocial Oncology, 2*, 71–91.

Cook, J. A. (1988). Dad's double binds: Rethinking fathers' bereavement from a men's studies perspective. *Journal of Contemporary Ethnography, 17*, 285–308.

Helmrath, T. A., & Steinitz, E. M. (1978). Death of an infant: Parental grieving and the failure of social support. *The Journal of Family Practice, 6*, 785–790.

Johnson, S. (1984–85). Sexual intimacy and replacement children after the death of a child. *Omega, 15*, 109–118.

Klass, D. (1986–87). Marriage and divorce among bereaved parents in a self-help group. *Omega, 17*, 237–249.

Nixon, J., & Pearn, J. (1977). Emotional sequelae of parents and sibs following the drowning or near-drowning of a child. *Australian and New Zealand Journal of Psychiatry, 11*, 265–268.

Schwab, R. (1986). *Differences in maternal and paternal mourning and coping behaviors: The final report.* Unpublished manuscript. Old Dominion University Research Foundation, Norfolk, VA.

Schwab, R. (1990). Paternal and maternal coping with the death of a child. *Death Studies, 14*, 407–422.

Shanfield, S. B., & Swain, B. J. (1984). Death of adult children in traffic accidents. *Journal of Nervous and Mental Disease, 172*, 533–538.

Credits/ Acknowledgments

Cover design by Charles Vitelli

1. The American Way of Dying and Death
Facing overview—United Nations photo by P. Sudhakaran.

2. Developmental Aspects of Dying and Death
Facing overview—United Nations photo by John Isaac.

3. The Dying Process
Facing overview—Middlesex Memorial Hospital photo.

4. Ethical Issues of Dying, Death, and Suicide
Facing overview—WHO photo by T. Farkas

5. Funeral and Burial Rites
Facing overview—EPA-Documerica photo.

6. Bereavement
Facing overview—*Children Today* photo by Jacquine Roland.

ANNUAL EDITIONS ARTICLE REVIEW FORM

■ NAME: _____ DATE: _____

■ TITLE AND NUMBER OF ARTICLE: _____

■ BRIEFLY STATE THE MAIN IDEA OF THIS ARTICLE: _____

_____

_____

_____

_____

■ LIST THREE IMPORTANT FACTS THAT THE AUTHOR USES TO SUPPORT THE MAIN IDEA:

_____

_____

_____

_____

_____

■ WHAT INFORMATION OR IDEAS DISCUSSED IN THIS ARTICLE ARE ALSO DISCUSSED IN YOUR TEXTBOOK OR OTHER READING YOU HAVE DONE? LIST THE TEXTBOOK CHAPTERS AND PAGE NUMBERS:

_____

_____

_____

_____

_____

_____

■ LIST ANY EXAMPLES OF BIAS OR FAULTY REASONING THAT YOU FOUND IN THE ARTICLE:

_____

_____

_____

_____

■ LIST ANY NEW TERMS/CONCEPTS THAT WERE DISCUSSED IN THE ARTICLE AND WRITE A SHORT DEFINITION:

_____

_____

_____

_____

_____

*Your instructor may require you to use this Annual Editions Article Review Form in any number of ways: for articles that are assigned, for extra credit, as a tool to assist in developing assigned papers, or simply for your own reference. Even if it is not required, we encourage you to photocopy and use this page; you'll find that reflecting on the articles will greatly enhance the information from your text.

ANNUAL EDITIONS:
DYING, DEATH, AND BEREAVEMENT, Third Edition
Article Rating Form

Here is an opportunity for you to have direct input into the next revision of this volume. We would like you to rate each of the 49 articles listed below, using the following scale:

1. **Excellent: should definitely be retained**
2. **Above average: should probably be retained**
3. **Below average: should probably be deleted**
4. **Poor: should definitely be deleted**

Your ratings will play a vital part in the next revision. So please mail this prepaid form to us just as soon as you complete it.
Thanks for your help!

Annual Editions revisions depend on two major opinion sources: one is our Advisory Board, listed in the front of this volume, which works with us in scanning the thousands of articles published in the public press each year; the other is you—the person actually using the book. Please help us and the users of the next edition by completing the prepaid article rating form on this page and returning it to us. Thank you.

Rating	Article	Rating	Article
	1. Death and Dying		26. Doctor, I Want to Die. Will You Help Me?
	2. American Death and Burial Custom Derivation from Medieval European Cultures		27. Medicine's Position Is Both Pivotal and Precarious in Assisted-Suicide Debate
	3. Constructing AIDS Policy in the Public Schools		28. Always to Care, Never to Kill: A Declaration on Euthanasia
	4. Current Models of Death, Dying, and Bereavement		29. Euthanasia: To Cease upon the Midnight
	5. Rewriting the End: Elisabeth Kübler-Ross		30. Suicide
	6. Psychology and Death: Meaningful Rediscovery		31. Attitudes toward Suicidal Behavior: A Review of the Literature
	7. Sunny Side Up		32. "We Have a Problem"
	8. Organizational Responses to Death in the Military		33. The Contemporary American Funeral
	9. Communication among Children, Parents, and Funeral Directors		34. Rituals: [Five] Ways Americans Deal with Death
	10. Death of a Friend		35. Psychocultural Influences on African-American Attitudes towards Death, Dying and Funeral Rites
	11. First Childhood Death Experiences		
	12. Detachment Revisited: The Child's Reconstruction of a Dead Parent		36. How Different Religions Pay Their Final Respects
	13. Reflections on the Death of My Daughter-in-Law		37. She Plans Funerals That Celebrate Life
	14. Feeling Something: When a Father Dies		38. It's Your Funeral
	15. Old No More		39. Burying the Ungrateful Dead
	16. The Naturalness of Dying		40. Burying Tradition, More People Opt for 'Fun' Funerals
	17. A Conversation with My Mother		41. Mourners Will Please Pay Respects at Speeds Not Exceeding 15 MPH
	18. Planning to Die		42. The Grieving Process
	19. The Art of Dying		43. Coping with Bereavement
	20. Dimensions of Dying		44. Disenfranchised Grief
	21. A Decade beyond Medical School: A Longitudinal Study of Physicians' Attitudes toward Death and Terminally-Ill Patients		45. The Increasing Prevalence of Complicated Mourning: The Onslaught Is Just Beginning
			46. The Spiritual Crisis of Bereavement
	22. Attitudes to Death and Bereavement among Cultural Minority Groups		47. Adolescent Mourning: The Sudden Death of a Peer
	23. The Spiritual Needs of the Dying		48. Solace and Immortality: Bereaved Parents' Continuing Bond with Their Children
	24. Spiritual Aspects of Death and Dying		
	25. Hospice Care for the 1990s: A Concept Coming of Age		49. Effects of a Child's Death on the Marital Relationship: A Preliminary Study

(Continued on next page)

ABOUT YOU

Name_____ Date_____

Are you a teacher? ☐   Or student? ☐

Your School Name _____

Department _____

Address _____

City _____ State _____ Zip _____

School Telephone # _____

YOUR COMMENTS ARE IMPORTANT TO US!

Please fill in the following information:

For which course did you use this book? _____

Did you use a text with this Annual Edition?   ☐ yes   ☐ no

The title of the text? _____

What are your general reactions to the Annual Editions concept?

Have you read any particular articles recently that you think should be included in the next edition?

Are there any articles you feel should be replaced in the next edition? Why?

Are there other areas that you feel would utilize an Annual Edition?

May we contact you for editorial input?

May we quote you from above?

ANNUAL EDITIONS: DYING, DEATH, AND BEREAVEMENT, Third Edition